ROYAL
COMMISSION
ON THE HISTORICAL
MONUMENTS
OF ENGLAND

THESAURUS OF MONUMENT TYPES

A STANDARD FOR USE IN
ARCHAEOLOGICAL AND ARCHITECTURAL RECORDS

ROYAL COMMISSION ON THE HISTORICAL MONUMENTS OF ENGLAND
ENGLISH HERITAGE

Published by the Royal Commission on the Historical Monuments of England, National Monuments Record Centre, Kemble Drive, Swindon SN2 2GZ

© Crown copyright 1995 and English Heritage 1995
Applications for reproduction should be made to the RCHME

First published 1995

ISBN 1 873592 20 5

British Library Cataloguing in Publication Data
A CIP catalogue record for this book is available from the British Library

Cover picture:
Arch of Hadrian, Shugborough Hall, Colwich, Staffordshire

CONTENTS

FOREWORD

The Royal Commission on the Historical Monuments of England (RCHME) and English Heritage (EH) jointly published the *Revised Thesaurus of Architectural Terms* in 1989 and the *Thesaurus of Archaeological Site Types* in 1992. This joint development of thesaurus standards has now been extended to the preparation of a thesaurus covering both disciplines, integrating the archaeological and architectural vocabulary for monument types.

The new Thesaurus will support the development and curation of national record systems within the RCHME and EH by setting standards and controlling the form in which information is held, assisting indexing and maximising retrieval of information. It will also be used as a standard for implementing the data capture and the indexing of listed buildings information in the computerisation of the statutory lists of historic buildings, part of the Heritage Database Project funded by the Department of National Heritage.

It is also hoped that the Thesaurus of Monument Types will further an overall consistency of approach between national and local records and thus facilitate the collection and exchange of information between record systems, and also assist other bodies and individuals recording archaeological or architectural monuments.

The new Thesaurus is not a definitive document and amendments and enhancements are welcomed for inclusion in the computerised database held by the RCHME and in any future edition of this Thesaurus. Future revision of the Thesaurus will take place in the context of continuing consultation between the RCHME, EH, the Association of County Archaeological Officers (ACAO) and others, on information standards for archaeological and architectural records.

The compilation of the Thesaurus was the responsibility of Catherine Steeves, Anna Eavis and Robin Bourne in turn, under the supervision of Neil Beagrie and Diana Hale. The project was directed by a working party including Neil Beagrie, Diana Hale, Dawn Abercromby (formerly EH), Nigel Clubb, Felicity Gilmour, Andrew Williams and Simon Walton from the RCHME, Philip Ellis from EH, Paul Gilman and Andrew Pike from ACAO, and Jeremy Oetgen from the British Archaeological Bibliography.

Many others have contributed to the work in a number of ways and we are indebted to them.

Tom Hassall, Royal Commission on the Historical Monuments of England

Jennifer Page, English Heritage

INTRODUCTION

1. The purpose of a thesaurus

A thesaurus is not primarily a classification system. It is a tool used to standardise terminology and to set up conceptual relationships between terms in order to assist indexing and to maximise the retrieval of information. Where sets of data relate to the same or similar subjects, for example archaeological sites and monuments and historical buildings, a thesaurus can help to standardise terminology and maximise retrieval across a number of data sets managed by different organisations. It can provide guidance to all bodies with interests in that subject area and contribute to establishing and maintaining national and international standards.

This Thesaurus is concerned with aiding the indexing and retrieval of architectural and archaeological monument type terms. It seeks to establish the relationships of the source terms and then develop these into a set of classes such as Domestic, Commercial, etc. based primarily on the functions of the monument.

Although its construction is more work intensive than word or subject heading lists, a thesaurus has a number of major strengths in dealing with site terms for archaeological or architectural monuments. The hierarchical structure of a thesaurus is ideally suited to retrieval from different information sources using different levels of indexing, whether general or specific: eg, MONASTERY as opposed to BENEDICTINE MONASTERY.

The ability to show associative relationships (ie related terms) through a thesaurus structure is also important in improving retrieval from sources using different levels of monument site definition, ie, by showing the typical components of monument complexes and vice versa: eg, by relating SPA to its possible components such as PUMP ROOMS or BATHS, or by prompting users towards monument types that are closely related, eg, ROUND BARROW and RING DITCH, or PARK and GARDEN.

Archaeological and architectural information can be incomplete and its interpretation will have varying levels of certainty. The ability to increase retrieval, while eliminating redundant data, through use of the different levels of the hierarchy and the related terms mechanism is, therefore, an important one in improving access to computerised information, particularly in large databases.

The Thesaurus is not intended to be definitive or comprehensive, as it is based primarily on existing terms used in the sources (see section 3 below), but it does seek to provide a structure and to establish guidelines for standardising monument type terminology for information purposes, without imposing a rigid classification or taxonomy of monuments. It is a dynamic terminology, which will continue to develop both in depth and breadth and in response to user need.

Potential users may make use of the Thesaurus as a manual guide or in a disk format which may be linked to a computerised record system. It is available in a fully computerised form as an integrated part of a software package for monument recording (MONARCH) which has been developed by the RCHME (see section 9 below).

2. Subject coverage

The scope of this Thesaurus is limited to archaeological and architectural monument types i
England. It includes over 7,000 terms. It is concerned primarily with suggesting preferred term
for describing monuments and establishing relationships between these terms, which can then b
classified at a higher level by function. There are 18 functional classes (see page xxvi for a ful
list with definitions showing the scope of each), for example CIVIL, DOMESTIC an
MARITIME.

Object names which are merely indicative of a site are generally excluded from this thesaurus
These terms now form a separate classification scheme which will be the subject of furthe
development. However terms such as URN or BATTLESHIP which may be considered a
monument types in their own right are included.

Monument type terms which express form rather than function are included where they ar
considered useful or necessary: eg, either to aid retrieval within large functional groupings, suc
as TIMBER FRAMED HOUSE as a narrow term of HOUSE < BY FORM >, or where they ar
the sole means of describing imperfectly understood monuments, such as RECTANGULAI
ENCLOSURE. Terms which are sometimes only components of structures may be included fo
the latter reason but may also be regarded as individual monuments in some cases : eg, WALL
ARCH. Components are sometimes re-used, forming free-standing architectural features an
terms may have been included to accommodate this situation. Components or elements c
buildings as such are however generally excluded.

Terms for components meaning the individual structures found within a complex are include
although some record compilers may not wish to record those individually. Terms for complexe
as such are not specifically distinguished from or linked to their component structures but wi
usually be linked as related terms or by a grouping within a class such as POTTER'
MANUFACTURING SITE. Terms relating to areas of buildings are only included where the
may be found as a detached physical entity or where it may sometimes be necessary to distinguis
the functional use of that area from that of the overall monument type: eg, KITCHEN.

Natural features are only included where they could be misinterpreted as archaeological sites, o
form part of a landscaped area, or where they may be of significance to archaeological sites c
contain archaeological deposits, eg, OXBOW LAKE, CAVE.

Most other concepts also used to describe monuments, such as period and materials are exclude
from this thesaurus, as they have an integrity of their own and are generally recorded separatel
from the monument type, particularly in computerised record systems. For an example of
period word list see *Recording England's Past. A Data Standard for the Extended Nationa
Archaeological Record* (RCHME 1993). However, concepts such as industrial product an
religious order tend not to be separated out and have been retained in the thesaurus as qualifiel
of broader monument types, as with form mentioned above.

Only terms which relate to monuments found in England or within its maritime territory ar
included. Some important architectural and archaeological terms are therefore not included here
Terms of specifically Scottish, Welsh, Irish or American significance, and foreign languag
terms, are excluded unless they have been adopted in England. Regional terms are only include
where they provide the sole description for a unique regional phenomenon (eg, PLAIN Al
GWARRY), or where the regional term has been adopted nationally. Where a regional term doe

not serve such a function the user will be guided to a term with a wider currency nationally, which is synonymous with the regional term: eg, Shippon USE COW HOUSE.

3. Sources

The terms included are derived both from the *Thesaurus of Archaeological Site Types* (RCHME and English Heritage 1992) and the *Revised Thesaurus of Architectural Terms* (RCHME and English Heritage 1989). As well as the proposals from the Thesaurus Working Party in its role as Steering Group for the production of this integrated version, many others have suggested additions and revisions since the publication of the two previous thesauri. Suggestions have come from RCHME recording staff in the field and in the National Monuments Record and from staff of English Heritage, particularly in the Records Office, reflecting the ongoing requirements of the Monument Protection Programme and List Review. Other organisations and individuals have also contributed, including county Sites and Monuments Records, the Association for Industrial Archaeology, the Institute for Advanced Architectural Studies and the Fortress Studies Group.

Work begun on comparing architectural and archaeological terminology at an international level, both under the auspices of the Council of Europe, and in collaboration with the Getty Art History Information Programme, has provided a broader framework within which to review both terms and structure for this version.

4. Structure

The structure of the Thesaurus follows the British and International Standards incorporated in the second edition of *Thesaurus Construction*, published by ASLIB (Aitchison and Gilchrist 1987). It deviates from these standards in using terms in the singular form rather than the plural. This decision was based on the fact that most heritage recording bodies use the singular form in their databases.

The construction of this Thesaurus was based upon establishing the four basic relationships outlined in the British Standard for the source terms.

These relationships are as follows:

i) The equivalence relationship

This is the first relationship to be established where terms are analysed and given preferred or non-preferred status. Preferred terms are those that will be used in the database records to index and which will also be recommended for use in retrieving records. Non-preferred terms are useful 'lead-in' terms which will indicate the appropriate preferred terms. The assignation of preferred or non-preferred status is based on current usage and acceptance. Non-preferred status is usually given in the following instances:

a) for synonyms: eg, Slaughter House USE ABATTOIR

b) for quasi-synonyms, ie, treated as synonyms for this particular subject area: eg, Tribunal USE COURT HOUSE

c) for upward posting, ie, where a term is treated as non-preferred and 'posted up' to broader term. This technique is used where the level of detail in a narrow term is thought to be beyond the scope of the current thesaurus: eg, Trout Farm USE FISH FARM

d) for certain archaic terms: eg, Bridewell USE PRISON

e) for complex compound terms: eg, Trackway Field System USE FIELD SYSTEM

f) for foreign terms, unless in common usage to describe English monuments: eg GRUBENHAUS

g) for regional terms: eg, Coe USE MINERS HUT, except where they represent the descriptive term for a unique regional phenomenon, eg, PLAIN AN GWARRY.

In some instances a non-preferred term will not equate to one preferred term and a choice of terms will be given: eg, Dike USE DYKE (DEFENCE), FLOOD DEFENCES, WATER CHANNEL. Advice on the selection of the preferred term to use, if not obvious, will be given in the scope note (see 4 (iv) below) eg, Dike SN Use DYKE (DEFENCE), FLOOD DEFENCE or WATER CHANNEL as appropriate. In addition for this example there is a scope note under DYKE (DEFENCE) SN Defensive or boundary earthwork.

ii) The hierarchical relationship

The preferred terms are then grouped hierarchically, by concept, into broad terms and narrow terms under a top term or class term: eg, FIELD BARN has the broader term BARN, which is in the class AGRICULTURE AND SUBSISTENCE.

The hierarchy is usually generic, ie the narrower term is a type of, or example of, the broader term, as with FIELD BARN and BARN above.

A broad term can have many subordinate or narrow terms. The levels of broad and narrow terms are flexible and so the Thesaurus is multi-level. The number of levels is decided by known and anticipated needs for retrieval: eg, BENEDICTINE GRANGE and CARTHUSIAN GRANGE are narrow terms of GRANGE, which in turn has a broader term of LAND USE SITE, which belongs to the class of AGRICULTURE AND SUBSISTENCE and of RELIGIOUS HOUSE which belongs to the class of RELIGIOUS, RITUAL AND FUNERARY. PILLOW MOUND has only one term above it, the class term itself, AGRICULTURE AND SUBSISTENCE.

It is sometimes necessary to specify on what basis the terms have been grouped into a hierarchy. In these instances the broadest term of the hierarchy is given a facet indicator, eg HOUSE <BY FORM>, HOUSE <BY FUNCTION>. This gives the user an indication of why the terms have been brought together. These terms are not index terms. Another type of broad term is one used to draw together terms of like concept, but which is not suitable for use as an index term, eg TEXTILE INDUSTRY SITE. These terms are differentiated in the Thesaurus from index terms, see section on Thesaurus Display.

The Thesaurus is poly-hierarchical, ie, a term can have more than one broad term and can appear in more than one hierarchy and more than one class. The same broad term may have different narrow terms where it appears in more than one class: eg, GARDEN has the narrow terms HOME GARDEN, KITCHEN GARDEN, MARKET GARDEN and NURSERY GARDEN in the

AGRICULTURE AND SUBSISTENCE class. In the GARDENS, PARKS AND URBAN SPACES class GARDEN has many more narrow terms including eg, ITALIAN GARDEN, SUNKEN GARDEN, WALLED GARDEN.

iii) The associative relationship

Relationships between terms that cannot be shown hierarchically can be expressed by the associative relationship which involves relating terms. Relating terms links terms that are similar in concept but where the relationship is not inherent within the hierarchy to which the terms belong. Thus, related terms normally link preferred terms in different classes or hierarchies, eg MINERS READING ROOM is related to COLLIERY; the first is in the EDUCATION class, whereas the second is in the INDUSTRIAL class. Related terms in this Thesaurus can be context specific, so if a term appears in more than one class or grouping, its related terms may vary.

Where a strong relationship exists between several terms among a larger grouping even within the same broader term, it may be useful to relate those terms: eg, BURIAL VAULT and MAUSOLEUM are made related terms, to each other, but they are both narrow terms of FUNERARY SITE. There is a closer link between BURIAL VAULT and MAUSOLEUM than between either of those terms and BARROW or LONG MOUND which are also narrow terms of FUNERARY SITE. They may be near synonyms for example.

iv) Scope notes

Guidance on the use or meaning of a term is provided by a scope note where necessary. This can both provide advice and define ambiguous terms or relationships. It is hoped that the use of scope notes can be developed further in the future.

5. Vocabulary control rules

The rules that have been adopted regarding the choice and form of terms in this thesaurus are as follows:

Synonyms

> The thesaurus controls the use of synonyms, quasi-synonyms and archaic terms to improve indexing and retrieval, by the use of preferred and non-preferred terms. Where non-preferred terms have several meanings, there can be more than one preferred term and guidance on their use may be given by a scope note.

Homographs

> The use of homographs has been avoided where possible. Where they do appear, they are distinguished from each other by a qualifier in brackets following each instance of the term, eg, BANK (FINANCIAL) and BANK (EARTHWORK). The effect this may have on computerised retrieval should be noted and recommendations made in the manual, as necessary for the particular system used, to ensure adequate retrieval, eg, by always querying using a wild card symbol following the term.

Punctuation

There is no punctuation in the Thesaurus apart from the use of the comma etc within scope notes.

Spelling

Spelling follows the 2 volume Oxford English Dictionary (*The Shorter Oxford Dictionary* 3rd edition 1986), apart from rare exceptions where common practice in the field of archaeological or architectural recording differs from this.

Hyphens

Hyphenated words are treated as two words.

Singular/Plural

Terms are used in the singular apart from instances where the plural is the common usage or where the singular changes the meaning.

Compound terms

Complex compound terms are split into unitary concepts: eg, Cave Burial USE CAVE and BURIAL, except where this affects the meaning, or where the use of such a term is well established: eg, RIDGE AND FURROW. (For other comments on multiple-keying, ie using multiple terms, see section 6 below)

Language order

Natural language order is used for all preferred and non-preferred terms.

Changes of meaning

Terms which have changed meaning over time will have to be identified through retrieval using period or date fields where possible, but clarification may sometimes be found in scope notes in the Thesaurus.

Alphabetisation

Word-by-word alphabetisation is used throughout.

6. The classes

The classes represent the top terms, ie the highest level broad terms in the hierarchical structure of the Thesaurus. They are primarily concerned with the classification of monument types by function. Multi-functional monument types may be assigned to more than one class. Similarly, where there are alternative interpretations of function, a monument type may be assigned to several classes.

Monument types will be included in a class on the basis of the criteria set out in the class definitions. The function of ancillary monuments will often be independent of their context: eg, a GRANARY can be a component monument of many sites, but its function, and therefore its class, will always be AGRICULTURE AND SUBSISTENCE. The Thesaurus does not aim to show the context or associations of individual monuments as these relationships vary in each case. They should be shown by cross-referencing fields in the records, if available, or by multiple-keying if the record structure does not allow for this. Many terms which appear in the UNASSIGNED class, for example, can be keyed in addition to terms from other classes to give the appropriate functional context for that particular monument: eg, GATEHOUSE may be keyed in addition to MONASTERY if the monument being recorded is a part of a monastic site.

Within each class groups of broad terms may be used to further sub-divide terms. These broad terms reflect the overall conceptual framework of classification by function and also other concepts used regularly for classification and retrieval within individual subject areas. Some examples for individual classes are described in more detail below.

Industrial class

The structure of the industrial class is based on a synthesis of ideas on industrial groupings and categories taken from a wide range of technological and industrial literature and specialised thesauri. The present structure and range of terms are not intended to be definitive but will be further developed in the future as a result of ongoing discussions with specialists recording in this field.

The current industrial class is structured largely by broad industry sub-groupings as follows:

ANIMAL PRODUCT SITE
ARMAMENTS MANUFACTURING SITE
CHEMICAL INDUSTRY SITE
CLOTHING INDUSTRY SITE
CRAFT INDUSTRY SITE
ENGINEERING INDUSTRY SITE
FOOD AND DRINK INDUSTRY SITE
FUEL PRODUCTION SITE
MARINE CONSTRUCTION SITE
METAL INDUSTRY SITE
MINERAL EXTRACTION SITE
MINERAL PRODUCT SITE
MINING INDUSTRY SITE
PAPER INDUSTRY SITE
POWER GENERATION SITE
TEXTILE INDUSTRY SITE
WASTE DISPOSAL SITE
WOOD PROCESSING SITE

These are further sub-divided in some cases, eg FUEL PRODUCTION SITE has sub-groupings of CHARCOAL PRODUCTION SITE, COAL MINING SITE, OIL REFINING SITE and PEAT WORKINGS, all including narrower indexing terms.

There are also a limited number of hierarchies by general monument types such as MILL ‹ FACTORY. Such terms are often ambiguous in meaning. No attempt has been made to defir the use of such terms in the scope notes, as the usage is so variable, although FACTORY h; groupings < BY FORM > and < BY PRODUCT >. These hierarchies will allow retrieval by tl broad terms, which frequently appear on maps and in other sources, as well as by the narro terms that are industry specific: eg, PAPER MILL or CAR FACTORY.

Some terms which have a more general application and are not restricted to one or two branch‹ of industry only, such as GRINDSTONE and ENGINE, are placed within the hierarchy at tl same level as the groupings for particular industries.

It is possible to classify industrial sites by a number of concepts, principally: product; proces power; form and type. Each concept could be recorded in a separate field in a specialis‹ database. Alternatively, concepts can be combined into single terms and/or using multiple-keyir in a monument type field. This Thesaurus has followed the latter course as it is the practice ‹ most architectural and archaeological databases. It has also suggested in scope notes where usir multiple terms is particularly recommended: eg, that the form of extraction such as DRIFT MIN or BELL PIT should be keyed as well as product types such as LEAD MINE or COA WORKINGS where known. This should assist consistent retrieval by different concepts from database.

The Association for Industrial Archaeology is currently testing a wordlist and recording syste‹ (IRIS) developed by them specifically for the industrial period. There has been, and will continu to be, consultation between those involved in developing terminologies within the AIA and th project, to ensure that compatibility, particularly for purposes of data exchange, is maintainec

The IRIS wordlist will use indexing terms from this Thesaurus and add terms as required for i specific purposes. As IRIS is being used for a specific period and specialised application, it ca include more specialist terms than it is feasible to include in a more wide-ranging thesaurus suc as this, covering the whole range of monuments from prehistory to the present day.

A separate field will be used to record classification in the AIA database. This uses a sing hierarchy structure, is period specific, has no related terms and will therefore use more broa terms for classifying entry terms than are used here. The structure of this Thesaurus shou‹ however allow comparable groupings of monuments to be retrieved.

Considerable recording work is now being carried out on industrial monuments and it anticipated that this will justify further review of the vocabulary before the next publishe revisions of both terminologies.

Religious, Ritual and Funerary

The major hierarchies found within this class are FUNERARY SITE, PLACE OF WORSHI and RELIGIOUS HOUSE. The terms found under PLACE OF WORSHIP may indicate religiou denominations: eg, ANGLICAN CHURCH, BUDDHIST TEMPLE, or other concepts such ‹ specific function or location: eg, LADY CHAPEL, PARISH CHURCH, CEMETERY CHAPEL It is recommended that terms denoting different concepts are all used for a record whe‹ appropriate.

The terms appearing under the broad term RELIGIOUS HOUSE can be defined as largely pre-dissolution, monastic or religious communities. These range from major centres with subordinate communities to smaller independent establishments, often without dependencies. There are as many as six possible valid concepts for classifying religious houses:

    i) monastic or religious *community*; eg, monastery, convent;
    ii) *status* of house; eg, abbey, priory;
    iii) monastic or religious *order*; eg, Augustinian, Benedictine;
    iv) *gender* of community - male, female, mixed (nuns, monks);
    v) *dependency* - especially alien houses dependent on a foreign mother house;
    vi) *rule* of house; eg, regular, observant, etc.

The classification given here attempts to meet the requirements of most users of earlier versions of this Thesaurus and specialists consulted in facilitating retrieval by community and gender: eg, FRIARY, NUNNERY, which can be combined with order where known or relevant through the use of narrow terms: eg, BENEDICTINE NUNNERY. As an additional level of indexing, the status of ABBEY or PRIORY are also available as preferred terms. These can be keyed in addition to FRIARY, NUNNERY etc, or their narrow terms. Scope notes are given to help the user determine what is appropriate: eg, CLUNIAC NUNNERY SN Abbeys and priories of Cluniac nuns. The monastic or religious communities/holdings of GRANGE and CELL are both broad terms. Their subordinate narrow terms are qualified by monastic or religious order, and, in the case of cells, whether they are alien houses, but no attempt has been made to indicate ownership by gender or specialisation.

It is recommended that indexers should indicate each change of community, monastic order, or status separately when compiling records.

Certain index terms have been purposely excluded from the broad term RELIGIOUS HOUSE: eg, HOSPITAL, ALMONRY, MANOR, etc, despite having strong monastic associations in many instances. As far as possible, these have been related to terms appearing under RELIGIOUS HOUSE.

Domestic

As HOUSE is such a common building type, the term soon becomes of limited value for retrieving records on a large database. One solution is to recommend the use of more specific terms wherever these are applicable and possible, dependent on the information available. A selection of such terms have here been grouped within facets of HOUSE <BY FORM> and HOUSE <BY FUNCTION>. Terms for housing relating to specific functional classes form subgroups within HOUSE <BY FUNCTION> here in the Domestic class, rather than appearing in those other related classes. Examples are terms found under CLERICAL DWELLING, eg, DEANERY, VICARAGE; TRANSPORT WORKERS HOUSE, eg, COACHMANS COTTAGE, FERRYKEEPERS COTTAGE; and MARITIME HOUSE, eg, COASTGUARDS COTTAGE, NAVAL OFFICERS HOUSE.

An exception is made for terms in the INDUSTRIAL HOUSE grouping, which appear in both the Domestic class and the Industrial class when the industrial process is likely to be carried out in the home itself. The additional function is intrinsic to the monument. Similarly, many of the terms for residential buildings appear in both the Domestic class and one or more other classes, such as Commercial, eg, HOTEL and its narrow terms. SPA HOTEL additionally appears in the Health and Welfare class.

7. Using the Thesaurus for indexing

Good indexing policies and a commitment to improving the quality of indexes are central to th successful operation of the Thesaurus on computerised databases. The following guidelines ar suggested to obtain maximum advantage from use of the Thesaurus:

i) Validation - the validation of indexing terms as they are entered on to a database is one of th most effective forms of vocabulary control and of increasing retrieval from the database. Th Thesaurus can serve as a master vocabulary file to check the indexing terms used by indexers an searchers. The system can reject non-preferred terms and, if desired, the preferred terms can b automatically substituted, except where there is more than one alternative. A browsing facilit can easily lead the indexer to valid terms in a broad, or more restricted, subject area. In additio a facility for proposing candidate terms can allow users to index records temporarily with a terr not at present included in the Thesaurus. Obviously this process needs careful control (see sectio 10 below for information on updating of the Thesaurus).

ii) Compilers' manual - It is recommended that sections on indexing policy reflecting th requirements of the system's end-users are included in the compilers' manual for the database together with instructions for the use of the Thesaurus.

iii) Levels of indexing - the Thesaurus is designed for use at the most specific level o information available when indexing. Indexers should therefore use the most specific term (ie narrow term) appropriate for indexing. The detail to which 'sites' should be indexed where the may have multiple component buildings or structures will reflect user requirements and availabl resources. The Thesaurus allows for a flexible approach as it places no restrictions on what ma constitute a component building or structure for any particular site or complex. The inclusion o related terms does however give an indication of associations commonly found.

iv) Monitoring retrieval - The Thesaurus is intimately linked to indexing and retrieval needs an its effective application will benefit from the monitoring of enquiries to the database and th efficiency of retrieval. The recording of enquiries and retrieval problems, together with thei regular review, should therefore help to improve the Thesaurus and the indexing of the database

8. Using the Thesaurus for retrieval

The Thesaurus is specifically designed to assist users in maximising the retrieval of informatio from a database. The hierarchical arrangement allows the user to retrieve information at differen levels or by different concepts according to their requirements. The amount of informatio retrieved may be expanded or contracted by structuring queries in different ways, eg, b including or excluding records indexed with narrow terms of a particular term, or including thos indexed with related terms, or including narrow and related terms.

In using the classes for retrieval from databases it should be remembered that the higher leve classifications by function apply to monument types generally and that the nature of evidence particularly archaeological evidence, for some monuments will often give rise to alternativ interpretations of function. Similarly, some monument types may be strongly associated with particular function, eg, barrows and funerary rites, but the function of individual sites within monument type may vary; eg, some barrows are known to have had no funerary function. I should be remembered, therefore, that the functional classifications are intended to assist themati searches and to provide the user with a range of monument types of interest to the enquiry whicl can be used to retrieve records of particular monuments from a database. It will then be necessary for the user to evaluate the evidence of function in the record for each particular monument.

Full guidance on retrieval and the use of the Thesaurus should be included in any user guide for a system. It may also be helpful for users to have an alphabetical listing of terms with the number of occurrences on the database. This information will assist users in making their enquiry at the appropriate level for their needs. It should be updated at regular intervals.

This Thesaurus covers terms for monument types but will frequently be most effective in retrieval when used with other database fields with controlled entries, eg, period or date, to refine the search. Clear guidance on such fields, their use in combination with the Thesaurus, and examples of effective searching techniques should be included in any user guide.

9. The use and future development of the Thesaurus

The Thesaurus has been developed utilising ORACLE database software and forms an element of the MONARCH database package being used by the RCHME's National Monuments Record and other heritage bodies including, for example, some county Sites and Monuments Records. It will also be used in database form for the indexing project of the Heritage Programme which will provide computerised access to listed buildings information. The Heritage Programme is a joint project involving the RCHME, English Heritage and the Department of National Heritage. The Thesaurus will also be implemented in the Records Office of English Heritage for architectural and archaeological records held by them.

As several of these uses are planned to create large numbers of records over the next two years, it is likely that considerable numbers of candidate terms will be proposed for inclusion in the Thesaurus. With other revisions anticipated in particular subject areas such as the industrial, it is anticipated that a revised publication of the Thesaurus may be necessary in a few years.

It is intended that the Thesaurus will help set the standard for monument type indexing and retrieval terminology for architectural and archaeological records at a national level, and it will also aid the further development of and agreement on terminology in this subject area at an international and multilingual level.

The level of detail included in the Thesaurus reflects that which is considered by the RCHME and English Heritage to be appropriate for recording monument types at a national level, based on the current indexing requirements of the databases held by them. It is recognised that greater levels of detail may be desirable at a local level and also where users have a more specialist interest in a particular area of vocabulary within the whole and such requirements will be reviewed as necessary and appropriate action taken, particularly where data exchange may be involved at a national level. The Thesaurus can provide rules and a broad term structure which could form a basis for a more detailed linked vocabulary for use for specialised projects or to meet local requirements.

At present it is intended to make the Thesaurus available in a word processed (or ASCII) file format as well as the hard copy publication. In database form it will at present only be available as part of the MONARCH package, but it is hoped that it may be available as an independent module at some future date.

It is intended that other related areas of vocabulary, some of which were included in previor versions of the architectural and archaeological thesauri, will eventually be published as separar thesauri or standards. Archaeological objects and construction materials are two areas terminology currently under further discussion. *Recording England's Past. A Data Standard f the Extended National Archaeological Record*, issued by the RCHME and the Association County Archaeological Officers provides guidance on standards for terminology for periods ar dates as well as other many other types of information used in archaeological records.

10. Updating and maintenance

The Thesaurus is a dynamic indexing tool and will evolve with further use and the developme of architectural and archaeological terminology and databases. It should be stressed therefore th this published version of the Thesaurus is only a paper copy of its contents current at the tim of publication and will be subject to addition or amendment.

The Thesaurus Working Party will continue to meet at regular intervals to consider new term or amendments to the Thesaurus, both from users in the organisations involved and others. W welcome suggestions for additions or amendments from external users and these should be se to the Working Party using the Comment Form or Candidate Term Form included in th publication. We particularly welcome consultation on the indexing and retrieval requirements archaeological and architectural recording projects at the earliest possible stage. Every attem will be made to respond to any suggestions within a reasonable period of time. It is intended issue a list of changes on a regular basis. Anyone wishing to receive such updates or requirir any further information on the Thesaurus or its availability in other formats should write to th address below:

Robin Bourne, Thesaurus Manager
Thesaurus Working Party
National Monuments Record Centre
Kemble Drive
Swindon SN2 2GZ

Tel: (01793) 414824

GLOSSARY

BROAD TERM (BT) A superordinate term that represents a parent to subordinates (NARROW TERM) within a CLASS. Their relationship is GENERIC or WHOLE-PART. A BROAD TERM may have many NARROW TERMS, which in themselves can be broken down into smaller arrangements of BROAD and NARROW TERMS. This means the Thesaurus is MULTI-LEVEL; eg, **FARM BUILDING** is the broad term to **BARN**, which in turn is the broad term to **TITHE BARN**.

CANDIDATE TERM A new term proposed by users for inclusion in the Thesaurus. The Thesaurus Working Party will periodically review these candidate terms and decide whether they are PREFERRED or NON-PREFERRED and if the former place them in the appropriate HIERARCHY.

CLASS (CL) The highest BROAD TERMS (TOP TERMS) in the Thesaurus hierarchies, eg, DOMESTIC or INDUSTRIAL.

COMPOUND TERM eg, **HUT CIRCLE SETTLEMENT**. Most compound terms are not allowed in common with standard thesaurus guidelines. The exceptions are where the splitting of the term would affect the meaning or where the use of the term is well established.

FACET INDICATOR A term or phrase qualifying a term which is then used as a guide term, ie a NON-INDEX TERM, indicating the concept by which narrower terms are grouped within that facet. In this Thesaurus the qualifier appears in angle brackets, eg, HOUSE <BY FORM>.

GENERIC RELATIONSHIP The principal link between a CLASS or a BROAD TERM and its members or NARROW TERMS.

HIERARCHY An arrangement of terms showing broader-narrower relationships between them.

HOMOGRAPHS or HOMONYMS Terms that are spelt alike but have different meanings. In this Thesaurus they are distinguished from each other by a qualifier in brackets after each occurence of the term, eg, **BANK (FINANCIAL)** and **BANK (EARTHWORK)**.

INDEX TERM A term or keyword that can be used to describe the monument type in records on a database, eg, **HOUSE**; a PREFERRED TERM in the Thesaurus. In this Thesaurus index terms appear in upper case and in bold type in the class list and in the alphabetical entry for that term.

MULTI-LEVEL A thesaurus structure with varying numbers of levels of BROAD or NARROW TERMS.

MULTIPLE-KEYING or MULTIPLE-INDEXING To retrieve and record different facets of particular sites it is possible to index with more than one PREFERRED TERM, eg, **BENEDICTINE NUNNERY** together with **ABBEY**. Multiple-indexing or multiple-keying can also be used where there is some uncertainty as to what the monument type is, and in these examples all alternatives can be entered.

NARROW TERM (NT) A term that is subordinate to a parent term, ie, a BROAD TERM or CLASS TERM; eg, **FUNICULAR RAILWAY** is a narrow term of **RAILWAY**. The relationship is usually GENERIC.

NON-INDEX TERM A PREFERRED TERM, which cannot be used as an INDEX TERM, but is useful in the Thesaurus as a grouping for retrieval purposes only, eg, WATER TRANSPORT SITE. Also known as a guide term. Distinguished in this Thesaurus by appearing in non-bold type in the class lists and in the alphabetical entry for that term.

NON-PREFERRED TERM Terms not selected for indexing or retrieval, eg, synonyms, but serving a function in the Thesaurus as lead-in terms to the PREFERRED TERM, eg, Fortlace USE FORTLET.

POLYHIERARCHICAL A classification allowing a PREFERRED TERM to belong to more than one CLASS or to have more than one BROAD TERM.

POST CO-ORDINATION The separation of two or more concepts when indexing and their combination at the time of retrieval, normally using Boolean operators to formulate a query on more than one field in a database, eg, **HILLFORT** and IRON AGE.

PRE CO-ORDINATION The combining of two or more concepts in a single term in order to formulate a description of site type, eg, **BENEDICTINE MONASTERY**.

PREFERRED TERM A term selected for retrieval in the Thesaurus, eg, **FORTLET** or WATER TRANSPORT SITE. A PREFERRED TERM can be an INDEX or NON-INDEX TERM. Appear in upper case in this Thesaurus.

RELATED TERM (RT) A relationship found between PREFERRED TERMS, which are linked conceptually but not hierarchically, eg, **RING DITCH** and **ROUND BARROW**. The Thesaurus allows for terms to be related in the same hierarchy when a particularly strong link occurs, eg, **BELVEDERE** and **GAZEBO**.

SCOPE NOTE (SN) A limited definition of a term and/or guidance on its use.

SYNONYM A term having a different form but the same or nearly the same meaning as another term.

UPWARD POSTING The treatment of NARROW TERMS as if they are equivalent to, rather than the species of, BROAD TERMS. Used where the level of detail suggested by a term is considered too specific for this Thesaurus. The term is upward-posted to a broader PREFERRED TERM, eg, spa well USE SPA.

USE A link indicating the PREFERRED TERM(S) for a NON-PREFERRED TERM, eg, Cairn Circle USE ROUND CAIRN.

USE FOR (UF) Indicates the NON-PREFERRED TERMS covered by a PREFERRED TERM.

WHOLE-PART RELATIONSHIP This is where the name of the part implies the name of the whole. This type of relationship is included here where some NON-PREFERRED TERMS have been upward posted to a PREFERRED TERM covering the whole.

SELECT BIBLIOGRAPHY

Aitchison, J and Gilchrist, A, 1987. *Thesaurus Construction*, 2nd edn

Association for Industrial Archaeology, 1993. *Index Record for Industrial Sites, Recording th Industrial Heritage, A Handbook*

British Standards Institution, 1987. *British Standard Guide to Establishment and Development c Monolingual Thesauri*

Curl, James Stevens, 1993. *Encyclopaedia of Architectural Terms*

Knowles, D and Hadcock, R N, 1971. *Medieval Religious Houses in England and Wales*, 2nd edn

Lavell, C, 1989. *British Archaeological Thesaurus*

Oxford University Press, 1986. *The Shorter Oxford English Dictionary*, 3rd edn

Oxford University Press, on behalf of The Getty Art History Information Programme, 1994. *Ar and Architecture Thesaurus*, 2nd edn

Oxford University Press, on behalf of The Getty Art History Information Programme, 1994 *Guide to Indexing and Cataloguing with the Art and Architecture Thesaurus*

RCHME and Association of County Archaeological Officers, 1993. *Recording England's Past A Data Standard for the Extended National Archaeological Record*

RCHME and English Heritage, 1989. *Revised Thesaurus of Architectural Terms*

RCHME and English Heritage, 1992. *Thesaurus of Archaeological Site Types*, 2nd edn

Trinder, Barrie, 1992. *The Blackwell Encyclopedia of Industrial Archaeology*

CANDIDATE TERM FORM

PROPOSED BY   Name   _ _ _ _ _ _ _ _ _ _ _ _ _ _ _
             Organisation   _ _ _ _ _ _ _ _ _ _ _ _ _ _ _
       Date Submitted   _ _/_ _/_ _

CANDIDATE TERM   _

SOURCE OF TERM   _
(Published references, etc.
   Please include photocopy.)   _

OPTIONAL INFORMATION
Suggested relationships for Candidate term are
      Class(es)   _ _ _ _ _ _ _ _ _ _ _ _ _ _ _ _ _ _
      Scope Note   _ _ _ _ _ _ _ _ _ _ _ _ _ _ _ _ _ _
      Non-Preferred Term(s)   _ _ _ _ _ _ _ _ _ _ _ _ _ _ _ _ _ _
      Broad Term(s)   _ _ _ _ _ _ _ _ _ _ _ _ _ _ _ _ _ _
      Narrow Term(s)   _ _ _ _ _ _ _ _ _ _ _ _ _ _ _ _ _ _
      Related Term(s)   _ _ _ _ _ _ _ _ _ _ _ _ _ _ _ _

      Comments   _

_ _

_ _

Please copy this form and return it to:

Robin Bourne, Thesaurus Manager, Thesaurus Working Party,
National Monuments Record Centre, Kemble Drive, Swindon, SN2 2GZ

Telephone: (01793) 414824   Fax: (01793) 414606

Date considered by Working Party _ _/_ _/_ _

Decision _

Reasons _

_ _

Reply sent on date   _ _/_ _/_ _
             by   _

COMMENT FORM

SUBMITTED BY   Name   _ _ _ _ _ _ _ _ _ _ _ _ _ _ _
           Organisation   _ _ _ _ _ _ _ _ _ _ _ _ _ _

           Date   _ _/_ _/_ _

COMMENTS

Please copy this form and return it to:

    Robin Bourne, Thesaurus Manager, Thesaurus Working Party
    National Monuments Record Centre, Kemble Drive, Swindon, SN2 2GZ.

    Telephone: (01793) 414824   Fax: (01793) 414606

Date considered by Working Party _ _/_ _/_ _

Decision   _

Reasons   _
_ _
_ _
_ _
_ _

Reply sent on date   _ _/_ _/_ _
          by   _

THESAURUS DISPLAY

The Thesaurus display is divided into two: an alphabetical list and the class lists, both using word-by-word arrangement.

It is anticipated that users of the Thesaurus will have differing levels of expertise and experience in using Thesaurus displays. Users who are unfamiliar with hierarchical displays and the general structure of a thesaurus are urged to read carefully all previous sections of the Introduction.

The alphabetical list

The alphabetical list shows the terms in alphabetical order and provides detailed information on their status and relationships.

Examples of alphabetical display

MARKET HALL		TERM (preferred and index term)
UF	Covered Market	USE FOR
SN	A purpose built covered market hall, usually 19th century.	SCOPE NOTE
CL	COMMERCIAL	CLASS (top term)
BT	MARKET	BROAD TERM
NT	CLOTH HALL	NARROW TERM(S)
RT	COINAGE HALL }	RELATED TERM(S)
	EXCHANGE }	

Tavern		TERM (non-preferred)
USE	PUBLIC HOUSE	USE [preferred term]

UNASSIGNED		TERM (preferred and non-index)
SN	Top term for the class. See UNASSIGNED class list for narrow terms.	

Terms can be preferred or non-preferred. Preferred terms are those selected for retrieval and appear in capitals. If a preferred term is intended for use in indexing records it is an index term and is shown alphabetically in bold type and capitals, eg, **MARKET HALL**. If a preferred term is only for retrieval via the Thesaurus, it is a non-index term and is shown in normal type and capitals, eg, UNASSIGNED.

Non-preferred terms are used only as 'lead in terms' to a preferred term in the Thesaurus and will not be used for indexing or retrieval. They are always shown in lower case type with initial capitals, eg, Tavern.

Entries listed underneath the term will be selected where relevant from the following:

USE	a link indicating the preferred term(s) for a non-preferred term, eg Tavern USE PUBLIC HOUSE
SN (Scope Note)	this gives limited definitions and indexing guidance where required
UF (Use For)	this indicates the non-preferred term(s) covered by a preferred term
CL (Class)	the top term of a hierarchy, eg, COMMERCIAL
BT (Broad Term)	Superordinate term(s) in the hierarchy, eg, MARKET is the broad term of MARKET HALL.
NT (Narrow Term)	Subordinate term(s) in the hierarchy, eg, CLOTH HALL is narrow term of MARKET HALL.
RT (Related Term)	This shows terms which are associated with but have no generic relationship to the term and which may also be of interest for retrieval, eg, COINAGE HALL and EXCHANGE are related terms of MARKET HALL.

The full hierarchy is not given in the alphabetical list but just the class term and one hierarchical level above and below the term if applicable. To see the full context of a term within a hierarchy users should consult the relevant class list.

If a term belongs to more than one class, then that term will be repeated in the alphabetical list ordered alphabetically by its class terms; eg,

BASILICA
    CL CIVIL
    RT FORUM

BASILICA
    CL COMMERCIAL
    RT FORUM

Where a term has more than one broader term, other than the class term, it is also repeated in the alphabetical list; eg,

BOUNDARY DITCH
    CL UNASSIGNED
    BT BOUNDARY

BOUNDARY DITCH
      CL UNASSIGNED
      BT DITCH

As only one level of broad term is displayed in each alphabetical list entry, some terms may appear to repeat erroneously. Scope notes indicate where this applies.

The class lists

The class list gives all the preferred terms belonging to the class and shows their superordinate and subordinate relationships. The same conventions are used in the class and alphabetical displays so that all terms in the class list are in capitals (preferred terms), with indexing terms shown in bold and non-index grouping terms in normal type. However, the class term is, in this list, displayed in bold in the header. The full multiple levels of the class can be viewed in this section.

Example of class list display

DEFENCE
                                                      CLASS
- - - - - - - - - -   TABULATION LINE
      SENTRY BOX   Narrow term of DEFENCE

      SERGEANTS MESS   Narrow term of DEFENCE

      SIEGEWORK   Narrow term of DEFENCE
         SAP   }   Narrow terms of SIEGEWORK
         SIEGE CASTLE   }

      SIGNAL STATION   Broad term of SEMAPHORE STATION
         SEMAPHORE STATION

      TANK TRAP   Narrow term of DEFENCE
- - - - - - - - - -   TABULATION LINE

Indentations under the class term reflect the broad to narrow relationships. The broad terms under the class term are indented six character spaces with subsequent narrow terms indented a further three character spaces at each level. A tabulation line appears at the top and bottom of each page to guide the user. The class term always appears above the tabulation line at the top of the page and is aligned on the first tab. The class term is repeated in this position if there is more than one page to the list. Terms immediately under the class term are aligned on the third tab; narrow terms of these terms on the fourth tab, and so on. A line space is also inserted between the first level broad terms as shown in the example above.

CLASS DEFINITIONS

AGRICULTURE AND SUBSISTENCE

Sites, buildings, structures, features and areas of land associated with cultivation, the rearing of livestock, gathering, hunting and fishing. This grouping includes farm based processing of foodstuffs and storage of agricultural produce.

CIVIL

Sites, buildings, structures and features associated with civil administration and law enforcement. This grouping includes local and central government, settlement specifically granted by the Crown or ruling administration but does not include manorial or seignorial settlement.

COMMEMORATIVE

Sites, buildings, structures and features or areas of land commemorating an historical event or personage.

COMMERCIAL

Sites, buildings, structures and features related to the sale or exchange and storage of goods or services. This grouping includes commercially operated catering and lodging premises, eg, hotel inn.

COMMUNICATIONS

Sites, buildings, structures and features associated with the transmission of information. This group includes signalling, broadcasting and telecommunications, but does not include transport except where there is a specific connection with communication.

DEFENCE

Sites, buildings, structures and features for the defence of, or offence against, civilian populations or armed forces. This grouping includes siege works, the storage of weaponry and ammunition defence training and military signalling.

DOMESTIC

Single dwellings or groups of dwellings for permanent, seasonal or temporary habitation together with related ancillary buildings, structures or features associated with occupation. This grouping includes commercial, military or religious residential sites. It also includes housing associated with industrial and transport workers. Where industrial activity may often be carried out in such premises the terms also appear in the industrial class, eg, weaver's cottage.

EDUCATION

Sites, buildings, structures and features relating to the provision of knowledge and skills.

GARDENS, PARKS AND URBAN SPACES

Planned urban or landscaped areas designed for aesthetic or recreational purposes, including all buildings, structures or features normally found therein and used for such purposes. Street furniture is also included here.

HEALTH AND WELFARE

Sites, buildings and structures associated with health (eg, treatment of the sick) or social welfare (eg, the alleviation of poverty), including all charitable foundations, such as almshouses, and all forms of social welfare defined by the state, such as workhouses, old people's homes etc.

INDUSTRIAL

Sites, buildings, structures or features related to the extraction or processing of raw materials and the manufacturing of finished goods, or the supply, storage and transmission of power.

INSTITUTIONAL

Sites, buildings and structures associated with private, political or professional organisations.

MARITIME

Sites, buildings, structures, features and craft (vessels) related to all maritime construction, navigation and shipping, including commercial shipping and the navy.

RECREATIONAL

Buildings, structures, features and areas of land related to sport (including hunting), leisure and entertainment.

RELIGIOUS, RITUAL AND FUNERARY

Sites, buildings, structures and features related to the practice of rituals and religious beliefs including funerary rites. This grouping includes ancillary buildings, structures, etc, associate with religious, ritual or funerary sites.

TRANSPORT

Sites, buildings, structures and features related to the conveyance of goods, or passengers. This grouping includes man-made routeways, and mechanical structures. Some terms for vehicles ar included for use when it is necessary to record such as monuments. Water craft are included i the maritime class.

UNASSIGNED

Buildings, structures, natural and man-made features that cannot be assigned to any one particula class, or whose function is unknown.

WATER SUPPLY AND DRAINAGE

Sites, buildings, structures and features relating to water supply, drainage and sewage disposal

AGRICULTURE AND SUBSISTENCE

- - - - - - - - - - - - - - - - - - -

AGRICULTURAL BUILDING
    APIARY
    ASH HOUSE
    BACK HOUSE
    BARK HOUSE
    BARK PEELERS HUT
    DOVECOTE
    DUCK HOUSE
    FARM BUILDING
        ANIMAL SHED
            CALF HOUSE
            CATTLE SHELTER
            CATTLE UNIT
            COW HOUSE
            DONKEY HOUSE
            OXHOUSE
            PIGSTY
            SHEEP HOUSE
            SHEEP SHEARING SHED
            SHELTER SHED
            STABLE
            STALLION HOUSE
        BARN
            BANK BARN
            BARN PLATFORM
            COMBINATION BARN
            COPPICE BARN
            FIELD BARN
            GRANGE BARN
            HAY BARN
            HOP BARN
            MIXING HOUSE BARN
            THRESHING BARN
            TITHE BARN
        BOILING HOUSE
        CHAFF HOUSE
        CHITTING HOUSE
        COMBINATION FARM BUILDING
        FARMHOUSE
        FODDER STORE
        GRAIN DRIER
        GRAIN SILO
        GRASS DRYING SHED
        HAYLOFT
        HUNGER HOUSE
        LAITHE
        LAITHE HOUSE
        LINHAY
        LONG HOUSE
        THRESHING MILL
    FOOD AND DRINK PROCESSING SITE
        BREWHOUSE
        BUTTERY
        CIDER MILL
        CIDER PRESS
        CIDER VAULT
        DAIRY
        FATTENING HOUSE
        FISH CELLAR
        FISH HOUSE
        FISH PROCESSING SITE
        GRANARY
        HOP HOUSE
        HOP KILN
        HOP STORE
        MALT HOUSE
        MALT KILN
        MILKING PARLOUR

- - - - - - - - - - - - - - - - - - -

AGRICULTURE AND SUBSISTENCE

MILKING SHED
OASTHOUSE
GREENHOUSE
HEMMEL
HEN BATTERY
HULL
POULTRY HOUSE
SHEPHERDS HUT

ANIMAL WASH
CATTLE WASH
HORSE WASH
SHEEP DIP
WASHFOLD

BEE BOLE

BEEHIVE
BEE SKEP

BIELD

CHURN STAND

CREW YARD

FARMYARD

FARMYARD CAUSEWAY

FISHING SITE
EEL TRAP
FISH FARM
FISH POND
FISHERY
FISH GARTH
FISH LADDER
FISH LOCK
FISH TRAP
FISH WEIR
COASTAL FISH WEIR
FISHERY MOUND
FISHING BAULK
NET HOUSE
NET LOFT
OYSTER BEDS

HEATED WALL

HILLTOP ENCLOSURE

HOGGERY

HUNTING SITE
DECOY POND
DEER COTE
DEER HOUSE
DEER LEAP
DEER PARK
DEER POUND
DEER SHELTER
FALCONRY
HUNTING FOREST
HUNTING LODGE
KENNELS
KILL SITE
PARK PALE
SHOOTING STAND

AGRICULTURE AND SUBSISTENCE

KELP PIT

LAND USE SITE
    ALLOTMENT
    CAIRN
        CLEARANCE CAIRN
    CAIRNFIELD
    COMMON LAND
    COPSE
    CROFT
    CULTIVATION MARKS
        PLOUGH MARKS
    CULTIVATION TERRACE
    FARM
        FARMSTEAD
        FERME ORNEE
        MANOR FARM
        MODEL FARM
        SILKWORM FARM
    FIELD
        CORD RIG
        FIELD BOUNDARY
        LYNCHET
            STRIP LYNCHET
        PLOUGH HEADLAND
        RIDGE AND FURROW
            BROAD RIDGE AND FURROW
            NARROW RIDGE AND FURROW
            STEAM PLOUGHED RIG
    FIELD SYSTEM
        AGGREGATE FIELD SYSTEM
        CELTIC FIELD SYSTEM
        CENTURIATED AREA
        COAXIAL FIELD SYSTEM
        ENCLOSED FIELD SYSTEM
        OPEN FIELD
        WATER MEADOW
    GARDEN
        BEE GARDEN
        HOP GARDEN
        KITCHEN GARDEN
        MARKET GARDEN
        NURSERY GARDEN
    GRANGE
        AUGUSTINIAN GRANGE
        BENEDICTINE GRANGE
        CARTHUSIAN GRANGE
        CISTERCIAN GRANGE
        CLUNIAC GRANGE
        GILBERTINE GRANGE
        PREMONSTRATENSIAN GRANGE
        TEMPLARS GRANGE
        TIRONIAN GRANGE
    INTERRUPTED DITCH SYSTEM
    LAZY BEDS
    MANOR
    MEADOW
    MESSUAGE
    ORCHARD
    OSIER BED
    PLANTATION
    PLANTATION BANK
    RANCH BOUNDARY
    REAVE
    SHIELING
    SMALLHOLDING
    VILLA (ROMAN)
    VINEYARD

WATERCRESS BED
WOOD BANK
WOODLAND
WOOD

MIDDEN
SHELL MIDDEN

OUTFARM

OX BOW STONE

PEN
BOAR PEN
BULL PEN

PILLOW MOUND

POUND
DEER POUND

RABBIT TYPE

RABBIT WARREN

SERPENTINE WALL

SHEEP FOLD

STACK STAND

STACK YARD

STADDLE STONE

STOCK ENCLOSURE

STORAGE PIT
GRAIN STORAGE PIT

SWANNERY

THRESHING FLOOR

TROUGH
CATTLE TROUGH
HORSE TROUGH

TURF STACK

VACCARY

VERMIN TRAP

CIVIL

· ·

BASILICA

BURH

CIVIC CENTRE

COASTGUARD STATION

COINAGE HALL

COMMUNITY CENTRE

CONFERENCE CENTRE

CONSTABLES OFFICE

CUSTOM HOUSE

CUSTOMS LOOKOUT

EMBASSY

FIRE STATION

FORUM

GOVERNMENT OFFICE
    LOCAL GOVERNMENT OFFICE
        COUNTY HALL

HOSE TOWER

HOUSES OF PARLIAMENT

LABOUR EXCHANGE

LEGAL SITE
    INNS OF CHANCERY
    INNS OF COURT
    JUDGES LODGING
    LAW COURT
        ASSIZE COURT
        CONSISTORY COURT
        CORONERS COURT
        COUNTY COURT
        COURT HOUSE
        COURT ROOM
        CROWN COURT
        DEBTORS COURT
        JUVENILE COURT
        MAGISTRATES COURT
        STANNARY COURT
    LEGAL CHAMBERS
    LEGAL OFFICE
    POLICE STATION
    PRISON
        CELL BLOCK
        DEBTORS PRISON
        HIGH SECURITY PRISON
        HOUSE OF DETENTION
        JUVENILE PRISON
        LOCK UP
        OPEN PRISON
        PRISON HULK
    PUNISHMENT PLACE
        DUCKING POND
        DUCKING STOOL
        EXECUTION SITE

· ·

GALLOWS
GALLOWS MOUND
GIBBET
SCAFFOLD
PILLORY
PRISON TREADMILL
STOCKS
WHIPPING POST

LIFEBOAT STATION

MANSIO

MANSION HOUSE

MAYORS RESIDENCE

MINT

MOOT

MUNIMENT HOUSE

OPPIDUM
ENCLOSED OPPIDUM
UNENCLOSED OPPIDUM

PARISH BOUNDARY

PUBLIC BUILDING
ASSEMBLY ROOMS
MARKET HOUSE
MEETING HALL
ASSEMBLY HALL
CHURCH HALL
CHURCH HOUSE
EGYPTIAN HALL
GUILDHALL
LEET HALL
LIVERY HALL
MARRIAGE FEAST HOUSE
MOOT HALL
PUBLIC HALL
SHIRE HALL
TOWN HALL
VERDERERS HALL
VILLAGE HALL
RECORD OFFICE

REGISTER OFFICE

TOWN
CIVITAS CAPITAL
COLONIA
MUNICIPIUM

TRINITY HOUSE

VICUS

WATCH HOUSE

- -

BATTLEFIELD

COMMEMORATIVE MONUMENT
    ANIMAL MEMORIAL
    CENOTAPH
    COAT OF ARMS
    COMMEMORATIVE BRASS
    COMMEMORATIVE STONE
        CENTURIAL STONE
        CORONATION STONE
        DATE STONE
        DEDICATION STONE
    EFFIGY
    ELEANOR CROSS
    HILL FIGURE
    NAMED TREE
    OBELISK
    PLAGUE MEMORIAL
    QUADRIGA
    ROSTRAL COLUMN
    TRIUMPHAL ARCH
    WALL MONUMENT
    WAR MEMORIAL

HISTORICAL SITE

- -

AUCTION HOUSE

BAKERY

BANK (FINANCIAL)

BASILICA

CHAMBER OF COMMERCE

CHANDLERY

CLEARING HOUSE

COBBLERS STALL

COINAGE HALL

COMMERCIAL ART GALLERY

COMMERCIAL OFFICE
    ASSAY OFFICE
    BOOKING OFFICE
    DRAWING OFFICE
    LEGAL OFFICE
    NEWSPAPER OFFICE
    PAY OFFICE
    TIMEKEEPERS OFFICE

CONFERENCE CENTRE

COUNTING HOUSE

EATING AND DRINKING ESTABLISHMENT
    BUFFET
    CAFE
    CHOCOLATE HOUSE
    COFFEE BAR
    COFFEE HOUSE
    EATING HOUSE
    LICENSED PREMISES
        BEER HOUSE
        CIDER HOUSE
        GIN PALACE
        PUBLIC HOUSE
            WINE LODGE
        WINE BAR
    PIE AND MASH SHOP
    RAILWAY BUFFET
    REFRESHMENT ROOMS
    RESTAURANT
    TEA ROOM
    TEMPERANCE PUBLIC HOUSE

EEL STALL

EXCHANGE
    COAL EXCHANGE
    CORN EXCHANGE
    COTTON EXCHANGE
    HOP EXCHANGE
    STOCK EXCHANGE
    WOOL EXCHANGE

EXHIBITION HALL
    AGRICULTURAL HALL
    HORTICULTURAL HALL

FISH STONE

FORUM

GUEST HOUSE

GUILDHALL

HOTEL
    GRAND HOTEL
    MOTEL
    RAILWAY HOTEL
    SPA HOTEL
    TEMPERANCE HOTEL

INN
    COACHING INN
    DROVERS INN

KIOSK

LAUNDRETTE

LAUNDRY

LEGAL CHAMBERS

LIVERY HALL

MANSIO

MARKET
    ANTIQUE MARKET
    BUTTER MARKET
    CHEESE MARKET
    CLOTH MARKET
    FISH MARKET
    FLEA MARKET
    FLOWER MARKET
    FRUIT AND VEGETABLE MARKET
    LEATHER MARKET
    LIVESTOCK MARKET
    MARKET HALL
        CLOTH HALL
    MARKET HOUSE
    MARKET PLACE
    MARKET STALL
    MEAT MARKET
    METAL MARKET
    TIMBER MARKET
    WHOLESALE MARKET
    WOOL STAPLE

MILK DEPOT

PAWNSHOP
    PLEDGE DEPOT

PETROL STATION

PHOTOGRAPHIC GALLERY

POST OFFICE

SERVICE STATION

SHAMBLES

- - - - - - - - - - - - - - - - - - - -

SHOP
    BAKERS SHOP
    BARBERS SHOP
    BEER SHOP
    BOOKSHOP
    BUTCHERS SHOP
    CHEMISTS SHOP
    CLOCK SHOP
    CLOTHING SHOP
    CONFECTIONERS SHOP
    COOKSHOP
    COOPERATIVE STORE
    DELICATESSEN
    DEPARTMENT STORE
    DRAPERS SHOP
    FISHMONGERS SHOP
    FLORISTS SHOP
    GENERAL STORE
    GREENGROCERS SHOP
    GROCERS SHOP
    HAIRDRESSERS SALON
    HARDWARE SHOP
    MILLINERS SHOP
    OFF LICENCE
    PERFUMERY
    PIE AND MASH SHOP
    SUPERMARKET
    TAILORS SHOP
    TAKE AWAY
        FISH AND CHIP SHOP
    TOBACCONISTS SHOP
    WIGMAKERS SHOP

SHOPPING ARCADE

SHOPPING CENTRE

SHOPPING PARADE

SHOPPING PRECINCT

SHOWROOM
    MOTOR VEHICLE SHOWROOM
    PORCELAIN SHOWROOM

SMUGGLERS CACHE

STEELYARD

WAREHOUSE
    BONDED WAREHOUSE
    FISH WAREHOUSE
    GRAIN WAREHOUSE
    LEATHER WAREHOUSE
    RAILWAY WAREHOUSE
    RUM WAREHOUSE
    TEA WAREHOUSE
    TEXTILE WAREHOUSE
    TOBACCO WAREHOUSE
    WHOLESALE WAREHOUSE
    WOOL WAREHOUSE

WINE CELLARS

- - - - - - - - - - - - - - - - - -

FILM STUDIO

POSTAL SYSTEM STRUCTURE
    MAIL BAG NET
    PILLAR BOX
    POST BOX
    POST OFFICE
    SORTING OFFICE

RAILWAY LOOKOUT TOWER

RECORDING STUDIO

SIGNALLING STRUCTURE
    BEACON
        RADAR BEACON
        REFUGE BEACON
        SEA BEACON
    LIGHTHOUSE
    RAILWAY SIGNAL
    SIGNAL BOX
    SIGNAL STATION
        SEMAPHORE STATION
        SHUTTER TELEGRAPH
        SHUTTER TELEGRAPH STATION
    SIGNAL TOWER
        TIMEBALL TOWER
    TRAFFIC LIGHTS

TELECOMMUNICATION BUILDING
    BROADCASTING HOUSE
    RADIO STATION
    TELEGRAPH OFFICE
        CABLE REPEATER OFFICE
    TELEGRAPH STATION
    TELEPHONE EXCHANGE
    TELEPHONE REPEATER STATION

TELECOMMUNICATION STRUCTURE
    BROADCASTING CONTROL ROOM
    BROADCASTING TRANSMITTER
    POLICE BOX
    POLICE TELEPHONE PILLAR
    RADIO BROADCASTING STUDIO
    RADIO STUDIO
    RADIO TELESCOPE
    SATELLITE DISH
    TELEGRAPH POLE
    TELEPHONE BOOTH
    TELEPHONE BOX
    TELEPHONE POLE
    TELEVISION STUDIO

WATCH TOWER

DEFENCE

AIR RAID SHELTER

AIRCRAFT OBSTRUCTION

AMPHITHEATRE

ANGLE TOWER

ARMAMENT STORE
    ARMAMENT DEPOT
    ARMOURY
    ARSENAL
    MAGAZINE
        POWDER MAGAZINE
    MUNITION HOUSE
    ORDNANCE STORE

ARMY OFFICE

ARTILLERY GROUND

ARTILLERY SCHOOL

ARTILLERY TOWER

BAILEY

BARBICAN

BARMKIN

BARRACKS

BARRAGE BALLOON SITE

BASTION
    BASTION OUTWORK

BATTERY
    ANTI AIRCRAFT BATTERY
    COASTAL BATTERY
    SALUTING BATTERY
    SEARCHLIGHT BATTERY

BATTLEFIELD

BEACON

BLOCKHOUSE

BOOM TOWER

BREASTWORK

BUTTS
    ARCHERY BUTTS
    RIFLE BUTTS

CASTLE
    ADULTERINE CASTLE
    ARTILLERY CASTLE
    CONCENTRIC CASTLE
    KEEP
        SHELL KEEP
        TOWER KEEP
    KEEP AND BAILEY CASTLE
    MOTTE
    MOTTE AND BAILEY

DEFENCE

- -

      QUADRANGULAR CASTLE
      RINGWORK
      RINGWORK AND BAILEY
      SIEGE CASTLE

CHEMISE

CHEVAUX DE FRISE

CURTAIN WALL

DOME TRAINER

DRILL HALL

DYKE (DEFENCE)
      CROSS DYKE

EARLY WARNING STATION

ENCLOSED SETTLEMENT
      BURH
      HILLFORT
          BIVALLATE HILLFORT
          MINI HILL FORT
          MULTIPLE ENCLOSURE FORT
          MULTIVALLATE HILLFORT
          UNIVALLATE HILLFORT
      HILLTOP ENCLOSURE
          PALISADED HILLTOP ENCLOSURE
      MULTIPLE DITCH SYSTEM
      OPPIDUM
      PALISADED ENCLOSURE
      PROMONTORY FORT
          CLIFF CASTLE
      ROUND

FIELD KITCHEN

FIELDWORK

FIRING RANGE

FLANKER

FLANKING TOWER

FORT
      ARTILLERY FORT
      AUXILIARY FORT
      BASTION TRACE FORT
      FORT ANNEXE
      SAXON SHORE FORT
      STAR FORT
      VEXILLATION FORT

FORTIFICATION

FORTIFIED HOUSE
      BASTLE
      FORTIFIED MANOR HOUSE
      PELE TOWER
      TOWER HOUSE

FORTLET
      MILECASTLE
      MILEFORTLET

FORTRESS

- - - - - - - - - - - - - - - - - - - -

LEGIONARY FORTRESS

FRONTIER DEFENCE
CENTURIAL STONE
MILECASTLE
MILEFORTLET
TURRET
VALLUM

GATE TOWER

GLACIS

GUARDHOUSE

GUN EMPLACEMENT

GUNPOST

GYRUS

HORNWORK

INTERVAL TOWER

LISTENING POST

MARTELLO TOWER

MILITARY BASE

MILITARY CAMP
ARMY CAMP

MILITARY CANAL

MILITARY COLLEGE

MILITARY ROAD

MISSILE BASE

NUCLEAR BUNKER

OFFICERS MESS

ORDNANCE FACTORY

PALISADE

PARADE GROUND

PILLBOX

POSTERN

PRISONER OF WAR CAMP

RADAR STATION

RAMPART

RECRUITING STATION

REGIMENTAL DEPOT

RETENTURA

SCARP

DEFENCE

- - - - - - - - - - - - - - - - - - - -

       SCONCE

       SENTRY BOX

       SERGEANTS MESS

       SIEGEWORK
          SAP
          SIEGE CASTLE

       SIGNAL STATION
          SEMAPHORE STATION

       TANK TRAP

       TARGET

       TEMPORARY CAMP
          MARCHING CAMP
          PRACTICE CAMP

       TOWN DEFENCES
          TOWN GATE
          TOWN WALL

       TRENCH
          SLIT TRENCH

       UNDERGROUND MILITARY HEADQUARTERS

       WATCH TOWER

       WATER GATE

- - - - - - - - - - - - - - - - - - - -

DOMESTIC

- - - - - - - - - - - - - - - - - - - -

    ASH PIT

    BAILEY

    BAKEHOUSE
        COMMUNAL BAKEHOUSE

    BURNT MOUND

    BUTTER WELL

    CALEFACTORY

    CASTLE
        ADULTERINE CASTLE
        CONCENTRIC CASTLE
        KEEP
            SHELL KEEP
            TOWER KEEP
        KEEP AND BAILEY CASTLE
        MOTTE
        MOTTE AND BAILEY
        QUADRANGULAR CASTLE
        RINGWORK
        RINGWORK AND BAILEY

    COOKHOUSE

    COOKING PIT

    COTTAGE ORNEE

    DORTER

    DWELLING
        APARTMENT
        COUNCIL FLAT
        CRANNOG
        HOUSE
            HOUSE < BY FORM >
                A FRAME HOUSE
                BUNGALOW
                CHALET
                COURTYARD HOUSE
                DETACHED HOUSE
                END CHIMNEY HOUSE
                FORTIFIED HOUSE
                    BASTLE
                    FORTIFIED MANOR HOUSE
                    PELE TOWER
                    TOWER HOUSE
                GABLED HOUSE
                    END GABLED HOUSE
                    FRONT GABLED HOUSE
                HALL HOUSE
                    AISLED HALL
                    AISLED HOUSE
                        QUASI AISLED HOUSE
                        SINGLE AISLED HOUSE
                    CROSS PASSAGE HOUSE
                    CROSS WING HOUSE
                        DOUBLE ENDED HALL HOUSE
                        SINGLE ENDED HALL HOUSE
                    END HALL HOUSE
                    FIRST FLOOR HALL HOUSE
                    HALL AND CELLAR HOUSE
                    HALL AND PARLOUR HOUSE
                    OPEN HALL HOUSE

- - - - - - - - - - - - - - - - - - - -

     WEALDEN HOUSE
      SINGLE ENDED WEALDEN HOUSE
    HOUSE PLATFORM
    PILE DWELLING
    ROCK CUT DWELLING
    ROW HOUSE
     GALLERIED ROW HOUSE
    SEMI DETACHED HOUSE
    SPLIT LEVEL HOUSE
    STUDIO HOUSE
    TERRACED HOUSE
     BACK TO BACK HOUSE
      THROUGH BY LIGHT
     BACK TO EARTH HOUSE
     BLIND BACK HOUSE
    TIMBER FRAMED HOUSE
     BOX FRAME HOUSE
     CRUCK HOUSE
      BASE CRUCK HOUSE
     JETTIED HOUSE
      CONTINUOUS JETTY HOUSE
      END JETTY HOUSE
     WEALDEN HOUSE
      SINGLE ENDED WEALDEN HOUSE
    TOFT
    TOWN HOUSE
    VILLA (NON ROMAN)
    VILLA (ROMAN)
  HOUSE <BY FUNCTION>
    CARETAKERS HOUSE
    CHARTIST COLONY HOUSE
    CHORISTERS HOUSE
    CLERICAL DWELLING
     ABBOTS HOUSE
     ARCHBISHOPS MANOR HOUSE
     ARCHDEACONRY
     CLERGY HOUSE
     DEANERY
     MANCIPLES HOUSE
     MANSE
     PARSONAGE
     PRESBYTERY
     PRIESTS HOUSE
     PRIORS HOUSE
     PRISON CHAPLAINS HOUSE
     PROVOSTS HOUSE
     RECTORY
     SUBDEANERY
     VERGERS HOUSE
     VICARAGE
    COMMANDER IN CHIEFS HOUSE
    COMMISSIONERS HOUSE
    COUNCIL HOUSE
    COUNTRY HOUSE
    CURATORS HOUSE
    DOWER HOUSE
    ESTATE COTTAGE
    FARM LABOURERS COTTAGE
    FARMHOUSE
    FOREMANS HOUSE
    GRADUATE HOUSE
    GREAT HOUSE
    GROOMS COTTAGE
    GUEST COTTAGE
    HEADMASTERS HOUSE
    HEALTH WORKERS HOUSE
     DOCTORS HOUSE
     MATRONS HOUSE
     MEDICAL ATTENDANTS HOUSE

MEDICAL SUPERINTENDENTS HOUSE
SISTERS HOUSE
WORKHOUSE MASTERS HOUSE
INDUSTRIAL HOUSE
    APPRENTICE HOUSE
    CLOTHIERS HOUSE
    FOREMANS HOUSE
    FRAMEWORK KNITTERS COTTAGE
    HOSIERS COTTAGE
    LACEMAKERS COTTAGE
    MASTER HOSIERS HOUSE
    MASTER WEAVERS HOUSE
    MILL HOUSE
    MINE CAPTAINS HOUSE
    SMITHS COTTAGE
    WEAVERS COTTAGE
    WORKERS COTTAGE
LAITHE HOUSE
LONG HOUSE
MANAGERS HOUSE
MANOR HOUSE
MARITIME HOUSE
    BOATSWAINS HOUSE
    COASTGUARDS COTTAGE
    DOCK WORKERS COTTAGE
    DOCKMASTERS HOUSE
    FISHERMANS HOUSE
    LASCAR HOUSE
    LIGHTHOUSE
    LIGHTKEEPERS HOUSE
    MARINERS COTTAGE
    MASTER ROPEMAKERS HOUSE
    NAVAL CAPTAINS HOUSE
    NAVAL OFFICERS HOUSE
    ORDNANCE STOREKEEPERS HOUSE
    PIERMASTERS HOUSE
    PORT ADMIRALS HOUSE
    WHARFINGERS COTTAGE
MERCHANTS HOUSE
PRISON GOVERNORS HOUSE
RANGERS HOUSE
REGISTRARS HOUSE
SQUATTERS COTTAGE
STEWARDS HOUSE
TEACHERS HOUSE
TRANSPORT WORKERS HOUSE
    BRIDGE KEEPERS COTTAGE
    CANAL WORKERS COTTAGE
    COACHMANS COTTAGE
    CROSSING KEEPERS COTTAGE
    FERRYKEEPERS COTTAGE
    INCLINE KEEPERS COTTAGE
    LENGTHMANS COTTAGE
    LOCK KEEPERS COTTAGE
    RAILWAY WORKERS COTTAGE
    RAILWAY WORKERS HOUSE
    STATION MASTERS HOUSE
    TOLL HOUSE
    WHARFINGERS COTTAGE
TREASURERS HOUSE
VERDERERS COTTAGE
WATERWORKS COTTAGE
HOVEL
HUT
    BARK PEELERS HUT
    CHARCOAL BURNERS HUT
    HUT CIRCLE
    HUT PLATFORM
    SHEPHERDS HUT

DOMESTIC

        TRANSHUMANCE HUT
        WOODWORKERS HUT
    LOG CABIN
    MAISONETTE
    MODEL DWELLING
    MULTIPLE DWELLING
        CLUSTER BLOCK
        CLUSTER HOUSE
        FLATS
            COUNCIL FLATS
            MANSION FLATS
        MEWS
        ROW
            GALLERIED ROW
            NAILERS ROW
        TENEMENT BLOCK
        TENEMENT HOUSE
        TERRACE
            BACK TO BACK TERRACE
            BACK TO EARTH TERRACE
            BLIND BACK TERRACE
            STEPPED TERRACE
            WEALDEN TERRACE
    PALACE
        ABBOTS SUMMER PALACE
        ARCHBISHOPS PALACE
        BISHOPS PALACE
            BISHOPS SUMMER PALACE
        ROYAL PALACE
    PREFAB
    ROCK SHELTER

ESTATE LAUNDRY

FISH TANK

FOGOU

FRATER

GRUBENHAUS

HUNTING LODGE

HYPOCAUST

ICEHOUSE

KENNELS

KITCHEN

LARDER
    GAME LARDER

MIDDEN
    SHELL MIDDEN

MOAT

REFECTORY

RESIDENTIAL BUILDING
    ALMSHOUSE
    BARRACKS
    BOTHY
        MINERS BOTHY
    CHILDRENS HOME
        HANDICAPPED CHILDRENS HOME

DOMESTIC

    CONVALESCENT HOME
    COTTAGE HOME
    GUEST HOUSE
    HALL OF RESIDENCE
    HOSTEL
        CHRISTIAN ASSOCIATION HOSTEL
        DOCTORS HOSTEL
        HOMELESS HOSTEL
        JAGGERS HOSTEL
        WORKERS HOSTEL
        YOUTH HOSTEL
    HOTEL
        GRAND HOTEL
        MOTEL
        RAILWAY HOTEL
        SPA HOTEL
        TEMPERANCE HOTEL
    INN
        COACHING INN
        DROVERS INN
    JUDGES LODGINGS
    LODGING HOUSE
    LODGINGS
        COLLEGE LODGINGS
        STABLEHANDS LODGINGS
    MAYORS RESIDENCE
    NURSES HOSTEL
    NURSING HOME
    ORPHANAGE
    SERVICES HOME
    TENANTS HALL
    WORKHOUSE

RUBBISH PIT

SADDLERY

SETTLEMENT
    CONSTRUCTION CAMP
    ENCLOSED SETTLEMENT
        BANJO ENCLOSURE
        BURH
        CLOTHES LINE ENCLOSURE
        ENCLOSED HUT CIRCLE SETTLEMENT
        ENCLOSED OPPIDUM
        ENCLOSED PLATFORM SETTLEMENT
        HILLFORT
            BIVALLATE HILLFORT
            MINI HILL FORT
            MULTIPLE ENCLOSURE FORT
            MULTIVALLATE HILLFORT
            UNIVALLATE HILLFORT
        HILLTOP ENCLOSURE
            PALISADED HILLTOP ENCLOSURE
        PALISADED HOMESTEAD
        PALISADED SETTLEMENT
        PROMONTORY FORT
            CLIFF CASTLE
        ROUND
    HAMLET
    HOUSING ESTATE
    HUT CIRCLE SETTLEMENT
        ENCLOSED HUT CIRCLE SETTLEMENT
        UNENCLOSED HUT CIRCLE SETTLEMENT
    LINEAR SETTLEMENT
    MODEL SETTLEMENT
        CHARTIST LAND COLONY
        ESTATE VILLAGE
        GARDEN SUBURB

- -

            GARDEN VILLAGE
            MORAVIAN SETTLEMENT
            RESORT VILLAGE
            UTOPIAN COMMUNITY VILLAGE
            WORKERS VILLAGE
OPEN SITE
OPPIDUM
            ENCLOSED OPPIDUM
            UNENCLOSED OPPIDUM
PALISADED ENCLOSURE
            PALISADED HILLTOP ENCLOSURE
PLATFORM SETTLEMENT
            ENCLOSED PLATFORM SETTLEMENT
            UNENCLOSED PLATFORM SETTLEMENT
SCOOPED SETTLEMENT
SQUATTER SETTLEMENT
TENEMENT
TOWN
            CIVITAS CAPITAL
            COLONIA
            MUNICIPIUM
UNENCLOSED SETTLEMENT
            LAKE VILLAGE
            UNENCLOSED HUT CIRCLE SETTLEMENT
            UNENCLOSED OPPIDUM
            UNENCLOSED PLATFORM SETTLEMENT
VICUS
VILL
VILLAGE
            AGGREGATE VILLAGE
            DESERTED VILLAGE
            GARDEN VILLAGE
            MIGRATED VILLAGE
            RESORT VILLAGE
            SHIFTED VILLAGE
            SHRUNKEN VILLAGE
            UTOPIAN COMMUNITY VILLAGE
            WORKERS VILLAGE

SHIELING

SOUTERRAIN

STILLING HOUSE

TACK ROOM

WASH HOUSE

- -

EDUCATION

ART GALLERY

CRAFT CENTRE

EXAMINATION HALL

EXHIBITION HALL

FACULTY BUILDING

GRADUATE HOUSE

GYMNASIUM (SCHOOL)

HANDICAPPED CHILDRENS HOME

HEADMASTERS HOUSE

INSTITUTE
  CHURCH INSTITUTE
  COLLIERY INSTITUTE
  COOPERATIVE INSTITUTE
  DEAF AND DUMB INSTITUTE
  FOREIGN LANGUAGE INSTITUTE
  LEARNED SOCIETY BUILDING
  LITERARY AND SCIENTIFIC INSTITUTE
    ATHENAEUM
    SCIENTIFIC INSTITUTE
  MATHEMATICAL INSTITUTE
  MECHANICS INSTITUTE
  ORIENTAL INSTITUTE
  PROFESSIONAL INSTITUTE
  RURAL INSTITUTE
  TECHNOLOGY INSTITUTE
  WORKING MENS INSTITUTE

LABORATORY
  MARINE LABORATORY

LIBRARY
  LENDING LIBRARY
  PUBLIC LIBRARY
  REFERENCE LIBRARY

MUSEUM

OBSERVATORY
  TELESCOPE (CELESTIAL)

POLYTECHNIC

READING ROOM
  MINERS READING ROOM

RESEARCH STATION

SCHOOL
  BOARD SCHOOL
  BOARDING SCHOOL
  CHARTIST COLONY SCHOOL
  CHURCH SCHOOL
  CONVENT SCHOOL
  ELEMENTARY SCHOOL
    DAME SCHOOL
    FREE SCHOOL
      BENEFICIAL SCHOOL
      CHARITY SCHOOL
      HOSPITAL SCHOOL

EDUCATION

· · · · · · · · · · · · · · · · · ·

           ORPHAN SCHOOL
           PAUPER SCHOOL
           RAGGED SCHOOL
        INFANT SCHOOL
        NURSERY SCHOOL
        PRIMARY SCHOOL
    PARISH SCHOOL
    PRIVATE SCHOOL
        PREPARATORY SCHOOL
        PROPRIETARY SCHOOL
        PUBLIC SCHOOL
    SCHOOL FOR THE BLIND
    SECONDARY SCHOOL
        COMPREHENSIVE SCHOOL
        GRAMMAR SCHOOL
        HIGHER GRADE SCHOOL
        SECONDARY MODERN SCHOOL
    SUNDAY SCHOOL
    TRAINING SCHOOL
        ARCHITECTURE SCHOOL
        ART SCHOOL
        ARTILLERY SCHOOL
        BALLET SCHOOL
        CHOIR SCHOOL
        COMMERCIAL TRAVELLERS SCHOOL
        DENTAL SCHOOL
        DIVINITY SCHOOL
        DOMESTIC SCIENCE SCHOOL
        DRAMA SCHOOL
        EXAMINATION SCHOOL
        FENCING SCHOOL
        INDUSTRIAL SCHOOL
        MUSIC SCHOOL
        PHILOLOGICAL SCHOOL
        RIDING SCHOOL
        TECHNICAL SCHOOL
        TRADE SCHOOL
    VOLUNTARY SCHOOL

SCHOOL HOUSE

SCHOOLROOM
    CLASSROOM

STUDENTS UNION

TEACHERS CENTRE

TELESCOPE DOME

TRAINING CENTRE

TRAINING COLLEGE
    AGRICULTURAL COLLEGE
    COMMERCIAL COLLEGE
    FURTHER EDUCATION COLLEGE
    HORTICULTURAL COLLEGE
    LADIES COLLEGE
    MEDICAL COLLEGE
    MILITARY COLLEGE
    NAVAL COLLEGE
    PEOPLES COLLEGE
    TEACHER TRAINING COLLEGE
    TECHNICAL COLLEGE
    THEOLOGICAL COLLEGE
    THEOSOPHICAL COLLEGE
    VILLAGE COLLEGE
    WORKING MENS COLLEGE

· · · · · · · · · · · · · · · · ·

EDUCATION

UNIVERSITY

UNIVERSITY ADMINISTRATION OFFICE

UNIVERSITY COLLEGE

GARDENS, PARKS AND URBAN SPACES

- - - - - - - - - - - - - - - - - - - -

ALLOTMENT

ARTIFICIAL MOUND
    PROSPECT MOUND

AVIARY

BACKYARD

BALUSTRADE

BANDSTAND

BORDER
    HERBACEOUS BORDER
    MIXED BORDER
    ROSE BORDER
    SHRUB BORDER

CASCADE

CATHEDRAL CLOSE

COMMON LAND

COURTYARD

CRESCENT

CUL DE SAC

DRIVE

FLORAL CLOCK

FLOWER BED
    CARPET BED
    RAISED BED

FOUNTAIN
    ORNAMENTAL FOUNTAIN
    SHELL FOUNTAIN
    TRICK FOUNTAIN

GARDEN
    ALPINE GARDEN
    AMERICAN GARDEN
    ARBORETUM
    BAMBOO GARDEN
    BOG GARDEN
    BOTANIC GARDEN
    BUTTERFLY GARDEN
    CABINET
    CHINESE GARDEN
    COLLEGE GARDEN
    COMMUNITY GARDEN
    COTTAGE GARDEN
    DUTCH GARDEN
    EGYPTIAN GARDEN
    FERNERY (GARDEN)
    FLOWER GARDEN
        ROSE GARDEN
    FORMAL GARDEN
    FRAGRANCE GARDEN
    HEATHER GARDEN
    HERB GARDEN
    ITALIAN GARDEN
    JAPANESE GARDEN

- - - - - - - - - - - - - - - - - - - -

GARDENS, PARKS AND URBAN SPACES

        KITCHEN GARDEN
        KNOT GARDEN
        MINIATURE GARDEN
        MOORISH GARDEN
        NURSERY GARDEN
        ORNAMENTAL GARDEN
        PARTERRE
        PHYSIC GARDEN
        PINETUM
        ROCK GARDEN
        SCULPTURE GARDEN
        SPRING GARDEN
        SUNKEN GARDEN
        SWISS GARDEN
        TERRACED GARDEN
        TOPIARY GARDEN
        TUDOR GARDEN
        VEGETABLE GARDEN
        WALLED GARDEN
        WATER GARDEN
        WHITE GARDEN
        WILD GARDEN
        WINTER GARDEN
        WOODLAND GARDEN
        YEW GARDEN

GARDEN BASIN

GARDEN BUILDING
    BANQUETING HOUSE
    BELVEDERE
    BOAT HOUSE
    CASCADE HOUSE
    COTTAGE ORNEE
    EXEDRA
    FERME ORNEE
    FISHING LODGE
    FOLLY
    FOUNTAIN HOUSE
    GARDEN HOUSE
    GARDEN SHED
    GARDEN TEMPLE
        DORIC TEMPLE
        IONIC TEMPLE
        OCTAGONAL TEMPLE
    GATE LODGE
    GAZEBO
    GLASSHOUSE
        CAMELLIA HOUSE
        CONSERVATORY
        FERNERY (GLASSHOUSE)
        GREENHOUSE
        HOTHOUSE
        ORANGERY
        ORCHARD HOUSE
        PALM HOUSE
        PINERY
        TEMPERATE HOUSE
        VINERY
        WATER LILY HOUSE
    HERBARIUM
    HERMITAGE
    ICEHOUSE
    LAITERIE
    LOGGIA
    MOSS HOUSE
    PAGODA
    POTTING SHED
    PROSPECT TOWER

GARDENS, PARKS AND URBAN SPACES

$\cdot \quad \cdot \quad \cdot \quad \cdot \quad \cdot \quad \cdot \quad \cdot \quad \cdot \quad \cdot \quad \cdot \quad \cdot \quad \cdot \quad \cdot \quad \cdot \quad \cdot \quad \cdot \quad \cdot \quad \cdot$

     ROOT HOUSE
     ROTUNDA
         IONIC ROTUNDA
     SUMMERHOUSE
     SWISS COTTAGE
     TREE HOUSE

GARDEN FEATURE

GARDEN ORNAMENT
     BIRD BATH
     GARDEN SEAT
         CAMOMILE SEAT
         TURFED SEAT
     HERM
     OBELISK
     SCULPTURE
         BUST
         STATUE
     SPHINX
     SUNDIAL
     SUNSHINE RECORDER
     URN
     VASE

GARDEN PATH

GARDEN RETREAT
     ARBOUR
         TUNNEL ARBOUR

GARDEN STEPS
     TURFED STEPS

GARDEN TERRACE

GARDEN WALL

GRILLE

GROTTO
     NYMPHAEUM
     SHELL GROTTO

HA HA

HEATED WALL

ISLAND

KISSING GATE

LAKE
     BOATING LAKE
     ORNAMENTAL LAKE

LAWN
     CAMOMILE LAWN
     CROQUET LAWN
     TERRACED LAWN

MAZE
     HEDGE MAZE
     TURF MAZE

OPEN AIR THEATRE

ORNAMENTAL CANAL

$\cdot \quad \cdot \quad \cdot \quad \cdot \quad \cdot \quad \cdot \quad \cdot \quad \cdot \quad \cdot \quad \cdot \quad \cdot \quad \cdot \quad \cdot \quad \cdot \quad \cdot \quad \cdot \quad \cdot \quad \cdot$

GARDENS, PARKS AND URBAN SPACES

ORNAMENTAL POND

PALISSADE

PARK
    DEER PARK
    HUNTING PARK
    LANDSCAPE PARK
    PUBLIC PARK
    ROYAL PARK

PARK PALE

PARK SHELTER

PARK WALL

PATIO

PAVILION
    BOWLING GREEN PAVILION
    CHINESE PAVILION
    FISHING PAVILION
    MOORISH PAVILION
    REFRESHMENT PAVILION
    SPORTS PAVILION
    WATER PAVILION

PERGOLA

PLANTATION

POOL
    SWIMMING POOL

PORTERS REST

ROCK BRIDGE

ROCKERY

SERPENTINE WALL

SHELL BRIDGE

SHRUBBERY
    BOSQUET

STREET FURNITURE
    BENCH
    BOLLARD
    BOOT SCRAPER
    BUS SHELTER
    CANNON
    CANNON BOLLARD
    COAL HOLE COVER
    DUTY POST
        COAL TAX POST
    FIRE HYDRANT
    FLAGPOLE
    HOARDING
    INN SIGN
    LAMP BRACKET
    LAMP POST
    LETTER BOX
        PILLAR BOX
    LIGHT HOLDER
    MILEPOST

GARDENS, PARKS AND URBAN SPACES

· ·

      MILESTONE
      MOUNTING BLOCK
      PARKING METER
      PEDESTRIAN CROSSING
         ZEBRA CROSSING
      PLAGUE STONE
      POLICE BOX
      POLICE TELEPHONE PILLAR
      ROAD SIGN
      ROADSIDE LIGHTHOUSE
      SEDAN CHAIR LIFT
      SNUFFER
      STREET LAMP
         GAS LAMP
      TELEGRAPH POLE
      TELEPHONE BOOTH
      TELEPHONE BOX
      TELEPHONE POLE
      TELESCOPE (TERRESTRIAL)
      TETHERING POST
      TRAFFIC LIGHTS
      TRAM SHELTER
      TROUGH
         DOG TROUGH
         HORSE TROUGH
      WATCHMANS BOX
      WAYSIDE PUMP
      WEIGHING MACHINE

TOPIARY AVENUE

TREE AVENUE

TREE ENCLOSURE RING

TREE MOUND

TREE RING

TRELLIS
    BERCEAU

URBAN SPACE
    CIRCUS (URBAN)
    MARKET PLACE
    PEDESTRIAN PRECINCT
    ROND POINT
    SHOPPING PRECINCT
    SQUARE
        PRIVATE SQUARE
        PUBLIC SQUARE

VILLAGE GREEN

WALK
    ALLEE
    ETOILE
    LIME WALK
    PERCEE
    PROMENADE
    SERPENTINE PATH
    SERPENTINE WALK
    TERRACED WALK
    YEW WALK

WATERFALL

WOODLAND
    BELT

GARDENS, PARKS AND URBAN SPACES

- - - - - - - - - - - - - - - - - - -

        CONIFEROUS WOODLAND
        COPSE
        DECIDUOUS WOODLAND
        GROVE
           ILEX GROVE
        MIXED WOODLAND
        ORCHARD

    ZOO

- - - - CONIFEROUS WOODLAND - - - - - - - - - - - -

- -

ALMONRY

ALMSHOUSE

AMBULANCE GARAGE

AMBULANCE STATION

ANIMAL WELFARE SITE
    DOGS HOME
    VETERINARY HOSPITAL
        HORSE HOSPITAL

BATH HOUSE

BATHS
    MINERAL BATHS
    PITHEAD BATHS
    SALT BATHS
    SLIPPER BATHS
    THERMAL BATHS
    TURKISH BATHS

CHILDRENS HOME
    HANDICAPPED CHILDRENS HOME
    ORPHANAGE

CLINIC
    MATERNITY CLINIC
    SCHOOL CLINIC

CONVALESCENT HOME

COTTAGE HOME

CRECHE

DAY CENTRE

DEAF AND DUMB INSTITUTE

DISINFECTOR HOUSE

DISPENSARY

EXERCISE YARD

HOMELESS HOSTEL

HOSPICE

HOSPITAL
    ACCIDENT HOSPITAL
    ADMISSION HOSPITAL
    CONVALESCENT HOSPITAL
    COTTAGE HOSPITAL
    DAY HOSPITAL
    GENERAL HOSPITAL
    HOSPITAL SHIP
    HYDROPATHIC INSTITUTE
    INCURABLES HOSPITAL
    MENTAL HOSPITAL
        HOSPITAL FOR EPILEPTICS
        HOSPITAL FOR THE MENTALLY HANDICAPPED
    MILITARY HOSPITAL
    NAVAL HOSPITAL
    ROYAL AIR FORCE HOSPITAL
    SANATORIUM

- -

HEALTH AND WELFARE

- - - - - - - - - - - - - - - - - - - -

SPECIALIST HOSPITAL
    CANCER HOSPITAL
    CHEST HOSPITAL
    CHILDRENS HOSPITAL
    DENTAL HOSPITAL
    EAR HOSPITAL
    EAR NOSE AND THROAT HOSPITAL
    EYE AND EAR HOSPITAL
    EYE HOSPITAL
    FOOT HOSPITAL
    GERIATRIC HOSPITAL
    HEART HOSPITAL
    HOMOEOPATHIC HOSPITAL
    HOSPITAL FOR FISTULA AND RECTAL DISEASES
    HOSPITAL FOR URINARY DISEASES
    INFECTIOUS DISEASES HOSPITAL
    LEPER HOSPITAL
    LOCK HOSPITAL
    MATERNITY HOSPITAL
    MINERAL WATER HOSPITAL
    NEPHROLOGY HOSPITAL
    NERVOUS DISEASES HOSPITAL
    NEUROLOGY HOSPITAL
    ORTHOPAEDIC HOSPITAL
    SEA BATHING HOSPITAL
    SKIN DISEASE HOSPITAL
    WOMEN AND CHILDRENS HOSPITAL
    WOMENS HOSPITAL
TEACHING HOSPITAL

HOSPITAL BLOCK
    ANTENATAL BLOCK
    CASUAL WARD BLOCK
    CHILDRENS WARD BLOCK
    CUBICLE BLOCK
    DAYROOM BLOCK
    DISCHARGE BLOCK
    EMERGENCY WARD BLOCK
    ISOLATION BLOCK
    MATERNITY BLOCK
    MENTAL WARD BLOCK
    PAVILION WARD BLOCK
    PRIVATE PATIENTS BLOCK
    PRIVATE PATIENTS WARD BLOCK
    RECEIVING BLOCK
    WARD BLOCK

HOSPITAL BUILDING

HOSPITAL DEPARTMENT
    CASUALTY DEPARTMENT
    DENTAL DEPARTMENT
    EAR NOSE AND THROAT DEPARTMENT
    EYE DEPARTMENT
    ORTHODONTICS DEPARTMENT
    ORTHOPAEDIC DEPARTMENT
    OUTPATIENTS DEPARTMENT
    PATHOLOGY DEPARTMENT
    PHYSIOTHERAPY DEPARTMENT

HOSPITAL LAUNDRY

INFIRMARY

LEECH HOUSE

MEDICAL CENTRE

MEDICAL COLLEGE

- - - - - - - - - - - - - - - - - - - -

MISSION HALL

NURSERY

NURSES TRAINING SCHOOL

NURSING HOME

OCCUPATIONAL THERAPY UNIT

OPERATING THEATRE

PATIENTS VILLA

PHARMACY

PLAGUE STONE

PUBLIC CONVENIENCE

PUMP ROOMS

RADIUM INSTITUTE

SOUP KITCHEN

SPA

SPA HOTEL

SPA PAVILION

STONE BREAKING YARD
    BUNK

SURGERY

TUBERCULOSIS CHALET

VENEREAL DISEASE UNIT

WASH HOUSE
    PUBLIC WASH HOUSE

WORKHOUSE

ANIMAL PRODUCT SITE
    BONE MILL
    FLEECING SHOP
    GLUE FACTORY
    HORN WORKING SITE
        HORNCORE PIT
    HORSEHAIR FACTORY
    LEATHER INDUSTRY SITE
        CURRIERY
        LEATHER DRYING SHED
        LEATHER FACTORY
        LEATHER WORKERS SHOP
        LEATHER WORKING SITE
        STEEPING PIT
        TANNERY
        TANNING PIT
        WASHING PIT
    SMOKE HOUSE
    SOAKING PIT
    SOAP FACTORY
    TALLOW FACTORY

ARMAMENT MANUFACTURING SITE
    ARSENAL
    CANNON BORING MILL
    GUN TESTING SHOP
    GUNPOWDER MIXING HOUSE
    GUNPOWDER WORKS
    MUNITIONS FACTORY
    ORDNANCE FACTORY
    ORDNANCE YARD
    PROVING HOUSE
    SHOT TOWER

CASTING HOUSE

CHARCOAL STORE

CHEMICAL INDUSTRY SITE
    CHEMICAL PRODUCT SITE
        BLACKING FACTORY
        CANDLE FACTORY
        CANDLE WORKS
        PERFUMERY
        PLASTICS FACTORY
        RUBBER WORKS
        SOAP FACTORY
        TAR WORKS
        WAX FACTORY
        WOOD CHEMICAL WORKS
    CHEMICAL PRODUCTION SITE
        ACID TOWER
        ACID WORKS
        AGRICULTURAL CHEMICAL SITE
            FERTILISER STOREHOUSE
            FERTILISER WORKS
                SUPERPHOSPHATE FACTORY
            LIME KILN
            NITRATE WORKS
            POTASH KILN
            POTASH MINE
        ALKALI WORKS
        ARSENIC WORKS
        BLEACH WORKS
        CHEMICAL WORKS
        DISTILLATION PLANT
        DYE AND PIGMENT SITE
            ALUM HOUSE

INDUSTRIAL

ALUM WORKS
    STEEPING TANK
COLOUR HOUSE
COLOUR MILL
COPPERAS WORKS
DYE WORKS
    ARTIFICAL DYE WORKS
FULLERS EARTH PIT
MARL PIT
OCHRE PIT
PAINT FACTORY
ELLING HEARTH
EXPLOSIVES SITE
    CORNING HOUSE
    EXPLOSIVES FACTORY
    GLAZE AND REEL HOUSE
    GREEN CHARGE HOUSE
    GUNPOWDER DRYING HOUSE
    GUNPOWDER WORKS
    INCORPORATING MILL
    NITRE BED
    NITROGLYCERINE WORKS
    ORDNANCE FACTORY
    POWDER MAGAZINE
    PRESS HOUSE
    RIPE CHARGE HOUSE
    SALTPETRE STORE
    SULPHUR STORE
    TESTING RANGE
LIME WORKS
PETROCHEMICAL SITE
    ETHER PLANT
    OIL DISTILLERY
    PLASTICS FACTORY
PHARMACEUTICAL CHEMICAL SITE
    HERB DISTILLERY
    PHARMACEUTICAL WORKS
PIPE BRIDGE
SALT WORKS
SODA KILN
SODA WORKS
LABORATORY
SALT STORE

CLOTHING INDUSTRY SITE
ARTIFICIAL TEXTILE FACTORY
BUTTON MILL
CLOG MILL
CLOTH CUTTERS WORKSHOP
CLOTHIERS WORKSHOP
CLOTHING FACTORY
CLOTHING WORKSHOP
COBBLERS WORKSHOP
GLOVE FACTORY
HAT FACTORY
HATTERS WORKSHOP
HOSIERY FACTORY
SHOE FACTORY
TAILORS WORKSHOP

CRAFT INDUSTRY SITE
ARCHITECTURAL ORNAMENT WORKSHOP
BASKET MAKERS WORKSHOP
BINDERY
BLACKSMITHS WORKSHOP
BRUSHMAKERS WORKSHOP
BUILDERS YARD
CARPENTERS WORKSHOP
CLOTH CUTTERS WORKSHOP

INDUSTRIAL

- - - - - - - - - - - - - - - - - - - -

       CLOTHIERS HOUSE
       CLOTHIERS WORKSHOP
       CRAFT CENTRE
       CRATEMAKERS SHOP
       CUTLERY WORKSHOP
       FRAMEWORK KNITTERS COTTAGE
       GOLDSMITHS WORKSHOP
       HATTERS WORKSHOP
       HOSIERS COTTAGE
       HOSIERY WORKSHOP
       JEWELLERY WORKS
       JEWELLERY WORKSHOP
       JOINERS SHOP
       LACEMAKERS COTTAGE
       LEATHER WORKERS SHOP
       LOCKSMITHS WORKSHOP
       NAILERS ROW
       POTTERS WORKSHOP
       SILVERSMITHS WORKSHOP
       STAINED GLASS WORKSHOP
       STATUE FOUNDRY
       TAPESTRY WEAVING WORKSHOP
       TILEMAKING WORKSHOP
       TOPSHOP
       WATCHMAKERS WORKSHOP
       WEAVERS COTTAGE
       WEAVERS WORKSHOP

DRESSING FLOOR

DRESSING MILL

DRESSING SHED

DRY HOUSE

DRYING HOUSE

ENGINE
       GAS ENGINE
       OIL ENGINE
       STEAM ENGINE
       TURBINE
           GAS TURBINE
           STEAM TURBINE
           WATER TURBINE
       WIND ENGINE

ENGINEERING INDUSTRY SITE
       AGRICULTURAL ENGINEERING WORKS
       ASSEMBLY PLANT
       ENGINEERING WORKS
       ENGINEERING WORKSHOP
       ERECTING SHOP
       FABRICATION SHED
       HEAVY ENGINEERING SITE
           BOILER SHOP
           BOILER WORKS
           FITTERS WORKSHOP
           FORGE
           FOUNDRY
           WHITESMITHS WORKSHOP
       LIGHT ENGINEERING SITE
           ELECTRICAL ENGINEERING WORKS
           INSTRUMENT ENGINEERING WORKS
           LIGHT ENGINEERING WORKS
           MACHINE TOOL ENGINEERING WORKS
           RADIO VALVE WORKS
       MACHINE SHOP

- - - - - - - - - - - - - - - - - - - -

INDUSTRIAL

- -

      PAINT SHOP
      PATTERN SHOP
      PLATERS SHOP
      POLISHING SHOP
      RAILWAY ENGINEERING SITE
          RAILWAY CARRIAGE WORKS
          RAILWAY ENGINEERING WORKS
          RAILWAY ENGINEERING WORKSHOP
          RAILWAY WAGON WORKS
          RAILWAY WORKS
          RAILWAY WORKSHOP
      SPRING SHOP
      TURNING SHOP
      VEHICLE ENGINEERING SITE
          AIRCRAFT ENGINEERING SITE
             AIRCRAFT ENGINE FACTORY
             AIRCRAFT FACTORY
             ROCKET MOTOR FACTORY
          BICYCLE FACTORY
          MOTOR VEHICLE ENGINEERING SITE
             CAR FACTORY
             CARRIAGE WORKS
             COACH WORKS
             LORRY FACTORY
             MOTOR CYCLE FACTORY

EXTRACTIVE PIT
   BELL PIT
   BRICK PIT
   BRICKEARTH PIT
   CHALK PIT
   CLAY WORKINGS
   COAL PIT
   COAL WORKINGS
   COPPER WORKINGS
   DENE HOLE
   FULLERS EARTH PIT
   GRAVEL PIT
   IRONSTONE WORKINGS
      IRONSTONE PIT
   JET WORKINGS
   LEAD WORKINGS
   MARL PIT
   MINERAL PIT
   OCHRE PIT
   SAND PIT
   STONE AXE FACTORY

FACTORY
   FACTORY <BY FORM>
      FACTORY UNIT
      FIREPROOF FACTORY
      MODEL FACTORY
      NORTH LIGHT FACTORY
      TENEMENT FACTORY
   FACTORY <BY PRODUCT>
      AIRCRAFT FACTORY
      BICYCLE FACTORY
      BLACKING FACTORY
      BRUSH FACTORY
      CANDLE FACTORY
      CANNING FACTORY
      CAR FACTORY
      CHEESE FACTORY
      CHINA FACTORY
      CHOCOLATE FACTORY
      CLOTHING FACTORY
      FISH PROCESSING FACTORY
      FLOORCLOTH FACTORY

- -

FOOD PROCESSING PLANT
FURNITURE FACTORY
GLOVE FACTORY
GLUE FACTORY
HAT FACTORY
HORSEHAIR FACTORY
HOSIERY FACTORY
LEATHER FACTORY
LINOLEUM FACTORY
LORRY FACTORY
MATCH FACTORY
MINERAL WATER FACTORY
MOTOR CYCLE FACTORY
MUNITIONS FACTORY
MUSICAL INSTRUMENT FACTORY
   ORGAN FACTORY
   PIANO FACTORY
NAIL FACTORY
NEEDLE FACTORY
ORDNANCE FACTORY
PAINT FACTORY
PIN FACTORY
PLASTICS FACTORY
RIBBON FACTORY
SCREW FACTORY
SHOE FACTORY
SOAP FACTORY
SUPERPHOSPHATE FACTORY
SWORD FACTORY
TALLOW FACTORY
TOBACCO FACTORY
TOY FACTORY
WALLPAPER FACTORY
WAX FACTORY

FOOD AND DRINK INDUSTRY SITE
BREWING AND MALTING SITE
   ALE STORE
   BREWERY
      VINEGAR BREWERY
   COOLING ROOM
   COOPERAGE
   COPPER ROOM
   FERMENTING BLOCK
   HOP KILN
   HOP STORE
   MALT HOUSE
   MALT KILN
   MALTINGS
   OASTHOUSE
   RACKING ROOM
   UNION ROOM
   VAT HALL
DISTILLING SITE
   DISTILLATION BLOCK
   DISTILLERY
   MASH HOUSE
   STILL HOUSE
FOOD PRESERVING SITE
   BOTTLING PLANT
   CANNING FACTORY
   COLD STORE
   CURING HOUSE
   FISH CELLAR
   FOOD DRYING KILN
      CHICORY KILN
   FOOD PRESERVING FACTORY
   ICE WORKS
   REFRIGERATED STORE

SMOKE HOUSE
FOOD PROCESSING SITE
    ABATTOIR
    BAKERY
    CONDENSERY
    CORN DRYING KILN
    CORN DRYING OVEN
    CORN MILL
    CURING HOUSE
    FLOUR MILL
    FOOD PROCESSING PLANT
    OIL MILL
    SUGAR HOUSE
    SUGAR REFINERY
FOOD PRODUCTION SITE
    CHEESE FACTORY
    CHOCOLATE FACTORY
    CONFECTIONERY WORKS
    MUSTARD MILL
MINERAL WATER FACTORY
MINERAL WATER WORKS
WINE AND CIDERMAKING SITE
    CIDER FACTORY
    CIDER MILL
    CIDER PRESS
    CIDER VAULT
    WINE PRESS
    WINERY

FUEL PRODUCTION SITE
CHARCOAL PRODUCTION SITE
    CHARCOAL BURNERS HUT
    CHARCOAL BURNERS SITE
    CHARCOAL BURNING PLATFORM
COAL MINING SITE
    COAL BUNKER
    COAL CLEANING PLANT
    COAL CRUSHER HOUSE
    COAL DROP
    COAL PIT
    COAL PREPARATION PLANT
    COAL SCREEN
    COAL TIPPLER
    COAL WORKINGS
    COALITE PLANT
    COKE OVEN
    COKE QUENCHING TOWER
    COLLIERY
    COLLIERY RAILWAY
    DUST EXTRACTION PLANT
    SCREENING PLANT
OIL REFINING SITE
    OIL DISTILLERY
    OIL PUMP
    OIL REFINERY
    OIL RIG
    OIL SILO
    OIL WELL
PEAT WORKINGS
    PEAT CUTTING
    PEAT STAND

FURNACE
ANNEALING FURNACE
GLASS FURNACE
    FRITTING FURNACE
METAL PRODUCTION FURNACE
    BLAST FURNACE
    BOLEHILL

INDUSTRIAL

- -

          BOWL FURNACE
          CEMENTATION FURNACE
          CRUCIBLE FURNACE
          CUPELLATION FURNACE
          ELECTRIC ARC FURNACE
          INDUCTION FURNACE
          IRON FURNACE
          LEAD FURNACE
          OPEN HEARTH FURNACE
          ORE HEARTH
          ROASTING HEARTH
          SHAFT FURNACE
              BLOOMERY
              CUPOLA FURNACE (SHAFT)
          SILVER HEARTH
          SLAG HEARTH
       REVERBERATORY FURNACE
          CUPOLA FURNACE (REVERBERATORY)
          PUDDLING FURNACE
          TANK FURNACE
       VENTILATION FURNACE

GRINDSTONE

HAMMER
    HELVE HAMMER
    TILT HAMMER

INDUSTRIAL BUILDING
    CHIMNEY
        VENTILATION CHIMNEY
    FIREPROOF BUILDING
    MILL
        BARK MILL
        BATTERY MILL
        BOBBIN MILL
        BONE MILL
        CANNON BORING MILL
        CLAY MILL
        COMB MILL
        CORN MILL
        CRAZING MILL
        CRUSHING MILL
        DRESSING MILL
        FEED MILL
        FLINT MILL
        FLOUR MILL
        INCORPORATING MILL
        LOGWOOD MILL
        LUMBER MILL
        MORTAR MILL
        MUSTARD MILL
        NEEDLE MILL
        OIL MILL
        PAPER MILL
        PLANING MILL
        PLASTER MILL
        PUG MILL
        ROLLING MILL
        SAW MILL
        SCREW MILL
        SCYTHE MILL
        SLITTING MILL
        SMELT MILL
        SNUFF MILL
        STAMPING MILL
        STARCH MILL
        STEAM MILL
        TEXTILE MILL

- -

INDUSTRIAL

THIMBLE MILL
THRESHING MILL
TIDEMILL
TIN MILL
TUBE MILL
WATERMILL
WINDMILL
WIRE MILL

INDUSTRIAL ESTATE

INDUSTRIAL HOUSE
APPRENTICE HOUSE
CLOTHIERS HOUSE
FOREMANS HOUSE
FRAMEWORK KNITTERS COTTAGE
HOSIERS COTTAGE
LACEMAKERS COTTAGE
MASTER HOSIERS HOUSE
MASTER WEAVERS HOUSE
MILL HOUSE
MINE CAPTAINS HOUSE
SMITHS COTTAGE
WEAVERS COTTAGE
WORKERS COTTAGE

INDUSTRIAL SITE

KILN
KILN <BY FORM>
BOTTLE KILN
CIRCULAR KILN
CLAMP KILN
COCKLE KILN
DOWNDRAUGHT KILN
HOFFMAN KILN
HORIZONTAL KILN
OCTAGONAL KILN
PYRAMIDAL KILN
ROMAN KILN
ROTARY KILN
SCOTCH KILN
SHAFT KILN
SPLIT SHAFT KILN
TRANSVERSE ARCH KILN
TUNNEL KILN
UPDRAUGHT KILN
KILN <BY FUNCTION>
BRICK KILN
CALCINER
ARSENIC CALCINER
IRON ORE CALCINER
CALCINING KILN
CHICORY KILN
CLAY PIPE KILN
COKE OVEN
DRYING KILN
CORN DRYING KILN
FOOD DRYING KILN
GYPSUM DRYING KILN
WOOD DRYING KILN
ELLING HEARTH
ENAMELLING KILN
HOP KILN
LIME KILN
MALT KILN
OASTHOUSE
POTASH KILN
POTTERY KILN

INDUSTRIAL

SODA KILN
TILE KILN
WASTER KILN

MARINE CONSTRUCTION SITE
    BOAT YARD
    CAMBER
    CHAIN PROVING HOUSE
    CHAIN WORKS
    DOCKYARD
        NAVAL DOCKYARD
    DRY DOCK
    FABRICATION SHED
    FLOATING CRANE
    GRIDIRON
    HALF TIDE DOCK
    HATCHELLING HOUSE
    HEMP STORE
    MARINE ENGINEERING WORKS
    MARINE WORKSHOP
        BLOCK MILL
        COLOUR LOFT
        HOOP HOUSE
        MAST HOUSE
        MOULD LOFT
        RIGGING HOUSE
        SAIL LOFT
        SHIPWRIGHTS WORKSHOP
        SLIP SHED
    MAST POND
    MASTING SHEAR
    PLATE RACK
    PLATERS SHOP
    RIVET AND TOOL SHOP
    RIVET AND TOOL STORE
    SHEER HULK
    SHEER LEGS
    SHIP REPAIR WORKS
    SHIPHOUSE FRAME
    SHIPYARD
    WET DOCK

METAL INDUSTRY SITE
    CASTING FLOOR
    FERROUS METAL EXTRACTION SITE
        IRONSTONE MINE
        IRONSTONE PIT
        IRONSTONE WORKINGS
    FERROUS METAL PRODUCT SITE
        CHAIN PROVING HOUSE
        CHAIN SHOP
        CHAIN WORKS
        COMB MILL
        CUTLERY WORKS
        EDGE TOOL WORKS
        IRON FOUNDRY
        LOCKSMITHS WORKSHOP
        NAIL FACTORY
        NAIL SHOP
        NEEDLE MILL
        PIN MILL
        SCRAP YARD
        SCREW FACTORY
        SCREW MILL
        SCYTHE MILL
        SHEET METAL WORKS
        SPRING SHOP
        SPRING WORKS
        STEEL WORKS

<pre>
                    CEMENTATION STEEL WORKS
                    CRUCIBLE STEEL WORKS
                SWORD FACTORY
                TUBE MILL
        FERROUS METAL SMELTING SITE
            BELLOWS HOUSE
            CEMENTATION FURNACE
            CUPOLA FURNACE (SHAFT)
            FORGE
                CHAFERY
                FINERY
            IRON ORE CALCINER
            IRON WORKING SITE
            IRON WORKS
            SLAG HEAP
        INDUCTION HEARTH
        NON FERROUS METAL EXTRACTION SITE
            ANTIMONY MINE
            ARSENIC MINE
            COPPER MINE
            COPPER WORKINGS
            GOLD MINE
            HUSH
            LEAD MINE
            LEAD WORKINGS
            MANGANESE MINE
            PROSPECTING PIT
            PROSPECTING TRENCH
            SILVER MINE
            STREAM WORKS
            TUNGSTEN MINE
            ZINC MINE
        NON FERROUS METAL PROCESSING SITE
            BOUSE TEAM
            BUDDLE
            BUDDLE HOUSE
            CRAZING MILL
            CRUSHING CIRCLE
            CRUSHING FLOOR
            CRUSHING MILL
            KNOCK STONE
            MEERSTONE
            ORE STONE
            ORE WASHING PLANT
            SETTLING PIT
            STAMPING MILL
            STAMPS
            TIN MILL
            TIN WORKS
                STREAM WORKS
            TINNERS CACHE
            TINNERS HUT
            WASH KILN
            WASHING FLOOR
        NON FERROUS METAL PRODUCT SITE
            ALUMINIUM SMELTER
            BATTERY MILL
            BELL CASTING PIT
            BELL FOUNDRY
            BRASS WORKS
            BRITANNIA METAL WORKS
            BRONZE FOUNDRY
            BRONZE WORKING SITE
            COPPER WORKING SITE
            COPPER WORKS
            GALVANIZING WORKSHOP
            GOLDSMITHS WORKSHOP
            JEWELLERY WORKS
            JEWELLERY WORKSHOP
</pre>

INDUSTRIAL

- -

    LEAD WORKS
    MINT
    PEWTER WORKS
    PLATING WORKS
    POLISHING SHOP
    SHOT TOWER
    SILVERSMITHS WORKSHOP
    TIN WORKS
    WATCHMAKERS WORKSHOP
    WHITESMITHS WORKSHOP
    ZINC WORKS
  NON FERROUS METAL SMELTING SITE
    ARSENIC CALCINER
    BLOWING HOUSE
    BRASS FOUNDRY
    BRASS WORKS
    BRONZE WORKING SITE
    CONDENSING CHIMNEY
    CONDENSING FLUE
    COPPER WORKING SITE
    COPPER WORKS
    CUPOLA FURNACE (REVERBERATORY)
    LEAD WORKING SITE
    LEAD WORKS
    SILVER HEARTH
    SILVER WORKING SITE
    SLAG HEARTH
    SMELT MILL
    SMELTER
      ALUMINIUM SMELTER
    SMELTERY
      SMELTING HOUSE
    ZINC WORKS
  ORE STORE
  ROLLING MILL
  SLITTING MILL
  WIRE MILL

MINERAL EXTRACTION SITE
  ALUM QUARRY
  ALUM WORKS
  BRINE PIT
  CHALK PIT
  CLAY EXTRACTION SITE
    BALL CLAY WORKS
    CHINA CLAY WORKS
    CLAY MINE
    CLAY PIT
  FLUORSPAR MINE
  FLUORSPAR WORKINGS
  GRAPHITE MINE
  GYPSUM MINE
  JET WORKINGS
  OCHRE PIT
  POTASH MINE
  SALT MINE
  SALTERN
  SAND AND GRAVEL EXTRACTION SITE
    GRAVEL PIT
    SAND PIT
    SAND WORKINGS
  STONE EXTRACTION SITE
    QUARRY
      STONE QUARRY
        GRANITE QUARRY
        GYPSUM QUARRY
        LIMESTONE QUARRY
        MARBLE QUARRY
        SANDSTONE QUARRY

- - - - - - - - - - - - - - - - - - - -

SHALE QUARRY
SLATE QUARRY
QUARRY HOIST
STONE CRUSHING PLANT
STONE DISPATCH BUILDING
STONE DRESSING FLOOR
STONE GRUBBING SITE
STONE WORKING SITE
FLINT WORKING SITE
JET WORKING SITE
MILLSTONE WORKING SITE
QUERN WORKING SITE
SHALE WORKING SITE
STONE AXE FACTORY
STONEMASONS YARD
STONE WORKS
UMBER WORKINGS
WITHERITE MINE

MINERAL PRODUCT SITE
ABRASIVES MANUFACTURING SITE
BRICK AND TILEMAKING SITE
BLUNGING PIT
BRICK DRYING SHED
BRICK KILN
BRICK PIT
BRICKEARTH PIT
BRICKFIELD
BRICKWORKS
BRICKYARD
CLAY MILL
CLAY PIT
CLAY PUDDLING PIT
FIRE CLAY WORKS
MOULDING HOUSE
PUG MILL
TILE WORKS
TILEMAKING WORKSHOP
CEMENT MANUFACTURING SITE
CEMENT KILN
CEMENT SILO
CEMENT WORKS
CONCRETE WORKS
GLASSMAKING SITE
BOTTLE WORKS
GLASS CONE
GLASS WORKING SITE
GLASS WORKS
PLATE GLASS WORKS
STAINED GLASS WORKSHOP
PLASTER MANUFACTURING SITE
MORTAR MILL
PLASTER MILL
PLASTER WORKS
ROTARY KILN
POTTERY MANUFACTURING SITE
BALL CLAY WORKS
BLUNGING PIT
CHINA CLAY WORKS
CHINA FACTORY
CLAY DRAINAGE PIPE WORKS
CLAY PIPE KILN
CLAY PIT
CLAY PUDDLING PIT
CLAY TOBACCO PIPE FACTORY
CRATEMAKERS SHOP
DECORATING SHOP
DIPPING HOUSE
FIRE CLAY WORKS

FLINT MILL
HANDLING HOUSE
MOULD STORE
MOULDMAKERS SHOP
MUFFLE KILN
MUG HOUSE
PIPE WORKSHOP
POT HOUSE
POTTERY KILN
POTTERY WORKS
POTTERY WORKSHOP
PUG MILL
SAGGAR MAKERS WORKSHOP
THROWING HOUSE
WASTER TIP
TERRACOTTA WORKS
WASTER KILN

MINING INDUSTRY SITE
DRIFT
HEAPSTEAD
METHANE PLANT
MINE
ANTIMONY MINE
ARSENIC MINE
BARYTES MINE
CALAMINE MINE
CLAY MINE
COLLIERY
COPPER MINE
DRIFT MINE
FLINT MINE
FLUORSPAR MINE
GOLD MINE
GRAPHITE MINE
GYPSUM MINE
IRONSTONE MINE
LEAD MINE
MANGANESE MINE
NICKEL MINE
OPEN CAST MINE
POTASH MINE
SALT MINE
SILVER MINE
TIN MINE
TUNGSTEN MINE
WITHERITE MINE
ZINC MINE
MINE BUILDING
LAMPHOUSE
MINERS BOTHY
MINERS CHANGING HOUSE
MINERS HUT
MINES RESCUE STATION
PITHEAD BATHS
MINE DRAINAGE AND VENTILATION SITE
ADIT
EXHAUSTER HOUSE
MINE PUMPING SHAFT
MINE PUMPING WORKS
MINE SHAFT
MINE LIFTING AND WINDING STRUCTURE
AERIAL ROPEWAY
HAULAGE ENGINE HOUSE
HORSE WHIM
MAN ENGINE
STEAM WINDER
STOWE
WINDER HOUSE

INDUSTRIAL

    WINDING CIRCLE
    WINDING GEAR
    WINDLASS
   SPOIL HEAP

  PACKING HOUSE

  PAPER INDUSTRY SITE
   BOARD MILL
   PAPER MILL
   PRINTING AND PUBLISHING SITE
    BINDERY
    PRINT SHOP
    PRINTING WORKS
   PULP MILL
   WALLPAPER FACTORY

  POWER GENERATION SITE
   ANIMAL POWER SITE
    CRANEWHEEL
    DONKEY WHEEL
    HORSE ENGINE
    HORSE ENGINE HOUSE
    HORSE WHEEL
    HORSE WHIM
    TREADMILL
     PRISON TREADMILL
    TREADWHEEL
    WINDLASS
   COAL GAS STRUCTURE
    GAS HOLDER
    GAS HOUSE
    GAS STORAGE TANK
    GAS WORKS
    PRODUCER GAS HOUSE
    PURIFIER HOUSE
    RETORT HOUSE
   ELECTRICITY PRODUCTION SITE
    ACCUMULATOR HOUSE
    ACCUMULATOR TOWER
    COOLING TOWER
    ELECTRICITY PYLON
    ELECTRICITY SUB STATION
    POWER STATION
     COAL FIRED POWER STATION
     GAS FIRED POWER STATION
     HYDROELECTRIC POWER STATION
     NUCLEAR POWER STATION
     OIL FIRED POWER STATION
     REFUSE DESTRUCTOR STATION
     STEAM TURBINE POWER STATION
    SWITCH HOUSE
    TRANSFORMER BOX
    TRANSFORMER STATION
     TRAM TRANSFORMER STATION
   ENGINE HOUSE
    ATMOSPHERIC ENGINE HOUSE
    ATMOSPHERIC RAILWAY ENGINE HOUSE
    BLOWING ENGINE HOUSE
    GAS ENGINE HOUSE
    HAULAGE ENGINE HOUSE
    HORSE ENGINE HOUSE
    HYDRAULIC ENGINE HOUSE
    STEAM ENGINE HOUSE
     BEAM ENGINE HOUSE
    TURBINE HOUSE
   HYDRAULIC POWER SITE
    HYDRAULIC ACCUMULATOR TOWER
    HYDRAULIC CRANE

- -

        HYDRAULIC BOX CRANE
        HYDRAULIC PILLAR CRANE
       HYDRAULIC ENGINE HOUSE
       HYDRAULIC JIGGER
       HYDRAULIC PIPEWORK
       HYDRAULIC PUMPING STATION
       HYDRAULIC RAM
       HYDRAULIC TIPPLER
STEAM POWER PRODUCTION SITE
       BOILER HOUSE
       COMPRESSOR HOUSE
       ECONOMISER HOUSE
       STEAM ENGINE
          BEAM ENGINE
             ROTATIVE BEAM ENGINE
          COMPOUND STEAM ENGINE
          HORIZONTAL STEAM ENGINE
          TRACTION STEAM ENGINE
          VERTICAL STEAM ENGINE
      STEAM MILL
      STEAM PLANT
      STEAM PUMP
      STEAM TURBINE
      STEAM WHIM
      STEAM WHIM HOUSE
      STEAM WINCH
      STEAM WINDER
      TURBINE HOUSE
TRANSMISSION RODS
WATER POWER PRODUCTION SITE
      DAM
        MILL DAM
      DRAINAGE MILL
      HAMMER POND
      LEAT
      MILL POND
      MILL RACE
        HEAD RACE
        TAIL RACE
      PEN POND
      PUMP HOUSE
      TIDEMILL
      TURBINE MILL
      WATER TURBINE
      WATERCOURSE
      WATERMILL
      WATERWHEEL
        WATERWHEEL <BY FORM>
          BREASTSHOT WHEEL
            HIGH BREASTSHOT WHEEL
            LOW BREASTSHOT WHEEL
          OVERSHOT WHEEL
          PITCHBACK WHEEL
          SCOOP WHEEL
          UNDERSHOT WHEEL
     WEIR
       TUMBLING WEIR
     WHEEL HOUSE
     WHEEL PIT
WIND POWER SITE
     WIND ENGINE
     WIND PUMP
     WINDMILL
       WINDMILL <BY FORM>
         HORIZONTAL AIR MILL
         POST MILL
         SMOCK MILL
         TOWER MILL
     WINDMILL MOUND

- - - - - - - - - - - - - - - -

SETTLING TANK

TEXTILE INDUSTRY SITE
    TEXTILE MILL
        ALPACA MILL
        ARTIFICIAL TEXTILE FACTORY
        BEETLING MILL
        BLANKET MILL
        BOMBASINE MILL
        CALENDER MILL
        CALICO MILL
        CALICO PRINTING WORKS
        CANVAS WORKS
        CARDING MILL
        CARPET MILL
        CLOTH DRESSING MILL
        COMBING WORKS
        COTTON MILL
        CREPE MILL
        DOUBLING MILL
        DRABBET FACTORY
        FELT MILL
        FINISHING WORKS
        FLAX DRESSING SHOP
        FLAX MILL
        FLOCK MILL
        FULLING MILL
        HEMP MILL
        JUTE MILL
        LACE FACTORY
        LINEN MILL
        MUNGO MILL
        RAG GRINDING MILL
        SAILMAKING WORKS
        SCRIBBLING MILL
        SCUTCHING MILL
        SERGE FACTORY
        SHODDY MILL
        SILK MILL
        SPINNING MILL
        TAPE MILL
        TAPESTRY MILL
        THROWING MILL
        TWEED MILL
        TWIST MILL
        WEAVING MILL
        WOOLLEN MILL
        WORSTED MILL
        YARN MILL
    TEXTILE PRODUCT SITE
        BLANKET MILL
        CARPET MANUFACTURING SITE
            CARPET MILL
            CARPET WEAVERS WORKSHOP
            FLOORCLOTH FACTORY
            LINOLEUM FACTORY
        FLOCK MILL
        LACE MANUFACTURING SITE
            LACE DRYING HOUSE
            LACE FACTORY
        RIBBON FACTORY
        ROPE MANUFACTURING SITE
            ROPERY
            ROPEWALK
            TAR HOUSE
            YARN HOUSE
        SAILMAKING WORKS
        TAPE MILL

TEXTILE SITE <BY PROCESS/PRODUCT>
    CARDING MILL
    COMBING SHED
    COMBING WORKS
    COTTON MANUFACTURING SITE
        COTTON MILL
            CALICO MILL
            CANVAS WORKS
    CREPE MILL
    DOUBLING MILL
    LINEN OR FLAX MANUFACTURING SITE
        DRABBET FACTORY
        FLAX BEATING STONE
        FLAX DRESSING SHOP
        FLAX DRY HOUSE
        FLAX DRY SHED
        FLAX MILL
        HEMP MILL
        JUTE MILL
        LINEN MILL
        RETTING PIT
        SCUTCHING MILL
    LOOMSHOP
    PICKER HOUSE
    PRESS SHOP
    RAG GRINDING SHED
    RAG MILL
    SCRIBBLING MILL
    SILK MANUFACTURING SITE
        REELING SHED
        SILK MILL
        THROWING MILL
    SPINNING MILL
    SPINNING SHED
    SPINNING SHOP
    TENTER GROUND
    TENTER POST
    TEXTILE FINISHING SITE
        BEETLING MILL
        BLEACHERY
        BLEACHFIELD
        CALENDER MILL
        CALICO PRINTING WORKS
        CLOTH DRESSING MILL
        CLOTH DRY HOUSE
        COLOUR HOUSE
        COLOUR MILL
        DYE HOUSE
        DYE WORKS
        FINISHING HOUSE
        FINISHING WORKS
        PRINTING SHOP
        TEXTILE CONDITIONING HOUSE
        TOPSHOP
        WASHING SHOP
        WEAVERS WORKSHOP
        WEAVING MILL
        WEAVING SHED
    TWIST MILL
    WILLEY SHED
    WOOL MANUFACTURING SITE
        ALPACA MILL
        BOMBASINE MILL
        FELT MILL
        FULLING MILL
        FULLING STOCKS
        GREASE WORKS
        HANDLE HOUSE
        MUNGO MILL

- -

          SERGE FACTORY
          SHODDY MILL
          TEAZLE SHOP
          TWEED MILL
          WOOL BARN
          WOOL DRY HOUSE
          WOOL STOVE
          WOOL WALL
          WOOLCOMBERS SHOP
          WOOLLEN MILL
          WORSTED MILL
      YARN DRY HOUSE
      YARN MILL

WASTE DISPOSAL SITE
    INCINERATOR
    REFUSE DEPOT
      REFUSE TRANSFER DEPOT
    REFUSE DESTRUCTOR STATION
    REFUSE DISPOSAL PLANT
    REFUSE DISPOSAL SITE

WOOD PROCESSING SITE
    TIMBER PROCESSING SITE
      LUMBER MILL
      PLANING MILL
      SAW MILL
      SAW PIT
      TIMBER SEASONING SHED
      TIMBER YARD
    TIMBER PRODUCT SITE
      BLOCK MILL
      BOBBIN MILL
      CARPENTERS WORKSHOP
      CLOG MILL
      COOPERAGE
      FURNITURE FACTORY
      JOINERS SHOP
      MATCH FACTORY
      SHIPYARD
      WHEEL MOULD
      WHEELWRIGHTS WORKSHOP
    WOOD PRODUCT SITE
      BARK HOUSE
      BARK MILL
      BARK PEELERS HUT
      BASKET MAKERS WORKSHOP
      BOARD MILL
      BRUSH FACTORY
      BRUSHMAKERS WORKSHOP
      COPPICE BARN
      LOGWOOD MILL
      PULP MILL
      WITHY BOILER
      WOOD CHEMICAL WORKS
      WOOD DRYING KILN
      WOODWORKERS HUT
      WOODWORKING SITE

WORKS

WORKSHOP

- -

CLUB
    GENTLEMENS CLUB
    POLITICAL CLUB
    SERVICES CLUB
    SOCIAL CLUB
    WORKING MENS CLUB
    YOUTH CLUB

INSTITUTE
    CHURCH INSTITUTE
    COLLIERY INSTITUTE
    COOPERATIVE INSTITUTE
    DEAF AND DUMB INSTITUTE
    FOREIGN LANGUAGE INSTITUTE
    LEARNED SOCIETY BUILDING
    LITERARY AND SCIENTIFIC INSTITUTE
        ATHENAEUM
    MATHEMATICAL INSTITUTE
    MECHANICS INSTITUTE
    ORIENTAL INSTITUTE
    PROFESSIONAL INSTITUTE
    RURAL INSTITUTE
    TECHNOLOGY INSTITUTE
    WORKING MENS INSTITUTE

MEETING HALL
    BRITISH LEGION HALL
    FREEMASONS HALL
    ODDFELLOWS HALL
    SECULAR HALL
    TEMPERANCE HALL
    TRADES UNION HALL

TRADES UNION BUILDING

MARITIME

- - - - - - - - - - - - - - - - - - - -

BEACH DEFENCE

CHANDLERY

DOCK AND HARBOUR INSTALLATION
    BOAT HOUSE
    BOAT STORE
    BUOY STORE
    CAPSTAN
        HAND CAPSTAN
    CAPSTAN HOUSE
    CUSTOMS LOOKOUT
    CUSTOMS POST
    DOCK
        DOUBLE DOCK
        DRAW DOCK
        DRY DOCK
        FLOATING DOCK
        HALF TIDE DOCK
        WET DOCK
    DOCK BASIN
    DOCK FLOOR
    DOCK PASSAGE
    DOCK SILL
    DOCKYARD RAILWAY
    DOLPHIN
    FAIRLEAD
    HARBOUR
        FLOATING BREAKWATER
        FLOATING HARBOUR
    KEEL BLOCK
    MARINA
    MOORING BOLLARD
    PORT
        CANAL PORT
        RIVER PORT
        SEAPORT
    PROMENADE
    SEA TERMINAL
        CONTAINER TERMINAL
        FERRY TERMINAL
        HOVERCRAFT TERMINAL
        OCEAN LINER TERMINAL
    SHIFTING HOUSE

FISHERMENS FASTENER

LANDING POINT
    BERTH
        CONTAINER BERTH
        OIL FUEL BERTH
    JETTY
        COAL JETTY
    LANDING HOUSE
    LANDING STAGE
    LANDING STEPS
    PIER
        LANDING PIER
    QUAY
        FALSE QUAY
    STAITH
    WHARF

MARINE CONSTRUCTION SITE
    BOAT YARD
    CAMBER
    CHAIN PROVING HOUSE
    CHAIN WORKS

- - - - - - - - - - - - - - - - - - - -

MARITIME

- -

DOCKYARD
  NAVAL DOCKYARD
DRY DOCK
FABRICATION SHED
FLOATING CRANE
GRIDIRON
HALF TIDE DOCK
HATCHELLING HOUSE
HEMP STORE
MARINE ENGINEERING WORKS
MARINE WORKSHOP
  BLOCK MILL
  COLOUR LOFT
  HOOP HOUSE
  MAST HOUSE
  MOULD LOFT
  RIGGING HOUSE
  SAIL LOFT
  SHIPWRIGHTS WORKSHOP
  SLIP SHED
MAST POND
MASTING SHEAR
PLATE RACK
PLATERS SHOP
RIVET AND TOOL SHOP
RIVET AND TOOL STORE
SHEER HULK
SHEER LEGS
SHIP REPAIR WORKS
SHIPHOUSE FRAME
SHIPYARD
WET DOCK

MARINE LABORATORY

MARITIME CRAFT
  COASTGUARD CRAFT
    REVENUE CUTTER
  COMMUNICATIONS CRAFT
    CABLE LAYER
    PACKET
    TELEGRAPH SHIP
  EXPERIMENTAL CRAFT
  FISHERIES PROTECTION CRAFT
    FISHERIES PROTECTION VESSEL
  FISHING VESSEL
    FACTORY SHIP
      FISH PROCESSING VESSEL
      WHALE PROCESSING SHIP
    FISHERMANS MISSION VESSEL
    FISHING DREDGER
      OYSTER DREDGER
    LINE FISHING VESSEL
      LONG LINER
    NET FISHING VESSEL
      DRIFTER
      SEINER
      TRAWLER
    POT HAULER
    SEAL FISHERIES VESSEL
    WHALER
      WHALE CATCHER
      WHALE PROCESSING SHIP
  HOUSE BOAT
  LEISURE CRAFT
    CRUISE BOAT
    CRUISE SHIP
    RACING CRAFT
  SAFETY CRAFT

- -

- - - - - - - - - - - - - - - - - - - -

        CHANNEL CLEARANCE VESSEL
          DREDGER
             BUCKET DREDGER
             CUTTER DREDGER
             GRAB DREDGER
             HOPPER DREDGER
             SUCTION DREDGER
          ICE BREAKER
        FIRE FIGHTING VESSEL
          FIRE FIGHTING TUG
        LIFEBOAT
        LIGHT SHIP
        PILOT VESSEL
        REFUGE BUOY
        RESCUE TUG
    SERVICE CRAFT
        ANCHOR HANDLING CRAFT
        BARRAGE BALLOON VESSEL
        DIVING SUPPORT VESSEL
        FUELER
        HARBOUR SERVICES VESSEL
          BUM BOAT
          DEPOT SHIP
          FLOATING DOCK
          HULK
             PRISON HULK
             SHEER HULK
             STORAGE HULK
        HOSPITAL SHIP
        SALVAGE VESSEL
        SURVEY VESSEL
        TENDER
        TUG
          FIRE FIGHTING TUG
          RESCUE TUG
          SALVAGE TUG
        VICTUALLER
        WATER CARRIER
    TRAINING SHIP
        CADET TRAINING SHIP
    TRANSPORT CRAFT
        CARGO VESSEL
          BARGE
             HOPPER BARGE
             LIGHTER
          COLLIER
          DRY BULK CARGO CARRIER
          FREIGHTER
             LIVESTOCK SHIP
             REFRIGERATED FREIGHTER
          TANKER
        CEREMONIAL CRAFT
        PASSENGER VESSEL
          CRUISE SHIP
          EMIGRANT SHIP
          FERRY
          LINER
          WATER TAXI
        STORESHIP
        TROOP SHIP
    UNASSIGNED CRAFT
        CANOE
        CORACLE
        CRAFT
          BOAT
          SHIP
        LOGBOAT
        RAFT
    UNMANNED CRAFT

- - - - - - - - - - - - - - - - - - - -

BLOCK SHIP
BOOM DEFENCE
PONTOON BRIDGE
PONTOON
PONTOON PIER
PONTOON
REFUGE BUOY
TARGET CRAFT
WARSHIP
AIRCRAFT CARRIER
AMPHIBIOUS OPERATIONS VESSEL
LANDING CRAFT
LANDING CRAFT INFANTRY
LANDING CRAFT SUPPORT
LANDING CRAFT TANK
LANDING CRAFT VEHICLE
CAPITAL WARSHIP
BATTLECRUISER
BATTLESHIP
DREADNOUGHT
FIRST RATE SHIP OF THE LINE
FLAG SHIP
GREAT SHIP
SECOND RATE SHIP OF THE LINE
THIRD RATE SHIP OF THE LINE
DECOY VESSEL
DUMMY WARSHIP
ESCORT
FIRESHIP
MINELAYER
MINESWEEPER
MINOR WARSHIP
BOMB VESSEL
CORVETTE
CRUISER
ANTI AIRCRAFT CRUISER
AUXILIARY CRUISER
BELTED CRUISER
LIGHT CRUISER
MASTED CRUISER
THIRD CLASS CRUISER
DESTROYER
FIFTH RATE SHIP OF THE LINE
FOURTH RATE SHIP OF THE LINE
FRIGATE
GALLEASSE
GALLEY
SIXTH RATE SHIP OF THE LINE
TORPEDO BOAT CARRIER
PATROL BOAT
MOTOR GUNBOAT
MOTOR TORPEDO BOAT
PRIVATEER
SHIP OF THE LINE
FIFTH RATE SHIP OF THE LINE
FIRST RATE SHIP OF THE LINE
FOURTH RATE SHIP OF THE LINE
SECOND RATE SHIP OF THE LINE
SIXTH RATE SHIP OF THE LINE
THIRD RATE SHIP OF THE LINE
SUBMARINE
FLEET SUBMARINE
HOLLAND SUBMARINE
MIDGET SUBMARINE
MINE LAYING SUBMARINE
SUBMARINE SEAPLANE CARRIER
WASTE DISPOSAL VESSEL
SEWAGE DUMPING VESSEL

MARITIME

- -

MARITIME OFFICE
 CUSTOM HOUSE
 DOCKMASTERS OFFICE
 EXCISE OFFICE
 HARBOUR MASTERS OFFICE
 PILOT OFFICE
 PORT AUTHORITY OFFICE

MILITARY COASTAL DEFENCES
 COASTAL BATTERY
 MARTELLO TOWER
 SALUTING BATTERY
 SAXON SHORE FORT

NAVAL COLLEGE

NAVAL OFFICERS MESS

NAVAL STOREHOUSE

NAVIGATION AID
 BEACON
  REFUGE BEACON
  SEA BEACON
 COAST LIGHT
 COASTGUARD STATION
 COASTGUARD TOWER
 LANDMARK TOWER
 LIFEBOAT STATION
 LIGHTHOUSE
  HIGH LIGHT
  LOW LIGHT
 SEA MARK
 TIMEBALL TOWER

NET HOUSE

NET LOFT

SCAVELLMANS CABIN

SEA DEFENCES
 BREAKWATER
 BULWARK
 GROYNE
 MOLE

SEAMENS CHURCH

SHIP BISCUIT SHOP

SHIPWRECK GRAVE

SLIPWAY

TRINITY HOUSE

WATER REGULATION INSTALLATION
 BALANCE BEAM
 CULVERT
  DOCK CULVERT
 DOCK BASIN
 DOCK GATE
 GAUGE HOUSE
 IMPOUNDING STATION
 LOCK
 LOCK CHAMBER
 LOCK GATE

- - - - - - - - - - - - - - - - - - - -

MARITIME

- - - - - - - - - - - - - - - - - - - -

LOCK SILL
SETTLING RESERVOIR
SLUICE
TIDAL BASIN
TIDAL DOOR
TIDAL LOCK
TIDE GAUGE

- - - - - **LOCK SILL** - - - - - - - - - - - - -

- -

AMPHITHEATRE

ANIMAL DWELLING
    ANIMAL CAGE
    ANIMAL HOUSE
        AQUARIUM
        AVIARY
        BEAR PIT
        DOLPHINARIUM
        ELEPHANT HOUSE
        GIRAFFE HOUSE
        KENNELS
        MONKEY HOUSE
        PARROT HOUSE
        PENGUIN POOL
        REPTILE HOUSE
        SEA LION POOL
    ZOO

ART AND EDUCATION VENUE
    ART GALLERY
    ARTS CENTRE
    CAMERA OBSCURA
    DIORAMA
    EXHIBITION HALL
    EXHIBITION PAVILION
    LIBRARY
    MUSEUM
    PANORAMA
    PHOTOGRAPHIC GALLERY
    PLANETARIUM

ASSEMBLY ROOMS

BAITING PLACE
    BADGER PIT
    BULLRING
    COCKPIT

BEACH HUT

BOATING LAKE

CINEMA

CIRCUS (RECREATIONAL)

CLUB
    GENTLEMENS CLUB
    SERVICES CLUB
    SOCIAL CLUB
    WORKING MENS CLUB
    YOUTH CLUB

CLUBHOUSE

EATING AND DRINKING ESTABLISHMENT
    BANQUETING HOUSE
    PUBLIC HOUSE
    REFRESHMENT PAVILION
    TEA HOUSE

FAIR

FISHERY

FISHING LODGE

- -

RECREATIONAL

GAMBLING SITE
    AMUSEMENT ARCADE
    BETTING OFFICE
    BINGO HALL
    CASINO (GAMBLING)
    GAMING HOUSE

HEALTH ESTABLISHMENT
    KURSAAL
    PUMP ROOMS
    SPA PAVILION

HUNTING SITE
    DECOY POND
    DEER COTE
    DEER HOUSE
    DEER LEAP
    DEER PARK
    DEER POUND
    DEER SHELTER
    FALCONRY
    HUNTING CLUB
    HUNTING FOREST
    HUNTING LODGE
    KILL SITE
    SHOOTING STAND

MUSIC AND DANCE VENUE
    BANDSTAND
    CONCERT HALL
    DANCE HALL
    DANCE STUDIO
    DISCOTHEQUE
    JAZZ CLUB
    MUSIC HALL
    OPERA HOUSE
    THEATRE
        OPEN AIR THEATRE
        STUDIO THEATRE

PIER PAVILION

PLAIN AN GWARRY

PLAYGROUND SHELTER

PLEASURE PIER

RECREATIONAL HALL

SCOUT HUT

SEASIDE PAVILION

SPORTS SITE
    ATHLETICS TRACK
    BOWLING CLUB
    BOWLING GREEN
    BOXING ARENA
    BUTTS
        ARCHERY BUTTS
        RIFLE BUTTS
    CHANGING ROOMS
    CROQUET LAWN
    FIRING RANGE
    FIVES COURT
    FOOTBALL PITCH
    FOOTBALL TERRACE

RECREATIONAL

GOLF CLUB
GOLF COURSE
HOCKEY PITCH
HOPSCOTCH COURT
NETBALL COURT
QUINTAIN
RACE TRACK
RACECOURSE
RACING CIRCUIT
RECREATION GROUND
    ADVENTURE PLAYGROUND
    ALL WEATHER PITCH
    CHILDRENS PLAYGROUND
    PLAYING FIELD
      POLO FIELD
    SPORTS GROUND
      CRICKET GROUND
      FOOTBALL GROUND
RIDING SCHOOL
ROWING CLUB
RUGBY PITCH
SAILING CLUB
SKATING RINK
SPORTS BUILDING
    BOWLING GREEN PAVILION
    CRICKET PAVILION
    CROQUET SHED
    FENCING SCHOOL
    GRANDSTAND
    GYMNASIUM (SPORTS)
    RACECOURSE PAVILION
    RACING STABLE
    SPORTS CENTRE
    SPORTS PAVILION
    TILTYARD TOWER
SQUASH COURT
STADIUM
SWIMMING POOL
TENNIS CLUB
TENNIS COURT
TILTYARD
WATER CHUTE

TELESCOPE (TERRESTRIAL)

YOUTH HOSTEL

ALMONRY

ALMSHOUSE

ALTAR

AMPHITHEATRE

BAPTISTERY

BELL TOWER
    CURFEW BELL TOWER

BIER HOUSE

CAIRN ALIGNMENT

CALVARY

CATHEDRAL PRECINCT

CAUSEWAYED ENCLOSURE

CAUSEWAYED RING DITCH

CEMETERY LODGE

CHAPTER HOUSE

CLOISTER
    DOUBLE CLOISTER

CLOISTER GARTH

COFFIN STONE

COLLEGE OF SECULAR PRIESTS
    CHANTRY COLLEGE
    COLLEGE OF THE VICARS CHORAL

COVE

CROSS
    BOUNDARY CROSS
    ELEANOR CROSS
    HIGH CROSS
    MARKET CROSS
    PREACHING CROSS
    TOWN CROSS
    VILLAGE CROSS
    WAYSIDE CROSS

CROSS INCISED STONE

CUP AND RING MARKED STONE

CUP MARKED STONE

CURSUS

EMBANKED AVENUE

FOGOU

FONT

FUNERARY SITE
    BARROW

        BANK BARROW
        CHAMBERED BARROW
            CHAMBERED LONG BARROW
            CHAMBERED ROUND BARROW
        D SHAPED BARROW
        LONG BARROW
            CHAMBERED LONG BARROW
        OVAL BARROW
        POND BARROW
        RING BARROW
        ROUND BARROW
            BELL BARROW
            BOWL BARROW
            CHAMBERED ROUND BARROW
            FANCY BARROW
                BELL DISC BARROW
                DISC BARROW
                SAUCER BARROW
        SQUARE BARROW
BURIAL
        ANIMAL BURIAL
        BAG BURIAL
        BASKET BURIAL
        BEAKER BURIAL
        BOAT BURIAL
        BOG BURIAL
        BUCKET BURIAL
        CART BURIAL
        CHARCOAL BURIAL
        CREMATION
            CINERARY URN
        GYPSUM BURIAL
        INHUMATION
            CONTRACTED INHUMATION
            CROUCHED INHUMATION
            EXTENDED INHUMATION
            FLEXED INHUMATION
        SHIP BURIAL
        TILE BURIAL
BURIAL PIT
        CHARNEL PIT
        CREMATION PIT
        PLAGUE PIT
BURIAL VAULT
        FAMILY VAULT
CAIRN
        BURIAL CAIRN
            CHAMBERED CAIRN
                CHAMBERED LONG CAIRN
                CHAMBERED ROUND CAIRN
            LONG CAIRN
                CHAMBERED LONG CAIRN
            RING CAIRN
            ROUND CAIRN
                CHAMBERED ROUND CAIRN
            SQUARE CAIRN
            TOR CAIRN
CATACOMB (FUNERARY)
CEMETERY
        BARROW CEMETERY
        CAIRN CEMETERY
        CREMATION CEMETERY
            ENCLOSED CREMATION CEMETERY
            URNFIELD
                ENCLOSED URNFIELD
        INHUMATION CEMETERY
            ANIMAL CEMETERY
            BAPTIST BURIAL GROUND
            CHURCHYARD

RELIGIOUS, RITUAL AND FUNERARY

· ·

           CIST GRAVE CEMETERY
           EASTERN ORTHODOX CEMETERY
           FRIENDS BURIAL GROUND
           HUGUENOT BURIAL GROUND
           JEWISH CEMETERY
           MILITARY CEMETERY
           MIXED CEMETERY
           PLAGUE CEMETERY
           ROMAN CATHOLIC CEMETERY
   CHAMBERED TOMB
      CHAMBERED BARROW
         CHAMBERED LONG BARROW
         CHAMBERED ROUND BARROW
      CHAMBERED CAIRN
         CHAMBERED LONG CAIRN
         CHAMBERED ROUND CAIRN
      ENTRANCE GRAVE
      GALLERY GRAVE
         TRANSEPTED GALLERY GRAVE
      PASSAGE GRAVE
      PORTAL DOLMEN
   CHARNEL HOUSE
   CIST
      LINTEL GRAVE
      LONG CIST
   COFFIN
      SARCOPHAGUS
      TREE TRUNK COFFIN
   COLUMBARIUM
   CREMATORIUM
   CRYPT
   GRAVE
      GRAVE SLAB
         CROSS SLAB
      GRAVESTONE
      PILLOW STONE
      SHIPWRECK GRAVE
   HOGBACK STONE
   HUMAN REMAINS
   LONG MOUND
   MAUSOLEUM
   MORT SAFE
   MORTUARY
   MORTUARY ENCLOSURE
   MORTUARY HOUSE
   OSSUARY
   TOMB
      ALTAR TOMB
      CANOPIED TOMB
      CHEST TOMB
      TABLE TOMB
      TOMBSTONE

GRAVESIDE SHELTER

GUEST HOUSE

HENGE

HENGE ENCLOSURE

HENGIFORM MONUMENT

HERMITAGE

HILL FIGURE

HOLY WELL

· ·

HOSPITAL
    LEPER HOSPITAL

INSCRIBED STONE

KERB CAIRN

KERBED BOULDER

LYCH GATE

MAYPOLE

MAZE
    HEDGE MAZE
    TURF MAZE

MISSION HALL

MONASTIC PRECINCT

MONUMENTAL MOUND

OGHAM STONE

PIT CIRCLE

PLACE OF WORSHIP
    CATHEDRAL
        ANGLICAN CATHEDRAL
        EASTERN ORTHODOX CATHEDRAL
        ROMAN CATHOLIC CATHEDRAL
        SECULAR CATHEDRAL
    CHAPEL
        BRIDGE CHAPEL
        CAUSEWAY CHAPEL
        CEMETERY CHAPEL
        CHANTRY CHAPEL
        CHAPEL OF EASE
        COLLEGIATE CHAPEL
        DOMESTIC CHAPEL
        GALILEE
        GUILD CHAPEL
        LADY CHAPEL
        MILITARY CHAPEL
        MORTUARY CHAPEL
        NONCONFORMIST CHAPEL
            BAPTIST CHAPEL
                GENERAL BAPTIST CHAPEL
                PARTICULAR BAPTIST CHAPEL
                SCOTCH BAPTIST CHAPEL
                STRICT BAPTIST CHAPEL
            CONGREGATIONAL CHAPEL
            INDEPENDENT CHAPEL
            METHODIST CHAPEL
                BIBLE CHRISTIAN CHAPEL
                CALVINISTIC METHODIST CHAPEL
                COUNTESS OF HUNTINGDONS CHAPEL
                FREE METHODIST CHAPEL
                METHODIST NEW CONNEXION CHAPEL
                PRIMITIVE METHODIST CHAPEL
                WESLEYAN METHODIST CHAPEL
            MORAVIAN CHAPEL
            PRESBYTERIAN CHAPEL
                SCOTTISH PRESBYTERIAN CHAPEL
                WELSH PRESBYTERIAN CHAPEL
            UNITARIAN CHAPEL
        PRIVATE CHAPEL

RELIGIOUS, RITUAL AND FUNERARY

- -

        ROMAN CATHOLIC CHAPEL
        ROYAL CHAPEL
    CHURCH
        ANGLICAN CHURCH
        CHRISTIAN SCIENCE CHURCH
        COLLEGIATE CHURCH
        DUTCH REFORMED CHURCH
        FORTIFIED CHURCH
        FRENCH PROTESTANT CHURCH
        HOSPITALLERS CHURCH
        HUGUENOT CHURCH
        MISSION CHURCH
        ORTHODOX CHURCH
            EASTERN ORTHODOX CHURCH
            SERBIAN ORTHODOX CHURCH
        PARISH CHURCH
        PENTECOSTALIST CHURCH
        REDEMPTIONISTS CHURCH
        ROMAN CATHOLIC CHURCH
        SEAMENS CHURCH
        SEVENTH DAY ADVENTISTS CHURCH
        SWEDENBORGIAN CHURCH
        SWISS PROTESTANT CHURCH
        TEMPLARS CHURCH
        UNITED REFORMED CHURCH
    MINSTER
    MOSQUE
    NONCONFORMIST MEETING HOUSE
        BRETHREN MEETING HOUSE
        FRIENDS MEETING HOUSE
        MEETING HOUSE OF JEHOVAHS WITNESSES
    PREACHING PIT
    SYNAGOGUE
    TEMPLE
        BUDDHIST TEMPLE
        MITHRAEUM

PLAIN AN GWARRY

POOR SOULS LIGHT

PRIEST HOLE

RECUMBENT STONE

RELIGIOUS HOUSE
    ABBEY
    CAMERA
        HOSPITALLERS CAMERA
        TEMPLARS CAMERA
    CELL
        ALIEN CELL
            AUGUSTINIAN ALIEN CELL
            BENEDICTINE ALIEN CELL
            CISTERCIAN ALIEN CELL
            PREMONSTRATENSIAN ALIEN CELL
            TIRONIAN ALIEN CELL
        ANCHORITE CELL
        AUGUSTINIAN CELL
        BENEDICTINE CELL
        CARTHUSIAN CELL
        CISTERCIAN CELL
        CLUNIAC CELL
        GILBERTINE CELL
        PREMONSTRATENSIAN CELL
    DOUBLE HOUSE
        AUGUSTINIAN DOUBLE HOUSE
        BENEDICTINE DOUBLE HOUSE
        BRIDGETTINE DOUBLE HOUSE

- - - - - - - - - - - - - - - - - - -

          FONTEVRAULTINE DOUBLE HOUSE
          GILBERTINE DOUBLE HOUSE
     FRIARY
          AUSTIN FRIARY
          CARMELITE FRIARY
          DOMINICAN FRIARY
          FRANCISCAN FRIARY
          FRIARY OF CRUTCHED FRIARS
          FRIARY OF FRIARS OF THE SACK
          FRIARY OF PIED FRIARS
     GRANGE
          AUGUSTINIAN GRANGE
          BENEDICTINE GRANGE
          CARTHUSIAN GRANGE
          CISTERCIAN GRANGE
          CLUNIAC GRANGE
          GILBERTINE GRANGE
          PREMONSTRATENSIAN GRANGE
          TEMPLARS GRANGE
          TIRONIAN GRANGE
     LAY BRETHREN SETTLEMENT
          COURERY
     MONASTERY
          AUGUSTINIAN MONASTERY
          BENEDICTINE MONASTERY
          BONHOMMES MONASTERY
          CARTHUSIAN MONASTERY
          CISTERCIAN MONASTERY
          CLUNIAC MONASTERY
          GILBERTINE MONASTERY
          GRANDMONTINE MONASTERY
          PREMONSTRATENSIAN MONASTERY
          SAVIGNIAC MONASTERY
          TIRONIAN MONASTERY
          TRINITARIAN MONASTERY
     NUNNERY
          ANGLICAN NUNNERY
          AUGUSTINIAN NUNNERY
          BENEDICTINE NUNNERY
          CISTERCIAN NUNNERY
          CLUNIAC NUNNERY
          DOMINICAN NUNNERY
          FRANCISCAN NUNNERY
          PREMONSTRATENSIAN NUNNERY
          SISTERS OF ST JOHN NUNNERY
     PRECEPTORY
          HOSPITALLERS PRECEPTORY
          TEMPLARS PRECEPTORY
     PRIORY
          ALIEN PRIORY

RITUAL PIT

RITUAL SHAFT

ROCK CARVING

RUNE STONE

SACRISTY

SANCTUARY

SHEILA NA GIG

SHRINE

STANDING STONE

RELIGIOUS, RITUAL AND FUNERARY

STATIONAL MONUMENT

STOCKADED ENCLOSURE

STONE ALIGNMENT

STONE AVENUE

STONE CIRCLE
    EMBANKED STONE CIRCLE
    FOUR POSTER STONE CIRCLE
    RECUMBENT STONE CIRCLE

STONE SETTING

SYNODAL HALL

TIMBER CIRCLE

VESTRY

VIERECKSCHANZEN

VOTIVE PIT

VOTIVE SHAFT

WESTWORK

AIR TRANSPORT SITE
    AIR TERMINAL
    AIRCRAFT
    AIRFIELD
    AIRPORT
        CIVIL AIRPORT
    AIRSHIP MOORING MAST
    AIRSHIP STATION
    CONTROL TOWER
    DISPERSAL
    FOG DISPERSAL PLANT
    HANGAR
        AIRCRAFT HANGAR
        AIRSHIP HANGAR
    HARD STANDING
    MILITARY AIRFIELD
    PERIMETER TRACK
    RUNWAY
    TAXIWAY
    TEST HOUSE

BRIDGE
    BRIDGE < BY FORM >
        CLAPPER BRIDGE
        DRAWBRIDGE
        LIFTING BRIDGE
        PACKHORSE BRIDGE
        SUSPENSION BRIDGE
        SWING BRIDGE
        TRANSPORTER BRIDGE
    BRIDGE < BY FUNCTION >
        ACCOMMODATION BRIDGE
        CANAL BRIDGE
        FOOTBRIDGE
        RAILWAY BRIDGE
        ROAD BRIDGE
        ROVING BRIDGE
        TOLL BRIDGE
        TOWING PATH BRIDGE
        TRAMWAY BRIDGE

CAPSTAN HOUSE

CATTLE DOCKS

CAUSEWAY

CRANE HOUSE

FIRE ENGINE HOUSE

FIRE STATION

INCLINED PLANE
    CANAL INCLINED PLANE
    RAILWAY INCLINED PLANE

LIFTING AND WINDING STRUCTURE
    CAPSTAN
        HAND CAPSTAN
    COAL DROP
    CRANE
        CRANE < BY FORM >
            FLOATING CRANE
            GANTRY CRANE
            HAMMERHEAD CRANE
            JIB CRANE
                FAIRBAIRN JIB CRANE

         LUFFING CRANE
         MOVING CRANE
          MOVING QUAY CRANE
         ROOF CRANE
          TRAVELLING ROOF CRANE
         TRAVELLING CRANE
          TRAVELLING OVERHEAD CRANE
          TRAVELLING ROOF CRANE
         TREADWHEEL CRANE
         WALL CRANE
        CRANE <BY FUNCTION>
         COALING CRANE
         HAND CRANE
         QUAY CRANE
          FIXED QUAY CRANE
          MOVING QUAY CRANE
         STEAM CRANE
      CRANEWHEEL
      DERRICK
      GANTRY
      GRAIN ELEVATOR
       FLOATING GRAIN ELEVATOR
      HOIST
       TEAGLE
      LIFT
       BOAT LIFT
       CANAL LIFT
       CLIFF LIFT
       RAILWAY LIFT
       RISE LIFT
      LIFT SHAFT
      WINCH
       BARGE WINCH
       ELECTRIC WINCH
      WINDING ENGINE
       INCLINE WINDING ENGINE

MILE PLATE

MILEPOST
  CANAL MILEPOST

MILESTONE

MILK DEPOT

PEDESTRIAN TRANSPORT SITE
  FOOTBRIDGE
  FOOTPATH
  PATH
   GRAVEL PATH
  PEDESTRIAN CROSSING
   ZEBRA CROSSING
  PEDESTRIAN TUNNEL
  RIDGEWAY
  STEPPING STONES
  STEPS
  STILE
  SUBWAY

RAILWAY TRANSPORT SITE
  ATMOSPHERIC RAILWAY ENGINE HOUSE
  ENGINE SHED
  GOODS SHED
  GOODS STATION
  GOODS YARD
  HOLDING SHED
  LEVEL CROSSING
  LEVEL CROSSING GATE

LOCOMOTIVE DEPOT
MAIL BAG NET
MARSHALLING YARD
RAILWAY
    ATMOSPHERIC RAILWAY
    CLIFF RAILWAY
    COLLIERY RAILWAY
    DOCKYARD RAILWAY
    FUNICULAR RAILWAY
    MINERAL RAILWAY
    MINIATURE RAILWAY
    OVERHEAD RAILWAY
    UNDERGROUND RAILWAY
RAILWAY BRIDGE
RAILWAY BUFFET
RAILWAY CUTTING
RAILWAY EMBANKMENT
RAILWAY HOTEL
RAILWAY INCLINED PLANE
RAILWAY JUNCTION
RAILWAY LIFT
RAILWAY LOOKOUT TOWER
RAILWAY OFFICE
RAILWAY PLATFORM
RAILWAY SHED
RAILWAY SIDING
RAILWAY SIGNAL
RAILWAY STABLE
RAILWAY STATION
    UNDERGROUND RAILWAY STATION
RAILWAY STOREHOUSE
RAILWAY TUNNEL
    UNDERGROUND RAILWAY TUNNEL
RAILWAY TURNTABLE
RAILWAY VIADUCT
RAILWAY WORKS
    RAILWAY CARRIAGE WORKS
ROUNDHOUSE (RAILWAY)
SIGNAL BOX
TRAIN SHED
TRANSIT SHED
TRAVERSER
WAGON SHED

REFUSE TRANSFER DEPOT

ROAD TRANSPORT SITE
    AMBULANCE GARAGE
    AMBULANCE STATION
    BUS DEPOT
    BUS SHELTER
    BUS STATION
    CABMENS SHELTER
    CAR PARK
        MULTI STOREY CAR PARK
        UNDERGROUND CAR PARK
    CARRIAGE HOUSE
    CART SHED
    CLAPPER BRIDGE
    COACH HOUSE
    COACHING INN STABLE
    DIRECTION STONE
    FLYOVER
    FORD
    GARAGE
    GOODS CLEARING HOUSE
    HACKNEY STABLE
    HORSE TROUGH
    MEWS

TRANSPORT

- - - - - - - - - - - - - - - - - - - -

        MOUNTING BLOCK
        PACKHORSE BRIDGE
        PARKING METER
        PETROL PUMP
        PETROL STATION
        RAMP
           CAR RAMP
           CARRIAGE RAMP
        ROAD
           ALLEY
           APPROACH ROAD
           CARRIAGEWAY
           COBBLED ROAD
           DROVE ROAD
           HOLLOW WAY
           PACKHORSE ROAD
           TOLL ROAD
           TRACKWAY
               BRIDLEWAY
           WOODEN ROAD
        ROAD BRIDGE
        ROAD JUNCTION
        ROAD TUNNEL
        ROAD VIADUCT
        ROADSIDE LIGHTHOUSE
        SEDAN CHAIR LIFT
        SERVICE STATION
        SIGNPOST
        TERMINUS STONE
        TETHERING POST
        TOLL BOARD
        TOLL BOUNDARY MARKER
        TOLL BRIDGE
        TOLL GATE
        TOLL HOUSE
        TOLLBOOTH
        TRAMWAY TRANSPORT SITE
           TRAM DEPOT
           TRAM SHELTER
           TRAM TRANSFORMER STATION
           TRAMWAY
               PLATEWAY
               STREET TRAMWAY
               WAGONWAY
           TRAMWAY BRIDGE
           TRAMWAY EMBANKMENT
           TRAMWAY REVERSING TRIANGLE
           TRAMWAY STABLE
           TRAMWAY TUNNEL
           TRAMWAY TUNNEL PORTAL
        TRANSPORTER BRIDGE
        TRAP HOUSE
        UNDERPASS

    STABLE
        COACHING INN STABLE
        HACKNEY STABLE
        LIVERY STABLE
        MULTI STOREY STABLE
        RAILWAY STABLE
        TRAMWAY STABLE

    SURVEY TOWER

    TRANSPORT TUNNEL
        CANAL TUNNEL
        HORSE TUNNEL
        PEDESTRIAN TUNNEL
        RAILWAY TUNNEL

- - - - - - - - - - - - - - - - -

TRANSPORT

       ROAD TUNNEL
       TRAMWAY TUNNEL
       UNDERGROUND RAILWAY TUNNEL

TUNNEL PORTAL
       CANAL TUNNEL PORTAL
       RAILWAY TUNNEL PORTAL
       ROAD TUNNEL PORTAL
       TRAMWAY TUNNEL PORTAL

VIADUCT
       RAILWAY VIADUCT
       ROAD VIADUCT

WAITING ROOM

WATER TRANSPORT SITE
    AQUEDUCT
    BALANCE BEAM
    BAULK
    BOAT HOUSE
    BOAT LIFT
    BOAT YARD
    CANAL TRANSPORT SITE
       ACCOMMODATION BRIDGE
       CANAL
           MILITARY CANAL
           SHIP CANAL
       CANAL BASIN
       CANAL BOAT YARD
       CANAL BRIDGE
       CANAL DOCKYARD
       CANAL FEEDER
       CANAL GATEHOUSE
       CANAL INCLINED PLANE
       CANAL LIFT
       CANAL LOCK
       CANAL MILEPOST
       CANAL OFFICE
       CANAL RESERVOIR
       CANAL SLUICE
       CANAL TUNNEL
       CANAL WAREHOUSE
       CANAL WHARF
       HORSE TUNNEL
       ROVING BRIDGE
    DOCK
       CANAL DOCK
           CANAL DRY DOCK
       DRY DOCK
       RIVER DOCK
    DOCKYARD
    GAUGE HOUSE
    HARBOUR
    JETTY
       COAL JETTY
    LANDING PIER
    LANDING STAGE
    LANDING STEPS
    LOCK
       CANAL LOCK
       FLASH LOCK
       FLOOD LOCK
       GUILLOTINE LOCK
       JUNCTION LOCK
       MITRE LOCK
       POUND LOCK
       RIVER LOCK
       STOP LOCK

TIDAL LOCK
LOCK CHAMBER
LOCK GATE
LOCK SILL
MOORING BOLLARD
QUAY
RIVER INTAKE GAUGE
RIVER NAVIGATION
SLIPWAY
STAITH
STAUNCH
TIDAL DOOR
TIDE GAUGE
TOW PATH
TOWING PATH BRIDGE
WATER GATE
WEIR
TUMBLING WEIR
WHARF
CANAL WHARF
RIVER WHARF

WEIGH HOUSE

WEIGHBRIDGE

UNASSIGNED

. . . .

ARCH

BASEMENT

BEAM SLOT

BOMB CRATER

BOUNDARY
    BOUNDARY BANK
    BOUNDARY CAIRN
    BOUNDARY DITCH
    BOUNDARY MARKER
    BOUNDARY MOUND
    BOUNDARY PLATE
    BOUNDARY POST
    BOUNDARY STONE
    BOUNDARY WALL

BUILDING
    GATEHOUSE
    GATEMANS HUT
    OFFICE
    OUTBUILDING
    PORTERS LODGE
    SHED
    STOREHOUSE
    TOWER
        CLOCK TOWER
    TOWER BLOCK

CACHE

CANTEEN

CARVED STONE

CARVING

CELLAR

COLONNADE

COLUMN

CONSTRUCTION WORKS

CONTROL ROOM

DITCH
    BOUNDARY DITCH

EARTHWORK
    BANK (EARTHWORK)
        RING BANK
    LINEAR EARTHWORK

EMBANKMENT

EMBANKMENT CROSS

ENCLOSURE
    CURVILINEAR ENCLOSURE
        CIRCULAR ENCLOSURE
        D SHAPED ENCLOSURE
        OVAL ENCLOSURE
        SPECTACLE ENCLOSURE
        SUB CIRCULAR ENCLOSURE

. . . .

UNASSIGNED

. . . .

    DITCHED ENCLOSURE
        DOUBLE DITCHED ENCLOSURE
    PIT DEFINED ENCLOSURE
    RECTILINEAR ENCLOSURE
        GOAL POST ENCLOSURE
        POLYGONAL ENCLOSURE
        RECTANGULAR ENCLOSURE
        SQUARE ENCLOSURE
        TRAPEZOIDAL ENCLOSURE

FEATURE
    LINEAR FEATURE
    NATURAL FEATURE
        CAVE
        FUNGUS RING
        GEOLOGICAL MARKS
        OXBOW LAKE
        REED BED
        ROCK BASIN
        STONE
        SUBMARINE FOREST
        TREE
        TREE HOLE
        TREE STUMP

FENCE

FLINT SCATTER

FLOOR
    TESSELATED FLOOR

FUEL STORE
    COAL SHED
    PEAT STORE

GATE

GATE PIER

GRAFFITI

HEARTH

HEDGE

HOLLOW

LAND RECLAMATION

LINEAR SYSTEM

MACULA

MARKER CAIRN

MOSAIC

MOUND
    BOUNDARY MOUND

OVEN

PAVEMENT
    RAISED PAVEMENT

PILE

PIPELINE

. . . .

PIT

PIT ALIGNMENT

PIT CLUSTER

PLAQUE

PLATFORM
    BUILDING PLATFORM
    CIRCULAR PLATFORM

PORTAL

POST HOLE

PRECINCT

RAILINGS

RING DITCH

ROBBER TRENCH

ROCK CUT CHAMBER

SCRATCH DIAL

SHAFT
    AIR SHAFT
    VENTILATION SHAFT

SHELTER
    LABOURERS SHELTER

SITE

STONE BLOCK

STRUCTURE
    UNDERGROUND STRUCTURE

TERRACED GROUND

TUNNEL

TUNNEL CHAMBER

UNDERCROFT

VAULT

WALL
    BOUNDARY WALL
    PRECINCT WALL
    REVETMENT

WALL PAINTING

WOOD SHED

YARD

BATH HOUSE

BATHS

CESS PIT
    CESS POOL

CONDUIT

CONDUIT HEAD

CONDUIT HOUSE

DAM
    MILL DAM

DRAIN
    CULVERT
    DRAIN SYPHON
    FIELD DRAIN

DRAINAGE DITCH

DRAINAGE LEVEL

DRAINAGE MILL

DRAINAGE SYSTEM

FILTER BED

FILTER HOUSE

FLOOD DEFENCES

FOUNTAIN
    DRINKING FOUNTAIN
    ORNAMENTAL FOUNTAIN
    SHELL FOUNTAIN
    TRICK FOUNTAIN

LATRINE

MILL RACE
    HEAD RACE
    TAIL RACE

MOAT

POND
    DECOY POND
    DEWPOND
    DUCKING POND
    FISH POND
    FURNACE POND
    HAMMER POND
    LILY POND
    MAST POND
    MILL POND
    ORNAMENTAL POND
    PEN POND
    SWANNERY POND
    TIMBER POND

POND BAY

PRIVY HOUSE

WATER SUPPLY AND DRAINAGE

· ·

PUBLIC CONVENIENCE

PUMP
  HAND PUMP
  WATER PUMP
  WAYSIDE PUMP
  WIND PUMP

PUMP HOUSE
  PUMP ROOM

PUMPING STATION
  SEWAGE PUMPING STATION
  WATER PUMPING STATION

PURIFIER

RAINWATER HEAD

RESERVOIR
  CANAL RESERVOIR

RESERVOIR INSPECTION CHAMBER

SCREENS HOUSE

SEPTIC TANK

SEWAGE WORKS

SEWER
  INTERCEPTOR
  OUTFALL SEWER

SLUICE

SLUICE GATE

SPA

SPRING

TOILET

TROUGH
  CATTLE TROUGH
  DOG TROUGH
  HORSE TROUGH

VALVE TOWER

WATER POINT

WATER TANK
  CISTERN

WATER TOWER

WATERCOURSE
  AQUEDUCT
  CANAL
    FLOOD RELIEF CANAL
  STREAM
  WATER CHANNEL
    GULLY
    LEAT
  WATER PIPE
  WATER TUNNEL

· ·

WATERWORKS

WEIR

WELL
    DIPPING WELL

WELL COVER

WELL HEAD

WELL HOUSE

WELL SHAFT

4% Industrial Dwellings
  USE LODGING HOUSE

5% Industrial Dwellings
  USE MODEL DWELLING

A FRAME HOUSE
  CL   DOMESTIC
  BT   HOUSE <BY FORM>

A P Enclosure
  USE ENCLOSURE

A P Linear Feature
  USE LINEAR FEATURE

A P Linear System
  USE LINEAR SYSTEM

A P Macula
  USE MACULA

A P Site
  USE SITE

ABATTOIR
  UF   Butching House
       Slaughter House
  CL   INDUSTRIAL
  BT   FOOD PROCESSING SITE
  RT   GLUE FACTORY
       HORSEHAIR FACTORY
       SHAMBLES
       SMOKE HOUSE
       TANNERY

ABBEY
  UF   Abbey Barn
       Abbey Bridge
       Abbey Church
       Abbey Gate
       Abbey Gatehouse
       Abbey Kitchen
       Arrouiasian Abbey
       Augustinian Abbey
       Benedictine Abbey
       Bridgettine Abbey
       Cistercian Abbey
       Cluniac Abbey
       Convent Chapel
       Conventual Chapel
       Conventual Church
       Farmery
       Franciscan Abbey
       Independent Abbey
       Premonstratensian Abbey
       Savigniac Abbey
       Tironensian Abbey
       Tironian Abbey
       Victorine Abbey
  SN   Use with narrow terms of DOUBLE HOUSE, MONASTERY
       or NUNNERY.
  CL   RELIGIOUS, RITUAL AND FUNERARY
  BT   RELIGIOUS HOUSE
  RT   ABBOTS HOUSE
       ALMONRY
       CATHEDRAL
       CHAPTER HOUSE
       CONVENT SCHOOL
       CURFEW BELL TOWER
       DOUBLE HOUSE
       FRATER
       FRIARY
       GATEHOUSE
       GUEST HOUSE
       KITCHEN
       MANCIPLES HOUSE
       MONASTERY

       NUNNERY
       PRECEPTORY
       PRECINCT WALL
       PRIORY
       REFECTORY

Abbey Barn
  USE ABBEY
      BARN
  SN Use both terms.

Abbey Bridge
  USE ABBEY
      BRIDGE
  SN Use both terms.

Abbey Church
  USE ABBEY
      CHURCH
  SN Use both terms.

Abbey Gate
  USE ABBEY
      GATE
  SN Use both terms.

Abbey Gatehouse
  USE ABBEY
      GATEHOUSE
  SN Use both terms.

Abbey Kitchen
  USE ABBEY
      KITCHEN
  SN Use both terms.

Abbey Wall
  USE PRECINCT WALL

ABBOTS HOUSE
  UF   Abbots Lodging
  CL   DOMESTIC
  BT   CLERICAL DWELLING
  RT   ABBEY
       ABBOTS SUMMER PALACE
       MONASTERY

Abbots Lodging
  USE ABBOTS HOUSE

ABBOTS SUMMER PALACE
  CL   DOMESTIC
  BT   PALACE
  RT   ABBOTS HOUSE
       ARCHBISHOPS MANOR HOUSE

ABRASIVES MANUFACTURING SITE
  CL   INDUSTRIAL
  BT   MINERAL PRODUCT SITE

Academy
  USE SCHOOL

Academy Of Art
  USE ART SCHOOL

Academy Of Music
  USE MUSIC SCHOOL

ACCIDENT HOSPITAL
  CL   HEALTH AND WELFARE
  BT   HOSPITAL

ACCOMMODATION BRIDGE
  CL   TRANSPORT
  BT   BRIDGE <BY FUNCTION>

ACCOMMODATION BRIDGE
  CL   TRANSPORT

BT CANAL TRANSPORT SITE

ACCUMULATOR HOUSE
    SN Storage for large lead-acid batteries
         (accumulators).
    CL INDUSTRIAL
    BT ELECTRICITY PRODUCTION SITE

ACCUMULATOR TOWER
    CL INDUSTRIAL
    BT ELECTRICITY PRODUCTION SITE

ACID TOWER
    SN Coke-filled tower for dissolving and neutralising
         the acid produced by alkali-making processes.
    CL INDUSTRIAL
    BT CHEMICAL PRODUCTION SITE
    RT SODA WORKS

ACID WORKS
    CL INDUSTRIAL
    BT CHEMICAL PRODUCTION SITE

Acoustic Detection Post
    USE LISTENING POST

Acoustic Mirror
    USE LISTENING POST

Acoustic Wall
    USE LISTENING POST

ADIT
    UF Adit Portal
         Tar Tunnel
    SN Horizontal tunnel opening from the surface used
         for haulage or access to a mine. It can also be
         used for drainage.
    CL INDUSTRIAL
    BT MINE DRAINAGE AND VENTILATION SITE
    RT DRAINAGE LEVEL
         EXTRACTIVE PIT
         MINE
         SHAFT
         TUNNEL
         TUNNEL CHAMBER
         UNDERGROUND STRUCTURE

Adit Portal
    USE ADIT
         PORTAL
    SN Use both terms.

Administration Block
    USE OFFICE

Admiralty
    USE GOVERNMENT OFFICE

ADMISSION HOSPITAL
    CL HEALTH AND WELFARE
    BT HOSPITAL

ADULTERINE CASTLE
    CL DOMESTIC
    BT CASTLE
    RT MOTTE

ADULTERINE CASTLE
    CL DEFENCE
    BT CASTLE
    RT MOTTE

ADVENTURE PLAYGROUND
    CL RECREATIONAL
    BT RECREATION GROUND

AERIAL ROPEWAY
    UF Overhead Cableway

    CL INDUSTRIAL
    BT MINE LIFTING AND WINDING STRUCTURE
    RT EXTRACTIVE PIT
         MINE

Aerodrome
    USE AIRFIELD

Aged Miners Home
    USE ALMSHOUSE

Aged Persons Home
    USE ALMSHOUSE

Aged Pilgrims Home
    USE ALMSHOUSE

Aged Womens Asylum
    USE ALMSHOUSE

Agger
    USE ROAD

AGGREGATE FIELD SYSTEM
    UF Irregular Aggregate Field System
         Regular Aggregate Field System
    CL AGRICULTURE AND SUBSISTENCE
    BT FIELD SYSTEM

AGGREGATE VILLAGE
    CL DOMESTIC
    BT VILLAGE

AGRICULTURAL BUILDING
    UF Crow
    CL AGRICULTURE AND SUBSISTENCE
    NT APIARY
         ASH HOUSE
         BACK HOUSE
         BARK HOUSE
         BARK PEELERS HUT
         DOVECOTE
         DUCK HOUSE
         FARM BUILDING
         FOOD AND DRINK PROCESSING SITE
         GREENHOUSE
         HEMMEL
         HEN BATTERY
         HULL
         POULTRY HOUSE
         SHEPHERDS HUT

AGRICULTURAL CHEMICAL SITE
    CL INDUSTRIAL
    BT CHEMICAL PRODUCTION SITE
    NT FERTILISER STOREHOUSE
         FERTILISER WORKS
         LIME KILN
         NITRATE WORKS
         POTASH KILN
         POTASH MINE
    RT LIME WORKS

AGRICULTURAL COLLEGE
    CL EDUCATION
    BT TRAINING COLLEGE
    RT HORTICULTURAL COLLEGE
         RURAL INSTITUTE

AGRICULTURAL ENGINEERING WORKS
    SN Small engineering works specialising in the
         production of items such as ploughs and threshing
         machinery.
    CL INDUSTRIAL
    BT ENGINEERING INDUSTRY SITE
    RT FOUNDRY
         MACHINE SHOP
         PAINT SHOP
         VEHICLE ENGINEERING SITE

AGRICULTURAL HALL
  CL COMMERCIAL
  BT EXHIBITION HALL

Agricultural Research Station
  USE RESEARCH STATION

Agricultural Workers Cottage
  USE FARM LABOURERS COTTAGE

AGRICULTURE AND SUBSISTENCE
  SN This is the top term for the class. See
      AGRICULTURE AND SUBSISTENCE Class List for narrow
      terms.

Air Force Barracks
  USE BARRACKS

Air Force Base
  USE MILITARY AIRFIELD

Air Mill
  USE WINDMILL

AIR RAID SHELTER
  UF Bomb Shelter
  CL DEFENCE
  RT NUCLEAR BUNKER
      PILLBOX
      UNDERGROUND MILITARY HEADQUARTERS
      UNDERGROUND STRUCTURE

AIR SHAFT
  UF Air Shaft Tower
      Air Vent House
  SN Separate shaft to the main working shaft in a
      colliery/mine. Sunk to ensure the adequate
      circulation of air through the mine.
  CL UNASSIGNED
  BT SHAFT
  RT EXHAUSTER HOUSE
      MINE SHAFT

Air Shaft Tower
  USE AIR SHAFT
       VENTILATION SHAFT
  SN Use both terms.

AIR TERMINAL
  CL TRANSPORT
  BT AIR TRANSPORT SITE

Air Traffic Control Tower
  USE CONTROL TOWER

AIR TRANSPORT SITE
  CL TRANSPORT
  NT AIR TERMINAL
      AIRCRAFT
      AIRFIELD
      AIRPORT
      AIRSHIP MOORING MAST
      AIRSHIP STATION
      CONTROL TOWER
      DISPERSAL
      FOG DISPERSAL PLANT
      HANGAR
      HARD STANDING
      MILITARY AIRFIELD
      PERIMETER TRACK
      RUNWAY
      TAXIWAY
      TEST HOUSE

Air Vent House
  USE AIR SHAFT
       VENTILATION SHAFT
  SN Use both terms.

AIRCRAFT
  SN Use for aircraft crash sites.
  CL TRANSPORT
  BT AIR TRANSPORT SITE

Aircraft Assembly Plant
  USE AIRCRAFT FACTORY

AIRCRAFT CARRIER
  CL MARITIME
  BT WARSHIP

AIRCRAFT ENGINE FACTORY
  CL INDUSTRIAL
  BT AIRCRAFT ENGINEERING SITE
  RT TURNING SHOP

AIRCRAFT ENGINEERING SITE
  CL INDUSTRIAL
  BT VEHICLE ENGINEERING SITE
  NT AIRCRAFT ENGINE FACTORY
      AIRCRAFT FACTORY
      ROCKET MOTOR FACTORY

AIRCRAFT FACTORY
  UF Aircraft Assembly Plant
      Aircraft Works
  CL INDUSTRIAL
  BT AIRCRAFT ENGINEERING SITE
  RT FABRICATION SHED

AIRCRAFT FACTORY
  UF Aircraft Assembly Plant
      Aircraft Works
  CL INDUSTRIAL
  BT FACTORY <BY PRODUCT>

AIRCRAFT HANGAR
  CL TRANSPORT
  BT HANGAR

AIRCRAFT OBSTRUCTION
  UF Anti Glider Ditch
  CL DEFENCE

Aircraft Works
  USE AIRCRAFT FACTORY

AIRFIELD
  UF Aerodrome
  CL TRANSPORT
  BT AIR TRANSPORT SITE

Airing Yard
  USE EXERCISE YARD

Airmens Graveyard
  USE MILITARY CEMETERY

AIRPORT
  CL TRANSPORT
  BT AIR TRANSPORT SITE
  NT CIVIL AIRPORT

Airport Control Tower
  USE CONTROL TOWER

Airport Test House
  USE TEST HOUSE

AIRSHIP HANGAR
  CL TRANSPORT
  BT HANGAR

AIRSHIP MOORING MAST
  CL TRANSPORT
  BT AIR TRANSPORT SITE

AIRSHIP STATION

SN   One with no hangars; simply an anchorage point
     with ancillary structures.
CL   TRANSPORT
BT   AIR TRANSPORT SITE

AISLED HALL
SN   Use where the aisles are open to the hall.
CL   DOMESTIC
BT   HALL HOUSE

AISLED HOUSE
SN   Use where the intervening arcade is closed but
     timber-framed.
CL   DOMESTIC
BT   HALL HOUSE
NT   QUASI AISLED HOUSE
     SINGLE AISLED HOUSE

Alcoholic Ladies Home
USE COTTAGE HOME

Ale House
USE BEER HOUSE

ALE STORE
CL   INDUSTRIAL
BT   BREWING AND MALTING SITE
RT   BEER HOUSE
     BREWHOUSE
     INN
     PUBLIC HOUSE

Alhambra
USE MOORISH PAVILION

ALIEN CELL
UF   Alien Priory Cell
CL   RELIGIOUS, RITUAL AND FUNERARY
BT   CELL
NT   AUGUSTINIAN ALIEN CELL
     BENEDICTINE ALIEN CELL
     CISTERCIAN ALIEN CELL
     PREMONSTRATENSIAN ALIEN CELL
     TIRONIAN ALIEN CELL
RT   ALIEN PRIORY

Alien Grange
USE GRANGE

ALIEN PRIORY
UF   Augustinian Alien Priory
     Benedictine Alien Priory
     Cluniac Alien Priory
     Fontevraultine Alien Priory
     Grandmontine Alien Priory
     Premonstratensian Alien Priory
     Tironian Alien Priory
SN   Use with narrow terms of DOUBLE HOUSE, MONASTERY
     or NUNNERY.
CL   RELIGIOUS, RITUAL AND FUNERARY
BT   PRIORY
RT   ALIEN CELL

Alien Priory Cell
USE ALIEN CELL

ALKALI WORKS
CL   INDUSTRIAL
BT   CHEMICAL PRODUCTION SITE

ALL WEATHER PITCH
CL   RECREATIONAL
BT   RECREATION GROUND

ALLEE
SN   A walk bordered by trees or clipped hedges in a
     garden or park. Made of gravel, sand or turf, it
     is different from a path or avenue.
CL   GARDENS, PARKS AND URBAN SPACES

BT   WALK

ALLEY
CL   TRANSPORT
BT   ROAD

ALLOTMENT
CL   GARDENS, PARKS AND URBAN SPACES
RT   GARDEN
     SMALLHOLDING
     VEGETABLE GARDEN

ALLOTMENT
CL   AGRICULTURE AND SUBSISTENCE
BT   LAND USE SITE
RT   GARDEN
     SMALLHOLDING
     VEGETABLE GARDEN

ALMONRY
CL   RELIGIOUS, RITUAL AND FUNERARY
RT   ABBEY
     ALMSHOUSE
     DISPENSARY
     FRIARY
     MONASTERY
     NUNNERY
     RELIGIOUS HOUSE

ALMONRY
CL   HEALTH AND WELFARE
RT   ABBEY
     ALMSHOUSE
     DISPENSARY
     FRIARY
     MONASTERY
     NUNNERY
     RELIGIOUS HOUSE

ALMSHOUSE
UF   Aged Miners Home
     Aged Persons Home
     Aged Pilgrims Home
     Aged Womens Asylum
     Almshouse Chapel
     Asylum For Aged And Decayed Freemasons
     Bead House
     Bead House Chapel
     Bedehouse
     Bedehouse Chapel
     Charity House
     Freemasons Asylum
     Maison Dieu
     Old Peoples Asylum
     Sailors Home
     Widows Home
CL   RELIGIOUS, RITUAL AND FUNERARY
RT   ALMONRY
     COTTAGE HOME
     HOSPITAL
     HOSPITAL SCHOOL
     LEPER HOSPITAL
     ORPHANAGE
     WORKHOUSE

ALMSHOUSE
UF   Aged Miners Home
     Aged Persons Home
     Aged Pilgrims Home
     Aged Womens Asylum
     Almshouse Chapel
     Asylum For Aged And Decayed Freemasons
     Bead House
     Bead House Chapel
     Bedehouse
     Bedehouse Chapel
     Charity House
     Freemasons Asylum
     Maison Dieu

Old Peoples Asylum
Sailors Home
Widows Home
CL   HEALTH AND WELFARE
RT   CHILDRENS HOME
      COTTAGE HOME
      HOSPITAL SCHOOL
      LEPER HOSPITAL
      WORKHOUSE

ALMSHOUSE
UF   Aged Miners Home
      Aged Persons Home
      Aged Pilgrims Home
      Aged Womens Asylum
      Almshouse Chapel
      Asylum For Aged And Decayed Freemasons
      Bead House
      Bead House Chapel
      Bedehouse
      Bedehouse Chapel
      Charity House
      Freemasons Asylum
      Maison Dieu
      Old Peoples Asylum
      Sailors Home
      Widows Home
CL   DOMESTIC
BT   RESIDENTIAL BUILDING
RT   ALMONRY
      COTTAGE HOME
      HOSPITAL SCHOOL
      ORPHANAGE

Almshouse Chapel
USE ALMSHOUSE
      CHAPEL
SN   Use both terms.

Alpaca Factory
USE ALPACA MILL

ALPACA MILL
UF   Alpaca Factory
SN   Long-staple hair, often from llamas, treated like
      worsted.
CL   INDUSTRIAL
BT   TEXTILE MILL

ALPACA MILL
UF   Alpaca Factory
SN   Long-staple hair, often from llamas, treated like
      worsted.
CL   INDUSTRIAL
BT   WOOL MANUFACTURING SITE

ALPINE GARDEN
CL   GARDENS, PARKS AND URBAN SPACES
BT   GARDEN
RT   ROCK GARDEN
      ROCKERY

ALTAR
CL   RELIGIOUS, RITUAL AND FUNERARY
RT   SHRINE

ALTAR TOMB
CL   RELIGIOUS, RITUAL AND FUNERARY
BT   TOMB

ALUM HOUSE
CL   INDUSTRIAL
BT   DYE AND PIGMENT SITE
RT   ALUM QUARRY
      ALUM WORKS

Alum Mine
USE ALUM WORKS

ALUM QUARRY

CL   INDUSTRIAL
BT   MINERAL EXTRACTION SITE
RT   ALUM HOUSE
      ALUM WORKS
      COPPERAS WORKS
      SHALE QUARRY

ALUM WORKS
UF   Alum Mine
SN   Works for the evaporation and crystallisation of
      sodium aluminium sulphate solution.
CL   INDUSTRIAL
BT   DYE AND PIGMENT SITE
NT   STEEPING TANK
RT   ALUM HOUSE
      ALUM QUARRY
      CHEMICAL WORKS
      COPPERAS WORKS
      DYE WORKS
      LEATHER FACTORY
      PAPER MILL
      TANNERY

ALUM WORKS
UF   Alum Mine
SN   Works for the evaporation and crystallisation of
      sodium aluminium sulphate solution.
CL   INDUSTRIAL
BT   MINERAL EXTRACTION SITE

ALUMINIUM SMELTER
CL   INDUSTRIAL
BT   SMELTER
RT   ELECTRIC ARC FURNACE

ALUMINIUM SMELTER
CL   INDUSTRIAL
BT   NON FERROUS METAL PRODUCT SITE

AMBULANCE GARAGE
CL   HEALTH AND WELFARE
RT   AMBULANCE STATION

AMBULANCE GARAGE
CL   TRANSPORT
BT   ROAD TRANSPORT SITE

AMBULANCE STATION
CL   TRANSPORT
BT   ROAD TRANSPORT SITE
RT   HOSPITAL

AMBULANCE STATION
CL   HEALTH AND WELFARE
RT   AMBULANCE GARAGE
      HOSPITAL

AMERICAN GARDEN
SN   A concept dating in England from the second half
      of the 18th century, when hardy North American
      plants were relatively easy to obtain.
CL   GARDENS, PARKS AND URBAN SPACES
BT   GARDEN

AMPHIBIOUS OPERATIONS VESSEL
CL   MARITIME
BT   WARSHIP
NT   LANDING CRAFT

AMPHITHEATRE
UF   Arena
CL   RECREATIONAL
RT   PLAIN AN GWARRY
      THEATRE

AMPHITHEATRE
UF   Arena
CL   RELIGIOUS, RITUAL AND FUNERARY
RT   PLAIN AN GWARRY

THEATRE

AMPHITHEATRE
- UF Arena
- CL DEFENCE
- RT GYRUS

AMUSEMENT ARCADE
- CL RECREATIONAL
- BT GAMBLING SITE

ANCHOR HANDLING CRAFT
- CL MARITIME
- BT SERVICE CRAFT

Anchorage
- USE ANCHORITE CELL

Anchoret Cell
- USE ANCHORITE CELL

ANCHORITE CELL
- UF Anchorage
  - Anchoret Cell
- SN Use ANCHORITE CELL if religious site or HARBOUR if ship anchorage.
- CL RELIGIOUS, RITUAL AND FUNERARY
- BT CELL
- RT CHURCH
  - HERMITAGE

ANGLE TOWER
- UF Corner Tower
  - Drum Tower
- CL DEFENCE
- RT FLANKING TOWER
  - TOWER

ANGLICAN CATHEDRAL
- CL RELIGIOUS, RITUAL AND FUNERARY
- BT CATHEDRAL
- RT ANGLICAN CHURCH

ANGLICAN CHURCH
- UF Protestant Church
- CL RELIGIOUS, RITUAL AND FUNERARY
- BT CHURCH
- RT ANGLICAN CATHEDRAL
  - MISSION HALL

Anglican College
- USE THEOLOGICAL COLLEGE

ANGLICAN NUNNERY
- CL RELIGIOUS, RITUAL AND FUNERARY
- BT NUNNERY

Anglican School
- USE CHURCH SCHOOL

ANIMAL BURIAL
- CL RELIGIOUS, RITUAL AND FUNERARY
- BT BURIAL

ANIMAL CAGE
- CL RECREATIONAL
- BT ANIMAL DWELLING

ANIMAL CEMETERY
- UF Dogs Cemetery
  - Pet Cemetery
- CL RELIGIOUS, RITUAL AND FUNERARY
- BT INHUMATION CEMETERY
- RT ANIMAL MEMORIAL

ANIMAL DWELLING
- SN Including accommodation for animals, birds, reptiles and fish in captivity.
- CL RECREATIONAL

- NT ANIMAL CAGE
  - ANIMAL HOUSE
  - ZOO

ANIMAL HOUSE
- SN Living quarters for animals, birds, etc, as pets or for observation, entertainment, etc.
- CL RECREATIONAL
- BT ANIMAL DWELLING
- NT AQUARIUM
  - AVIARY
  - BEAR PIT
  - DOLPHINARIUM
  - ELEPHANT HOUSE
  - GIRAFFE HOUSE
  - KENNELS
  - MONKEY HOUSE
  - PARROT HOUSE
  - PENGUIN POOL
  - REPTILE HOUSE
  - SEA LION POOL
- RT ANIMAL SHED

ANIMAL MEMORIAL
- UF Cat Memorial
  - Dogs Gravestone
- CL COMMEMORATIVE
- BT COMMEMORATIVE MONUMENT
- RT ANIMAL CEMETERY

Animal Pound
- USE POUND

ANIMAL POWER SITE
- CL INDUSTRIAL
- BT POWER GENERATION SITE
- NT CRANEWHEEL
  - DONKEY WHEEL
  - HORSE ENGINE
  - HORSE ENGINE HOUSE
  - HORSE WHEEL
  - HORSE WHIM
  - TREADMILL
  - TREADWHEEL
  - WINDLASS
- RT WINDING CIRCLE

ANIMAL PRODUCT SITE
- CL INDUSTRIAL
- NT BONE MILL
  - FLEECING SHOP
  - GLUE FACTORY
  - HORN WORKING SITE
  - HORSEHAIR FACTORY
  - LEATHER INDUSTRY SITE
  - SMOKE HOUSE
  - SOAKING PIT
  - SOAP FACTORY
  - TALLOW FACTORY

ANIMAL SHED
- UF Beasthouse
  - Stock House
  - Stock Shed
- SN For non agricultural use see ANIMAL HOUSE and narrow terms in RECREATIONAL class.
- CL AGRICULTURE AND SUBSISTENCE
- BT FARM BUILDING
- NT CALF HOUSE
  - CATTLE SHELTER
  - CATTLE UNIT
  - COW HOUSE
  - DONKEY HOUSE
  - OXHOUSE
  - PIGSTY
  - SHEEP HOUSE
  - SHEEP SHEARING SHED
  - SHELTER SHED
  - STABLE

STALLION HOUSE
RT ANIMAL HOUSE
   SHED

ANIMAL WASH
CL AGRICULTURE AND SUBSISTENCE
NT CATTLE WASH
   HORSE WASH
   SHEEP DIP
   WASHFOLD

ANIMAL WELFARE SITE
CL HEALTH AND WELFARE
NT DOGS HOME
   VETERINARY HOSPITAL

ANNEALING FURNACE
UF Annealing Oven
SN For reheating of worked metal or glass to make it
   malleable or to harden it after use for
   toolmaking, etc.
CL INDUSTRIAL
BT FURNACE
RT NON FERROUS METAL SMELTING SITE

Annealing Oven
USE ANNEALING FURNACE

Annuellars Hall
USE CHANTRY COLLEGE

Annular Enclosure
USE CURVILINEAR ENCLOSURE

ANTENATAL BLOCK
CL HEALTH AND WELFARE
BT HOSPITAL BLOCK
RT MATERNITY CLINIC
   MATERNITY HOSPITAL

Anthaeum
USE CONSERVATORY

ANTI AIRCRAFT BATTERY
CL DEFENCE
BT BATTERY
RT LISTENING POST

ANTI AIRCRAFT CRUISER
CL MARITIME
BT CRUISER

Anti Glider Ditch
USE AIRCRAFT OBSTRUCTION

Anti Tank Block
USE TANK TRAP

ANTIMONY MINE
SN When secondary product use with major product and
   MINE, eg. COPPER MINE.
CL INDUSTRIAL
BT NON FERROUS METAL EXTRACTION SITE
RT COPPER MINE

ANTIMONY MINE
SN When secondary product use with major product and
   MINE, eg. COPPER MINE.
CL INDUSTRIAL
BT MINE
RT COPPER MINE

Antique Auction Rooms
USE AUCTION HOUSE

ANTIQUE MARKET
CL COMMERCIAL
BT MARKET

APARTMENT

UF Flat
CL DOMESTIC
BT DWELLING
RT LODGINGS

APIARY
UF Bee House
CL AGRICULTURE AND SUBSISTENCE
BT AGRICULTURAL BUILDING
RT BEE BOLE
   BEE GARDEN
   BEE SKEP
   BEEHIVE

Apple Crusher
USE CIDER PRESS

Applecrusher
USE CIDER PRESS

APPRENTICE HOUSE
UF Mill Apprentice House
CL DOMESTIC
BT INDUSTRIAL HOUSE

APPRENTICE HOUSE
UF Mill Apprentice House
CL INDUSTRIAL
BT INDUSTRIAL HOUSE

APPROACH ROAD
UF Bridge Approach Road
CL TRANSPORT
BT ROAD
RT BRIDGE
   CAUSEWAY

Approved School
USE JUVENILE PRISON

Aquaduct
USE AQUEDUCT

AQUARIUM
CL RECREATIONAL
BT ANIMAL HOUSE

AQUEDUCT
UF Aquaduct
   Aquaduct Bridge
   Canal Aquaduct
   Canal Aqueduct
   Canal Viaduct
CL WATER SUPPLY AND DRAINAGE
BT WATERCOURSE
RT BRIDGE
   BRIDGE KEEPERS COTTAGE
   CANAL
   CANAL BRIDGE
   CONDUIT
   ROVING BRIDGE
   VIADUCT
   WATER CHANNEL
   WATERWORKS

AQUEDUCT
UF Aquaduct
   Aquaduct Bridge
   Canal Aquaduct
   Canal Aqueduct
   Canal Viaduct
CL TRANSPORT
BT WATER TRANSPORT SITE
RT BRIDGE
   BRIDGE KEEPERS COTTAGE
   CANAL
   CANAL BRIDGE
   CONDUIT
   ROVING BRIDGE

VIADUCT
WATER CHANNEL
WATERWORKS

Aqueduct Bridge
USE AQUEDUCT

Araucaria House
USE ARBORETUM

ARBORETUM
UF Araucaria House
    Arboretum Rooms
CL GARDENS, PARKS AND URBAN SPACES
BT GARDEN
RT BOTANIC GARDEN

Arboretum Rooms
USE ARBORETUM

ARBOUR
SN A lattice work bower or shady retreat covered with
    climbing plants.
CL GARDENS, PARKS AND URBAN SPACES
BT GARDEN RETREAT
NT TUNNEL ARBOUR
RT GARDEN SEAT
    PERGOLA
    ROOT HOUSE
    TRELLIS

ARCH
UF Archway
    Ceremonial Arch
    Commemorative Arch
    Monumental Arch
CL UNASSIGNED
RT TRIUMPHAL ARCH

ARCHBISHOPS MANOR HOUSE
CL DOMESTIC
BT CLERICAL DWELLING
RT ABBOTS SUMMER PALACE
    MANOR HOUSE

ARCHBISHOPS PALACE
CL DOMESTIC
BT PALACE
RT BISHOPS PALACE

ARCHDEACONRY
CL DOMESTIC
BT CLERICAL DWELLING

ARCHERY BUTTS
CL DEFENCE
BT BUTTS

ARCHERY BUTTS
CL RECREATIONAL
BT BUTTS

Architects Drawing Office
USE DRAWING OFFICE

ARCHITECTURAL ORNAMENT WORKSHOP
CL INDUSTRIAL
BT CRAFT INDUSTRY SITE

ARCHITECTURE SCHOOL
UF Naval Architecture School
CL EDUCATION
BT TRAINING SCHOOL

Archway
USE ARCH

Ardmarks
USE PLOUGH MARKS

Arena
USE AMPHITHEATRE

ARMAMENT DEPOT
UF Munitions Depot
    Naval Armament Depot
CL DEFENCE
BT ARMAMENT STORE
RT ARMY CAMP
    ORDNANCE YARD

ARMAMENT MANUFACTURING SITE
CL INDUSTRIAL
NT ARSENAL
    CANNON BORING MILL
    GUN TESTING SHOP
    GUNPOWDER MIXING HOUSE
    GUNPOWDER WORKS
    MUNITIONS FACTORY
    ORDNANCE FACTORY
    ORDNANCE YARD
    PROVING HOUSE
    SHOT TOWER

ARMAMENT STORE
CL DEFENCE
NT ARMAMENT DEPOT
    ARMOURY
    ARSENAL
    MAGAZINE
    MUNITION HOUSE
    ORDNANCE STORE
RT MILITARY BASE
    ORDNANCE FACTORY

Armaments Factory
USE ORDNANCE FACTORY

ARMOURY
CL DEFENCE
BT ARMAMENT STORE
RT ORDNANCE YARD

Army And Navy Club
USE SERVICES CLUB

Army Barracks
USE BARRACKS

ARMY CAMP
CL DEFENCE
BT MILITARY CAMP
RT ARMAMENT DEPOT
    BARRACKS
    COOKHOUSE
    FIRING RANGE
    OFFICERS MESS
    PRISONER OF WAR CAMP
    REGIMENTAL DEPOT
    SERGEANTS MESS

Army Hospital
USE MILITARY HOSPITAL

ARMY OFFICE
CL DEFENCE
RT OFFICE
    RECRUITING STATION

Arrouiasian Abbey
USE ABBEY
    AUGUSTINIAN MONASTERY
SN Use ABBEY with AUGUSTINIAN MONASTERY.

Arrouiasian Priory
USE AUGUSTINIAN MONASTERY
    PRIORY
SN Use PRIORY with AUGUSTINIAN MONASTERY.

ARSENAL
  UF   Naval Arsenal
  CL   INDUSTRIAL
  BT   ARMAMENT MANUFACTURING SITE
  RT   FOUNDRY
       GUNPOWDER DRYING HOUSE
       ORDNANCE FACTORY
       SHIFTING HOUSE

ARSENAL
  UF   Naval Arsenal
  CL   DEFENCE
  BT   ARMAMENT STORE
  RT   CANNON BORING MILL
       FOUNDRY
       GUN TESTING SHOP
       ORDNANCE FACTORY
       ORDNANCE YARD
       SHIFTING HOUSE

ARSENIC CALCINER
  CL   INDUSTRIAL
  BT   CALCINER
  RT   ARSENIC WORKS

ARSENIC CALCINER
  CL   INDUSTRIAL
  BT   NON FERROUS METAL SMELTING SITE
  RT   CONDENSING CHIMNEY
       CONDENSING FLUE

Arsenic Flue
  USE CONDENSING FLUE

ARSENIC MINE
  SN   When secondary product use with major product and
       MINE, eg. COPPER MINE.
  CL   INDUSTRIAL
  BT   NON FERROUS METAL EXTRACTION SITE
  RT   ARSENIC WORKS

ARSENIC MINE
  SN   When secondary product use with major product and
       MINE, eg. COPPER MINE.
  CL   INDUSTRIAL
  BT   MINE

ARSENIC WORKS
  CL   INDUSTRIAL
  BT   CHEMICAL PRODUCTION SITE
  RT   ARSENIC CALCINER
       ARSENIC MINE
       CONDENSING CHIMNEY
       CONDENSING FLUE

Art Academy
  USE ART SCHOOL

ART AND EDUCATION VENUE
  CL   RECREATIONAL
  NT   ART GALLERY
       ARTS CENTRE
       CAMERA OBSCURA
       DIORAMA
       EXHIBITION HALL
       EXHIBITION PAVILION
       LIBRARY
       MUSEUM
       PANORAMA
       PHOTOGRAPHIC GALLERY
       PLANETARIUM

ART GALLERY
  UF   Public Gallery
  CL   EDUCATION
  RT   ARTS CENTRE
       COMMERCIAL ART GALLERY
       EXHIBITION HALL

       MUSEUM

ART GALLERY
  UF   Public Gallery
  CL   RECREATIONAL
  BT   ART AND EDUCATION VENUE
  RT   COMMERCIAL ART GALLERY

ART SCHOOL
  UF   Academy Of Art
       Art Academy
       College Of Art
       Fine Art Academy
       School Of Arts And Crafts
  CL   EDUCATION
  BT   TRAINING SCHOOL

ARTIFICAL DYE WORKS
  CL   INDUSTRIAL
  BT   DYE WORKS
  RT   COPPERAS WORKS

ARTIFICIAL MOUND
  UF   Mount
  CL   GARDENS, PARKS AND URBAN SPACES
  NT   PROSPECT MOUND
  RT   MOUND

Artificial Ruin
  USE FOLLY

ARTIFICIAL TEXTILE FACTORY
  UF   Rayon Factory
       Synthetic Textile Factory
  SN   For chemical processes making nylon, rayon, etc.
  CL   INDUSTRIAL
  BT   CLOTHING INDUSTRY SITE
  RT   PLASTICS FACTORY

ARTIFICIAL TEXTILE FACTORY
  UF   Rayon Factory
       Synthetic Textile Factory
  SN   For chemical processes making nylon, rayon, etc.
  CL   INDUSTRIAL
  BT   TEXTILE MILL

ARTILLERY CASTLE
  SN   Castles constructed between 1481 and 1561 for
       defence using heavy guns.
  CL   DEFENCE
  BT   CASTLE
  RT   ARTILLERY TOWER
       BATTERY
       BLOCKHOUSE
       FORT
       MARTELLO TOWER
       STAR FORT

ARTILLERY FORT
  SN   Artillery positions from the Civil War to the 19th
       century.
  CL   DEFENCE
  BT   FORT
  RT   GUN EMPLACEMENT
       GYRUS
       SCONCE

ARTILLERY GROUND
  CL   DEFENCE
  RT   ARTILLERY SCHOOL
       FIRING RANGE
       PARADE GROUND

Artillery Hospital
  USE MILITARY HOSPITAL

Artillery Mound
  USE SCONCE

ARTILLERY SCHOOL

CL DEFENCE
RT ARTILLERY GROUND
    MILITARY COLLEGE
    NAVAL COLLEGE

ARTILLERY SCHOOL
CL EDUCATION
BT TRAINING SCHOOL
RT ARTILLERY GROUND
    MILITARY COLLEGE
    NAVAL COLLEGE

ARTILLERY TOWER
UF Gun Tower
CL DEFENCE
RT ARTILLERY CASTLE
    BLOCKHOUSE
    MARTELLO TOWER

Artisans Dwelling
USE LODGING HOUSE

Artists House
USE STUDIO HOUSE

ARTS CENTRE
CL RECREATIONAL
BT ART AND EDUCATION VENUE
RT ART GALLERY
    CONCERT HALL
    THEATRE

ASH HOUSE
CL AGRICULTURE AND SUBSISTENCE
BT AGRICULTURAL BUILDING

ASH PIT
CL DOMESTIC
RT RUBBISH PIT

ASSAY OFFICE
CL COMMERCIAL
BT COMMERCIAL OFFICE
RT COINAGE HALL
    GOLDSMITHS WORKSHOP
    MARKET HALL
    MINE
    MOOT HALL
    OFFICE
    PROVING HOUSE
    SILVERSMITHS WORKSHOP
    WEIGH HOUSE

ASSEMBLY HALL
CL CIVIL
BT MEETING HALL
RT ASSEMBLY ROOMS

ASSEMBLY PLANT
CL INDUSTRIAL
BT ENGINEERING INDUSTRY SITE
RT FACTORY
    PATTERN SHOP
    PLASTICS FACTORY
    VEHICLE ENGINEERING SITE
    WORKS

Assembly Room
USE ASSEMBLY ROOMS

ASSEMBLY ROOMS
UF Assembly Room
CL CIVIL
BT PUBLIC BUILDING
RT ASSEMBLY HALL
    BANQUETING HOUSE
    CONCERT HALL
    PUMP ROOMS

ASSEMBLY ROOMS

UF Assembly Room
CL RECREATIONAL
RT ASSEMBLY HALL
    BANQUETING HOUSE
    CONCERT HALL
    PUMP ROOMS

ASSIZE COURT
CL CIVIL
BT LAW COURT
RT JUDGES LODGINGS

Assurance Office
USE COMMERCIAL OFFICE

Asylum
USE MENTAL HOSPITAL

Asylum For Aged And Decayed Freemasons
USE ALMSHOUSE

Asylum For Pauper Imbeciles
USE MENTAL HOSPITAL

ATHENAEUM
CL EDUCATION
BT LITERARY AND SCIENTIFIC INSTITUTE
RT LEARNED SOCIETY BUILDING
    PROFESSIONAL INSTITUTE

ATHENAEUM
CL INSTITUTIONAL
BT LITERARY AND SCIENTIFIC INSTITUTE

ATHLETICS TRACK
CL RECREATIONAL
BT SPORTS SITE

ATMOSPHERIC ENGINE HOUSE
SN Building housing a form of early steam engine
    using steam at atmospheric pressure. Chiefly
    employed in mine pumping.
CL INDUSTRIAL
BT ENGINE HOUSE
RT MINE PUMPING SHAFT
    STEAM ENGINE

ATMOSPHERIC RAILWAY
CL TRANSPORT
BT RAILWAY
RT ATMOSPHERIC RAILWAY ENGINE HOUSE

ATMOSPHERIC RAILWAY ENGINE HOUSE
UF Atmospheric Railway Pumping Station
CL INDUSTRIAL
BT ENGINE HOUSE
RT ATMOSPHERIC RAILWAY
    STEAM ENGINE
    STEAM ENGINE HOUSE

ATMOSPHERIC RAILWAY ENGINE HOUSE
UF Atmospheric Railway Pumping Station
CL TRANSPORT
BT RAILWAY TRANSPORT SITE
RT ATMOSPHERIC RAILWAY

Atmospheric Railway Pumping Station
USE ATMOSPHERIC RAILWAY ENGINE HOUSE

Atomic Power Station
USE NUCLEAR POWER STATION

Attic Workshop
USE TOPSHOP

AUCTION HOUSE
UF Antique Auction Rooms
    Auction Rooms
    Horse And Carriage Auction Rooms

CL   COMMERCIAL

Auction Rooms
USE   AUCTION HOUSE

Augustinian Abbey
USE   ABBEY
        AUGUSTINIAN MONASTERY
        AUGUSTINIAN NUNNERY
        AUGUSTINIAN DOUBLE HOUSE
SN   Use ABBEY with AUGUSTINIAN DOUBLE
        HOUSE/MONASTERY/NUNNERY.

AUGUSTINIAN ALIEN CELL
UF   Augustinian Alien Priory Cell
CL   RELIGIOUS, RITUAL AND FUNERARY
BT   ALIEN CELL

Augustinian Alien Priory
USE   AUGUSTINIAN MONASTERY
        AUGUSTINIAN NUNNERY
        ALIEN PRIORY
        AUGUSTINIAN DOUBLE HOUSE
SN   Use ALIEN PRIORY with AUGUSTINIAN DOUBLE
        HOUSE/MONASTERY or NUNNERY.

Augustinian Alien Priory Cell
USE   AUGUSTINIAN ALIEN CELL

Augustinian Cathedral Priory
USE   CATHEDRAL
        AUGUSTINIAN MONASTERY
        PRIORY
SN   Use all terms.

AUGUSTINIAN CELL
UF   Augustinian Priory Cell
CL   RELIGIOUS, RITUAL AND FUNERARY
BT   CELL
RT   AUGUSTINIAN DOUBLE HOUSE
        AUGUSTINIAN GRANGE
        AUGUSTINIAN MONASTERY
        AUGUSTINIAN NUNNERY

AUGUSTINIAN DOUBLE HOUSE
UF   Augustinian Abbey
        Augustinian Alien Priory
SN   Mixed house of Augustinian nuns, canonesses and
        canons.
CL   RELIGIOUS, RITUAL AND FUNERARY
BT   DOUBLE HOUSE
RT   AUGUSTINIAN CELL
        AUGUSTINIAN GRANGE
        AUGUSTINIAN MONASTERY
        AUGUSTINIAN NUNNERY

AUGUSTINIAN GRANGE
CL   RELIGIOUS, RITUAL AND FUNERARY
BT   GRANGE
RT   AUGUSTINIAN CELL
        AUGUSTINIAN DOUBLE HOUSE
        AUGUSTINIAN MONASTERY
        AUGUSTINIAN NUNNERY

AUGUSTINIAN GRANGE
CL   AGRICULTURE AND SUBSISTENCE
BT   GRANGE

AUGUSTINIAN MONASTERY
UF   Arrouiasian Abbey
        Arrouiasian Priory
        Augustinian Abbey
        Augustinian Alien Priory
        Augustinian Cathedral Priory
        Augustinian Priory
        Holy Sepulchre Priory
        Victorine Abbey
        Victorine Priory
SN   Abbeys and priories of Augustinian canons.
CL   RELIGIOUS, RITUAL AND FUNERARY

BT   MONASTERY
RT   AUGUSTINIAN CELL
        AUGUSTINIAN DOUBLE HOUSE
        AUGUSTINIAN GRANGE
        AUGUSTINIAN NUNNERY

AUGUSTINIAN NUNNERY
UF   Augustinian Abbey
        Augustinian Alien Priory
        Augustinian Priory
SN   Abbeys and priories of Augustinian canonesses.
CL   RELIGIOUS, RITUAL AND FUNERARY
BT   NUNNERY
RT   AUGUSTINIAN CELL
        AUGUSTINIAN DOUBLE HOUSE
        AUGUSTINIAN GRANGE
        AUGUSTINIAN MONASTERY

Augustinian Priory
USE   AUGUSTINIAN MONASTERY
        AUGUSTINIAN NUNNERY
        PRIORY
SN   Use PRIORY with AUGUSTINIAN MONASTERY or
        AUGUSTINIAN NUNNERY.

Augustinian Priory Cell
USE   AUGUSTINIAN CELL

AUSTIN FRIARY
SN   Austin or Augustinian friars.
CL   RELIGIOUS, RITUAL AND FUNERARY
BT   FRIARY

Automata
USE   TRICK FOUNTAIN

AUXILIARY CRUISER
CL   MARITIME
BT   CRUISER

AUXILIARY FORT
CL   DEFENCE
BT   FORT
RT   FORTLET
        GYRUS

Avenue
USE   STONE AVENUE
        TREE AVENUE
        EMBANKED AVENUE
SN   Use appropriate term, eg. TREE AVENUE.

AVIARY
UF   Bird House
CL   GARDENS, PARKS AND URBAN SPACES

AVIARY
UF   Bird House
CL   RECREATIONAL
BT   ANIMAL HOUSE

Axe Factory
USE   STONE AXE FACTORY

BACK HOUSE
UF   Backhouse
SN   A brewing or baking house attached to a vernacular
        house, 16/17th century.
CL   AGRICULTURE AND SUBSISTENCE
BT   AGRICULTURAL BUILDING
RT   BAKEHOUSE
        BREWHOUSE

Back To Back
USE   BACK TO BACK HOUSE

Back To Back Cottage
USE   BACK TO BACK HOUSE

BACK TO BACK HOUSE

UF   Back To Back
      Back To Back Cottage
CL   DOMESTIC
BT   TERRACED HOUSE
NT   THROUGH BY LIGHT
RT   BACK TO BACK TERRACE
      BACK TO EARTH HOUSE
      BLIND BACK HOUSE
      CLUSTER HOUSE

BACK TO BACK TERRACE
CL   DOMESTIC
BT   TERRACE
RT   BACK TO BACK HOUSE

BACK TO EARTH HOUSE
CL   DOMESTIC
BT   TERRACED HOUSE
RT   BACK TO BACK HOUSE
      BACK TO EARTH TERRACE
      BLIND BACK HOUSE
      CLUSTER HOUSE

BACK TO EARTH TERRACE
CL   DOMESTIC
BT   TERRACE
RT   BACK TO EARTH HOUSE

Backhouse
      USE BACK HOUSE

BACKYARD
CL   GARDENS, PARKS AND URBAN SPACES
RT   HOUSE
      YARD

Bacon Factory
      USE FOOD PROCESSING PLANT

Baconer House
      USE FATTENING HOUSE

BADGER PIT
CL   RECREATIONAL
BT   BAITING PLACE

BAG BURIAL
CL   RELIGIOUS, RITUAL AND FUNERARY
BT   BURIAL

BAILEY
UF   Inner Bailey
      Outer Bailey
SN   Component. Use with wider site type where known.
CL   DOMESTIC
RT   CASTLE
      ENCLOSURE
      MOTTE
      MOTTE AND BAILEY
      RINGWORK
      RINGWORK AND BAILEY

BAILEY
UF   Inner Bailey
      Outer Bailey
SN   Component. Use with wider site type where known.
CL   DEFENCE
RT   CASTLE
      ENCLOSURE
      MOTTE
      MOTTE AND BAILEY
      RINGWORK
      RINGWORK AND BAILEY

BAITING PLACE
UF   Gaming Pit
SN   Use more specific site type where known.
CL   RECREATIONAL
NT   BADGER PIT

      BULLRING
      COCKPIT
RT   GAMING HOUSE

BAKEHOUSE
UF   Bakern
SN   If commercial premises use BAKERY.
CL   DOMESTIC
NT   COMMUNAL BAKEHOUSE
RT   BACK HOUSE
      BAKERY
      BREWHOUSE
      COUNTRY HOUSE
      KITCHEN

Bakern
      USE BAKEHOUSE

BAKERS SHOP
CL   COMMERCIAL
BT   SHOP
RT   BAKERY

BAKERY
SN   If domestic use BAKEHOUSE.
CL   INDUSTRIAL
BT   FOOD PROCESSING SITE
RT   BAKEHOUSE
      BAKERS SHOP
      FLOUR MILL
      GRANARY

BAKERY
SN   If domestic use BAKEHOUSE.
CL   COMMERCIAL
RT   BAKEHOUSE
      BAKERS SHOP

BALANCE BEAM
SN   The horizontal beam on a lock gate.
CL   TRANSPORT
BT   WATER TRANSPORT SITE
RT   LOCK

BALANCE BEAM
SN   The horizontal beam on a lock gate.
CL   MARITIME
BT   WATER REGULATION INSTALLATION

Balk Yard
      USE TIMBER YARD

Ball Clay Mine
      USE BALL CLAY WORKS

BALL CLAY WORKS
UF   Ball Clay Mine
SN   Works producing a clay of high plasticity and
      firmness, used as a basic raw material for
      porcelain.
CL   INDUSTRIAL
BT   POTTERY MANUFACTURING SITE

BALL CLAY WORKS
UF   Ball Clay Mine
SN   Works producing a clay of high plasticity and
      firmness, used as a basic raw material for
      porcelain.
CL   INDUSTRIAL
BT   CLAY EXTRACTION SITE

BALLET SCHOOL
CL   EDUCATION
BT   TRAINING SCHOOL
RT   DANCE STUDIO

BALUSTRADE
CL   GARDENS, PARKS AND URBAN SPACES

BAMBOO GARDEN

CL GARDENS, PARKS AND URBAN SPACES
BT GARDEN

BANDSTAND
    CL GARDENS, PARKS AND URBAN SPACES
    RT PUBLIC PARK
           TEA HOUSE

BANDSTAND
    CL RECREATIONAL
    BT MUSIC AND DANCE VENUE
    RT PUBLIC PARK
           TEA HOUSE

BANJO ENCLOSURE
    CL DOMESTIC
    BT ENCLOSED SETTLEMENT

BANK (EARTHWORK)
    SN Use specific site type where known.
    CL UNASSIGNED
    BT EARTHWORK
    NT RING BANK

BANK (FINANCIAL)
    CL COMMERCIAL
    RT CLEARING HOUSE

BANK BARN
    CL AGRICULTURE AND SUBSISTENCE
    BT BARN
    RT CATTLE SHELTER
           COMBINATION BARN
           COW HOUSE
           FIELD BARN
           HAYLOFT
           LINHAY
           VACCARY

BANK BARROW
    CL RELIGIOUS, RITUAL AND FUNERARY
    BT BARROW
    RT LONG BARROW

Bank Chambers
    USE COMMERCIAL OFFICE

Bank Office
    USE COMMERCIAL OFFICE

Banquet Hall
    USE BANQUETING HOUSE

Banquet House
    USE BANQUETING HOUSE

Banqueting Hall
    USE BANQUETING HOUSE

BANQUETING HOUSE
    UF Banquet Hall
           Banquet House
           Banqueting Hall
    CL GARDENS, PARKS AND URBAN SPACES
    BT GARDEN BUILDING
    RT ASSEMBLY ROOMS
           MARRIAGE FEAST HOUSE
           PALACE
           ROYAL PALACE

BANQUETING HOUSE
    UF Banquet Hall
           Banquet House
           Banqueting Hall
    CL RECREATIONAL
    BT EATING AND DRINKING ESTABLISHMENT
    RT ASSEMBLY ROOMS
           MARRIAGE FEAST HOUSE
           PALACE

           ROYAL PALACE

BAPTIST BURIAL GROUND
    CL RELIGIOUS, RITUAL AND FUNERARY
    BT INHUMATION CEMETERY

BAPTIST CHAPEL
    UF Baptist Meeting House
           Baptist Tabernacle
    CL RELIGIOUS, RITUAL AND FUNERARY
    BT NONCONFORMIST CHAPEL
    NT GENERAL BAPTIST CHAPEL
           PARTICULAR BAPTIST CHAPEL
           SCOTCH BAPTIST CHAPEL
           STRICT BAPTIST CHAPEL

Baptist College
    USE THEOLOGICAL COLLEGE

Baptist Meeting House
    USE BAPTIST CHAPEL

Baptist Tabernacle
    USE BAPTIST CHAPEL

BAPTISTERY
    UF Baptistry
    SN Free-standing building.
    CL RELIGIOUS, RITUAL AND FUNERARY
    RT FONT
           NONCONFORMIST CHAPEL

Baptistry
    USE BAPTISTERY

Bar
    USE TOWN GATE

Bar Gate
    USE TOWN GATE

BARBERS SHOP
    CL COMMERCIAL
    BT SHOP
    RT HAIRDRESSERS SALON

BARBICAN
    SN Any earthworks, walling, bastion or fortified
           outwork, or combination of these, generally with
           ditch or moat.
    CL DEFENCE
    RT CASTLE
           GATE
           GATE TOWER
           GATEHOUSE
           TOWN DEFENCES

BARGE
    SN Shallow draft cargo vessel, often broad beamed and
           flat bottomed, powered by engine or sail.
    CL MARITIME
    BT CARGO VESSEL
    NT HOPPER BARGE
           LIGHTER

BARGE WINCH
    CL TRANSPORT
    BT WINCH
    RT CANAL
           CANAL LIFT
           INCLINE WINDING ENGINE
           INCLINED PLANE

BARK HOUSE
    SN Storage place for tree bark.
    CL INDUSTRIAL
    BT WOOD PRODUCT SITE
    RT BARK MILL
           BARK PEELERS HUT

BARK HOUSE
- SN Storage place for tree bark.
- CL AGRICULTURE AND SUBSISTENCE
- BT AGRICULTURAL BUILDING
- RT BARK MILL
  - BARK PEELERS HUT
  - TANNERY

BARK MILL
- SN Mill for stripping the bark from sawn tree trunks.
  - Use with power type(s), eg. WATERMILL where known.
- CL INDUSTRIAL
- BT MILL
- RT BARK HOUSE
  - BARK PEELERS HUT
  - GRINDSTONE

BARK MILL
- SN Mill for stripping the bark from sawn tree trunks.
  - Use with power type(s), eg. WATERMILL where known.
- CL INDUSTRIAL
- BT WOOD PRODUCT SITE
- RT BARK HOUSE
  - LOGWOOD MILL
  - PAPER INDUSTRY SITE
  - TANNERY

BARK PEELERS HUT
- CL DOMESTIC
- BT HUT
- RT BARK HOUSE
  - BARK MILL
  - INDUSTRIAL HOUSE

BARK PEELERS HUT
- CL AGRICULTURE AND SUBSISTENCE
- BT AGRICULTURAL BUILDING
- RT BARK HOUSE
  - BARK MILL

BARK PEELERS HUT
- CL INDUSTRIAL
- BT WOOD PRODUCT SITE
- RT BARK HOUSE
  - WOODWORKERS HUT
  - WOODWORKING SITE

Barmekin
USE BARMKIN

BARMKIN
- UF Barmekin
- SN A defensive cattle enclosure added to fortified towers.
- CL DEFENCE
- RT PELE TOWER
  - TOWER HOUSE

BARN
- UF Abbey Barn
  - Monastery Barn
  - Priory Barn
- CL AGRICULTURE AND SUBSISTENCE
- BT FARM BUILDING
- NT BANK BARN
  - BARN PLATFORM
  - COMBINATION BARN
  - COPPICE BARN
  - FIELD BARN
  - GRANGE BARN
  - HAY BARN
  - HOP BARN
  - MIXING HOUSE BARN
  - THRESHING BARN
  - TITHE BARN
- RT COPPICE BARN
  - GRANARY
  - GRANGE

LAITHE
LONG HOUSE
STADDLE STONE
THRESHING FLOOR

BARN PLATFORM
- CL AGRICULTURE AND SUBSISTENCE
- BT BARN
- RT BUILDING PLATFORM
  - PLATFORM
  - STACK STAND

Barrack Block
USE BARRACKS

BARRACKS
- UF Air Force Barracks
  - Army Barracks
  - Barrack Block
  - Cavalry Barracks
  - Naval Barracks
- CL DEFENCE
- RT FORT
  - MILITARY BASE
  - MILITARY CAMP
  - PARADE GROUND

BARRACKS
- UF Air Force Barracks
  - Army Barracks
  - Barrack Block
  - Cavalry Barracks
  - Naval Barracks
- CL DOMESTIC
- BT RESIDENTIAL BUILDING
- RT ARMY CAMP
  - BLOCKHOUSE
  - COOKHOUSE
  - DRILL HALL
  - OFFICERS MESS
  - SERGEANTS MESS

BARRAGE BALLOON SITE
- CL DEFENCE

BARRAGE BALLOON VESSEL
- CL MARITIME
- BT SERVICE CRAFT

Barristers Office
USE LEGAL OFFICE

BARROW
- UF Burial Mound
  - Hlaew
  - Howe
  - Knowe
  - Tumulus
- CL RELIGIOUS, RITUAL AND FUNERARY
- BT FUNERARY SITE
- NT BANK BARROW
  - CHAMBERED BARROW
  - D SHAPED BARROW
  - LONG BARROW
  - OVAL BARROW
  - POND BARROW
  - RING BARROW
  - ROUND BARROW
  - SQUARE BARROW
- RT BARROW CEMETERY
  - BURIAL CAIRN
  - MORTUARY ENCLOSURE
  - MORTUARY HOUSE
  - MOUND

BARROW CEMETERY
- UF Barrow Field
  - Round Barrow Cemetery
  - Square Barrow Cemetery

CL RELIGIOUS, RITUAL AND FUNERARY
BT CEMETERY
RT BARROW

Barrow Field
    USE BARROW CEMETERY

Barth
    USE CATTLE SHELTER

Barton
    USE FARMHOUSE

BARYTES MINE
CL INDUSTRIAL
BT MINE
RT LEAD MINE
    WITHERITE MINE

BASE CRUCK HOUSE
CL DOMESTIC
BT CRUCK HOUSE

BASEMENT
SN Component. Use wider site type where known.
CL UNASSIGNED

BASILICA
CL CIVIL
RT FORUM

BASILICA
CL COMMERCIAL
RT FORUM

BASKET BURIAL
CL RELIGIOUS, RITUAL AND FUNERARY
BT BURIAL

BASKET MAKERS WORKSHOP
UF Basket Works
    Spale Makers Workshop
    Spelk Makers Workshop
    Swill Makers Workshop
CL INDUSTRIAL
BT WOOD PRODUCT SITE

BASKET MAKERS WORKSHOP
UF Basket Works
    Spale Makers Workshop
    Spelk Makers Workshop
    Swill Makers Workshop
CL INDUSTRIAL
BT CRAFT INDUSTRY SITE

Basket Works
    USE BASKET MAKERS WORKSHOP

Bastel House
    USE BASTLE

BASTION
UF Beak Bastion
    Boccarum
    Cavalier
    Demi Bastion
    Horn Bastion
    Orillon
    Pointed Bastion
    Tour En Bec
CL DEFENCE
NT BASTION OUTWORK
RT CASTLE
    CURTAIN WALL
    FLANKER
    FORT
    FORTRESS
    SCONCE
    TOWN DEFENCES

BASTION OUTWORK
UF Half Moon
    Lunette
    Ravelin
    Redan
    Redoubt
    Tenaille
    Tenaillon
CL DEFENCE
BT BASTION

BASTION TRACE FORT
CL DEFENCE
BT FORT
RT STAR FORT

BASTLE
UF Bastel House
    Bastle House
CL DOMESTIC
BT FORTIFIED HOUSE
RT FARMHOUSE

BASTLE
UF Bastel House
    Bastle House
CL DEFENCE
BT FORTIFIED HOUSE

Bastle House
    USE BASTLE

BATH HOUSE
UF Bathing House
    Bathing Pavilion
SN A building equipped with facilities for bathing,
    and occasionally public baths.
CL WATER SUPPLY AND DRAINAGE
RT BATHS
    COUNTRY HOUSE
    FORT
    HYPOCAUST
    WASH HOUSE

BATH HOUSE
UF Bathing House
    Bathing Pavilion
SN A building equipped with facilities for bathing,
    and occasionally public baths.
CL HEALTH AND WELFARE
RT BATHS
    COUNTRY HOUSE
    FORT
    HYPOCAUST
    WASH HOUSE

Bathing House
    USE BATH HOUSE

Bathing Hut
    USE BEACH HUT

Bathing Pavilion
    USE BATH HOUSE

BATHS
UF City Baths
    Municipal Baths
    Public Baths
    Swimming Baths
SN A building containing a number of areas for
    bathing.
CL HEALTH AND WELFARE
NT MINERAL BATHS
    PITHEAD BATHS
    SALT BATHS
    SLIPPER BATHS
    THERMAL BATHS

TURKISH BATHS
RT BATH HOUSE
HYPOCAUST
KURSAAL
PUBLIC WASH HOUSE
PUMP ROOMS
SPA
SPA HOTEL

BATHS
UF City Baths
Municipal Baths
Public Baths
Swimming Baths
SN A building containing a number of areas for bathing.
CL WATER SUPPLY AND DRAINAGE
RT BATH HOUSE
HYPOCAUST
KURSAAL
PUBLIC WASH HOUSE
PUMP ROOMS
SPA
SPA HOTEL

BATTERY
UF Gun Battery
SN Use specific type where known.
CL DEFENCE
NT ANTI AIRCRAFT BATTERY
COASTAL BATTERY
SALUTING BATTERY
SEARCHLIGHT BATTERY
RT ARTILLERY CASTLE
BLOCKHOUSE
FLANKER
GUN EMPLACEMENT
PILLBOX
SCONCE
SIEGEWORK
TANK TRAP

BATTERY MILL
SN Mill incorporating water-powered hammers for beating brass sheet, etc. into vessels, pots, etc.
CL INDUSTRIAL
BT MILL
RT BRASS WORKS

BATTERY MILL
SN Mill incorporating water-powered hammers for beating brass sheet, etc. into vessels, pots, etc.
CL INDUSTRIAL
BT NON FERROUS METAL PRODUCT SITE
RT BRASS WORKS

BATTLECRUISER
CL MARITIME
BT CAPITAL WARSHIP

BATTLEFIELD
CL DEFENCE
RT HISTORICAL SITE

BATTLEFIELD
CL COMMEMORATIVE
RT HISTORICAL SITE

BATTLESHIP
CL MARITIME
BT CAPITAL WARSHIP
NT DREADNOUGHT

BAULK
CL TRANSPORT
BT WATER TRANSPORT SITE

Bazaar
USE MARKET

SHOPPING ARCADE
SN Use both terms.

BEACH DEFENCE
CL MARITIME

BEACH HUT
UF Bathing Hut
CL RECREATIONAL

BEACON
UF Fire Beacon
SN Use for beacon sites or surviving beacon structures.
CL DEFENCE
RT SIGNAL STATION
WATCH TOWER

BEACON
UF Fire Beacon
SN Use for beacon sites or surviving beacon structures.
CL MARITIME
BT NAVIGATION AID
NT REFUGE BEACON
SEA BEACON
RT LIGHTHOUSE
TIMEBALL TOWER

BEACON
UF Fire Beacon
SN Use for beacon sites or surviving beacon structures.
CL COMMUNICATIONS
BT SIGNALLING STRUCTURE
NT RADAR BEACON
REFUGE BEACON
SEA BEACON
RT LIGHTHOUSE
SIGNAL STATION
TIMEBALL TOWER
WATCH TOWER

Bead House
USE ALMSHOUSE

Bead House Chapel
USE ALMSHOUSE
CHAPEL
SN Use both terms.

Beak Bastion
USE BASTION

BEAKER BURIAL
CL RELIGIOUS, RITUAL AND FUNERARY
BT BURIAL

BEAM ENGINE
SN A steam engine with a horizontal beam connecting the piston and crank.
CL INDUSTRIAL
BT STEAM ENGINE
NT ROTATIVE BEAM ENGINE
RT COMPOUND STEAM ENGINE
MINE PUMPING WORKS
PUMPING STATION
STEAM PUMP
VERTICAL STEAM ENGINE

BEAM ENGINE HOUSE
CL INDUSTRIAL
BT STEAM ENGINE HOUSE

BEAM SLOT
SN Component. Use wider site type where known.
CL UNASSIGNED

Beam Station

USE RADIO STATION

Beam Winder House
USE WINDER HOUSE

BEAR PIT
SN   Animal house, rather than baiting place.
CL   RECREATIONAL
BT   ANIMAL HOUSE
RT   PIT

Beast Pond
USE POND

Beasthouse
USE ANIMAL SHED

Bedehouse
USE ALMSHOUSE

Bedehouse Chapel
USE ALMSHOUSE
CHAPEL
SN   Use both terms.

Bedlam
USE MENTAL HOSPITAL

BEE BOLE
UF   Bee Hole
SN   A recess in a wall, in which a bee skepp is
placed.
CL   AGRICULTURE AND SUBSISTENCE
RT   APIARY
BEE GARDEN
BEE SKEP
BEEHIVE

BEE GARDEN
SN   A garden in which bees are kept.
CL   AGRICULTURE AND SUBSISTENCE
BT   GARDEN
RT   APIARY
BEE BOLE
BEE SKEP
BEEHIVE

Bee Hole
USE BEE BOLE

Bee House
USE APIARY

BEE SKEP
SN   A portable beehive, often made of straw.
CL   AGRICULTURE AND SUBSISTENCE
BT   BEEHIVE
RT   APIARY
BEE BOLE
BEE GARDEN

Beef Market
USE MEAT MARKET

BEEHIVE
CL   AGRICULTURE AND SUBSISTENCE
NT   BEE SKEP
RT   APIARY
BEE BOLE
BEE GARDEN

Beehive Hut
USE HUT

Beehive Kiln
USE DOWNDRAUGHT KILN

BEER HOUSE
UF   Ale House

CL   COMMERCIAL
BT   LICENSED PREMISES
RT   ALE STORE
BEER SHOP
INN

BEER SHOP
CL   COMMERCIAL
BT   SHOP
RT   BEER HOUSE
INN
PUBLIC HOUSE

BEETLING MILL
SN   A finishing process for cloth involving the
pounding of the cloth with heavy weights.
CL   INDUSTRIAL
BT   TEXTILE MILL

BEETLING MILL
SN   A finishing process for cloth involving the
pounding of the cloth with heavy weights.
CL   INDUSTRIAL
BT   TEXTILE FINISHING SITE
RT   CALENDER MILL
CLOTH DRY HOUSE
DRABBET FACTORY
FLAX MILL
LINEN MILL

Belfry
USE BELL TOWER

Belgic Oppidum
USE OPPIDUM

BELL BARROW
CL   RELIGIOUS, RITUAL AND FUNERARY
BT   ROUND BARROW

BELL CASTING PIT
CL   INDUSTRIAL
BT   NON FERROUS METAL PRODUCT SITE
RT   BELL FOUNDRY

BELL DISC BARROW
CL   RELIGIOUS, RITUAL AND FUNERARY
BT   FANCY BARROW

BELL FOUNDRY
CL   INDUSTRIAL
BT   NON FERROUS METAL PRODUCT SITE
RT   BELL CASTING PIT

Bell House
USE BELL TOWER

BELL PIT
SN   Use with functional type if known, eg. COAL
WORKINGS.
CL   INDUSTRIAL
BT   EXTRACTIVE PIT
RT   COAL PIT
LEAD WORKINGS
MARL PIT

BELL TOWER
UF   Belfry
Bell House
Campanile
Clocher
CL   RELIGIOUS, RITUAL AND FUNERARY
NT   CURFEW BELL TOWER
RT   CHURCH
TOWER

BELLOWS HOUSE
CL   INDUSTRIAL
BT   FERROUS METAL SMELTING SITE

RT   BLOWING ENGINE HOUSE
      STEEL WORKS

BELT
SN   A narrow plantation of trees around the perimeter
      of a park.
CL   GARDENS, PARKS AND URBAN SPACES
BT   WOODLAND

BELTED CRUISER
CL   MARITIME
BT   CRUISER

BELVEDERE
UF   Standing
SN   A turret, tower or look out occupying a prominent
      position to provide a view, either a separate
      building, or part of a villa.
CL   GARDENS, PARKS AND URBAN SPACES
BT   GARDEN BUILDING
RT   GAZEBO
      PROSPECT TOWER
      TOWER

BENCH
CL   GARDENS, PARKS AND URBAN SPACES
BT   STREET FURNITURE

Benedictine Abbey
USE   ABBEY
      BENEDICTINE MONASTERY
      BENEDICTINE NUNNERY
SN   Use ABBEY and BENEDICTINE MONASTERY/NUNNERY.

BENEDICTINE ALIEN CELL
CL   RELIGIOUS, RITUAL AND FUNERARY
BT   ALIEN CELL

Benedictine Alien Priory
USE   BENEDICTINE MONASTERY
      BENEDICTINE NUNNERY
      ALIEN PRIORY
SN   Use ALIEN PRIORY with BENEDICTINE
      MONASTERY/NUNNERY.

Benedictine Cathedral Priory
USE   CATHEDRAL
      BENEDICTINE MONASTERY
      PRIORY
SN   Use all terms.

BENEDICTINE CELL
UF   Benedictine Priory Cell
CL   RELIGIOUS, RITUAL AND FUNERARY
BT   CELL
RT   BENEDICTINE DOUBLE HOUSE
      BENEDICTINE GRANGE
      BENEDICTINE MONASTERY
      BENEDICTINE NUNNERY

BENEDICTINE DOUBLE HOUSE
CL   RELIGIOUS, RITUAL AND FUNERARY
BT   DOUBLE HOUSE
RT   BENEDICTINE CELL
      BENEDICTINE GRANGE
      BENEDICTINE MONASTERY
      BENEDICTINE NUNNERY

BENEDICTINE GRANGE
CL   RELIGIOUS, RITUAL AND FUNERARY
BT   GRANGE
RT   BENEDICTINE CELL
      BENEDICTINE DOUBLE HOUSE
      BENEDICTINE MONASTERY
      BENEDICTINE NUNNERY

BENEDICTINE GRANGE
CL   AGRICULTURE AND SUBSISTENCE
BT   GRANGE

BENEDICTINE MONASTERY
UF   Benedictine Abbey
      Benedictine Alien Priory
      Benedictine Cathedral Priory
      Benedictine Priory
SN   Abbeys and Priories of Benedictine monks.
CL   RELIGIOUS, RITUAL AND FUNERARY
BT   MONASTERY
RT   BENEDICTINE CELL
      BENEDICTINE DOUBLE HOUSE
      BENEDICTINE GRANGE
      BENEDICTINE NUNNERY

BENEDICTINE NUNNERY
UF   Benedictine Abbey
      Benedictine Alien Priory
      Benedictine Priory
SN   Abbeys and Priories of Benedictine nuns.
CL   RELIGIOUS, RITUAL AND FUNERARY
BT   NUNNERY
RT   BENEDICTINE CELL
      BENEDICTINE DOUBLE HOUSE
      BENEDICTINE GRANGE
      BENEDICTINE MONASTERY

Benedictine Priory
USE   BENEDICTINE MONASTERY
      BENEDICTINE NUNNERY
      PRIORY
SN   Use PRIORY and BENEDICTINE MONASTERY or
      BENEDICTINE NUNNERY.

Benedictine Priory Cell
USE   BENEDICTINE CELL

BENEFICIAL SCHOOL
CL   EDUCATION
BT   FREE SCHOOL

Bercarie
USE   SHEEP HOUSE

BERCEAU
SN   A vault shaped trellis on which climbing plants
      are trained.
CL   GARDENS, PARKS AND URBAN SPACES
BT   TRELLIS

BERTH
CL   MARITIME
BT   LANDING POINT
NT   CONTAINER BERTH
      OIL FUEL BERTH

BETTING OFFICE
UF   Betting Shop
      Book Makers
      Turf Accountants
CL   RECREATIONAL
BT   GAMBLING SITE
RT   OFFICE

Betting Shop
USE   BETTING OFFICE

BIBLE CHRISTIAN CHAPEL
SN   Chapel used by a Protestant sect founded in 1815.
      Found chiefly in the South West.
CL   RELIGIOUS, RITUAL AND FUNERARY
BT   METHODIST CHAPEL

BICYCLE FACTORY
CL   INDUSTRIAL
BT   VEHICLE ENGINEERING SITE

BICYCLE FACTORY
CL   INDUSTRIAL
BT   FACTORY <BY PRODUCT>

BIELD
  SN   Wall built to give shelter to sheep.
  CL   AGRICULTURE AND SUBSISTENCE
  RT   SHEEP FOLD

BIER HOUSE
  CL   RELIGIOUS, RITUAL AND FUNERARY
  RT   CHURCHYARD

BINDERY
  CL   INDUSTRIAL
  BT   CRAFT INDUSTRY SITE
  RT   LEATHER WORKERS SHOP

BINDERY
  CL   INDUSTRIAL
  BT   PRINTING AND PUBLISHING SITE
  RT   PRINT SHOP

BINGO HALL
  CL   RECREATIONAL
  BT   GAMBLING SITE

BIRD BATH
  CL   GARDENS, PARKS AND URBAN SPACES
  BT   GARDEN ORNAMENT

Bird House
  USE AVIARY

Biscuit Kiln
  USE POTTERY KILN

BISHOPS PALACE
  UF   Ecclesiastical Palace
        Episcopal Palace
  CL   DOMESTIC
  BT   PALACE
  NT   BISHOPS SUMMER PALACE
  RT   ARCHBISHOPS PALACE
        SYNODAL HALL

BISHOPS SUMMER PALACE
  CL   DOMESTIC
  BT   BISHOPS PALACE

BIVALLATE HILLFORT
  CL   DOMESTIC
  BT   HILLFORT

BIVALLATE HILLFORT
  CL   DEFENCE
  BT   HILLFORT

Black Yarn House
  USE YARN HOUSE

BLACKING FACTORY
  CL   INDUSTRIAL
  BT   CHEMICAL PRODUCT SITE
  RT   PAINT FACTORY

BLACKING FACTORY
  CL   INDUSTRIAL
  BT   FACTORY <BY PRODUCT>

Blacksmiths Cottage
  USE SMITHS COTTAGE

Blacksmiths Shop
  USE BLACKSMITHS WORKSHOP

BLACKSMITHS WORKSHOP
  UF   Blacksmiths Shop
        Smithery
        Smithy
        Stiddy
        Stithy

  SN   Place where a smith works iron. May be for small
        scale local use or within a larger industrial
        complex.
  CL   INDUSTRIAL
  BT   CRAFT INDUSTRY SITE
  RT   SMITHS COTTAGE

Blade Works
  USE EDGE TOOL WORKS

BLANKET MILL
  CL   INDUSTRIAL
  BT   TEXTILE MILL
  RT   WEAVING MILL

BLANKET MILL
  CL   INDUSTRIAL
  BT   TEXTILE PRODUCT SITE

BLAST FURNACE
  UF   Charcoal Blast Furnace
  SN   Smelting furnace into which compressed hot air is
        driven.
  CL   INDUSTRIAL
  BT   METAL PRODUCTION FURNACE
  RT   BLOWING ENGINE HOUSE
        FERROUS METAL SMELTING SITE
        FOUNDRY
        HAMMER POND
        NON FERROUS METAL SMELTING SITE
        OPEN HEARTH FURNACE

Bleach Croft
  USE BLEACHFIELD

Bleach Green
  USE BLEACHFIELD

Bleach Grounds
  USE BLEACHFIELD

BLEACH WORKS
  SN   Works where bleach is made.
  CL   INDUSTRIAL
  BT   CHEMICAL PRODUCTION SITE
  RT   SODA WORKS

Bleach Yard
  USE BLEACHFIELD

BLEACHERY
  UF   Bleaching Factory
        Bleaching House
  SN   Bleach works or bleach house for bleaching of
        textiles, etc.
  CL   INDUSTRIAL
  BT   TEXTILE FINISHING SITE

BLEACHFIELD
  UF   Bleach Croft
        Bleach Green
        Bleach Grounds
        Bleach Yard
        Bleaching
  SN   Large field used to lay fabrics out ready for
        bleaching.
  CL   INDUSTRIAL
  BT   TEXTILE FINISHING SITE
  RT   TENTER GROUND

Bleaching
  USE BLEACHFIELD

Bleaching Factory
  USE BLEACHERY

Bleaching House
  USE BLEACHERY

BLIND BACK HOUSE

CL DOMESTIC
BT TERRACED HOUSE
RT BACK TO BACK HOUSE
BACK TO EARTH HOUSE
BLIND BACK TERRACE
CLUSTER HOUSE

BLIND BACK TERRACE
CL DOMESTIC
BT TERRACE
RT BLIND BACK HOUSE

Blind School
USE SCHOOL FOR THE BLIND

Block Dwellings
USE MODEL DWELLING

BLOCK MILL
SN Building housing machinery used in the production of wooden pulley blocks for the rigging of sailing ships.
CL INDUSTRIAL
BT TIMBER PRODUCT SITE
RT PLANING MILL
TIMBER SEASONING SHED

BLOCK MILL
SN Building housing machinery used in the production of wooden pulley blocks for the rigging of sailing ships.
CL MARITIME
BT MARINE WORKSHOP

BLOCK MILL
SN Building housing machinery used in the production of wooden pulley blocks for the rigging of sailing ships.
CL INDUSTRIAL
BT MARINE WORKSHOP

Block Of Flats
USE FLATS

BLOCK SHIP
CL MARITIME
BT UNMANNED CRAFT

BLOCKHOUSE
CL DEFENCE
RT ARTILLERY CASTLE
ARTILLERY TOWER
BARRACKS
BATTERY
FORTRESS
PILLBOX
TRENCH

Blockmakers Workshop
USE MARINE WORKSHOP

Blockstone
USE NAVAL STOREHOUSE

Bloom Hearth
USE BLOOMERY

Bloomary
USE BLOOMERY

BLOOMERY
UF Bloom Hearth
Bloomary
Bloomsmithy
String Hearth
SN A charcoal fired shaft furnace used for the direct reduction of iron ore to produce wrought iron.
CL INDUSTRIAL
BT SHAFT FURNACE

Bloomsmithy
USE BLOOMERY

BLOWING ENGINE HOUSE
SN Steam engine, usually, driving a centrifugal fan to provide an air blast for a blast furnace.
CL INDUSTRIAL
BT ENGINE HOUSE
RT BELLOWS HOUSE
BLAST FURNACE
IRON WORKS
STEAM ENGINE

Blowing Furnace
USE GLASS FURNACE

BLOWING HOUSE
UF Jews House
SN A building containing a small stone cylindrical furnace, eg. used for tin smelting in Cornwall.
CL INDUSTRIAL
BT NON FERROUS METAL SMELTING SITE
RT COINAGE HALL
METAL PRODUCTION FURNACE
PEAT STORE
TIN WORKS
TUBE MILL

Blue John Mine
USE FLUORSPAR MINE

Bluecoat School
USE CHARITY SCHOOL

Blunger
USE BLUNGING PIT

BLUNGING PIT
UF Blunger
SN Pit for mixing raw materials with water in the preparation of a clay body.
CL INDUSTRIAL
BT BRICK AND TILEMAKING SITE

BLUNGING PIT
UF Blunger
SN Pit for mixing raw materials with water in the preparation of a clay body.
CL INDUSTRIAL
BT POTTERY MANUFACTURING SITE

BOAR PEN
CL AGRICULTURE AND SUBSISTENCE
BT PEN
RT PIGSTY

BOARD MILL
SN Production of cardboard and other similar products.
CL INDUSTRIAL
BT WOOD PRODUCT SITE

BOARD MILL
SN Production of cardboard and other similar products.
CL INDUSTRIAL
BT PAPER INDUSTRY SITE

BOARD SCHOOL
SN 19th century school administered by a school board.
CL EDUCATION
BT SCHOOL

BOARDING SCHOOL
CL EDUCATION
BT SCHOOL

BOAT

SN A vessel of non specific function up to 30 metres
    long.
CL MARITIME
BT CRAFT
RT BOAT BURIAL

Boat Building Yard
    USE BOAT YARD

BOAT BURIAL
SN Use with barrow type where relevant.
CL RELIGIOUS, RITUAL AND FUNERARY
BT BURIAL
RT BOAT
    SHIP BURIAL

BOAT HOUSE
UF Boating Lodge
    Punt Shelter
    Yachting Lodge
CL GARDENS, PARKS AND URBAN SPACES
BT GARDEN BUILDING
RT BOATING LAKE
    ROWING CLUB
    SAILING CLUB

BOAT HOUSE
UF Boating Lodge
    Punt Shelter
    Yachting Lodge
CL TRANSPORT
BT WATER TRANSPORT SITE
RT ROWING CLUB
    SAILING CLUB

BOAT HOUSE
UF Boating Lodge
    Punt Shelter
    Yachting Lodge
CL MARITIME
BT DOCK AND HARBOUR INSTALLATION
RT SLIP SHED

BOAT LIFT
CL TRANSPORT
BT LIFT

BOAT LIFT
CL TRANSPORT
BT WATER TRANSPORT SITE
RT CANAL

BOAT STORE
CL MARITIME
BT DOCK AND HARBOUR INSTALLATION

BOAT YARD
UF Boat Building Yard
CL MARITIME
BT MARINE CONSTRUCTION SITE
RT HARBOUR

BOAT YARD
UF Boat Building Yard
CL TRANSPORT
BT WATER TRANSPORT SITE
RT HARBOUR
    SLIPWAY

BOAT YARD
UF Boat Building Yard
CL INDUSTRIAL
BT MARINE CONSTRUCTION SITE
RT HARBOUR

BOATING LAKE
UF Boating Pool
CL GARDENS, PARKS AND URBAN SPACES
BT LAKE

RT BOAT HOUSE
    PUBLIC PARK

BOATING LAKE
UF Boating Pool
CL RECREATIONAL
RT BOAT HOUSE
    PUBLIC PARK

Boating Lodge
    USE BOAT HOUSE

Boating Pool
    USE BOATING LAKE

BOATSWAINS HOUSE
CL DOMESTIC
BT MARITIME HOUSE

BOBBIN MILL
CL INDUSTRIAL
BT MILL

BOBBIN MILL
CL INDUSTRIAL
BT TIMBER PRODUCT SITE
RT LUMBER MILL
    SAW MILL

Boccarum
    USE BASTION

BOG BURIAL
CL RELIGIOUS, RITUAL AND FUNERARY
BT BURIAL

BOG GARDEN
CL GARDENS, PARKS AND URBAN SPACES
BT GARDEN

Boiler Erecting Workshop
    USE BOILER SHOP

BOILER HOUSE
CL INDUSTRIAL
BT STEAM POWER PRODUCTION SITE
RT COMPRESSOR HOUSE
    ECONOMISER HOUSE
    ENGINE
    STEAM ENGINE

BOILER SHOP
UF Boiler Erecting Workshop
SN Workshop for the construction and maintenance of
    boilers within an industrial complex.
CL INDUSTRIAL
BT HEAVY ENGINEERING SITE
RT ENGINEERING WORKSHOP
    FOUNDRY
    MARINE ENGINEERING WORKS
    PLATERS SHOP
    RAILWAY ENGINEERING SITE
    SHIPYARD

BOILER WORKS
UF Boilermaking Works
SN Engineering works dedicated solely to the
    manufacture and repair of boilers.
CL INDUSTRIAL
BT HEAVY ENGINEERING SITE
RT PLATERS SHOP

Boilermaking Works
    USE BOILER WORKS

BOILING HOUSE
UF Pigswill Boiling House
CL AGRICULTURE AND SUBSISTENCE
BT FARM BUILDING

Boiling Mound
USE BURNT MOUND

BOLEHILL
SN   An early form of lead furnace, set upon a hilltop
       or crest to utilise winds in smelting.
CL   INDUSTRIAL
BT   METAL PRODUCTION FURNACE
RT   LEAD WORKING SITE
       NON FERROUS METAL SMELTING SITE

BOLLARD
UF   Carriage Post
       Stump
CL   GARDENS, PARKS AND URBAN SPACES
BT   STREET FURNITURE
RT   MOORING BOLLARD

Bolting House
USE FLOUR MILL

BOMB CRATER
CL   UNASSIGNED

Bomb Shelter
USE AIR RAID SHELTER

BOMB VESSEL
SN   Vessel armed with mortars for land bombardment,
       provided with minimum rig for ease of firing.
CL   MARITIME
BT   MINOR WARSHIP

BOMBASINE MILL
SN   Twilled dress material of worsted with or without
       a mixture of cotton or silk.
CL   INDUSTRIAL
BT   TEXTILE MILL

BOMBASINE MILL
SN   Twilled dress material of worsted with or without
       a mixture of cotton or silk.
CL   INDUSTRIAL
BT   WOOL MANUFACTURING SITE

Bonded Store
USE BONDED WAREHOUSE

BONDED WAREHOUSE
UF   Bonded Store
CL   COMMERCIAL
BT   WAREHOUSE
RT   CUSTOM HOUSE
       DISTILLERY
       TRANSIT SHED

Bone House
USE CHARNEL HOUSE

BONE MILL
SN   A mill for grinding or crushing bones, in the
       process of making bone china, for example.
CL   INDUSTRIAL
BT   ANIMAL PRODUCT SITE
RT   CHINA FACTORY
       FERTILISER WORKS

BONE MILL
SN   A mill for grinding or crushing bones, in the
       process of making bone china, for example.
CL   INDUSTRIAL
BT   MILL

Bonhommes College
USE BONHOMMES MONASTERY

BONHOMMES MONASTERY
UF   Bonhommes College

       Bonshommes College
       Bonshommes Monastery
SN   Bonhomme brethren following the rule of St
       Augustine.
CL   RELIGIOUS, RITUAL AND FUNERARY
BT   MONASTERY

Bonshommes College
USE BONHOMMES MONASTERY

Bonshommes Monastery
USE BONHOMMES MONASTERY

Book Makers
USE BETTING OFFICE

BOOKING OFFICE
UF   Ticket Office
CL   COMMERCIAL
BT   COMMERCIAL OFFICE
RT   OFFICE
       RAILWAY STATION
       WAITING ROOM

BOOKSHOP
CL   COMMERCIAL
BT   SHOP

BOOM DEFENCE
CL   MARITIME
BT   UNMANNED CRAFT
RT   BOOM TOWER

BOOM TOWER
UF   Chain Tower
SN   A tower at the mouth of the harbour to defend the
       end of the harbour boom.
CL   DEFENCE
RT   BOOM DEFENCE
       CASTLE
       TOWER

Boot And Shoe Factory
USE SHOE FACTORY

BOOT SCRAPER
UF   Foot Scraper
CL   GARDENS, PARKS AND URBAN SPACES
BT   STREET FURNITURE

BORDER
CL   GARDENS, PARKS AND URBAN SPACES
NT   HERBACEOUS BORDER
       MIXED BORDER
       ROSE BORDER
       SHRUB BORDER
RT   GARDEN

Borough Hall
USE TOWN HALL

Borough Library
USE PUBLIC LIBRARY

Borough Stone
USE BOUNDARY STONE

Borstal
USE JUVENILE PRISON

Bosco
USE ILEX GROVE

BOSQUET
SN   An ornamental grove, thicket or shrubbery pierced
       by walks.
CL   GARDENS, PARKS AND URBAN SPACES
BT   SHRUBBERY

BOTANIC GARDEN

UF   Botanic Gardens
     Botanical Gardens
SN   A garden designed to provide living material for
     the study of botany and horticulture.
CL   GARDENS, PARKS AND URBAN SPACES
BT   GARDEN
RT   ARBORETUM
     CONSERVATORY
     PALM HOUSE
     PHYSIC GARDEN
     ZOO

Botanic Gardens
     USE BOTANIC GARDEN

Botanical Gardens
     USE BOTANIC GARDEN

Botanical House
     USE CONSERVATORY

Bothie
     USE BOTHY

BOTHY
UF   Bothie
     Cabin
SN   A one-roomed building in which unmarried labourers
     lodge together.
CL   DOMESTIC
BT   RESIDENTIAL BUILDING
NT   MINERS BOTHY
RT   HUT
     WORKERS COTTAGE
     WORKERS HOSTEL

BOTTLE KILN
UF   Bottle Oven
CL   INDUSTRIAL
BT   KILN <BY FORM>
RT   LIME KILN
     POTTERY KILN
     TILE KILN
     UPDRAUGHT KILN

Bottle Oven
     USE BOTTLE KILN

BOTTLE WORKS
CL   INDUSTRIAL
BT   GLASSMAKING SITE

BOTTLING PLANT
CL   INDUSTRIAL
BT   FOOD PRESERVING SITE
RT   BREWERY
     DAIRY
     DISTILLERY
     MINERAL WATER FACTORY
     MINERAL WATER WORKS

Boulevard
     USE ROAD

Boulting House
     USE FLOUR MILL

BOUNDARY
UF   Boundary Feature
     Boundary Fence
     Estate Boundary
     Linear Boundary
     Property Boundary
SN   Unspecified function. Use specific type where
     known.
CL   UNASSIGNED
NT   BOUNDARY BANK
     BOUNDARY CAIRN
     BOUNDARY DITCH

       BOUNDARY MARKER
       BOUNDARY MOUND
       BOUNDARY PLATE
       BOUNDARY POST
       BOUNDARY STONE
       BOUNDARY WALL
RT   BOUNDARY CROSS
       DYKE (DEFENCE)
       FENCE
       FIELD BOUNDARY
       HA HA
       HEDGE
       LINEAR EARTHWORK
       LINEAR FEATURE
       PARISH BOUNDARY
       PARK PALE
       PIT ALIGNMENT
       PLANTATION BANK
       RAILINGS
       RANCH BOUNDARY
       REAVE
       WALL
       WOOD BANK

BOUNDARY BANK
CL   UNASSIGNED
BT   BOUNDARY

BOUNDARY CAIRN
CL   UNASSIGNED
BT   BOUNDARY
RT   CAIRN

BOUNDARY CROSS
CL   RELIGIOUS, RITUAL AND FUNERARY
BT   CROSS
RT   BOUNDARY

BOUNDARY DITCH
CL   UNASSIGNED
BT   BOUNDARY

BOUNDARY DITCH
CL   UNASSIGNED
BT   DITCH

Boundary Feature
     USE BOUNDARY

Boundary Fence
     USE FENCE
         BOUNDARY

BOUNDARY MARKER
CL   UNASSIGNED
BT   BOUNDARY
RT   COAL TAX POST
     MEERSTONE
     TOLL BOUNDARY MARKER

BOUNDARY MOUND
CL   UNASSIGNED
BT   BOUNDARY

BOUNDARY MOUND
CL   UNASSIGNED
BT   MOUND

BOUNDARY PLATE
CL   UNASSIGNED
BT   BOUNDARY
RT   COAL TAX POST

BOUNDARY POST
CL   UNASSIGNED
BT   BOUNDARY
RT   COAL TAX POST

BOUNDARY STONE

UF   Borough Stone
        County Stone
        Estate Stone
        Hoar Stone
        Hundred Stone
        Markstone
CL   UNASSIGNED
BT   BOUNDARY
RT   COAL TAX POST
        MEERSTONE
        STONE

BOUNDARY WALL
UF   Dockyard Boundary Wall
CL   UNASSIGNED
BT   BOUNDARY
RT   PRECINCT WALL
        PRISON

BOUNDARY WALL
UF   Dockyard Boundary Wall
CL   UNASSIGNED
BT   WALL

BOUSE TEAM
SN   Term for ore store/ore hopper, used particularly in Yorkshire and Derbyshire.
CL   INDUSTRIAL
BT   NON FERROUS METAL PROCESSING SITE

Boutique
    USE CLOTHING SHOP

Bovile
    USE COW HOUSE

Bower
    USE HERMITAGE

BOWL BARROW
CL   RELIGIOUS, RITUAL AND FUNERARY
BT   ROUND BARROW

BOWL FURNACE
CL   INDUSTRIAL
BT   METAL PRODUCTION FURNACE
RT   FERROUS METAL SMELTING SITE

BOWLING CLUB
CL   RECREATIONAL
BT   SPORTS SITE
RT   BOWLING GREEN
        BOWLING GREEN PAVILION

BOWLING GREEN
CL   RECREATIONAL
BT   SPORTS SITE
RT   BOWLING CLUB
        BOWLING GREEN PAVILION
        CROQUET LAWN

BOWLING GREEN PAVILION
CL   GARDENS, PARKS AND URBAN SPACES
BT   PAVILION
RT   BOWLING CLUB
        BOWLING GREEN
        CROQUET SHED

BOWLING GREEN PAVILION
CL   RECREATIONAL
BT   SPORTS BUILDING
RT   BOWLING CLUB
        BOWLING GREEN
        CROQUET SHED

Bowre
    USE HERMITAGE

BOX FRAME HOUSE
CL   DOMESTIC
BT   TIMBER FRAMED HOUSE

BOXING ARENA
CL   RECREATIONAL
BT   SPORTS SITE

Boys Club
    USE YOUTH CLUB

Boys Home
    USE ORPHANAGE

Boys Refuge
    USE ORPHANAGE

Brasiatorio
    USE BREWHOUSE

BRASS FOUNDRY
CL   INDUSTRIAL
BT   NON FERROUS METAL SMELTING SITE

Brass Mill
    USE BRASS WORKS

BRASS WORKS
UF   Brass Mill
SN   A brass manufacturing complex incorporating battery mill furnaces, hammers, etc.
CL   INDUSTRIAL
BT   NON FERROUS METAL SMELTING SITE
RT   BATTERY MILL
        ROLLING MILL
        SLITTING MILL
        TUBE MILL

BRASS WORKS
UF   Brass Mill
SN   A brass manufacturing complex incorporating battery mill furnaces, hammers, etc.
CL   INDUSTRIAL
BT   NON FERROUS METAL PRODUCT SITE
RT   BATTERY MILL
        BRITANNIA METAL WORKS
        PIN MILL
        WIRE MILL

Brasserie
    USE RESTAURANT

Brassinium
    USE BREWHOUSE

BREAKWATER
UF   Harbour Wall
SN   A structure which protects a beach or harbour by breaking the force of the waves.
CL   MARITIME
BT   SEA DEFENCES
RT   CAUSEWAY
        HARBOUR
        PROMENADE

BREASTSHOT WHEEL
CL   INDUSTRIAL
BT   WATERWHEEL <BY FORM>
NT   HIGH BREASTSHOT WHEEL
        LOW BREASTSHOT WHEEL

BREASTWORK
CL   DEFENCE
RT   TRENCH

BRETHREN MEETING HOUSE
UF   Plymouth Brethren Meeting House
CL   RELIGIOUS, RITUAL AND FUNERARY
BT   NONCONFORMIST MEETING HOUSE

Brew House

USE BREWHOUSE

Brew House Garden
USE HOP GARDEN

Brewers House
USE MANAGERS HOUSE

BREWERY
- UF Brewery Stable
- CL INDUSTRIAL
- BT BREWING AND MALTING SITE
- NT VINEGAR BREWERY
- RT BOTTLING PLANT
  BREWHOUSE
  STABLE

Brewery Office
USE OFFICE

Brewery Stable
USE BREWERY
STABLE
- SN Use both terms.

Brewery Vat Hall
USE VAT HALL

BREWHOUSE
- UF Brasiatorio
  Brassinium
  Brew House
  Yelling House
  Yielding House
- CL AGRICULTURE AND SUBSISTENCE
- BT FOOD AND DRINK PROCESSING SITE
- RT ALE STORE
  BACK HOUSE
  BAKEHOUSE
  BREWERY
  COOPERAGE
  COUNTRY HOUSE
  MALTINGS
  STILLING HOUSE

Brewhouse Garden
USE HOP GARDEN

BREWING AND MALTING SITE
- CL INDUSTRIAL
- BT FOOD AND DRINK INDUSTRY SITE
- NT ALE STORE
  BREWERY
  COOLING ROOM
  COOPERAGE
  COPPER ROOM
  FERMENTING BLOCK
  HOP KILN
  HOP STORE
  MALT HOUSE
  MALT KILN
  MALTINGS
  OASTHOUSE
  RACKING ROOM
  UNION ROOM
  VAT HALL

BRICK AND TILEMAKING SITE
- SN Includes earth extraction and preparation.
- CL INDUSTRIAL
- BT MINERAL PRODUCT SITE
- NT BLUNGING PIT
  BRICK DRYING SHED
  BRICK KILN
  BRICK PIT
  BRICKEARTH PIT
  BRICKFIELD
  BRICKWORKS
  BRICKYARD

CLAY MILL
CLAY PIT
CLAY PUDDLING PIT
FIRE CLAY WORKS
MOULDING HOUSE
PUG MILL
TILE WORKS
TILEMAKING WORKSHOP

BRICK DRYING SHED
- CL INDUSTRIAL
- BT BRICK AND TILEMAKING SITE
- RT SHED

BRICK KILN
- CL INDUSTRIAL
- BT KILN <BY FUNCTION>
- RT CIRCULAR KILN
  CLAMP KILN
  HOFFMAN KILN

BRICK KILN
- CL INDUSTRIAL
- BT BRICK AND TILEMAKING SITE

BRICK PIT
- CL INDUSTRIAL
- BT BRICK AND TILEMAKING SITE

BRICK PIT
- CL INDUSTRIAL
- BT EXTRACTIVE PIT

BRICKEARTH PIT
- UF Brickearth Quarry
- CL INDUSTRIAL
- BT BRICK AND TILEMAKING SITE

BRICKEARTH PIT
- UF Brickearth Quarry
- CL INDUSTRIAL
- BT EXTRACTIVE PIT

Brickearth Quarry
USE BRICKEARTH PIT

BRICKFIELD
- SN A site where clay is both extracted and fired to produce bricks.
- CL INDUSTRIAL
- BT BRICK AND TILEMAKING SITE

Brickworkers Cottage
USE WORKERS COTTAGE

BRICKWORKS
- SN Industrial manufacturing complex producing bricks.
- CL INDUSTRIAL
- BT BRICK AND TILEMAKING SITE
- RT CLAY DRAINAGE PIPE WORKS
  TERRACOTTA WORKS

BRICKYARD
- UF Dummy Yard
- SN Small scale enterprise producing bricks but not at the same site as the extraction of clay.
- CL INDUSTRIAL
- BT BRICK AND TILEMAKING SITE

Bridewell
USE PRISON

BRIDGE
- UF Abbey Bridge
  Brigg
  Monastery Bridge
  Multi Span Bridge
  Single Span Bridge
- SN Use specific type where known.
- CL TRANSPORT

NT BRIDGE <BY FORM>
    BRIDGE <BY FUNCTION>
RT APPROACH ROAD
    AQUEDUCT
    BRIDGE CHAPEL
    BRIDGE KEEPERS COTTAGE
    CAUSEWAY
    FLYOVER
    SHELL BRIDGE
    SURVEY TOWER
    VIADUCT

BRIDGE <BY FORM>
CL TRANSPORT
BT BRIDGE
NT CLAPPER BRIDGE
    DRAWBRIDGE
    LIFTING BRIDGE
    PACKHORSE BRIDGE
    SUSPENSION BRIDGE
    SWING BRIDGE
    TRANSPORTER BRIDGE

BRIDGE <BY FUNCTION>
CL TRANSPORT
BT BRIDGE
NT ACCOMMODATION BRIDGE
    CANAL BRIDGE
    FOOTBRIDGE
    RAILWAY BRIDGE
    ROAD BRIDGE
    ROVING BRIDGE
    TOLL BRIDGE
    TOWING PATH BRIDGE
    TRAMWAY BRIDGE

Bridge Approach Road
  USE APPROACH ROAD

BRIDGE CHAPEL
CL RELIGIOUS, RITUAL AND FUNERARY
BT CHAPEL
RT BRIDGE

Bridge House
  USE BRIDGE KEEPERS COTTAGE

BRIDGE KEEPERS COTTAGE
UF Bridge House
    Weighbridge House
CL DOMESTIC
BT TRANSPORT WORKERS HOUSE
RT AQUEDUCT
    BRIDGE
    CANAL
    CANAL GATEHOUSE
    WEIGHBRIDGE
    WHARFINGERS COTTAGE

Bridgettine Abbey
  USE ABBEY
      BRIDGETTINE DOUBLE HOUSE
SN Use both terms.

BRIDGETTINE DOUBLE HOUSE
UF Bridgettine Abbey
SN Abbeys of Bridgettine double order of nuns and
    religious men.
CL RELIGIOUS, RITUAL AND FUNERARY
BT DOUBLE HOUSE

BRIDLEWAY
CL TRANSPORT
BT TRACKWAY

Brigg
  USE BRIDGE

Brine Baths

  USE SALT BATHS

BRINE PIT
CL INDUSTRIAL
BT MINERAL EXTRACTION SITE
RT EXTRACTIVE PIT
    PIT
    SALT WORKS
    SALTERN

BRITANNIA METAL WORKS
SN An alloy of tin, antimony and copper used as a
    replacement for pewter.
CL INDUSTRIAL
BT NON FERROUS METAL PRODUCT SITE
RT BRASS WORKS
    CUTLERY WORKS
    CUTLERY WORKSHOP
    PLATING WORKS

British And Foreign School
  USE CHURCH SCHOOL

British And Foreign Society School
  USE CHURCH SCHOOL

British Legion Club
  USE SERVICES CLUB

BRITISH LEGION HALL
CL INSTITUTIONAL
BT MEETING HALL
RT SERVICES CLUB

BROAD RIDGE AND FURROW
CL AGRICULTURE AND SUBSISTENCE
BT RIDGE AND FURROW

BROADCASTING CONTROL ROOM
CL COMMUNICATIONS
BT TELECOMMUNICATION STRUCTURE

BROADCASTING HOUSE
CL COMMUNICATIONS
BT TELECOMMUNICATION BUILDING
RT RADIO BROADCASTING STUDIO
    TELEVISION STUDIO

BROADCASTING TRANSMITTER
UF Radio Beacon
    Radio Mast
    Television Mast
CL COMMUNICATIONS
BT TELECOMMUNICATION STRUCTURE

BRONZE FOUNDRY
CL INDUSTRIAL
BT NON FERROUS METAL PRODUCT SITE
RT BRONZE WORKING SITE

BRONZE WORKING SITE
SN Use only where evidence is specific, ie.
    copper/tin alloy. For working of copper based
    alloys of unknown composition use COPPER WORKING
    SITE.
CL INDUSTRIAL
BT NON FERROUS METAL SMELTING SITE
RT BRONZE FOUNDRY

BRONZE WORKING SITE
SN Use only where evidence is specific, ie.
    copper/tin alloy. For working of copper based
    alloys of unknown composition use COPPER WORKING
    SITE.
CL INDUSTRIAL
BT NON FERROUS METAL PRODUCT SITE
RT BRONZE FOUNDRY

Brotherhood House

USE GUILDHALL

BRUSH FACTORY
 CL INDUSTRIAL
 BT FACTORY <BY PRODUCT>

BRUSH FACTORY
 CL INDUSTRIAL
 BT WOOD PRODUCT SITE

BRUSHMAKERS WORKSHOP
 CL INDUSTRIAL
 BT CRAFT INDUSTRY SITE
 RT WORKSHOP

BRUSHMAKERS WORKSHOP
 CL INDUSTRIAL
 BT WOOD PRODUCT SITE

Brushwood Trackway
 USE TRACKWAY

BUCKET BURIAL
 CL RELIGIOUS, RITUAL AND FUNERARY
 BT BURIAL

BUCKET DREDGER
 CL MARITIME
 BT DREDGER

Buckstall
 USE DEER POUND

BUDDHIST TEMPLE
 CL RELIGIOUS, RITUAL AND FUNERARY
 BT TEMPLE

BUDDLE
 UF Buddle Pit
 SN A machine or feature for concentrating ores by
   sedimentation.
 CL INDUSTRIAL
 BT NON FERROUS METAL PROCESSING SITE
 RT BUDDLE HOUSE
   CRUSHING MILL
   LEAD MINE
   ORE WASHING PLANT
   SETTLING PIT
   STAMPS
   WASHING FLOOR

BUDDLE HOUSE
 SN Building or structure housing a buddle.
 CL INDUSTRIAL
 BT NON FERROUS METAL PROCESSING SITE
 RT BUDDLE
   CRAZING MILL
   CRUSHING MILL
   SETTLING PIT
   STAMPS

Buddle Pit
 USE BUDDLE

BUFFET
 CL COMMERCIAL
 BT EATING AND DRINKING ESTABLISHMENT
 RT CANTEEN

BUILDERS YARD
 CL INDUSTRIAL
 BT CRAFT INDUSTRY SITE
 RT TIMBER YARD

BUILDING
 UF Foundation
   Terminal Building
 SN Use specific type where known.
 CL UNASSIGNED

 NT GATEHOUSE
   GATEMANS HUT
   OFFICE
   OUTBUILDING
   PORTERS LODGE
   SHED
   STOREHOUSE
   TOWER
   TOWER BLOCK
 RT STRUCTURE

BUILDING PLATFORM
 SN Use only where specific function is unknown.
 CL UNASSIGNED
 BT PLATFORM
 RT BARN PLATFORM
   HOUSE PLATFORM
   HUT PLATFORM

Building Society Office
 USE COMMERCIAL OFFICE

BULL PEN
 CL AGRICULTURE AND SUBSISTENCE
 BT PEN

BULLRING
 SN An arena for bull-baiting, not a tethering ring.
 CL RECREATIONAL
 BT BAITING PLACE

BULWARK
 CL MARITIME
 BT SEA DEFENCES
 RT CAUSEWAY
   PROMENADE

BUM BOAT
 CL MARITIME
 BT HARBOUR SERVICES VESSEL

BUNGALOW
 CL DOMESTIC
 BT HOUSE <BY FORM>

BUNK
 SN Working area for an individual pauper in the
   stone-breaking yard. Usually covered.
 CL HEALTH AND WELFARE
 BT STONE BREAKING YARD

Bunker
 USE UNDERGROUND MILITARY HEADQUARTERS

Buon Retiro
 USE GARDEN RETREAT

BUOY STORE
 CL MARITIME
 BT DOCK AND HARBOUR INSTALLATION

BURH
 CL DOMESTIC
 BT ENCLOSED SETTLEMENT
 RT TOWN

BURH
 CL CIVIL
 RT TOWN

BURH
 CL DEFENCE
 BT ENCLOSED SETTLEMENT
 RT TOWN

BURIAL
 UF Cave Burial
   Interment
 SN Use specific type where known. If component use
   with wider site type. Use FUNERARY SITE for
   optimum retrieval in searches.
 CL RELIGIOUS, RITUAL AND FUNERARY

BT   FUNERARY SITE
NT   ANIMAL BURIAL
     BAG BURIAL
     BASKET BURIAL
     BEAKER BURIAL
     BOAT BURIAL
     BOG BURIAL
     BUCKET BURIAL
     CART BURIAL
     CHARCOAL BURIAL
     CREMATION
     GYPSUM BURIAL
     INHUMATION
     SHIP BURIAL
     TILE BURIAL
RT   OSSUARY

BURIAL CAIRN
UF   Burial Mound
CL   RELIGIOUS, RITUAL AND FUNERARY
BT   CAIRN
NT   CHAMBERED CAIRN
     LONG CAIRN
     RING CAIRN
     ROUND CAIRN
     SQUARE CAIRN
     TOR CAIRN
RT   BARROW
     CAIRN CEMETERY

Burial Chamber
USE CHAMBERED TOMB

Burial Ground
USE CEMETERY
SN   Use specific type of cemetry where known.

Burial Mound
USE BARROW
     BURIAL CAIRN
SN   Use both terms.

BURIAL PIT
CL   RELIGIOUS, RITUAL AND FUNERARY
BT   FUNERARY SITE
NT   CHARNEL PIT
     CREMATION PIT
     PLAGUE PIT
RT   PIT

BURIAL VAULT
CL   RELIGIOUS, RITUAL AND FUNERARY
BT   FUNERARY SITE
NT   FAMILY VAULT
RT   MAUSOLEUM

Burial Yard
USE CEMETERY

BURNT MOUND
UF   Boiling Mound
CL   DOMESTIC
RT   COOKING PIT
     HEARTH
     MOUND

BUS DEPOT
UF   Bus Garage
     Omnibus Depot
     Trolleybus Depot
CL   TRANSPORT
BT   ROAD TRANSPORT SITE
RT   BUS STATION

Bus Garage
USE BUS DEPOT

BUS SHELTER
CL   GARDENS, PARKS AND URBAN SPACES

BT   STREET FURNITURE
RT   TRAM SHELTER

BUS SHELTER
CL   TRANSPORT
BT   ROAD TRANSPORT SITE
RT   BUS STATION
     TRAM SHELTER

BUS STATION
UF   Coach Station
     Omnibus Staton
CL   TRANSPORT
BT   ROAD TRANSPORT SITE
RT   BUS DEPOT
     BUS SHELTER
     WAITING ROOM

BUST
CL   GARDENS, PARKS AND URBAN SPACES
BT   SCULPTURE
RT   COLUMN
     HERM
     OBELISK
     SPHINX
     STATUE

Butchers Market
USE MEAT MARKET

BUTCHERS SHOP
CL   COMMERCIAL
BT   SHOP

Butching House
USE ABATTOIR

Butter Cross
USE MARKET CROSS

BUTTER MARKET
CL   COMMERCIAL
BT   MARKET

BUTTER WELL
SN   A small stone structure, usually at a spring or
     bog, in which dairy products were kept cool on
     slate shelves.
CL   DOMESTIC

BUTTERFLY GARDEN
CL   GARDENS, PARKS AND URBAN SPACES
BT   GARDEN

BUTTERY
SN   Primarily a storeroom for domestic food and drink.
CL   AGRICULTURE AND SUBSISTENCE
BT   FOOD AND DRINK PROCESSING SITE

BUTTON MILL
CL   INDUSTRIAL
BT   CLOTHING INDUSTRY SITE

BUTTS
SN   Use specific type where known.
CL   DEFENCE
NT   ARCHERY BUTTS
     RIFLE BUTTS
RT   FIRING RANGE

BUTTS
SN   Use specific type where known.
CL   RECREATIONAL
BT   SPORTS SITE
NT   ARCHERY BUTTS
     RIFLE BUTTS

Byre
USE COW HOUSE

Byre House
  USE LONG HOUSE

Cabbies Shelter
  USE CABMENS SHELTER

Cabin
  USE BOTHY

CABINET
  SN   A small garden enclosure within a BOSQUET or
       surrounded by clipped hedges.
  CL   GARDENS, PARKS AND URBAN SPACES
  BT   GARDEN

Cabinetmakers
  USE CARPENTERS WORKSHOP

CABLE LAYER
  CL   MARITIME
  BT   COMMUNICATIONS CRAFT

CABLE REPEATER OFFICE
  SN   Cross channel telegraph office.
  CL   COMMUNICATIONS
  BT   TELEGRAPH OFFICE
  RT   OFFICE
       TELEGRAPH STATION

Cabmans Shelter
  USE CABMENS SHELTER

CABMENS SHELTER
  UF   Cabbies Shelter
       Cabmans Shelter
       Hansom Cabmans Shelter
  CL   TRANSPORT
  BT   ROAD TRANSPORT SITE
  RT   SHELTER

CACHE
  SN   Use specific type where known.
  CL   UNASSIGNED
  RT   SMUGGLERS CACHE
       TINNERS CACHE

CADET TRAINING SHIP
  CL   MARITIME
  BT   TRAINING SHIP

CAFE
  UF   Cafeteria
       Snack Bar
  CL   COMMERCIAL
  BT   EATING AND DRINKING ESTABLISHMENT
  RT   CANTEEN

Cafeteria
  USE CAFE

Cage
  USE PRISON

Cage Shop
  USE COLLIERY
       WORKSHOP
  SN   Use both terms.

CAIRN
  SN   Use specific type where known.
  CL   RELIGIOUS, RITUAL AND FUNERARY
  BT   FUNERARY SITE
  NT   BURIAL CAIRN
  RT   BOUNDARY CAIRN
       MARKER CAIRN

CAIRN
  SN   Use specific type where known.
  CL   AGRICULTURE AND SUBSISTENCE

  BT   LAND USE SITE
  NT   CLEARANCE CAIRN
  RT   BOUNDARY CAIRN
       CAIRNFIELD
       MARKER CAIRN

CAIRN ALIGNMENT
  SN   Long alignment of cairns lying between two large
       cairns; first recognised as a site type on Sourton
       Tor, Dartmoor.
  CL   RELIGIOUS, RITUAL AND FUNERARY

CAIRN CEMETERY
  CL   RELIGIOUS, RITUAL AND FUNERARY
  BT   CEMETERY
  RT   BURIAL CAIRN
       CAIRNFIELD

Cairn Circle
  USE ROUND CAIRN

CAIRNFIELD
  CL   AGRICULTURE AND SUBSISTENCE
  BT   LAND USE SITE
  RT   CAIRN
       CAIRN CEMETERY
       CLEARANCE CAIRN
       FIELD SYSTEM

Calamine Cavern
  USE CALAMINE MINE

CALAMINE MINE
  UF   Calamine Cavern
  SN   Where secondary product use with major product and
       MINE, eg. LEAD MINE.
  CL   INDUSTRIAL
  BT   MINE
  RT   LEAD MINE
       ZINC MINE

CALCINER
  UF   Calcining Furnace
  CL   INDUSTRIAL
  BT   KILN <BY FUNCTION>
  NT   ARSENIC CALCINER
       IRON ORE CALCINER
  RT   CHIMNEY
       CLAMP KILN
       METAL INDUSTRY SITE

Calcining Furnace
  USE CALCINER

Calcining House
  USE CALCINING KILN

CALCINING KILN
  UF   Calcining House
  CL   INDUSTRIAL
  BT   KILN <BY FUNCTION>
  RT   CEMENT WORKS
       METAL INDUSTRY SITE
       POTTERY MANUFACTURING SITE

CALEFACTORY
  UF   Common House
  SN   A heated common room in a monastery.
  CL   DOMESTIC
  RT   MONASTERY

CALENDER MILL
  SN   Finishing process for cloth, especially linen,
       running the cloth between heavy rollers.
  CL   INDUSTRIAL
  BT   TEXTILE MILL

CALENDER MILL
  SN   Finishing process for cloth, especially linen,
       running the cloth between heavy rollers.
  CL   INDUSTRIAL

BT   TEXTILE FINISHING SITE
RT   BEETLING MILL
     CLOTH DRY HOUSE
     DRABBET FACTORY
     FLAX MILL
     LINEN MILL

CALF HOUSE
SN   One large room for calves.
CL   AGRICULTURE AND SUBSISTENCE
BT   ANIMAL SHED

CALICO MILL
UF   Calico Works
SN   Textile mill producing calico, ie. coarse cotton
     cloth.
CL   INDUSTRIAL
BT   TEXTILE MILL

CALICO MILL
UF   Calico Works
SN   Textile mill producing calico, ie. coarse cotton
     cloth.
CL   INDUSTRIAL
BT   COTTON MILL

CALICO PRINTING WORKS
CL   INDUSTRIAL
BT   TEXTILE MILL

CALICO PRINTING WORKS
CL   INDUSTRIAL
BT   TEXTILE FINISHING SITE

Calico Works
   USE CALICO MILL

CALVARY
SN   A representation of the crucifixion of Christ or
     related scenes as a sculpture in a churchyard,
     etc.
CL   RELIGIOUS, RITUAL AND FUNERARY

CALVINISTIC METHODIST CHAPEL
CL   RELIGIOUS, RITUAL AND FUNERARY
BT   METHODIST CHAPEL

CAMBER
SN   Dock for small boats.
CL   MARITIME
BT   MARINE CONSTRUCTION SITE
RT   MAST POND

CAMBER
SN   Dock for small boats.
CL   INDUSTRIAL
BT   MARINE CONSTRUCTION SITE

CAMELLIA HOUSE
CL   GARDENS, PARKS AND URBAN SPACES
BT   GLASSHOUSE

CAMERA
SN   A subsidiary form of Knights Templar or
     Hospitallers' preceptories provided with a chapel.
     Use specific type where known.
CL   RELIGIOUS, RITUAL AND FUNERARY
BT   RELIGIOUS HOUSE
NT   HOSPITALLERS CAMERA
     TEMPLARS CAMERA
RT   CELL
     GRANGE
     MANOR
     MONASTERY
     NUNNERY
     PRECEPTORY
     SISTERS OF ST JOHN NUNNERY

CAMERA OBSCURA

CL   RECREATIONAL
BT   ART AND EDUCATION VENUE
RT   OBSERVATORY

CAMOMILE LAWN
CL   GARDENS, PARKS AND URBAN SPACES
BT   LAWN

CAMOMILE SEAT
CL   GARDENS, PARKS AND URBAN SPACES
BT   GARDEN SEAT

Campanile
   USE BELL TOWER

CANAL
UF   Canal Bank
     Canal Cutting
     Canal Depository
     Canal Embankment
     Canal Toll House
     Canal Tollhouse
CL   WATER SUPPLY AND DRAINAGE
BT   WATERCOURSE
NT   FLOOD RELIEF CANAL
RT   AQUEDUCT
     BARGE WINCH
     BRIDGE KEEPERS COTTAGE
     CANAL PORT
     INCLINE KEEPERS COTTAGE
     INCLINED PLANE
     JUNCTION LOCK
     LENGTHMANS COTTAGE
     ORNAMENTAL CANAL
     POUND LOCK
     SHIP CANAL
     TOW PATH
     WATER CHANNEL
     WEIR
     WHARFINGERS COTTAGE

CANAL
UF   Canal Bank
     Canal Cutting
     Canal Depository
     Canal Embankment
     Canal Toll House
     Canal Tollhouse
CL   TRANSPORT
BT   CANAL TRANSPORT SITE
NT   MILITARY CANAL
     SHIP CANAL
RT   AQUEDUCT
     BARGE WINCH
     BOAT LIFT
     CANAL PORT
     INCLINE KEEPERS COTTAGE
     INCLINE WINDING ENGINE
     INCLINED PLANE
     JUNCTION LOCK
     LENGTHMANS COTTAGE
     LOCK
     POUND LOCK
     RIVER NAVIGATION
     VIADUCT
     WEIR
     WHARFINGERS COTTAGE

Canal Aquaduct
   USE AQUEDUCT

Canal Aqueduct
   USE AQUEDUCT

Canal Bank
   USE CANAL

CANAL BASIN
CL   TRANSPORT

BT CANAL TRANSPORT SITE

CANAL BOAT YARD
    CL   TRANSPORT
    BT   CANAL TRANSPORT SITE

CANAL BRIDGE
    CL   TRANSPORT
    BT   BRIDGE <BY FUNCTION>
    RT   AQUEDUCT
          ROVING BRIDGE
          TOWING PATH BRIDGE

CANAL BRIDGE
    CL   TRANSPORT
    BT   CANAL TRANSPORT SITE
    RT   AQUEDUCT
          ROVING BRIDGE
          TOWING PATH BRIDGE

Canal Company Office
    USE CANAL OFFICE

Canal Cutting
    USE CANAL

Canal Depository
    USE CANAL
          WAREHOUSE
    SN   Use both terms.

CANAL DOCK
    CL   TRANSPORT
    BT   DOCK
    NT   CANAL DRY DOCK
    RT   DOCK

CANAL DOCKYARD
    CL   TRANSPORT
    BT   CANAL TRANSPORT SITE
    RT   DOCKYARD
          LENGTHMANS COTTAGE
          STAITH
          WHARFINGERS COTTAGE

CANAL DRY DOCK
    CL   TRANSPORT
    BT   CANAL DOCK

Canal Embankment
    USE CANAL

CANAL FEEDER
    CL   TRANSPORT
    BT   CANAL TRANSPORT SITE
    RT   LEAT

CANAL GATEHOUSE
    SN   A gatehouse bridging a canal.
    CL   TRANSPORT
    BT   CANAL TRANSPORT SITE
    RT   BRIDGE KEEPERS COTTAGE
          GATEHOUSE
          GAUGE HOUSE
          INCLINE KEEPERS COTTAGE
          LENGTHMANS COTTAGE
          WHARFINGERS COTTAGE

Canal Incline
    USE CANAL INCLINED PLANE

CANAL INCLINED PLANE
    UF   Canal Incline
    CL   TRANSPORT
    BT   CANAL TRANSPORT SITE

CANAL INCLINED PLANE
    UF   Canal Incline
    CL   TRANSPORT

BT INCLINED PLANE

Canal Keepers House
    USE CANAL WORKERS COTTAGE

CANAL LIFT
    CL   TRANSPORT
    BT   LIFT
    RT   BARGE WINCH
          INCLINE KEEPERS COTTAGE
          INCLINE WINDING ENGINE
          INCLINED PLANE

CANAL LIFT
    CL   TRANSPORT
    BT   CANAL TRANSPORT SITE
    RT   BARGE WINCH
          INCLINE KEEPERS COTTAGE
          INCLINE WINDING ENGINE
          INCLINED PLANE

CANAL LOCK
    CL   TRANSPORT
    BT   LOCK
    RT   RIVER LOCK

CANAL LOCK
    CL   TRANSPORT
    BT   CANAL TRANSPORT SITE

Canal Lock Keepers Cottage
    USE LOCK KEEPERS COTTAGE

CANAL MILEPOST
    CL   TRANSPORT
    BT   MILEPOST

CANAL MILEPOST
    CL   TRANSPORT
    BT   CANAL TRANSPORT SITE

CANAL OFFICE
    UF   Canal Company Office
    CL   TRANSPORT
    BT   CANAL TRANSPORT SITE
    RT   LENGTHMANS COTTAGE
          OFFICE
          WHARFINGERS COTTAGE

CANAL PORT
    CL   MARITIME
    BT   PORT
    RT   CANAL

CANAL RESERVOIR
    CL   WATER SUPPLY AND DRAINAGE
    BT   RESERVOIR

CANAL RESERVOIR
    CL   TRANSPORT
    BT   CANAL TRANSPORT SITE

CANAL SLUICE
    CL   TRANSPORT
    BT   CANAL TRANSPORT SITE
    RT   LOCK

Canal Toll House
    USE TOLL HOUSE
          CANAL
    SN   Use both terms.

Canal Tollhouse
    USE TOLL HOUSE
          CANAL
    SN   Use both terms.

CANAL TRANSPORT SITE
    CL   TRANSPORT

BT WATER TRANSPORT SITE
NT ACCOMMODATION BRIDGE
   CANAL
   CANAL BASIN
   CANAL BOAT YARD
   CANAL BRIDGE
   CANAL DOCKYARD
   CANAL FEEDER
   CANAL GATEHOUSE
   CANAL INCLINED PLANE
   CANAL LIFT
   CANAL LOCK
   CANAL MILEPOST
   CANAL OFFICE
   CANAL RESERVOIR
   CANAL SLUICE
   CANAL TUNNEL
   CANAL WAREHOUSE
   CANAL WHARF
   HORSE TUNNEL
   ROVING BRIDGE
RT CANAL WORKERS COTTAGE

CANAL TUNNEL
CL TRANSPORT
BT TRANSPORT TUNNEL
RT CANAL TUNNEL PORTAL
   TUNNEL

CANAL TUNNEL
CL TRANSPORT
BT CANAL TRANSPORT SITE
RT CANAL TUNNEL PORTAL
   TUNNEL

CANAL TUNNEL PORTAL
CL TRANSPORT
BT TUNNEL PORTAL
RT CANAL TUNNEL
   PORTAL

Canal Viaduct
USE AQUEDUCT

CANAL WAREHOUSE
CL TRANSPORT
BT CANAL TRANSPORT SITE

CANAL WHARF
CL TRANSPORT
BT WHARF
RT MOORING BOLLARD
   STAITH

CANAL WHARF
CL TRANSPORT
BT CANAL TRANSPORT SITE
RT MOORING BOLLARD
   STAITH

CANAL WORKERS COTTAGE
UF Canal Keepers House
CL DOMESTIC
BT TRANSPORT WORKERS HOUSE
RT CANAL TRANSPORT SITE

CANCER HOSPITAL
CL HEALTH AND WELFARE
BT SPECIALIST HOSPITAL

CANDLE FACTORY
CL INDUSTRIAL
BT FACTORY <BY PRODUCT>

CANDLE FACTORY
CL INDUSTRIAL
BT CHEMICAL PRODUCT SITE
RT CANDLE WORKS
   TALLOW FACTORY

WAX FACTORY

CANDLE WORKS
CL INDUSTRIAL
BT CHEMICAL PRODUCT SITE
RT CANDLE FACTORY
   WAX FACTORY

Cannery
USE CANNING FACTORY

CANNING FACTORY
UF Cannery
CL INDUSTRIAL
BT FACTORY <BY PRODUCT>

CANNING FACTORY
UF Cannery
CL INDUSTRIAL
BT FOOD PRESERVING SITE
RT COOPERAGE
   FOOD PROCESSING PLANT

CANNON
CL GARDENS, PARKS AND URBAN SPACES
BT STREET FURNITURE

CANNON BOLLARD
CL GARDENS, PARKS AND URBAN SPACES
BT STREET FURNITURE

CANNON BORING MILL
CL INDUSTRIAL
BT ARMAMENT MANUFACTURING SITE
RT ARSENAL
   FOUNDRY
   GUN TESTING SHOP
   IRON WORKS

CANNON BORING MILL
CL INDUSTRIAL
BT MILL

Cannon Foundry
USE FOUNDRY

CANOE
CL MARITIME
BT UNASSIGNED CRAFT

Canonical House
USE CLERGY HOUSE

Canonry
USE CLERGY HOUSE

Canons House
USE CLERGY HOUSE

Canons Summer House
USE CLERGY HOUSE

CANOPIED TOMB
UF Dresser Tomb
   Tester Tomb
CL RELIGIOUS, RITUAL AND FUNERARY
BT TOMB

CANTEEN
UF Factory Canteen
   Hospital Canteen
   Miners Canteen
   School Canteen
   Works Canteen
CL UNASSIGNED
RT BUFFET
   CAFE
   FACTORY
   HOSPITAL

OFFICE
REFECTORY
RESTAURANT
SCHOOL

CANVAS WORKS
CL INDUSTRIAL
BT TEXTILE MILL
RT FLOORCLOTH FACTORY
SAILMAKING WORKS

CANVAS WORKS
CL INDUSTRIAL
BT COTTON MILL

CAPITAL WARSHIP
CL MARITIME
BT WARSHIP
NT BATTLECRUISER
BATTLESHIP
FIRST RATE SHIP OF THE LINE
FLAG SHIP
GREAT SHIP
SECOND RATE SHIP OF THE LINE
THIRD RATE SHIP OF THE LINE

CAPSTAN
SN An apparatus around which cables or hawsers are
wound for hoisting anchors, lifting weights, etc.
CL TRANSPORT
BT LIFTING AND WINDING STRUCTURE
NT HAND CAPSTAN
RT DOCKYARD
DRY DOCK

CAPSTAN
SN An apparatus around which cables or hawsers are
wound for hoisting anchors, lifting weights, etc.
CL MARITIME
BT DOCK AND HARBOUR INSTALLATION
NT HAND CAPSTAN
RT CAPSTAN HOUSE

CAPSTAN HOUSE
CL TRANSPORT
RT CAPSTAN

CAPSTAN HOUSE
CL MARITIME
BT DOCK AND HARBOUR INSTALLATION
RT CAPSTAN

CAR FACTORY
UF Motor Works
CL INDUSTRIAL
BT MOTOR VEHICLE ENGINEERING SITE
RT FOUNDRY
SHEET METAL WORKS

CAR FACTORY
UF Motor Works
CL INDUSTRIAL
BT FACTORY <BY PRODUCT>

CAR PARK
CL TRANSPORT
BT ROAD TRANSPORT SITE
NT MULTI STOREY CAR PARK
UNDERGROUND CAR PARK

Car Port
USE GARAGE

CAR RAMP
CL TRANSPORT
BT RAMP
RT MULTI STOREY CAR PARK
ROAD

Car Showroom

USE MOTOR VEHICLE SHOWROOM

CARDING MILL
UF Woollen Carding Mill
CL INDUSTRIAL
BT TEXTILE MILL

CARDING MILL
UF Woollen Carding Mill
CL INDUSTRIAL
BT TEXTILE SITE <BY PROCESS/PRODUCT>

CARETAKERS HOUSE
CL DOMESTIC
BT HOUSE <BY FUNCTION>

CARGO VESSEL
CL MARITIME
BT TRANSPORT CRAFT
NT BARGE
COLLIER
DRY BULK CARGO CARRIER
FREIGHTER
TANKER

CARMELITE FRIARY
CL RELIGIOUS, RITUAL AND FUNERARY
BT FRIARY

Carnary
USE CHARNEL HOUSE

CARPENTERS WORKSHOP
UF Cabinetmakers
Wood Turners Shop
Woodworking Shop
CL INDUSTRIAL
BT CRAFT INDUSTRY SITE
RT WORKSHOP

CARPENTERS WORKSHOP
UF Cabinetmakers
Wood Turners Shop
Woodworking Shop
CL INDUSTRIAL
BT TIMBER PRODUCT SITE
RT SHIPYARD

CARPET BED
CL GARDENS, PARKS AND URBAN SPACES
BT FLOWER BED

CARPET MANUFACTURING SITE
SN Includes any textile floor covering.
CL INDUSTRIAL
BT TEXTILE PRODUCT SITE
NT CARPET MILL
CARPET WEAVERS WORKSHOP
FLOORCLOTH FACTORY
LINOLEUM FACTORY

CARPET MILL
UF Carpet Works
CL INDUSTRIAL
BT TEXTILE MILL

CARPET MILL
UF Carpet Works
CL INDUSTRIAL
BT CARPET MANUFACTURING SITE
RT FELT MILL
WEAVING MILL
WOOLLEN MILL

CARPET WEAVERS WORKSHOP
CL INDUSTRIAL
BT CARPET MANUFACTURING SITE
RT TAPESTRY WEAVING WORKSHOP

Carpet Works

USE CARPET MILL

Carport
    USE GARAGE

CARRIAGE HOUSE
    UF   Carriage Shed
           Carriage Shelter
           Gig House
    CL   TRANSPORT
    BT   ROAD TRANSPORT SITE
    RT   COACH HOUSE
           COUNTRY HOUSE
           TRAP HOUSE

Carriage Post
    USE BOLLARD

CARRIAGE RAMP
    CL   TRANSPORT
    BT   RAMP
    RT   CARRIAGEWAY

Carriage Shed
    USE CARRIAGE HOUSE

Carriage Shelter
    USE CARRIAGE HOUSE

CARRIAGE WORKS
    SN   Use RAILWAY CARRIAGE WORKS if railway carriages.
    CL   INDUSTRIAL
    BT   MOTOR VEHICLE ENGINEERING SITE

CARRIAGEWAY
    CL   TRANSPORT
    BT   ROAD
    RT   CARRIAGE RAMP

CART BURIAL
    UF   Chariot Burial
           Wagon Burial
    CL   RELIGIOUS, RITUAL AND FUNERARY
    BT   BURIAL
    RT   SQUARE BARROW

Cart House
    USE CART SHED

Cart Lodge
    USE CART SHED

CART SHED
    UF   Cart House
           Cart Lodge
           Wagon Stable
    CL   TRANSPORT
    BT   ROAD TRANSPORT SITE
    RT   SHED
           WAGON SHED

CARTHUSIAN CELL
    CL   RELIGIOUS, RITUAL AND FUNERARY
    BT   CELL
    RT   CARTHUSIAN GRANGE
           CARTHUSIAN MONASTERY
           COURERY

CARTHUSIAN GRANGE
    UF   Charterhouse Grange
    CL   RELIGIOUS, RITUAL AND FUNERARY
    BT   GRANGE
    RT   CARTHUSIAN CELL
           CARTHUSIAN GRANGE
           COURERY

CARTHUSIAN GRANGE
    UF   Charterhouse Grange
    CL   AGRICULTURE AND SUBSISTENCE

    BT   GRANGE
    RT   CARTHUSIAN GRANGE
           CARTHUSIAN MONASTERY

CARTHUSIAN MONASTERY
    UF   Carthusian Priory
           Charterhouse
    SN   Priories of Carthusian monks.
    CL   RELIGIOUS, RITUAL AND FUNERARY
    BT   MONASTERY
    RT   CARTHUSIAN CELL
           CARTHUSIAN GRANGE
           COURERY

Carthusian Priory
    USE CARTHUSIAN MONASTERY
           PRIORY
    SN   Use both terms.

CARVED STONE
    CL   UNASSIGNED
    RT   CARVING
           CROSS INCISED STONE
           CUP AND RING MARKED STONE
           ROCK CARVING
           STONE

CARVING
    CL   UNASSIGNED
    RT   CARVED STONE
           ROCK CARVING

Caryatid Terminal
    USE HERM

CASCADE
    SN   Fall of water sometimes taking the form of a water
           staircase.
    CL   GARDENS, PARKS AND URBAN SPACES
    RT   CASCADE HOUSE
           FOUNTAIN
           FOUNTAIN HOUSE
           ORNAMENTAL CANAL
           WATER GARDEN
           WATERFALL

CASCADE HOUSE
    CL   GARDENS, PARKS AND URBAN SPACES
    BT   GARDEN BUILDING
    RT   CASCADE
           FOUNTAIN
           FOUNTAIN HOUSE
           WATER GARDEN
           WATER PAVILION

CASINO (GAMBLING)
    CL   RECREATIONAL
    BT   GAMBLING SITE

Casino (Garden)
    USE SUMMERHOUSE

CASTING FLOOR
    CL   INDUSTRIAL
    BT   METAL INDUSTRY SITE

CASTING HOUSE
    UF   Casting Shop
    SN   Building or structure covering a casting floor or
           pit.
    CL   INDUSTRIAL
    RT   METAL INDUSTRY SITE

Casting Shop
    USE CASTING HOUSE

CASTLE
    UF   Castle Gate
           Castle Gatehouse

Citadel
Enclosure Castle
CL DOMESTIC
NT ADULTERINE CASTLE
CONCENTRIC CASTLE
KEEP
KEEP AND BAILEY CASTLE
MOTTE
MOTTE AND BAILEY
QUADRANGULAR CASTLE
RINGWORK
RINGWORK AND BAILEY
RT FORTIFIED HOUSE
FORTRESS

CASTLE
UF Castle Gate
Castle Gatehouse
Citadel
Enclosure Castle
CL DEFENCE
NT ADULTERINE CASTLE
ARTILLERY CASTLE
CONCENTRIC CASTLE
KEEP
KEEP AND BAILEY CASTLE
MOTTE
MOTTE AND BAILEY
QUADRANGULAR CASTLE
RINGWORK
RINGWORK AND BAILEY
SIEGE CASTLE
RT BAILEY
BARBICAN
BASTION
BOOM TOWER
CHEMISE
CURTAIN WALL
GATE TOWER
GATEHOUSE
POSTERN
WATER GATE

Castle Gate
USE CASTLE
GATE
SN Use both terms.

Castle Gatehouse
USE CASTLE
GATEHOUSE
SN Use both terms.

Castle Keep
USE KEEP

Castle Motte
USE MOTTE

Castle Mound
USE MOTTE

Castle Wall
USE CURTAIN WALL

CASUAL WARD BLOCK
UF Tramp Ward
SN For tramps.
CL HEALTH AND WELFARE
BT HOSPITAL BLOCK
RT WORKHOUSE

CASUALTY DEPARTMENT
CL HEALTH AND WELFARE
BT HOSPITAL DEPARTMENT

Cat Memorial
USE ANIMAL MEMORIAL

CATACOMB (FUNERARY)

SN An underground site for the depositing of the dead.
CL RELIGIOUS, RITUAL AND FUNERARY
BT FUNERARY SITE

Catacomb (Wine Storage)
USE WINE CELLARS

Catadrome
USE TILTYARD

CATHEDRAL
UF Augustinian Cathedral Priory
Benedictine Cathedral Priory
Cathedral Church
Cathedral Priory
Monastic Cathedral
Offertorium
CL RELIGIOUS, RITUAL AND FUNERARY
BT PLACE OF WORSHIP
NT ANGLICAN CATHEDRAL
EASTERN ORTHODOX CATHEDRAL
ROMAN CATHOLIC CATHEDRAL
SECULAR CATHEDRAL
RT ABBEY
CATHEDRAL CLOSE
CATHEDRAL PRECINCT
CHAPTER HOUSE
CHOIR SCHOOL
CHORISTERS HOUSE
CLERGY HOUSE
CRYPT
FRIARY
MONASTERY
NUNNERY
PRECINCT WALL
PRIORY
TREASURERS HOUSE

Cathedral Choir School
USE CHOIR SCHOOL

Cathedral Church
USE CATHEDRAL

CATHEDRAL CLOSE
CL GARDENS, PARKS AND URBAN SPACES
RT CATHEDRAL
CATHEDRAL PRECINCT

CATHEDRAL PRECINCT
CL RELIGIOUS, RITUAL AND FUNERARY
RT CATHEDRAL
CATHEDRAL CLOSE
MONASTIC PRECINCT

Cathedral Priory
USE CATHEDRAL
PRIORY
SN Use both terms.

Catholic Cathedral
USE ROMAN CATHOLIC CATHEDRAL

Catholic Chapel
USE ROMAN CATHOLIC CHAPEL

Catholic Church
USE ROMAN CATHOLIC CHURCH

Catholic College
USE THEOLOGICAL COLLEGE

Catholic School
USE CHURCH SCHOOL

CATTLE DOCKS
SN Pens for housing cattle awaiting transportation.
CL TRANSPORT

RT   LIVESTOCK MARKET
     RAILWAY STATION

Cattle Fodder Factory
   USE FOOD PROCESSING PLANT

Cattle Market
   USE LIVESTOCK MARKET

Cattle Shed
   USE COW HOUSE

CATTLE SHELTER
   UF   Barth
   SN   An open sided building known to have been used for
        sheltering cattle.
   CL   AGRICULTURE AND SUBSISTENCE
   BT   ANIMAL SHED
   RT   BANK BARN
        COMBINATION BARN
        COW HOUSE
        FIELD BARN
        HOVEL
        LINHAY
        SHELTER
        SHELTER SHED
        VACCARY

CATTLE TROUGH
   CL   AGRICULTURE AND SUBSISTENCE
   BT   TROUGH

CATTLE TROUGH
   CL   WATER SUPPLY AND DRAINAGE
   BT   TROUGH

CATTLE UNIT
   SN   Modern farm building.
   CL   AGRICULTURE AND SUBSISTENCE
   BT   ANIMAL SHED

CATTLE WASH
   CL   AGRICULTURE AND SUBSISTENCE
   BT   ANIMAL WASH

CAUSEWAY
   CL   TRANSPORT
   RT   APPROACH ROAD
        BREAKWATER
        BRIDGE
        BULWARK
        EMBANKMENT
        PROMENADE
        SLIPWAY

CAUSEWAY CHAPEL
   CL   RELIGIOUS, RITUAL AND FUNERARY
   BT   CHAPEL

Causewayed Camp
   USE CAUSEWAYED ENCLOSURE

CAUSEWAYED ENCLOSURE
   UF   Causewayed Camp
        Interrupted Ditch Enclosure
   CL   RELIGIOUS, RITUAL AND FUNERARY
   RT   ENCLOSURE
        HENGE ENCLOSURE
        HENGIFORM MONUMENT

CAUSEWAYED RING DITCH
   CL   RELIGIOUS, RITUAL AND FUNERARY
   RT   ENCLOSURE
        HENGE ENCLOSURE
        HENGIFORM MONUMENT

Cavalier
   USE BASTION
   SN   Raised earth platform built on bastion or curtain
        wall.

Cavalry Barracks
   USE BARRACKS

Cavalry Club
   USE SERVICES CLUB

Cavalry Riding School
   USE RIDING SCHOOL

CAVE
   UF   Cave Burial
        Cave Settlement
   SN   Natural cave utilised by man. Use with functional
        site type(s) to indicate use where known, eg.
        SETTLEMENT.
   CL   UNASSIGNED
   BT   NATURAL FEATURE
   RT   ROCK CUT CHAMBER
        ROCK CUT DWELLING
        ROCK SHELTER

Cave Burial
   USE BURIAL
        CAVE
   SN   Use both terms.

Cave Settlement
   USE SETTLEMENT
        CAVE
   SN   Use both terms.

CELL
   UF   Priory Cell
   SN   A monastic enclave dependent on a mother house.
   CL   RELIGIOUS, RITUAL AND FUNERARY
   BT   RELIGIOUS HOUSE
   NT   ALIEN CELL
        ANCHORITE CELL
        AUGUSTINIAN CELL
        BENEDICTINE CELL
        CARTHUSIAN CELL
        CISTERCIAN CELL
        CLUNIAC CELL
        GILBERTINE CELL
        PREMONSTRATENSIAN CELL
   RT   CAMERA
        CHAPEL
        DOUBLE HOUSE
        FARM
        GRANGE
        MANOR
        MONASTERY
        NUNNERY
        PRECEPTORY

CELL BLOCK
   CL   CIVIL
   BT   PRISON

CELLAR
   UF   Town Cellars
   SN   A room or group of rooms usually below the ground
        level and usually under a building, often used for
        storing fuel, provisions or wines.
   CL   UNASSIGNED
   RT   CIDER VAULT
        CRYPT
        HULL
        WINE CELLARS

Celluloid Works
   USE CHEMICAL WORKS

CELTIC FIELD SYSTEM
   CL   AGRICULTURE AND SUBSISTENCE
   BT   FIELD SYSTEM

Celtic Monastery

USE RELIGIOUS HOUSE
  DOUBLE HOUSE
  MONASTERY
  NUNNERY
SN Use DOUBLE HOUSE, MONASTERY, NUNNERY or
  RELIGIOUS HOUSE.

CEMENT KILN
  CL INDUSTRIAL
  BT CEMENT MANUFACTURING SITE
  RT ROTARY KILN
    SHAFT KILN
    SPLIT SHAFT KILN

CEMENT MANUFACTURING SITE
  CL INDUSTRIAL
  BT MINERAL PRODUCT SITE
  NT CEMENT KILN
    CEMENT SILO
    CEMENT WORKS
    CONCRETE WORKS

CEMENT SILO
  SN Large storage structure for powdered cement.
  CL INDUSTRIAL
  BT CEMENT MANUFACTURING SITE

CEMENT WORKS
  CL INDUSTRIAL
  BT CEMENT MANUFACTURING SITE
  RT CALCINING KILN
    CLAY PIT
    LIME KILN

CEMENTATION FURNACE
  UF Huntsman Furnace
    Huntsman Kiln
  SN Large open hearth furnace often located inside a
    brick cone for use in steelmaking.
  CL INDUSTRIAL
  BT METAL PRODUCTION FURNACE
  RT FERROUS METAL SMELTING SITE
    OPEN HEARTH FURNACE

CEMENTATION FURNACE
  UF Huntsman Furnace
    Huntsman Kiln
  SN Large open hearth furnace often located inside a
    brick cone for use in steelmaking.
  CL INDUSTRIAL
  BT FERROUS METAL SMELTING SITE
  RT CEMENTATION STEEL WORKS
    FERROUS METAL SMELTING SITE

CEMENTATION STEEL WORKS
  SN Production of steel by reheating wrought iron in
    charcoal filled containers.
  CL INDUSTRIAL
  BT STEEL WORKS
  RT CEMENTATION FURNACE
    CRUCIBLE STEEL WORKS

CEMETERY
  UF Burial Ground
    Burial Yard
    Cemetery Garden
    Detached Cemetery
    Execution Cemetery
    Flat Grave Cemetery
    Graveyard
    Necropolis
  CL RELIGIOUS, RITUAL AND FUNERARY
  BT FUNERARY SITE
  NT BARROW CEMETERY
    CAIRN CEMETERY
    CREMATION CEMETERY
    INHUMATION CEMETERY
  RT CEMETERY CHAPEL
    CEMETERY LODGE

  MORTUARY CHAPEL
  REGISTRARS HOUSE

CEMETERY CHAPEL
  UF Dissenters Cemetery Chapel
    Eastern Orthodox Cemetery Chapel
    Greek Orthodox Cemetery Chapel
  CL RELIGIOUS, RITUAL AND FUNERARY
  BT CHAPEL
  RT CEMETERY
    CEMETERY LODGE
    MORTUARY CHAPEL

Cemetery Garden
  USE GARDEN
    CEMETERY
  SN Use both terms.

CEMETERY LODGE
  UF Lodge
  CL RELIGIOUS, RITUAL AND FUNERARY
  RT CEMETERY
    CEMETERY CHAPEL

CENOTAPH
  CL COMMEMORATIVE
  BT COMMEMORATIVE MONUMENT
  RT TOMB
    WAR MEMORIAL

CENTURIAL STONE
  SN An inscribed marker stone found on Hadrian's Wall.
  CL DEFENCE
  BT FRONTIER DEFENCE
  RT INSCRIBED STONE

CENTURIAL STONE
  SN An inscribed marker stone found on Hadrian's Wall.
  CL COMMEMORATIVE
  BT COMMEMORATIVE STONE

CENTURIATED AREA
  UF Centuriation
  CL AGRICULTURE AND SUBSISTENCE
  BT FIELD SYSTEM

Centuriation
  USE CENTURIATED AREA

Ceramics Factory
  USE POTTERY WORKS

Ceremonial Arch
  USE COMMEMORATIVE MONUMENT
    ARCH
  SN Use both terms.

CEREMONIAL CRAFT
  CL MARITIME
  BT TRANSPORT CRAFT

CESS PIT
  CL WATER SUPPLY AND DRAINAGE
  NT CESS POOL
  RT LATRINE
    PIT
    SEWER

CESS POOL
  CL WATER SUPPLY AND DRAINAGE
  BT CESS PIT
  RT SEWER

CHAFERY
  SN Reheating of iron from a finery, for rolling or
    slitting.
  CL INDUSTRIAL
  BT FORGE
  RT FERROUS METAL PRODUCT SITE

ROLLING MILL

CHAFF HOUSE
- CL AGRICULTURE AND SUBSISTENCE
- BT FARM BUILDING
- RT FODDER STORE
      GRASS DRYING SHED

Chain Bridge
  USE SUSPENSION BRIDGE

Chain Ferry
  USE FERRY

CHAIN PROVING HOUSE
- UF Chain Testing House
- SN Building housing apparatus for testing chain links.
- CL INDUSTRIAL
- BT MARINE CONSTRUCTION SITE
- RT CHAIN WORKS

CHAIN PROVING HOUSE
- UF Chain Testing House
- SN Building housing apparatus for testing chain links.
- CL INDUSTRIAL
- BT FERROUS METAL PRODUCT SITE
- RT CHAIN WORKS
      HYDRAULIC ENGINE HOUSE
      RAILWAY ENGINEERING WORKS

CHAIN PROVING HOUSE
- UF Chain Testing House
- SN Building housing apparatus for testing chain links.
- CL MARITIME
- BT MARINE CONSTRUCTION SITE

CHAIN SHOP
- UF Chainmakers Workshop
      Chainmaking Workshop
      Chainshop
- CL INDUSTRIAL
- BT FERROUS METAL PRODUCT SITE
- RT CHAIN WORKS
      FORGE
      TILT HAMMER

Chain Testing House
  USE CHAIN PROVING HOUSE

Chain Tower
  USE BOOM TOWER

CHAIN WORKS
- CL INDUSTRIAL
- BT MARINE CONSTRUCTION SITE
- RT CHAIN PROVING HOUSE
      CHAIN SHOP
      DOCKYARD
      FORGE
      MARINE ENGINEERING WORKS
      SHIP REPAIR WORKS

CHAIN WORKS
- CL INDUSTRIAL
- BT FERROUS METAL PRODUCT SITE

CHAIN WORKS
- CL MARITIME
- BT MARINE CONSTRUCTION SITE

Chainmakers Workshop
  USE CHAIN SHOP

Chainmaking Workshop
  USE CHAIN SHOP

Chainshop
  USE CHAIN SHOP

CHALET
- CL DOMESTIC
- BT HOUSE <BY FORM>

Chalk Figure
  USE HILL FIGURE

Chalk Horse
  USE HILL FIGURE

CHALK PIT
- CL INDUSTRIAL
- BT MINERAL EXTRACTION SITE
- RT DENE HOLE
      GRAVEL PIT
      MARL PIT

CHALK PIT
- CL INDUSTRIAL
- BT EXTRACTIVE PIT

Chalk Quarry
  USE STONE QUARRY

CHAMBER OF COMMERCE
- CL COMMERCIAL
- RT EXCHANGE

CHAMBERED BARROW
- CL RELIGIOUS, RITUAL AND FUNERARY
- BT BARROW
- NT CHAMBERED LONG BARROW
      CHAMBERED ROUND BARROW

CHAMBERED BARROW
- CL RELIGIOUS, RITUAL AND FUNERARY
- BT CHAMBERED TOMB
- NT CHAMBERED LONG BARROW
      CHAMBERED ROUND BARROW

CHAMBERED CAIRN
- CL RELIGIOUS, RITUAL AND FUNERARY
- BT BURIAL CAIRN
- NT CHAMBERED LONG CAIRN
      CHAMBERED ROUND CAIRN
- RT PASSAGE GRAVE

CHAMBERED CAIRN
- CL RELIGIOUS, RITUAL AND FUNERARY
- BT CHAMBERED TOMB
- NT CHAMBERED LONG CAIRN
      CHAMBERED ROUND CAIRN

CHAMBERED LONG BARROW
- SN Differences between occurrences of term may be at a higher broad term level than that displayed here. See RELIGIOUS, RITUAL AND FUNERARY Class List for context.
- CL RELIGIOUS, RITUAL AND FUNERARY
- BT LONG BARROW

CHAMBERED LONG BARROW
- SN Differences between occurrences of term may be at a higher broad term level than that displayed here. See RELIGIOUS, RITUAL AND FUNERARY Class List for context.
- CL RELIGIOUS, RITUAL AND FUNERARY
- BT CHAMBERED BARROW

CHAMBERED LONG BARROW
- SN Differences between occurrences of term may be at a higher broad term level than that displayed here. See RELIGIOUS, RITUAL AND FUNERARY Class List for context.
- CL RELIGIOUS, RITUAL AND FUNERARY
- BT CHAMBERED BARROW

CHAMBERED LONG CAIRN

SN Differences between occurrences of term may be at
    a higher broad term level than that displayed
    here. See RELIGIOUS, RITUAL ANd FUNERARY Class
    List for context.
CL RELIGIOUS, RITUAL AND FUNERARY
BT CHAMBERED CAIRN

CHAMBERED LONG CAIRN
SN Differences between occurrences of term may be at
    a higher broad term level than that displayed
    here. See RELIGIOUS, RITUAL ANd FUNERARY Class
    List for context.
CL RELIGIOUS, RITUAL AND FUNERARY
BT LONG CAIRN

CHAMBERED LONG CAIRN
SN Differences between occurrences of term may be at
    a higher broad term level than that displayed
    here. See RELIGIOUS, RITUAL ANd FUNERARY Class
    List for context.
CL RELIGIOUS, RITUAL AND FUNERARY
BT CHAMBERED CAIRN

Chambered Mound
    USE CHAMBERED TOMB

CHAMBERED ROUND BARROW
SN Differences between occurrences of term may be at
    a higher broad term level than that displayed
    here. See RELIGIOUS, RITUAL AND FUNERARY Class
    List for context.
CL RELIGIOUS, RITUAL AND FUNERARY
BT CHAMBERED BARROW

CHAMBERED ROUND BARROW
SN Differences between occurrences of term may be at
    a higher broad term level than that displayed
    here. See RELIGIOUS, RITUAL AND FUNERARY Class
    List for context.
CL RELIGIOUS, RITUAL AND FUNERARY
BT ROUND BARROW

CHAMBERED ROUND BARROW
SN Differences between occurrences of term may be at
    a higher broad term level than that displayed
    here. See RELIGIOUS, RITUAL AND FUNERARY Class
    List for context.
CL RELIGIOUS, RITUAL AND FUNERARY
BT CHAMBERED BARROW

CHAMBERED ROUND CAIRN
SN Differences between occurrences of term may be at
    a higher broad term level than that displayed
    here. See RELIGIOUS, RITUAL AND FUNERARY Class
    List for context.
CL RELIGIOUS, RITUAL AND FUNERARY
BT CHAMBERED CAIRN

CHAMBERED ROUND CAIRN
SN Differences between occurrences of term may be at
    a higher broad term level than that displayed
    here. See RELIGIOUS, RITUAL AND FUNERARY Class
    List for context.
CL RELIGIOUS, RITUAL AND FUNERARY
BT ROUND CAIRN

CHAMBERED ROUND CAIRN
SN Differences between occurrences of term may be at
    a higher broad term level than that displayed
    here. See RELIGIOUS, RITUAL AND FUNERARY Class
    List for context.
CL RELIGIOUS, RITUAL AND FUNERARY
BT CHAMBERED CAIRN

CHAMBERED TOMB
UF Burial Chamber
    Chambered Mound
    Corbelled Tomb
    Cromlech

    Dolmen
    Megalithic Tomb
    Quoit
SN Use specific type where known.
CL RELIGIOUS, RITUAL AND FUNERARY
BT FUNERARY SITE
NT CHAMBERED BARROW
    CHAMBERED CAIRN
    ENTRANCE GRAVE
    GALLERY GRAVE
    PASSAGE GRAVE
    PORTAL DOLMEN

Chamois Leather Works
    USE LEATHER FACTORY

Chandlers Shop
    USE CHANDLERY

CHANDLERY
UF Chandlers Shop
    Ship Chandlery
CL COMMERCIAL

CHANDLERY
UF Chandlers Shop
    Ship Chandlery
CL MARITIME
RT SHIP BISCUIT SHOP
    WAREHOUSE

Changing House
    USE CHANGING ROOMS

CHANGING ROOMS
UF Changing House
CL RECREATIONAL
BT SPORTS SITE
RT RACECOURSE PAVILION
    SPORTS PAVILION

CHANNEL CLEARANCE VESSEL
CL MARITIME
BT SAFETY CRAFT
NT DREDGER
    ICE BREAKER

Chantry
    USE CHANTRY CHAPEL

CHANTRY CHAPEL
UF Chantry
CL RELIGIOUS, RITUAL AND FUNERARY
BT CHAPEL
RT COLLEGIATE CHAPEL
    COLLEGIATE CHURCH

CHANTRY COLLEGE
UF Annuellars Hall
    Chantry House
    College
    College Library
CL RELIGIOUS, RITUAL AND FUNERARY
BT COLLEGE OF SECULAR PRIESTS
RT CLERGY HOUSE
    COLLEGIATE CHAPEL
    COLLEGIATE CHURCH

Chantry House
    USE CHANTRY COLLEGE

CHAPEL
UF Almshouse Chapel
    Bead House Chapel
    Bedehouse Chapel
    Convent Chapel
    Conventual Chapel
    Crematorium Chapel
    Foundling Hospital Chapel

Funeral Chapel
Gate Chapel
Gatehouse Chapel
Hospital Chapel
Keeill
Memorial Chapel
Non Parochial Chapel
Orphanage Chapel
School Chapel
Swedenborgian Chapel
Tabernacle
University Chapel
War Memorial Chapel
Workhouse Chapel
CL RELIGIOUS, RITUAL AND FUNERARY
BT PLACE OF WORSHIP
NT BRIDGE CHAPEL
   CAUSEWAY CHAPEL
   CEMETERY CHAPEL
   CHANTRY CHAPEL
   CHAPEL OF EASE
   COLLEGIATE CHAPEL
   DOMESTIC CHAPEL
   GALILEE
   GUILD CHAPEL
   LADY CHAPEL
   MILITARY CHAPEL
   MORTUARY CHAPEL
   NONCONFORMIST CHAPEL
   PRIVATE CHAPEL
   ROMAN CATHOLIC CHAPEL
   ROYAL CHAPEL
RT CELL
   COAST LIGHT
   COURERY

CHAPEL OF EASE
CL RELIGIOUS, RITUAL AND FUNERARY
BT CHAPEL

CHAPTER HOUSE
SN The building attached to a cathedral or collegiate church where the dean, prebendaries or monks and canons met for the transaction of business.
CL RELIGIOUS, RITUAL AND FUNERARY
RT ABBEY
   CATHEDRAL
   FRIARY
   MONASTERY
   NUNNERY
   PRIORY
   RELIGIOUS HOUSE
   SYNODAL HALL

Charcoal Blast Furnace
USE BLAST FURNACE

CHARCOAL BURIAL
CL RELIGIOUS, RITUAL AND FUNERARY
BT BURIAL

CHARCOAL BURNERS HUT
CL DOMESTIC
BT HUT

CHARCOAL BURNERS HUT
CL INDUSTRIAL
BT CHARCOAL PRODUCTION SITE

CHARCOAL BURNERS SITE
CL INDUSTRIAL
BT CHARCOAL PRODUCTION SITE

CHARCOAL BURNING PLATFORM
CL INDUSTRIAL
BT CHARCOAL PRODUCTION SITE

CHARCOAL PRODUCTION SITE
CL INDUSTRIAL

BT FUEL PRODUCTION SITE
NT CHARCOAL BURNERS HUT
   CHARCOAL BURNERS SITE
   CHARCOAL BURNING PLATFORM
RT WOOD CHEMICAL WORKS

CHARCOAL STORE
CL INDUSTRIAL
RT EXPLOSIVES SITE
   METAL INDUSTRY SITE

Chariot Burial
USE CART BURIAL

Charity House
USE ALMSHOUSE

CHARITY SCHOOL
UF Bluecoat School
   Greycoat School
CL EDUCATION
BT FREE SCHOOL

CHARNEL HOUSE
UF Bone House
   Carnary
SN A building where the bones of the dead were stored.
CL RELIGIOUS, RITUAL AND FUNERARY
BT FUNERARY SITE
RT CHARNEL PIT
   CREMATION
   MAUSOLEUM
   MORTUARY CHAPEL
   MORTUARY HOUSE

CHARNEL PIT
CL RELIGIOUS, RITUAL AND FUNERARY
BT BURIAL PIT
RT CHARNEL HOUSE
   CHURCHYARD
   CREMATION

Chartered Institute Office
USE PROFESSIONAL INSTITUTE

Charterhouse
USE CARTHUSIAN MONASTERY

Charterhouse Grange
USE CARTHUSIAN GRANGE

CHARTIST COLONY HOUSE
UF Chartist Cottage
CL DOMESTIC
BT HOUSE <BY FUNCTION>
RT CHARTIST LAND COLONY

CHARTIST COLONY SCHOOL
CL EDUCATION
BT SCHOOL
RT CHARTIST LAND COLONY

Chartist Cottage
USE CHARTIST COLONY HOUSE

CHARTIST LAND COLONY
CL DOMESTIC
BT MODEL SETTLEMENT
RT CHARTIST COLONY HOUSE
   CHARTIST COLONY SCHOOL
   UTOPIAN COMMUNITY VILLAGE

Chase
USE HUNTING FOREST

CHEESE FACTORY
CL INDUSTRIAL
BT FACTORY <BY PRODUCT>

CHEESE FACTORY
  CL   INDUSTRIAL
  BT   FOOD PRODUCTION SITE
  RT   DAIRY

CHEESE MARKET
  CL   COMMERCIAL
  BT   MARKET

Chemical Factory
  USE CHEMICAL WORKS

CHEMICAL INDUSTRY SITE
  CL   INDUSTRIAL
  NT   CHEMICAL PRODUCT SITE
       CHEMICAL PRODUCTION SITE
       LABORATORY
       SALT STORE

CHEMICAL PRODUCT SITE
  CL   INDUSTRIAL
  BT   CHEMICAL INDUSTRY SITE
  NT   BLACKING FACTORY
       CANDLE FACTORY
       CANDLE WORKS
       PERFUMERY
       PLASTICS FACTORY
       RUBBER WORKS
       SOAP FACTORY
       TAR WORKS
       WAX FACTORY
       WOOD CHEMICAL WORKS

CHEMICAL PRODUCTION SITE
  CL   INDUSTRIAL
  BT   CHEMICAL INDUSTRY SITE
  NT   ACID TOWER
       ACID WORKS
       AGRICULTURAL CHEMICAL SITE
       ALKALI WORKS
       ARSENIC WORKS
       BLEACH WORKS
       CHEMICAL WORKS
       DISTILLATION PLANT
       DYE AND PIGMENT SITE
       ELLING HEARTH
       EXPLOSIVES SITE
       LIME WORKS
       PETROCHEMICAL SITE
       PHARMACEUTICAL CHEMICAL SITE
       PIPE BRIDGE
       SALT WORKS
       SODA KILN
       SODA WORKS

CHEMICAL WORKS
  UF   Celluloid Works
       Chemical Factory
  SN   Industrial complex involved in the production of a
       range of chemicals.
  CL   INDUSTRIAL
  BT   CHEMICAL PRODUCTION SITE
  RT   ALUM WORKS
       PLASTICS FACTORY

CHEMISE
  SN   An outer wall or moat.
  CL   DEFENCE
  RT   CASTLE
       CURTAIN WALL

CHEMISTS SHOP
  CL   COMMERCIAL
  BT   SHOP
  RT   DISPENSARY

Chepyn
  USE COW HOUSE

CHEST HOSPITAL
  SN   Pre sanatoria.
  CL   HEALTH AND WELFARE
  BT   SPECIALIST HOSPITAL

CHEST TOMB
  UF   Tomb Chest
  CL   RELIGIOUS, RITUAL AND FUNERARY
  BT   TOMB

CHEVAUX DE FRISE
  CL   DEFENCE
  RT   HILLFORT

Chicken House
  USE POULTRY HOUSE

CHICORY KILN
  UF   Liquorice Kiln
  CL   INDUSTRIAL
  BT   FOOD DRYING KILN

CHICORY KILN
  UF   Liquorice Kiln
  CL   INDUSTRIAL
  BT   KILN <BY FUNCTION>

Chief Constables Office
  USE CONSTABLES OFFICE

CHILDRENS HOME
  UF   Girls Home
       Home For Girls
  CL   HEALTH AND WELFARE
  NT   HANDICAPPED CHILDRENS HOME
       ORPHANAGE
  RT   ALMSHOUSE
       COTTAGE HOME
       MISSION HALL
       ORPHAN SCHOOL

CHILDRENS HOME
  UF   Girls Home
       Home For Girls
  CL   DOMESTIC
  BT   RESIDENTIAL BUILDING
  NT   HANDICAPPED CHILDRENS HOME

CHILDRENS HOSPITAL
  UF   Sick Childrens Hospital
  CL   HEALTH AND WELFARE
  BT   SPECIALIST HOSPITAL
  RT   CHILDRENS WARD BLOCK

CHILDRENS PLAYGROUND
  UF   Playground
  CL   RECREATIONAL
  BT   RECREATION GROUND
  RT   PLAYGROUND SHELTER

CHILDRENS WARD BLOCK
  CL   HEALTH AND WELFARE
  BT   HOSPITAL BLOCK
  RT   CHILDRENS HOSPITAL

CHIMNEY
  UF   Colliery Chimney
  SN   Industrial chimney.
  CL   INDUSTRIAL
  BT   INDUSTRIAL BUILDING
  NT   VENTILATION CHIMNEY
  RT   CALCINER
       CIRCULAR KILN
       CONDENSING CHIMNEY
       CONDENSING FLUE
       ECONOMISER HOUSE
       ENGINE HOUSE
       FACTORY

GLASS CONE
HOFFMAN KILN
KILN
POWER STATION
STEAM ENGINE
TEXTILE MILL
TUNNEL KILN

CHINA CLAY WORKS
- SN Works producing a refractory clay, kaolin. An essential raw material of porcelain and some types of papermaking.
- CL INDUSTRIAL
- BT POTTERY MANUFACTURING SITE

CHINA CLAY WORKS
- SN Works producing a refractory clay, kaolin. An essential raw material of porcelain and some types of papermaking.
- CL INDUSTRIAL
- BT CLAY EXTRACTION SITE

CHINA FACTORY
- UF Porcelain Factory
- CL INDUSTRIAL
- BT POTTERY MANUFACTURING SITE
- RT BONE MILL

CHINA FACTORY
- UF Porcelain Factory
- CL INDUSTRIAL
- BT FACTORY <BY PRODUCT>
- RT BONE MILL

CHINESE GARDEN
- CL GARDENS, PARKS AND URBAN SPACES
- BT GARDEN

CHINESE PAVILION
- CL GARDENS, PARKS AND URBAN SPACES
- BT PAVILION

Chipping Floor
USE FLINT WORKING SITE

CHITTING HOUSE
- SN A building in which potatoes can sprout and germinate.
- CL AGRICULTURE AND SUBSISTENCE
- BT FARM BUILDING

CHOCOLATE FACTORY
- CL INDUSTRIAL
- BT FACTORY <BY PRODUCT>
- RT CONFECTIONERY WORKS

CHOCOLATE FACTORY
- CL INDUSTRIAL
- BT FOOD PRODUCTION SITE
- RT CONFECTIONERY WORKS

CHOCOLATE HOUSE
- CL COMMERCIAL
- BT EATING AND DRINKING ESTABLISHMENT
- RT COFFEE HOUSE
       GENTLEMENS CLUB

CHOIR SCHOOL
- UF Cathedral Choir School
       Choristers School
       Plainsong School
       Song School
- CL EDUCATION
- BT TRAINING SCHOOL
- RT CATHEDRAL
       CHORISTERS HOUSE
       CLERGY HOUSE

Cholera Hospital

USE INFECTIOUS DISEASES HOSPITAL

Chop House
USE EATING HOUSE

CHORISTERS HOUSE
- UF Queristers House
- CL DOMESTIC
- BT HOUSE <BY FUNCTION>
- RT CATHEDRAL
       CHOIR SCHOOL

Choristers School
USE CHOIR SCHOOL

CHRISTIAN ASSOCIATION HOSTEL
- UF Ymca Hostel
       Ywca Hostel
- CL DOMESTIC
- BT HOSTEL

CHRISTIAN SCIENCE CHURCH
- CL RELIGIOUS, RITUAL AND FUNERARY
- BT CHURCH

CHURCH
- UF Abbey Church
       Church Tower
       Conventual Church
       Friars Church
       Friary Church
       Kirk
       Nuns Church
       Priory Church
       University Church
- CL RELIGIOUS, RITUAL AND FUNERARY
- BT PLACE OF WORSHIP
- NT ANGLICAN CHURCH
       CHRISTIAN SCIENCE CHURCH
       COLLEGIATE CHURCH
       DUTCH REFORMED CHURCH
       FORTIFIED CHURCH
       FRENCH PROTESTANT CHURCH
       HOSPITALLERS CHURCH
       HUGUENOT CHURCH
       MISSION CHURCH
       ORTHODOX CHURCH
       PARISH CHURCH
       PENTECOSTALIST CHURCH
       REDEMPTIONISTS CHURCH
       ROMAN CATHOLIC CHURCH
       SEAMENS CHURCH
       SEVENTH DAY ADVENTISTS CHURCH
       SWEDENBORGIAN CHURCH
       SWISS PROTESTANT CHURCH
       TEMPLARS CHURCH
       UNITED REFORMED CHURCH
- RT ANCHORITE CELL
       BELL TOWER
       CHURCHYARD
       CRYPT
       GALILEE
       LYCH GATE
       PRESBYTERY
       SACRISTY
       SHRINE
       SUNDAY SCHOOL
       VESTRY
       WESTWORK

CHURCH HALL
- CL CIVIL
- BT MEETING HALL
- RT CHURCH HOUSE
       VILLAGE HALL

CHURCH HOUSE
- SN House owned by the church, often used for meetings.
- CL CIVIL

BT   MEETING HALL
RT   CHURCH HALL
       GUILDHALL
       MARKET HOUSE
       MARRIAGE FEAST HOUSE
       TOWN HALL

CHURCH INSTITUTE
CL   EDUCATION
BT   INSTITUTE
RT   LEARNED SOCIETY BUILDING
       MINERS READING ROOM
       PEOPLES COLLEGE
       PROFESSIONAL INSTITUTE
       WORKING MENS COLLEGE

CHURCH INSTITUTE
CL   INSTITUTIONAL
BT   INSTITUTE
RT   MECHANICS INSTITUTE
       MINERS READING ROOM
       PEOPLES COLLEGE
       WORKING MENS COLLEGE

Church Of England School
USE CHURCH SCHOOL

Church Organ Factory
USE ORGAN FACTORY

CHURCH SCHOOL
UF   Anglican School
       British And Foreign School
       British And Foreign Society School
       Catholic School
       Church Of England School
       Congregational School
       Dissenters Grammar School
       Dissenters Proprietary School
       Dissenters School
       French Protestant School
       Lancasterian School
       Madras School
       Methodist School
       Moravian School
       National School
       National Society School
       Nonconformist Academy
       Nonconformist Proprietary School
       Nonconformist School
       Protestant School
       Roman Catholic School
       Scottish National School
CL   EDUCATION
BT   SCHOOL
RT   MORAVIAN SETTLEMENT

Church Tower
USE CHURCH

CHURCHYARD
UF   Churchyard Cross
       Churchyard Gate
       Churchyard Wall
CL   RELIGIOUS, RITUAL AND FUNERARY
BT   INHUMATION CEMETERY
RT   BIER HOUSE
       CHARNEL PIT
       CHURCH
       GRAVE
       GRAVESIDE SHELTER
       GRAVESTONE
       LYCH GATE
       SARCOPHAGUS
       TOMB
       TOMBSTONE
       WATCH HOUSE

Churchyard Cross

USE CROSS
       CHURCHYARD
SN   Use both terms.

Churchyard Gate
USE GATE
       CHURCHYARD
SN   Use both terms.

Churchyard Wall
USE WALL
       CHURCHYARD
SN   Use both terms.

CHURN STAND
CL   AGRICULTURE AND SUBSISTENCE

Cider Brewery
USE CIDER FACTORY

CIDER FACTORY
UF   Cider Brewery
       Cider Works
CL   INDUSTRIAL
BT   WINE AND CIDERMAKING SITE

CIDER HOUSE
UF   Ciderhouse
CL   COMMERCIAL
BT   LICENSED PREMISES
RT   CIDER MILL
       CIDER PRESS
       CIDER VAULT

CIDER MILL
SN   In which apples are broken down for pressing. May
       be animal drawn.
CL   INDUSTRIAL
BT   WINE AND CIDERMAKING SITE
RT   CIDER PRESS

CIDER MILL
SN   In which apples are broken down for pressing. May
       be animal drawn.
CL   AGRICULTURE AND SUBSISTENCE
BT   FOOD AND DRINK PROCESSING SITE
RT   CIDER HOUSE
       CIDER PRESS
       HORSE ENGINE HOUSE
       WINE PRESS

CIDER PRESS
UF   Apple Crusher
       Applecrusher
SN   In which crushed apples are pressed.
CL   INDUSTRIAL
BT   WINE AND CIDERMAKING SITE
RT   CIDER MILL

CIDER PRESS
UF   Apple Crusher
       Applecrusher
SN   In which crushed apples are pressed.
CL   AGRICULTURE AND SUBSISTENCE
BT   FOOD AND DRINK PROCESSING SITE
RT   CIDER HOUSE
       CIDER MILL
       CIDER VAULT
       FARM
       WINE PRESS

CIDER VAULT
SN   For the storage of cider.
CL   INDUSTRIAL
BT   WINE AND CIDERMAKING SITE
RT   CELLAR

CIDER VAULT
SN   For the storage of cider.
CL   AGRICULTURE AND SUBSISTENCE

BT   FOOD AND DRINK PROCESSING SITE
RT   CELLAR
     CIDER HOUSE
     CIDER PRESS

Cider Works
   USE CIDER FACTORY

Ciderhouse
   USE CIDER HOUSE

Cigarette Factory
   USE TOBACCO FACTORY

CINEMA
UF   Cinematograph Theatre
     Electric Theatre
     Picture House
     Picture Palace
CL   RECREATIONAL
RT   THEATRE

Cinematograph Theatre
   USE CINEMA

CINERARY URN
UF   Urned Cremation
SN   Urn containing a cremation. Where component use
     with wider site type.
CL   RELIGIOUS, RITUAL AND FUNERARY
BT   CREMATION
RT   COLUMBARIUM
     CREMATION CEMETERY
     OSSUARY
     URN
     URNFIELD

CIRCULAR ENCLOSURE
UF   Ring Enclosure
CL   UNASSIGNED
BT   CURVILINEAR ENCLOSURE

CIRCULAR KILN
UF   Conical Kiln
CL   INDUSTRIAL
BT   KILN <BY FORM>
RT   BRICK KILN
     CHIMNEY
     POTTERY KILN

CIRCULAR PLATFORM
CL   UNASSIGNED
BT   PLATFORM

Circumvallation
   USE SIEGEWORK

CIRCUS (RECREATIONAL)
UF   Circus Tent
CL   RECREATIONAL

Circus (Roman)
   USE EARTHWORK
SN   Use more specific type where known.

CIRCUS (URBAN)
CL   GARDENS, PARKS AND URBAN SPACES
BT   URBAN SPACE
RT   CRESCENT
     ROAD JUNCTION
     ROND POINT
     SQUARE

Circus Tent
   USE CIRCUS (RECREATIONAL)

CIST
UF   Kist
     Kistvaen

CL   RELIGIOUS, RITUAL AND FUNERARY
BT   FUNERARY SITE
NT   LINTEL GRAVE
     LONG CIST

CIST GRAVE CEMETERY
CL   RELIGIOUS, RITUAL AND FUNERARY
BT   INHUMATION CEMETERY

Cistercian Abbey
   USE ABBEY
       CISTERCIAN MONASTERY
       CISTERCIAN NUNNERY
SN   Use ABBEY and CISTERCIAN MONASTERY/NUNNER

CISTERCIAN ALIEN CELL
CL   RELIGIOUS, RITUAL AND FUNERARY
BT   ALIEN CELL
RT   CISTERCIAN MONASTERY

CISTERCIAN CELL
CL   RELIGIOUS, RITUAL AND FUNERARY
BT   CELL
RT   CISTERCIAN GRANGE
     CISTERCIAN MONASTERY
     CISTERCIAN NUNNERY

CISTERCIAN GRANGE
CL   RELIGIOUS, RITUAL AND FUNERARY
BT   GRANGE
RT   CISTERCIAN CELL
     CISTERCIAN MONASTERY
     CISTERCIAN NUNNERY

CISTERCIAN GRANGE
CL   AGRICULTURE AND SUBSISTENCE
BT   GRANGE

CISTERCIAN MONASTERY
UF   Cistercian Abbey
     Cistercian Priory
SN   Abbeys of Cistercian monks.
CL   RELIGIOUS, RITUAL AND FUNERARY
BT   MONASTERY
RT   CISTERCIAN ALIEN CELL
     CISTERCIAN CELL
     CISTERCIAN GRANGE
     CISTERCIAN NUNNERY
     SAVIGNIAC MONASTERY

CISTERCIAN NUNNERY
UF   Cistercian Abbey
     Cistercian Priory
SN   Abbeys and Priories of Cistercian nuns.
CL   RELIGIOUS, RITUAL AND FUNERARY
BT   NUNNERY
RT   CISTERCIAN CELL
     CISTERCIAN GRANGE
     CISTERCIAN MONASTERY

Cistercian Priory
   USE CISTERCIAN MONASTERY
       CISTERCIAN NUNNERY
       PRIORY
SN   Use PRIORY and CISTERCIAN MONASTERY/NUNNE

CISTERN
CL   WATER SUPPLY AND DRAINAGE
BT   WATER TANK
RT   CONDUIT HEAD
     RESERVOIR
     WATER PIPE

Citadel
   USE CASTLE

City Baths
   USE BATHS

City Cross

USE TOWN CROSS

City Defences
USE TOWN DEFENCES

City Education Office
USE LOCAL GOVERNMENT OFFICE

City Gate
USE TOWN GATE

City Hall
USE TOWN HALL

City Transport Office
USE LOCAL GOVERNMENT OFFICE

City Treasurers Office
USE LOCAL GOVERNMENT OFFICE

City Wall
USE TOWN WALL

CIVIC CENTRE
    CL   CIVIL
    RT   COUNTY HALL
          SHIRE HALL
          TOWN HALL

Civic Hall
USE TOWN HALL

CIVIL
    SN   This is the top term for the class. See CIVIL
          Class List for narrow terms.

CIVIL AIRPORT
    UF   International Airport
    CL   TRANSPORT
    BT   AIRPORT

Civil War Defences
USE SIEGEWORK

Civil War Siegework
USE SIEGEWORK

CIVITAS CAPITAL
    CL   DOMESTIC
    BT   TOWN

CIVITAS CAPITAL
    CL   CIVIL
    BT   TOWN

CLAMP KILN
    CL   INDUSTRIAL
    BT   KILN <BY FORM>
    RT   BRICK KILN
          CALCINER
          TILE KILN

CLAPPER BRIDGE
    CL   TRANSPORT
    BT   BRIDGE <BY FORM>

CLAPPER BRIDGE
    CL   TRANSPORT
    BT   ROAD TRANSPORT SITE

CLASSROOM
    CL   EDUCATION
    BT   SCHOOLROOM
    RT   SCHOOL

Claustral Buildings
USE CLOISTER

CLAY DRAINAGE PIPE WORKS

    CL   INDUSTRIAL
    BT   POTTERY MANUFACTURING SITE
    RT   BRICKWORKS

CLAY EXTRACTION SITE
    CL   INDUSTRIAL
    BT   MINERAL EXTRACTION SITE
    NT   BALL CLAY WORKS
          CHINA CLAY WORKS
          CLAY MINE
          CLAY PIT

CLAY MILL
    CL   INDUSTRIAL
    BT   BRICK AND TILEMAKING SITE
    RT   CLAY PIT
          PUG MILL
          TILE WORKS

CLAY MILL
    CL   INDUSTRIAL
    BT   MILL

CLAY MINE
    CL   INDUSTRIAL
    BT   CLAY EXTRACTION SITE
    RT   DRIFT MINE
          OPEN CAST MINE

CLAY MINE
    CL   INDUSTRIAL
    BT   MINE

CLAY PIPE KILN
    UF   Pipe Kiln
    SN   For the production of clay tobacco pipes.
    CL   INDUSTRIAL
    BT   POTTERY MANUFACTURING SITE
    RT   CLAY TOBACCO PIPE FACTORY
          POTTERY KILN

CLAY PIPE KILN
    UF   Pipe Kiln
    SN   For the production of clay tobacco pipes.
    CL   INDUSTRIAL
    BT   KILN <BY FUNCTION>

CLAY PIT
    CL   INDUSTRIAL
    BT   BRICK AND TILEMAKING SITE
    RT   CEMENT WORKS
          CLAY MILL
          CLAY PUDDLING PIT
          MARL PIT

CLAY PIT
    CL   INDUSTRIAL
    BT   POTTERY MANUFACTURING SITE

CLAY PIT
    CL   INDUSTRIAL
    BT   CLAY EXTRACTION SITE
    RT   DENE HOLE
          EXTRACTIVE PIT
          GRAVEL PIT
          MARL PIT

CLAY PUDDLING PIT
    CL   INDUSTRIAL
    BT   BRICK AND TILEMAKING SITE
    RT   CLAY PIT

CLAY PUDDLING PIT
    CL   INDUSTRIAL
    BT   POTTERY MANUFACTURING SITE
    RT   PUG MILL
          SAGGAR MAKERS WORKSHOP

CLAY TOBACCO PIPE FACTORY

CL INDUSTRIAL
BT POTTERY MANUFACTURING SITE
RT CLAY PIPE KILN
    WASTER TIP

CLAY WORKINGS
CL INDUSTRIAL
BT EXTRACTIVE PIT

Claypipe Workshop
USE PIPE WORKSHOP

CLEARANCE CAIRN
UF Field Clearance Cairn
CL AGRICULTURE AND SUBSISTENCE
BT CAIRN
RT CAIRNFIELD
    FIELD SYSTEM

CLEARING HOUSE
CL COMMERCIAL
RT BANK (FINANCIAL)

CLERGY HOUSE
UF Canonical House
    Canonry
    Canons House
    Canons Summer House
    Prebendal House
    Residentiary
    Wiccamical Prebendaries House
CL DOMESTIC
BT CLERICAL DWELLING
RT CATHEDRAL
    CHANTRY COLLEGE
    CHOIR SCHOOL
    TREASURERS HOUSE

CLERICAL DWELLING
CL DOMESTIC
BT HOUSE <BY FUNCTION>
NT ABBOTS HOUSE
    ARCHBISHOPS MANOR HOUSE
    ARCHDEACONRY
    CLERGY HOUSE
    DEANERY
    MANCIPLES HOUSE
    MANSE
    PARSONAGE
    PRESBYTERY
    PRIESTS HOUSE
    PRIORS HOUSE
    PRISON CHAPLAINS HOUSE
    PROVOSTS HOUSE
    RECTORY
    SUBDEANERY
    VERGERS HOUSE
    VICARAGE

CLIFF CASTLE
CL DOMESTIC
BT PROMONTORY FORT

CLIFF CASTLE
CL DEFENCE
BT PROMONTORY FORT

CLIFF LIFT
CL TRANSPORT
BT LIFT

CLIFF RAILWAY
CL TRANSPORT
BT RAILWAY
RT FUNICULAR RAILWAY

CLINIC
UF Health Centre
    Health Clinic
CL HEALTH AND WELFARE
NT MATERNITY CLINIC
    SCHOOL CLINIC
RT DISPENSARY
    DOCTORS HOUSE
    HOSPITAL

Clink
USE PRISON

Clipping Floor
USE FLINT WORKING SITE

Clocher
USE BELL TOWER

Clock House
USE CLOCK TOWER

CLOCK SHOP
CL COMMERCIAL
BT SHOP

CLOCK TOWER
UF Clock House
CL UNASSIGNED
BT TOWER

CLOG MILL
UF Clogmaking Works
CL INDUSTRIAL
BT CLOTHING INDUSTRY SITE

CLOG MILL
UF Clogmaking Works
CL INDUSTRIAL
BT TIMBER PRODUCT SITE

Clogmaking Works
USE CLOG MILL

CLOISTER
UF Claustral Buildings
CL RELIGIOUS, RITUAL AND FUNERARY
NT DOUBLE CLOISTER
RT CLOISTER GARTH
    MONASTERY

CLOISTER GARTH
CL RELIGIOUS, RITUAL AND FUNERARY
RT CLOISTER

Closing Stile
USE STILE

CLOTH CUTTERS WORKSHOP
UF Fustian Cutters Shop
    Velvet Cutters Workshop
CL INDUSTRIAL
BT CRAFT INDUSTRY SITE
RT HATTERS WORKSHOP
    WORKSHOP

CLOTH CUTTERS WORKSHOP
UF Fustian Cutters Shop
    Velvet Cutters Workshop
CL INDUSTRIAL
BT CLOTHING INDUSTRY SITE

CLOTH DRESSING MILL
SN Cloth finishing process using machinery to raise
    the nap of the cloth before shearing.
CL INDUSTRIAL
BT TEXTILE MILL

CLOTH DRESSING MILL
SN Cloth finishing process using machinery to raise
    the nap of the cloth before shearing.
CL INDUSTRIAL

BT   TEXTILE FINISHING SITE
RT   CLOTH DRY HOUSE
     FINISHING HOUSE
     FINISHING WORKS
     FULLING MILL
     WASHING SHOP

CLOTH DRY HOUSE
UF   Tenter House
CL   INDUSTRIAL
BT   TEXTILE FINISHING SITE
RT   BEETLING MILL
     CALENDER MILL
     CLOTH DRESSING MILL
     DRY HOUSE
     TENTER GROUND

CLOTH HALL
UF   Coloured Cloth Hall
     Piece Hall
     Tammy Hall
     White Cloth Hall
SN   A market hall built for the exchange of textiles.
CL   COMMERCIAL
BT   MARKET HALL
RT   CLOTH MARKET
     GUILDHALL

CLOTH MARKET
UF   Lace Market
     Lace Warehouse
     Yarn Market
SN   An open market used for the exchange of textiles.
CL   COMMERCIAL
BT   MARKET
RT   CLOTH HALL

CLOTHES LINE ENCLOSURE
SN   A small rectangular or sub circular area bounded
     by an earthwork in which one side is formed by an
     existing linear boundary.
CL   DOMESTIC
BT   ENCLOSED SETTLEMENT
RT   D SHAPED ENCLOSURE

CLOTHIERS HOUSE
CL   DOMESTIC
BT   INDUSTRIAL HOUSE

CLOTHIERS HOUSE
CL   INDUSTRIAL
BT   CRAFT INDUSTRY SITE

CLOTHIERS HOUSE
CL   INDUSTRIAL
BT   INDUSTRIAL HOUSE

CLOTHIERS WORKSHOP
CL   INDUSTRIAL
BT   CRAFT INDUSTRY SITE

CLOTHIERS WORKSHOP
CL   INDUSTRIAL
BT   CLOTHING INDUSTRY SITE
RT   FLAX BEATING STONE
     LACE DRYING HOUSE
     WOOL WALL

CLOTHING FACTORY
UF   Tailoring Factory
CL   INDUSTRIAL
BT   FACTORY <BY PRODUCT>
RT   TEXTILE MILL

CLOTHING FACTORY
UF   Tailoring Factory
CL   INDUSTRIAL
BT   CLOTHING INDUSTRY SITE

CLOTHING INDUSTRY SITE

CL   INDUSTRIAL
NT   ARTIFICIAL TEXTILE FACTORY
     BUTTON MILL
     CLOG MILL
     CLOTH CUTTERS WORKSHOP
     CLOTHIERS WORKSHOP
     CLOTHING FACTORY
     CLOTHING WORKSHOP
     COBBLERS WORKSHOP
     GLOVE FACTORY
     HAT FACTORY
     HATTERS WORKSHOP
     HOSIERY FACTORY
     SHOE FACTORY
     TAILORS WORKSHOP
RT   TEXTILE PRODUCT SITE

CLOTHING SHOP
UF   Boutique
CL   COMMERCIAL
BT   SHOP
RT   TAILORS SHOP

CLOTHING WORKSHOP
CL   INDUSTRIAL
BT   CLOTHING INDUSTRY SITE
RT   TAILORS SHOP

Clow
  USE SLUICE

CLUB
CL   INSTITUTIONAL
NT   GENTLEMENS CLUB
     POLITICAL CLUB
     SERVICES CLUB
     SOCIAL CLUB
     WORKING MENS CLUB
     YOUTH CLUB
RT   CLUBHOUSE
     JAZZ CLUB

CLUB
CL   RECREATIONAL
NT   GENTLEMENS CLUB
     SERVICES CLUB
     SOCIAL CLUB
     WORKING MENS CLUB
     YOUTH CLUB
RT   CLUBHOUSE
     JAZZ CLUB

Club Building
  USE CLUBHOUSE

CLUBHOUSE
UF   Club Building
CL   RECREATIONAL
RT   CLUB

Cludgie
  USE TOILET

Cluniac Abbey
  USE ABBEY
      CLUNIAC MONASTERY
      CLUNIAC NUNNERY
  SN   Use ABBEY and CLUNIAC MONASTERY or CLUNIAC
       NUNNERY.

Cluniac Alien Priory
  USE CLUNIAC MONASTERY
      CLUNIAC NUNNERY
      ALIEN PRIORY
  SN   Use ALIEN PRIORY and CLUNIAC MONASTERY
       /NUNNERY.

Cluniac Alien Priory Cell
  USE CLUNIAC ALIEN CELL

127

CLUNIAC CELL
    UF   Cluniac Priory Cell
    CL   RELIGIOUS, RITUAL AND FUNERARY
    BT   CELL
    RT   CLUNIAC GRANGE
            CLUNIAC MONASTERY
            CLUNIAC NUNNERY

CLUNIAC GRANGE
    CL   RELIGIOUS, RITUAL AND FUNERARY
    BT   GRANGE
    RT   CLUNIAC CELL
            CLUNIAC MONASTERY
            CLUNIAC NUNNERY

CLUNIAC GRANGE
    CL   AGRICULTURE AND SUBSISTENCE
    BT   GRANGE
    RT   CLUNIAC CELL

CLUNIAC MONASTERY
    UF   Cluniac Abbey
            Cluniac Alien Priory
            Cluniac Priory
    SN   Abbeys and Priories of Cluniac monks.
    CL   RELIGIOUS, RITUAL AND FUNERARY
    BT   MONASTERY
    RT   CLUNIAC CELL
            CLUNIAC GRANGE
            CLUNIAC NUNNERY

CLUNIAC NUNNERY
    UF   Cluniac Abbey
            Cluniac Alien Priory
            Cluniac Priory
    SN   Abbeys and Priories of Cluniac nuns.
    CL   RELIGIOUS, RITUAL AND FUNERARY
    BT   NUNNERY
    RT   CLUNIAC CELL
            CLUNIAC GRANGE
            CLUNIAC MONASTERY

Cluniac Priory
    USE CLUNIAC MONASTERY
            CLUNIAC NUNNERY
            PRIORY
    SN   Use PRIORY and CLUNIAC MONASTERY/NUNNERY.

Cluniac Priory Cell
    USE CLUNIAC CELL

CLUSTER BLOCK
    CL   DOMESTIC
    BT   MULTIPLE DWELLING
    RT   FLATS

CLUSTER HOUSE
    CL   DOMESTIC
    BT   MULTIPLE DWELLING
    RT   BACK TO BACK HOUSE
            BACK TO EARTH HOUSE
            BLIND BACK HOUSE
            TERRACED HOUSE
            THROUGH BY LIGHT

Coach Building Works
    USE COACH WORKS

COACH HOUSE
    CL   TRANSPORT
    BT   ROAD TRANSPORT SITE
    RT   CARRIAGE HOUSE
            COACHING INN
            COACHING INN STABLE
            COACHMANS COTTAGE
            HACKNEY STABLE
            LIVERY STABLE
            STABLE

TRAP HOUSE

Coach Station
    USE BUS STATION

COACH WORKS
    UF   Coach Building Works
    CL   INDUSTRIAL
    BT   MOTOR VEHICLE ENGINEERING SITE

COACHING INN
    UF   Livery Tavern
    CL   COMMERCIAL
    BT   INN
    RT   COACH HOUSE
            COACHING INN STABLE
            DROVERS INN
            HACKNEY STABLE
            JAGGERS HOSTEL
            LIVERY STABLE

COACHING INN
    UF   Livery Tavern
    CL   DOMESTIC
    BT   INN
    RT   COACH HOUSE
            COACHING INN STABLE
            DROVERS INN
            HACKNEY STABLE
            JAGGERS HOSTEL
            LIVERY STABLE

COACHING INN STABLE
    CL   TRANSPORT
    BT   ROAD TRANSPORT SITE
    RT   COACH HOUSE
            COACHING INN
            HACKNEY STABLE
            LIVERY STABLE

COACHING INN STABLE
    CL   TRANSPORT
    BT   STABLE
    RT   COACHING INN

COACHMANS COTTAGE
    CL   DOMESTIC
    BT   TRANSPORT WORKERS HOUSE
    RT   COACH HOUSE
            ESTATE COTTAGE
            GROOMS COTTAGE
            MEWS
            STABLE

COAL BUNKER
    CL   INDUSTRIAL
    BT   COAL MINING SITE
    RT   COALING CRANE

COAL CLEANING PLANT
    UF   Coal Washery
            Washery
    CL   INDUSTRIAL
    BT   COAL MINING SITE

COAL CRUSHER HOUSE
    CL   INDUSTRIAL
    BT   COAL MINING SITE
    RT   COKE OVEN
            SCREENING PLANT

COAL DROP
    UF   Coal Waggon Hoist
    CL   TRANSPORT
    BT   LIFTING AND WINDING STRUCTURE
    RT   COAL JETTY
            COALING CRANE
            STAITH

COAL DROP

UF   Coal Waggon Hoist
CL   INDUSTRIAL
BT   COAL MINING SITE
RT   MINE LIFTING AND WINDING STRUCTURE

Coal Duty Boundary Marker
USE COAL TAX POST

COAL EXCHANGE
CL   COMMERCIAL
BT   EXCHANGE

COAL FIRED POWER STATION
CL   INDUSTRIAL
BT   POWER STATION

COAL GAS STRUCTURE
CL   INDUSTRIAL
BT   POWER GENERATION SITE
NT   GAS HOLDER
        GAS HOUSE
        GAS STORAGE TANK
        GAS WORKS
        PRODUCER GAS HOUSE
        PURIFIER HOUSE
        RETORT HOUSE

COAL HOLE COVER
CL   GARDENS, PARKS AND URBAN SPACES
BT   STREET FURNITURE

Coal House
USE COAL SHED

COAL JETTY
UF   Coal Staith
        Coal Staithe
CL   TRANSPORT
BT   JETTY
RT   COAL DROP
        COALING CRANE
        STAITH

COAL JETTY
UF   Coal Staith
        Coal Staithe
CL   MARITIME
BT   JETTY
RT   COAL DROP
        COALING CRANE
        STAITH

Coal Mine
USE COLLIERY

Coal Miners Cottage
USE WORKERS COTTAGE

Coal Miners Village
USE WORKERS VILLAGE

COAL MINING SITE
SN   Includes terms for components of site. See also
        terms in MINING INDUSTRY SITE grouping.
CL   INDUSTRIAL
BT   FUEL PRODUCTION SITE
NT   COAL BUNKER
        COAL CLEANING PLANT
        COAL CRUSHER HOUSE
        COAL DROP
        COAL PIT
        COAL PREPARATION PLANT
        COAL SCREEN
        COAL TIPPLER
        COAL WORKINGS
        COALITE PLANT
        COKE OVEN
        COKE QUENCHING TOWER
        COLLIERY

        COLLIERY RAILWAY
        DUST EXTRACTION PLANT
        SCREENING PLANT
RT   MINING INDUSTRY SITE

COAL PIT
CL   INDUSTRIAL
BT   EXTRACTIVE PIT
RT   BELL PIT

COAL PIT
CL   INDUSTRIAL
BT   COAL MINING SITE
RT   BELL PIT
        DRIFT MINE

COAL PREPARATION PLANT
CL   INDUSTRIAL
BT   COAL MINING SITE

COAL SCREEN
SN   Series of wire mesh screens used for grading lumps
        of coal according to size.
CL   INDUSTRIAL
BT   COAL MINING SITE

COAL SHED
UF   Coal House
        Coal Store
CL   UNASSIGNED
BT   FUEL STORE
RT   SHED

Coal Staith
USE COAL JETTY
        STAITH
SN   Use both terms.

Coal Staithe
USE COAL JETTY
        STAITH
SN   Use both terms.

Coal Store
USE COAL SHED

COAL TAX POST
UF   Coal Duty Boundary Marker
CL   GARDENS, PARKS AND URBAN SPACES
BT   DUTY POST
RT   BOUNDARY MARKER
        BOUNDARY PLATE
        BOUNDARY POST
        BOUNDARY STONE
        TOLL BOUNDARY MARKER

Coal Tip
USE SPOIL HEAP

COAL TIPPLER
UF   Tippler
SN   Loading machinery tipping coal into railway wagons
        usually at a pithead.
CL   INDUSTRIAL
BT   COAL MINING SITE
RT   HYDRAULIC TIPPLER

Coal Waggon Hoist
USE COAL DROP

Coal Washery
USE COAL CLEANING PLANT

COAL WORKINGS
UF   Open Cast Coal Workings
SN   Use with form of extraction where known.
CL   INDUSTRIAL
BT   EXTRACTIVE PIT
RT   COLLIERY

COAL WORKINGS
- UF Open Cast Coal Workings
- SN Use with form of extraction where known.
- CL INDUSTRIAL
- BT COAL MINING SITE
- RT COLLIERY

COALING CRANE
- CL TRANSPORT
- BT CRANE <BY FUNCTION>
- RT COAL BUNKER
  - COAL DROP
  - COAL JETTY
  - STAITH

COALITE PLANT
- SN Production of smokeless domestic fuel by roasting anthracite in a type of kiln.
- CL INDUSTRIAL
- BT COAL MINING SITE
- RT COKE QUENCHING TOWER

Coalminers Union Hall
  USE TRADES UNION HALL

COAST LIGHT
- CL MARITIME
- BT NAVIGATION AID
- RT CHAPEL

COASTAL BATTERY
- CL DEFENCE
- BT BATTERY

COASTAL BATTERY
- CL MARITIME
- BT MILITARY COASTAL DEFENCES

COASTAL FISH WEIR
- CL AGRICULTURE AND SUBSISTENCE
- BT FISH WEIR

Coastal Fort
  USE FORTRESS

Coastal Landmark Tower
  USE LANDMARK TOWER

COASTGUARD CRAFT
- CL MARITIME
- BT MARITIME CRAFT
- NT REVENUE CUTTER

COASTGUARD STATION
- CL CIVIL
- RT COASTGUARD TOWER
  - COASTGUARDS COTTAGE
  - CUSTOM HOUSE
  - LIFEBOAT STATION
  - LIGHTHOUSE

COASTGUARD STATION
- CL MARITIME
- BT NAVIGATION AID
- RT COASTGUARD TOWER
  - COASTGUARDS COTTAGE
  - CUSTOM HOUSE
  - LIGHTHOUSE

COASTGUARD TOWER
- CL MARITIME
- BT NAVIGATION AID
- RT COASTGUARD STATION
  - COASTGUARDS COTTAGE

COASTGUARDS COTTAGE
- CL DOMESTIC
- BT MARITIME HOUSE

- RT COASTGUARD STATION
  - COASTGUARD TOWER
  - FISHERMANS HOUSE
  - LIGHTKEEPERS HOUSE
  - MARINERS COTTAGE

COAT OF ARMS
- UF Crest
- SN Includes crests, hatchments and supporters.
- CL COMMEMORATIVE
- BT COMMEMORATIVE MONUMENT

COAXIAL FIELD SYSTEM
- CL AGRICULTURE AND SUBSISTENCE
- BT FIELD SYSTEM

COBBLED ROAD
- UF Cobbled Street
- CL TRANSPORT
- BT ROAD

Cobbled Street
  USE COBBLED ROAD

Cobbled Surface
  USE FEATURE

COBBLERS STALL
- CL COMMERCIAL
- RT COBBLERS WORKSHOP

COBBLERS WORKSHOP
- CL INDUSTRIAL
- BT CLOTHING INDUSTRY SITE
- RT COBBLERS STALL
  - LEATHER WORKERS SHOP

COCKLE KILN
- CL INDUSTRIAL
- BT KILN <BY FORM>

COCKPIT
- CL RECREATIONAL
- BT BAITING PLACE
- RT PIT

Cocoa Tavern
  USE TEMPERANCE PUBLIC HOUSE

Coe
  USE MINERS HUT

COFFEE BAR
- CL COMMERCIAL
- BT EATING AND DRINKING ESTABLISHMENT

COFFEE HOUSE
- CL COMMERCIAL
- BT EATING AND DRINKING ESTABLISHMENT
- RT CHOCOLATE HOUSE
  - GENTLEMENS CLUB

Coffee Palace
  USE TEMPERANCE PUBLIC HOUSE

Coffee Public House
  USE TEMPERANCE PUBLIC HOUSE

Coffee Tavern
  USE TEMPERANCE PUBLIC HOUSE

COFFIN
- CL RELIGIOUS, RITUAL AND FUNERARY
- BT FUNERARY SITE
- NT SARCOPHAGUS
  - TREE TRUNK COFFIN

COFFIN STONE
- SN A stone found on route to a churchyard on which the coffin is rested during transportation.
- CL RELIGIOUS, RITUAL AND FUNERARY

Cog And Rung Gin
USE HORSE ENGINE

COINAGE HALL
SN Civil building in Cornwall and Devon for assay and sale of tin ingots.
CL CIVIL
RT ASSAY OFFICE
BLOWING HOUSE
MARKET HALL
STANNARY COURT
TIN MINE

COINAGE HALL
SN Civil building in Cornwall and Devon for assay and sale of tin ingots.
CL COMMERCIAL
RT ASSAY OFFICE
BLOWING HOUSE
MARKET HALL
STANNARY COURT
TIN MINE

Coke Furnace
USE COKE OVEN

COKE OVEN
UF Coke Furnace
SN Oven for roasting coal to drive off chemical constituents and reduce it to almost pure carbon, ie. coke.
CL INDUSTRIAL
BT COAL MINING SITE
RT COAL CRUSHER HOUSE
COKE QUENCHING TOWER
TAR WORKS

COKE OVEN
UF Coke Furnace
SN Oven for roasting coal to drive off chemical constituents and reduce it to almost pure carbon, ie. coke.
CL INDUSTRIAL
BT KILN <BY FUNCTION>
RT OVEN
PRODUCER GAS HOUSE
STEEL WORKS

COKE QUENCHING TOWER
SN Water spraying tower for cooling coke after it emerges from the furnace.
CL INDUSTRIAL
BT COAL MINING SITE
RT COALITE PLANT
COKE OVEN

COLD STORE
CL INDUSTRIAL
BT FOOD PRESERVING SITE
RT FISH WAREHOUSE
ICEHOUSE
REFRIGERATED STORE
WAREHOUSE

College
USE UNIVERSITY COLLEGE
CHANTRY COLLEGE
TRAINING COLLEGE
SN Use appropriate term.

COLLEGE GARDEN
CL GARDENS, PARKS AND URBAN SPACES
BT GARDEN

College Library
USE LIBRARY
UNIVERSITY COLLEGE
CHANTRY COLLEGE

TRAINING COLLEGE
SN Use LIBRARY with other appropriate term.

COLLEGE LODGINGS
UF College Wardens Lodgings
Hospitium
Provosts Lodgings
Tutors Lodgings
CL DOMESTIC
BT LODGINGS
RT HALL OF RESIDENCE

College Of Arms
USE PROFESSIONAL INSTITUTE

College Of Art
USE ART SCHOOL

COLLEGE OF SECULAR PRIESTS
CL RELIGIOUS, RITUAL AND FUNERARY
NT CHANTRY COLLEGE
COLLEGE OF THE VICARS CHORAL
RT COLLEGIATE CHAPEL

COLLEGE OF THE VICARS CHORAL
CL RELIGIOUS, RITUAL AND FUNERARY
BT COLLEGE OF SECULAR PRIESTS

College Wardens Lodgings
USE COLLEGE LODGINGS

COLLEGIATE CHAPEL
CL RELIGIOUS, RITUAL AND FUNERARY
BT CHAPEL
RT CHANTRY CHAPEL
CHANTRY COLLEGE
COLLEGE OF SECULAR PRIESTS
COLLEGIATE CHURCH

COLLEGIATE CHURCH
CL RELIGIOUS, RITUAL AND FUNERARY
BT CHURCH
RT CHANTRY CHAPEL
CHANTRY COLLEGE
COLLEGIATE CHAPEL

COLLIER
CL MARITIME
BT CARGO VESSEL

COLLIERY
UF Cage Shop
Coal Mine
Colliery Chimney
Colliery Pumphouse
Colliery Repair Shop
Colliery Winding House
Pit Prop Shop
CL INDUSTRIAL
BT COAL MINING SITE
RT COLLIERY INSTITUTE
MINES RESCUE STATION
PITHEAD BATHS
SPOIL HEAP
WORKERS VILLAGE

COLLIERY
UF Cage Shop
Coal Mine
Colliery Chimney
Colliery Pumphouse
Colliery Repair Shop
Colliery Winding House
Pit Prop Shop
CL INDUSTRIAL
BT MINE
RT COAL WORKINGS

Colliery Baths

USE PITHEAD BATHS

Colliery Chimney
  USE COLLIERY
      CHIMNEY
  SN Use both terms.

COLLIERY INSTITUTE
  CL EDUCATION
  BT INSTITUTE
  RT MINERS READING ROOM
      PEOPLES COLLEGE
      WORKERS VILLAGE
      WORKING MENS COLLEGE

COLLIERY INSTITUTE
  CL INSTITUTIONAL
  BT INSTITUTE
  RT COLLIERY
      MINERS READING ROOM
      PEOPLES COLLEGE
      WORKERS VILLAGE
      WORKING MENS COLLEGE

Colliery Pumphouse
  USE COLLIERY
      MINE PUMPING WORKS
  SN Use both terms.

COLLIERY RAILWAY
  SN Railway constructed specifically for the movement
      of coal around the pithead of a coal mine.
  CL INDUSTRIAL
  BT COAL MINING SITE
  RT HAULAGE ENGINE HOUSE
      HEAPSTEAD

COLLIERY RAILWAY
  SN Railway constructed specifically for the movement
      of coal around the pithead of a coal mine.
  CL TRANSPORT
  BT RAILWAY
  RT HAULAGE ENGINE HOUSE

Colliery Repair Shop
  USE COLLIERY
      WORKSHOP
  SN Use both terms.

Colliery Village
  USE WORKERS VILLAGE

Colliery Winding House
  USE COLLIERY
      WINDER HOUSE
  SN Use both terms.

COLONIA
  CL DOMESTIC
  BT TOWN

COLONIA
  CL CIVIL
  BT TOWN

Colonial Office
  USE GOVERNMENT OFFICE

COLONNADE
  SN A row of columns supporting an entablature.
  CL UNASSIGNED

COLOUR HOUSE
  SN Small dye works.
  CL INDUSTRIAL
  BT DYE AND PIGMENT SITE
  RT COLOUR MILL
      DYE HOUSE
      DYE WORKS

COLOUR HOUSE
  SN Small dye works.
  CL INDUSTRIAL
  BT TEXTILE FINISHING SITE
  RT COLOUR MILL
      DYE HOUSE
      DYE WORKS

COLOUR LOFT
  SN A naval dockyard building used for the manufacture
      of flags.
  CL MARITIME
  BT MARINE WORKSHOP

COLOUR LOFT
  SN A naval dockyard building used for the manufacture
      of flags.
  CL INDUSTRIAL
  BT MARINE WORKSHOP

COLOUR MILL
  SN Grinding mill for producing dyes and pigments from
      natural materials.
  CL INDUSTRIAL
  BT DYE AND PIGMENT SITE
  RT FLINT MILL
      LOGWOOD MILL
      SALT WORKS

COLOUR MILL
  SN Grinding mill for producing dyes and pigments from
      natural materials.
  CL INDUSTRIAL
  BT TEXTILE FINISHING SITE
  RT COLOUR HOUSE
      DYE WORKS

Coloured Cloth Hall
  USE CLOTH HALL

COLUMBARIUM
  CL RELIGIOUS, RITUAL AND FUNERARY
  BT FUNERARY SITE
  RT CINERARY URN
      CREMATION CEMETERY
      CREMATORIUM

Columbary
  USE DOVECOTE

COLUMN
  UF Commemorative Column
  SN Use for free standing column.
  CL UNASSIGNED
  RT BUST
      HERM
      OBELISK
      STATUE
      URN

COMB MILL
  CL INDUSTRIAL
  BT MILL
  RT WIRE MILL

COMB MILL
  CL INDUSTRIAL
  BT FERROUS METAL PRODUCT SITE

COMBINATION BARN
  UF Lancashire Barn
  SN A barn accommodating livestock and crops, the
      former being in an aisle, outshut or at one end of
      the building.
  CL AGRICULTURE AND SUBSISTENCE
  BT BARN
  RT BANK BARN
      CATTLE SHELTER

COW HOUSE
FIELD BARN
HAYLOFT
LINHAY
VACCARY

COMBINATION FARM BUILDING
SN   Any multi-purpose farm building, other than
     COMBINATION BARN.
CL   AGRICULTURE AND SUBSISTENCE
BT   FARM BUILDING

COMBING SHED
CL   INDUSTRIAL
BT   TEXTILE SITE < BY PROCESS/PRODUCT >
RT   COMBING WORKS
     SCRIBBLING MILL
     SHED
     WILLEY SHED
     WORSTED MILL
     YARN MILL

COMBING WORKS
CL   INDUSTRIAL
BT   TEXTILE MILL

COMBING WORKS
CL   INDUSTRIAL
BT   TEXTILE SITE < BY PROCESS/PRODUCT >
RT   COMBING SHED
     GREASE WORKS
     WILLEY SHED
     WOOLCOMBERS SHOP
     WORSTED MILL

COMMANDER IN CHIEFS HOUSE
CL   DOMESTIC
BT   HOUSE < BY FUNCTION >
RT   COMMISSIONERS HOUSE
     NAVAL OFFICERS HOUSE

Commandery
USE HOSPITALLERS PRECEPTORY

COMMEMORATIVE
SN   This is the top term for the class. See
     COMMEMORATIVE Class List for narrow terms.

Commemorative Arch
USE COMMEMORATIVE MONUMENT
     ARCH
SN   Use both terms.

COMMEMORATIVE BRASS
UF   Memorial Brass
CL   COMMEMORATIVE
BT   COMMEMORATIVE MONUMENT

Commemorative Column
USE COLUMN
     COMMEMORATIVE MONUMENT
SN   Use both terms.

COMMEMORATIVE MONUMENT
UF   Ceremonial Arch
     Commemorative Arch
     Commemorative Column
     Commemorative Plaque
     Commemorative Tablet
     Hall Of Memory
     Memorial
     Memorial Chapel
     Memorial Garden
     Memorial Hall
     Memorial Seat
     Monument
     Monumental Arch
CL   COMMEMORATIVE
NT   ANIMAL MEMORIAL

CENOTAPH
COAT OF ARMS
COMMEMORATIVE BRASS
COMMEMORATIVE STONE
EFFIGY
ELEANOR CROSS
HILL FIGURE
NAMED TREE
OBELISK
PLAGUE MEMORIAL
QUADRIGA
ROSTRAL COLUMN
TRIUMPHAL ARCH
WALL MONUMENT
WAR MEMORIAL

Commemorative Plaque
USE COMMEMORATIVE MONUMENT
     PLAQUE
SN   Use both terms.

COMMEMORATIVE STONE
UF   Memorial Stone
CL   COMMEMORATIVE
BT   COMMEMORATIVE MONUMENT
NT   CENTURIAL STONE
     CORONATION STONE
     DATE STONE
     DEDICATION STONE
RT   INSCRIBED STONE

Commemorative Tablet
USE COMMEMORATIVE MONUMENT
     PLAQUE
SN   Use both terms.

COMMERCIAL
SN   This is the top term for the class. See COMMERCIAL
     Class list for narrow terms.

COMMERCIAL ART GALLERY
UF   Commercial Gallery
     Private Art Gallery
CL   COMMERCIAL
RT   ART GALLERY

COMMERCIAL COLLEGE
CL   EDUCATION
BT   TRAINING COLLEGE

Commercial Gallery
USE COMMERCIAL ART GALLERY

COMMERCIAL OFFICE
UF   Assurance Office
     Bank Chambers
     Bank Office
     Building Society Office
     Estate Agent
     Fire Office
     Insurance Office
     Life Assurance Office
     Shipping Insurance Office
CL   COMMERCIAL
NT   ASSAY OFFICE
     BOOKING OFFICE
     DRAWING OFFICE
     LEGAL OFFICE
     NEWSPAPER OFFICE
     PAY OFFICE
     TIMEKEEPERS OFFICE
RT   OFFICE

COMMERCIAL TRAVELLERS SCHOOL
CL   EDUCATION
BT   TRAINING SCHOOL

COMMISSIONERS HOUSE
CL   DOMESTIC

BT HOUSE <BY FUNCTION>
RT COMMANDER IN CHIEFS HOUSE
NAVAL OFFICERS HOUSE

Common
USE COMMON LAND

Common House
USE CALEFACTORY

COMMON LAND
UF Common
CL GARDENS, PARKS AND URBAN SPACES

COMMON LAND
UF Common
CL AGRICULTURE AND SUBSISTENCE
BT LAND USE SITE

COMMUNAL BAKEHOUSE
CL DOMESTIC
BT BAKEHOUSE
RT FLATS
VILLAGE

COMMUNICATIONS
SN This is the top term for the class. See
COMMUNICATIONS Class List for narrow terms.

COMMUNICATIONS CRAFT
CL MARITIME
BT MARITIME CRAFT
NT CABLE LAYER
PACKET
TELEGRAPH SHIP

COMMUNITY CENTRE
UF Community Hall
Neighbourhood Centre
CL CIVIL
RT RECREATIONAL HALL
TENANTS HALL

COMMUNITY GARDEN
CL GARDENS, PARKS AND URBAN SPACES
BT GARDEN

Community Hall
USE COMMUNITY CENTRE

Company Hall
USE LIVERY HALL

COMPOUND STEAM ENGINE
SN A steam engine that uses the same steam
successively to drive pistons in high and then low
pressure cylinders.
CL INDUSTRIAL
BT STEAM ENGINE
RT BEAM ENGINE

COMPREHENSIVE SCHOOL
CL EDUCATION
BT SECONDARY SCHOOL

COMPRESSOR HOUSE
CL INDUSTRIAL
BT STEAM POWER PRODUCTION SITE
RT BOILER HOUSE
ENGINE

CONCENTRIC CASTLE
CL DOMESTIC
BT CASTLE

CONCENTRIC CASTLE
CL DEFENCE
BT CASTLE

Concentric Stone Circle

USE STONE CIRCLE

CONCERT HALL
UF Concert Rooms
Music House
Symphony Hall
CL RECREATIONAL
BT MUSIC AND DANCE VENUE
RT ARTS CENTRE
ASSEMBLY ROOMS
MUSIC HALL
OPERA HOUSE
THEATRE

Concert Rooms
USE CONCERT HALL

CONCRETE WORKS
CL INDUSTRIAL
BT CEMENT MANUFACTURING SITE
RT LIME WORKS
SAND PIT

Condenser Flue
USE CONDENSING FLUE

CONDENSERY
CL INDUSTRIAL
BT FOOD PROCESSING SITE
RT DAIRY

CONDENSING CHIMNEY
UF Smelt Mill Chimney
SN Chimney used to extract metal from the smoke
produced by a lead smelter.
CL INDUSTRIAL
BT NON FERROUS METAL SMELTING SITE
RT ARSENIC CALCINER
ARSENIC WORKS
CHIMNEY
LEAD WORKS
SMELTING HOUSE

CONDENSING FLUE
UF Arsenic Flue
Condenser Flue
Lead Condensing Flue
Lead Precipitation Flue
Lead Smelting Chimney
Smelt Mill Flue
SN Flue employed from the mid-19th century to extract
metal from the smoke produced by a lead smelter.
CL INDUSTRIAL
BT NON FERROUS METAL SMELTING SITE
RT ARSENIC CALCINER
ARSENIC WORKS
CHIMNEY
LEAD WORKS

CONDUIT
CL WATER SUPPLY AND DRAINAGE
RT AQUEDUCT
CONDUIT HEAD
CONDUIT HOUSE
GULLY
LEAT
WATER CHANNEL
WATER PUMPING STATION

CONDUIT HEAD
CL WATER SUPPLY AND DRAINAGE
RT CISTERN
CONDUIT
CONDUIT HOUSE

CONDUIT HOUSE
CL WATER SUPPLY AND DRAINAGE
RT CONDUIT HEAD
ENGINE HOUSE

PUMP HOUSE
PUMPING STATION
WATER TOWER
WATERWORKS
WELL HOUSE

Coney Garth
USE RABBIT WARREN

CONFECTIONERS SHOP
CL COMMERCIAL
BT SHOP

Confectionery Factory
USE CONFECTIONERY WORKS

CONFECTIONERY WORKS
UF Confectionery Factory
CL INDUSTRIAL
BT FOOD PRODUCTION SITE
RT CHOCOLATE FACTORY
SUGAR REFINERY

CONFERENCE CENTRE
CL CIVIL

CONFERENCE CENTRE
CL COMMERCIAL

CONGREGATIONAL CHAPEL
UF Congregational Church
CL RELIGIOUS, RITUAL AND FUNERARY
BT NONCONFORMIST CHAPEL

Congregational Church
USE CONGREGATIONAL CHAPEL

Congregational College
USE THEOLOGICAL COLLEGE

Congregational Hall
USE NONCONFORMIST MEETING HOUSE

Congregational School
USE CHURCH SCHOOL

Conical Kiln
USE CIRCULAR KILN

Conical Mound
USE MOUND

CONIFEROUS WOODLAND
CL GARDENS, PARKS AND URBAN SPACES
BT WOODLAND

Conservative Club
USE POLITICAL CLUB

CONSERVATORY
UF Anthaeum
Botanical House
Flower Conservatory
SN A glasshouse used to grow and display tender
decorative plants. May be either an extension to a
house or freestanding.
CL GARDENS, PARKS AND URBAN SPACES
BT GLASSHOUSE
RT BOTANIC GARDEN
COUNTRY HOUSE
LOGGIA

CONSISTORY COURT
CL CIVIL
BT LAW COURT

CONSTABLES OFFICE
UF Chief Constables Office
CL CIVIL

RT OFFICE
POLICE STATION

Constitutional Club
USE GENTLEMENS CLUB

CONSTRUCTION CAMP
SN Temporary settlement relating to the construction
of railways, viaducts, dams, etc.
CL DOMESTIC
BT SETTLEMENT

CONSTRUCTION WORKS
CL UNASSIGNED

CONTAINER BERTH
CL MARITIME
BT BERTH

CONTAINER TERMINAL
CL MARITIME
BT SEA TERMINAL

CONTINUOUS JETTY HOUSE
CL DOMESTIC
BT JETTIED HOUSE

Contour Fort
USE HILLFORT

Contour Reave
USE REAVE

CONTRACTED INHUMATION
SN Inhumation with knees brought up against the
chest.
CL RELIGIOUS, RITUAL AND FUNERARY
BT INHUMATION

Contravallation
USE SIEGEWORK

CONTROL ROOM
CL UNASSIGNED

CONTROL TOWER
UF Air Traffic Control Tower
Airport Control Tower
Watch Office
CL TRANSPORT
BT AIR TRANSPORT SITE
RT FOG DISPERSAL PLANT
TEST HOUSE

CONVALESCENT HOME
UF Rest Home
CL HEALTH AND WELFARE
RT NURSING HOME
SANATORIUM

CONVALESCENT HOME
UF Rest Home
CL DOMESTIC
BT RESIDENTIAL BUILDING
RT NURSING HOME
SANATORIUM

CONVALESCENT HOSPITAL
CL HEALTH AND WELFARE
BT HOSPITAL
RT SANATORIUM

Convent
USE RELIGIOUS HOUSE
DOUBLE HOUSE
MONASTERY
NUNNERY
SN Use NUNNERY, DOUBLE HOUSE, MONASTERY or
RELIGIOUS HOUSE. Use with order if known.

Convent Chapel
USE ABBEY
CHAPEL
PRIORY
SN Use CHAPEL and ABBEY or PRIORY.

CONVENT SCHOOL
CL EDUCATION
BT SCHOOL
RT ABBEY
NUNNERY

Conventual Chapel
USE ABBEY
CHAPEL
PRIORY
SN Use CHAPEL and ABBEY or PRIORY.

Conventual Church
USE ABBEY
CHURCH
PRIORY
SN Use CHURCH and ABBEY or PRIORY.

Convocation House
USE UNIVERSITY ADMINISTRATION OFFICE

COOKHOUSE
CL DOMESTIC
RT ARMY CAMP
BARRACKS
OFFICERS MESS
SERGEANTS MESS

Cooking Hearth
USE HEARTH

COOKING PIT
CL DOMESTIC
RT BURNT MOUND

Cooking Place
USE HEARTH
OVEN
SN Use HEARTH or OVEN as appropriate.

COOKSHOP
SN Medieval.
CL COMMERCIAL
BT SHOP

COOLING ROOM
CL INDUSTRIAL
BT BREWING AND MALTING SITE

COOLING TOWER
SN Wooden or ferro-concrete tower for cooling waste
hot water from a power station. The water cascades
from the top of the tower to a pond in the bottom.
CL INDUSTRIAL
BT ELECTRICITY PRODUCTION SITE
RT POWER STATION
STEAM TURBINE POWER STATION

COOPERAGE
UF Coopers Workshop
Dry Cooperage
Electric Cooperage
Steam Cooperage
Wet Cooperage
CL INDUSTRIAL
BT BREWING AND MALTING SITE
RT BREWHOUSE
CANNING FACTORY
DISTILLERY

COOPERAGE
UF Coopers Workshop

Dry Cooperage
Electric Cooperage
Steam Cooperage
Wet Cooperage
CL INDUSTRIAL
BT TIMBER PRODUCT SITE
RT BREWHOUSE
GUNPOWDER WORKS
SAW MILL
TIMBER SEASONING SHED

COOPERATIVE INSTITUTE
CL EDUCATION
BT INSTITUTE
RT COOPERATIVE STORE
MINERS READING ROOM
PEOPLES COLLEGE
WORKING MENS COLLEGE

COOPERATIVE INSTITUTE
CL INSTITUTIONAL
BT INSTITUTE
RT COOPERATIVE STORE

COOPERATIVE STORE
CL COMMERCIAL
BT SHOP
RT COOPERATIVE INSTITUTE

Coopers Workshop
USE COOPERAGE

Copper Mill
USE SMELT MILL

COPPER MINE
SN Where several minerals produced, use with other
products and MINE, eg. ARSENIC MINE.
CL INDUSTRIAL
BT NON FERROUS METAL EXTRACTION SITE
RT ANTIMONY MINE
COPPER WORKINGS
ORE HEARTH
TIN MINE

COPPER MINE
SN Where several minerals produced, use with other
products and MINE, eg. ARSENIC MINE.
CL INDUSTRIAL
BT MINE
RT COPPER WORKINGS

COPPER ROOM
CL INDUSTRIAL
BT BREWING AND MALTING SITE

Copper Smelting Works
USE SMELT MILL

COPPER WORKING SITE
SN For copper or copper based alloys of unknown
composition.
CL INDUSTRIAL
BT NON FERROUS METAL SMELTING SITE
RT COPPER WORKS

COPPER WORKING SITE
SN For copper or copper based alloys of unknown
composition.
CL INDUSTRIAL
BT NON FERROUS METAL PRODUCT SITE
RT COPPER WORKS

COPPER WORKINGS
UF Open Cast Copper Workings
CL INDUSTRIAL
BT EXTRACTIVE PIT
RT COPPER MINE

COPPER WORKINGS

UF   Open Cast Copper Workings
CL   INDUSTRIAL
BT   NON FERROUS METAL EXTRACTION SITE
RT   COPPER MINE

COPPER WORKS
CL   INDUSTRIAL
BT   NON FERROUS METAL SMELTING SITE
RT   COPPER WORKING SITE

COPPER WORKS
CL   INDUSTRIAL
BT   NON FERROUS METAL PRODUCT SITE
RT   COPPER WORKING SITE

COPPERAS WORKS
SN   Producing copperas: green iron sulphate crushed in
      hot water and used as a dye.
CL   INDUSTRIAL
BT   DYE AND PIGMENT SITE
RT   ALUM QUARRY
      ALUM WORKS
      ARTIFICAL DYE WORKS
      DYE WORKS

Coppice
USE   COPSE

COPPICE BARN
SN   Open sided barn for the storage of wood produced
      by the periodic cutting of small trees.
CL   INDUSTRIAL
BT   WOOD PRODUCT SITE
RT   BARN

COPPICE BARN
SN   Open sided barn for the storage of wood produced
      by the periodic cutting of small trees.
CL   AGRICULTURE AND SUBSISTENCE
BT   BARN

COPSE
UF   Coppice
CL   GARDENS, PARKS AND URBAN SPACES
BT   WOODLAND

COPSE
UF   Coppice
CL   AGRICULTURE AND SUBSISTENCE
BT   LAND USE SITE
RT   WOOD

CORACLE
CL   MARITIME
BT   UNASSIGNED CRAFT

Corbelled Tomb
USE   CHAMBERED TOMB

CORD RIG
CL   AGRICULTURE AND SUBSISTENCE
BT   FIELD
RT   RIDGE AND FURROW

Cordage House
USE   RIGGING HOUSE

Corduroy Road
USE   TRACKWAY

Corn Drier
USE   CORN DRYING OVEN

CORN DRYING KILN
CL   INDUSTRIAL
BT   DRYING KILN
RT   CORN DRYING OVEN

CORN DRYING KILN

CL   INDUSTRIAL
BT   FOOD PROCESSING SITE
RT   CORN DRYING OVEN
      CORN MILL
      WATERMILL

CORN DRYING OVEN
UF   Corn Drier
      Corn Oven
CL   INDUSTRIAL
BT   FOOD PROCESSING SITE
RT   CORN DRYING KILN
      CORN MILL
      GRANARY
      WATERMILL

CORN EXCHANGE
CL   COMMERCIAL
BT   EXCHANGE

CORN MILL
UF   Grist Mill
SN   Use with power type where known.
CL   INDUSTRIAL
BT   MILL
RT   TIDEMILL
      WATERMILL
      WINDMILL

CORN MILL
UF   Grist Mill
SN   Use with power type where known.
CL   INDUSTRIAL
BT   FOOD PROCESSING SITE
RT   CORN DRYING KILN
      CORN DRYING OVEN
      GRANARY
      MILL HOUSE
      TIDEMILL
      WATERMILL
      WINDMILL

Corn Millers House
USE   MILL HOUSE

Corn Oven
USE   CORN DRYING OVEN

Corn Store
USE   GRAIN WAREHOUSE

Corn Warehouse
USE   GRAIN WAREHOUSE

Corner Tower
USE   ANGLE TOWER

CORNING HOUSE
CL   INDUSTRIAL
BT   EXPLOSIVES SITE

CORONATION STONE
CL   COMMEMORATIVE
BT   COMMEMORATIVE STONE

CORONERS COURT
CL   CIVIL
BT   LAW COURT

Corporation Chapel
USE   GUILD CHAPEL

Corporation Office
USE   LOCAL GOVERNMENT OFFICE

Corridor Villa
USE   VILLA (ROMAN)

Cortile

USE COURTYARD

Cortina
USE CURTAIN WALL

CORVETTE
    CL   MARITIME
    BT   MINOR WARSHIP

Cote
    USE FARM LABOURERS COTTAGE

Cottage
    USE HOUSE

COTTAGE GARDEN
    CL   GARDENS, PARKS AND URBAN SPACES
    BT   GARDEN

COTTAGE HOME
    UF   Alcoholic Ladies Home
          Cottage Home For Alcoholic Ladies
          Cottage Home Hospital
          Poor Law Guardians Home
    SN   Established under the Poor Law to provide more
          suitable accommodation for classes of the
          "deserving" poor, eg. children, aged couples.
    CL   HEALTH AND WELFARE
    RT   ALMSHOUSE
          CHILDRENS HOME
          ORPHANAGE

COTTAGE HOME
    UF   Alcoholic Ladies Home
          Cottage Home For Alcoholic Ladies
          Cottage Home Hospital
          Poor Law Guardians Home
    SN   Established under the Poor Law to provide more
          suitable accommodation for classes of the
          "deserving" poor, eg. children, aged couples.
    CL   DOMESTIC
    BT   RESIDENTIAL BUILDING
    RT   ALMSHOUSE
          CHILDRENS HOME
          ORPHANAGE

Cottage Home For Alcoholic Ladies
    USE COTTAGE HOME

Cottage Home Hospital
    USE COTTAGE HOME
          HOSPITAL
    SN   Use both terms.

COTTAGE HOSPITAL
    SN   Can include small pre-Cranleigh institutions, eg:
          dispensaries with in-patients.
    CL   HEALTH AND WELFARE
    BT   HOSPITAL

COTTAGE ORNEE
    SN   A rustic building of picturesque design.
    CL   GARDENS, PARKS AND URBAN SPACES
    BT   GARDEN BUILDING
    RT   FERME ORNEE
          HERMITAGE

COTTAGE ORNEE
    SN   A rustic building of picturesque design.
    CL   DOMESTIC
    RT   FERME ORNEE
          HERMITAGE

COTTON EXCHANGE
    CL   COMMERCIAL
    BT   EXCHANGE

COTTON MANUFACTURING SITE
    CL   INDUSTRIAL

    BT   TEXTILE SITE < BY PROCESS/PRODUCT >
    NT   COTTON MILL

COTTON MILL
    CL   INDUSTRIAL
    BT   TEXTILE MILL

COTTON MILL
    CL   INDUSTRIAL
    BT   COTTON MANUFACTURING SITE
    NT   CALICO MILL
          CANVAS WORKS

COUNCIL FLAT
    CL   DOMESTIC
    BT   DWELLING
    RT   COUNCIL HOUSE

COUNCIL FLATS
    CL   DOMESTIC
    BT   FLATS
    RT   COUNCIL HOUSE

COUNCIL HOUSE
    CL   DOMESTIC
    BT   HOUSE < BY FUNCTION >
    RT   COUNCIL FLAT
          COUNCIL FLATS

Council Office
    USE LOCAL GOVERNMENT OFFICE

COUNTESS OF HUNTINGDONS CHAPEL
    CL   RELIGIOUS, RITUAL AND FUNERARY
    BT   METHODIST CHAPEL

COUNTING HOUSE
    UF   Telling House
    CL   COMMERCIAL
    RT   OFFICE
          PAY OFFICE
          TIMEKEEPERS OFFICE

Country Hall
    USE COUNTRY HOUSE

COUNTRY HOUSE
    UF   Country Hall
          Country Mansion
          Mansion
    CL   DOMESTIC
    BT   HOUSE < BY FUNCTION >
    RT   BAKEHOUSE
          BATH HOUSE
          BREWHOUSE
          CARRIAGE HOUSE
          CONSERVATORY
          DEER PARK
          DOMESTIC CHAPEL
          DOVECOTE
          ESTATE COTTAGE
          ESTATE LAUNDRY
          GARDEN BUILDING
          GARDEN HOUSE
          GARDEN RETREAT
          GREAT HOUSE
          GUEST COTTAGE
          HUNTING LODGE
          KITCHEN
          KITCHEN GARDEN
          LAITERIE
          MANOR HOUSE
          PALACE
          REFRESHMENT PAVILION
          RIDING SCHOOL
          ROYAL PALACE
          SADDLERY
          STABLE
          TACK ROOM

TEA HOUSE
TOWN HOUSE
VILLA (NON ROMAN)

Country Mansion
USE COUNTRY HOUSE

COUNTY COURT
CL CIVIL
BT LAW COURT

County Education Office
USE LOCAL GOVERNMENT OFFICE

County Gaol
USE PRISON

COUNTY HALL
CL CIVIL
BT LOCAL GOVERNMENT OFFICE
RT CIVIC CENTRE
SHIRE HALL
TOWN HALL

County Library
USE PUBLIC LIBRARY

County Stone
USE BOUNDARY STONE

COURERY
SN Subsidiary settlement of lay brothers attached to
some Carthusian monasteries.
CL RELIGIOUS, RITUAL AND FUNERARY
BT LAY BRETHREN SETTLEMENT
RT CARTHUSIAN CELL
CARTHUSIAN GRANGE
CARTHUSIAN MONASTERY
CHAPEL

Court Hall
USE COURT HOUSE

COURT HOUSE
UF Court Hall
Courthouse
Speech House
Tribunal
CL CIVIL
BT LAW COURT
RT JUDGES LODGINGS
LEET HALL
MOOT HALL

Court Of Speech
USE MOOT HALL

COURT ROOM
CL CIVIL
BT LAW COURT

Courthouse
USE COURT HOUSE

Courting
USE FARMYARD

COURTYARD
UF Cortile
CL GARDENS, PARKS AND URBAN SPACES
RT PATIO
YARD

COURTYARD HOUSE
UF Yard House
CL DOMESTIC
BT HOUSE <BY FORM>

Courtyard Villa

USE VILLA (ROMAN)

COVE
SN Prehistoric structure consisting of three or more
standing stones in close proximity to each other,
forming an unroofed approximately rectangular
structure open in one direction.
CL RELIGIOUS, RITUAL AND FUNERARY
RT STANDING STONE
STONE CIRCLE
STONE SETTING

Covered Market
USE MARKET HALL

COW HOUSE
UF Bovile
Byre
Cattle Shed
Chepyn
Cow Shed
Cowhouse
Cowshed
Hammel
Mistal
Shippon
CL AGRICULTURE AND SUBSISTENCE
BT ANIMAL SHED
RT BANK BARN
CATTLE SHELTER
COMBINATION BARN
FIELD BARN
LAITHE
LINHAY
VACCARY

Cow Shed
USE COW HOUSE

Cowhouse
USE COW HOUSE

Cowshed
USE COW HOUSE

CRAFT
SN A sea or river going vessel of uncertain size and
function.
CL MARITIME
BT UNASSIGNED CRAFT
NT BOAT
SHIP

CRAFT CENTRE
UF Industrial Craft Centre
CL INDUSTRIAL
BT CRAFT INDUSTRY SITE
RT FACTORY UNIT
INDUSTRIAL ESTATE

CRAFT CENTRE
UF Industrial Craft Centre
CL EDUCATION

CRAFT INDUSTRY SITE
SN Site of small scale industrial production often
involving hand work and craft skills.
CL INDUSTRIAL
NT ARCHITECTURAL ORNAMENT WORKSHOP
BASKET MAKERS WORKSHOP
BINDERY
BLACKSMITHS WORKSHOP
BRUSHMAKERS WORKSHOP
BUILDERS YARD
CARPENTERS WORKSHOP
CLOTH CUTTERS WORKSHOP
CLOTHIERS HOUSE
CLOTHIERS WORKSHOP
CRAFT CENTRE

CRATEMAKERS SHOP
CUTLERY WORKSHOP
FRAMEWORK KNITTERS COTTAGE
GOLDSMITHS WORKSHOP
HATTERS WORKSHOP
HOSIERS COTTAGE
HOSIERY WORKSHOP
JEWELLERY WORKS
JEWELLERY WORKSHOP
JOINERS SHOP
LACEMAKERS COTTAGE
LEATHER WORKERS SHOP
LOCKSMITHS WORKSHOP
NAILERS ROW
POTTERS WORKSHOP
SILVERSMITHS WORKSHOP
STAINED GLASS WORKSHOP
STATUE FOUNDRY
TAPESTRY WEAVING WORKSHOP
TILEMAKING WORKSHOP
TOPSHOP
WATCHMAKERS WORKSHOP
WEAVERS COTTAGE
WEAVERS WORKSHOP

CRANE
- CL   TRANSPORT
- BT   LIFTING AND WINDING STRUCTURE
- NT   CRANE <BY FORM>
  CRANE <BY FUNCTION>
- RT   DERRICK
  ENGINE
  HARBOUR
  HYDRAULIC CRANE
  HYDRAULIC ENGINE HOUSE
  HYDRAULIC PILLAR CRANE
  SHIPYARD

CRANE <BY FORM>
- CL   TRANSPORT
- BT   CRANE
- NT   FLOATING CRANE
  GANTRY CRANE
  HAMMERHEAD CRANE
  JIB CRANE
  LUFFING CRANE
  MOVING CRANE
  ROOF CRANE
  TRAVELLING CRANE
  TREADWHEEL CRANE
  WALL CRANE

CRANE <BY FUNCTION>
- CL   TRANSPORT
- BT   CRANE
- NT   COALING CRANE
  HAND CRANE
  QUAY CRANE
  STEAM CRANE

CRANE HOUSE
- CL   TRANSPORT

CRANEWHEEL
- CL   INDUSTRIAL
- BT   ANIMAL POWER SITE

CRANEWHEEL
- CL   TRANSPORT
- BT   LIFTING AND WINDING STRUCTURE
- RT   TREADWHEEL
  TREADWHEEL CRANE

CRANNOG
- UF   Lake Dwelling
- CL   DOMESTIC
- BT   DWELLING
- RT   HOUSE
  LAKE VILLAGE

PILE DWELLING

CRATEMAKERS SHOP
- SN   Workshop for producing crates, particularly for the packing of pottery.
- CL   INDUSTRIAL
- BT   CRAFT INDUSTRY SITE
- RT   JOINERS SHOP

CRATEMAKERS SHOP
- SN   Workshop for producing crates, particularly for the packing of pottery.
- CL   INDUSTRIAL
- BT   POTTERY MANUFACTURING SITE
- RT   MOULDMAKERS SHOP
  PACKING HOUSE
  POTTERY WORKS

CRAZING MILL
- SN   Mill for fine grinding of tin ore between millstones.
- CL   INDUSTRIAL
- BT   NON FERROUS METAL PROCESSING SITE
- RT   BUDDLE HOUSE
  CRUSHING MILL
  STAMPING MILL
  TIN MILL
  TIN MINE
  TIN WORKS
  WASHING FLOOR

CRAZING MILL
- SN   Mill for fine grinding of tin ore between millstones.
- CL   INDUSTRIAL
- BT   MILL

Creamery
  USE DAIRY

CRECHE
- CL   HEALTH AND WELFARE
- RT   NURSERY
  NURSERY SCHOOL

CREMATION
- CL   RELIGIOUS, RITUAL AND FUNERARY
- BT   BURIAL
- NT   CINERARY URN
- RT   CHARNEL HOUSE
  CHARNEL PIT
  CREMATION CEMETERY
  CREMATION PIT
  CREMATORIUM
  OSSUARY

CREMATION CEMETERY
- UF   Unenclosed Cremation Cemetery
- CL   RELIGIOUS, RITUAL AND FUNERARY
- BT   CEMETERY
- NT   ENCLOSED CREMATION CEMETERY
  URNFIELD
- RT   CINERARY URN
  COLUMBARIUM
  CREMATION
  CREMATORIUM
  OSSUARY

CREMATION PIT
- CL   RELIGIOUS, RITUAL AND FUNERARY
- BT   BURIAL PIT
- RT   CREMATION

CREMATORIUM
- UF   Crematorium Chapel
- CL   RELIGIOUS, RITUAL AND FUNERARY
- BT   FUNERARY SITE
- RT   COLUMBARIUM
  CREMATION

CREMATION CEMETERY
MORTUARY CHAPEL

Crematorium Chapel
USE CHAPEL
      CREMATORIUM
SN   Use both terms.

CREPE MILL
SN   Fine cloth particularly silk or mixture of silk
      and cotton.
CL   INDUSTRIAL
BT   TEXTILE MILL

CREPE MILL
SN   Fine cloth particularly silk or mixture of silk
      and cotton.
CL   INDUSTRIAL
BT   TEXTILE SITE <BY PROCESS/PRODUCT>

CRESCENT
CL   GARDENS, PARKS AND URBAN SPACES
RT   CIRCUS (URBAN)
      SQUARE
      TERRACE

Crest
USE COAT OF ARMS

CREW YARD
SN   Open yard for keeping cattle in during winter.
      Used from the mid-14th century in drier, Eastern,
      arable counties.
CL   AGRICULTURE AND SUBSISTENCE
RT   FARMYARD

CRICKET GROUND
CL   RECREATIONAL
BT   SPORTS GROUND
RT   CRICKET PAVILION
      GRANDSTAND
      SPORTS PAVILION
      STADIUM

CRICKET PAVILION
CL   RECREATIONAL
BT   SPORTS BUILDING
RT   CRICKET GROUND

Cricket Stand
USE GRANDSTAND

Criminal Courts
USE LAW COURT

Crinkle Crankle Wall
USE SERPENTINE WALL

Crippled Childrens Home
USE HANDICAPPED CHILDRENS HOME

CROFT
CL   AGRICULTURE AND SUBSISTENCE
BT   LAND USE SITE
RT   FARM
      FARMSTEAD
      MESSUAGE
      SMALLHOLDING
      TOFT

Cromlech
USE CHAMBERED TOMB

Crop Mark
USE SITE
SN   Use a more specific site type where known, eg.
      ENCLOSURE.

Croquet House

USE CROQUET SHED

CROQUET LAWN
CL   GARDENS, PARKS AND URBAN SPACES
BT   LAWN
RT   BOWLING GREEN
      CROQUET SHED

CROQUET LAWN
CL   RECREATIONAL
BT   SPORTS SITE
RT   BOWLING GREEN
      CROQUET SHED

CROQUET SHED
UF   Croquet House
CL   RECREATIONAL
BT   SPORTS BUILDING
RT   BOWLING GREEN PAVILION
      CROQUET LAWN
      PAVILION
      SHED

CROSS
UF   Churchyard Cross
      Cross Base
      Cross Shaft
      Cross Socket
      Lantern Cross
      Sanctuary Cross
      Sepulchral Cross
      Standing Cross
      Wheel Cross
SN   Free standing.
CL   RELIGIOUS, RITUAL AND FUNERARY
NT   BOUNDARY CROSS
      ELEANOR CROSS
      HIGH CROSS
      MARKET CROSS
      PREACHING CROSS
      TOWN CROSS
      VILLAGE CROSS
      WAYSIDE CROSS
RT   CROSS INCISED STONE
      CROSS SLAB
      INSCRIBED STONE
      OGHAM STONE
      RUNE STONE

Cross Base
USE CROSS

CROSS DYKE
UF   Cross Ridge Dyke
CL   DEFENCE
BT   DYKE (DEFENCE)
RT   EARTHWORK

CROSS INCISED STONE
UF   Cross Stone
CL   RELIGIOUS, RITUAL AND FUNERARY
RT   CARVED STONE
      CROSS
      CROSS SLAB
      INSCRIBED STONE

CROSS PASSAGE HOUSE
CL   DOMESTIC
BT   HALL HOUSE

Cross Ridge Dyke
USE CROSS DYKE

Cross Shaft
USE CROSS

CROSS SLAB
CL   RELIGIOUS, RITUAL AND FUNERARY
BT   GRAVE SLAB

RT CROSS
   CROSS INCISED STONE

Cross Socket
   USE CROSS

Cross Stone
   USE CROSS INCISED STONE

CROSS WING HOUSE
CL DOMESTIC
BT HALL HOUSE
NT DOUBLE ENDED HALL HOUSE
   SINGLE ENDED HALL HOUSE

CROSSING KEEPERS COTTAGE
UF Level Crossing Cottage
   Railway Crossing Keepers Cottage
CL DOMESTIC
BT TRANSPORT WORKERS HOUSE
RT LEVEL CROSSING
   LEVEL CROSSING GATE
   RAILWAY STATION
   RAILWAY WORKERS COTTAGE
   STATION MASTERS HOUSE

CROUCHED INHUMATION
SN Inhumation with leg joints bent through angle
   greater than ninety degrees.
CL RELIGIOUS, RITUAL AND FUNERARY
BT INHUMATION

Crow
   USE AGRICULTURAL BUILDING
SN Small agricultural structure built into field
   walls in Cornwall.

CROWN COURT
CL CIVIL
BT LAW COURT

Crucible
   USE CRUCIBLE FURNACE

CRUCIBLE FURNACE
UF Crucible
SN Furnace composed of two fire brick boxes: the fire
   was in the lower box and the upper box held the
   crucibles.
CL INDUSTRIAL
BT METAL PRODUCTION FURNACE
RT FERROUS METAL SMELTING SITE

CRUCIBLE STEEL WORKS
SN Production of high quality steel by reheating
   cementation steel in a refractory crucible.
CL INDUSTRIAL
BT STEEL WORKS
RT CEMENTATION STEEL WORKS

Cruciferi
   USE FRIARY OF CRUTCHED FRIARS

CRUCK HOUSE
CL DOMESTIC
BT TIMBER FRAMED HOUSE
NT BASE CRUCK HOUSE

CRUISE BOAT
CL MARITIME
BT LEISURE CRAFT

CRUISE SHIP
CL MARITIME
BT LEISURE CRAFT

CRUISE SHIP
CL MARITIME
BT PASSENGER VESSEL

CRUISER
CL MARITIME
BT MINOR WARSHIP
NT ANTI AIRCRAFT CRUISER
   AUXILIARY CRUISER
   BELTED CRUISER
   LIGHT CRUISER
   MASTED CRUISER
   THIRD CLASS CRUISER

CRUSHING CIRCLE
SN Horse powered ore crusher, consisting of a stone
   wheel running over a circular iron or stone bed.
CL INDUSTRIAL
BT NON FERROUS METAL PROCESSING SITE
RT CRUSHING FLOOR
   CRUSHING MILL
   GRINDSTONE

CRUSHING FLOOR
SN Floor for mounting mechanically powered ore
   crushers.
CL INDUSTRIAL
BT NON FERROUS METAL PROCESSING SITE
RT CRUSHING CIRCLE
   CRUSHING MILL
   MINE
   STAMPING MILL
   STAMPS

CRUSHING MILL
UF Lead Crushing Mill
   Ore Crushing Mill
SN A building containing mechanically powered ore
   crushers or rollers.
CL INDUSTRIAL
BT NON FERROUS METAL PROCESSING SITE
RT BUDDLE HOUSE
   CRAZING MILL
   CRUSHING CIRCLE
   CRUSHING FLOOR
   STAMPING MILL

CRUSHING MILL
UF Lead Crushing Mill
   Ore Crushing Mill
SN A building containing mechanically powered ore
   crushers or rollers.
CL INDUSTRIAL
BT MILL
RT BUDDLE
   BUDDLE HOUSE

Crutched Friars House
   USE FRIARY OF CRUTCHED FRIARS

CRYPT
CL RELIGIOUS, RITUAL AND FUNERARY
BT FUNERARY SITE
RT CATHEDRAL
   CELLAR
   CHURCH

CUBICLE BLOCK
SN Block for the treatment of separate diseases.
CL HEALTH AND WELFARE
BT HOSPITAL BLOCK

Cucking Stool
   USE DUCKING STOOL

CUL DE SAC
CL GARDENS, PARKS AND URBAN SPACES
RT ROAD

CULTIVATION MARKS
CL AGRICULTURE AND SUBSISTENCE
BT LAND USE SITE

NT   PLOUGH MARKS
RT   FIELD
       FIELD SYSTEM

CULTIVATION TERRACE
CL   AGRICULTURE AND SUBSISTENCE
BT   LAND USE SITE
RT   FIELD SYSTEM
       STRIP LYNCHET
       TERRACED GROUND

Culverhouse
   USE DOVECOTE

CULVERT
CL   WATER SUPPLY AND DRAINAGE
BT   DRAIN
RT   DRAINAGE DITCH
       SEWER
       SLUICE

CULVERT
CL   MARITIME
BT   WATER REGULATION INSTALLATION
NT   DOCK CULVERT

CUP AND RING MARKED STONE
SN   Includes earth-fast rocks.
CL   RELIGIOUS, RITUAL AND FUNERARY
RT   CARVED STONE
       CUP MARKED STONE
       ROCK CARVING

CUP MARKED STONE
CL   RELIGIOUS, RITUAL AND FUNERARY
RT   CUP AND RING MARKED STONE
       ROCK CARVING

CUPELLATION FURNACE
SN   Small cupola type furnace for the extraction of
       precious metals.
CL   INDUSTRIAL
BT   METAL PRODUCTION FURNACE
RT   FERROUS METAL SMELTING SITE
       GOLDSMITHS WORKSHOP
       JEWELLERY WORKSHOP
       NON FERROUS METAL SMELTING SITE
       SILVERSMITHS WORKSHOP

CUPOLA FURNACE (REVERBERATORY)
SN   A reverberatory furnace used for smelting lead,
       employed from the 18th century onwards.
CL   INDUSTRIAL
BT   REVERBERATORY FURNACE
RT   NON FERROUS METAL SMELTING SITE
       ORE HEARTH

CUPOLA FURNACE (REVERBERATORY)
SN   A reverberatory furnace used for smelting lead,
       employed from the 18th century onwards.
CL   INDUSTRIAL
BT   NON FERROUS METAL SMELTING SITE
RT   NON FERROUS METAL SMELTING SITE

CUPOLA FURNACE (SHAFT)
SN   A shaft furnace for remelting pig or scrap iron in
       a foundry.
CL   INDUSTRIAL
BT   FERROUS METAL SMELTING SITE
RT   FERROUS METAL SMELTING SITE
       IRON WORKS
       ROLLING MILL

CUPOLA FURNACE (SHAFT)
SN   A shaft furnace for remelting pig or scrap iron in
       a foundry.
CL   INDUSTRIAL
BT   SHAFT FURNACE
RT   FERROUS METAL SMELTING SITE

CURATORS HOUSE
CL   DOMESTIC
BT   HOUSE <BY FUNCTION>
RT   MUSEUM

CURFEW BELL TOWER
CL   RELIGIOUS, RITUAL AND FUNERARY
BT   BELL TOWER
RT   ABBEY
       NUNNERY
       PRIORY

CURING HOUSE
CL   INDUSTRIAL
BT   FOOD PRESERVING SITE
RT   SMOKE HOUSE

CURING HOUSE
CL   INDUSTRIAL
BT   FOOD PROCESSING SITE
RT   FISH PROCESSING FACTORY
       SMOKE HOUSE

CURRIERY
SN   Place where tanned leather is dressed and
       coloured.
CL   INDUSTRIAL
BT   LEATHER INDUSTRY SITE
RT   GLOVE FACTORY
       SHOE FACTORY
       TALLOW FACTORY

CURSUS
SN   Long narrow earthwork enclosures whose proximity
       to henge monuments suggests that their function
       was primarily religious.
CL   RELIGIOUS, RITUAL AND FUNERARY
RT   EMBANKED AVENUE

Curtain
   USE CURTAIN WALL

Curtain Frontier Works
   USE FRONTIER DEFENCE

Curtain Frontiers
   USE FRONTIER DEFENCE

CURTAIN WALL
UF   Castle Wall
       Cortina
       Curtain
       Screen Wall
SN   A wall between two towers or pavilions.
CL   DEFENCE
RT   BASTION
       CASTLE
       CHEMISE
       WALL

CURVILINEAR ENCLOSURE
UF   Annular Enclosure
       Penannular Enclosure
CL   UNASSIGNED
BT   ENCLOSURE
NT   CIRCULAR ENCLOSURE
       D SHAPED ENCLOSURE
       OVAL ENCLOSURE
       SPECTACLE ENCLOSURE
       SUB CIRCULAR ENCLOSURE
RT   RING DITCH

CUSTOM HOUSE
CL   CIVIL
RT   BONDED WAREHOUSE
       COASTGUARD STATION
       CUSTOMS LOOKOUT
       CUSTOMS POST

DOCKMASTERS HOUSE
PILOT OFFICE
TRINITY HOUSE

CUSTOM HOUSE
CL   MARITIME
BT   MARITIME OFFICE
RT   BONDED WAREHOUSE
      COASTGUARD STATION
      CUSTOMS LOOKOUT
      DOCKMASTERS HOUSE
      PILOT OFFICE
      TRINITY HOUSE

Customs And Excise Office
   USE GOVERNMENT OFFICE

CUSTOMS LOOKOUT
CL   CIVIL
RT   CUSTOM HOUSE
      CUSTOMS POST
      WATCH TOWER

CUSTOMS LOOKOUT
CL   MARITIME
BT   DOCK AND HARBOUR INSTALLATION
RT   CUSTOM HOUSE
      CUSTOMS POST
      WATCH TOWER

CUSTOMS POST
CL   MARITIME
BT   DOCK AND HARBOUR INSTALLATION
RT   CUSTOM HOUSE
      CUSTOMS LOOKOUT
      QUAY

CUTLERY WORKS
UF   Fork Factory
      Knife Factory
      Knife Works
      Spoon Factory
CL   INDUSTRIAL
BT   FERROUS METAL PRODUCT SITE
RT   BRITANNIA METAL WORKS
      CUTLERY WORKSHOP
      EDGE TOOL WORKS
      GRINDSTONE
      PLATING WORKS
      STEEL WORKS

CUTLERY WORKSHOP
CL   INDUSTRIAL
BT   CRAFT INDUSTRY SITE
RT   BRITANNIA METAL WORKS
      CUTLERY WORKS
      EDGE TOOL WORKS
      GRINDSTONE
      PLATING WORKS
      STEEL WORKS

CUTTER DREDGER
CL   MARITIME
BT   DREDGER

D SHAPED BARROW
SN   Not a round barrow ploughed out at one end, but a
      specific type, the flat edge being additionally
      defined by stone slabs.
CL   RELIGIOUS, RITUAL AND FUNERARY
BT   BARROW

D SHAPED ENCLOSURE
CL   UNASSIGNED
BT   CURVILINEAR ENCLOSURE
RT   CLOTHES LINE ENCLOSURE

Dahlia Garden
   USE FLOWER GARDEN

DAIRY
UF   Creamery
      Dish House
      Milk House
      Milk Processing Plant
CL   AGRICULTURE AND SUBSISTENCE
BT   FOOD AND DRINK PROCESSING SITE
RT   BOTTLING PLANT
      CHEESE FACTORY
      CONDENSERY
      LAITERIE
      MILK DEPOT
      MILKING SHED

DAM
CL   INDUSTRIAL
BT   WATER POWER PRODUCTION SITE
NT   MILL DAM
RT   HYDROELECTRIC POWER STATION
      POND BAY
      WEIR

DAM
CL   WATER SUPPLY AND DRAINAGE
NT   MILL DAM
RT   HAMMER POND
      RESERVOIR
      WEIR

DAME SCHOOL
CL   EDUCATION
BT   ELEMENTARY SCHOOL

DANCE HALL
CL   RECREATIONAL
BT   MUSIC AND DANCE VENUE
RT   DISCOTHEQUE
      JAZZ CLUB

DANCE STUDIO
UF   Studio
CL   RECREATIONAL
BT   MUSIC AND DANCE VENUE
RT   BALLET SCHOOL

Danish Camp
   USE EARTHWORK

DATE STONE
CL   COMMEMORATIVE
BT   COMMEMORATIVE STONE
RT   PLAQUE

DAY CENTRE
CL   HEALTH AND WELFARE

DAY HOSPITAL
SN   For geriatrics.
CL   HEALTH AND WELFARE
BT   HOSPITAL

DAYROOM BLOCK
CL   HEALTH AND WELFARE
BT   HOSPITAL BLOCK

DEAF AND DUMB INSTITUTE
CL   EDUCATION
BT   INSTITUTE

DEAF AND DUMB INSTITUTE
CL   HEALTH AND WELFARE

DEAF AND DUMB INSTITUTE
CL   INSTITUTIONAL
BT   INSTITUTE

Dean Hole
   USE PRIEST HOLE

SN   Not DENE HOLE.

DEANERY
UF   Deans House
      Deans Lodgings
CL   DOMESTIC
BT   CLERICAL DWELLING
RT   SUBDEANERY

Deans House
USE DEANERY

Deans Lodgings
USE DEANERY

DEBTORS COURT
UF   Insolvent Debtors Court
CL   CIVIL
BT   LAW COURT

DEBTORS PRISON
CL   CIVIL
BT   PRISON

DECIDUOUS WOODLAND
CL   GARDENS, PARKS AND URBAN SPACES
BT   WOODLAND

DECORATING SHOP
CL   INDUSTRIAL
BT   POTTERY MANUFACTURING SITE

Decoy
USE DECOY POND

DECOY POND
UF   Decoy
      Duck Decoy Pond
SN   Including water feeder channels.
CL   WATER SUPPLY AND DRAINAGE
BT   POND

DECOY POND
UF   Decoy
      Duck Decoy Pond
SN   Including water feeder channels.
CL   AGRICULTURE AND SUBSISTENCE
BT   HUNTING SITE

DECOY POND
UF   Decoy
      Duck Decoy Pond
SN   Including water feeder channels.
CL   RECREATIONAL
BT   HUNTING SITE

DECOY VESSEL
CL   MARITIME
BT   WARSHIP

DEDICATION STONE
CL   COMMEMORATIVE
BT   COMMEMORATIVE STONE

DEER COTE
CL   AGRICULTURE AND SUBSISTENCE
BT   HUNTING SITE

DEER COTE
CL   RECREATIONAL
BT   HUNTING SITE

DEER HOUSE
CL   AGRICULTURE AND SUBSISTENCE
BT   HUNTING SITE
RT   DEER PARK

DEER HOUSE
CL   RECREATIONAL

BT   HUNTING SITE

DEER LEAP
SN   Bank to let deer cross fences or roads.
CL   AGRICULTURE AND SUBSISTENCE
BT   HUNTING SITE

DEER LEAP
SN   Bank to let deer cross fences or roads.
CL   RECREATIONAL
BT   HUNTING SITE

DEER PARK
CL   GARDENS, PARKS AND URBAN SPACES
BT   PARK
RT   COUNTRY HOUSE
      DEER HOUSE
      DEER POUND
      DEER SHELTER
      HUNTING FOREST
      HUNTING LODGE
      PARK PALE

DEER PARK
CL   RECREATIONAL
BT   HUNTING SITE
RT   COUNTRY HOUSE
      DEER HOUSE
      DEER POUND
      DEER SHELTER
      HUNTING FOREST
      HUNTING LODGE
      PARK PALE

DEER PARK
CL   AGRICULTURE AND SUBSISTENCE
BT   HUNTING SITE
RT   COUNTRY HOUSE
      DEER POUND
      DEER SHELTER
      HUNTING FOREST
      HUNTING LODGE
      PARK PALE

DEER POUND
UF   Buckstall
      Deerhay
CL   AGRICULTURE AND SUBSISTENCE
BT   HUNTING SITE
RT   DEER PARK

DEER POUND
UF   Buckstall
      Deerhay
CL   AGRICULTURE AND SUBSISTENCE
BT   POUND
RT   DEER PARK

DEER POUND
UF   Buckstall
      Deerhay
CL   RECREATIONAL
BT   HUNTING SITE

DEER SHELTER
SN   For hunters.
CL   RECREATIONAL
BT   HUNTING SITE
RT   DEER PARK
      HUNTING LODGE

DEER SHELTER
SN   For hunters.
CL   AGRICULTURE AND SUBSISTENCE
BT   HUNTING SITE
RT   DEER PARK
      HUNTING LODGE

Deerhay

USE DEER POUND

DEFENCE
SN   This is the top term for the class. See DEFENCE
     Class List for narrow terms.

DELICATESSEN
CL   COMMERCIAL
BT   SHOP

Demi Bastion
USE BASTION

DENE HOLE
SN   The name of a class of excavations, found in chalk
     formations in England, consisting of a shaft sunk
     to the chalk, and there widening out into one or
     more chambers.
CL   INDUSTRIAL
BT   EXTRACTIVE PIT
RT   CHALK PIT
     CLAY PIT

DENTAL DEPARTMENT
CL   HEALTH AND WELFARE
BT   HOSPITAL DEPARTMENT

DENTAL HOSPITAL
CL   HEALTH AND WELFARE
BT   SPECIALIST HOSPITAL

DENTAL SCHOOL
CL   EDUCATION
BT   TRAINING SCHOOL

Dental Surgery
USE SURGERY

DEPARTMENT STORE
CL   COMMERCIAL
BT   SHOP

Depository
USE WAREHOUSE

DEPOT SHIP
CL   MARITIME
BT   HARBOUR SERVICES VESSEL

Depression
USE HOLLOW

DERRICK
CL   TRANSPORT
BT   LIFTING AND WINDING STRUCTURE
RT   CRANE
     SHEER LEGS

Deserted Medieval Village
USE DESERTED VILLAGE

DESERTED VILLAGE
UF   Deserted Medieval Village
SN   Use in conjuction with Medieval in a period field
     if possible.
CL   DOMESTIC
BT   VILLAGE

Despence
USE LARDER

DESTROYER
CL   MARITIME
BT   MINOR WARSHIP

Detached Cemetery
USE CEMETERY

DETACHED HOUSE

CL   DOMESTIC
BT   HOUSE <BY FORM>

Detention Centre
USE JUVENILE PRISON

DEWPOND
CL   WATER SUPPLY AND DRAINAGE
BT   POND

Dike
USE FLOOD DEFENCES
    WATER CHANNEL
    DYKE (DEFENCE)
SN   Use DYKE (DEFENCE), FLOOD DEFENCES or WATE
     CHANNEL as appropriate.

Dining Hall
USE REFECTORY

DIORAMA
CL   RECREATIONAL
BT   ART AND EDUCATION VENUE
RT   PANORAMA

DIPPING HOUSE
SN   Finishing of raw pottery by dipping it in glaze.
CL   INDUSTRIAL
BT   POTTERY MANUFACTURING SITE

DIPPING WELL
CL   WATER SUPPLY AND DRAINAGE
BT   WELL

DIRECTION STONE
CL   TRANSPORT
BT   ROAD TRANSPORT SITE
RT   SIGNPOST

DISC BARROW
CL   RELIGIOUS, RITUAL AND FUNERARY
BT   FANCY BARROW

DISCHARGE BLOCK
CL   HEALTH AND WELFARE
BT   HOSPITAL BLOCK

DISCOTHEQUE
CL   RECREATIONAL
BT   MUSIC AND DANCE VENUE
RT   DANCE HALL
     JAZZ CLUB

Dish House
USE DAIRY

DISINFECTOR HOUSE
CL   HEALTH AND WELFARE

Dispence
USE LARDER

DISPENSARY
CL   HEALTH AND WELFARE
RT   ALMONRY
     CHEMISTS SHOP
     CLINIC
     HOSPITAL
     PHARMACY

DISPERSAL
SN   Concrete hardstanding for parking aircraft around
     the perimeter of an airfield to avoid damage by
     bombing.
CL   TRANSPORT
BT   AIR TRANSPORT SITE

Dissenters Cemetery Chapel
USE CEMETERY CHAPEL

Dissenters Chapel
  USE NONCONFORMIST CHAPEL

Dissenters Grammar School
  USE CHURCH SCHOOL

Dissenters Meeting House
  USE NONCONFORMIST MEETING HOUSE

Dissenters Proprietary School
  USE CHURCH SCHOOL

Dissenters School
  USE CHURCH SCHOOL

DISTILLATION BLOCK
  CL INDUSTRIAL
  BT DISTILLING SITE

DISTILLATION PLANT
  SN Distillation is a chemical process used in the
      production of a range of different chemicals.
  CL INDUSTRIAL
  BT CHEMICAL PRODUCTION SITE
  RT PHARMACEUTICAL WORKS
      PIPE BRIDGE
      WOOD CHEMICAL WORKS

DISTILLERY
  UF Distilling Mill
      Still
  CL INDUSTRIAL
  BT DISTILLING SITE
  RT BONDED WAREHOUSE
      BOTTLING PLANT
      COOPERAGE
      GRANARY
      MALTINGS

Distilling Mill
  USE DISTILLERY

DISTILLING SITE
  CL INDUSTRIAL
  BT FOOD AND DRINK INDUSTRY SITE
  NT DISTILLATION BLOCK
      DISTILLERY
      MASH HOUSE
      STILL HOUSE

District Library
  USE PUBLIC LIBRARY

DITCH
  CL UNASSIGNED
  NT BOUNDARY DITCH
  RT EARTHWORK

DITCHED ENCLOSURE
  CL UNASSIGNED
  BT ENCLOSURE
  NT DOUBLE DITCHED ENCLOSURE

DIVING SUPPORT VESSEL
  CL MARITIME
  BT SERVICE CRAFT

DIVINITY SCHOOL
  CL EDUCATION
  BT TRAINING SCHOOL
  RT THEOLOGICAL COLLEGE

DOCK
  UF Dock Engine House
      Dock Pumphouse
      Dock Pumping Station
      Dock Railway
      Dock Tower
      Dock Wall
      Dock Warehouse
  CL TRANSPORT
  BT WATER TRANSPORT SITE
  NT CANAL DOCK
      DRY DOCK
      RIVER DOCK
  RT DOCKYARD
      WHARF

DOCK
  UF Dock Engine House
      Dock Pumphouse
      Dock Pumping Station
      Dock Railway
      Dock Tower
      Dock Wall
      Dock Warehouse
  CL MARITIME
  BT DOCK AND HARBOUR INSTALLATION
  NT DOUBLE DOCK
      DRAW DOCK
      DRY DOCK
      FLOATING DOCK
      HALF TIDE DOCK
      WET DOCK
  RT CANAL DOCK

DOCK AND HARBOUR INSTALLATION
  SN Excludes terms specific to MARINE CONSTRUCTION
      SITE.
  CL MARITIME
  NT BOAT HOUSE
      BOAT STORE
      BUOY STORE
      CAPSTAN
      CAPSTAN HOUSE
      CUSTOMS LOOKOUT
      CUSTOMS POST
      DOCK
      DOCK BASIN
      DOCK FLOOR
      DOCK PASSAGE
      DOCK SILL
      DOCKYARD RAILWAY
      DOLPHIN
      FAIRLEAD
      HARBOUR
      KEEL BLOCK
      MARINA
      MOORING BOLLARD
      PORT
      PROMENADE
      SEA TERMINAL
      SHIFTING HOUSE
  RT DOCKYARD
      MARINE CONSTRUCTION SITE
      MARITIME HOUSE
      MARITIME OFFICE

DOCK BASIN
  CL MARITIME
  BT DOCK AND HARBOUR INSTALLATION

DOCK BASIN
  CL MARITIME
  BT WATER REGULATION INSTALLATION

DOCK CULVERT
  CL MARITIME
  BT CULVERT

Dock Engine House
  USE DOCK
       ENGINE HOUSE
  SN Use both terms.

DOCK FLOOR
  CL MARITIME

BT   DOCK AND HARBOUR INSTALLATION

DOCK GATE
CL   MARITIME
BT   WATER REGULATION INSTALLATION

DOCK PASSAGE
CL   MARITIME
BT   DOCK AND HARBOUR INSTALLATION

Dock Pumphouse
USE DOCK
     PUMP HOUSE
SN   Use both terms.

Dock Pumping Station
USE DOCK
     PUMPING STATION
SN   Use both terms.

Dock Railway
USE DOCK
     RAILWAY
SN   Use both terms.

DOCK SILL
CL   MARITIME
BT   DOCK AND HARBOUR INSTALLATION

Dock Superintendents House
USE DOCKMASTERS HOUSE

Dock Tower
USE TOWER
     DOCK
SN   Use both terms

Dock Traffic Office
USE PILOT OFFICE

Dock Wall
USE WALL
     DOCK
SN   Use both terms.

Dock Warehouse
USE DOCK
     WAREHOUSE
SN   Use both terms.

Dock Watch House
USE WATCH HOUSE

DOCK WORKERS COTTAGE
CL   DOMESTIC
BT   MARITIME HOUSE
RT   SHIPYARD

DOCKMASTERS HOUSE
UF   Dock Superintendents House
CL   DOMESTIC
BT   MARITIME HOUSE
RT   CUSTOM HOUSE

DOCKMASTERS OFFICE
CL   MARITIME
BT   MARITIME OFFICE
RT   OFFICE

Docks
USE DOCKYARD

DOCKYARD
UF   Docks
     Dockyard Boundary Wall
     Dockyard Gate
     Dockyard Gatehouse
     Dockyard Office
     Dockyard Stable

SN   An enclosure in which ships are built and
     repaired.
CL   INDUSTRIAL
BT   MARINE CONSTRUCTION SITE
NT   NAVAL DOCKYARD
RT   CAPSTAN
     CHAIN WORKS
     DOCK
     DOCK AND HARBOUR INSTALLATION
     FLOATING CRANE
     GATEHOUSE
     SHIPYARD
     SLIP SHED
     SLIPWAY
     STABLE

DOCKYARD
UF   Docks
     Dockyard Boundary Wall
     Dockyard Gate
     Dockyard Gatehouse
     Dockyard Office
     Dockyard Stable
SN   An enclosure in which ships are built and
     repaired.
CL   TRANSPORT
BT   WATER TRANSPORT SITE
RT   CANAL DOCKYARD
     DOCK
     GATEHOUSE
     SLIP SHED

DOCKYARD
UF   Docks
     Dockyard Boundary Wall
     Dockyard Gate
     Dockyard Gatehouse
     Dockyard Office
     Dockyard Stable
SN   An enclosure in which ships are built and
     repaired.
CL   MARITIME
BT   MARINE CONSTRUCTION SITE
NT   NAVAL DOCKYARD
RT   CANAL DOCKYARD
     DOCK AND HARBOUR INSTALLATION

Dockyard Boundary Wall
USE BOUNDARY WALL
     DOCKYARD
SN   Use both terms.

Dockyard Church
USE SEAMENS CHURCH

Dockyard Gate
USE GATE
     DOCKYARD
SN   Use both terms.

Dockyard Gatehouse
USE DOCKYARD
     GATEHOUSE
SN   Use both terms.

Dockyard Office
USE DOCKYARD
     OFFICE
SN   Use both terms.

DOCKYARD RAILWAY
CL   TRANSPORT
BT   RAILWAY

DOCKYARD RAILWAY
CL   MARITIME
BT   DOCK AND HARBOUR INSTALLATION

Dockyard Stable

USE DOCKYARD
    STABLE
SN Use both terms.

DOCTORS HOSTEL
SN To include blocks of self-contained flats.
CL DOMESTIC
BT HOSTEL
RT HOSPITAL

DOCTORS HOUSE
CL DOMESTIC
BT HEALTH WORKERS HOUSE
RT CLINIC

Doctors Surgery
USE SURGERY

DOG TROUGH
CL GARDENS, PARKS AND URBAN SPACES
BT TROUGH

DOG TROUGH
CL WATER SUPPLY AND DRAINAGE
BT TROUGH

Doghouse
USE KENNELS

Dogs Cemetery
USE ANIMAL CEMETERY

Dogs Gravestone
USE ANIMAL MEMORIAL

DOGS HOME
CL HEALTH AND WELFARE
BT ANIMAL WELFARE SITE

Dolmen
USE CHAMBERED TOMB

DOLPHIN
SN A cluster of piles for mooring a vessel.
CL MARITIME
BT DOCK AND HARBOUR INSTALLATION
RT MOORING BOLLARD

DOLPHINARIUM
CL RECREATIONAL
BT ANIMAL HOUSE

DOME TRAINER
SN Building housing a training aid for aircraft
    gunners (WWII).
CL DEFENCE

DOMESTIC
SN This is the top term for the class. See DOMESTIC
    Class List for narrow terms.

DOMESTIC CHAPEL
UF Manor House Chapel
CL RELIGIOUS, RITUAL AND FUNERARY
BT CHAPEL
RT COUNTRY HOUSE
    MANOR HOUSE
    PALACE

Domestic Dwelling
USE HOUSE

DOMESTIC SCIENCE SCHOOL
CL EDUCATION
BT TRAINING SCHOOL

DOMINICAN FRIARY
CL RELIGIOUS, RITUAL AND FUNERARY
BT FRIARY

RT DOMINICAN NUNNERY

DOMINICAN NUNNERY
UF Dominican Priory
SN Priory of Dominican nuns, Dartford.
CL RELIGIOUS, RITUAL AND FUNERARY
BT NUNNERY
RT DOMINICAN FRIARY

Dominican Priory
USE DOMINICAN NUNNERY
    PRIORY
SN Use both terms.

Domus Longa
USE LONG HOUSE

Donjon
USE KEEP

DONKEY HOUSE
CL AGRICULTURE AND SUBSISTENCE
BT ANIMAL SHED

Donkey Mill
USE DONKEY WHEEL

DONKEY WHEEL
UF Donkey Mill
CL INDUSTRIAL
BT ANIMAL POWER SITE
RT HORSE ENGINE
    HORSE ENGINE HOUSE
    WELL
    WELL HOUSE

DORIC TEMPLE
CL GARDENS, PARKS AND URBAN SPACES
BT GARDEN TEMPLE

DORTER
CL DOMESTIC
RT MONASTERY

DOUBLE CLOISTER
CL RELIGIOUS, RITUAL AND FUNERARY
BT CLOISTER

Double Cottage
USE SEMI DETACHED HOUSE

DOUBLE DITCHED ENCLOSURE
CL UNASSIGNED
BT DITCHED ENCLOSURE

DOUBLE DOCK
CL MARITIME
BT DOCK

DOUBLE ENDED HALL HOUSE
CL DOMESTIC
BT CROSS WING HOUSE
RT SINGLE ENDED HALL HOUSE

DOUBLE HOUSE
UF Celtic Monastery
    Convent
SN Mixed house of nuns and religious men.
CL RELIGIOUS, RITUAL AND FUNERARY
BT RELIGIOUS HOUSE
NT AUGUSTINIAN DOUBLE HOUSE
    BENEDICTINE DOUBLE HOUSE
    BRIDGETTINE DOUBLE HOUSE
    FONTEVRAULTINE DOUBLE HOUSE
    GILBERTINE DOUBLE HOUSE
RT ABBEY
    CELL
    FARM
    FRIARY

GRANGE
MANOR
MONASTERY
NUNNERY
PRIORY

Double Moated Garden
USE MOAT
     GARDEN
SN   Use both terms.

Double Ropehouse
USE ROPERY

DOUBLING MILL
CL   INDUSTRIAL
BT   TEXTILE MILL
RT   SPINNING MILL
     TWIST MILL
     YARN MILL

DOUBLING MILL
CL   INDUSTRIAL
BT   TEXTILE SITE <BY PROCESS/PRODUCT>
RT   SPINNING MILL
     TWIST MILL
     YARN MILL

Dovecot
USE DOVECOTE

DOVECOTE
UF   Columbary
     Culverhouse
     Dovecot
     Pigeon House
CL   AGRICULTURE AND SUBSISTENCE
BT   AGRICULTURAL BUILDING
RT   COUNTRY HOUSE
     MANOR HOUSE

DOWER HOUSE
CL   DOMESTIC
BT   HOUSE <BY FUNCTION>

DOWNDRAUGHT KILN
UF   Beehive Kiln
CL   INDUSTRIAL
BT   KILN <BY FORM>
RT   HOFFMAN KILN
     TUNNEL KILN
     UPDRAUGHT KILN

DRABBET FACTORY
SN   A factory producing drabbet, a type of linen
     cloth.
CL   INDUSTRIAL
BT   TEXTILE MILL
RT   BEETLING MILL
     LINEN MILL

DRABBET FACTORY
SN   A factory producing drabbet, a type of linen
     cloth.
CL   INDUSTRIAL
BT   LINEN OR FLAX MANUFACTURING SITE
RT   BEETLING MILL
     CALENDER MILL
     LINEN MILL

DRAIN
UF   Gutter
     Land Drain
CL   WATER SUPPLY AND DRAINAGE
NT   CULVERT
     DRAIN SYPHON
     FIELD DRAIN
RT   DRAINAGE DITCH
     DRAINAGE SYSTEM

LEAT
SEWER
SLUICE
UNDERGROUND STRUCTURE

DRAIN SYPHON
CL   WATER SUPPLY AND DRAINAGE
BT   DRAIN
RT   FIELD DRAIN

DRAINAGE DITCH
CL   WATER SUPPLY AND DRAINAGE
RT   CULVERT
     DRAIN
     DRAINAGE SYSTEM
     LINEAR EARTHWORK

DRAINAGE LEVEL
UF   Drainpipe Tunnel
     Mine Drainage Tunnel
     Sough
     Sough Tunnel
SN   A horizontal tunnel dug specifically for draining,
     for example, a mine.
CL   WATER SUPPLY AND DRAINAGE
RT   ADIT
     MINE

DRAINAGE MILL
SN   Wind or water-powered mill for pumping water.
CL   INDUSTRIAL
BT   WATER POWER PRODUCTION SITE
RT   WIND PUMP
     WINDMILL

DRAINAGE MILL
SN   Wind or water-powered mill for pumping water.
CL   WATER SUPPLY AND DRAINAGE
RT   WIND PUMP
     WINDMILL

DRAINAGE SYSTEM
UF   Land Drainage
CL   WATER SUPPLY AND DRAINAGE
RT   DRAIN
     DRAINAGE DITCH

Drainage Works
USE PUMPING STATION

Drainpipe Tunnel
USE DRAINAGE LEVEL
SN   Drainage tunnel used in mine drainage.

DRAMA SCHOOL
UF   Theatre School
     Theatrical School
CL   EDUCATION
BT   TRAINING SCHOOL

DRAPERS SHOP
UF   Drapery Shop
CL   COMMERCIAL
BT   SHOP

Drapery Shop
USE DRAPERS SHOP

DRAW DOCK
CL   MARITIME
BT   DOCK

DRAWBRIDGE
SN   Bridge type over canals, etc. Otherwise a
     component, use wider site type.
CL   TRANSPORT
BT   BRIDGE <BY FORM>

DRAWING OFFICE

UF   Architects Drawing Office
     Surveyors Office
CL   COMMERCIAL
BT   COMMERCIAL OFFICE
RT   OFFICE

DREADNOUGHT
CL   MARITIME
BT   BATTLESHIP

DREDGER
CL   MARITIME
BT   CHANNEL CLEARANCE VESSEL
NT   BUCKET DREDGER
     CUTTER DREDGER
     GRAB DREDGER
     HOPPER DREDGER
     SUCTION DREDGER

Dresser Tomb
  USE   CANOPIED TOMB

DRESSING FLOOR
CL   INDUSTRIAL
RT   STONE EXTRACTION SITE

DRESSING MILL
CL   INDUSTRIAL
RT   MINE
     STONE EXTRACTION SITE

DRESSING MILL
CL   INDUSTRIAL
BT   MILL
RT   STONE EXTRACTION SITE

DRESSING SHED
CL   INDUSTRIAL
RT   SHED
     STONE EXTRACTION SITE

DRIFT
CL   INDUSTRIAL
BT   MINING INDUSTRY SITE

DRIFT MINE
SN   Use with product(s) extracted and MINE where
     known, eg. COAL MINE.
CL   INDUSTRIAL
BT   MINE
RT   CLAY MINE
     COAL PIT

DRIFTER
CL   MARITIME
BT   NET FISHING VESSEL

DRILL HALL
CL   DEFENCE
RT   BARRACKS

DRINKING FOUNTAIN
UF   Pant
CL   WATER SUPPLY AND DRAINAGE
BT   FOUNTAIN
RT   WELL

Drinking Trough
  USE   TROUGH

DRIVE
SN   A road/carriage way giving access from the main
     road to the house, stables.
CL   GARDENS, PARKS AND URBAN SPACES

Drop Forge Stamps
  USE   STAMPS

DROVE ROAD

UF   Droveway
     Greenway
CL   TRANSPORT
BT   ROAD
RT   DROVERS INN

DROVERS INN
CL   COMMERCIAL
BT   INN
RT   COACHING INN
     DROVE ROAD
     JAGGERS HOSTEL

DROVERS INN
CL   DOMESTIC
BT   INN
RT   COACHING INN
     DROVE ROAD
     JAGGERS HOSTEL

Droveway
  USE   DROVE ROAD

Drum Tower
  USE   ANGLE TOWER

Dry
  USE   MALT KILN

DRY BULK CARGO CARRIER
CL   MARITIME
BT   CARGO VESSEL

Dry Cooperage
  USE   COOPERAGE

DRY DOCK
UF   Graving Dock
CL   INDUSTRIAL
BT   MARINE CONSTRUCTION SITE
RT   CAPSTAN
     GRIDIRON
     SHIP REPAIR WORKS

DRY DOCK
UF   Graving Dock
CL   TRANSPORT
BT   DOCK

DRY DOCK
UF   Graving Dock
CL   MARITIME
BT   DOCK

DRY DOCK
UF   Graving Dock
CL   MARITIME
BT   MARINE CONSTRUCTION SITE

DRY HOUSE
CL   INDUSTRIAL
RT   CLOTH DRY HOUSE
     FLAX DRY HOUSE
     LACE DRYING HOUSE
     WOOL DRY HOUSE
     YARN DRY HOUSE

DRYING HOUSE
UF   Drying Shed
     Tarpaulin Drying Shed
CL   INDUSTRIAL
RT   DRYING KILN
     TEXTILE MILL

DRYING KILN
UF   Drying Oven
CL   INDUSTRIAL
BT   KILN <BY FUNCTION>
NT   CORN DRYING KILN

FOOD DRYING KILN
GYPSUM DRYING KILN
WOOD DRYING KILN
RT DRYING HOUSE

Drying Oven
USE DRYING KILN

Drying Shed
USE DRYING HOUSE

Duck Decoy Pond
USE DECOY POND

DUCK HOUSE
CL AGRICULTURE AND SUBSISTENCE
BT AGRICULTURAL BUILDING

DUCKING POND
CL CIVIL
BT PUNISHMENT PLACE
RT DUCKING STOOL

DUCKING POND
CL WATER SUPPLY AND DRAINAGE
BT POND
RT DUCKING STOOL

DUCKING STOOL
UF Cucking Stool
CL CIVIL
BT PUNISHMENT PLACE
RT DUCKING POND

Dugout Boat
USE LOGBOAT

Dugout Canoe
USE LOGBOAT

DUMMY WARSHIP
CL MARITIME
BT WARSHIP

Dummy Yard
USE BRICKYARD

DUST EXTRACTION PLANT
SN Washing down and removal of dust from freshly
    mined coal before loading for transport away from
    the colliery.
CL INDUSTRIAL
BT COAL MINING SITE

Dutch Barn
USE HAY BARN

DUTCH GARDEN
CL GARDENS, PARKS AND URBAN SPACES
BT GARDEN

DUTCH REFORMED CHURCH
CL RELIGIOUS, RITUAL AND FUNERARY
BT CHURCH

DUTY POST
SN Boundary marker for the payment of tax or duty.
CL GARDENS, PARKS AND URBAN SPACES
BT STREET FURNITURE
NT COAL TAX POST

DWELLING
CL DOMESTIC
NT APARTMENT
    COUNCIL FLAT
    CRANNOG
    HOUSE
    HOVEL
    HUT

LOG CABIN
MAISONETTE
MODEL DWELLING
MULTIPLE DWELLING
PALACE
PREFAB
ROCK SHELTER
RT GRUBENHAUS
    MOAT
    RESIDENTIAL BUILDING
    SETTLEMENT
    TENEMENT

DYE AND PIGMENT SITE
CL INDUSTRIAL
BT CHEMICAL PRODUCTION SITE
NT ALUM HOUSE
    ALUM WORKS
    COLOUR HOUSE
    COLOUR MILL
    COPPERAS WORKS
    DYE WORKS
    FULLERS EARTH PIT
    MARL PIT
    OCHRE PIT
    PAINT FACTORY

DYE HOUSE
UF Dyehouse
    Dyeing Shop
    Dyeshop
CL INDUSTRIAL
BT TEXTILE FINISHING SITE
RT COLOUR HOUSE
    DYE WORKS
    FINISHING WORKS
    FULLING MILL
    LOGWOOD MILL
    PICKER HOUSE
    PRESS SHOP

DYE WORKS
CL INDUSTRIAL
BT DYE AND PIGMENT SITE
NT ARTIFICAL DYE WORKS
RT COPPERAS WORKS

DYE WORKS
CL INDUSTRIAL
BT TEXTILE FINISHING SITE
RT ALUM WORKS
    COLOUR HOUSE
    COLOUR MILL
    COPPERAS WORKS
    DYE HOUSE
    FULLERS EARTH PIT
    FULLING MILL

Dyehouse
USE DYE HOUSE

Dyeing Shop
USE DYE HOUSE

Dyeshop
USE DYE HOUSE

DYKE (DEFENCE)
UF Dike
SN Defensive or boundary earthwork.
CL DEFENCE
NT CROSS DYKE
RT BOUNDARY
    EARTHWORK
    LINEAR EARTHWORK
    OPPIDUM

Dyke (Water)
USE FLOOD DEFENCES

WATER CHANNEL
SN   Use WATER CHANNEL where drain or other
      water-filled ditch. Use FLOOD DEFENCES where flood
      defence embankment.

EAR HOSPITAL
CL   HEALTH AND WELFARE
BT   SPECIALIST HOSPITAL

EAR NOSE AND THROAT DEPARTMENT
CL   HEALTH AND WELFARE
BT   HOSPITAL DEPARTMENT

EAR NOSE AND THROAT HOSPITAL
CL   HEALTH AND WELFARE
BT   SPECIALIST HOSPITAL

Early Christian Memorial Stone
USE INSCRIBED STONE

EARLY WARNING STATION
CL   DEFENCE
RT   MISSILE BASE
      RADAR STATION

Earthen Artillery Fort
USE FORT

Earthen Long Barrow
USE LONG BARROW

Earthenware Works
USE POTTERY WORKS

EARTHWORK
UF   Circus (Roman)
      Danish Camp
CL   UNASSIGNED
NT   BANK (EARTHWORK)
      LINEAR EARTHWORK
RT   CROSS DYKE
      DITCH
      DYKE (DEFENCE)
      ENCLOSURE
      FIELDWORK
      MOUND

EASTERN ORTHODOX CATHEDRAL
CL   RELIGIOUS, RITUAL AND FUNERARY
BT   CATHEDRAL
RT   EASTERN ORTHODOX CEMETERY
      EASTERN ORTHODOX CHURCH

EASTERN ORTHODOX CEMETERY
CL   RELIGIOUS, RITUAL AND FUNERARY
BT   INHUMATION CEMETERY
RT   EASTERN ORTHODOX CATHEDRAL

Eastern Orthodox Cemetery Chapel
USE CEMETERY CHAPEL

EASTERN ORTHODOX CHURCH
UF   Greek Orthodox Church
      Russian Orthodox Church
CL   RELIGIOUS, RITUAL AND FUNERARY
BT   ORTHODOX CHURCH
RT   EASTERN ORTHODOX CATHEDRAL

EATING AND DRINKING ESTABLISHMENT
SN   For commercial or non commercial use. See narrow
      terms in each class.
CL   COMMERCIAL
NT   BUFFET
      CAFE
      CHOCOLATE HOUSE
      COFFEE BAR
      COFFEE HOUSE
      EATING HOUSE
      LICENSED PREMISES

PIE AND MASH SHOP
RAILWAY BUFFET
REFRESHMENT ROOMS
RESTAURANT
TEA ROOM
TEMPERANCE PUBLIC HOUSE

EATING AND DRINKING ESTABLISHMENT
SN   For commercial or non commercial use. See narrow
      terms in each class.
CL   RECREATIONAL
NT   BANQUETING HOUSE
      PUBLIC HOUSE
      REFRESHMENT PAVILION
      TEA HOUSE

EATING HOUSE
UF   Chop House
CL   COMMERCIAL
BT   EATING AND DRINKING ESTABLISHMENT
RT   FISH AND CHIP SHOP

Ecclesiastical Palace
USE BISHOPS PALACE

ECONOMISER HOUSE
CL   INDUSTRIAL
BT   STEAM POWER PRODUCTION SITE
RT   BOILER HOUSE
      CHIMNEY
      ENGINE HOUSE
      TEXTILE MILL

EDGE TOOL WORKS
UF   Blade Works
      Spade And Shovel Works
      Spade Forge
SN   Forging and sharpening of a variety of tools
      including scythes, spades, etc.
CL   INDUSTRIAL
BT   FERROUS METAL PRODUCT SITE
RT   CUTLERY WORKS
      CUTLERY WORKSHOP
      FORGE
      GRINDSTONE
      SCYTHE MILL

Editorial Office
USE NEWSPAPER OFFICE

EDUCATION
SN   This is the top term for the class. See EDUCATION
      Class List for narrow terms.

Education Office
USE LOCAL GOVERNMENT OFFICE

Eel And Pie Shop
USE PIE AND MASH SHOP

EEL STALL
CL   COMMERCIAL

EEL TRAP
CL   AGRICULTURE AND SUBSISTENCE
BT   FISHING SITE
RT   FISH LADDER
      FISH LOCK
      FISH WEIR
      WEIR

EFFIGY
UF   Memorial Effigy
CL   COMMEMORATIVE
BT   COMMEMORATIVE MONUMENT

EGYPTIAN GARDEN
CL   GARDENS, PARKS AND URBAN SPACES
BT   GARDEN

EGYPTIAN HALL
- SN   Hall with an internal peristyle.
- CL   CIVIL
- BT   MEETING HALL

ELEANOR CROSS
- UF   Queen Eleanor Cross
- CL   COMMEMORATIVE
- BT   COMMEMORATIVE MONUMENT

ELEANOR CROSS
- UF   Queen Eleanor Cross
- CL   RELIGIOUS, RITUAL AND FUNERARY
- BT   CROSS

ELECTRIC ARC FURNACE
- SN   A refractory lined furnace in which an electric arc is struck between the electrode and the metal to be melted.
- CL   INDUSTRIAL
- BT   METAL PRODUCTION FURNACE
- RT   ALUMINIUM SMELTER
       FERROUS METAL SMELTING SITE
       NON FERROUS METAL SMELTING SITE

Electric Cooperage
   USE COOPERAGE

Electric Generating Station
   USE POWER STATION

Electric Light Works
   USE POWER STATION

Electric Theatre
   USE CINEMA

ELECTRIC WINCH
- CL   TRANSPORT
- BT   WINCH
- RT   HAULAGE ENGINE HOUSE

ELECTRICAL ENGINEERING WORKS
- CL   INDUSTRIAL
- BT   LIGHT ENGINEERING SITE

Electrical Valve Works
   USE RADIO VALVE WORKS

Electricity Plant
   USE POWER STATION

ELECTRICITY PRODUCTION SITE
- CL   INDUSTRIAL
- BT   POWER GENERATION SITE
- NT   ACCUMULATOR HOUSE
       ACCUMULATOR TOWER
       COOLING TOWER
       ELECTRICITY PYLON
       ELECTRICITY SUB STATION
       POWER STATION
       SWITCH HOUSE
       TRANSFORMER BOX
       TRANSFORMER STATION

ELECTRICITY PYLON
- UF   Pylon
- CL   INDUSTRIAL
- BT   ELECTRICITY PRODUCTION SITE
- RT   ELECTRICITY SUB STATION

ELECTRICITY SUB STATION
- UF   Sub Station
- SN   Building containing transformers to reduce the high voltage of the National Grid to the lower voltage of domestic supply.
- CL   INDUSTRIAL
- BT   ELECTRICITY PRODUCTION SITE

- RT   ELECTRICITY PYLON
       POWER STATION
       TRANSFORMER STATION

Electricity Works
   USE POWER STATION

Electro Plating Works
   USE PLATING WORKS

ELEMENTARY SCHOOL
- CL   EDUCATION
- BT   SCHOOL
- NT   DAME SCHOOL
       FREE SCHOOL
       INFANT SCHOOL
       NURSERY SCHOOL
       PRIMARY SCHOOL
- RT   PREPARATORY SCHOOL

ELEPHANT HOUSE
- CL   RECREATIONAL
- BT   ANIMAL HOUSE

ELLING HEARTH
- SN   Small stone hearth set up in a shallow pit. Burns vegetation and coppiced twigs to produce potash.
- CL   INDUSTRIAL
- BT   KILN <BY FUNCTION>
- RT   POTASH KILN
       SILVER HEARTH
       SOAP FACTORY

ELLING HEARTH
- SN   Small stone hearth set up in a shallow pit. Burns vegetation and coppiced twigs to produce potash.
- CL   INDUSTRIAL
- BT   CHEMICAL PRODUCTION SITE

EMBANKED AVENUE
- UF   Avenue
- SN   Use for prehistoric avenues such as Stonehenge.
- CL   RELIGIOUS, RITUAL AND FUNERARY
- RT   CURSUS

EMBANKED STONE CIRCLE
- CL   RELIGIOUS, RITUAL AND FUNERARY
- BT   STONE CIRCLE
- RT   ENCLOSURE

EMBANKMENT
- CL   UNASSIGNED
- RT   CAUSEWAY
       FLOOD RELIEF CANAL
       RAISED PAVEMENT

EMBANKMENT CROSS
- CL   UNASSIGNED

Embankment Steps
   USE LANDING STEPS

EMBASSY
- UF   High Commission Building
- CL   CIVIL
- RT   GOVERNMENT OFFICE

Emergency Hospital
   USE GENERAL HOSPITAL
- SN   Emergency Medical Scheme Hospital (WWII). For epidemics use INFECTIOUS DISEASES HOSPITAL.

Emergency Medical Scheme Hospital
   USE GENERAL HOSPITAL

EMERGENCY WARD BLOCK
- SN   Use for blocks in Emergency Medical Scheme hospitals (WWII).
- CL   HEALTH AND WELFARE

BT   HOSPITAL BLOCK

EMIGRANT SHIP
  CL   MARITIME
  BT   PASSENGER VESSEL

Emporium
  USE SHOP

ENAMELLING KILN
  CL   INDUSTRIAL
  BT   KILN <BY FUNCTION>
  RT   POTTERY MANUFACTURING SITE

ENCLOSED CREMATION CEMETERY
  CL   RELIGIOUS, RITUAL AND FUNERARY
  BT   CREMATION CEMETERY
  RT   ENCLOSURE

ENCLOSED FIELD SYSTEM
  UF   Irregular Enclosed Field System
        Regular Enclosed Field System
  SN   System of individually enclosed fields.
  CL   AGRICULTURE AND SUBSISTENCE
  BT   FIELD SYSTEM

ENCLOSED HUT CIRCLE SETTLEMENT
  UF   Enclosed Stone Hut Circle Settlement
  CL   DOMESTIC
  BT   ENCLOSED SETTLEMENT

ENCLOSED HUT CIRCLE SETTLEMENT
  UF   Enclosed Stone Hut Circle Settlement
  CL   DOMESTIC
  BT   HUT CIRCLE SETTLEMENT

ENCLOSED OPPIDUM
  CL   DOMESTIC
  BT   ENCLOSED SETTLEMENT

ENCLOSED OPPIDUM
  CL   CIVIL
  BT   OPPIDUM

ENCLOSED OPPIDUM
  CL   DOMESTIC
  BT   OPPIDUM

ENCLOSED PLATFORM SETTLEMENT
  CL   DOMESTIC
  BT   ENCLOSED SETTLEMENT

ENCLOSED PLATFORM SETTLEMENT
  CL   DOMESTIC
  BT   PLATFORM SETTLEMENT

Enclosed Port
  USE PORT

ENCLOSED SETTLEMENT
  UF   Gussage Style Settlement
        Homestead
        Itford Hill Style Enclosure
        Martin Down Style Enclosure
        Rams Hill Style Enclosure
        Springfield Style Enclosure
        Wootton Hill Style Enclosure
  CL   DOMESTIC
  BT   SETTLEMENT
  NT   BANJO ENCLOSURE
        BURH
        CLOTHES LINE ENCLOSURE
        ENCLOSED HUT CIRCLE SETTLEMENT
        ENCLOSED OPPIDUM
        ENCLOSED PLATFORM SETTLEMENT
        HILLFORT
        HILLTOP ENCLOSURE
        PALISADED HOMESTEAD
        PALISADED SETTLEMENT

        PROMONTORY FORT
        ROUND
  RT   ENCLOSURE

ENCLOSED SETTLEMENT
  UF   Gussage Style Settlement
        Homestead
        Itford Hill Style Enclosure
        Martin Down Style Enclosure
        Rams Hill Style Enclosure
        Springfield Style Enclosure
        Wootton Hill Style Enclosure
  CL   DEFENCE
  NT   BURH
        HILLFORT
        HILLTOP ENCLOSURE
        MULTIPLE DITCH SYSTEM
        OPPIDUM
        PALISADED ENCLOSURE
        PROMONTORY FORT
        ROUND
  RT   ENCLOSURE

Enclosed Stone Hut Circle Settlement
  USE ENCLOSED HUT CIRCLE SETTLEMENT

ENCLOSED URNFIELD
  CL   RELIGIOUS, RITUAL AND FUNERARY
  BT   URNFIELD
  RT   ENCLOSURE

ENCLOSURE
  UF   A P Enclosure
        Garth
        Irregular Enclosure
  CL   UNASSIGNED
  NT   CURVILINEAR ENCLOSURE
        DITCHED ENCLOSURE
        PIT DEFINED ENCLOSURE
        RECTILINEAR ENCLOSURE
  RT   BAILEY
        CAUSEWAYED ENCLOSURE
        CAUSEWAYED RING DITCH
        EARTHWORK
        EMBANKED STONE CIRCLE
        ENCLOSED CREMATION CEMETERY
        ENCLOSED SETTLEMENT
        ENCLOSED URNFIELD
        HENGE ENCLOSURE
        HENGIFORM MONUMENT
        MORTUARY ENCLOSURE
        RINGWORK
        STOCK ENCLOSURE
        STOCKADED ENCLOSURE
        TREE ENCLOSURE RING

Enclosure Castle
  USE CASTLE

END CHIMNEY HOUSE
  CL   DOMESTIC
  BT   HOUSE <BY FORM>

END GABLED HOUSE
  CL   DOMESTIC
  BT   GABLED HOUSE

End Hall
  USE END HALL HOUSE

END HALL HOUSE
  UF   End Hall
  CL   DOMESTIC
  BT   HALL HOUSE

END JETTY HOUSE
  CL   DOMESTIC
  BT   JETTIED HOUSE

Endowed Grammar School

USE GRAMMAR SCHOOL

ENGINE
- SN   Industrial rather than transport use.
- CL   INDUSTRIAL
- NT   GAS ENGINE
  OIL ENGINE
  STEAM ENGINE
  TURBINE
  WIND ENGINE
- RT   BOILER HOUSE
  COMPRESSOR HOUSE
  CRANE
  ENGINE HOUSE

ENGINE HOUSE
- UF   Dock Engine House
  Incline House
- CL   INDUSTRIAL
- BT   POWER GENERATION SITE
- NT   ATMOSPHERIC ENGINE HOUSE
  ATMOSPHERIC RAILWAY ENGINE HOUSE
  BLOWING ENGINE HOUSE
  GAS ENGINE HOUSE
  HAULAGE ENGINE HOUSE
  HORSE ENGINE HOUSE
  HYDRAULIC ENGINE HOUSE
  STEAM ENGINE HOUSE
  TURBINE HOUSE
- RT   CHIMNEY
  ECONOMISER HOUSE
  ENGINE
  FACTORY
  MINE
  PUMP HOUSE
  PUMPING STATION
  TEXTILE MILL
  WATER PUMPING STATION
  WATERWORKS
  WORKS

Engine Manufactory
  USE ENGINEERING WORKS

ENGINE SHED
- UF   Locomotive Shed
  Railway Engine Shed
- CL   TRANSPORT
- BT   RAILWAY TRANSPORT SITE
- RT   ROUNDHOUSE (RAILWAY)
  SHED

Engine Works
  USE ENGINEERING WORKS

Engineering College
  USE TECHNICAL COLLEGE

ENGINEERING INDUSTRY SITE
- CL   INDUSTRIAL
- NT   AGRICULTURAL ENGINEERING WORKS
  ASSEMBLY PLANT
  ENGINEERING WORKS
  ENGINEERING WORKSHOP
  ERECTING SHOP
  FABRICATION SHED
  HEAVY ENGINEERING SITE
  LIGHT ENGINEERING SITE
  MACHINE SHOP
  PAINT SHOP
  PATTERN SHOP
  PLATERS SHOP
  POLISHING SHOP
  RAILWAY ENGINEERING SITE
  SPRING SHOP
  TURNING SHOP
  VEHICLE ENGINEERING SITE
- RT   TRAVELLING OVERHEAD CRANE

ENGINEERING WORKS

- UF   Engine Manufactory
  Engine Works
  Traction Engine Works
- CL   INDUSTRIAL
- BT   ENGINEERING INDUSTRY SITE

ENGINEERING WORKSHOP
- CL   INDUSTRIAL
- BT   ENGINEERING INDUSTRY SITE
- RT   BOILER SHOP
  FITTERS WORKSHOP
  FORGE
  MACHINE SHOP
  PATTERN SHOP
  TURNING SHOP
  WHITESMITHS WORKSHOP

ENTRANCE GRAVE
- CL   RELIGIOUS, RITUAL AND FUNERARY
- BT   CHAMBERED TOMB

Entrance Lodge
  USE GATE LODGE

Entrenchment
  USE TRENCH

Epileptic Colony
  USE HOSPITAL FOR EPILEPTICS

Episcopal Palace
  USE BISHOPS PALACE

Equestrian Statue
  USE STATUE

ERECTING SHOP
- SN   Engineering workshop used for the final assembly
  of vehicles or structures from parts produced
  elsewhere in an engineering works.
- CL   INDUSTRIAL
- BT   ENGINEERING INDUSTRY SITE
- RT   SPRING SHOP

ESCORT
- CL   MARITIME
- BT   WARSHIP

Estate Agent
  USE COMMERCIAL OFFICE

Estate Boundary
  USE BOUNDARY

ESTATE COTTAGE
- UF   Estate House
  Estate Workers Cottage
  Estate Workers House
  Gamekeepers Cottage
  Gamekeepers House
  Gamekeepers Lodge
  Garden Cottage
  Gardeners Cottage
  Gardeners House
  Tied Cottage
- CL   DOMESTIC
- BT   HOUSE <BY FUNCTION>
- RT   COACHMANS COTTAGE
  COUNTRY HOUSE
  ESTATE LAUNDRY
  ESTATE VILLAGE
  GROOMS COTTAGE
  RANGERS HOUSE

Estate House
  USE ESTATE COTTAGE

ESTATE LAUNDRY
- CL   DOMESTIC

RT COUNTRY HOUSE
    ESTATE COTTAGE
    ESTATE VILLAGE
    LAUNDRETTE
    LAUNDRY

Estate Managers House
  USE MANAGERS HOUSE

Estate Office
  USE OFFICE

Estate Stone
  USE BOUNDARY STONE

ESTATE VILLAGE
  CL DOMESTIC
  BT MODEL SETTLEMENT
  RT ESTATE COTTAGE
    ESTATE LAUNDRY
    GARDEN SUBURB

Estate Workers Cottage
  USE ESTATE COTTAGE

Estate Workers House
  USE ESTATE COTTAGE

ETHER PLANT
  SN For production of anaesthetic gas.
  CL INDUSTRIAL
  BT PETROCHEMICAL SITE
  RT PHARMACEUTICAL WORKS

Ethical Society Hall
  USE SECULAR HALL

ETOILE
  SN An intersection of straight walks in a wooded
    area.
  CL GARDENS, PARKS AND URBAN SPACES
  BT WALK

Eton Fives Court
  USE FIVES COURT

EXAMINATION HALL
  CL EDUCATION
  RT SCHOOL

EXAMINATION SCHOOL
  CL EDUCATION
  BT TRAINING SCHOOL

EXCHANGE
  CL COMMERCIAL
  NT COAL EXCHANGE
    CORN EXCHANGE
    COTTON EXCHANGE
    HOP EXCHANGE
    STOCK EXCHANGE
    WOOL EXCHANGE
  RT CHAMBER OF COMMERCE
    GUILDHALL
    MARKET HALL

EXCISE OFFICE
  CL MARITIME
  BT MARITIME OFFICE
  RT OFFICE

Execution Cemetery
  USE CEMETERY

EXECUTION SITE
  CL CIVIL
  BT PUNISHMENT PLACE
  NT GALLOWS
    GALLOWS MOUND

    GIBBET
    SCAFFOLD

EXEDRA
  SN A semi-circular or rectangular recess with raised
    seats.
  CL GARDENS, PARKS AND URBAN SPACES
  BT GARDEN BUILDING

EXERCISE YARD
  UF Airing Yard
  CL HEALTH AND WELFARE
  RT PRISON
    WORKHOUSE

EXHAUSTER HOUSE
  UF Fanhouse
    Ventilating Fanhouse
  SN Part of colliery ventilation system exhausting
    stale air from shafts and headings.
  CL INDUSTRIAL
  BT MINE DRAINAGE AND VENTILATION SITE
  RT AIR SHAFT
    VENTILATION SHAFT

Exhibition Cottage
  USE MODEL DWELLING

EXHIBITION HALL
  CL EDUCATION
  RT ART GALLERY
    MUSEUM

EXHIBITION HALL
  CL RECREATIONAL
  BT ART AND EDUCATION VENUE
  RT ART GALLERY

EXHIBITION HALL
  CL COMMERCIAL
  NT AGRICULTURAL HALL
    HORTICULTURAL HALL
  RT ART GALLERY
    EXHIBITION PAVILION
    MUSEUM

EXHIBITION PAVILION
  UF Exhibition Tent
  SN For example, the exhibition pavilions at the Great
    Empire Exhibition, Wembley, 1925.
  CL RECREATIONAL
  BT ART AND EDUCATION VENUE
  RT EXHIBITION HALL

Exhibition Tent
  USE EXHIBITION PAVILION

EXPERIMENTAL CRAFT
  CL MARITIME
  BT MARITIME CRAFT

Experimental Research Station
  USE RESEARCH STATION

EXPLOSIVES FACTORY
  CL INDUSTRIAL
  BT EXPLOSIVES SITE

EXPLOSIVES SITE
  CL INDUSTRIAL
  BT CHEMICAL PRODUCTION SITE
  NT CORNING HOUSE
    EXPLOSIVES FACTORY
    GLAZE AND REEL HOUSE
    GREEN CHARGE HOUSE
    GUNPOWDER DRYING HOUSE
    GUNPOWDER WORKS
    INCORPORATING MILL
    NITRE BED

NITROGLYCERINE WORKS
ORDNANCE FACTORY
POWDER MAGAZINE
PRESS HOUSE
RIPE CHARGE HOUSE
SALTPETRE STORE
SULPHUR STORE
TESTING RANGE
RT CHARCOAL STORE
    ROCKET MOTOR FACTORY

EXTENDED INHUMATION
CL RELIGIOUS, RITUAL AND FUNERARY
BT INHUMATION

EXTRACTIVE PIT
UF Minepits
    Open Cast Workings
    Open Pit Mining
    Open Work
SN Surface workings including shallow shafts, lode
    workings, open-pit methods and quarrying including
    some mines of stone, clays, compounds, etc. See
    also MINERAL EXTRACTION SITE.
CL INDUSTRIAL
NT BELL PIT
    BRICK PIT
    BRICKEARTH PIT
    CHALK PIT
    CLAY WORKINGS
    COAL PIT
    COAL WORKINGS
    COPPER WORKINGS
    DENE HOLE
    FULLERS EARTH PIT
    GRAVEL PIT
    IRONSTONE WORKINGS
    JET WORKINGS
    LEAD WORKINGS
    MARL PIT
    MINERAL PIT
    OCHRE PIT
    SAND PIT
    STONE AXE FACTORY
RT ADIT
    AERIAL ROPEWAY
    BRINE PIT
    CLAY PIT
    PIT
    QUARRY

EYE AND EAR HOSPITAL
CL HEALTH AND WELFARE
BT SPECIALIST HOSPITAL

EYE DEPARTMENT
UF Ophthalmic Department
CL HEALTH AND WELFARE
BT HOSPITAL DEPARTMENT

EYE HOSPITAL
UF Ophthalmic Hospital
CL HEALTH AND WELFARE
BT SPECIALIST HOSPITAL

Eyecatcher
    USE FOLLY

Fabric Mill
    USE TEXTILE MILL

FABRICATION SHED
SN Covered area for making large engineered
    constructions such as sections of ships or
    bridges.
CL INDUSTRIAL
BT ENGINEERING INDUSTRY SITE
RT AIRCRAFT FACTORY
    MOULD LOFT

PLATE RACK
PLATERS SHOP
RIVET AND TOOL SHOP
SHED
SHIPHOUSE FRAME

FABRICATION SHED
SN Covered area for making large engineered
    constructions such as sections of ships or
    bridges.
CL INDUSTRIAL
BT MARINE CONSTRUCTION SITE

FABRICATION SHED
SN Covered area for making large engineered
    constructions such as sections of ships or
    bridges.
CL MARITIME
BT MARINE CONSTRUCTION SITE

FACTORY
UF Factory Gate
    Factory Gate Lodge
    Manufactory
    Mill Lodge
SN Use specific monument type where known.
CL INDUSTRIAL
NT FACTORY <BY FORM>
    FACTORY <BY PRODUCT>
RT ASSEMBLY PLANT
    CANTEEN
    CHIMNEY
    ENGINE HOUSE
    FIRE ENGINE HOUSE
    FOOD AND DRINK INDUSTRY SITE
    FOREMANS HOUSE
    INDUSTRIAL ESTATE
    INDUSTRIAL SITE
    LIGHT ENGINEERING WORKS
    MANAGERS HOUSE
    PAY OFFICE
    RECREATIONAL HALL
    STEAM ENGINE
    TIMEKEEPERS OFFICE
    WATCH HOUSE
    WORKERS VILLAGE
    WORKS

FACTORY <BY FORM>
CL INDUSTRIAL
BT FACTORY
NT FACTORY UNIT
    FIREPROOF FACTORY
    MODEL FACTORY
    NORTH LIGHT FACTORY
    TENEMENT FACTORY

FACTORY <BY PRODUCT>
CL INDUSTRIAL
BT FACTORY
NT AIRCRAFT FACTORY
    BICYCLE FACTORY
    BLACKING FACTORY
    BRUSH FACTORY
    CANDLE FACTORY
    CANNING FACTORY
    CAR FACTORY
    CHEESE FACTORY
    CHINA FACTORY
    CHOCOLATE FACTORY
    CLOTHING FACTORY
    FISH PROCESSING FACTORY
    FLOORCLOTH FACTORY
    FOOD PROCESSING PLANT
    FURNITURE FACTORY
    GLOVE FACTORY
    GLUE FACTORY
    HAT FACTORY
    HORSEHAIR FACTORY

HOSIERY FACTORY
LEATHER FACTORY
LINOLEUM FACTORY
LORRY FACTORY
MATCH FACTORY
MINERAL WATER FACTORY
MOTOR CYCLE FACTORY
MUNITIONS FACTORY
MUSICAL INSTRUMENT FACTORY
NAIL FACTORY
NEEDLE FACTORY
ORDNANCE FACTORY
PAINT FACTORY
PIN FACTORY
PLASTICS FACTORY
RIBBON FACTORY
SCREW FACTORY
SHOE FACTORY
SOAP FACTORY
SUPERPHOSPHATE FACTORY
SWORD FACTORY
TALLOW FACTORY
TOBACCO FACTORY
TOY FACTORY
WALLPAPER FACTORY
WAX FACTORY

Factory Canteen
    USE CANTEEN

Factory Foremans House
    USE FOREMANS HOUSE

Factory Gate
    USE GATE
         FACTORY
    SN   Use both terms.

Factory Gate Lodge
    USE GATE LODGE
         FACTORY
    SN   Use both terms.

Factory Managers House
    USE MANAGERS HOUSE

Factory Masters House
    USE MANAGERS HOUSE

Factory Model Village
    USE WORKERS VILLAGE

FACTORY SHIP
    CL   MARITIME
    BT   FISHING VESSEL
    NT   FISH PROCESSING VESSEL
         WHALE PROCESSING SHIP

FACTORY UNIT
    CL   INDUSTRIAL
    BT   FACTORY <BY FORM>
    RT   CRAFT CENTRE
         LIGHT ENGINEERING WORKS

FACULTY BUILDING
    CL   EDUCATION
    RT   POLYTECHNIC
         TRAINING COLLEGE
         UNIVERSITY

FAIR
    UF   Fairground
         Funfair
    CL   RECREATIONAL

FAIRBAIRN JIB CRANE
    UF   Swanneck Crane
    CL   TRANSPORT
    BT   JIB CRANE

Fairground
    USE FAIR

FAIRLEAD
    SN   A pulley block and metal ring used to guide a line
         or rope and cause it to run easily without
         chafing.
    CL   MARITIME
    BT   DOCK AND HARBOUR INSTALLATION

FALCONRY
    CL   RECREATIONAL
    BT   HUNTING SITE

FALCONRY
    CL   AGRICULTURE AND SUBSISTENCE
    BT   HUNTING SITE

False Jetty
    USE FALSE QUAY

FALSE QUAY
    UF   False Jetty
         Hewn Jetty
    CL   MARITIME
    BT   QUAY

FAMILY VAULT
    CL   RELIGIOUS, RITUAL AND FUNERARY
    BT   BURIAL VAULT

FANCY BARROW
    CL   RELIGIOUS, RITUAL AND FUNERARY
    BT   ROUND BARROW
    NT   BELL DISC BARROW
         DISC BARROW
         SAUCER BARROW

Fanhouse
    USE EXHAUSTER HOUSE

FARM
    CL   AGRICULTURE AND SUBSISTENCE
    BT   LAND USE SITE
    NT   FARMSTEAD
         FERME ORNEE
         MANOR FARM
         MODEL FARM
         SILKWORM FARM
    RT   CELL
         CIDER PRESS
         CROFT
         DOUBLE HOUSE
         FARM BUILDING
         FARM LABOURERS COTTAGE
         FARMYARD
         FARMYARD CAUSEWAY
         GRANGE
         MANOR
         MESSUAGE
         MONASTERY
         NUNNERY
         PRECEPTORY
         SHEPHERDS HUT
         SHIELING
         SMALLHOLDING
         STACK STAND
         TOFT
         VILL
         VILLA (ROMAN)

FARM BUILDING
    CL   AGRICULTURE AND SUBSISTENCE
    BT   AGRICULTURAL BUILDING
    NT   ANIMAL SHED
         BARN
         BOILING HOUSE
         CHAFF HOUSE

CHITTING HOUSE
COMBINATION FARM BUILDING
FARMHOUSE
FODDER STORE
GRAIN DRIER
GRAIN SILO
GRASS DRYING SHED
HAYLOFT
HUNGER HOUSE
LAITHE
LAITHE HOUSE
LINHAY
LONG HOUSE
THRESHING MILL
RT FARM
OIL MILL
SHIELING

FARM LABOURERS COTTAGE
UF Agricultural Workers Cottage
Cote
Farm Workers Cottage
CL DOMESTIC
BT HOUSE <BY FUNCTION>
RT FARM
FARMHOUSE
LAITHE HOUSE
LONG HOUSE

Farm Workers Cottage
USE FARM LABOURERS COTTAGE

Farmery
USE ABBEY
PRIORY
INFIRMARY
SN Use INFIRMARY with ABBEY or PRIORY.

FARMHOUSE
UF Barton
CL DOMESTIC
BT HOUSE <BY FUNCTION>
RT BASTLE
FARM LABOURERS COTTAGE
GRANGE
LAITHE HOUSE
LONG HOUSE

FARMHOUSE
UF Barton
CL AGRICULTURE AND SUBSISTENCE
BT FARM BUILDING
RT BASTLE
FARM LABOURERS COTTAGE
GRANGE
LAITHE HOUSE
LONG HOUSE

FARMSTEAD
UF Steading
CL AGRICULTURE AND SUBSISTENCE
BT FARM
RT CROFT
VILL

FARMYARD
UF Courting
Fold Garth
Fold Yard
CL AGRICULTURE AND SUBSISTENCE
RT CREW YARD
FARM

FARMYARD CAUSEWAY
CL AGRICULTURE AND SUBSISTENCE
RT FARM

FATTENING HOUSE
UF Baconer House

CL AGRICULTURE AND SUBSISTENCE
BT FOOD AND DRINK PROCESSING SITE
RT HUNGER HOUSE

FEATURE
UF Cobbled Surface
SN Small areas of indeterminate function.
CL UNASSIGNED
NT LINEAR FEATURE
NATURAL FEATURE

FEED MILL
CL INDUSTRIAL
BT MILL

FELT MILL
CL INDUSTRIAL
BT TEXTILE MILL

FELT MILL
CL INDUSTRIAL
BT WOOL MANUFACTURING SITE
RT CARPET MILL
HAT FACTORY

FENCE
UF Boundary Fence
CL UNASSIGNED
RT BOUNDARY
RAILINGS

FENCING SCHOOL
CL RECREATIONAL
BT SPORTS BUILDING

FENCING SCHOOL
CL EDUCATION
BT TRAINING SCHOOL

FERME ORNEE
SN A rustic building of picturesque design, often associated with a model farm, country house, estate, etc.
CL GARDENS, PARKS AND URBAN SPACES
BT GARDEN BUILDING
RT COTTAGE ORNEE

FERME ORNEE
SN A rustic building of picturesque design, often associated with a model farm, country house, estate, etc.
CL AGRICULTURE AND SUBSISTENCE
BT FARM
RT COTTAGE ORNEE

FERMENTING BLOCK
UF Fermenting Tower
CL INDUSTRIAL
BT BREWING AND MALTING SITE
RT RACKING ROOM

Fermenting Tower
USE FERMENTING BLOCK

FERNERY (GARDEN)
SN Area of a garden for the cultivation of ferns.
CL GARDENS, PARKS AND URBAN SPACES
BT GARDEN

FERNERY (GLASSHOUSE)
SN A glasshouse for the cultivation of ferns.
CL GARDENS, PARKS AND URBAN SPACES
BT GLASSHOUSE

FERROUS METAL EXTRACTION SITE
SN Includes preliminary processing.
CL INDUSTRIAL
BT METAL INDUSTRY SITE
NT IRONSTONE MINE

IRONSTONE PIT
IRONSTONE WORKINGS
RT   IRONSTONE WORKINGS

FERROUS METAL PRODUCT SITE
SN   Manufacturing of products from ferrous metals.
CL   INDUSTRIAL
BT   METAL INDUSTRY SITE
NT   CHAIN PROVING HOUSE
CHAIN SHOP
CHAIN WORKS
COMB MILL
CUTLERY WORKS
EDGE TOOL WORKS
IRON FOUNDRY
LOCKSMITHS WORKSHOP
NAIL FACTORY
NAIL SHOP
NEEDLE MILL
PIN MILL
SCRAP YARD
SCREW FACTORY
SCREW MILL
SCYTHE MILL
SHEET METAL WORKS
SPRING SHOP
SPRING WORKS
STEEL WORKS
SWORD FACTORY
TUBE MILL
RT   CHAFERY
FINERY

FERROUS METAL SMELTING SITE
SN   Includes refining processes.
CL   INDUSTRIAL
BT   METAL INDUSTRY SITE
NT   BELLOWS HOUSE
CEMENTATION FURNACE
CUPOLA FURNACE (SHAFT)
FORGE
IRON ORE CALCINER
IRON WORKING SITE
IRON WORKS
SLAG HEAP
RT   BLAST FURNACE
BOWL FURNACE
CEMENTATION FURNACE
CRUCIBLE FURNACE
CUPELLATION FURNACE
CUPOLA FURNACE (SHAFT)
ELECTRIC ARC FURNACE
IRON FURNACE
OPEN HEARTH FURNACE
REVERBERATORY FURNACE
SHAFT FURNACE

FERRY
UF   Chain Ferry
SN   Includes associated structures.
CL   MARITIME
BT   PASSENGER VESSEL
RT   FERRYKEEPERS COTTAGE

FERRY TERMINAL
CL   MARITIME
BT   SEA TERMINAL

FERRYKEEPERS COTTAGE
CL   DOMESTIC
BT   TRANSPORT WORKERS HOUSE
RT   FERRY

Fertiliser Plant
USE FERTILISER WORKS

FERTILISER STOREHOUSE
CL   INDUSTRIAL
BT   AGRICULTURAL CHEMICAL SITE

RT   FERTILISER WORKS
STOREHOUSE

FERTILISER WORKS
UF   Fertiliser Plant
Guano Works
Manure Works
CL   INDUSTRIAL
BT   AGRICULTURAL CHEMICAL SITE
NT   SUPERPHOSPHATE FACTORY
RT   BONE MILL
FERTILISER STOREHOUSE
LIME KILN
LIME WORKS
NITRATE WORKS
POTASH KILN

Fever Hospital
USE INFECTIOUS DISEASES HOSPITAL

FIELD
CL   AGRICULTURE AND SUBSISTENCE
BT   LAND USE SITE
NT   CORD RIG
FIELD BOUNDARY
LYNCHET
PLOUGH HEADLAND
RIDGE AND FURROW
RT   CULTIVATION MARKS
FIELD BARN
FIELD SYSTEM

FIELD BARN
UF   Field House
CL   AGRICULTURE AND SUBSISTENCE
BT   BARN
RT   BANK BARN
CATTLE SHELTER
COMBINATION BARN
COW HOUSE
FIELD
HAYLOFT
LINHAY
OUTFARM
SHELTER SHED
VACCARY

FIELD BOUNDARY
UF   Field Wall
CL   AGRICULTURE AND SUBSISTENCE
BT   FIELD
RT   BOUNDARY
LYNCHET
RANCH BOUNDARY
REAVE

Field Clearance Cairn
USE CLEARANCE CAIRN

FIELD DRAIN
CL   WATER SUPPLY AND DRAINAGE
BT   DRAIN
RT   DRAIN SYPHON

Field House
USE FIELD BARN

FIELD KITCHEN
UF   Military Field Kitchen
SN   Use with MILITARY CAMP if existence of this is
known.
CL   DEFENCE

FIELD SYSTEM
UF   Trackway Field System
CL   AGRICULTURE AND SUBSISTENCE
BT   LAND USE SITE
NT   AGGREGATE FIELD SYSTEM
CELTIC FIELD SYSTEM

CENTURIATED AREA
COAXIAL FIELD SYSTEM
ENCLOSED FIELD SYSTEM
OPEN FIELD
WATER MEADOW
RT CAIRNFIELD
CLEARANCE CAIRN
CULTIVATION MARKS
CULTIVATION TERRACE
FIELD
LAZY BEDS

Field Wall
USE WALL
FIELD BOUNDARY
SN Use both terms.

FIELDWORK
UF Military Earthwork
SN Military earthwork of unspecifiable type.
CL DEFENCE
RT EARTHWORK
FORTIFICATION

FIFTH RATE SHIP OF THE LINE
CL MARITIME
BT SHIP OF THE LINE

FIFTH RATE SHIP OF THE LINE
CL MARITIME
BT MINOR WARSHIP

Filling Station
USE PETROL STATION

FILM STUDIO
UF Studio
CL COMMUNICATIONS
RT TELEVISION STUDIO

FILTER BED
CL WATER SUPPLY AND DRAINAGE
RT FILTER HOUSE
PURIFIER
SEWAGE WORKS
WATERWORKS

FILTER HOUSE
CL WATER SUPPLY AND DRAINAGE
RT FILTER BED
PURIFIER
SEWAGE WORKS
WATERWORKS

Fine Art Academy
USE ART SCHOOL

FINERY
SN Decarburizing of pig iron in a hearth to produce
wrought iron.
CL INDUSTRIAL
BT FORGE
RT FERROUS METAL PRODUCT SITE
TILT HAMMER

Finger Post
USE SIGNPOST

FINISHING HOUSE
SN Building or area where processes like bleaching,
dressing, etc, are conducted under one roof.
CL INDUSTRIAL
BT TEXTILE FINISHING SITE
RT CLOTH DRESSING MILL
FINISHING WORKS
FULLING MILL

FINISHING WORKS
SN Large scale works for cloth finishing processes.
CL INDUSTRIAL

BT TEXTILE MILL

FINISHING WORKS
SN Large scale works for cloth finishing processes.
CL INDUSTRIAL
BT TEXTILE FINISHING SITE
RT CLOTH DRESSING MILL
DYE HOUSE
FINISHING HOUSE

Fire Beacon
USE BEACON

FIRE CLAY WORKS
SN Production of bricks, principally, but also other
items, from a clay with refractory properties.
CL INDUSTRIAL
BT BRICK AND TILEMAKING SITE

FIRE CLAY WORKS
SN Production of bricks, principally, but also other
items, from a clay with refractory properties.
CL INDUSTRIAL
BT POTTERY MANUFACTURING SITE
RT PIPE WORKSHOP
POTTERY WORKS

FIRE ENGINE HOUSE
CL TRANSPORT
RT FACTORY
FIRE STATION
GUNPOWDER WORKS

FIRE FIGHTING TUG
CL MARITIME
BT FIRE FIGHTING VESSEL

FIRE FIGHTING TUG
CL MARITIME
BT TUG

FIRE FIGHTING VESSEL
CL MARITIME
BT SAFETY CRAFT
NT FIRE FIGHTING TUG

FIRE HYDRANT
CL GARDENS, PARKS AND URBAN SPACES
BT STREET FURNITURE

Fire Office
USE COMMERCIAL OFFICE

FIRE STATION
CL CIVIL
RT FIRE ENGINE HOUSE
HOSE TOWER

FIRE STATION
CL TRANSPORT
RT FIRE ENGINE HOUSE
HOSE TOWER

FIREPROOF BUILDING
CL INDUSTRIAL
BT INDUSTRIAL BUILDING
RT FIREPROOF FACTORY
TEXTILE MILL

FIREPROOF FACTORY
UF Fireproof Mill
CL INDUSTRIAL
BT FACTORY <BY FORM>
RT FIREPROOF BUILDING
MATCH FACTORY
TEXTILE MILL

Fireproof Mill
USE FIREPROOF FACTORY

FIRESHIP
CL MARITIME
BT WARSHIP

FIRING RANGE
UF Rifle Range
CL DEFENCE
RT BUTTS

FIRING RANGE
UF Rifle Range
CL RECREATIONAL
BT SPORTS SITE
RT ARMY CAMP
    ARTILLERY GROUND
    BUTTS

Firing Target
USE TARGET

FIRST FLOOR HALL HOUSE
UF Upper Floor Hall House
CL DOMESTIC
BT HALL HOUSE

FIRST RATE SHIP OF THE LINE
CL MARITIME
BT SHIP OF THE LINE

FIRST RATE SHIP OF THE LINE
CL MARITIME
BT CAPITAL WARSHIP

FISH AND CHIP SHOP
CL COMMERCIAL
BT TAKE AWAY
RT EATING HOUSE
    RESTAURANT

FISH CELLAR
CL AGRICULTURE AND SUBSISTENCE
BT FOOD AND DRINK PROCESSING SITE

FISH CELLAR
CL INDUSTRIAL
BT FOOD PRESERVING SITE

Fish Curing House
USE SMOKE HOUSE

Fish Factory
USE FOOD PROCESSING PLANT

FISH FARM
UF Trout Farm
SN A farm which is artificially stocked with fish.
CL AGRICULTURE AND SUBSISTENCE
BT FISHING SITE

FISH GARTH
UF Garth
CL AGRICULTURE AND SUBSISTENCE
BT FISHERY

FISH HOUSE
CL AGRICULTURE AND SUBSISTENCE
BT FOOD AND DRINK PROCESSING SITE
RT GAME LARDER
    ICEHOUSE
    LARDER
    SMOKE HOUSE

FISH LADDER
UF Salmon Ladder
CL AGRICULTURE AND SUBSISTENCE
BT FISHERY
RT EEL TRAP
    WEIR

FISH LOCK
CL AGRICULTURE AND SUBSISTENCE
BT FISHERY
RT EEL TRAP

FISH MARKET
CL COMMERCIAL
BT MARKET
RT FISH STONE

FISH POND
UF Fish Sorting Tank
    Stew
    Stews
    Vivarium
SN Includes various types of pond used in fish breeding, sorting and storing.
CL WATER SUPPLY AND DRAINAGE
BT POND
RT MOAT

FISH POND
UF Fish Sorting Tank
    Stew
    Stews
    Vivarium
SN Includes various types of pond used in fish breeding, sorting and storing.
CL AGRICULTURE AND SUBSISTENCE
BT FISHING SITE

FISH PROCESSING FACTORY
CL INDUSTRIAL
BT FACTORY <BY PRODUCT>
RT CURING HOUSE
    FOOD PROCESSING PLANT

FISH PROCESSING SITE
CL AGRICULTURE AND SUBSISTENCE
BT FOOD AND DRINK PROCESSING SITE

Fish Processing Unit
USE FOOD PROCESSING PLANT

FISH PROCESSING VESSEL
CL MARITIME
BT FACTORY SHIP

Fish Smoking House
USE SMOKE HOUSE

Fish Sorting Tank
USE FISH POND

FISH STONE
CL COMMERCIAL
RT FISH MARKET

FISH TANK
SN A small brick structure attached to house for keeping fish prior to cooking.
CL DOMESTIC

FISH TRAP
CL AGRICULTURE AND SUBSISTENCE
BT FISHERY

FISH WAREHOUSE
CL COMMERCIAL
BT WAREHOUSE
RT COLD STORE
    SMOKE HOUSE

FISH WEIR
CL AGRICULTURE AND SUBSISTENCE
BT FISHERY
NT COASTAL FISH WEIR
RT EEL TRAP

FISHERIES PROTECTION CRAFT
  CL MARITIME
  BT MARITIME CRAFT
  NT FISHERIES PROTECTION VESSEL

FISHERIES PROTECTION VESSEL
  CL MARITIME
  BT FISHERIES PROTECTION CRAFT

FISHERMANS HOUSE
  CL DOMESTIC
  BT MARITIME HOUSE
  RT COASTGUARDS COTTAGE
      MARINERS COTTAGE
      NET HOUSE

FISHERMANS MISSION VESSEL
  CL MARITIME
  BT FISHING VESSEL

FISHERMENS FASTENER
  SN An unidentified feature on the seabed recorded by
      fishermen as an obstruction to trawling.
  CL MARITIME

FISHERY
  UF River Fishery
  SN Where fish are naturally present, eg. part of a
      river.
  CL RECREATIONAL

FISHERY
  UF River Fishery
  SN Where fish are naturally present, eg. part of a
      river.
  CL AGRICULTURE AND SUBSISTENCE
  BT FISHING SITE
  NT FISH GARTH
      FISH LADDER
      FISH LOCK
      FISH TRAP
      FISH WEIR
      FISHERY MOUND
      FISHING BAULK

FISHERY MOUND
  CL AGRICULTURE AND SUBSISTENCE
  BT FISHERY
  RT MOUND

FISHING BAULK
  CL AGRICULTURE AND SUBSISTENCE
  BT FISHERY

FISHING DREDGER
  CL MARITIME
  BT FISHING VESSEL
  NT OYSTER DREDGER

FISHING LODGE
  UF Fishing Temple
      Lodge
  CL GARDENS, PARKS AND URBAN SPACES
  BT GARDEN BUILDING
  RT WATER PAVILION

FISHING LODGE
  UF Fishing Temple
      Lodge
  CL RECREATIONAL

FISHING PAVILION
  CL GARDENS, PARKS AND URBAN SPACES
  BT PAVILION
  RT WATER PAVILION

FISHING SITE
  CL AGRICULTURE AND SUBSISTENCE

  NT EEL TRAP
      FISH FARM
      FISH POND
      FISHERY
      NET HOUSE
      NET LOFT
      OYSTER BEDS

Fishing Temple
  USE FISHING LODGE

FISHING VESSEL
  CL MARITIME
  BT MARITIME CRAFT
  NT FACTORY SHIP
      FISHERMANS MISSION VESSEL
      FISHING DREDGER
      LINE FISHING VESSEL
      NET FISHING VESSEL
      POT HAULER
      SEAL FISHERIES VESSEL
      WHALER

FISHMONGERS SHOP
  CL COMMERCIAL
  BT SHOP

FITTERS WORKSHOP
  SN Engineering workshop intended either for final
      adjustments of new machinery or the fitting of
      replacement parts to machinery under repair.
  CL INDUSTRIAL
  BT HEAVY ENGINEERING SITE
  RT ENGINEERING WORKSHOP
      FORGE
      MACHINE SHOP
      TURNING SHOP

FIVES COURT
  UF Eton Fives Court
  CL RECREATIONAL
  BT SPORTS SITE

FIXED QUAY CRANE
  CL TRANSPORT
  BT QUAY CRANE

Flag Pole
  USE FLAGPOLE

FLAG SHIP
  CL MARITIME
  BT CAPITAL WARSHIP

FLAGPOLE
  UF Flag Pole
  CL GARDENS, PARKS AND URBAN SPACES
  BT STREET FURNITURE

FLANKER
  CL DEFENCE
  RT BASTION
      BATTERY

FLANKING TOWER
  SN Small tower projecting from a castle wall, or
      other fortified wall. Allows defenders to fire
      along the length of the wall.
  CL DEFENCE
  RT ANGLE TOWER

FLASH LOCK
  CL TRANSPORT
  BT LOCK
  RT STAUNCH
      WEIR

Flat
  USE APARTMENT

Flat Grave Cemetery
  USE CEMETERY

FLATS
  UF Block Of Flats
  CL DOMESTIC
  BT MULTIPLE DWELLING
  NT COUNCIL FLATS
      MANSION FLATS
  RT CLUSTER BLOCK
      COMMUNAL BAKEHOUSE
      MAISONETTE
      RECREATIONAL HALL
      TENANTS HALL
      TENEMENT BLOCK
      TENEMENT HOUSE

Flatted Factory
  USE TENEMENT FACTORY

FLAX BEATING STONE
  CL INDUSTRIAL
  BT LINEN OR FLAX MANUFACTURING SITE
  RT CLOTHIERS WORKSHOP
      HOSIERY WORKSHOP
      LACE DRYING HOUSE
      LOOMSHOP
      TENTER GROUND
      TENTER POST
      WEAVERS COTTAGE
      WOOL WALL

FLAX DRESSING SHOP
  UF Heckling Shop
  CL INDUSTRIAL
  BT TEXTILE MILL

FLAX DRESSING SHOP
  UF Heckling Shop
  CL INDUSTRIAL
  BT LINEN OR FLAX MANUFACTURING SITE

FLAX DRY HOUSE
  CL INDUSTRIAL
  BT LINEN OR FLAX MANUFACTURING SITE
  RT DRY HOUSE
      TENTER GROUND

FLAX DRY SHED
  CL INDUSTRIAL
  BT LINEN OR FLAX MANUFACTURING SITE
  RT SCUTCHING MILL
      SHED

FLAX MILL
  UF Flax Spinning Mill
  CL INDUSTRIAL
  BT TEXTILE MILL

FLAX MILL
  UF Flax Spinning Mill
  CL INDUSTRIAL
  BT LINEN OR FLAX MANUFACTURING SITE
  RT BEETLING MILL
      CALENDER MILL
      SCUTCHING MILL
      THROWING MILL

Flax Retting Pit
  USE RETTING PIT

Flax Spinning Mill
  USE FLAX MILL

FLEA MARKET
  CL COMMERCIAL
  BT MARKET

FLEECING SHOP

  CL INDUSTRIAL
  BT ANIMAL PRODUCT SITE
  RT TANNERY

FLEET SUBMARINE
  CL MARITIME
  BT SUBMARINE

Flesh Market
  USE MEAT MARKET

Flexed Burial
  USE FLEXED INHUMATION

FLEXED INHUMATION
  UF Flexed Burial
  SN Inhumation with leg joints bent by angle of less
      than ninety degrees.
  CL RELIGIOUS, RITUAL AND FUNERARY
  BT INHUMATION

Flint Knapping Site
  USE FLINT WORKING SITE

FLINT MILL
  CL INDUSTRIAL
  BT POTTERY MANUFACTURING SITE
  RT COLOUR MILL
      POTTERY WORKS
      SALT WORKS

FLINT MILL
  CL INDUSTRIAL
  BT MILL
  RT GRINDSTONE

FLINT MINE
  CL INDUSTRIAL
  BT MINE

FLINT SCATTER
  CL UNASSIGNED
  RT FLINT WORKING SITE

FLINT WORKING SITE
  UF Chipping Floor
      Clipping Floor
      Flint Knapping Site
      Knapping Site
  CL INDUSTRIAL
  BT STONE WORKING SITE
  RT FLINT SCATTER

FLOATING BREAKWATER
  CL MARITIME
  BT HARBOUR

FLOATING CRANE
  CL INDUSTRIAL
  BT MARINE CONSTRUCTION SITE
  RT DOCKYARD
      MARINE ENGINEERING WORKS
      SHIP REPAIR WORKS

FLOATING CRANE
  CL TRANSPORT
  BT CRANE <BY FORM>

FLOATING CRANE
  CL MARITIME
  BT MARINE CONSTRUCTION SITE

FLOATING DOCK
  UF Floating Platform
  CL MARITIME
  BT DOCK

FLOATING DOCK
  UF Floating Platform

CL   MARITIME
BT   HARBOUR SERVICES VESSEL

FLOATING GRAIN ELEVATOR
CL   TRANSPORT
BT   GRAIN ELEVATOR

FLOATING HARBOUR
UF   Phoenix Unit
CL   MARITIME
BT   HARBOUR

Floating Platform
USE FLOATING DOCK

FLOCK MILL
CL   INDUSTRIAL
BT   TEXTILE MILL

FLOCK MILL
CL   INDUSTRIAL
BT   TEXTILE PRODUCT SITE
RT   MUNGO MILL
     PAPER MILL
     SHODDY MILL
     WOOLLEN MILL

Flood Bank
USE FLOOD DEFENCES

Flood Barrier
USE FLOOD DEFENCES

FLOOD DEFENCES
UF   Dike
     Dyke (Water)
     Flood Bank
     Flood Barrier
     River Bank
     River Defences
     River Embankment
     River Wall
CL   WATER SUPPLY AND DRAINAGE
RT   SEA DEFENCES

FLOOD LOCK
CL   TRANSPORT
BT   LOCK

FLOOD RELIEF CANAL
CL   WATER SUPPLY AND DRAINAGE
BT   CANAL
RT   EMBANKMENT

FLOOR
CL   UNASSIGNED
NT   TESSELATED FLOOR

FLOORCLOTH FACTORY
CL   INDUSTRIAL
BT   FACTORY <BY PRODUCT>

FLOORCLOTH FACTORY
CL   INDUSTRIAL
BT   CARPET MANUFACTURING SITE
RT   CANVAS WORKS
     LINOLEUM FACTORY

FLORAL CLOCK
CL   GARDENS, PARKS AND URBAN SPACES

Floral Market
USE FLOWER MARKET

FLORISTS SHOP
CL   COMMERCIAL
BT   SHOP

FLOUR MILL

UF   Bolting House
     Boulting House
CL   INDUSTRIAL
BT   FOOD PROCESSING SITE
RT   BAKERY
     GRANARY

FLOUR MILL
UF   Bolting House
     Boulting House
CL   INDUSTRIAL
BT   MILL

FLOWER BED
CL   GARDENS, PARKS AND URBAN SPACES
NT   CARPET BED
     RAISED BED
RT   MIXED BORDER

Flower Conservatory
USE CONSERVATORY

FLOWER GARDEN
UF   Dahlia Garden
     Hyacinth Garden
CL   GARDENS, PARKS AND URBAN SPACES
BT   GARDEN
NT   ROSE GARDEN

FLOWER MARKET
UF   Floral Market
CL   COMMERCIAL
BT   MARKET

Flue
USE SHAFT

FLUORSPAR MINE
UF   Blue John Mine
SN   When a secondary mineral, use term for product
     type, eg. LEAD MINE.
CL   INDUSTRIAL
BT   MINERAL EXTRACTION SITE
RT   FLUORSPAR WORKINGS
     LEAD MINE
     ZINC MINE

FLUORSPAR MINE
UF   Blue John Mine
SN   When a secondary mineral, use term for product
     type, eg. LEAD MINE.
CL   INDUSTRIAL
BT   MINE

FLUORSPAR WORKINGS
CL   INDUSTRIAL
BT   MINERAL EXTRACTION SITE
RT   FLUORSPAR MINE
     LEAD WORKINGS

Flying Boat Warehouse
USE HANGAR

FLYOVER
CL   TRANSPORT
BT   ROAD TRANSPORT SITE
RT   BRIDGE
     ROAD
     ROAD BRIDGE
     ROAD JUNCTION
     ROAD TUNNEL
     ROAD VIADUCT
     UNDERPASS

Fodder Preparation Area
USE FODDER STORE

FODDER STORE
UF   Fodder Preparation Area

Provender Store
Root Room
CL   AGRICULTURE AND SUBSISTENCE
BT   FARM BUILDING
RT   CHAFF HOUSE
     GRASS DRYING SHED

FOG DISPERSAL PLANT
CL   TRANSPORT
BT   AIR TRANSPORT SITE
RT   CONTROL TOWER
     TEST HOUSE

FOGOU
UF   Fougou
SN   Underground chambers and stone passages of Iron
     Age date found in South West England.
CL   DOMESTIC
RT   HULL
     SOUTERRAIN
     UNDERGROUND STRUCTURE

FOGOU
UF   Fougou
SN   Underground chambers and stone passages of Iron
     Age date found in South West England.
CL   RELIGIOUS, RITUAL AND FUNERARY
RT   HULL
     SOUTERRAIN
     UNDERGROUND STRUCTURE

Fold Garth
USE FARMYARD

Fold Yard
USE FARMYARD

Folk Moot
USE MOOT

FOLLY
UF   Artificial Ruin
     Eyecatcher
     Sham Castle
     Sham Ruin
     Vista Closer
CL   GARDENS, PARKS AND URBAN SPACES
BT   GARDEN BUILDING
RT   GROTTO

FONT
SN   Use a broader monument type if possible.
CL   RELIGIOUS, RITUAL AND FUNERARY
RT   BAPTISTERY

Fontevraultine Alien Priory
USE FONTEVRAULTINE DOUBLE HOUSE
    ALIEN PRIORY
SN   Use both terms.

FONTEVRAULTINE DOUBLE HOUSE
UF   Fontevraultine Alien Priory
     Fontevraultine Priory
SN   Priories of double order of Fontevrault nuns and
     brethren.
CL   RELIGIOUS, RITUAL AND FUNERARY
BT   DOUBLE HOUSE

Fontevraultine Priory
USE FONTEVRAULTINE DOUBLE HOUSE
    PRIORY
SN   Use both terms.

FOOD AND DRINK INDUSTRY SITE
CL   INDUSTRIAL
NT   BREWING AND MALTING SITE
     DISTILLING SITE
     FOOD PRESERVING SITE
     FOOD PROCESSING SITE

FOOD PRODUCTION SITE
MINERAL WATER FACTORY
MINERAL WATER WORKS
WINE AND CIDERMAKING SITE
RT   FACTORY

FOOD AND DRINK PROCESSING SITE
SN   Terms included here are for small scale
     agricultural production. See also FOOD AND DRINK
     INDUSTRY SITE grouping in INDUSTRIAL class.
CL   AGRICULTURE AND SUBSISTENCE
BT   AGRICULTURAL BUILDING
NT   BREWHOUSE
     BUTTERY
     CIDER MILL
     CIDER PRESS
     CIDER VAULT
     DAIRY
     FATTENING HOUSE
     FISH CELLAR
     FISH HOUSE
     FISH PROCESSING SITE
     GRANARY
     HOP HOUSE
     HOP KILN
     HOP STORE
     MALT HOUSE
     MALT KILN
     MILKING PARLOUR
     MILKING SHED
     OASTHOUSE

FOOD DRYING KILN
CL   INDUSTRIAL
BT   FOOD PRESERVING SITE
NT   CHICORY KILN
RT   FOOD PROCESSING PLANT

FOOD DRYING KILN
CL   INDUSTRIAL
BT   DRYING KILN

FOOD PRESERVING FACTORY
CL   INDUSTRIAL
BT   FOOD PRESERVING SITE

FOOD PRESERVING SITE
CL   INDUSTRIAL
BT   FOOD AND DRINK INDUSTRY SITE
NT   BOTTLING PLANT
     CANNING FACTORY
     COLD STORE
     CURING HOUSE
     FISH CELLAR
     FOOD DRYING KILN
     FOOD PRESERVING FACTORY
     ICE WORKS
     REFRIGERATED STORE
     SMOKE HOUSE

FOOD PROCESSING PLANT
UF   Bacon Factory
     Cattle Fodder Factory
     Fish Factory
     Fish Processing Unit
     Margarine Factory
CL   INDUSTRIAL
BT   FACTORY <BY PRODUCT>

FOOD PROCESSING PLANT
UF   Bacon Factory
     Cattle Fodder Factory
     Fish Factory
     Fish Processing Unit
     Margarine Factory
CL   INDUSTRIAL
BT   FOOD PROCESSING SITE
RT   CANNING FACTORY
     FISH PROCESSING FACTORY

FOOD DRYING KILN

FOOD PROCESSING SITE
    CL   INDUSTRIAL
    BT   FOOD AND DRINK INDUSTRY SITE
    NT   ABATTOIR
          BAKERY
          CONDENSERY
          CORN DRYING KILN
          CORN DRYING OVEN
          CORN MILL
          CURING HOUSE
          FLOUR MILL
          FOOD PROCESSING PLANT
          OIL MILL
          SUGAR HOUSE
          SUGAR REFINERY

FOOD PRODUCTION SITE
    CL   INDUSTRIAL
    BT   FOOD AND DRINK INDUSTRY SITE
    NT   CHEESE FACTORY
          CHOCOLATE FACTORY
          CONFECTIONERY WORKS
          MUSTARD MILL

Foot Bridge
    USE FOOTBRIDGE

FOOT HOSPITAL
    CL   HEALTH AND WELFARE
    BT   SPECIALIST HOSPITAL

Foot Scraper
    USE BOOT SCRAPER

Foot Tunnel
    USE PEDESTRIAN TUNNEL

FOOTBALL GROUND
    CL   RECREATIONAL
    BT   SPORTS GROUND
    RT   FOOTBALL PITCH
          FOOTBALL TERRACE
          GRANDSTAND
          STADIUM

FOOTBALL PITCH
    CL   RECREATIONAL
    BT   SPORTS SITE
    RT   FOOTBALL GROUND

Football Stadium
    USE STADIUM

Football Stand
    USE GRANDSTAND

FOOTBALL TERRACE
    CL   RECREATIONAL
    BT   SPORTS SITE
    RT   FOOTBALL GROUND
          GRANDSTAND

FOOTBRIDGE
    UF   Foot Bridge
          Pedestrian Bridge
    CL   TRANSPORT
    BT   BRIDGE <BY FUNCTION>

FOOTBRIDGE
    UF   Foot Bridge
          Pedestrian Bridge
    CL   TRANSPORT
    BT   PEDESTRIAN TRANSPORT SITE

FOOTPATH
    CL   TRANSPORT
    BT   PEDESTRIAN TRANSPORT SITE

    RT   PAVEMENT
          STEPS
          TOW PATH

FORD
    CL   TRANSPORT
    BT   ROAD TRANSPORT SITE
    RT   STEPPING STONES
          WEIR

FOREIGN LANGUAGE INSTITUTE
    UF   French Institute
          German Institute
    CL   EDUCATION
    BT   INSTITUTE

FOREIGN LANGUAGE INSTITUTE
    UF   French Institute
          German Institute
    CL   INSTITUTIONAL
    BT   INSTITUTE

Foreign Office
    USE GOVERNMENT OFFICE

FOREMANS HOUSE
    UF   Factory Foremans House
          Overlookers House
          Overseers House
    CL   DOMESTIC
    BT   HOUSE <BY FUNCTION>
    RT   FACTORY
          MANAGERS HOUSE
          WORKERS COTTAGE

FOREMANS HOUSE
    UF   Factory Foremans House
          Overlookers House
          Overseers House
    CL   DOMESTIC
    BT   INDUSTRIAL HOUSE
    RT   FACTORY
          WORKERS COTTAGE

FOREMANS HOUSE
    UF   Factory Foremans House
          Overlookers House
          Overseers House
    CL   INDUSTRIAL
    BT   INDUSTRIAL HOUSE

Forest Court
    USE LAW COURT

FORGE
    UF   Forge House
          Forge Mill
          Iron Forge
          Steel Forge
    CL   INDUSTRIAL
    BT   HEAVY ENGINEERING SITE
    RT   CHAIN SHOP
          CHAIN WORKS
          EDGE TOOL WORKS
          ENGINEERING WORKSHOP
          FITTERS WORKSHOP
          FOUNDRY
          HAMMER
          HAMMER POND
          HELVE HAMMER
          IRON WORKS
          NAIL FACTORY
          NAIL SHOP
          RAILWAY ENGINEERING SITE
          SLITTING MILL
          SMITHS COTTAGE
          TUMBLING WEIR
          WEIR

FORGE

UF   Forge House
      Forge Mill
      Iron Forge
      Steel Forge
CL   INDUSTRIAL
BT   FERROUS METAL SMELTING SITE
NT   CHAFERY
      FINERY
RT   SCYTHE MILL
      TUMBLING WEIR

Forge House
   USE FORGE

Forge Mill
   USE FORGE

Fork Factory
   USE CUTLERY WORKS

FORMAL GARDEN
CL   GARDENS, PARKS AND URBAN SPACES
BT   GARDEN
RT   GARDEN TERRACE
      HA HA
      PARTERRE

FORT
UF   Earthen Artillery Fort
      Praetentura
      Praetorium
      Roman Fort
SN   Permanently occupied by military forces.
CL   DEFENCE
NT   ARTILLERY FORT
      AUXILIARY FORT
      BASTION TRACE FORT
      FORT ANNEXE
      SAXON SHORE FORT
      STAR FORT
      VEXILLATION FORT
RT   ARTILLERY CASTLE
      BARRACKS
      BASTION
      BATH HOUSE
      FORTRESS
      FRONTIER DEFENCE
      GUN EMPLACEMENT
      PARADE GROUND
      TEMPORARY CAMP
      VICUS

FORT ANNEXE
CL   DEFENCE
BT   FORT

FORTIFICATION
SN   Unspecified type. Use specific type(s) where
      known. Use FIELDWORK for unspecified military
      earthworks.
CL   DEFENCE
RT   FIELDWORK

FORTIFIED CHURCH
CL   RELIGIOUS, RITUAL AND FUNERARY
BT   CHURCH

FORTIFIED HOUSE
CL   DOMESTIC
BT   HOUSE < BY FORM >
NT   BASTLE
      FORTIFIED MANOR HOUSE
      PELE TOWER
      TOWER HOUSE
RT   CASTLE

FORTIFIED HOUSE
CL   DEFENCE
NT   BASTLE

FORTIFIED MANOR HOUSE
PELE TOWER
TOWER HOUSE

FORTIFIED MANOR HOUSE
CL   DOMESTIC
BT   FORTIFIED HOUSE
RT   MANOR HOUSE

FORTIFIED MANOR HOUSE
CL   DEFENCE
BT   FORTIFIED HOUSE

Fortilace
   USE FORTLET

FORTLET
UF   Fortilace
      Roman Fortlet
CL   DEFENCE
NT   MILECASTLE
      MILEFORTLET
RT   AUXILIARY FORT
      FRONTIER DEFENCE
      SIGNAL STATION

FORTRESS
UF   Coastal Fort
      Land Fort
SN   If Roman use LEGIONARY FORTRESS.
CL   DEFENCE
NT   LEGIONARY FORTRESS
RT   BASTION
      BLOCKHOUSE
      CASTLE
      FORT
      GUN EMPLACEMENT
      GUNPOST
      SCONCE
      SHIFTING HOUSE
      TOWN DEFENCES

FORUM
CL   CIVIL
RT   BASILICA

FORUM
CL   COMMERCIAL
RT   BASILICA

Fougou
   USE FOGOU

Foundation
   USE BUILDING
SN   Where building foundation use specific site type
      where known.

Foundling Hospital
   USE ORPHANAGE

Foundling Hospital Chapel
   USE CHAPEL
        ORPHANAGE
SN   Use both terms.

Foundling Hospital School
   USE ORPHAN SCHOOL

FOUNDRY
UF   Cannon Foundry
      Gun Foundry
CL   INDUSTRIAL
BT   HEAVY ENGINEERING SITE
RT   AGRICULTURAL ENGINEERING WORKS
      ARSENAL
      BLAST FURNACE
      BOILER SHOP
      CANNON BORING MILL

CAR FACTORY
FORGE
FURNACE
GUN TESTING SHOP
IRON FOUNDRY
LORRY FACTORY
MINT
ORDNANCE FACTORY
PATTERN SHOP
STEEL WORKS

FOUNTAIN
- CL GARDENS, PARKS AND URBAN SPACES
- NT ORNAMENTAL FOUNTAIN
  SHELL FOUNTAIN
  TRICK FOUNTAIN
- RT CASCADE
  FOUNTAIN HOUSE
  GARDEN ORNAMENT
  WATER GARDEN

FOUNTAIN
- CL WATER SUPPLY AND DRAINAGE
- NT DRINKING FOUNTAIN
  ORNAMENTAL FOUNTAIN
  SHELL FOUNTAIN
  TRICK FOUNTAIN
- RT CASCADE
  CASCADE HOUSE
  FOUNTAIN HOUSE
  WATER GARDEN

FOUNTAIN HOUSE
- CL GARDENS, PARKS AND URBAN SPACES
- BT GARDEN BUILDING
- RT CASCADE
  CASCADE HOUSE
  FOUNTAIN
  WATER GARDEN
  WATER PAVILION

Four Poster
  USE FOUR POSTER STONE CIRCLE

FOUR POSTER STONE CIRCLE
- UF Four Poster
- CL RELIGIOUS, RITUAL AND FUNERARY
- BT STONE CIRCLE

FOURTH RATE SHIP OF THE LINE
- CL MARITIME
- BT SHIP OF THE LINE

FOURTH RATE SHIP OF THE LINE
- CL MARITIME
- BT MINOR WARSHIP

Fowl House
  USE POULTRY HOUSE

FRAGRANCE GARDEN
- CL GARDENS, PARKS AND URBAN SPACES
- BT GARDEN

Frame Knitters Workshop
  USE FRAMEWORK KNITTERS COTTAGE

Frameshop
  USE FRAMEWORK KNITTERS COTTAGE

FRAMEWORK KNITTERS COTTAGE
- UF Frame Knitters Workshop
  Frameshop
  Framework Knitters House
  Knitters Workshop
- CL DOMESTIC
- BT INDUSTRIAL HOUSE
- RT HOSIERS COTTAGE
  HOSIERY WORKSHOP

TOPSHOP

FRAMEWORK KNITTERS COTTAGE
- UF Frame Knitters Workshop
  Frameshop
  Framework Knitters House
  Knitters Workshop
- CL INDUSTRIAL
- BT CRAFT INDUSTRY SITE
- RT HOSIERS COTTAGE
  TOPSHOP

FRAMEWORK KNITTERS COTTAGE
- UF Frame Knitters Workshop
  Frameshop
  Framework Knitters House
  Knitters Workshop
- CL INDUSTRIAL
- BT INDUSTRIAL HOUSE

Framework Knitters House
  USE FRAMEWORK KNITTERS COTTAGE

Franciscan Abbey
  USE ABBEY
      FRANCISCAN NUNNERY
- SN Use both terms.

FRANCISCAN FRIARY
- UF Minories
- SN Includes houses of both Friars Minor and Friars
  Observant or Capuchins.
- CL RELIGIOUS, RITUAL AND FUNERARY
- BT FRIARY
- RT FRANCISCAN NUNNERY

FRANCISCAN NUNNERY
- UF Franciscan Abbey
- SN Abbeys of Franciscan nuns also known as Minoresses
  or Poor Clares.
- CL RELIGIOUS, RITUAL AND FUNERARY
- BT NUNNERY
- RT FRANCISCAN FRIARY

FRATER
- CL DOMESTIC
- RT ABBEY
  FRIARY
  MONASTERY
  NUNNERY
  PRIORY
  REFECTORY

Free Grammar School
  USE GRAMMAR SCHOOL

Free Library
  USE PUBLIC LIBRARY

FREE METHODIST CHAPEL
- CL RELIGIOUS, RITUAL AND FUNERARY
- BT METHODIST CHAPEL

FREE SCHOOL
- CL EDUCATION
- BT ELEMENTARY SCHOOL
- NT BENEFICIAL SCHOOL
  CHARITY SCHOOL
  HOSPITAL SCHOOL
  ORPHAN SCHOOL
  PAUPER SCHOOL
  RAGGED SCHOOL

Freemasons Asylum
  USE ALMSHOUSE

FREEMASONS HALL
- UF Freemasons Lodge
  Freemasons Temple

Masonic Hall
Masonic Lodge
Masons Hall
Masons Lodge
Masons Temple
CL   INSTITUTIONAL
BT   MEETING HALL

Freemasons Lodge
USE FREEMASONS HALL

Freemasons Temple
USE FREEMASONS HALL

Freestore
USE WAREHOUSE

FREIGHTER
CL   MARITIME
BT   CARGO VESSEL
NT   LIVESTOCK SHIP
         REFRIGERATED FREIGHTER

French Institute
USE FOREIGN LANGUAGE INSTITUTE

FRENCH PROTESTANT CHURCH
UF   Protestant Church
CL   RELIGIOUS, RITUAL AND FUNERARY
BT   CHURCH

French Protestant School
USE CHURCH SCHOOL

Friars Church
USE CHURCH
         FRIARY
SN   Use both terms.

FRIARY
UF   Friars Church
         Friary Church
         Friary De Ordine Martyrum
         Friary Gatehouse
SN   Houses specifically for men and of chiefly
         mendicant religious orders. The status of priory
         is represented in several friaries. Use with
         PRIORY if required.
CL   RELIGIOUS, RITUAL AND FUNERARY
BT   RELIGIOUS HOUSE
NT   AUSTIN FRIARY
         CARMELITE FRIARY
         DOMINICAN FRIARY
         FRANCISCAN FRIARY
         FRIARY OF CRUTCHED FRIARS
         FRIARY OF FRIARS OF THE SACK
         FRIARY OF PIED FRIARS
RT   ABBEY
         ALMONRY
         CATHEDRAL
         CHAPTER HOUSE
         DOUBLE HOUSE
         FRATER
         GATEHOUSE
         GUEST HOUSE
         MONASTERY
         NUNNERY
         PRECEPTORY
         PRIORY
         REFECTORY

Friary Church
USE CHURCH
         FRIARY
SN   Use both terms.

Friary De Ordine Martyrum
USE FRIARY

Friary Gatehouse

USE FRIARY
         GATEHOUSE
SN   Use both terms.

FRIARY OF CRUTCHED FRIARS
UF   Cruciferi
         Crutched Friars House
SN   Crutched Friars also known as Crosiers or Fratres.
CL   RELIGIOUS, RITUAL AND FUNERARY
BT   FRIARY

FRIARY OF FRIARS OF THE SACK
SN   Friars of the Sack also known as Friars of Penance
         or Penitentia.
CL   RELIGIOUS, RITUAL AND FUNERARY
BT   FRIARY

FRIARY OF PIED FRIARS
SN   Pied Friars also known as Friars of Blessed Mary
         or St Mary de Arens.
CL   RELIGIOUS, RITUAL AND FUNERARY
BT   FRIARY

FRIENDS BURIAL GROUND
UF   Quaker Burial Ground
         Quaker Graveyard
CL   RELIGIOUS, RITUAL AND FUNERARY
BT   INHUMATION CEMETERY

FRIENDS MEETING HOUSE
UF   Quaker Meeting House
CL   RELIGIOUS, RITUAL AND FUNERARY
BT   NONCONFORMIST MEETING HOUSE
RT   MEETING HALL

FRIGATE
SN   Use only to classify modern warships (post 1939),
         usually large escort vessels.
CL   MARITIME
BT   MINOR WARSHIP

FRITTING FURNACE
CL   INDUSTRIAL
BT   GLASS FURNACE

FRONT GABLED HOUSE
CL   DOMESTIC
BT   GABLED HOUSE

FRONTIER DEFENCE
UF   Curtain Frontier Works
         Curtain Frontiers
         Frontier Works
         Hadrians Wall
CL   DEFENCE
NT   CENTURIAL STONE
         MILECASTLE
         MILEFORTLET
         TURRET
         VALLUM
RT   FORT
         FORTLET
         LINEAR EARTHWORK
         MILITARY ROAD
         SIGNAL STATION
         WATCH TOWER

Frontier Works
USE FRONTIER DEFENCE

FRUIT AND VEGETABLE MARKET
UF   Fruit Exchange
CL   COMMERCIAL
BT   MARKET

Fruit Exchange
USE FRUIT AND VEGETABLE MARKET

FUEL PRODUCTION SITE

SN   Includes sites associated with extraction.
CL   INDUSTRIAL
NT   CHARCOAL PRODUCTION SITE
     COAL MINING SITE
     OIL REFINING SITE
     PEAT WORKINGS

FUEL STORE
UF   Peat House
     Turf House
CL   UNASSIGNED
NT   COAL SHED
     PEAT STORE
RT   PEAT STORE
     WOOD SHED

FUELER
CL   MARITIME
BT   SERVICE CRAFT

FULLERS EARTH PIT
CL   INDUSTRIAL
BT   EXTRACTIVE PIT
RT   DYE WORKS
     FULLING MILL
     MINERAL PIT

FULLERS EARTH PIT
CL   INDUSTRIAL
BT   DYE AND PIGMENT SITE

Fullery
     USE FULLING MILL

FULLING MILL
UF   Fullery
     Pecking Mill
     Tuck Mill
     Tucking Mill
     Walk Mill
     Waulk Mill
SN   Vigorous working of woollen cloth in a solution of
     water and fulling agent, eg. fuller's earth and
     soap.
CL   INDUSTRIAL
BT   TEXTILE MILL
RT   CLOTH DRESSING MILL
     DYE HOUSE
     DYE WORKS
     FULLERS EARTH PIT
     PICKER HOUSE
     SCRIBBLING MILL
     SPINNING MILL

FULLING MILL
UF   Fullery
     Pecking Mill
     Tuck Mill
     Tucking Mill
     Walk Mill
     Waulk Mill
SN   Vigorous working of woollen cloth in a solution of
     water and fulling agent, eg. fuller's earth and
     soap.
CL   INDUSTRIAL
BT   WOOL MANUFACTURING SITE
RT   FINISHING HOUSE
     FULLING STOCKS
     TEAZLE SHOP

FULLING STOCKS
SN   Large wooden hammer beams pounding cloth in a
     fulling solution.
CL   INDUSTRIAL
BT   WOOL MANUFACTURING SITE
RT   FULLING MILL
     TENTER GROUND

Funeral Chapel

USE CHAPEL

FUNERARY SITE
SN   Site types normally or frequently associated with
     burials which in some instances may have had
     solely religious or ritual functions.
CL   RELIGIOUS, RITUAL AND FUNERARY
NT   BARROW
     BURIAL
     BURIAL PIT
     BURIAL VAULT
     CAIRN
     CATACOMB (FUNERARY)
     CEMETERY
     CHAMBERED TOMB
     CHARNEL HOUSE
     CIST
     COFFIN
     COLUMBARIUM
     CREMATORIUM
     CRYPT
     GRAVE
     HOGBACK STONE
     HUMAN REMAINS
     LONG MOUND
     MAUSOLEUM
     MORT SAFE
     MORTUARY
     MORTUARY ENCLOSURE
     MORTUARY HOUSE
     OSSUARY
     TOMB

Funfair
     USE FAIR

FUNGUS RING
CL   UNASSIGNED
BT   NATURAL FEATURE

FUNICULAR RAILWAY
CL   TRANSPORT
BT   RAILWAY
RT   CLIFF RAILWAY
     OVERHEAD RAILWAY

Funnel
     USE SHAFT
SN   Where structure on an industrial site.

FURNACE
UF   Furnace House
CL   INDUSTRIAL
NT   ANNEALING FURNACE
     GLASS FURNACE
     METAL PRODUCTION FURNACE
     REVERBERATORY FURNACE
     VENTILATION FURNACE
RT   FOUNDRY

Furnace House
     USE FURNACE

FURNACE POND
CL   WATER SUPPLY AND DRAINAGE
BT   POND
RT   HAMMER POND
     METAL PRODUCTION FURNACE
     MILL POND

FURNITURE FACTORY
CL   INDUSTRIAL
BT   FACTORY <BY PRODUCT>

FURNITURE FACTORY
CL   INDUSTRIAL
BT   TIMBER PRODUCT SITE
RT   JOINERS SHOP

FURTHER EDUCATION COLLEGE

CL EDUCATION
BT TRAINING COLLEGE

Fustian Cutters Shop
USE CLOTH CUTTERS WORKSHOP

GABLED HOUSE
CL DOMESTIC
BT HOUSE <BY FORM>
NT END GABLED HOUSE
    FRONT GABLED HOUSE

GALILEE
CL RELIGIOUS, RITUAL AND FUNERARY
BT CHAPEL
RT CHURCH

GALLEASSE
CL MARITIME
BT MINOR WARSHIP

GALLERIED ROW
CL DOMESTIC
BT ROW

GALLERIED ROW HOUSE
CL DOMESTIC
BT ROW HOUSE

GALLERY GRAVE
CL RELIGIOUS, RITUAL AND FUNERARY
BT CHAMBERED TOMB
NT TRANSEPTED GALLERY GRAVE

GALLEY
CL MARITIME
BT MINOR WARSHIP

GALLOWS
CL CIVIL
BT EXECUTION SITE

GALLOWS MOUND
CL CIVIL
BT EXECUTION SITE
RT MOUND

GALVANIZING WORKSHOP
CL INDUSTRIAL
BT NON FERROUS METAL PRODUCT SITE

GAMBLING SITE
CL RECREATIONAL
NT AMUSEMENT ARCADE
    BETTING OFFICE
    BINGO HALL
    CASINO (GAMBLING)
    GAMING HOUSE

GAME LARDER
UF Game Store
    Venison House
    Venison Larder
CL DOMESTIC
BT LARDER
RT FISH HOUSE
    HUNTING SITE
    ICEHOUSE

Game Store
USE GAME LARDER

Gamekeepers Cottage
USE ESTATE COTTAGE

Gamekeepers House
USE ESTATE COTTAGE

Gamekeepers Lodge

USE ESTATE COTTAGE

Games Pavilion
USE SPORTS PAVILION

GAMING HOUSE
CL RECREATIONAL
BT GAMBLING SITE
RT BAITING PLACE

Gaming Pit
USE BAITING PLACE

Gang Mill
USE SAW MILL

GANTRY
CL TRANSPORT
BT LIFTING AND WINDING STRUCTURE

GANTRY CRANE
CL TRANSPORT
BT CRANE <BY FORM>

Gaol
USE PRISON

GARAGE
UF Car Port
    Carport
    Motor Repair Shop
    Motor Repair Workshop
    Vehicle Repair Shop
    Vehicle Repair Workshop
SN Use only for buildings which house motor vehicles.
    Includes garages for vehicle repair. For petrol
    sales use PETROL STATION.
CL TRANSPORT
BT ROAD TRANSPORT SITE
RT MOTOR VEHICLE SHOWROOM
    MULTI STOREY CAR PARK
    PETROL PUMP
    PETROL STATION

GARDEN
UF Cemetery Garden
    Double Moated Garden
    Garden Lake
    Garden Pool
    Memorial Garden
    Moated Garden
    Prison Garden
    Station Garden
    War Memorial Garden
CL GARDENS, PARKS AND URBAN SPACES
NT ALPINE GARDEN
    AMERICAN GARDEN
    ARBORETUM
    BAMBOO GARDEN
    BOG GARDEN
    BOTANIC GARDEN
    BUTTERFLY GARDEN
    CABINET
    CHINESE GARDEN
    COLLEGE GARDEN
    COMMUNITY GARDEN
    COTTAGE GARDEN
    DUTCH GARDEN
    EGYPTIAN GARDEN
    FERNERY (GARDEN)
    FLOWER GARDEN
    FORMAL GARDEN
    FRAGRANCE GARDEN
    HEATHER GARDEN
    HERB GARDEN
    ITALIAN GARDEN
    JAPANESE GARDEN
    KITCHEN GARDEN
    KNOT GARDEN

MINIATURE GARDEN
MOORISH GARDEN
NURSERY GARDEN
ORNAMENTAL GARDEN
PARTERRE
PHYSIC GARDEN
PINETUM
ROCK GARDEN
SCULPTURE GARDEN
SPRING GARDEN
SUNKEN GARDEN
SWISS GARDEN
TERRACED GARDEN
TOPIARY GARDEN
TUDOR GARDEN
VEGETABLE GARDEN
WALLED GARDEN
WATER GARDEN
WHITE GARDEN
WILD GARDEN
WINTER GARDEN
WOODLAND GARDEN
YEW GARDEN
RT   ALLOTMENT
BORDER
GARDEN BUILDING
GARDEN ORNAMENT
GARDEN PATH
GARDEN RETREAT
GARDEN STEPS
GARDEN TERRACE
GARDEN WALL
HA HA
LAWN
MOAT
PARK
PATIO
TEA HOUSE

GARDEN

UF   Cemetery Garden
Double Moated Garden
Garden Lake
Garden Pool
Memorial Garden
Moated Garden
Prison Garden
Station Garden
War Memorial Garden
CL   AGRICULTURE AND SUBSISTENCE
BT   LAND USE SITE
NT   BEE GARDEN
HOP GARDEN
KITCHEN GARDEN
MARKET GARDEN
NURSERY GARDEN
RT   ALLOTMENT
GARDEN WALL
HA HA
MOAT
PATIO

Garden Archway
USE PERGOLA

GARDEN BASIN

CL   GARDENS, PARKS AND URBAN SPACES

GARDEN BUILDING

SN   Includes some structures that are not strictly
buildings. Use a more specific term where
possible.
CL   GARDENS, PARKS AND URBAN SPACES
NT   BANQUETING HOUSE
BELVEDERE
BOAT HOUSE
CASCADE HOUSE
COTTAGE ORNEE
EXEDRA

FERME ORNEE
FISHING LODGE
FOLLY
FOUNTAIN HOUSE
GARDEN HOUSE
GARDEN SHED
GARDEN TEMPLE
GATE LODGE
GAZEBO
GLASSHOUSE
HERBARIUM
HERMITAGE
ICEHOUSE
LAITERIE
LOGGIA
MOSS HOUSE
PAGODA
POTTING SHED
PROSPECT TOWER
ROOT HOUSE
ROTUNDA
SUMMERHOUSE
SWISS COTTAGE
TREE HOUSE
RT   COUNTRY HOUSE
GARDEN
GARDEN RETREAT
PAVILION

Garden Cottage
USE ESTATE COTTAGE

GARDEN FEATURE

CL   GARDENS, PARKS AND URBAN SPACES

GARDEN HOUSE

UF   Garden Room
Pleasance
SN   Use a more specific term where known.
CL   GARDENS, PARKS AND URBAN SPACES
BT   GARDEN BUILDING
RT   COUNTRY HOUSE
GARDEN RETREAT
PAVILION

Garden Lake
USE GARDEN
LAKE
SN   Use both terms.

GARDEN ORNAMENT

CL   GARDENS, PARKS AND URBAN SPACES
NT   BIRD BATH
GARDEN SEAT
HERM
OBELISK
SCULPTURE
SPHINX
SUNDIAL
SUNSHINE RECORDER
URN
VASE
RT   FOUNTAIN
GARDEN

GARDEN PATH

CL   GARDENS, PARKS AND URBAN SPACES
RT   GARDEN

Garden Pool
USE GARDEN
POOL
SN   Use both terms.

GARDEN RETREAT

UF   Buon Retiro
CL   GARDENS, PARKS AND URBAN SPACES
NT   ARBOUR
RT   COUNTRY HOUSE

GARDEN
GARDEN BUILDING
GARDEN HOUSE
GARDEN SEAT

Garden Room
USE GARDEN HOUSE

GARDEN SEAT
CL GARDENS, PARKS AND URBAN SPACES
BT GARDEN ORNAMENT
NT CAMOMILE SEAT
TURFED SEAT
RT ARBOUR
GARDEN RETREAT
GAZEBO

GARDEN SHED
CL GARDENS, PARKS AND URBAN SPACES
BT GARDEN BUILDING
RT POTTING SHED
SHED

Garden Staircase
USE GARDEN STEPS

Garden Stairs
USE GARDEN STEPS

GARDEN STEPS
UF Garden Staircase
Garden Stairs
CL GARDENS, PARKS AND URBAN SPACES
NT TURFED STEPS
RT GARDEN
STEPS

GARDEN SUBURB
CL DOMESTIC
BT MODEL SETTLEMENT
RT ESTATE VILLAGE
GARDEN VILLAGE
HOUSING ESTATE
RECREATIONAL HALL

GARDEN TEMPLE
CL GARDENS, PARKS AND URBAN SPACES
BT GARDEN BUILDING
NT DORIC TEMPLE
IONIC TEMPLE
OCTAGONAL TEMPLE
RT ROTUNDA
TEMPLE

GARDEN TERRACE
UF Ornamental Terrace
CL GARDENS, PARKS AND URBAN SPACES
RT FORMAL GARDEN
GARDEN
PARTERRE
TERRACED GARDEN

GARDEN VILLAGE
CL DOMESTIC
BT VILLAGE
RT GARDEN SUBURB
RECREATIONAL HALL

GARDEN VILLAGE
CL DOMESTIC
BT MODEL SETTLEMENT

GARDEN WALL
CL GARDENS, PARKS AND URBAN SPACES
RT GARDEN
HA HA
WALL

Gardeners Cottage

USE ESTATE COTTAGE

Gardeners House
USE ESTATE COTTAGE

GARDENS, PARKS AND URBAN SPACES
SN This is the top term for the class. See GARDENS,
PARKS AND URBAN SPACES Class List for narrow
terms.

Garderobe
USE TOILET

Garrison Church
USE MILITARY CHAPEL

Garrison Chapel
USE MILITARY CHAPEL

Garrison Church
USE MILITARY CHAPEL

Garth
USE FISH GARTH
ENCLOSURE
SN Enclosed ground. Use either FISH GARTH or
ENCLOSURE as appropriate.

GAS ENGINE
SN A machine producing mechanical power by the
internal combustion of town gas.
CL INDUSTRIAL
BT ENGINE
RT GAS ENGINE HOUSE

GAS ENGINE HOUSE
CL INDUSTRIAL
BT ENGINE HOUSE
RT GAS ENGINE

GAS FIRED POWER STATION
CL INDUSTRIAL
BT POWER STATION
RT STEAM TURBINE POWER STATION

Gas Generator House
USE GAS HOUSE

GAS HOLDER
UF Gas Holder Building
Gasometer
SN Expanding storage tank for coal gas. Often
described as a gasometer which is incorrect.
CL INDUSTRIAL
BT COAL GAS STRUCTURE
RT GAS STORAGE TANK

Gas Holder Building
USE GAS HOLDER

GAS HOUSE
UF Gas Generator House
SN Houses the principal processes for the production
of coal gas.
CL INDUSTRIAL
BT COAL GAS STRUCTURE
RT GAS WORKS

GAS LAMP
CL GARDENS, PARKS AND URBAN SPACES
BT STREET LAMP
RT LAMP POST
LIGHT HOLDER
SNUFFER

GAS STORAGE TANK
SN Storage tank for coal gas and possibly other types
of gas .
CL INDUSTRIAL

BT   COAL GAS STRUCTURE
RT   GAS HOLDER

GAS TURBINE
   CL   INDUSTRIAL
   BT   TURBINE

GAS WORKS
   UF   Gasworks
   SN   Industrial complex concerned with the manufacture
        of gas for domestic use from coal and oil.
   CL   INDUSTRIAL
   BT   COAL GAS STRUCTURE
   RT   GAS HOUSE

Gasometer
   USE GAS HOLDER

Gasworks
   USE GAS WORKS

GATE
   UF   Abbey Gate
        Castle Gate
        Churchyard Gate
        Dockyard Gate
        Factory Gate
        Gate Chapel
        Gateway
        Monastery Gateway
        Priory Gate
   SN   Including gateway and gate post.
   CL   UNASSIGNED
   RT   BARBICAN
        GATE LODGE
        GATE PIER
        GATEHOUSE
        KISSING GATE
        LEVEL CROSSING GATE
        LYCH GATE
        PORTAL
        POSTERN
        RAILINGS
        TOLL GATE
        TOWN GATE
        WALL
        WATER GATE

Gate Chapel
   USE GATE
         CHAPEL
   SN   Use both terms.

GATE LODGE
   UF   Entrance Lodge
        Factory Gate Lodge
        Gatekeepers Cottage
        Gatekeepers House
        Gatekeepers Lodge
        Lodge
        Mill Lodge
        Park Lodge
        Park Rangers Lodge
   CL   GARDENS, PARKS AND URBAN SPACES
   BT   GARDEN BUILDING
   RT   GATE
        GATEHOUSE
        PORTERS LODGE

GATE PIER
   UF   Gate Post
   SN   A pier of brick, masonry, etc, to which the hinges
        of a gate are attached.
   CL   UNASSIGNED
   RT   GATE

Gate Post
   USE GATE PIER

GATE TOWER

GATEHOUSE
   UF   Abbey Gatehouse
        Castle Gatehouse
        Dockyard Gatehouse
        Friary Gatehouse
        Gatehouse Chapel
        Monastery Gatehouse
        Priory Gatehouse
   SN   Use with wider site type where known.
   CL   UNASSIGNED
   BT   BUILDING
   RT   ABBEY
        BARBICAN
        CANAL GATEHOUSE
        CASTLE
        DOCKYARD
        FRIARY
        GATE
        GATE LODGE
        GATE TOWER
        GATEMANS HUT
        GUARDHOUSE
        MONASTERY
        PORTERS LODGE
        PRIORY
        TOWN GATE

Gatehouse Chapel
   USE CHAPEL
         GATEHOUSE
   SN   Use both terms.

Gatekeepers Cottage
   USE GATE LODGE

Gatekeepers House
   USE GATE LODGE

Gatekeepers Lodge
   USE GATE LODGE

GATEMANS HUT
   CL   UNASSIGNED
   BT   BUILDING
   RT   GATEHOUSE

Gateway
   USE GATE

GAUGE HOUSE
   UF   Tide Gauge House
   CL   TRANSPORT
   BT   WATER TRANSPORT SITE
   RT   CANAL GATEHOUSE
        RIVER INTAKE GAUGE
        TIDE GAUGE
        TRANSPORT WORKERS HOUSE

GAUGE HOUSE
   UF   Tide Gauge House
   CL   MARITIME
   BT   WATER REGULATION INSTALLATION
   RT   TIDE GAUGE

GAZEBO
   SN   A garden house situated to provide a commanding
        view.
   CL   GARDENS, PARKS AND URBAN SPACES
   BT   GARDEN BUILDING
   RT   BELVEDERE
        GARDEN SEAT
        PROSPECT MOUND

GENERAL BAPTIST CHAPEL

CL   RELIGIOUS, RITUAL AND FUNERARY
BT   BAPTIST CHAPEL

GENERAL HOSPITAL
UF   Emergency Hospital
      Emergency Medical Scheme Hospital
      Voluntary Hospital
CL   HEALTH AND WELFARE
BT   HOSPITAL

General Post Office
USE POST OFFICE

GENERAL STORE
CL   COMMERCIAL
BT   SHOP

Generating Station
USE POWER STATION

GENTLEMENS CLUB
UF   Constitutional Club
      Junior Reform Club
      Reform Club
CL   INSTITUTIONAL
BT   CLUB
RT   CHOCOLATE HOUSE
      COFFEE HOUSE

GENTLEMENS CLUB
UF   Constitutional Club
      Junior Reform Club
      Reform Club
CL   RECREATIONAL
BT   CLUB
RT   CHOCOLATE HOUSE
      COFFEE HOUSE

Gentlemens Subscription Library
USE LENDING LIBRARY

GEOLOGICAL MARKS
CL   UNASSIGNED
BT   NATURAL FEATURE

GERIATRIC HOSPITAL
CL   HEALTH AND WELFARE
BT   SPECIALIST HOSPITAL

German Institute
USE FOREIGN LANGUAGE INSTITUTE

GIBBET
CL   CIVIL
BT   EXECUTION SITE

Gig House
USE CARRIAGE HOUSE

GILBERTINE CELL
UF   Gilbertine Priory Cell
CL   RELIGIOUS, RITUAL AND FUNERARY
BT   CELL
RT   GILBERTINE DOUBLE HOUSE
      GILBERTINE MONASTERY

GILBERTINE DOUBLE HOUSE
UF   Gilbertine Nunnery
      Gilbertine Priory
SN   Priories of Gilbertine double order of nuns and
      canons.
CL   RELIGIOUS, RITUAL AND FUNERARY
BT   DOUBLE HOUSE
RT   GILBERTINE CELL
      GILBERTINE MONASTERY

GILBERTINE GRANGE
CL   RELIGIOUS, RITUAL AND FUNERARY
BT   GRANGE

GILBERTINE GRANGE
CL   AGRICULTURE AND SUBSISTENCE
BT   GRANGE

GILBERTINE MONASTERY
UF   Gilbertine Priory
CL   RELIGIOUS, RITUAL AND FUNERARY
BT   MONASTERY
RT   GILBERTINE CELL
      GILBERTINE DOUBLE HOUSE

Gilbertine Nunnery
USE GILBERTINE DOUBLE HOUSE

Gilbertine Priory
USE GILBERTINE DOUBLE HOUSE
      GILBERTINE MONASTERY
      PRIORY
SN   Use PRIORY and GILBERTINE DOUBLE HOUSE or
      GILBERTINE MONASTERY.

Gilbertine Priory Cell
USE GILBERTINE CELL

Gin Case
USE HORSE ENGINE

Gin Circle
USE WINDING CIRCLE
      HORSE WHIM
SN   Use both terms.

GIN PALACE
SN   An ornate public house that developed in the 1830s
      after the passing of a law to encourage the
      drinking of beer in alehouses licensed for the
      sale of beer only.
CL   COMMERCIAL
BT   LICENSED PREMISES

Gin Wheel
USE HORSE WHEEL

Gingang
USE HORSE ENGINE

GIRAFFE HOUSE
CL   RECREATIONAL
BT   ANIMAL HOUSE

Girls Club
USE YOUTH CLUB

Girls Home
USE CHILDRENS HOME

GLACIS
SN   An artificial mound of earth outside a ditch or
      wall intended to deflect or absorb gunfire.
CL   DEFENCE
RT   RAMPART

GLASS CONE
CL   INDUSTRIAL
BT   GLASSMAKING SITE
RT   CHIMNEY
      WASTER KILN

Glass Factory
USE GLASS WORKS

Glass Foundry
USE GLASS WORKS

GLASS FURNACE
UF   Blowing Furnace
      Glass Kiln
CL   INDUSTRIAL

BT   FURNACE
NT   FRITTING FURNACE
RT   GLASSMAKING SITE

Glass Kiln
   USE GLASS FURNACE

GLASS WORKING SITE
CL   INDUSTRIAL
BT   GLASSMAKING SITE
RT   GLASS WORKS
       JEWELLERY WORKSHOP
       STAINED GLASS WORKSHOP

GLASS WORKS
UF   Glass Factory
       Glass Foundry
CL   INDUSTRIAL
BT   GLASSMAKING SITE
NT   PLATE GLASS WORKS
RT   GLASS WORKING SITE
       POTASH KILN
       REVERBERATORY FURNACE
       SAND PIT
       SODA KILN
       SODA WORKS
       STAINED GLASS WORKSHOP

GLASSHOUSE
CL   GARDENS, PARKS AND URBAN SPACES
BT   GARDEN BUILDING
NT   CAMELLIA HOUSE
       CONSERVATORY
       FERNERY (GLASSHOUSE)
       GREENHOUSE
       HOTHOUSE
       ORANGERY
       ORCHARD HOUSE
       PALM HOUSE
       PINERY
       TEMPERATE HOUSE
       VINERY
       WATER LILY HOUSE
RT   NURSERY GARDEN

GLASSMAKING SITE
CL   INDUSTRIAL
BT   MINERAL PRODUCT SITE
NT   BOTTLE WORKS
       GLASS CONE
       GLASS WORKING SITE
       GLASS WORKS
       STAINED GLASS WORKSHOP
RT   GLASS FURNACE
       WASTER KILN

GLAZE AND REEL HOUSE
CL   INDUSTRIAL
BT   EXPLOSIVES SITE

Glost Kiln
   USE POTTERY KILN

GLOVE FACTORY
CL   INDUSTRIAL
BT   FACTORY <BY PRODUCT>

GLOVE FACTORY
CL   INDUSTRIAL
BT   CLOTHING INDUSTRY SITE
RT   CURRIERY

GLUE FACTORY
CL   INDUSTRIAL
BT   ANIMAL PRODUCT SITE
RT   ABATTOIR
       TANNERY

GLUE FACTORY

CL   INDUSTRIAL
BT   FACTORY <BY PRODUCT>

GOAL POST ENCLOSURE
UF   Staple Enclosure
SN   Single ditched 3-sided rectilinear enclosure.
CL   UNASSIGNED
BT   RECTILINEAR ENCLOSURE

GOLD MINE
CL   INDUSTRIAL
BT   NON FERROUS METAL EXTRACTION SITE

GOLD MINE
CL   INDUSTRIAL
BT   MINE
RT   STREAM WORKS

GOLDSMITHS WORKSHOP
CL   INDUSTRIAL
BT   CRAFT INDUSTRY SITE
RT   ASSAY OFFICE
       CUPELLATION FURNACE
       JEWELLERY WORKS
       JEWELLERY WORKSHOP
       SILVERSMITHS WORKSHOP

GOLDSMITHS WORKSHOP
CL   INDUSTRIAL
BT   NON FERROUS METAL PRODUCT SITE

GOLF CLUB
CL   RECREATIONAL
BT   SPORTS SITE
RT   GOLF COURSE

GOLF COURSE
CL   RECREATIONAL
BT   SPORTS SITE
RT   GOLF CLUB

Gong
   USE TOILET

GOODS CLEARING HOUSE
UF   Goods Departure Warehouse
       Goods Warehouse
CL   TRANSPORT
BT   ROAD TRANSPORT SITE
RT   GOODS SHED
       GOODS STATION
       GOODS YARD

Goods Departure Warehouse
   USE GOODS CLEARING HOUSE

Goods Depot
   USE GOODS YARD

GOODS SHED
CL   TRANSPORT
BT   RAILWAY TRANSPORT SITE
RT   GOODS CLEARING HOUSE
       GOODS STATION
       GOODS YARD
       SHED

GOODS STATION
CL   TRANSPORT
BT   RAILWAY TRANSPORT SITE
RT   GOODS CLEARING HOUSE
       GOODS SHED
       GOODS YARD

Goods Station Office
   USE RAILWAY OFFICE

Goods Warehouse
   USE GOODS CLEARING HOUSE

GOODS YARD
- UF Goods Depot
- CL TRANSPORT
- BT RAILWAY TRANSPORT SITE
- RT GOODS CLEARING HOUSE
  - GOODS SHED
  - GOODS STATION
  - HOLDING SHED
  - MARSHALLING YARD
  - RAILWAY STABLE
  - RAILWAY WAREHOUSE

Goose House
- USE POULTRY HOUSE

Gospel Hall
- USE NONCONFORMIST MEETING HOUSE

Government Building
- USE GOVERNMENT OFFICE

GOVERNMENT OFFICE
- UF Admiralty
  - Colonial Office
  - Customs And Excise Office
  - Foreign Office
  - Government Building
  - Home Office
  - Inland Revenue Office
  - National Debt Redemption Office
  - Ordnance Office
  - Ordnance Survey Office
  - Patent Office
  - Paymaster Generals Office
  - Rolls Office
  - Scottish Office
  - Treasury
  - Treasury Office
  - War Office
  - Weights And Measures Office
  - Whips Office
- CL CIVIL
- NT LOCAL GOVERNMENT OFFICE
- RT EMBASSY
  - HOUSES OF PARLIAMENT
  - OFFICE
  - RECORD OFFICE

GRAB DREDGER
- CL MARITIME
- BT DREDGER

GRADUATE HOUSE
- CL DOMESTIC
- BT HOUSE <BY FUNCTION>
- RT UNIVERSITY

GRADUATE HOUSE
- CL EDUCATION
- RT UNIVERSITY

GRAFFITI
- CL UNASSIGNED

GRAIN DRIER
- CL AGRICULTURE AND SUBSISTENCE
- BT FARM BUILDING
- RT GRAIN SILO
  - GRANARY

GRAIN ELEVATOR
- CL TRANSPORT
- BT LIFTING AND WINDING STRUCTURE
- NT FLOATING GRAIN ELEVATOR
- RT GRAIN WAREHOUSE

GRAIN SILO
- UF Silo

- CL AGRICULTURE AND SUBSISTENCE
- BT FARM BUILDING
- RT GRAIN DRIER
  - GRANARY

GRAIN STORAGE PIT
- CL AGRICULTURE AND SUBSISTENCE
- BT STORAGE PIT
- RT GRAIN WAREHOUSE
  - GRANARY

Grain Store
- USE GRAIN WAREHOUSE

GRAIN WAREHOUSE
- UF Corn Store
  - Corn Warehouse
  - Grain Store
- CL COMMERCIAL
- BT WAREHOUSE
- RT GRAIN ELEVATOR
  - GRAIN STORAGE PIT

GRAMMAR SCHOOL
- UF Endowed Grammar School
  - Free Grammar School
- CL EDUCATION
- BT SECONDARY SCHOOL

GRANARY
- CL AGRICULTURE AND SUBSISTENCE
- BT FOOD AND DRINK PROCESSING SITE
- RT BAKERY
  - BARN
  - CORN DRYING OVEN
  - CORN MILL
  - DISTILLERY
  - FLOUR MILL
  - GRAIN DRIER
  - GRAIN SILO
  - GRAIN STORAGE PIT
  - STADDLE STONE

GRAND HOTEL
- CL COMMERCIAL
- BT HOTEL

GRAND HOTEL
- CL DOMESTIC
- BT HOTEL

Grandmontine Alien Priory
- USE GRANDMONTINE MONASTERY
  - ALIEN PRIORY
- SN Use both terms.

GRANDMONTINE MONASTERY
- UF Grandmontine Alien Priory
  - Grandmontine Priory
- SN Priories of Grandmontine monks.
- CL RELIGIOUS, RITUAL AND FUNERARY
- BT MONASTERY

Grandmontine Priory
- USE GRANDMONTINE MONASTERY
  - PRIORY
- SN Use both terms.

GRANDSTAND
- UF Cricket Stand
  - Football Stand
  - Stand
- CL RECREATIONAL
- BT SPORTS BUILDING
- RT CRICKET GROUND
  - FOOTBALL GROUND
  - FOOTBALL TERRACE
  - RACECOURSE
  - RACECOURSE PAVILION

SPORTS PAVILION
STADIUM

GRANGE
- UF   Alien Grange
-       Monastic Grange
- SN   Specifically related to core buildings and structures associated with monastic land holding. Use specific term where known.
- CL   RELIGIOUS, RITUAL AND FUNERARY
- BT   RELIGIOUS HOUSE
- NT   AUGUSTINIAN GRANGE
-       BENEDICTINE GRANGE
-       CARTHUSIAN GRANGE
-       CISTERCIAN GRANGE
-       CLUNIAC GRANGE
-       GILBERTINE GRANGE
-       PREMONSTRATENSIAN GRANGE
-       TEMPLARS GRANGE
-       TIRONIAN GRANGE
- RT   BARN
-       CAMERA
-       CELL
-       DOUBLE HOUSE
-       FARM
-       FARMHOUSE
-       GRANGE BARN
-       MANOR
-       MONASTERY
-       NUNNERY
-       PRECEPTORY

GRANGE
- UF   Alien Grange
-       Monastic Grange
- SN   Specifically related to core buildings and structures associated with monastic land holding. Use specific term where known.
- CL   AGRICULTURE AND SUBSISTENCE
- BT   LAND USE SITE
- NT   AUGUSTINIAN GRANGE
-       BENEDICTINE GRANGE
-       CARTHUSIAN GRANGE
-       CISTERCIAN GRANGE
-       CLUNIAC GRANGE
-       GILBERTINE GRANGE
-       PREMONSTRATENSIAN GRANGE
-       TEMPLARS GRANGE
-       TIRONIAN GRANGE
- RT   BARN

GRANGE BARN
- CL   AGRICULTURE AND SUBSISTENCE
- BT   BARN
- RT   GRANGE
-       TITHE BARN

GRANITE QUARRY
- CL   INDUSTRIAL
- BT   STONE QUARRY
- RT   MILLSTONE WORKING SITE

GRAPHITE MINE
- UF   Plumbago Mine
- CL   INDUSTRIAL
- BT   MINE

GRAPHITE MINE
- UF   Plumbago Mine
- CL   INDUSTRIAL
- BT   MINERAL EXTRACTION SITE

GRASS DRYING SHED
- CL   AGRICULTURE AND SUBSISTENCE
- BT   FARM BUILDING
- RT   CHAFF HOUSE
-       FODDER STORE
-       SHED

GRAVE

GRAVE (right column)
- CL   RELIGIOUS, RITUAL AND FUNERARY
- BT   FUNERARY SITE
- NT   GRAVE SLAB
-       GRAVESTONE
-       PILLOW STONE
-       SHIPWRECK GRAVE
- RT   CHURCHYARD
-       SARCOPHAGUS
-       SHIPWRECK GRAVE

Grave Cover
    USE GRAVE SLAB

GRAVE SLAB
- UF   Grave Cover
- CL   RELIGIOUS, RITUAL AND FUNERARY
- BT   GRAVE
- NT   CROSS SLAB

GRAVEL PATH
- CL   TRANSPORT
- BT   PATH

GRAVEL PIT
- CL   INDUSTRIAL
- BT   SAND AND GRAVEL EXTRACTION SITE
- RT   CHALK PIT
-       MARL PIT

GRAVEL PIT
- CL   INDUSTRIAL
- BT   EXTRACTIVE PIT
- RT   CHALK PIT
-       CLAY PIT
-       MARL PIT
-       SAND PIT

GRAVESIDE SHELTER
- UF   Graveyard Shelter
-       Hudd
- CL   RELIGIOUS, RITUAL AND FUNERARY
- RT   CHURCHYARD

GRAVESTONE
- UF   Headstone
- CL   RELIGIOUS, RITUAL AND FUNERARY
- BT   GRAVE
- RT   CHURCHYARD
-       INSCRIBED STONE
-       OGHAM STONE
-       SARCOPHAGUS

Graveyard
    USE CEMETERY

Graveyard Shelter
    USE GRAVESIDE SHELTER

Graving Dock
    USE DRY DOCK
- SN   Dry dock for the repair of ships.

GREASE WORKS
- SN   Recovery and removal of grease (lanolin) from raw wool.
- CL   INDUSTRIAL
- BT   WOOL MANUFACTURING SITE
- RT   COMBING WORKS
-       WORSTED MILL

GREAT HOUSE
- CL   DOMESTIC
- BT   HOUSE <BY FUNCTION>
- RT   COUNTRY HOUSE
-       ICEHOUSE
-       MANOR HOUSE
-       TOWN HOUSE

GREAT SHIP

CL MARITIME
BT CAPITAL WARSHIP

Great Tower
USE KEEP

Greek Orthodox Cemetery Chapel
USE CEMETERY CHAPEL

Greek Orthodox Church
USE EASTERN ORTHODOX CHURCH

GREEN CHARGE HOUSE
CL INDUSTRIAL
BT EXPLOSIVES SITE

GREENGROCERS SHOP
CL COMMERCIAL
BT SHOP

GREENHOUSE
SN Freestanding building used for propagation,
overwintering and growth of tender plants.
CL AGRICULTURE AND SUBSISTENCE
BT AGRICULTURAL BUILDING
RT MARKET GARDEN
NURSERY GARDEN

GREENHOUSE
SN Freestanding building used for propagation,
overwintering and growth of tender plants.
CL GARDENS, PARKS AND URBAN SPACES
BT GLASSHOUSE
RT MARKET GARDEN
NURSERY GARDEN

Greenway
USE DROVE ROAD

Grees
USE STEPS

Greycoat School
USE CHARITY SCHOOL

GRIDIRON
SN A heavy framework of parallel beams used to
support a ship in dock.
CL INDUSTRIAL
BT MARINE CONSTRUCTION SITE
RT DRY DOCK
SHIP REPAIR WORKS

GRIDIRON
SN A heavy framework of parallel beams used to
support a ship in dock.
CL MARITIME
BT MARINE CONSTRUCTION SITE

GRILLE
SN An open grating of wrought iron, bronze or wood,
forming a screen to a door, window or other
opening, or used as a divider.
CL GARDENS, PARKS AND URBAN SPACES

GRINDSTONE
CL INDUSTRIAL
RT BARK MILL
CRUSHING CIRCLE
CUTLERY WORKS
CUTLERY WORKSHOP
EDGE TOOL WORKS
FLINT MILL
MILLSTONE WORKING SITE
OIL MILL
PIN MILL
PLASTER MILL
SCYTHE MILL
STONE QUARRY

Grist Mill
USE CORN MILL

Gritstone Quarry
USE SANDSTONE QUARRY
MILLSTONE WORKING SITE
SN Use both terms.

GROCERS SHOP
UF Grocery Shop
CL COMMERCIAL
BT SHOP

Grocery Shop
USE GROCERS SHOP

GROOMS COTTAGE
CL DOMESTIC
BT HOUSE <BY FUNCTION>
RT COACHMANS COTTAGE
ESTATE COTTAGE
MEWS
STABLE
STABLEHANDS LODGINGS

Grot
USE GROTTO

GROTTO
UF Grot
SN A shady cavern built as a garden feature. In the
18th century it usually took the form of an
artificial rocky cave or apartment decorated with
stalactites and shells in a wild part of the
grounds.
CL GARDENS, PARKS AND URBAN SPACES
NT NYMPHAEUM
SHELL GROTTO
RT FOLLY
HERMITAGE
ROCK BRIDGE

GROVE
SN A group of trees, usually a single species, either
growing naturally or planted in formation.
CL GARDENS, PARKS AND URBAN SPACES
BT WOODLAND
NT ILEX GROVE

GROYNE
SN A structure extending into the sea for the purpose
of preventing further movement of washed up sand
and shingle.
CL MARITIME
BT SEA DEFENCES

GRUBENHAUS
UF Sunken Featured Building
Sunken Floored Building
SN A form of sunken hut dating back to the Roman
period.
CL DOMESTIC
RT DWELLING

Gryse
USE STEPS

Guano Works
USE FERTILISER WORKS

Guard Post
USE GUARDHOUSE

GUARDHOUSE
UF Guard Post
CL DEFENCE
RT GATEHOUSE
WATCH HOUSE

WATCH TOWER

Guards Chapel
USE MILITARY CHAPEL

GUEST COTTAGE
- SN Cottage provided for guests to a country house.
- CL DOMESTIC
- BT HOUSE <BY FUNCTION>
- RT COUNTRY HOUSE

GUEST HOUSE
- UF Pilgrims Rest House
- CL DOMESTIC
- BT RESIDENTIAL BUILDING
- RT HOTEL

GUEST HOUSE
- UF Pilgrims Rest House
- CL RELIGIOUS, RITUAL AND FUNERARY
- RT ABBEY
  - FRIARY
  - MONASTERY
  - NUNNERY
  - PRIORY

GUEST HOUSE
- UF Pilgrims Rest House
- CL COMMERCIAL

Guide Plate
USE SIGNPOST

Guide Post
USE SIGNPOST

Guide Stone
USE SIGNPOST

Guidepost
USE SIGNPOST

GUILD CHAPEL
- UF Corporation Chapel
  - Guild Of The Holy Cross Chapel
- CL RELIGIOUS, RITUAL AND FUNERARY
- BT CHAPEL

Guild House
USE GUILDHALL

Guild Of The Holy Cross Chapel
USE GUILD CHAPEL

GUILDHALL
- UF Brotherhood House
  - Guild House
  - Hanshus
- CL CIVIL
- BT MEETING HALL
- RT CHURCH HOUSE
  - CLOTH HALL
  - EXCHANGE
  - LIVERY HALL
  - MARKET HALL
  - MARKET HOUSE
  - STEELYARD
  - TOWN HALL
  - TRINITY HOUSE

GUILDHALL
- UF Brotherhood House
  - Guild House
  - Hanshus
- CL COMMERCIAL
- RT CLOTH HALL
  - EXCHANGE
  - LIVERY HALL
  - MARKET HALL

MARKET HOUSE
MARRIAGE FEAST HOUSE
MOOT HALL
STEELYARD

GUILLOTINE LOCK
- CL TRANSPORT
- BT LOCK

GULLY
- CL WATER SUPPLY AND DRAINAGE
- BT WATER CHANNEL
- RT CONDUIT
  - LEAT

Gun Barrel Proof House
USE GUN TESTING SHOP

Gun Battery
USE BATTERY

Gun Carriage Store
USE NAVAL STOREHOUSE

GUN EMPLACEMENT
- CL DEFENCE
- RT ARTILLERY FORT
  - BATTERY
  - FORT
  - FORTRESS
  - GUNPOST
  - PILLBOX
  - TANK TRAP

Gun Factory
USE ORDNANCE FACTORY

Gun Foundry
USE FOUNDRY

GUN TESTING SHOP
- UF Gun Barrel Proof House
- CL INDUSTRIAL
- BT ARMAMENT MANUFACTURING SITE
- RT ARSENAL
  - CANNON BORING MILL
  - FOUNDRY
  - ORDNANCE FACTORY
  - PROVING HOUSE

Gun Tower
USE ARTILLERY TOWER

Gun Wharf
USE WHARF

GUNPOST
- CL DEFENCE
- RT FORTRESS
  - GUN EMPLACEMENT

GUNPOWDER DRYING HOUSE
- CL INDUSTRIAL
- BT EXPLOSIVES SITE
- RT ARSENAL
  - RIPE CHARGE HOUSE

Gunpowder Factory
USE GUNPOWDER WORKS

Gunpowder Mill
USE GUNPOWDER WORKS

GUNPOWDER MIXING HOUSE
- UF Mixing House
- CL INDUSTRIAL
- BT ARMAMENT MANUFACTURING SITE

GUNPOWDER WORKS

UF   Gunpowder Factory
      Gunpowder Mill
      Powder Mill
CL   INDUSTRIAL
BT   EXPLOSIVES SITE
RT   COOPERAGE
      FIRE ENGINE HOUSE

GUNPOWDER WORKS
UF   Gunpowder Factory
      Gunpowder Mill
      Powder Mill
CL   INDUSTRIAL
BT   ARMAMENT MANUFACTURING SITE

Gussage Style Settlement
USE   ENCLOSED SETTLEMENT

Gutter
USE   DRAIN

GYMNASIUM (SCHOOL)
CL   EDUCATION
RT   SCHOOL

GYMNASIUM (SPORTS)
CL   RECREATIONAL
BT   SPORTS BUILDING

GYPSUM BURIAL
CL   RELIGIOUS, RITUAL AND FUNERARY
BT   BURIAL

GYPSUM DRYING KILN
CL   INDUSTRIAL
BT   DRYING KILN

GYPSUM MINE
SN   Includes anhydrate mining.
CL   INDUSTRIAL
BT   MINERAL EXTRACTION SITE
RT   PLASTER WORKS

GYPSUM MINE
SN   Includes anhydrate mining.
CL   INDUSTRIAL
BT   MINE

GYPSUM QUARRY
CL   INDUSTRIAL
BT   STONE QUARRY

GYRUS
SN   A sunken arena used by the Romans for training
      cavalry horses and recruits.
CL   DEFENCE
RT   AMPHITHEATRE
      ARTILLERY FORT
      AUXILIARY FORT

HA HA
UF   Sunken Wall
SN   A dry ditch or sunk fence which divided the formal
      garden from the landscaped park without
      interrupting the view.
CL   GARDENS, PARKS AND URBAN SPACES
RT   BOUNDARY
      FORMAL GARDEN
      GARDEN
      GARDEN WALL
      WALL

Habitation Site
USE   SETTLEMENT

HACKNEY STABLE
CL   TRANSPORT
BT   ROAD TRANSPORT SITE
RT   COACH HOUSE

COACHING INN
COACHING INN STABLE
LIVERY STABLE

HACKNEY STABLE
CL   TRANSPORT
BT   STABLE

Hadrians Wall
USE   FRONTIER DEFENCE
SN   Use Hadrian's Wall in a site name field. Use other
      terms, eg. VALLUM, FORT, TURRET as appropriate for
      components.

HAIRDRESSERS SALON
UF   Hairdressers Shop
CL   COMMERCIAL
BT   SHOP
RT   BARBERS SHOP

Hairdressers Shop
USE   HAIRDRESSERS SALON

Half Moon
USE   BASTION OUTWORK
SN   Also known as "Demi Lune", another type of outwork
      associated with the bastion system.

HALF TIDE DOCK
CL   MARITIME
BT   DOCK

HALF TIDE DOCK
CL   INDUSTRIAL
BT   MARINE CONSTRUCTION SITE

HALF TIDE DOCK
CL   MARITIME
BT   MARINE CONSTRUCTION SITE

Half Wealden House
USE   SINGLE ENDED WEALDEN HOUSE

Hall
USE   HALL HOUSE
SN   If not domestic use specific type, eg. CHURCH
      HALL.

HALL AND CELLAR HOUSE
CL   DOMESTIC
BT   HALL HOUSE

HALL AND PARLOUR HOUSE
CL   DOMESTIC
BT   HALL HOUSE

HALL HOUSE
UF   Hall
CL   DOMESTIC
BT   HOUSE <BY FORM>
NT   AISLED HALL
      AISLED HOUSE
      CROSS PASSAGE HOUSE
      CROSS WING HOUSE
      END HALL HOUSE
      FIRST FLOOR HALL HOUSE
      HALL AND CELLAR HOUSE
      HALL AND PARLOUR HOUSE
      OPEN HALL HOUSE
      WEALDEN HOUSE

Hall Of Memory
USE   COMMEMORATIVE MONUMENT
SN   Use COMMEMORATIVE MONUMENT with the relevant
      hall type.

HALL OF RESIDENCE
UF   Students Hostel
CL   DOMESTIC

BT   RESIDENTIAL BUILDING
RT   COLLEGE LODGINGS
     POLYTECHNIC
     UNIVERSITY

Halt
   USE RAILWAY STATION

HAMLET
   SN   Small settlement with no ecclesiastical or lay
        administrative function.
   CL   DOMESTIC
   BT   SETTLEMENT
   RT   VILLAGE

Hammel
   USE COW HOUSE

HAMMER
   CL   INDUSTRIAL
   NT   HELVE HAMMER
        TILT HAMMER
   RT   FORGE
        HAMMER POND
        IRON WORKS

HAMMER POND
   SN   Pond, created specifically for providing power to
        helve or other hammers.
   CL   WATER SUPPLY AND DRAINAGE
   BT   POND
   RT   BLAST FURNACE
        DAM
        FORGE
        FURNACE POND
        IRON WORKS
        MILL POND
        PEN POND
        POND BAY

HAMMER POND
   SN   Pond, created specifically for providing power to
        helve or other hammers.
   CL   INDUSTRIAL
   BT   WATER POWER PRODUCTION SITE
   RT   BLAST FURNACE
        DAM
        HAMMER
        IRON WORKS
        PEN POND

HAMMERHEAD CRANE
   CL   TRANSPORT
   BT   CRANE <BY FORM>

HAND CAPSTAN
   CL   TRANSPORT
   BT   CAPSTAN

HAND CAPSTAN
   CL   MARITIME
   BT   CAPSTAN

HAND CRANE
   CL   TRANSPORT
   BT   CRANE <BY FUNCTION>

HAND PUMP
   CL   WATER SUPPLY AND DRAINAGE
   BT   PUMP
   RT   WATER PUMP
        WAYSIDE PUMP
        WELL

HANDICAPPED CHILDRENS HOME
   UF   Crippled Childrens Home
   CL   EDUCATION
   RT   ORPHANAGE

HANDICAPPED CHILDRENS HOME

UF   Crippled Childrens Home
CL   HEALTH AND WELFARE
BT   CHILDRENS HOME
RT   ORPHANAGE

HANDICAPPED CHILDRENS HOME
   UF   Crippled Childrens Home
   CL   DOMESTIC
   BT   CHILDRENS HOME
   RT   ORPHANAGE

HANDLE HOUSE
   SN   Drying house for wooden frames containing teazles.
   CL   INDUSTRIAL
   BT   WOOL MANUFACTURING SITE
   RT   TEAZLE SHOP
        TEXTILE MILL
        WOOL BARN
        WOOL STOVE

HANDLING HOUSE
   SN   Workshop for placing handles on mugs, teapots,
        etc.
   CL   INDUSTRIAL
   BT   POTTERY MANUFACTURING SITE
   RT   MUG HOUSE
        POTTERY WORKS
        POTTERY WORKSHOP
        THROWING HOUSE

HANGAR
   UF   Flying Boat Warehouse
   CL   TRANSPORT
   BT   AIR TRANSPORT SITE
   NT   AIRCRAFT HANGAR
        AIRSHIP HANGAR

Hanshus
   USE GUILDHALL

Hansom Cabmans Shelter
   USE CABMENS SHELTER

HARBOUR
   UF   Hythe
   CL   TRANSPORT
   BT   WATER TRANSPORT SITE
   RT   CRANE

HARBOUR
   UF   Hythe
   CL   MARITIME
   BT   DOCK AND HARBOUR INSTALLATION
   NT   FLOATING BREAKWATER
        FLOATING HARBOUR
   RT   BOAT YARD
        BREAKWATER

Harbour Light
   USE LIGHTHOUSE

HARBOUR MASTERS OFFICE
   CL   MARITIME
   BT   MARITIME OFFICE
   RT   OFFICE

HARBOUR SERVICES VESSEL
   CL   MARITIME
   BT   SERVICE CRAFT
   NT   BUM BOAT
        DEPOT SHIP
        FLOATING DOCK
        HULK

Harbour Wall
   USE BREAKWATER

HARD STANDING
   CL   TRANSPORT

BT   AIR TRANSPORT SITE

HARDWARE SHOP
UF   Ironmongers Shop
CL   COMMERCIAL
BT   SHOP

HAT FACTORY
UF   Straw Hat Factory
CL   INDUSTRIAL
BT   CLOTHING INDUSTRY SITE
RT   FELT MILL
     HATTERS WORKSHOP

HAT FACTORY
UF   Straw Hat Factory
CL   INDUSTRIAL
BT   FACTORY <BY PRODUCT>

HATCHELLING HOUSE
CL   INDUSTRIAL
BT   MARINE CONSTRUCTION SITE
RT   ROPERY
     TAR HOUSE
     YARN HOUSE

HATCHELLING HOUSE
CL   MARITIME
BT   MARINE CONSTRUCTION SITE

Hatters Shop
USE   MILLINERS SHOP

HATTERS WORKSHOP
UF   Hatting Shop
CL   INDUSTRIAL
BT   CRAFT INDUSTRY SITE
RT   CLOTH CUTTERS WORKSHOP
     HAT FACTORY
     LEATHER WORKERS SHOP

HATTERS WORKSHOP
UF   Hatting Shop
CL   INDUSTRIAL
BT   CLOTHING INDUSTRY SITE

Hatting Shop
USE   HATTERS WORKSHOP

HAULAGE ENGINE HOUSE
SN   Engine driving a continuous wire rope for the
     haulage of tubs in a mine and at the heapstead.
CL   INDUSTRIAL
BT   MINE LIFTING AND WINDING STRUCTURE
RT   COLLIERY RAILWAY
     ELECTRIC WINCH
     STEAM ENGINE
     WINDER HOUSE
     WINDING GEAR

HAULAGE ENGINE HOUSE
SN   Engine driving a continuous wire rope for the
     haulage of tubs in a mine and at the heapstead.
CL   INDUSTRIAL
BT   ENGINE HOUSE
RT   STEAM ENGINE

Haulage Table Incline
USE   INCLINED PLANE

HAY BARN
UF   Dutch Barn
     Hay House
CL   AGRICULTURE AND SUBSISTENCE
BT   BARN
RT   HAYLOFT

Hay House
USE   HAY BARN

HAYLOFT
CL   AGRICULTURE AND SUBSISTENCE
BT   FARM BUILDING
RT   BANK BARN
     COMBINATION BARN
     FIELD BARN
     HAY BARN
     LINHAY

Head Brewers House
USE   MANAGERS HOUSE

HEAD RACE
SN   Water channel leading to water wheel.
CL   WATER SUPPLY AND DRAINAGE
BT   MILL RACE
RT   MILL POND
     TUMBLING WEIR
     WATERCOURSE
     WATERMILL

HEAD RACE
SN   Water channel leading to water wheel.
CL   INDUSTRIAL
BT   MILL RACE
RT   TUMBLING WEIR
     WATERWHEEL

Headgear
USE   WINDING GEAR

HEADMASTERS HOUSE
CL   DOMESTIC
BT   HOUSE <BY FUNCTION>

HEADMASTERS HOUSE
CL   EDUCATION
RT   SCHOOL

Headquarters
USE   OFFICE

Headstock
USE   WINDING GEAR

Headstone
USE   GRAVESTONE

Healing Well
USE   HOLY WELL

HEALTH AND WELFARE
SN   This is the top term for the class. See HEALTH AND
     WELFARE Class List for narrow terms.

Health Centre
USE   CLINIC

Health Clinic
USE   CLINIC

HEALTH ESTABLISHMENT
CL   RECREATIONAL
NT   KURSAAL
     PUMP ROOMS
     SPA PAVILION

HEALTH WORKERS HOUSE
CL   DOMESTIC
BT   HOUSE <BY FUNCTION>
NT   DOCTORS HOUSE
     MATRONS HOUSE
     MEDICAL ATTENDANTS HOUSE
     MEDICAL SUPERINTENDENTS HOUSE
     SISTERS HOUSE
     WORKHOUSE MASTERS HOUSE

HEAPSTEAD

SN Buildings and works around a mine shaft with an
    artificial embankment on which the winding gear
    etc, is located.
CL INDUSTRIAL
BT MINING INDUSTRY SITE
RT COLLIERY RAILWAY
    WINDING GEAR

HEART HOSPITAL
CL HEALTH AND WELFARE
BT SPECIALIST HOSPITAL

HEARTH
UF Cooking Hearth
    Cooking Place
SN The slab or place on which a fire is made.
CL UNASSIGNED
RT BURNT MOUND
    OVEN

HEATED WALL
CL AGRICULTURE AND SUBSISTENCE
RT WALL

HEATED WALL
CL GARDENS, PARKS AND URBAN SPACES
RT WALL

HEATHER GARDEN
CL GARDENS, PARKS AND URBAN SPACES
BT GARDEN

HEAVY ENGINEERING SITE
CL INDUSTRIAL
BT ENGINEERING INDUSTRY SITE
NT BOILER SHOP
    BOILER WORKS
    FITTERS WORKSHOP
    FORGE
    FOUNDRY
    WHITESMITHS WORKSHOP
RT MARINE ENGINEERING WORKS
    TURNING SHOP

Heckling Shop
USE FLAX DRESSING SHOP

HEDGE
CL UNASSIGNED
RT BOUNDARY
    HEDGE MAZE

HEDGE MAZE
CL GARDENS, PARKS AND URBAN SPACES
BT MAZE
RT HEDGE

HEDGE MAZE
CL RELIGIOUS, RITUAL AND FUNERARY
BT MAZE

HELVE HAMMER
SN A cast iron hammer used for shingling iron or
    making heavy forgings.
CL INDUSTRIAL
BT HAMMER
RT FORGE
    STEAM ENGINE
    WATERWHEEL

HEMMEL
SN A roofed shelter for cattle without tethering
    point or stalls, but with a small yard attached. It
    is often detached from the main range of farm
    buildings.
CL AGRICULTURE AND SUBSISTENCE
BT AGRICULTURAL BUILDING

HEMP MILL

CL INDUSTRIAL
BT TEXTILE MILL
RT ROPERY

HEMP MILL
CL INDUSTRIAL
BT LINEN OR FLAX MANUFACTURING SITE

HEMP STORE
CL INDUSTRIAL
BT MARINE CONSTRUCTION SITE
RT ROPERY
    ROPEWALK

HEMP STORE
CL MARITIME
BT MARINE CONSTRUCTION SITE

HEN BATTERY
CL AGRICULTURE AND SUBSISTENCE
BT AGRICULTURAL BUILDING
RT POULTRY HOUSE

Hen Cote
USE POULTRY HOUSE

Hen House
USE POULTRY HOUSE

HENGE
CL RELIGIOUS, RITUAL AND FUNERARY

HENGE ENCLOSURE
UF Mount Pleasant Enclosure
CL RELIGIOUS, RITUAL AND FUNERARY
RT CAUSEWAYED ENCLOSURE
    CAUSEWAYED RING DITCH
    ENCLOSURE

HENGIFORM MONUMENT
CL RELIGIOUS, RITUAL AND FUNERARY
RT CAUSEWAYED ENCLOSURE
    CAUSEWAYED RING DITCH
    ENCLOSURE
    STONE CIRCLE
    TIMBER CIRCLE

Heraldic Office
USE PROFESSIONAL INSTITUTE

Heralds College
USE PROFESSIONAL INSTITUTE

HERB DISTILLERY
UF Perfume Distillery
CL INDUSTRIAL
BT PHARMACEUTICAL CHEMICAL SITE
RT PERFUMERY

HERB GARDEN
CL GARDENS, PARKS AND URBAN SPACES
BT GARDEN
RT HERBARIUM
    KITCHEN
    KITCHEN GARDEN

HERBACEOUS BORDER
CL GARDENS, PARKS AND URBAN SPACES
BT BORDER

HERBARIUM
SN A building or room containing a collection of
    preserved plants (usually pressed and dried
    specimens).
CL GARDENS, PARKS AND URBAN SPACES
BT GARDEN BUILDING
RT HERB GARDEN

HERM

UF   Caryatid Terminal
      Hermes
      Term
      Terminal Figure
      Therm
SN   A pedestal terminating in a head or bust of Hermes
      or some other deity.
CL   GARDENS, PARKS AND URBAN SPACES
BT   GARDEN ORNAMENT
RT   BUST
      COLUMN
      SCULPTURE
      STATUE

Hermes
   USE HERM

HERMITAGE
UF   Bower
      Bowre
SN   A small hut or dwelling in a secluded spot,
      usually built in a park, as a resting place,
      retreat or viewing point.
CL   GARDENS, PARKS AND URBAN SPACES
BT   GARDEN BUILDING
RT   COTTAGE ORNEE
      GROTTO
      ROOT HOUSE

HERMITAGE
UF   Bower
      Bowre
SN   A small hut or dwelling in a secluded spot,
      usually built in a park, as a resting place,
      retreat or viewing point.
CL   RELIGIOUS, RITUAL AND FUNERARY
RT   ANCHORITE CELL
      COTTAGE ORNEE
      GROTTO
      ROOT HOUSE

Hewn Jetty
   USE FALSE QUAY

Hide And Skin Works
   USE TANNERY

HIGH BREASTSHOT WHEEL
CL   INDUSTRIAL
BT   BREASTSHOT WHEEL

High Commission Building
   USE EMBASSY

HIGH CROSS
CL   RELIGIOUS, RITUAL AND FUNERARY
BT   CROSS

HIGH LIGHT
CL   MARITIME
BT   LIGHTHOUSE

High Rise Block
   USE TOWER BLOCK

HIGH SECURITY PRISON
CL   CIVIL
BT   PRISON

Higher Elementary School
   USE SECONDARY SCHOOL

HIGHER GRADE SCHOOL
CL   EDUCATION
BT   SECONDARY SCHOOL

HILL FIGURE
UF   Chalk Figure
      Chalk Horse

      White Horse
CL   RELIGIOUS, RITUAL AND FUNERARY

HILL FIGURE
UF   Chalk Figure
      Chalk Horse
      White Horse
CL   COMMEMORATIVE
BT   COMMEMORATIVE MONUMENT

HILLFORT
UF   Contour Fort
CL   DOMESTIC
BT   ENCLOSED SETTLEMENT
NT   BIVALLATE HILLFORT
      MINI HILL FORT
      MULTIPLE ENCLOSURE FORT
      MULTIVALLATE HILLFORT
      UNIVALLATE HILLFORT
RT   CHEVAUX DE FRISE
      HILLTOP ENCLOSURE
      OPPIDUM
      PROMONTORY FORT

HILLFORT
UF   Contour Fort
CL   DEFENCE
BT   ENCLOSED SETTLEMENT
NT   BIVALLATE HILLFORT
      MINI HILL FORT
      MULTIPLE ENCLOSURE FORT
      MULTIVALLATE HILLFORT
      UNIVALLATE HILLFORT
RT   CHEVAUX DE FRISE
      HILLTOP ENCLOSURE
      OPPIDUM
      PROMONTORY FORT

HILLTOP ENCLOSURE
SN   Substantial area of ground surrounded by slight
      univallate earthwork often interpreted as stock
      enclosures or as sites where agricultural produce
      was stored.
CL   DOMESTIC
BT   ENCLOSED SETTLEMENT
NT   PALISADED HILLTOP ENCLOSURE
RT   HILLFORT

HILLTOP ENCLOSURE
SN   Substantial area of ground surrounded by slight
      univallate earthwork often interpreted as stock
      enclosures or as sites where agricultural produce
      was stored.
CL   AGRICULTURE AND SUBSISTENCE
RT   HILLFORT

HILLTOP ENCLOSURE
SN   Substantial area of ground surrounded by slight
      univallate earthwork often interpreted as stock
      enclosures or as sites where agricultural produce
      was stored.
CL   DEFENCE
BT   ENCLOSED SETTLEMENT
NT   PALISADED HILLTOP ENCLOSURE
RT   HILLFORT

HISTORICAL SITE
SN   Site with important historical association.
CL   COMMEMORATIVE
RT   BATTLEFIELD
      NAMED TREE

Hlaew
   USE BARROW

Hoar Stone
   USE BOUNDARY STONE

HOARDING

CL   GARDENS, PARKS AND URBAN SPACES
BT   STREET FURNITURE

HOCKEY PITCH
CL   RECREATIONAL
BT   SPORTS SITE

HOFFMAN KILN
CL   INDUSTRIAL
BT   KILN <BY FORM>
RT   BRICK KILN
     CHIMNEY
     DOWNDRAUGHT KILN
     LIME KILN

Hogback
USE HOGBACK STONE

HOGBACK STONE
UF   Hogback
CL   RELIGIOUS, RITUAL AND FUNERARY
BT   FUNERARY SITE

Hogg Cote
USE SHEEP FOLD
SN   A pen or enclosure for hoggs (yearling sheep, not
     pigs).

Hogg House
USE SHEEP HOUSE
SN   For the housing of hoggs (yearling sheep, not
     pigs).

HOGGERY
SN   A yard for pigs.
CL   AGRICULTURE AND SUBSISTENCE
RT   PIGSTY

HOIST
CL   TRANSPORT
BT   LIFTING AND WINDING STRUCTURE
NT   TEAGLE

HOLDING SHED
CL   TRANSPORT
BT   RAILWAY TRANSPORT SITE
RT   GOODS YARD
     RAILWAY WAREHOUSE
     SHED

HOLLAND SUBMARINE
CL   MARITIME
BT   SUBMARINE

HOLLOW
UF   Depression
CL   UNASSIGNED

HOLLOW WAY
CL   TRANSPORT
BT   ROAD

Holy Sepulchre Priory
USE AUGUSTINIAN MONASTERY
     PRIORY
SN   Use both terms.

HOLY WELL
UF   Healing Well
     Sacred Well
CL   RELIGIOUS, RITUAL AND FUNERARY
RT   SHRINE
     SPRING
     WELL

Home For Girls
USE CHILDRENS HOME

Home For The Elderly

USE NURSING HOME

Home Office
USE GOVERNMENT OFFICE

HOMELESS HOSTEL
UF   Oriental Strangers Home
     Salvation Army Hostel
CL   HEALTH AND WELFARE
RT   MISSION HALL

HOMELESS HOSTEL
UF   Oriental Strangers Home
     Salvation Army Hostel
CL   DOMESTIC
BT   HOSTEL

Homestead
USE ENCLOSED SETTLEMENT

Homestead Moat
USE MOAT

HOMOEOPATHIC HOSPITAL
CL   HEALTH AND WELFARE
BT   SPECIALIST HOSPITAL

HOOP HOUSE
SN   Where hoops (for masts) were heated.
CL   MARITIME
BT   MARINE WORKSHOP

HOOP HOUSE
SN   Where hoops (for masts) were heated.
CL   INDUSTRIAL
BT   MARINE WORKSHOP

HOP BARN
CL   AGRICULTURE AND SUBSISTENCE
BT   BARN
RT   HOP HOUSE
     HOP STORE
     OASTHOUSE

HOP EXCHANGE
CL   COMMERCIAL
BT   EXCHANGE

HOP GARDEN
UF   Brew House Garden
     Brewhouse Garden
     Hop Yard
CL   AGRICULTURE AND SUBSISTENCE
BT   GARDEN
RT   HOP KILN

HOP HOUSE
CL   AGRICULTURE AND SUBSISTENCE
BT   FOOD AND DRINK PROCESSING SITE
RT   HOP BARN
     HOP STORE
     OASTHOUSE

HOP KILN
CL   INDUSTRIAL
BT   BREWING AND MALTING SITE
RT   HOP GARDEN
     HOP STORE
     MALT KILN
     OASTHOUSE

HOP KILN
CL   INDUSTRIAL
BT   KILN <BY FUNCTION>

HOP KILN
CL   AGRICULTURE AND SUBSISTENCE
BT   FOOD AND DRINK PROCESSING SITE
RT   MALT KILN

OASTHOUSE

HOP STORE
- CL INDUSTRIAL
- BT BREWING AND MALTING SITE
- RT HOP BARN
    HOP HOUSE
    OASTHOUSE

HOP STORE
- CL AGRICULTURE AND SUBSISTENCE
- BT FOOD AND DRINK PROCESSING SITE
- RT HOP BARN
    HOP HOUSE
    HOP KILN
    OASTHOUSE

Hop Yard
  USE HOP GARDEN

HOPPER BARGE
- CL MARITIME
- BT BARGE

HOPPER DREDGER
- CL MARITIME
- BT DREDGER

HOPSCOTCH COURT
- CL RECREATIONAL
- BT SPORTS SITE
- RT SCHOOL

HORIZONTAL AIR MILL
- CL INDUSTRIAL
- BT WINDMILL <BY FORM>

HORIZONTAL KILN
- CL INDUSTRIAL
- BT KILN <BY FORM>

HORIZONTAL STEAM ENGINE
- SN A piston mounted horizontally supplying power via a valve gear directly to a crankshaft or flywheel.
- CL INDUSTRIAL
- BT STEAM ENGINE

Horizontal Watermill
  USE WATERMILL

Horn Bastion
  USE BASTION

HORN WORKING SITE
- CL INDUSTRIAL
- BT ANIMAL PRODUCT SITE
- NT HORNCORE PIT

HORNCORE PIT
- CL INDUSTRIAL
- BT HORN WORKING SITE
- RT PIT

HORNWORK
- SN An outwork joined to the mainwork by two parallel wings.
- CL DEFENCE

Horse And Carriage Auction Rooms
  USE AUCTION HOUSE

HORSE ENGINE
- UF Cog And Rung Gin
    Gin Case
    Gingang
    Horse Gin
    Whim Gin
- CL INDUSTRIAL
- BT ANIMAL POWER SITE

- RT DONKEY WHEEL
    HORSE ENGINE HOUSE
    HORSE WHEEL
    HORSE WHIM
    OIL MILL

HORSE ENGINE HOUSE
- UF Horse Gin House
    Horse Mill
    Horse Wheel House
    Round House (Horse Engine)
    Whim House
- CL INDUSTRIAL
- BT ANIMAL POWER SITE
- RT CIDER MILL
    DONKEY WHEEL
    HORSE ENGINE
    HORSE WHEEL
    HORSE WHIM
    MIXING HOUSE BARN
    THRESHING BARN

HORSE ENGINE HOUSE
- UF Horse Gin House
    Horse Mill
    Horse Wheel House
    Round House (Horse Engine)
    Whim House
- CL INDUSTRIAL
- BT ENGINE HOUSE

Horse Gin
  USE HORSE ENGINE

Horse Gin House
  USE HORSE ENGINE HOUSE

HORSE HOSPITAL
- CL HEALTH AND WELFARE
- BT VETERINARY HOSPITAL

Horse Mill
  USE HORSE ENGINE HOUSE

Horse Mounting Block
  USE MOUNTING BLOCK

Horse Mounting Stone
  USE MOUNTING BLOCK

HORSE TROUGH
- CL GARDENS, PARKS AND URBAN SPACES
- BT TROUGH

HORSE TROUGH
- CL AGRICULTURE AND SUBSISTENCE
- BT TROUGH

HORSE TROUGH
- CL TRANSPORT
- BT ROAD TRANSPORT SITE

HORSE TROUGH
- CL WATER SUPPLY AND DRAINAGE
- BT TROUGH

HORSE TUNNEL
- CL TRANSPORT
- BT TRANSPORT TUNNEL
- RT TUNNEL

HORSE TUNNEL
- CL TRANSPORT
- BT CANAL TRANSPORT SITE
- RT TUNNEL

Horse Walk
  USE WINDING CIRCLE

HORSE WASH

CL AGRICULTURE AND SUBSISTENCE
BT ANIMAL WASH

HORSE WHEEL
UF Gin Wheel
CL INDUSTRIAL
BT ANIMAL POWER SITE
RT HORSE ENGINE
    HORSE ENGINE HOUSE
    OIL MILL

Horse Wheel House
  USE HORSE ENGINE HOUSE

HORSE WHIM
UF Gin Circle
SN A horse-powered winding engine used at mining
    sites.
CL INDUSTRIAL
BT ANIMAL POWER SITE
RT HORSE ENGINE
    HORSE ENGINE HOUSE

HORSE WHIM
UF Gin Circle
SN A horse-powered winding engine used at mining
    sites.
CL INDUSTRIAL
BT MINE LIFTING AND WINDING STRUCTURE
RT WINDING CIRCLE
    WINDING GEAR

HORSEHAIR FACTORY
UF Horsehair Works
SN The cleaning and sorting of horse hair mainly for
    use in the upholstery trade.
CL INDUSTRIAL
BT ANIMAL PRODUCT SITE
RT ABATTOIR

HORSEHAIR FACTORY
UF Horsehair Works
SN The cleaning and sorting of horse hair mainly for
    use in the upholstery trade.
CL INDUSTRIAL
BT FACTORY <BY PRODUCT>

Horsehair Works
  USE HORSEHAIR FACTORY

HORTICULTURAL COLLEGE
CL EDUCATION
BT TRAINING COLLEGE
RT AGRICULTURAL COLLEGE
    RURAL INSTITUTE

HORTICULTURAL HALL
CL COMMERCIAL
BT EXHIBITION HALL

HOSE TOWER
CL CIVIL
RT FIRE STATION

HOSIERS COTTAGE
UF Stockingers Cottage
CL DOMESTIC
BT INDUSTRIAL HOUSE
RT FRAMEWORK KNITTERS COTTAGE
    HOSIERY WORKSHOP

HOSIERS COTTAGE
UF Stockingers Cottage
CL INDUSTRIAL
BT CRAFT INDUSTRY SITE
RT FRAMEWORK KNITTERS COTTAGE
    HOSIERY WORKSHOP

HOSIERS COTTAGE

UF Stockingers Cottage
CL INDUSTRIAL
BT INDUSTRIAL HOUSE

HOSIERY FACTORY
UF Hosiery Works
SN Mechanised knitting processes to produce stockings
    and socks.
CL INDUSTRIAL
BT CLOTHING INDUSTRY SITE
RT TEXTILE MILL

HOSIERY FACTORY
UF Hosiery Works
SN Mechanised knitting processes to produce stockings
    and socks.
CL INDUSTRIAL
BT FACTORY <BY PRODUCT>

Hosiery Works
  USE HOSIERY FACTORY

HOSIERY WORKSHOP
CL INDUSTRIAL
BT CRAFT INDUSTRY SITE
RT FLAX BEATING STONE
    FRAMEWORK KNITTERS COTTAGE
    HOSIERS COTTAGE
    LOOMSHOP
    TOPSHOP

HOSPICE
SN An establishment providing care for the terminally
    ill.
CL HEALTH AND WELFARE
RT HOSPITAL

HOSPITAL
UF Cottage Home Hospital
    Hospital Chapel
    Hospital Kitchen
SN Use narrower monument type if possible.
CL HEALTH AND WELFARE
NT ACCIDENT HOSPITAL
    ADMISSION HOSPITAL
    CONVALESCENT HOSPITAL
    COTTAGE HOSPITAL
    DAY HOSPITAL
    GENERAL HOSPITAL
    HOSPITAL SHIP
    HYDROPATHIC INSTITUTE
    INCURABLES HOSPITAL
    MENTAL HOSPITAL
    MILITARY HOSPITAL
    NAVAL HOSPITAL
    ROYAL AIR FORCE HOSPITAL
    SANATORIUM
    SPECIALIST HOSPITAL
    TEACHING HOSPITAL
RT ALMSHOUSE
    AMBULANCE STATION
    CANTEEN
    CLINIC
    DISPENSARY
    DOCTORS HOSTEL
    HOSPICE
    HOSPITAL BLOCK
    HOSPITAL BUILDING
    HOSPITAL DEPARTMENT
    HOSPITAL SCHOOL
    INFIRMARY
    ISOLATION BLOCK
    MEDICAL COLLEGE
    MONASTERY
    NURSES HOSTEL
    NURSES TRAINING SCHOOL
    OPERATING THEATRE
    PRECEPTORY
    RECEIVING BLOCK

RELIGIOUS HOUSE
WARD BLOCK

HOSPITAL
UF   Cottage Home Hospital
       Hospital Chapel
       Hospital Kitchen
SN   Use narrower monument type if possible.
CL   RELIGIOUS, RITUAL AND FUNERARY
NT   LEPER HOSPITAL

HOSPITAL BLOCK
SN   A specialist unit within a hospital complex. It
       may be a separate building or sometimes linked by
       a corridor or covered walkway to a main building.
CL   HEALTH AND WELFARE
NT   ANTENATAL BLOCK
       CASUAL WARD BLOCK
       CHILDRENS WARD BLOCK
       CUBICLE BLOCK
       DAYROOM BLOCK
       DISCHARGE BLOCK
       EMERGENCY WARD BLOCK
       ISOLATION BLOCK
       MATERNITY BLOCK
       MENTAL WARD BLOCK
       PAVILION WARD BLOCK
       PRIVATE PATIENTS BLOCK
       PRIVATE PATIENTS WARD BLOCK
       RECEIVING BLOCK
       WARD BLOCK
RT   HOSPITAL

HOSPITAL BUILDING
SN   Use more specific type if known.
CL   HEALTH AND WELFARE
RT   HOSPITAL

Hospital Canteen
USE CANTEEN

Hospital Chapel
USE CHAPEL
       HOSPITAL
SN   Use both terms.

HOSPITAL DEPARTMENT
SN   A separate functional unit of a hospital not
       necessarily on the same site.
CL   HEALTH AND WELFARE
NT   CASUALTY DEPARTMENT
       DENTAL DEPARTMENT
       EAR NOSE AND THROAT DEPARTMENT
       EYE DEPARTMENT
       ORTHODONTICS DEPARTMENT
       ORTHOPAEDIC DEPARTMENT
       OUTPATIENTS DEPARTMENT
       PATHOLOGY DEPARTMENT
       PHYSIOTHERAPY DEPARTMENT
RT   HOSPITAL

HOSPITAL FOR EPILEPTICS
UF   Epileptic Colony
SN   Originally epilepsy was seen as a mental illness.
CL   HEALTH AND WELFARE
BT   MENTAL HOSPITAL

HOSPITAL FOR FISTULA AND RECTAL DISEASES
CL   HEALTH AND WELFARE
BT   SPECIALIST HOSPITAL

HOSPITAL FOR THE MENTALLY HANDICAPPED
UF   Mental Deficiency Colony
SN   Modern use only.
CL   HEALTH AND WELFARE
BT   MENTAL HOSPITAL

HOSPITAL FOR URINARY DISEASES
CL   HEALTH AND WELFARE

BT   SPECIALIST HOSPITAL

Hospital Kitchen
USE KITCHEN
       HOSPITAL
SN   Use both terms.

HOSPITAL LAUNDRY
CL   HEALTH AND WELFARE
RT   LAUNDRY

HOSPITAL SCHOOL
SN   Charity school in almshouse.
CL   EDUCATION
BT   FREE SCHOOL
RT   ALMSHOUSE
       HOSPITAL

HOSPITAL SHIP
CL   MARITIME
BT   SERVICE CRAFT

HOSPITAL SHIP
CL   HEALTH AND WELFARE
BT   HOSPITAL

HOSPITALLERS CAMERA
UF   Knights Hospitallers Camera
CL   RELIGIOUS, RITUAL AND FUNERARY
BT   CAMERA
RT   HOSPITALLERS PRECEPTORY
       SISTERS OF ST JOHN NUNNERY

HOSPITALLERS CHURCH
UF   Knights Hospitallers Church
CL   RELIGIOUS, RITUAL AND FUNERARY
BT   CHURCH
RT   TEMPLARS CHURCH

HOSPITALLERS PRECEPTORY
UF   Commandery
       Hospitallers Priory
       Knights Hospitallers Commandery
       Knights Hospitallers Priory
SN   Includes the mother house styled Priory of St
       John, Clerkenwell.
CL   RELIGIOUS, RITUAL AND FUNERARY
BT   PRECEPTORY
RT   HOSPITALLERS CAMERA
       SISTERS OF ST JOHN NUNNERY
       TEMPLARS PRECEPTORY

Hospitallers Priory
USE HOSPITALLERS PRECEPTORY

Hospitium
USE COLLEGE LODGINGS

HOSTEL
SN   Use more specific term if known.
CL   DOMESTIC
BT   RESIDENTIAL BUILDING
NT   CHRISTIAN ASSOCIATION HOSTEL
       DOCTORS HOSTEL
       HOMELESS HOSTEL
       JAGGERS HOSTEL
       WORKERS HOSTEL
       YOUTH HOSTEL
RT   LODGING HOUSE

Hostelry
USE INN

HOTEL
CL   COMMERCIAL
NT   GRAND HOTEL
       MOTEL
       RAILWAY HOTEL
       SPA HOTEL

TEMPERANCE HOTEL
RT GUEST HOUSE
    INN
    LICENSED PREMISES
    TELEGRAPH OFFICE

HOTEL
CL DOMESTIC
BT RESIDENTIAL BUILDING
NT GRAND HOTEL
    MOTEL
    RAILWAY HOTEL
    SPA HOTEL
    TEMPERANCE HOTEL
RT GUEST HOUSE
    INN
    LICENSED PREMISES

HOTHOUSE
SN A glasshouse used for the cultivation of tropical
    plants.
CL GARDENS, PARKS AND URBAN SPACES
BT GLASSHOUSE

HOUSE
UF Cottage
    Domestic Dwelling
    Lobby Entry House
    Moated House
    Winged Corridor House
CL DOMESTIC
BT DWELLING
NT HOUSE <BY FORM>
    HOUSE <BY FUNCTION>
RT BACKYARD
    CRANNOG
    PATIO

HOUSE <BY FORM>
CL DOMESTIC
BT HOUSE
NT A FRAME HOUSE
    BUNGALOW
    CHALET
    COURTYARD HOUSE
    DETACHED HOUSE
    END CHIMNEY HOUSE
    FORTIFIED HOUSE
    GABLED HOUSE
    HALL HOUSE
    HOUSE PLATFORM
    PILE DWELLING
    ROCK CUT DWELLING
    ROW HOUSE
    SEMI DETACHED HOUSE
    SPLIT LEVEL HOUSE
    STUDIO HOUSE
    TERRACED HOUSE
    TIMBER FRAMED HOUSE
    TOFT
    TOWN HOUSE
    VILLA (NON ROMAN)
    VILLA (ROMAN)

HOUSE <BY FUNCTION>
CL DOMESTIC
BT HOUSE
NT CARETAKERS HOUSE
    CHARTIST COLONY HOUSE
    CHORISTERS HOUSE
    CLERICAL DWELLING
    COMMANDER IN CHIEFS HOUSE
    COMMISSIONERS HOUSE
    COUNCIL HOUSE
    COUNTRY HOUSE
    CURATORS HOUSE
    DOWER HOUSE
    ESTATE COTTAGE
    FARM LABOURERS COTTAGE

FARMHOUSE
FOREMANS HOUSE
GRADUATE HOUSE
GREAT HOUSE
GROOMS COTTAGE
GUEST COTTAGE
HEADMASTERS HOUSE
HEALTH WORKERS HOUSE
INDUSTRIAL HOUSE
LAITHE HOUSE
LONG HOUSE
MANAGERS HOUSE
MANOR HOUSE
MARITIME HOUSE
MERCHANTS HOUSE
PRISON GOVERNORS HOUSE
RANGERS HOUSE
REGISTRARS HOUSE
SQUATTERS COTTAGE
STEWARDS HOUSE
TEACHERS HOUSE
TRANSPORT WORKERS HOUSE
TREASURERS HOUSE
VERDERERS COTTAGE
WATERWORKS COTTAGE

HOUSE BOAT
CL MARITIME
BT MARITIME CRAFT

House Of Confinement
USE LOCK UP

House Of Correction
USE PRISON

HOUSE OF DETENTION
CL CIVIL
BT PRISON

House Of Industry
USE WORKHOUSE

House Of Institution
USE WORKHOUSE

House Of Recovery
USE INFECTIOUS DISEASES HOSPITAL

HOUSE PLATFORM
UF Platform House
CL DOMESTIC
BT HOUSE <BY FORM>
RT BUILDING PLATFORM
    PLATFORM
    TOFT

HOUSES OF PARLIAMENT
UF Parliament House
CL CIVIL
RT GOVERNMENT OFFICE

HOUSING ESTATE
CL DOMESTIC
BT SETTLEMENT
RT GARDEN SUBURB
    RECREATIONAL HALL

HOVEL
CL DOMESTIC
BT DWELLING
RT CATTLE SHELTER
    HUT
    SHELTER SHED

HOVERCRAFT TERMINAL
CL MARITIME
BT SEA TERMINAL

Howe

USE BARROW

Hudd
　　USE GRAVESIDE SHELTER

HUGUENOT BURIAL GROUND
　　CL　RELIGIOUS, RITUAL AND FUNERARY
　　BT　INHUMATION CEMETERY

HUGUENOT CHURCH
　　CL　RELIGIOUS, RITUAL AND FUNERARY
　　BT　CHURCH

HULK
　　CL　MARITIME
　　BT　HARBOUR SERVICES VESSEL
　　NT　PRISON HULK
　　　　SHEER HULK
　　　　STORAGE HULK

HULL
　　SN　Underground passage with storage chambers found in
　　　　South West England.
　　CL　AGRICULTURE AND SUBSISTENCE
　　BT　AGRICULTURAL BUILDING
　　RT　CELLAR
　　　　FOGOU
　　　　SOUTERRAIN
　　　　UNDERGROUND STRUCTURE

Human Bone
　　USE HUMAN REMAINS

HUMAN REMAINS
　　UF　Human Bone
　　　　Skeleton
　　SN　Unarticulated remains.
　　CL　RELIGIOUS, RITUAL AND FUNERARY
　　BT　FUNERARY SITE

Hundred Stone
　　USE BOUNDARY STONE

HUNGER HOUSE
　　CL　AGRICULTURE AND SUBSISTENCE
　　BT　FARM BUILDING
　　RT　FATTENING HOUSE

Hunting Box
　　USE HUNTING LODGE

HUNTING CLUB
　　UF　Huntsmans Club
　　CL　RECREATIONAL
　　BT　HUNTING SITE

HUNTING FOREST
　　UF　Chase
　　　　Royal Forest
　　CL　RECREATIONAL
　　BT　HUNTING SITE
　　RT　DEER PARK
　　　　HUNTING LODGE
　　　　WOOD

HUNTING FOREST
　　UF　Chase
　　　　Royal Forest
　　CL　AGRICULTURE AND SUBSISTENCE
　　BT　HUNTING SITE
　　RT　DEER PARK
　　　　HUNTING LODGE
　　　　WOOD

HUNTING LODGE
　　UF　Hunting Box
　　　　Lodge
　　　　Royal Hunting Lodge
　　　　Shooting Box

　　　　Shooting Lodge
　　CL　DOMESTIC
　　RT　COUNTRY HOUSE
　　　　DEER PARK
　　　　HUNTING FOREST
　　　　KENNELS
　　　　ROYAL PALACE
　　　　SHOOTING STAND

HUNTING LODGE
　　UF　Hunting Box
　　　　Lodge
　　　　Royal Hunting Lodge
　　　　Shooting Box
　　　　Shooting Lodge
　　CL　RECREATIONAL
　　BT　HUNTING SITE
　　RT　COUNTRY HOUSE
　　　　KENNELS
　　　　ROYAL PALACE

HUNTING LODGE
　　UF　Hunting Box
　　　　Lodge
　　　　Royal Hunting Lodge
　　　　Shooting Box
　　　　Shooting Lodge
　　CL　AGRICULTURE AND SUBSISTENCE
　　BT　HUNTING SITE
　　RT　COUNTRY HOUSE
　　　　DEER PARK
　　　　DEER SHELTER
　　　　HUNTING FOREST
　　　　HUNTING PARK
　　　　ROYAL PALACE
　　　　SHOOTING STAND

HUNTING PARK
　　CL　GARDENS, PARKS AND URBAN SPACES
　　BT　PARK
　　RT　HUNTING LODGE

HUNTING SITE
　　SN　Includes ancillary structures.
　　CL　AGRICULTURE AND SUBSISTENCE
　　NT　DECOY POND
　　　　DEER COTE
　　　　DEER HOUSE
　　　　DEER LEAP
　　　　DEER PARK
　　　　DEER POUND
　　　　DEER SHELTER
　　　　FALCONRY
　　　　HUNTING FOREST
　　　　HUNTING LODGE
　　　　KENNELS
　　　　KILL SITE
　　　　PARK PALE
　　　　SHOOTING STAND
　　RT　GAME LARDER
　　　　KENNELS

HUNTING SITE
　　SN　Includes ancillary structures.
　　CL　RECREATIONAL
　　NT　DECOY POND
　　　　DEER COTE
　　　　DEER HOUSE
　　　　DEER LEAP
　　　　DEER PARK
　　　　DEER POUND
　　　　DEER SHELTER
　　　　FALCONRY
　　　　HUNTING CLUB
　　　　HUNTING FOREST
　　　　HUNTING LODGE
　　　　KILL SITE
　　　　SHOOTING STAND
　　RT　KENNELS

Huntsman Furnace
USE CEMENTATION FURNACE

Huntsman Kiln
USE CEMENTATION FURNACE

Huntsmans Club
USE HUNTING CLUB

HUSH
UF   Lead Hush
SN   A ravine formed by using water to reveal or
     exploit a vein.
CL   INDUSTRIAL
BT   NON FERROUS METAL EXTRACTION SITE
RT   LEAT
     RESERVOIR

HUT
UF   Beehive Hut
SN   A dwelling of ruder and meaner construction, and
     usually smaller in size than a house. Often made
     of branches, turf or mud.
CL   DOMESTIC
BT   DWELLING
NT   BARK PEELERS HUT
     CHARCOAL BURNERS HUT
     HUT CIRCLE
     HUT PLATFORM
     SHEPHERDS HUT
     TRANSHUMANCE HUT
     WOODWORKERS HUT
RT   BOTHY
     HOVEL
     SHIELING

HUT CIRCLE
UF   Hut Walls
     Round House (Domestic)
     Stone Hut Circle
CL   DOMESTIC
BT   HUT
RT   HUT CIRCLE SETTLEMENT

HUT CIRCLE SETTLEMENT
UF   Hut Group
CL   DOMESTIC
BT   SETTLEMENT
NT   ENCLOSED HUT CIRCLE SETTLEMENT
     UNENCLOSED HUT CIRCLE SETTLEMENT
RT   HUT CIRCLE

Hut Group
USE HUT CIRCLE SETTLEMENT

HUT PLATFORM
CL   DOMESTIC
BT   HUT
RT   BUILDING PLATFORM
     PLATFORM

Hut Walls
USE HUT CIRCLE

Hyacinth Garden
USE FLOWER GARDEN

Hydrant
USE WATER PUMP

HYDRAULIC ACCUMULATOR TOWER
CL   INDUSTRIAL
BT   HYDRAULIC POWER SITE
RT   TOWER

HYDRAULIC BOX CRANE
CL   INDUSTRIAL
BT   HYDRAULIC CRANE

HYDRAULIC CRANE
CL   INDUSTRIAL
BT   HYDRAULIC POWER SITE
NT   HYDRAULIC BOX CRANE
     HYDRAULIC PILLAR CRANE
RT   CRANE

HYDRAULIC ENGINE HOUSE
CL   INDUSTRIAL
BT   ENGINE HOUSE
RT   CHAIN PROVING HOUSE
     CRANE
     LIFTING BRIDGE
     SHEET METAL WORKS

HYDRAULIC ENGINE HOUSE
CL   INDUSTRIAL
BT   HYDRAULIC POWER SITE

HYDRAULIC JIGGER
SN   A hydraulic machine used to magnify the stroke of
     a hydraulic piston. The pulleys and chains of a
     crane or other device are attached to the jigger.
CL   INDUSTRIAL
BT   HYDRAULIC POWER SITE

HYDRAULIC PILLAR CRANE
CL   INDUSTRIAL
BT   HYDRAULIC CRANE
RT   CRANE

HYDRAULIC PIPEWORK
SN   Pipes used to carry water or hydraulic fluid for
     power transmission within a hydraulic system.
CL   INDUSTRIAL
BT   HYDRAULIC POWER SITE

HYDRAULIC POWER SITE
CL   INDUSTRIAL
BT   POWER GENERATION SITE
NT   HYDRAULIC ACCUMULATOR TOWER
     HYDRAULIC CRANE
     HYDRAULIC ENGINE HOUSE
     HYDRAULIC JIGGER
     HYDRAULIC PIPEWORK
     HYDRAULIC PUMPING STATION
     HYDRAULIC RAM
     HYDRAULIC TIPPLER

Hydraulic Power Station
USE POWER STATION

HYDRAULIC PUMPING STATION
SN   A building in which water is pumped up a tower
     providing a head of water to maintain a working
     pressure in the hydraulic mains.
CL   INDUSTRIAL
BT   HYDRAULIC POWER SITE
RT   POWER STATION
     WELL HOUSE

HYDRAULIC RAM
SN   Large piston used to operate lifting bridges, lock
     gates, etc.
CL   INDUSTRIAL
BT   HYDRAULIC POWER SITE

HYDRAULIC TIPPLER
SN   A tippler, eg. a coal tippler, operated by
     hydraulic power.
CL   INDUSTRIAL
BT   HYDRAULIC POWER SITE
RT   COAL TIPPLER

Hydro (Hospital)
USE HYDROPATHIC INSTITUTE

Hydro (Power Station)

USE HYDROELECTRIC POWER STATION

Hydroelectric Power Plant
USE HYDROELECTRIC POWER STATION

HYDROELECTRIC POWER STATION
UF   Hydro (Power Station)
       Hydroelectric Power Plant
SN   Power generation by releasing stored water through
       a turbine driving a generator.
CL   INDUSTRIAL
BT   POWER STATION
RT   DAM
       TURBINE

Hydropathic Hospital
USE HYDROPATHIC INSTITUTE

HYDROPATHIC INSTITUTE
UF   Hydro (Hospital)
       Hydropathic Hospital
CL   HEALTH AND WELFARE
BT   HOSPITAL
RT   KURSAAL
       PUMP ROOMS
       SPA
       SPA HOTEL

Hypermarket
USE SUPERMARKET

HYPOCAUST
CL   DOMESTIC
RT   BATH HOUSE
       BATHS

Hythe
USE HARBOUR

ICE BREAKER
CL   MARITIME
BT   CHANNEL CLEARANCE VESSEL

Ice House
USE ICEHOUSE

Ice Rink
USE SKATING RINK

Ice Skating Rink
USE SKATING RINK

Ice Well
USE ICE WORKS

ICE WORKS
UF   Ice Well
CL   INDUSTRIAL
BT   FOOD PRESERVING SITE

ICEHOUSE
UF   Ice House
SN   A structure, partly underground, for the
       preservation of ice for use during warmer weather.
CL   DOMESTIC
RT   COLD STORE
       FISH HOUSE
       GAME LARDER
       GREAT HOUSE
       LARDER
       SMOKE HOUSE

ICEHOUSE
UF   Ice House
SN   A structure, partly underground, for the
       preservation of ice for use during warmer weather.
CL   GARDENS, PARKS AND URBAN SPACES
BT   GARDEN BUILDING
RT   FISH HOUSE

       GAME LARDER
       GREAT HOUSE
       SMOKE HOUSE

Idiots Asylum
USE MENTAL HOSPITAL

ILEX GROVE
UF   Bosco
CL   GARDENS, PARKS AND URBAN SPACES
BT   GROVE

Imbecile Ward
USE MENTAL WARD BLOCK

Implement Shed
USE SHED

IMPOUNDING STATION
CL   MARITIME
BT   WATER REGULATION INSTALLATION

INCINERATOR
CL   INDUSTRIAL
BT   WASTE DISPOSAL SITE
RT   REFUSE DESTRUCTOR STATION
       REFUSE DISPOSAL PLANT

Incline House
USE ENGINE HOUSE

INCLINE KEEPERS COTTAGE
CL   DOMESTIC
BT   TRANSPORT WORKERS HOUSE
RT   CANAL
       CANAL GATEHOUSE
       CANAL LIFT
       INCLINE WINDING ENGINE
       INCLINED PLANE
       LENGTHMANS COTTAGE
       WHARFINGERS COTTAGE

Incline Plane
USE INCLINED PLANE

INCLINE WINDING ENGINE
CL   TRANSPORT
BT   WINDING ENGINE
RT   BARGE WINCH
       CANAL
       CANAL LIFT
       INCLINE KEEPERS COTTAGE
       INCLINED PLANE

INCLINED PLANE
UF   Haulage Table Incline
       Incline Plane
CL   TRANSPORT
NT   CANAL INCLINED PLANE
       RAILWAY INCLINED PLANE
RT   BARGE WINCH
       CANAL
       CANAL LIFT
       INCLINE KEEPERS COTTAGE
       INCLINE WINDING ENGINE

INCORPORATING MILL
CL   INDUSTRIAL
BT   EXPLOSIVES SITE

INCORPORATING MILL
CL   INDUSTRIAL
BT   MILL

INCURABLES HOSPITAL
CL   HEALTH AND WELFARE
BT   HOSPITAL

Independent Abbey

USE ABBEY
SN Use order and type where known.

INDEPENDENT CHAPEL
CL RELIGIOUS, RITUAL AND FUNERARY
BT NONCONFORMIST CHAPEL

INDUCTION FURNACE
CL INDUSTRIAL
BT METAL PRODUCTION FURNACE
RT NON FERROUS METAL SMELTING SITE

INDUCTION HEARTH
CL INDUSTRIAL
BT METAL INDUSTRY SITE

INDUSTRIAL
SN This is the top term for the class. See INDUSTRIAL
    Class List for narrow terms.

INDUSTRIAL BUILDING
SN Any building designed or adapted to accommodate
    trades and manufacturing activity. Use more
    specific site where known.
CL INDUSTRIAL
NT CHIMNEY
    FIREPROOF BUILDING
    MILL

Industrial Craft Centre
USE CRAFT CENTRE

INDUSTRIAL ESTATE
UF Trading Estate
CL INDUSTRIAL
RT CRAFT CENTRE
    FACTORY
    WORKS

INDUSTRIAL HOUSE
CL DOMESTIC
BT HOUSE <BY FUNCTION>
NT APPRENTICE HOUSE
    CLOTHIERS HOUSE
    FOREMANS HOUSE
    FRAMEWORK KNITTERS COTTAGE
    HOSIERS COTTAGE
    LACEMAKERS COTTAGE
    MASTER HOSIERS HOUSE
    MASTER WEAVERS HOUSE
    MILL HOUSE
    MINE CAPTAINS HOUSE
    SMITHS COTTAGE
    WEAVERS COTTAGE
    WORKERS COTTAGE
RT BARK PEELERS HUT
    WOODWORKERS HUT
    WORKERS HOSTEL
    WORKERS VILLAGE

INDUSTRIAL HOUSE
CL INDUSTRIAL
NT APPRENTICE HOUSE
    CLOTHIERS HOUSE
    FOREMANS HOUSE
    FRAMEWORK KNITTERS COTTAGE
    HOSIERS COTTAGE
    LACEMAKERS COTTAGE
    MASTER HOSIERS HOUSE
    MASTER WEAVERS HOUSE
    MILL HOUSE
    MINE CAPTAINS HOUSE
    SMITHS COTTAGE
    WEAVERS COTTAGE
    WORKERS COTTAGE

Industrial Housing Estate
USE WORKERS VILLAGE

Industrial Model Village

USE WORKERS VILLAGE

INDUSTRIAL SCHOOL
UF School Of Industry
CL EDUCATION
BT TRAINING SCHOOL

INDUSTRIAL SITE
SN An area or defined space used for trades and
    manufacturing activity. Use more specific site
    where known.
CL INDUSTRIAL
RT FACTORY
    MILL
    WORKS

Infant Orphans Asylum
USE ORPHANAGE

INFANT SCHOOL
CL EDUCATION
BT ELEMENTARY SCHOOL

Infantry School
USE MILITARY COLLEGE

INFECTIOUS DISEASES HOSPITAL
UF Cholera Hospital
    Fever Hospital
    House Of Recovery
    Isolation Hospital
    Pest House
    Plague House
    Smallpox Hospital
    Tropical Diseases Hospital
CL HEALTH AND WELFARE
BT SPECIALIST HOSPITAL

INFIRMARY
UF Farmery
    Monastic Infirmary
    Poor Law Infirmary
    Poor Law Union Hospital
    Prison Infirmary
    School Infirmary
    Sick House
    Workhouse Infirmary
SN Only to be used where part of a complex, eg. a
    workhouse. In such cases use with appropriate
    monument type.
CL HEALTH AND WELFARE
RT HOSPITAL
    MONASTERY
    PRISON
    SCHOOL
    WORKHOUSE

Inhabited Medieval Village
USE VILLAGE

INHUMATION
UF Skeleton
CL RELIGIOUS, RITUAL AND FUNERARY
BT BURIAL
NT CONTRACTED INHUMATION
    CROUCHED INHUMATION
    EXTENDED INHUMATION
    FLEXED INHUMATION

INHUMATION CEMETERY
CL RELIGIOUS, RITUAL AND FUNERARY
BT CEMETERY
NT ANIMAL CEMETERY
    BAPTIST BURIAL GROUND
    CHURCHYARD
    CIST GRAVE CEMETERY
    EASTERN ORTHODOX CEMETERY
    FRIENDS BURIAL GROUND
    HUGUENOT BURIAL GROUND

JEWISH CEMETERY
MILITARY CEMETERY
MIXED CEMETERY
PLAGUE CEMETERY
ROMAN CATHOLIC CEMETERY

Inland Revenue Office
USE GOVERNMENT OFFICE

INN
UF Hostelry
Post Inn
CL COMMERCIAL
NT COACHING INN
DROVERS INN
RT ALE STORE
BEER HOUSE
BEER SHOP
HOTEL
INN SIGN
JAGGERS HOSTEL
LICENSED PREMISES
MANSIO
MOTEL
PUBLIC HOUSE

INN
UF Hostelry
Post Inn
CL DOMESTIC
BT RESIDENTIAL BUILDING
NT COACHING INN
DROVERS INN
RT ALE STORE
HOTEL
JAGGERS HOSTEL
MOTEL
PUBLIC HOUSE

INN SIGN
CL GARDENS, PARKS AND URBAN SPACES
BT STREET FURNITURE
RT INN

Inner Bailey
USE BAILEY

INNS OF CHANCERY
UF Legal Inn
CL CIVIL
BT LEGAL SITE

INNS OF COURT
CL CIVIL
BT LEGAL SITE

Insane Asylum
USE MENTAL HOSPITAL

Inscribed Slab
USE INSCRIBED STONE

INSCRIBED STONE
UF Early Christian Memorial Stone
Inscribed Slab
Pillar Stone
Pre Conquest Inscribed Stone
SN Early Medieval commemorative monument.
CL RELIGIOUS, RITUAL AND FUNERARY
RT CENTURIAL STONE
COMMEMORATIVE STONE
CROSS
CROSS INCISED STONE
GRAVESTONE
OGHAM STONE
RUNE STONE
STONE

Insolvent Debtors Court

USE DEBTORS COURT

INSTITUTE
UF Institution
CL EDUCATION
NT CHURCH INSTITUTE
COLLIERY INSTITUTE
COOPERATIVE INSTITUTE
DEAF AND DUMB INSTITUTE
FOREIGN LANGUAGE INSTITUTE
LEARNED SOCIETY BUILDING
LITERARY AND SCIENTIFIC INSTITUTE
MATHEMATICAL INSTITUTE
MECHANICS INSTITUTE
ORIENTAL INSTITUTE
PROFESSIONAL INSTITUTE
RURAL INSTITUTE
TECHNOLOGY INSTITUTE
WORKING MENS INSTITUTE

INSTITUTE
UF Institution
CL INSTITUTIONAL
NT CHURCH INSTITUTE
COLLIERY INSTITUTE
COOPERATIVE INSTITUTE
DEAF AND DUMB INSTITUTE
FOREIGN LANGUAGE INSTITUTE
LEARNED SOCIETY BUILDING
LITERARY AND SCIENTIFIC INSTITUTE
MATHEMATICAL INSTITUTE
MECHANICS INSTITUTE
ORIENTAL INSTITUTE
PROFESSIONAL INSTITUTE
RURAL INSTITUTE
TECHNOLOGY INSTITUTE
WORKING MENS INSTITUTE

Institution
USE INSTITUTE

INSTITUTIONAL
SN This is the top term for the class. See
INSTITUTIONAL Class List for narrow terms.

INSTRUMENT ENGINEERING WORKS
CL INDUSTRIAL
BT LIGHT ENGINEERING SITE
RT LIGHT ENGINEERING WORKS
WATCHMAKERS WORKSHOP

Insurance Office
USE COMMERCIAL OFFICE

INTERCEPTOR
CL WATER SUPPLY AND DRAINAGE
BT SEWER

Interment
USE BURIAL

International Airport
USE CIVIL AIRPORT

Interrupted Ditch Enclosure
USE CAUSEWAYED ENCLOSURE

INTERRUPTED DITCH SYSTEM
SN Ditches interrupted by wide, regular causeways.
Each section of ditch is about 30-40m long, and
each causeway is 10-15m wide. In some cases, a
network of fields has been created. To date (1993)
restricted to SE Kent.
CL AGRICULTURE AND SUBSISTENCE
BT LAND USE SITE

INTERVAL TOWER
CL DEFENCE

IONIC ROTUNDA

CL GARDENS, PARKS AND URBAN SPACES
BT ROTUNDA

IONIC TEMPLE
CL GARDENS, PARKS AND URBAN SPACES
BT GARDEN TEMPLE
RT TEMPLE

Iron Forge
USE FORGE

IRON FOUNDRY
CL INDUSTRIAL
BT FERROUS METAL PRODUCT SITE
RT FOUNDRY
    IRON WORKS
    SCRAP YARD

IRON FURNACE
CL INDUSTRIAL
BT METAL PRODUCTION FURNACE
RT FERROUS METAL SMELTING SITE

Iron Mine
USE IRONSTONE MINE

IRON ORE CALCINER
CL INDUSTRIAL
BT FERROUS METAL SMELTING SITE

IRON ORE CALCINER
CL INDUSTRIAL
BT CALCINER

Iron Slag Heap
USE SLAG HEAP

Iron Smelting Site
USE IRON WORKING SITE
SN Use more specific type of site where known, eg.
    BLOOMERY.

Iron Working
USE IRONSTONE WORKINGS

IRON WORKING SITE
UF Iron Smelting Site
CL INDUSTRIAL
BT FERROUS METAL SMELTING SITE
RT IRON WORKS

IRON WORKS
UF Ironworks
CL INDUSTRIAL
BT FERROUS METAL SMELTING SITE
RT BLOWING ENGINE HOUSE
    CANNON BORING MILL
    CUPOLA FURNACE (SHAFT)
    FORGE
    HAMMER
    HAMMER POND
    IRON FOUNDRY
    IRON WORKING SITE
    MANAGERS HOUSE
    PEN POND
    ROLLING MILL
    SLITTING MILL

Ironmasters House
USE MANAGERS HOUSE

Ironmongers Shop
USE HARDWARE SHOP

IRONSTONE MINE
UF Iron Mine
CL INDUSTRIAL
BT FERROUS METAL EXTRACTION SITE

IRONSTONE MINE

UF Iron Mine
CL INDUSTRIAL
BT MINE

IRONSTONE PIT
UF Ironstone Quarry
CL INDUSTRIAL
BT FERROUS METAL EXTRACTION SITE

IRONSTONE PIT
UF Ironstone Quarry
CL INDUSTRIAL
BT IRONSTONE WORKINGS

Ironstone Quarry
USE IRONSTONE PIT

IRONSTONE WORKINGS
UF Iron Working
    Open Cast Iron Workings
SN Open cast mining of iron ore.
CL INDUSTRIAL
BT FERROUS METAL EXTRACTION SITE

IRONSTONE WORKINGS
UF Iron Working
    Open Cast Iron Workings
SN Open cast mining of iron ore.
CL INDUSTRIAL
BT EXTRACTIVE PIT
NT IRONSTONE PIT
RT FERROUS METAL EXTRACTION SITE
    MINERAL EXTRACTION SITE

Ironworkers Cottage
USE WORKERS COTTAGE

Ironworks
USE IRON WORKS

Irregular Aggregate Field System
USE AGGREGATE FIELD SYSTEM

Irregular Enclosed Field System
USE ENCLOSED FIELD SYSTEM

Irregular Enclosure
USE ENCLOSURE

Irregular Open Field System
USE OPEN FIELD

ISLAND
SN A piece of land, sometimes man-made, completely
   surrounded by water.
CL GARDENS, PARKS AND URBAN SPACES

ISOLATION BLOCK
CL HEALTH AND WELFARE
BT HOSPITAL BLOCK
RT HOSPITAL
   LEPER HOSPITAL

Isolation Hospital
USE INFECTIOUS DISEASES HOSPITAL

ITALIAN GARDEN
CL GARDENS, PARKS AND URBAN SPACES
BT GARDEN

Itford Hill Style Enclosure
USE ENCLOSED SETTLEMENT

JAGGERS HOSTEL
CL DOMESTIC
BT HOSTEL
RT COACHING INN
   DROVERS INN
   INN

PACKHORSE BRIDGE

Jail
    USE PRISON

Jakes
    USE TOILET

JAPANESE GARDEN
    CL   GARDENS, PARKS AND URBAN SPACES
    BT   GARDEN

JAZZ CLUB
    CL   RECREATIONAL
    BT   MUSIC AND DANCE VENUE
    RT   CLUB
          DANCE HALL
          DISCOTHEQUE

Jesuit College
    USE THEOLOGICAL COLLEGE

Jet Mine
    USE JET WORKINGS

Jet Quarry
    USE JET WORKINGS

JET WORKING SITE
    CL   INDUSTRIAL
    BT   STONE WORKING SITE
    RT   JET WORKINGS
          JEWELLERY WORKSHOP

JET WORKINGS
    UF   Jet Mine
          Jet Quarry
    CL   INDUSTRIAL
    BT   MINERAL EXTRACTION SITE

JET WORKINGS
    UF   Jet Mine
          Jet Quarry
    CL   INDUSTRIAL
    BT   EXTRACTIVE PIT
    RT   JET WORKING SITE

JETTIED HOUSE
    CL   DOMESTIC
    BT   TIMBER FRAMED HOUSE
    NT   CONTINUOUS JETTY HOUSE
          END JETTY HOUSE

JETTY
    CL   TRANSPORT
    BT   WATER TRANSPORT SITE
    NT   COAL JETTY

JETTY
    CL   MARITIME
    BT   LANDING POINT
    NT   COAL JETTY

Jetty Staith
    USE STAITH

Jewellers Workshop
    USE JEWELLERY WORKSHOP

Jewellery Factory
    USE JEWELLERY WORKS

JEWELLERY WORKS
    UF   Jewellery Factory
    CL   INDUSTRIAL
    BT   CRAFT INDUSTRY SITE
    RT   GOLDSMITHS WORKSHOP
          JEWELLERY WORKSHOP
          SILVERSMITHS WORKSHOP

JEWELLERY WORKS
    UF   Jewellery Factory
    CL   INDUSTRIAL
    BT   NON FERROUS METAL PRODUCT SITE

JEWELLERY WORKSHOP
    UF   Jewellers Workshop
          Magenta Works
    CL   INDUSTRIAL
    BT   CRAFT INDUSTRY SITE
    RT   CUPELLATION FURNACE
          GLASS WORKING SITE
          GOLDSMITHS WORKSHOP
          JET WORKING SITE
          JEWELLERY WORKS
          SILVERSMITHS WORKSHOP
          WATCHMAKERS WORKSHOP

JEWELLERY WORKSHOP
    UF   Jewellers Workshop
          Magenta Works
    CL   INDUSTRIAL
    BT   NON FERROUS METAL PRODUCT SITE

JEWISH CEMETERY
    CL   RELIGIOUS, RITUAL AND FUNERARY
    BT   INHUMATION CEMETERY

Jewish Temple
    USE SYNAGOGUE

Jews House
    USE BLOWING HOUSE

JIB CRANE
    CL   TRANSPORT
    BT   CRANE <BY FORM>
    NT   FAIRBAIRN JIB CRANE

JOINERS SHOP
    UF   Joiners Workshop
    CL   INDUSTRIAL
    BT   CRAFT INDUSTRY SITE
    RT   CRATEMAKERS SHOP

JOINERS SHOP
    UF   Joiners Workshop
    CL   INDUSTRIAL
    BT   TIMBER PRODUCT SITE
    RT   FURNITURE FACTORY
          WHEELWRIGHTS WORKSHOP

Joiners Workshop
    USE JOINERS SHOP

Jougs
    USE PILLORY

Jube
    USE TOILET

JUDGES LODGING
    CL   CIVIL
    BT   LEGAL SITE
    RT   LODGINGS

JUDGES LODGINGS
    CL   DOMESTIC
    BT   RESIDENTIAL BUILDING
    RT   ASSIZE COURT
          COURT HOUSE
          LODGINGS

JUNCTION LOCK
    CL   TRANSPORT
    BT   LOCK
    RT   CANAL

Junior Reform Club

USE GENTLEMENS CLUB

JUTE MILL
- CL   INDUSTRIAL
- BT   TEXTILE MILL

JUTE MILL
- CL   INDUSTRIAL
- BT   LINEN OR FLAX MANUFACTURING SITE

JUVENILE COURT
- CL   CIVIL
- BT   LAW COURT

JUVENILE PRISON
- UF   Approved School
       Borstal
       Detention Centre
       Youth Custody Centre
- CL   CIVIL
- BT   PRISON

Keeill
   USE CHAPEL

KEEL BLOCK
- CL   MARITIME
- BT   DOCK AND HARBOUR INSTALLATION

KEEP
- UF   Castle Keep
       Donjon
       Great Tower
- CL   DOMESTIC
- BT   CASTLE
- NT   SHELL KEEP
       TOWER KEEP

KEEP
- UF   Castle Keep
       Donjon
       Great Tower
- CL   DEFENCE
- BT   CASTLE
- NT   SHELL KEEP
       TOWER KEEP

KEEP AND BAILEY CASTLE
- CL   DOMESTIC
- BT   CASTLE

KEEP AND BAILEY CASTLE
- CL   DEFENCE
- BT   CASTLE

KELP PIT
- CL   AGRICULTURE AND SUBSISTENCE

KENNELS
- UF   Doghouse
- CL   DOMESTIC
- RT   HUNTING LODGE

KENNELS
- UF   Doghouse
- CL   RECREATIONAL
- BT   ANIMAL HOUSE
- RT   HUNTING LODGE
       HUNTING SITE

KENNELS
- UF   Doghouse
- CL   AGRICULTURE AND SUBSISTENCE
- BT   HUNTING SITE
- RT   HUNTING LODGE

KERB CAIRN
- SN   A term used in Britain to describe a cairn
       featuring a mound with a diameter usually less
       than 6m, surrounded by large kerb stones standing
       considerably higher than the cairn mound.
- CL   RELIGIOUS, RITUAL AND FUNERARY

KERBED BOULDER
- SN   Prehistoric monument type in South West England in
       which a natural boulder is surrounded by a
       man-made kerb of stones.
- CL   RELIGIOUS, RITUAL AND FUNERARY

Key
   USE QUAY

KILL SITE
- CL   AGRICULTURE AND SUBSISTENCE
- BT   HUNTING SITE

KILL SITE
- CL   RECREATIONAL
- BT   HUNTING SITE

KILN
- UF   Kiln Debris
- SN   Use narrow term where known.
- CL   INDUSTRIAL
- NT   KILN <BY FORM>
       KILN <BY FUNCTION>
- RT   CHIMNEY
       OVEN

KILN <BY FORM>
- CL   INDUSTRIAL
- BT   KILN
- NT   BOTTLE KILN
       CIRCULAR KILN
       CLAMP KILN
       COCKLE KILN
       DOWNDRAUGHT KILN
       HOFFMAN KILN
       HORIZONTAL KILN
       OCTAGONAL KILN
       PYRAMIDAL KILN
       ROMAN KILN
       ROTARY KILN
       SCOTCH KILN
       SHAFT KILN
       TRANSVERSE ARCH KILN
       TUNNEL KILN
       UPDRAUGHT KILN

KILN <BY FUNCTION>
- CL   INDUSTRIAL
- BT   KILN
- NT   BRICK KILN
       CALCINER
       CALCINING KILN
       CHICORY KILN
       CLAY PIPE KILN
       COKE OVEN
       DRYING KILN
       ELLING HEARTH
       ENAMELLING KILN
       HOP KILN
       LIME KILN
       MALT KILN
       OASTHOUSE
       POTASH KILN
       POTTERY KILN
       SODA KILN
       TILE KILN
       WASTER KILN

Kiln Debris
   USE KILN

Kiln Waster
   USE WASTER KILN

KIOSK
- UF   Theatre Pay Box
- CL   COMMERCIAL
- RT   PUBLIC PARK

SHOP
SHOPPING CENTRE
THEATRE

Kippering Shed
USE SMOKE HOUSE

Kirk
USE CHURCH

KISSING GATE
CL GARDENS, PARKS AND URBAN SPACES
RT GATE
STILE

Kist
USE CIST

Kistvaen
USE CIST

KITCHEN
UF Abbey Kitchen
Hospital Kitchen
Monastery Kitchen
Priory Kitchen
Village Kitchen
CL DOMESTIC
RT ABBEY
BAKEHOUSE
COUNTRY HOUSE
HERB GARDEN
MONASTERY
PRIORY

KITCHEN GARDEN
CL GARDENS, PARKS AND URBAN SPACES
BT GARDEN
RT COUNTRY HOUSE
HERB GARDEN

KITCHEN GARDEN
CL AGRICULTURE AND SUBSISTENCE
BT GARDEN
RT COUNTRY HOUSE
HERB GARDEN

Knapping Site
USE FLINT WORKING SITE

Knife Factory
USE CUTLERY WORKS

Knife Works
USE CUTLERY WORKS

Knights Hospitallers Camera
USE HOSPITALLERS CAMERA

Knights Hospitallers Church
USE HOSPITALLERS CHURCH

Knights Hospitallers Commandery
USE HOSPITALLERS PRECEPTORY

Knights Hospitallers Priory
USE HOSPITALLERS PRECEPTORY

Knights Templars Camera
USE TEMPLARS CAMERA

Knights Templars Church
USE TEMPLARS CHURCH

Knights Templars Preceptory
USE TEMPLARS PRECEPTORY

Knitters Workshop
USE FRAMEWORK KNITTERS COTTAGE

KNOCK STONE
SN A stone or platform on which lumps of ore are manually broken up.
CL INDUSTRIAL
BT NON FERROUS METAL PROCESSING SITE
RT ORE STONE
WASHING FLOOR

Knocking Mill
USE STAMPING MILL

KNOT GARDEN
CL GARDENS, PARKS AND URBAN SPACES
BT GARDEN
RT MAZE

Knowe
USE BARROW

Koepe Winding Tower
USE WINDER HOUSE

KURSAAL
CL RECREATIONAL
BT HEALTH ESTABLISHMENT
RT BATHS
HYDROPATHIC INSTITUTE
PUMP ROOMS
SPA HOTEL

LABORATORY
UF Research Laboratory
School Laboratory
CL EDUCATION
NT MARINE LABORATORY
RT NITROGLYCERINE WORKS
PHARMACEUTICAL WORKS
PIPE BRIDGE
RESEARCH STATION

LABORATORY
UF Research Laboratory
School Laboratory
CL INDUSTRIAL
BT CHEMICAL INDUSTRY SITE

Labour Club
USE POLITICAL CLUB

LABOUR EXCHANGE
UF Sailors Exchange
Sailors Registry
CL CIVIL

LABOURERS SHELTER
SN Simple lean to structure, such as those built by the dock companies to provide shelter for dock workers waiting for work.
CL UNASSIGNED
BT SHELTER

Labyrinth
USE MAZE

Lace Drying Chamber
USE LACE DRYING HOUSE

LACE DRYING HOUSE
UF Lace Drying Chamber
CL INDUSTRIAL
BT LACE MANUFACTURING SITE
RT CLOTHIERS WORKSHOP
DRY HOUSE
FLAX BEATING STONE
LACE FACTORY
LACEMAKERS COTTAGE
TOPSHOP

LACE FACTORY

CL INDUSTRIAL
BT TEXTILE MILL
RT LACE DRYING HOUSE

LACE FACTORY
  CL INDUSTRIAL
  BT LACE MANUFACTURING SITE

LACE MANUFACTURING SITE
  CL INDUSTRIAL
  BT TEXTILE PRODUCT SITE
  NT LACE DRYING HOUSE
      LACE FACTORY
  RT LACEMAKERS COTTAGE

Lace Market
  USE CLOTH MARKET

Lace Warehouse
  USE CLOTH MARKET

LACEMAKERS COTTAGE
  CL INDUSTRIAL
  BT CRAFT INDUSTRY SITE
  RT LACE DRYING HOUSE
      LACE MANUFACTURING SITE

LACEMAKERS COTTAGE
  CL DOMESTIC
  BT INDUSTRIAL HOUSE
  RT LACE MANUFACTURING SITE

LACEMAKERS COTTAGE
  CL INDUSTRIAL
  BT INDUSTRIAL HOUSE

LADIES COLLEGE
  UF Ladies Seminary
  CL EDUCATION
  BT TRAINING COLLEGE
  RT PRIVATE SCHOOL
      PUBLIC SCHOOL

Ladies Seminary
  USE LADIES COLLEGE

LADY CHAPEL
  CL RELIGIOUS, RITUAL AND FUNERARY
  BT CHAPEL

LAITERIE
  SN A decorative building in the form of a dairy, used
      for recreation.
  CL GARDENS, PARKS AND URBAN SPACES
  BT GARDEN BUILDING
  RT COUNTRY HOUSE
      DAIRY

LAITHE
  SN A building combining a cow-house with crop storage
      space.
  CL AGRICULTURE AND SUBSISTENCE
  BT FARM BUILDING
  RT BARN
      COW HOUSE
      LAITHE HOUSE
      VACCARY

LAITHE HOUSE
  SN A laithe with an attached house.
  CL DOMESTIC
  BT HOUSE <BY FUNCTION>
  RT FARM LABOURERS COTTAGE
      FARMHOUSE
      LAITHE
      LONG HOUSE

LAITHE HOUSE
  SN A laithe with an attached house.
  CL AGRICULTURE AND SUBSISTENCE

BT FARM BUILDING
RT FARM LABOURERS COTTAGE
    FARMHOUSE
    LAITHE
    LONG HOUSE

LAKE
  UF Garden Lake
  CL GARDENS, PARKS AND URBAN SPACES
  NT BOATING LAKE
      ORNAMENTAL LAKE

Lake Dwelling
  USE CRANNOG

Lake Settlement
  USE LAKE VILLAGE

LAKE VILLAGE
  UF Lake Settlement
  CL DOMESTIC
  BT UNENCLOSED SETTLEMENT
  RT CRANNOG

LAMP BRACKET
  CL GARDENS, PARKS AND URBAN SPACES
  BT STREET FURNITURE

Lamp House
  USE LAMPHOUSE

LAMP POST
  UF Lamp Standard
  CL GARDENS, PARKS AND URBAN SPACES
  BT STREET FURNITURE
  RT GAS LAMP
      SNUFFER

Lamp Room
  USE LAMPHOUSE

Lamp Standard
  USE LAMP POST

LAMPHOUSE
  UF Lamp House
      Lamp Room
      Miners Lamphouse
  SN For the storage and recharging of battery-powered
      miners lamps.
  CL INDUSTRIAL
  BT MINE BUILDING
  RT MINERS CHANGING HOUSE
      PITHEAD BATHS

Lancashire Barn
  USE COMBINATION BARN

Lancasterian School
  USE CHURCH SCHOOL

Land Drain
  USE DRAIN

Land Drainage
  USE DRAINAGE SYSTEM

Land Fort
  USE FORTRESS

LAND RECLAMATION
  CL UNASSIGNED

Land Stewards Office
  USE OFFICE

LAND USE SITE
  SN Areas of land used primarily for agriculture. See
      also GARDENS, PARKS AND URBAN SPACES.
  CL AGRICULTURE AND SUBSISTENCE

NT ALLOTMENT
   CAIRN
   CAIRNFIELD
   COMMON LAND
   COPSE
   CROFT
   CULTIVATION MARKS
   CULTIVATION TERRACE
   FARM
   FIELD
   FIELD SYSTEM
   GARDEN
   GRANGE
   INTERRUPTED DITCH SYSTEM
   LAZY BEDS
   MANOR
   MEADOW
   MESSUAGE
   ORCHARD
   OSIER BED
   PLANTATION
   PLANTATION BANK
   RANCH BOUNDARY
   REAVE
   SHIELING
   SMALLHOLDING
   VILLA (ROMAN)
   VINEYARD
   WATERCRESS BED
   WOOD BANK
   WOODLAND

LANDING CRAFT
   CL MARITIME
   BT AMPHIBIOUS OPERATIONS VESSEL
   NT LANDING CRAFT INFANTRY
      LANDING CRAFT SUPPORT
      LANDING CRAFT TANK
      LANDING CRAFT VEHICLE

LANDING CRAFT INFANTRY
   CL MARITIME
   BT LANDING CRAFT

LANDING CRAFT SUPPORT
   CL MARITIME
   BT LANDING CRAFT

LANDING CRAFT TANK
   CL MARITIME
   BT LANDING CRAFT

LANDING CRAFT VEHICLE
   CL MARITIME
   BT LANDING CRAFT

LANDING HOUSE
   CL MARITIME
   BT LANDING POINT

LANDING PIER
   CL TRANSPORT
   BT WATER TRANSPORT SITE

LANDING PIER
   CL MARITIME
   BT PIER

LANDING POINT
   CL MARITIME
   NT BERTH
      JETTY
      LANDING HOUSE
      LANDING STAGE
      LANDING STEPS
      PIER
      QUAY
      STAITH
      WHARF

LANDING STAGE
   CL TRANSPORT
   BT WATER TRANSPORT SITE

LANDING STAGE
   CL MARITIME
   BT LANDING POINT

LANDING STEPS
   UF Embankment Steps
      River Stairs
      River Steps
   CL TRANSPORT
   BT WATER TRANSPORT SITE

LANDING STEPS
   UF Embankment Steps
      River Stairs
      River Steps
   CL MARITIME
   BT LANDING POINT

Landing Strip
   USE RUNWAY

LANDMARK TOWER
   UF Coastal Landmark Tower
   CL MARITIME
   BT NAVIGATION AID

Landscape Garden
   USE LANDSCAPE PARK

LANDSCAPE PARK
   UF Landscape Garden
   CL GARDENS, PARKS AND URBAN SPACES
   BT PARK

Lantern Cross
   USE CROSS

LARDER
   UF Despence
      Dispence
   CL DOMESTIC
   NT GAME LARDER
   RT FISH HOUSE
      ICEHOUSE

Large Irregular Stone Circle
   USE STONE CIRCLE

Large Multivallate Hillfort
   USE MULTIVALLATE HILLFORT

Large Regular Stone Circle
   USE STONE CIRCLE

Large Stone Circle
   USE STONE CIRCLE

Large Univallate Hillfort
   USE UNIVALLATE HILLFORT

LASCAR HOUSE
   CL DOMESTIC
   BT MARITIME HOUSE

LATRINE
   UF Latrine Pit
   CL WATER SUPPLY AND DRAINAGE
   RT CESS PIT
      MIDDEN
      TOILET

Latrine Pit
   USE LATRINE

LAUNDRETTE

CL COMMERCIAL
RT ESTATE LAUNDRY
   LAUNDRY

LAUNDRY
CL COMMERCIAL
RT ESTATE LAUNDRY
   HOSPITAL LAUNDRY
   LAUNDRETTE
   WASH HOUSE

Lavatory
USE TOILET

LAW COURT
UF Criminal Courts
   Forest Court
   Law Courts
CL CIVIL
BT LEGAL SITE
NT ASSIZE COURT
   CONSISTORY COURT
   CORONERS COURT
   COUNTY COURT
   COURT HOUSE
   COURT ROOM
   CROWN COURT
   DEBTORS COURT
   JUVENILE COURT
   MAGISTRATES COURT
   STANNARY COURT

Law Courts
USE LAW COURT

LAWN
CL GARDENS, PARKS AND URBAN SPACES
NT CAMOMILE LAWN
   CROQUET LAWN
   TERRACED LAWN
RT GARDEN

Lay Apart Store
USE NAVAL STOREHOUSE

LAY BRETHREN SETTLEMENT
CL RELIGIOUS, RITUAL AND FUNERARY
BT RELIGIOUS HOUSE
NT COURERY

Lazar House
USE LEPER HOSPITAL

Lazaretto
USE LEPER HOSPITAL

LAZY BEDS
CL AGRICULTURE AND SUBSISTENCE
BT LAND USE SITE
RT FIELD SYSTEM

Lead Condensing Flue
USE CONDENSING FLUE

Lead Crushing Mill
USE CRUSHING MILL

LEAD FURNACE
CL INDUSTRIAL
BT METAL PRODUCTION FURNACE
RT NON FERROUS METAL SMELTING SITE

Lead Hush
USE HUSH

Lead Mill
USE SMELT MILL

LEAD MINE

SN Use with form of extraction where known. Also use
   MINE and other ores extracted where relevant, eg.
   SILVER MINE.
CL INDUSTRIAL
BT NON FERROUS METAL EXTRACTION SITE
RT BUDDLE
   FLUORSPAR MINE
   LEAD WORKINGS
   MANGANESE MINE
   ORE HEARTH
   SILVER MINE
   WITHERITE MINE
   ZINC MINE

LEAD MINE
SN Use with form of extraction where known. Also use
   MINE and other ores extracted where relevant, eg.
   SILVER MINE.
CL INDUSTRIAL
BT MINE
RT BARYTES MINE
   CALAMINE MINE
   FLUORSPAR MINE
   MANGANESE MINE
   SILVER MINE
   WITHERITE MINE
   ZINC MINE

Lead Miners Cottage
USE WORKERS COTTAGE

Lead Precipitation Flue
USE CONDENSING FLUE

Lead Smelting Chimney
USE CONDENSING FLUE

Lead Smelting Mill
USE SMELT MILL

LEAD WORKING SITE
CL INDUSTRIAL
BT NON FERROUS METAL SMELTING SITE
RT BOLEHILL
   LEAD WORKS
   PEAT STORE
   SILVER HEARTH
   SLAG HEARTH

LEAD WORKINGS
UF Opencast Lead Workings
CL INDUSTRIAL
BT EXTRACTIVE PIT
RT BELL PIT

LEAD WORKINGS
UF Opencast Lead Workings
CL INDUSTRIAL
BT NON FERROUS METAL EXTRACTION SITE
RT BELL PIT
   FLUORSPAR WORKINGS
   LEAD MINE
   LEAD WORKS

LEAD WORKS
SN Production of red lead used in glass manufacture,
   or white lead used as the pigment in white paint.
CL INDUSTRIAL
BT NON FERROUS METAL SMELTING SITE
RT CONDENSING CHIMNEY
   CONDENSING FLUE
   LEAD WORKING SITE
   LEAD WORKINGS

LEAD WORKS
SN Production of red lead used in glass manufacture,
   or white lead used as the pigment in white paint.
CL INDUSTRIAL
BT NON FERROUS METAL PRODUCT SITE

RT   CONDENSING CHIMNEY

Leading Light
USE LIGHTHOUSE

LEARNED SOCIETY BUILDING
UF   Royal Institution
CL   INSTITUTIONAL
BT   INSTITUTE
RT   ATHENAEUM
     CHURCH INSTITUTE
     LITERARY AND SCIENTIFIC INSTITUTE

LEARNED SOCIETY BUILDING
UF   Royal Institution
CL   EDUCATION
BT   INSTITUTE

LEAT
SN   Artificial water channel, usually leading to a
     mill.
CL   WATER SUPPLY AND DRAINAGE
BT   WATER CHANNEL
RT   CANAL FEEDER
     CONDUIT
     DRAIN
     GULLY
     HUSH
     MILL
     MILL POND
     MILL RACE
     STREAM WORKS

LEAT
SN   Artificial water channel, usually leading to a
     mill.
CL   INDUSTRIAL
BT   WATER POWER PRODUCTION SITE

LEATHER DRYING SHED
CL   INDUSTRIAL
BT   LEATHER INDUSTRY SITE
RT   SHED
     TANNERY

LEATHER FACTORY
UF   Chamois Leather Works
     Leather Works
CL   INDUSTRIAL
BT   LEATHER INDUSTRY SITE
RT   ALUM WORKS
     POTASH KILN
     TANNERY

LEATHER FACTORY
UF   Chamois Leather Works
     Leather Works
CL   INDUSTRIAL
BT   FACTORY <BY PRODUCT>

LEATHER INDUSTRY SITE
CL   INDUSTRIAL
BT   ANIMAL PRODUCT SITE
NT   CURRIERY
     LEATHER DRYING SHED
     LEATHER FACTORY
     LEATHER WORKERS SHOP
     LEATHER WORKING SITE
     STEEPING PIT
     TANNERY
     TANNING PIT
     WASHING PIT

LEATHER MARKET
UF   Skin Market
CL   COMMERCIAL
BT   MARKET

LEATHER WAREHOUSE

CL   COMMERCIAL
BT   WAREHOUSE

LEATHER WORKERS SHOP
CL   INDUSTRIAL
BT   LEATHER INDUSTRY SITE
RT   BINDERY
     COBBLERS WORKSHOP
     SHOE FACTORY

LEATHER WORKERS SHOP
CL   INDUSTRIAL
BT   CRAFT INDUSTRY SITE
RT   HATTERS WORKSHOP

LEATHER WORKING SITE
CL   INDUSTRIAL
BT   LEATHER INDUSTRY SITE

Leather Works
USE LEATHER FACTORY

LEECH HOUSE
CL   HEALTH AND WELFARE

LEET HALL
CL   CIVIL
BT   MEETING HALL
RT   COURT HOUSE
     MOOT HALL

LEGAL CHAMBERS
UF   Serjeants Inn
CL   CIVIL
BT   LEGAL SITE

LEGAL CHAMBERS
UF   Serjeants Inn
CL   COMMERCIAL
RT   LEGAL OFFICE

Legal Inn
USE INNS OF CHANCERY

LEGAL OFFICE
UF   Barristers Office
     Solicitors Office
CL   CIVIL
BT   LEGAL SITE
RT   OFFICE

LEGAL OFFICE
UF   Barristers Office
     Solicitors Office
CL   COMMERCIAL
BT   COMMERCIAL OFFICE
RT   LEGAL CHAMBERS

LEGAL SITE
CL   CIVIL
NT   INNS OF CHANCERY
     INNS OF COURT
     JUDGES LODGING
     LAW COURT
     LEGAL CHAMBERS
     LEGAL OFFICE
     POLICE STATION
     PRISON
     PUNISHMENT PLACE

LEGIONARY FORTRESS
UF   Praetentura
     Praetorium
     Roman Fortress
CL   DEFENCE
BT   FORTRESS
RT   VEXILLATION FORT

LEISURE CRAFT

CL   MARITIME
BT   MARITIME CRAFT
NT   CRUISE BOAT
     CRUISE SHIP
     RACING CRAFT

LENDING LIBRARY
UF   Gentlemens Subscription Library
     Subscription Library
CL   EDUCATION
BT   LIBRARY

LENGTHMANS COTTAGE
UF   LENGTHMANS HOUSE
CL   DOMESTIC
BT   TRANSPORT WORKERS HOUSE
RT   CANAL
     CANAL DOCKYARD
     CANAL GATEHOUSE
     CANAL OFFICE
     INCLINE KEEPERS COTTAGE
     WHARFINGERS COTTAGE

LEPER HOSPITAL
UF   Lazar House
     Lazaretto
     Leper House
     Spital
     Spittle House
CL   HEALTH AND WELFARE
BT   SPECIALIST HOSPITAL
RT   ALMSHOUSE
     ISOLATION BLOCK

LEPER HOSPITAL
UF   Lazar House
     Lazaretto
     Leper House
     Spital
     Spittle House
CL   RELIGIOUS, RITUAL AND FUNERARY
BT   HOSPITAL
RT   ALMSHOUSE
     ISOLATION BLOCK

Leper House
  USE LEPER HOSPITAL

LETTER BOX
UF   Letter Box House
     POST BOX
CL   GARDENS, PARKS AND URBAN SPACES
BT   STREET FURNITURE
NT   PILLAR BOX

Letter Box House
  USE LETTER BOX

LEVEL CROSSING
UF   Railway Level Crossing
CL   TRANSPORT
BT   RAILWAY TRANSPORT SITE
RT   CROSSING KEEPERS COTTAGE
     LEVEL CROSSING GATE
     MAIL BAG NET

Level Crossing Cottage
  USE CROSSING KEEPERS COTTAGE

LEVEL CROSSING GATE
CL   TRANSPORT
BT   RAILWAY TRANSPORT SITE
RT   CROSSING KEEPERS COTTAGE
     GATE
     LEVEL CROSSING
     MAIL BAG NET

Liberal Club
  USE POLITICAL CLUB

Liberals Hall
  USE POLITICAL CLUB

LIBRARY
UF   College Library
     School Library
     University Library
CL   EDUCATION
NT   LENDING LIBRARY
     PUBLIC LIBRARY
     REFERENCE LIBRARY
RT   READING ROOM

LIBRARY
UF   College Library
     School Library
     University Library
CL   RECREATIONAL
BT   ART AND EDUCATION VENUE
RT   READING ROOM

LICENSED PREMISES
CL   COMMERCIAL
BT   EATING AND DRINKING ESTABLISHMENT
NT   BEER HOUSE
     CIDER HOUSE
     GIN PALACE
     PUBLIC HOUSE
     WINE BAR
RT   HOTEL
     INN
     OFF LICENCE

Life Assurance Office
  USE COMMERCIAL OFFICE

LIFEBOAT
CL   MARITIME
BT   SAFETY CRAFT

Lifeboat House
  USE LIFEBOAT STATION

LIFEBOAT STATION
UF   Lifeboat House
CL   CIVIL
RT   COASTGUARD STATION

LIFEBOAT STATION
UF   Lifeboat House
CL   MARITIME
BT   NAVIGATION AID
RT   COASTGUARD STATION
     SLIPWAY

LIFT
CL   TRANSPORT
BT   LIFTING AND WINDING STRUCTURE
NT   BOAT LIFT
     CANAL LIFT
     CLIFF LIFT
     RAILWAY LIFT
     RISE LIFT

Lift Bridge
  USE LIFTING BRIDGE

LIFT SHAFT
CL   TRANSPORT
BT   LIFTING AND WINDING STRUCTURE
RT   MAN ENGINE
     MINE SHAFT
     WINDING ENGINE

LIFTING AND WINDING STRUCTURE
CL   TRANSPORT
NT   CAPSTAN
     COAL DROP

CRANE
CRANEWHEEL
DERRICK
GANTRY
GRAIN ELEVATOR
HOIST
LIFT
LIFT SHAFT
WINCH
WINDING ENGINE
RT   MINE LIFTING AND WINDING STRUCTURE

LIFTING BRIDGE
UF   Lift Bridge
CL   TRANSPORT
BT   BRIDGE <BY FORM>
RT   HYDRAULIC ENGINE HOUSE

LIGHT CRUISER
CL   MARITIME
BT   CRUISER

LIGHT ENGINEERING SITE
CL   INDUSTRIAL
BT   ENGINEERING INDUSTRY SITE
NT   ELECTRICAL ENGINEERING WORKS
      INSTRUMENT ENGINEERING WORKS
      LIGHT ENGINEERING WORKS
      MACHINE TOOL ENGINEERING WORKS
      RADIO VALVE WORKS
RT   WORKS

LIGHT ENGINEERING WORKS
CL   INDUSTRIAL
BT   LIGHT ENGINEERING SITE
RT   FACTORY
      FACTORY UNIT
      INSTRUMENT ENGINEERING WORKS
      MACHINE TOOL ENGINEERING WORKS
      NORTH LIGHT FACTORY
      WORKS

LIGHT HOLDER
CL   GARDENS, PARKS AND URBAN SPACES
BT   STREET FURNITURE
RT   GAS LAMP
      SNUFFER

Light Railway
USE RAILWAY

LIGHT SHIP
CL   MARITIME
BT   SAFETY CRAFT

Light Snuffer
USE SNUFFER

Light Tower
USE LIGHTHOUSE

LIGHTER
SN   Unpowered shallow draft cargo vessel, often broad
      beamed and flat bottomed.
CL   MARITIME
BT   BARGE

LIGHTHOUSE
UF   Harbour Light
      Leading Light
      Light Tower
      Navigation Light
      Pharos
CL   DOMESTIC
BT   MARITIME HOUSE
RT   BEACON
      COASTGUARD STATION
      LIGHTKEEPERS HOUSE
      ROADSIDE LIGHTHOUSE

SIGNAL STATION
TIMEBALL TOWER
WATCH TOWER

LIGHTHOUSE
UF   Harbour Light
      Leading Light
      Light Tower
      Navigation Light
      Pharos
CL   MARITIME
BT   NAVIGATION AID
NT   HIGH LIGHT
      LOW LIGHT
RT   COASTGUARD STATION
      LIGHTKEEPERS HOUSE
      TIMEBALL TOWER
      WATCH TOWER

LIGHTHOUSE
UF   Harbour Light
      Leading Light
      Light Tower
      Navigation Light
      Pharos
CL   COMMUNICATIONS
BT   SIGNALLING STRUCTURE
RT   LIGHTKEEPERS HOUSE
      ROADSIDE LIGHTHOUSE
      WATCH TOWER

Lighthouse Keepers Cottage
USE LIGHTKEEPERS HOUSE

LIGHTKEEPERS HOUSE
UF   Lighthouse Keepers Cottage
CL   DOMESTIC
BT   MARITIME HOUSE
RT   COASTGUARDS COTTAGE
      LIGHTHOUSE
      MARINERS COTTAGE

LILY POND
CL   WATER SUPPLY AND DRAINAGE
BT   POND

LIME KILN
UF   Pye Kiln
CL   INDUSTRIAL
BT   KILN <BY FUNCTION>
RT   BOTTLE KILN
      CEMENT WORKS
      HOFFMAN KILN
      LIMESTONE QUARRY

LIME KILN
UF   Pye Kiln
CL   INDUSTRIAL
BT   AGRICULTURAL CHEMICAL SITE
RT   CEMENT WORKS
      FERTILISER WORKS
      LIME WORKS
      STEEL WORKS

LIME WALK
CL   GARDENS, PARKS AND URBAN SPACES
BT   WALK

LIME WORKS
CL   INDUSTRIAL
BT   CHEMICAL PRODUCTION SITE
RT   AGRICULTURAL CHEMICAL SITE
      CONCRETE WORKS
      FERTILISER WORKS
      LIME KILN
      LIMESTONE QUARRY

Limestone Dispatch Building
USE STONE DISPATCH BUILDING

LIMESTONE QUARRY
  CL INDUSTRIAL
  BT STONE QUARRY
  RT LIME KILN
      LIME WORKS

Linchet
  USE LYNCHET

LINE FISHING VESSEL
  CL MARITIME
  BT FISHING VESSEL
  NT LONG LINER

Linear Boundary
  USE BOUNDARY

Linear Crop Mark
  USE LINEAR FEATURE

Linear Ditch
  USE LINEAR EARTHWORK

LINEAR EARTHWORK
  UF Linear Ditch
      Meandering Linear Earthwork
  CL UNASSIGNED
  BT EARTHWORK
  RT BOUNDARY
      DRAINAGE DITCH
      DYKE (DEFENCE)
      FRONTIER DEFENCE
      LINEAR FEATURE
      MULTIPLE DITCH SYSTEM
      RANCH BOUNDARY
      REAVE

LINEAR FEATURE
  UF A P Linear Feature
      Linear Crop Mark
  CL UNASSIGNED
  BT FEATURE
  RT BOUNDARY
      LINEAR EARTHWORK

LINEAR SETTLEMENT
  UF Linear Village
  CL DOMESTIC
  BT SETTLEMENT

LINEAR SYSTEM
  UF A P Linear System
  CL UNASSIGNED

Linear Village
  USE LINEAR SETTLEMENT

LINEN MILL
  SN Weaving of the flax fibres into linen cloth.
  CL INDUSTRIAL
  BT TEXTILE MILL
  RT BEETLING MILL
      CALENDER MILL
      DRABBET FACTORY
      RETTING PIT

LINEN MILL
  SN Weaving of the flax fibres into linen cloth.
  CL INDUSTRIAL
  BT LINEN OR FLAX MANUFACTURING SITE
  RT BEETLING MILL
      CALENDER MILL
      DRABBET FACTORY

LINEN OR FLAX MANUFACTURING SITE
  CL INDUSTRIAL
  BT TEXTILE SITE <BY PROCESS/PRODUCT>
  NT DRABBET FACTORY

      FLAX BEATING STONE
      FLAX DRESSING SHOP
      FLAX DRY HOUSE
      FLAX DRY SHED
      FLAX MILL
      HEMP MILL
      JUTE MILL
      LINEN MILL
      RETTING PIT
      SCUTCHING MILL

LINER
  CL MARITIME
  BT PASSENGER VESSEL

LINHAY
  SN A double-storeyed open-sided structure comprising
      a cattle or cart shelter on the ground floor with
      a hayloft above. Most common in South West
      England.
  CL AGRICULTURE AND SUBSISTENCE
  BT FARM BUILDING
  RT BANK BARN
      CATTLE SHELTER
      COMBINATION BARN
      COW HOUSE
      FIELD BARN
      HAYLOFT
      VACCARY

LINOLEUM FACTORY
  CL INDUSTRIAL
  BT FACTORY <BY PRODUCT>

LINOLEUM FACTORY
  CL INDUSTRIAL
  BT CARPET MANUFACTURING SITE
  RT FLOORCLOTH FACTORY

LINTEL GRAVE
  CL RELIGIOUS, RITUAL AND FUNERARY
  BT CIST

Liquorice Kiln
  USE CHICORY KILN

LISTENING POST
  UF Acoustic Detection Post
      Acoustic Mirror
      Acoustic Wall
      Sound Dish
      Sound Mirror
  SN For the detection of enemy aircraft.
  CL DEFENCE
  RT ANTI AIRCRAFT BATTERY

Literary And Philosophical Society
  USE LITERARY AND SCIENTIFIC INSTITUTE

LITERARY AND SCIENTIFIC INSTITUTE
  UF Literary And Philosophical Society
      Literary Institute
      Lyceum
  CL EDUCATION
  BT INSTITUTE
  NT ATHENAEUM
      SCIENTIFIC INSTITUTE
  RT LEARNED SOCIETY BUILDING
      PEOPLES COLLEGE
      WORKING MENS COLLEGE

LITERARY AND SCIENTIFIC INSTITUTE
  UF Literary And Philosophical Society
      Literary Institute
      Lyceum
  CL INSTITUTIONAL
  BT INSTITUTE
  NT ATHENAEUM

Literary Institute

USE LITERARY AND SCIENTIFIC INSTITUTE

Little Boys Home
USE ORPHANAGE

Livery Company Hall
USE LIVERY HALL

LIVERY HALL
UF Company Hall
       Livery Company Hall
CL CIVIL
BT MEETING HALL
RT GUILDHALL

LIVERY HALL
UF Company Hall
       Livery Company Hall
CL COMMERCIAL
RT GUILDHALL

LIVERY STABLE
CL TRANSPORT
BT STABLE
RT COACH HOUSE
       COACHING INN
       COACHING INN STABLE
       HACKNEY STABLE

Livery Tavern
USE COACHING INN

LIVESTOCK MARKET
UF Cattle Market
       Pig Market
       Poultry Market
CL COMMERCIAL
BT MARKET
RT CATTLE DOCKS

LIVESTOCK SHIP
CL MARITIME
BT FREIGHTER

Lobby Entry House
USE HOUSE

LOCAL GOVERNMENT OFFICE
UF City Education Office
       City Transport Office
       City Treasurers Office
       Corporation Office
       Council Office
       County Education Office
       Education Office
       Municipal Office
       Parish Office
       Poor Law Guardians Office
       Poor Law Office
       School Board Office
       Transport Office
       Treasurers Office
       Urban District Office
CL CIVIL
BT GOVERNMENT OFFICE
NT COUNTY HALL
RT OFFICE
       TOWN HALL

LOCK
CL MARITIME
BT WATER REGULATION INSTALLATION

LOCK
CL TRANSPORT
BT WATER TRANSPORT SITE
NT CANAL LOCK
       FLASH LOCK
       FLOOD LOCK

       GUILLOTINE LOCK
       JUNCTION LOCK
       MITRE LOCK
       POUND LOCK
       RIVER LOCK
       STOP LOCK
       TIDAL LOCK
RT BALANCE BEAM
       CANAL
       CANAL SLUICE

LOCK CHAMBER
CL MARITIME
BT WATER REGULATION INSTALLATION

LOCK CHAMBER
CL TRANSPORT
BT WATER TRANSPORT SITE

LOCK GATE
CL MARITIME
BT WATER REGULATION INSTALLATION

LOCK GATE
CL TRANSPORT
BT WATER TRANSPORT SITE

LOCK HOSPITAL
CL HEALTH AND WELFARE
BT SPECIALIST HOSPITAL

Lock House
USE LOCK KEEPERS COTTAGE

LOCK KEEPERS COTTAGE
UF Canal Lock Keepers Cottage
       Lock House
       Lock Keepers House
CL DOMESTIC
BT TRANSPORT WORKERS HOUSE
RT WATER TRANSPORT SITE

Lock Keepers House
USE LOCK KEEPERS COTTAGE

LOCK SILL
CL MARITIME
BT WATER REGULATION INSTALLATION

LOCK SILL
CL TRANSPORT
BT WATER TRANSPORT SITE

LOCK UP
UF House Of Confinement
       Lock Up House
       Roundhouse (Lock Up)
       Station House
CL CIVIL
BT PRISON
RT WATCH HOUSE

Lock Up House
USE LOCK UP

Lockmakers Workshop
USE LOCKSMITHS WORKSHOP

LOCKSMITHS WORKSHOP
UF Lockmakers Workshop
CL INDUSTRIAL
BT CRAFT INDUSTRY SITE
RT WATCHMAKERS WORKSHOP

LOCKSMITHS WORKSHOP
UF Lockmakers Workshop
CL INDUSTRIAL
BT FERROUS METAL PRODUCT SITE

LOCOMOTIVE DEPOT

CL TRANSPORT
BT RAILWAY TRANSPORT SITE

Locomotive Shed
USE ENGINE SHED

Locomotive Works
USE RAILWAY ENGINEERING WORKS

Lodge
USE GATE LODGE
HUNTING LODGE
PORTERS LODGE
FISHING LODGE
CEMETERY LODGE
WINE LODGE
SN Use appropriate term.

LODGING HOUSE
UF 4% Industrial Dwellings
Artisans Dwelling
Model Lodging House
Sailors Hostel
Seamans Hostel
Single Mens Hostel
Working Ladies Hostel
Working Mens Hostel
Working Mens Lodgings
SN Purpose built workers' accommodation comprising
single rooms with communal eating and washing
facilities. Usually for short stay accommodation
only.
CL DOMESTIC
BT RESIDENTIAL BUILDING
RT HOSTEL
RECREATIONAL HALL
TENANTS HALL
TENEMENT BLOCK
TENEMENT HOUSE

LODGINGS
UF Quarters
CL DOMESTIC
BT RESIDENTIAL BUILDING
NT COLLEGE LODGINGS
STABLEHANDS LODGINGS
RT APARTMENT
JUDGES LODGING
JUDGES LODGINGS

LOG CABIN
CL DOMESTIC
BT DWELLING

LOGBOAT
UF Dugout Boat
Dugout Canoe
CL MARITIME
BT UNASSIGNED CRAFT

LOGGIA
SN A covered outdoor space for sitting or walking,
open on one or more sides.
CL GARDENS, PARKS AND URBAN SPACES
BT GARDEN BUILDING
RT CONSERVATORY
PERGOLA

LOGWOOD MILL
SN The inner red wood of a South American tree used
widely in dyeing. Imported in the form of logs and
cut and ground into dye by a mechanical process.
CL INDUSTRIAL
BT MILL

LOGWOOD MILL
SN The inner red wood of a South American tree used
widely in dyeing. Imported in the form of logs and
cut and ground into dye by a mechanical process.
CL INDUSTRIAL

BT WOOD PRODUCT SITE
RT BARK MILL
COLOUR MILL
DYE HOUSE
WOOD CHEMICAL WORKS

LONG BARROW
UF Earthen Long Barrow
CL RELIGIOUS, RITUAL AND FUNERARY
BT BARROW
NT CHAMBERED LONG BARROW
RT BANK BARROW
LONG CAIRN
LONG MOUND
OVAL BARROW

LONG CAIRN
CL RELIGIOUS, RITUAL AND FUNERARY
BT BURIAL CAIRN
NT CHAMBERED LONG CAIRN
RT LONG BARROW

LONG CIST
CL RELIGIOUS, RITUAL AND FUNERARY
BT CIST

LONG HOUSE
UF Byre House
Domus Longa
CL DOMESTIC
BT HOUSE <BY FUNCTION>
RT BARN
FARMHOUSE
LAITHE HOUSE

LONG HOUSE
UF Byre House
Domus Longa
CL AGRICULTURE AND SUBSISTENCE
BT FARM BUILDING
RT BARN
FARM LABOURERS COTTAGE
FARMHOUSE
LAITHE HOUSE

LONG LINER
CL MARITIME
BT LINE FISHING VESSEL

Long Mortuary Enclosure
USE MORTUARY ENCLOSURE

LONG MOUND
CL RELIGIOUS, RITUAL AND FUNERARY
BT FUNERARY SITE
RT LONG BARROW
MOUND

Long Stone
USE STANDING STONE

Look Out
USE LOOKOUT

Lookout House
USE LOOKOUT

LOOMSHOP
CL INDUSTRIAL
BT TEXTILE SITE <BY PROCESS/PRODUCT>
RT FLAX BEATING STONE
HOSIERY WORKSHOP
SILK MILL
SPINNING SHOP
TOPSHOP
WEAVERS COTTAGE
WEAVING MILL

Loose Box

USE STABLE

Lord Mayors Residence
USE MAYORS RESIDENCE

LORRY FACTORY
CL INDUSTRIAL
BT MOTOR VEHICLE ENGINEERING SITE
RT FOUNDRY

LORRY FACTORY
CL INDUSTRIAL
BT FACTORY < BY PRODUCT>

LOW BREASTSHOT WHEEL
CL INDUSTRIAL
BT BREASTSHOT WHEEL

LOW LIGHT
CL MARITIME
BT LIGHTHOUSE

LUFFING CRANE
CL TRANSPORT
BT CRANE < BY FORM>

LUMBER MILL
SN Timber sawn roughly into planks, ready for use by
     craftsmen.
CL INDUSTRIAL
BT MILL

LUMBER MILL
SN Timber sawn roughly into planks, ready for use by
     craftsmen.
CL INDUSTRIAL
BT TIMBER PROCESSING SITE
RT BOBBIN MILL
     PLANING MILL

Lunatic Asylum
USE MENTAL HOSPITAL

Lunatic Ward
USE MENTAL WARD BLOCK

Lunette
USE BASTION OUTWORK

Lyceum
USE LITERARY AND SCIENTIFIC INSTITUTE

LYCH GATE
UF Scallage
     Scallenge
CL RELIGIOUS, RITUAL AND FUNERARY
RT CHURCH
     CHURCHYARD
     GATE

Lye Kiln
USE POTASH KILN

Lying In Hospital
USE MATERNITY HOSPITAL

LYNCHET
UF Linchet
     Lynchet Field System
     Negative Lynchet
     Positive Lynchet
CL AGRICULTURE AND SUBSISTENCE
BT FIELD
NT STRIP LYNCHET
RT FIELD BOUNDARY

Lynchet Field System
USE LYNCHET

MACHINE SHOP

SN Engineering workshop housing specialised machinery
     such as lathes, presses, etc., for making
     machines.
CL INDUSTRIAL
BT ENGINEERING INDUSTRY SITE
RT AGRICULTURAL ENGINEERING WORKS
     ENGINEERING WORKSHOP
     FITTERS WORKSHOP
     TURNING SHOP

MACHINE TOOL ENGINEERING WORKS
CL INDUSTRIAL
BT LIGHT ENGINEERING SITE
RT LIGHT ENGINEERING WORKS

MACULA
UF A P Macula
SN Use a more specific site type where known.
CL UNASSIGNED

Madhouse
USE MENTAL HOSPITAL

Madras School
USE CHURCH SCHOOL

MAGAZINE
SN A building in which a supply of arms , ammunition
     and provisions for an army in time of war is
     stored.
CL DEFENCE
BT ARMAMENT STORE
NT POWDER MAGAZINE
RT MUNITIONS FACTORY

Magenta Works
USE JEWELLERY WORKSHOP

MAGISTRATES COURT
CL CIVIL
BT LAW COURT

MAIL BAG NET
CL TRANSPORT
BT RAILWAY TRANSPORT SITE
RT LEVEL CROSSING
     LEVEL CROSSING GATE
     RAILWAY SIGNAL
     WATER POINT

MAIL BAG NET
CL COMMUNICATIONS
BT POSTAL SYSTEM STRUCTURE
RT LEVEL CROSSING
     LEVEL CROSSING GATE
     RAILWAY SIGNAL
     WATER POINT

Maison Dieu
USE ALMSHOUSE

MAISONETTE
CL DOMESTIC
BT DWELLING
RT FLATS
     TENEMENT BLOCK

Majolica Works
USE POTTERY WORKS

Major Villa
USE VILLA (ROMAN)

MALT HOUSE
CL INDUSTRIAL
BT BREWING AND MALTING SITE
RT MALT KILN
     MALTINGS

MALT HOUSE

CL AGRICULTURE AND SUBSISTENCE
BT FOOD AND DRINK PROCESSING SITE
RT MALTINGS

MALT KILN
UF Dry
CL INDUSTRIAL
BT BREWING AND MALTING SITE
RT HOP KILN
MALT HOUSE
MALTINGS

MALT KILN
UF Dry
CL INDUSTRIAL
BT KILN <BY FUNCTION>

MALT KILN
UF Dry
CL AGRICULTURE AND SUBSISTENCE
BT FOOD AND DRINK PROCESSING SITE
RT HOP KILN
MALT HOUSE
MALTINGS

MALTINGS
CL INDUSTRIAL
BT BREWING AND MALTING SITE
RT BREWHOUSE
DISTILLERY
MALT HOUSE
MALT KILN
MANAGERS HOUSE

Maltsters House
USE MANAGERS HOUSE

MAN ENGINE
SN Early 19th century method of raising and lowering
miners to/from the pit bottom.
CL INDUSTRIAL
BT MINE LIFTING AND WINDING STRUCTURE
RT LIFT SHAFT
WINDER HOUSE

MANAGERS HOUSE
UF Brewers House
Estate Managers House
Factory Managers House
Factory Masters House
Head Brewers House
Ironmasters House
Maltsters House
Master Brewers House
Mill Managers House
Mill Masters House
Mine Managers House
Works Managers House
CL DOMESTIC
BT HOUSE <BY FUNCTION>
RT FACTORY
FOREMANS HOUSE
IRON WORKS
MALTINGS
TEXTILE MILL
WORKERS COTTAGE

MANCIPLES HOUSE
CL DOMESTIC
BT CLERICAL DWELLING
RT ABBEY
MONASTERY
PRIORY

MANGANESE MINE
UF Rhodonite Mine
SN Use with other ores extracted and MINE where
relevant.
CL INDUSTRIAL

BT NON FERROUS METAL EXTRACTION SITE
RT LEAD MINE
TIN MINE
UMBER WORKINGS

MANGANESE MINE
UF Rhodonite Mine
SN Use with other ores extracted and MINE where
relevant.
CL INDUSTRIAL
BT MINE

Manometer Tower
USE WATER TOWER

MANOR
CL AGRICULTURE AND SUBSISTENCE
BT LAND USE SITE
RT CAMERA
CELL
DOUBLE HOUSE
FARM
GRANGE
MANOR HOUSE
MONASTERY
NUNNERY
PRECEPTORY

MANOR FARM
CL AGRICULTURE AND SUBSISTENCE
BT FARM
RT MANOR HOUSE

MANOR HOUSE
UF Manorial Site
Moated Manor House
CL DOMESTIC
BT HOUSE <BY FUNCTION>
RT ARCHBISHOPS MANOR HOUSE
COUNTRY HOUSE
DOMESTIC CHAPEL
DOVECOTE
FORTIFIED MANOR HOUSE
GREAT HOUSE
MANOR
MANOR FARM
MOAT
PALACE
PRECEPTORY
TOWN HOUSE

Manor House Chapel
USE DOMESTIC CHAPEL

Manorial Site
USE MANOR HOUSE

MANSE
UF Ministers Cottage
CL DOMESTIC
BT CLERICAL DWELLING

MANSIO
SN A type of Roman lodging house, frequently sited
near the town gate.
CL CIVIL
RT INN

MANSIO
SN A type of Roman lodging house, frequently sited
near the town gate.
CL COMMERCIAL
RT INN

Mansion
USE COUNTRY HOUSE

MANSION FLATS
CL DOMESTIC

BT FLATS

MANSION HOUSE
    CL CIVIL
    RT MAYORS RESIDENCE

Manufactory
    USE FACTORY

Manure Works
    USE FERTILISER WORKS

MARBLE QUARRY
    CL INDUSTRIAL
    BT STONE QUARRY

Marble Works
    USE STONE WORKS

MARCHING CAMP
    CL DEFENCE
    BT TEMPORARY CAMP

Margarine Factory
    USE FOOD PROCESSING PLANT

MARINA
    CL MARITIME
    BT DOCK AND HARBOUR INSTALLATION

MARINE CONSTRUCTION SITE
    CL INDUSTRIAL
    NT BOAT YARD
       CAMBER
       CHAIN PROVING HOUSE
       CHAIN WORKS
       DOCKYARD
       DRY DOCK
       FABRICATION SHED
       FLOATING CRANE
       GRIDIRON
       HALF TIDE DOCK
       HATCHELLING HOUSE
       HEMP STORE
       MARINE ENGINEERING WORKS
       MARINE WORKSHOP
       MAST POND
       MASTING SHEAR
       PLATE RACK
       PLATERS SHOP
       RIVET AND TOOL SHOP
       RIVET AND TOOL STORE
       SHEER HULK
       SHEER LEGS
       SHIP REPAIR WORKS
       SHIPHOUSE FRAME
       SHIPYARD
       WET DOCK
    RT DOCK AND HARBOUR INSTALLATION

MARINE CONSTRUCTION SITE
    CL MARITIME
    NT BOAT YARD
       CAMBER
       CHAIN PROVING HOUSE
       CHAIN WORKS
       DOCKYARD
       DRY DOCK
       FABRICATION SHED
       FLOATING CRANE
       GRIDIRON
       HALF TIDE DOCK
       HATCHELLING HOUSE
       HEMP STORE
       MARINE ENGINEERING WORKS
       MARINE WORKSHOP
       MAST POND
       MASTING SHEAR
       PLATE RACK

PLATERS SHOP
RIVET AND TOOL SHOP
RIVET AND TOOL STORE
SHEER HULK
SHEER LEGS
SHIP REPAIR WORKS
SHIPHOUSE FRAME
SHIPYARD
WET DOCK
    RT DOCK AND HARBOUR INSTALLATION

MARINE ENGINEERING WORKS
    SN Specialised engineering workshop particularly for
       the production of marine engines or other large
       components of ships.
    CL INDUSTRIAL
    BT MARINE CONSTRUCTION SITE
    RT BOILER SHOP
       CHAIN WORKS
       FLOATING CRANE
       HEAVY ENGINEERING SITE
       RIVET AND TOOL SHOP
       SHIP REPAIR WORKS

MARINE ENGINEERING WORKS
    SN Specialised engineering workshop particularly for
       the production of marine engines or other large
       components of ships.
    CL MARITIME
    BT MARINE CONSTRUCTION SITE

MARINE LABORATORY
    CL EDUCATION
    BT LABORATORY
    RT RESEARCH STATION

MARINE LABORATORY
    CL MARITIME

Marine Sanatorium
    USE SANATORIUM

MARINE WORKSHOP
    UF Blockmakers Workshop
    CL INDUSTRIAL
    BT MARINE CONSTRUCTION SITE
    NT BLOCK MILL
       COLOUR LOFT
       HOOP HOUSE
       MAST HOUSE
       MOULD LOFT
       RIGGING HOUSE
       SAIL LOFT
       SHIPWRIGHTS WORKSHOP
       SLIP SHED
    RT MAST POND
       MASTING SHEAR

MARINE WORKSHOP
    UF Blockmakers Workshop
    CL MARITIME
    BT MARINE CONSTRUCTION SITE
    NT BLOCK MILL
       COLOUR LOFT
       HOOP HOUSE
       MAST HOUSE
       MOULD LOFT
       RIGGING HOUSE
       SAIL LOFT
       SHIPWRIGHTS WORKSHOP
       SLIP SHED
    RT MAST POND
       SHIPYARD

Mariners Church
    USE SEAMENS CHURCH

MARINERS COTTAGE
    UF Sailors Cottage

CL   DOMESTIC
BT   MARITIME HOUSE
RT   COASTGUARDS COTTAGE
     FISHERMANS HOUSE
     LIGHTKEEPERS HOUSE

MARITIME
  SN   This is the top term for the class. See MARITIME
       Class List for narrow terms.

MARITIME CRAFT
  CL   MARITIME
  NT   COASTGUARD CRAFT
       COMMUNICATIONS CRAFT
       EXPERIMENTAL CRAFT
       FISHERIES PROTECTION CRAFT
       FISHING VESSEL
       HOUSE BOAT
       LEISURE CRAFT
       SAFETY CRAFT
       SERVICE CRAFT
       TRAINING SHIP
       TRANSPORT CRAFT
       UNASSIGNED CRAFT
       UNMANNED CRAFT
       WARSHIP
       WASTE DISPOSAL VESSEL

MARITIME HOUSE
  CL   DOMESTIC
  BT   HOUSE <BY FUNCTION>
  NT   BOATSWAINS HOUSE
       COASTGUARDS COTTAGE
       DOCK WORKERS COTTAGE
       DOCKMASTERS HOUSE
       FISHERMANS HOUSE
       LASCAR HOUSE
       LIGHTHOUSE
       LIGHTKEEPERS HOUSE
       MARINERS COTTAGE
       MASTER ROPEMAKERS HOUSE
       NAVAL CAPTAINS HOUSE
       NAVAL OFFICERS HOUSE
       ORDNANCE STOREKEEPERS HOUSE
       PIERMASTERS HOUSE
       PORT ADMIRALS HOUSE
       WHARFINGERS COTTAGE
  RT   DOCK AND HARBOUR INSTALLATION

MARITIME OFFICE
  CL   MARITIME
  NT   CUSTOM HOUSE
       DOCKMASTERS OFFICE
       EXCISE OFFICE
       HARBOUR MASTERS OFFICE
       PILOT OFFICE
       PORT AUTHORITY OFFICE
  RT   DOCK AND HARBOUR INSTALLATION
       OFFICE

MARKER CAIRN
  CL   UNASSIGNED
  RT   CAIRN

MARKET
  UF   Bazaar
  CL   COMMERCIAL
  NT   ANTIQUE MARKET
       BUTTER MARKET
       CHEESE MARKET
       CLOTH MARKET
       FISH MARKET
       FLEA MARKET
       FLOWER MARKET
       FRUIT AND VEGETABLE MARKET
       LEATHER MARKET
       LIVESTOCK MARKET
       MARKET HALL
       MARKET HOUSE

       MARKET PLACE
       MARKET STALL
       MEAT MARKET
       METAL MARKET
       TIMBER MARKET
       WHOLESALE MARKET
       WOOL STAPLE
  RT   MARKET CROSS

MARKET CROSS
  UF   Butter Cross
       Market Cross Shelter
  CL   RELIGIOUS, RITUAL AND FUNERARY
  BT   CROSS
  RT   MARKET
       MARKET PLACE
       PREACHING CROSS
       TOWN CROSS
       VILLAGE CROSS
       WAYSIDE CROSS

Market Cross Shelter
  USE MARKET CROSS

MARKET GARDEN
  CL   AGRICULTURE AND SUBSISTENCE
  BT   GARDEN
  RT   GREENHOUSE

MARKET HALL
  UF   Covered Market
  SN   A purpose built covered market hall, usually 19th
       century (although earlier examples do exist, eg.
       the Piece Hall, Halifax, 1775).
  CL   COMMERCIAL
  BT   MARKET
  NT   CLOTH HALL
  RT   ASSAY OFFICE
       COINAGE HALL
       EXCHANGE
       GUILDHALL
       MARKET HOUSE

MARKET HOUSE
  SN   A market building, pre-19th century, incorporating
       other function rooms, eg. theatres, courtrooms,
       schoolrooms.
  CL   CIVIL
  BT   PUBLIC BUILDING
  RT   CHURCH HOUSE
       GUILDHALL
       MARKET HALL
       MARRIAGE FEAST HOUSE
       TOWN HALL

MARKET HOUSE
  SN   A market building, pre-19th century, incorporating
       other function rooms, eg. theatres, courtrooms,
       schoolrooms.
  CL   COMMERCIAL
  BT   MARKET
  RT   CHURCH HOUSE
       GUILDHALL
       MARKET HALL
       MARRIAGE FEAST HOUSE
       TOWN HALL

MARKET PLACE
  UF   Market Square
  CL   GARDENS, PARKS AND URBAN SPACES
  BT   URBAN SPACE
  RT   MARKET CROSS
       MARKET STALL

MARKET PLACE
  UF   Market Square
  CL   COMMERCIAL
  BT   MARKET

Market Square

USE MARKET PLACE

MARKET STALL
- CL COMMERCIAL
- BT MARKET
- RT MARKET PLACE

Markstone
USE BOUNDARY STONE

MARL PIT
- CL INDUSTRIAL
- BT EXTRACTIVE PIT
- RT BELL PIT
  CHALK PIT
  CLAY PIT
  GRAVEL PIT
  MUG HOUSE
  POTTERY WORKS
  POTTERY WORKSHOP
  SAND PIT
  THROWING HOUSE

MARL PIT
- CL INDUSTRIAL
- BT DYE AND PIGMENT SITE

MARRIAGE FEAST HOUSE
- CL CIVIL
- BT MEETING HALL
- RT BANQUETING HOUSE
  CHURCH HOUSE
  GUILDHALL
  MARKET HOUSE
  TOWN HALL

MARSHALLING YARD
- CL TRANSPORT
- BT RAILWAY TRANSPORT SITE
- RT GOODS YARD

Marshalsea
USE PRISON

MARTELLO TOWER
- CL DEFENCE
- RT ARTILLERY CASTLE
  ARTILLERY TOWER
  TOWER
  WATCH TOWER

MARTELLO TOWER
- CL MARITIME
- BT MILITARY COASTAL DEFENCES
- RT WATCH TOWER

Martin Down Style Enclosure
USE ENCLOSED SETTLEMENT

MASH HOUSE
- CL INDUSTRIAL
- BT DISTILLING SITE
- RT STILL HOUSE

Masonic Hall
USE FREEMASONS HALL

Masonic Lodge
USE FREEMASONS HALL

Masons Hall
USE FREEMASONS HALL

Masons Lodge
USE FREEMASONS HALL

Masons Temple
USE FREEMASONS HALL

MAST HOUSE

- CL INDUSTRIAL
- BT MARINE WORKSHOP
- RT MAST POND
  SHEER LEGS

MAST HOUSE
- CL MARITIME
- BT MARINE WORKSHOP
- RT MAST POND
  MASTING SHEAR
  SHEER HULK
  SHEER LEGS

MAST POND
- CL WATER SUPPLY AND DRAINAGE
- BT POND
- RT MAST HOUSE
  MASTING SHEAR

MAST POND
- CL MARITIME
- BT MARINE CONSTRUCTION SITE
- RT CAMBER
  MARINE WORKSHOP
  SHEER HULK
  SHEER LEGS

MAST POND
- CL INDUSTRIAL
- BT MARINE CONSTRUCTION SITE
- RT MARINE WORKSHOP
  MAST HOUSE

MASTED CRUISER
- CL MARITIME
- BT CRUISER

Master Brewers House
USE MANAGERS HOUSE

MASTER HOSIERS HOUSE
- CL DOMESTIC
- BT INDUSTRIAL HOUSE

MASTER HOSIERS HOUSE
- CL INDUSTRIAL
- BT INDUSTRIAL HOUSE

MASTER ROPEMAKERS HOUSE
- CL DOMESTIC
- BT MARITIME HOUSE

MASTER WEAVERS HOUSE
- CL DOMESTIC
- BT INDUSTRIAL HOUSE

MASTER WEAVERS HOUSE
- CL INDUSTRIAL
- BT INDUSTRIAL HOUSE

MASTING SHEAR
- CL INDUSTRIAL
- BT MARINE CONSTRUCTION SITE
- RT MAST HOUSE
  MILL POND

MASTING SHEAR
- CL MARITIME
- BT MARINE CONSTRUCTION SITE
- RT MARINE WORKSHOP
  MAST POND
  SHEER HULK
  SHEER LEGS

MATCH FACTORY
- CL INDUSTRIAL
- BT FACTORY <BY PRODUCT>
- RT FIREPROOF FACTORY

MATCH FACTORY

CL INDUSTRIAL
BT TIMBER PRODUCT SITE
RT SAW MILL

MATERNITY BLOCK
CL HEALTH AND WELFARE
BT HOSPITAL BLOCK

MATERNITY CLINIC
SN Self-contained establishment (out-patients).
CL HEALTH AND WELFARE
BT CLINIC
RT ANTENATAL BLOCK

Maternity Home
USE MATERNITY HOSPITAL

MATERNITY HOSPITAL
UF Lying In Hospital
Maternity Home
CL HEALTH AND WELFARE
BT SPECIALIST HOSPITAL
RT ANTENATAL BLOCK

MATHEMATICAL INSTITUTE
CL EDUCATION
BT INSTITUTE

MATHEMATICAL INSTITUTE
CL INSTITUTIONAL
BT INSTITUTE

MATRONS HOUSE
CL DOMESTIC
BT HEALTH WORKERS HOUSE

MAUSOLEUM
CL RELIGIOUS, RITUAL AND FUNERARY
BT FUNERARY SITE
RT BURIAL VAULT
CHARNEL HOUSE
MORTUARY HOUSE
TOMB

MAYORS RESIDENCE
UF Lord Mayors Residence
CL DOMESTIC
BT RESIDENTIAL BUILDING

MAYORS RESIDENCE
UF Lord Mayors Residence
CL CIVIL
RT MANSION HOUSE

MAYPOLE
CL RELIGIOUS, RITUAL AND FUNERARY

MAZE
UF Labyrinth
Mizmaze
CL GARDENS, PARKS AND URBAN SPACES
NT HEDGE MAZE
TURF MAZE
RT KNOT GARDEN

MAZE
UF Labyrinth
Mizmaze
CL RELIGIOUS, RITUAL AND FUNERARY
NT HEDGE MAZE
TURF MAZE
RT KNOT GARDEN

MEADOW
CL AGRICULTURE AND SUBSISTENCE
BT LAND USE SITE

Meandering Linear Earthwork
USE LINEAR EARTHWORK

MEAT MARKET
UF Beef Market
Butchers Market
Flesh Market
White Market
CL COMMERCIAL
BT MARKET
RT SHAMBLES

MECHANICS INSTITUTE
CL EDUCATION
BT INSTITUTE
RT CHURCH INSTITUTE
MINERS READING ROOM
PEOPLES COLLEGE
WORKING MENS COLLEGE

MECHANICS INSTITUTE
CL INSTITUTIONAL
BT INSTITUTE

MEDICAL ATTENDANTS HOUSE
CL DOMESTIC
BT HEALTH WORKERS HOUSE

MEDICAL CENTRE
CL HEALTH AND WELFARE

MEDICAL COLLEGE
UF Nursing College
CL EDUCATION
BT TRAINING COLLEGE
RT HOSPITAL

MEDICAL COLLEGE
UF Nursing College
CL HEALTH AND WELFARE
RT HOSPITAL

MEDICAL SUPERINTENDENTS HOUSE
CL DOMESTIC
BT HEALTH WORKERS HOUSE

Medieval Village
USE VILLAGE

MEERSTONE
CL INDUSTRIAL
BT NON FERROUS METAL PROCESSING SITE
RT BOUNDARY MARKER
BOUNDARY STONE

MEETING HALL
CL INSTITUTIONAL
NT BRITISH LEGION HALL
FREEMASONS HALL
ODDFELLOWS HALL
SECULAR HALL
TEMPERANCE HALL
TRADES UNION HALL
RT FRIENDS MEETING HOUSE

MEETING HALL
CL CIVIL
BT PUBLIC BUILDING
NT ASSEMBLY HALL
CHURCH HALL
CHURCH HOUSE
EGYPTIAN HALL
GUILDHALL
LEET HALL
LIVERY HALL
MARRIAGE FEAST HOUSE
MOOT HALL
PUBLIC HALL
SHIRE HALL
TOWN HALL
VERDERERS HALL

VILLAGE HALL
RT   FRIENDS MEETING HOUSE

Meeting House
USE NONCONFORMIST MEETING HOUSE

MEETING HOUSE OF JEHOVAHS WITNESSES
CL   RELIGIOUS, RITUAL AND FUNERARY
BT   NONCONFORMIST MEETING HOUSE
RT   NONCONFORMIST CHAPEL

Megalith
USE STANDING STONE

Megalithic Tomb
USE CHAMBERED TOMB

Memorial
USE COMMEMORATIVE MONUMENT

Memorial Brass
USE COMMEMORATIVE BRASS

Memorial Chapel
USE CHAPEL
     COMMEMORATIVE MONUMENT
SN   Use both terms.

Memorial Effigy
USE EFFIGY

Memorial Garden
USE GARDEN
     COMMEMORATIVE MONUMENT
SN   Use both terms.

Memorial Hall
USE COMMEMORATIVE MONUMENT
SN   Use COMMEMORATIVE MONUMENT with the relevant hall
     type.

Memorial Seat
USE COMMEMORATIVE MONUMENT

Memorial Stone
USE COMMEMORATIVE STONE

Menagerie
USE ZOO

Menhir
USE STANDING STONE

Mental Asylum
USE MENTAL HOSPITAL

Mental Deficiency Colony
USE HOSPITAL FOR THE MENTALLY HANDICAPPED

MENTAL HOSPITAL
UF   Asylum
     Asylum For Pauper Imbeciles
     Bedlam
     Idiots Asylum
     Insane Asylum
     Lunatic Asylum
     Madhouse
     Mental Asylum
     Military Asylum
     Military Mental Hospital
     Naval Asylum
     Pauper Lunatic Asylum
     Psychiatric Hospital
     Psychiatric Unit
SN   Used in historical sense.
CL   HEALTH AND WELFARE
BT   HOSPITAL
NT   HOSPITAL FOR EPILEPTICS
     HOSPITAL FOR THE MENTALLY HANDICAPPED

RT   WORKHOUSE

MENTAL WARD BLOCK
UF   Imbecile Ward
     Lunatic Ward
     Workhouse Mental Ward Block
CL   HEALTH AND WELFARE
BT   HOSPITAL BLOCK

MERCHANTS HOUSE
CL   DOMESTIC
BT   HOUSE < BY FUNCTION >

MESSUAGE
CL   AGRICULTURE AND SUBSISTENCE
BT   LAND USE SITE
RT   CROFT
     FARM
     SMALLHOLDING
     TOFT

METAL INDUSTRY SITE
CL   INDUSTRIAL
NT   CASTING FLOOR
     FERROUS METAL EXTRACTION SITE
     FERROUS METAL PRODUCT SITE
     FERROUS METAL SMELTING SITE
     INDUCTION HEARTH
     NON FERROUS METAL EXTRACTION SITE
     NON FERROUS METAL PROCESSING SITE
     NON FERROUS METAL PRODUCT SITE
     NON FERROUS METAL SMELTING SITE
     ORE STORE
     ROLLING MILL
     SLITTING MILL
     WIRE MILL
RT   CALCINER
     CALCINING KILN
     CASTING HOUSE
     CHARCOAL STORE
     METAL PRODUCTION FURNACE

METAL MARKET
CL   COMMERCIAL
BT   MARKET

METAL PRODUCTION FURNACE
CL   INDUSTRIAL
BT   FURNACE
NT   BLAST FURNACE
     BOLEHILL
     BOWL FURNACE
     CEMENTATION FURNACE
     CRUCIBLE FURNACE
     CUPELLATION FURNACE
     ELECTRIC ARC FURNACE
     INDUCTION FURNACE
     IRON FURNACE
     LEAD FURNACE
     OPEN HEARTH FURNACE
     ORE HEARTH
     ROASTING HEARTH
     SHAFT FURNACE
     SILVER HEARTH
     SLAG HEARTH
RT   BLOWING HOUSE
     FURNACE POND
     METAL INDUSTRY SITE

Meteorological Research Station
USE RESEARCH STATION

METHANE PLANT
SN   Collection of methane gas released by coal mining.
CL   INDUSTRIAL
BT   MINING INDUSTRY SITE

Methodist Central Hall
USE NONCONFORMIST MEETING HOUSE

METHODIST CHAPEL
UF Methodist Church
CL RELIGIOUS, RITUAL AND FUNERARY
BT NONCONFORMIST CHAPEL
NT BIBLE CHRISTIAN CHAPEL
    CALVINISTIC METHODIST CHAPEL
    COUNTESS OF HUNTINGDONS CHAPEL
    FREE METHODIST CHAPEL
    METHODIST NEW CONNEXION CHAPEL
    PRIMITIVE METHODIST CHAPEL
    WESLEYAN METHODIST CHAPEL

Methodist Church
USE METHODIST CHAPEL

Methodist College
USE THEOLOGICAL COLLEGE

Methodist Hall
USE NONCONFORMIST MEETING HOUSE

METHODIST NEW CONNEXION CHAPEL
CL RELIGIOUS, RITUAL AND FUNERARY
BT METHODIST CHAPEL

Methodist School
USE CHURCH SCHOOL

MEWS
CL DOMESTIC
BT MULTIPLE DWELLING
RT COACHMANS COTTAGE
    GROOMS COTTAGE
    STABLE
    STABLEHANDS LODGINGS
    TACK ROOM

MEWS
CL TRANSPORT
BT ROAD TRANSPORT SITE
RT COACHMANS COTTAGE
    GROOMS COTTAGE
    STABLE
    TACK ROOM

MIDDEN
CL DOMESTIC
NT SHELL MIDDEN
RT LATRINE
    RUBBISH PIT

MIDDEN
CL AGRICULTURE AND SUBSISTENCE
NT SHELL MIDDEN

MIDGET SUBMARINE
CL MARITIME
BT SUBMARINE

MIGRATED VILLAGE
CL DOMESTIC
BT VILLAGE

MILE PLATE
CL TRANSPORT
RT RAILWAY
    RIVER NAVIGATION
    ROAD
    SIGNPOST

MILECASTLE
CL DEFENCE
BT FORTLET

MILECASTLE
CL DEFENCE
BT FRONTIER DEFENCE

MILEFORTLET

CL DEFENCE
BT FORTLET

MILEFORTLET
CL DEFENCE
BT FRONTIER DEFENCE

MILEPOST
CL GARDENS, PARKS AND URBAN SPACES
BT STREET FURNITURE
RT MILESTONE
    ROADSIDE LIGHTHOUSE
    TERMINUS STONE

MILEPOST
CL TRANSPORT
NT CANAL MILEPOST
RT MILESTONE
    RAILWAY
    RIVER NAVIGATION
    ROAD
    ROADSIDE LIGHTHOUSE
    SIGNPOST
    TERMINUS STONE

MILESTONE
CL GARDENS, PARKS AND URBAN SPACES
BT STREET FURNITURE
RT MILEPOST
    ROADSIDE LIGHTHOUSE
    TERMINUS STONE

MILESTONE
CL TRANSPORT
RT MILEPOST
    RAILWAY
    RIVER NAVIGATION
    ROAD
    ROADSIDE LIGHTHOUSE
    SIGNPOST
    TERMINUS STONE

Military Academy
USE MILITARY COLLEGE

MILITARY AIRFIELD
UF Air Force Base
CL TRANSPORT
BT AIR TRANSPORT SITE

Military Asylum
USE MENTAL HOSPITAL

MILITARY BASE
UF Military Works Depot
CL DEFENCE
RT ARMAMENT STORE
    BARRACKS
    MILITARY CAMP

MILITARY CAMP
CL DEFENCE
NT ARMY CAMP
RT BARRACKS
    MILITARY BASE
    PARADE GROUND
    TEMPORARY CAMP

MILITARY CANAL
CL DEFENCE
RT TOWN DEFENCES

MILITARY CANAL
CL TRANSPORT
BT CANAL   -

MILITARY CEMETERY
UF Airmens Graveyard
CL RELIGIOUS, RITUAL AND FUNERARY

BT   INHUMATION CEMETERY
RT   WAR MEMORIAL

MILITARY CHAPEL
UF   Garrison Church
      Garrison Chapel
      Garrison Church
      Guards Chapel
      Military Church
CL   RELIGIOUS, RITUAL AND FUNERARY
BT   CHAPEL

Military Church
USE MILITARY CHAPEL

MILITARY COASTAL DEFENCES
CL   MARITIME
NT   COASTAL BATTERY
      MARTELLO TOWER
      SALUTING BATTERY
      SAXON SHORE FORT

MILITARY COLLEGE
UF   Infantry School
      Military Academy
      Royal Air Force College
CL   EDUCATION
BT   TRAINING COLLEGE
RT   ARTILLERY SCHOOL

MILITARY COLLEGE
UF   Infantry School
      Military Academy
      Royal Air Force College
CL   DEFENCE
RT   ARTILLERY SCHOOL
      NAVAL COLLEGE

Military Earthwork
USE FIELDWORK
SN   Military earthwork of unspecified type. Use
      specific site type where known.

Military Families Hospital
USE MILITARY HOSPITAL

Military Field Kitchen
USE FIELD KITCHEN

MILITARY HOSPITAL
UF   Army Hospital
      Artillery Hospital
      Military Families Hospital
      Military Isolation Hospital
      Regimental Hospital
CL   HEALTH AND WELFARE
BT   HOSPITAL

Military Isolation Hospital
USE MILITARY HOSPITAL

Military Mental Hospital
USE MENTAL HOSPITAL

Military Music School
USE MUSIC SCHOOL

MILITARY ROAD
CL   DEFENCE
RT   FRONTIER DEFENCE

Military Works Depot
USE MILITARY BASE

MILK DEPOT
CL   COMMERCIAL
RT   DAIRY

MILK DEPOT

CL   TRANSPORT

Milk House
USE DAIRY

Milk Processing Plant
USE DAIRY

MILKING PARLOUR
CL   AGRICULTURE AND SUBSISTENCE
BT   FOOD AND DRINK PROCESSING SITE
RT   MILKING SHED

MILKING SHED
CL   AGRICULTURE AND SUBSISTENCE
BT   FOOD AND DRINK PROCESSING SITE
RT   DAIRY
      MILKING PARLOUR
      SHED

MILL
SN   Use more specific mill type where known. See also
      TEXTILE MILL, for more narrow terms.
CL   INDUSTRIAL
BT   INDUSTRIAL BUILDING
NT   BARK MILL
      BATTERY MILL
      BOBBIN MILL
      BONE MILL
      CANNON BORING MILL
      CLAY MILL
      COMB MILL
      CORN MILL
      CRAZING MILL
      CRUSHING MILL
      DRESSING MILL
      FEED MILL
      FLINT MILL
      FLOUR MILL
      INCORPORATING MILL
      LOGWOOD MILL
      LUMBER MILL
      MORTAR MILL
      MUSTARD MILL
      NEEDLE MILL
      OIL MILL
      PAPER MILL
      PLANING MILL
      PLASTER MILL
      PUG MILL
      ROLLING MILL
      SAW MILL
      SCREW MILL
      SCYTHE MILL
      SLITTING MILL
      SMELT MILL
      SNUFF MILL
      STAMPING MILL
      STARCH MILL
      STEAM MILL
      TEXTILE MILL
      THIMBLE MILL
      THRESHING MILL
      TIDEMILL
      TIN MILL
      TUBE MILL
      WATERMILL
      WINDMILL
      WIRE MILL
RT   INDUSTRIAL SITE
      LEAT
      MILL HOUSE
      POND BAY
      TIMEKEEPERS OFFICE
      WATERCOURSE
      WORKS

Mill Apprentice House
USE APPRENTICE HOUSE

MILL DAM
- CL INDUSTRIAL
- BT DAM
- RT MILL POND
  - WATERMILL
  - WATERWHEEL
  - WEIR

MILL DAM
- CL WATER SUPPLY AND DRAINAGE
- BT DAM
- RT POND BAY
  - WATERMILL

MILL HOUSE
- UF Corn Millers House
  - Millers House
- CL DOMESTIC
- BT INDUSTRIAL HOUSE
- RT CORN MILL
  - MILL

MILL HOUSE
- UF Corn Millers House
  - Millers House
- CL INDUSTRIAL
- BT INDUSTRIAL HOUSE

Mill Lodge
- USE GATE LODGE
  - FACTORY
- SN Use both terms.

Mill Managers House
- USE MANAGERS HOUSE

Mill Masters House
- USE MANAGERS HOUSE

Mill Mound
- USE WINDMILL MOUND

MILL POND
- CL WATER SUPPLY AND DRAINAGE
- BT POND
- RT FURNACE POND
  - HAMMER POND
  - HEAD RACE
  - LEAT
  - MASTING SHEAR
  - MILL DAM
  - MILL RACE
  - SHEER HULK
  - SHEER LEGS
  - TAIL RACE
  - WATERMILL
  - WEIR

MILL POND
- CL INDUSTRIAL
- BT WATER POWER PRODUCTION SITE
- RT MILL DAM
  - MILL RACE
  - PEN POND
  - WATERMILL

MILL RACE
- CL INDUSTRIAL
- BT WATER POWER PRODUCTION SITE
- NT HEAD RACE
  - TAIL RACE
- RT LEAT
  - MILL POND
  - TUMBLING WEIR
  - WATERCOURSE
  - WATERMILL
  - WEIR

MILL RACE

- CL WATER SUPPLY AND DRAINAGE
- NT HEAD RACE
  - TAIL RACE
- RT LEAT
  - MILL POND
  - TUMBLING WEIR
  - WATER CHANNEL
  - WATERCOURSE
  - WATERMILL
  - WEIR

Mill Workers Cottage
- USE WORKERS COTTAGE

Mill Workers Village
- USE WORKERS VILLAGE

Millers House
- USE MILL HOUSE

MILLINERS SHOP
- UF Hatters Shop
- CL COMMERCIAL
- BT SHOP

MILLSTONE WORKING SITE
- UF Gritstone Quarry
- CL INDUSTRIAL
- BT STONE WORKING SITE
- RT GRANITE QUARRY
  - GRINDSTONE
  - QUARRY
  - QUERN WORKING SITE
  - SANDSTONE QUARRY

Millwheel
- USE WATERWHEEL

MINE
- UF Mine Pumphouse
  - Pit Pony Stable
  - Winding Gear Shop
- SN Use with term showing major products where known.
- CL INDUSTRIAL
- BT MINING INDUSTRY SITE
- NT ANTIMONY MINE
  - ARSENIC MINE
  - BARYTES MINE
  - CALAMINE MINE
  - CLAY MINE
  - COLLIERY
  - COPPER MINE
  - DRIFT MINE
  - FLINT MINE
  - FLUORSPAR MINE
  - GOLD MINE
  - GRAPHITE MINE
  - GYPSUM MINE
  - IRONSTONE MINE
  - LEAD MINE
  - MANGANESE MINE
  - NICKEL MINE
  - OPEN CAST MINE
  - POTASH MINE
  - SALT MINE
  - SILVER MINE
  - TIN MINE
  - TUNGSTEN MINE
  - WITHERITE MINE
  - ZINC MINE
- RT ADIT
  - AERIAL ROPEWAY
  - ASSAY OFFICE
  - CRUSHING FLOOR
  - DRAINAGE LEVEL
  - DRESSING MILL
  - ENGINE HOUSE
  - MINE BUILDING
  - MINE CAPTAINS HOUSE

MINE PUMPING SHAFT
MINERS CHANGING HOUSE
MINES RESCUE STATION
SPOIL HEAP
STEAM WHIM
STEAM WHIM HOUSE
STOWE
WINDER HOUSE
WINDING CIRCLE
WORKERS VILLAGE

MINE BUILDING
UF   Minehouse
SN   Use specific type where known.
CL   INDUSTRIAL
BT   MINING INDUSTRY SITE
NT   LAMPHOUSE
       MINERS BOTHY
       MINERS CHANGING HOUSE
       MINERS HUT
       MINES RESCUE STATION
       PITHEAD BATHS
RT   MINE

MINE CAPTAINS HOUSE
CL   DOMESTIC
BT   INDUSTRIAL HOUSE
RT   MINE
       WORKERS COTTAGE

MINE CAPTAINS HOUSE
CL   INDUSTRIAL
BT   INDUSTRIAL HOUSE

MINE DRAINAGE AND VENTILATION SITE
CL   INDUSTRIAL
BT   MINING INDUSTRY SITE
NT   ADIT
       EXHAUSTER HOUSE
       MINE PUMPING SHAFT
       MINE PUMPING WORKS
       MINE SHAFT
RT   VENTILATION FURNACE

Mine Drainage Tunnel
   USE DRAINAGE LEVEL

MINE LAYING SUBMARINE
CL   MARITIME
BT   SUBMARINE

MINE LIFTING AND WINDING STRUCTURE
CL   INDUSTRIAL
BT   MINING INDUSTRY SITE
NT   AERIAL ROPEWAY
       HAULAGE ENGINE HOUSE
       HORSE WHIM
       MAN ENGINE
       STEAM WINDER
       STOWE
       WINDER HOUSE
       WINDING CIRCLE
       WINDING GEAR
       WINDLASS
RT   COAL DROP
       LIFTING AND WINDING STRUCTURE

Mine Managers House
   USE MANAGERS HOUSE

Mine Pumphouse
   USE MINE
       PUMPING STATION
SN   Use both terms.

MINE PUMPING SHAFT
SN   Separate shaft to the main working shaft.
       Specifically for the pumping of water out of the
       mine workings.
CL   INDUSTRIAL

BT   MINE DRAINAGE AND VENTILATION SITE
RT   ATMOSPHERIC ENGINE HOUSE
       MINE
       MINE PUMPING WORKS
       MINE SHAFT

Mine Pumping Station
   USE MINE PUMPING WORKS

MINE PUMPING WORKS
UF   Colliery Pumphouse
       Mine Pumping Station
CL   INDUSTRIAL
BT   MINE DRAINAGE AND VENTILATION SITE
RT   BEAM ENGINE
       MINE PUMPING SHAFT
       PUMPING STATION

MINE SHAFT
CL   INDUSTRIAL
BT   MINE DRAINAGE AND VENTILATION SITE
RT   AIR SHAFT
       LIFT SHAFT
       MINE PUMPING SHAFT
       SHAFT
       TUNNEL CHAMBER
       VENTILATION SHAFT

Minehouse
   USE MINE BUILDING

MINELAYER
CL   MARITIME
BT   WARSHIP

Minepits
   USE EXTRACTIVE PIT

MINERAL BATHS
CL   HEALTH AND WELFARE
BT   BATHS
RT   PUMP ROOMS
       SPA
       SPA HOTEL
       THERMAL BATHS

MINERAL EXTRACTION SITE
CL   INDUSTRIAL
NT   ALUM QUARRY
       ALUM WORKS
       BRINE PIT
       CHALK PIT
       CLAY EXTRACTION SITE
       FLUORSPAR MINE
       FLUORSPAR WORKINGS
       GRAPHITE MINE
       GYPSUM MINE
       JET WORKINGS
       OCHRE PIT
       POTASH MINE
       SALT MINE
       SALTERN
       SAND AND GRAVEL EXTRACTION SITE
       STONE EXTRACTION SITE
       UMBER WORKINGS
       WITHERITE MINE
RT   IRONSTONE WORKINGS
       MINERAL PIT
       MINERAL RAILWAY

Mineral Line
   USE MINERAL RAILWAY

MINERAL PIT
CL   INDUSTRIAL
BT   EXTRACTIVE PIT
RT   FULLERS EARTH PIT
       MINERAL EXTRACTION SITE
       OCHRE PIT

MINERAL PRODUCT SITE
CL   INDUSTRIAL
NT   ABRASIVES MANUFACTURING SITE
     BRICK AND TILEMAKING SITE
     CEMENT MANUFACTURING SITE
     GLASSMAKING SITE
     PLASTER MANUFACTURING SITE
     POTTERY MANUFACTURING SITE
     TERRACOTTA WORKS
     WASTER KILN

MINERAL RAILWAY
UF   Mineral Line
CL   TRANSPORT
BT   RAILWAY
RT   MINERAL EXTRACTION SITE
     MINING INDUSTRY SITE

MINERAL WATER FACTORY
CL   INDUSTRIAL
BT   FACTORY <BY PRODUCT>
RT   BOTTLING PLANT

MINERAL WATER FACTORY
CL   INDUSTRIAL
BT   FOOD AND DRINK INDUSTRY SITE
RT   BOTTLING PLANT

MINERAL WATER HOSPITAL
CL   HEALTH AND WELFARE
BT   SPECIALIST HOSPITAL

MINERAL WATER WORKS
CL   INDUSTRIAL
BT   FOOD AND DRINK INDUSTRY SITE
RT   BOTTLING PLANT

Miners Baths
USE PITHEAD BATHS

MINERS BOTHY
SN   Hut or crude shelter for miners.
CL   DOMESTIC
BT   BOTHY

MINERS BOTHY
SN   Hut or crude shelter for miners.
CL   INDUSTRIAL
BT   MINE BUILDING

Miners Canteen
USE CANTEEN

MINERS CHANGING HOUSE
CL   INDUSTRIAL
BT   MINE BUILDING
RT   LAMPHOUSE
     MINE
     PITHEAD BATHS

Miners Cottage
USE WORKERS COTTAGE

Miners Hall
USE TRADES UNION HALL

MINERS HUT
UF   Coe
CL   INDUSTRIAL
BT   MINE BUILDING

Miners Lamphouse
USE LAMPHOUSE

MINERS READING ROOM
CL   EDUCATION
BT   READING ROOM
RT   CHURCH INSTITUTE

COLLIERY INSTITUTE
COOPERATIVE INSTITUTE
MECHANICS INSTITUTE
PEOPLES COLLEGE
WORKERS VILLAGE
WORKING MENS COLLEGE
WORKING MENS INSTITUTE

Miners Union Hall
USE TRADES UNION HALL

Miners Village
USE WORKERS VILLAGE

MINES RESCUE STATION
SN   A rescue station serving a number of mines in the
     immediate area.
CL   INDUSTRIAL
BT   MINE BUILDING
RT   COLLIERY
     MINE

MINESWEEPER
CL   MARITIME
BT   WARSHIP

MINI HILL FORT
SN   Late Bronze Age settlement consisting of large hut
     circle surrounded by bank and ditches, eg. Thwing.
CL   DOMESTIC
BT   HILLFORT

MINI HILL FORT
SN   Late Bronze Age settlement consisting of large hut
     circle surrounded by bank and ditches, eg. Thwing.
CL   DEFENCE
BT   HILLFORT

MINIATURE GARDEN
CL   GARDENS, PARKS AND URBAN SPACES
BT   GARDEN

MINIATURE RAILWAY
CL   TRANSPORT
BT   RAILWAY

MINING INDUSTRY SITE
CL   INDUSTRIAL
NT   DRIFT
     HEAPSTEAD
     METHANE PLANT
     MINE
     MINE BUILDING
     MINE DRAINAGE AND VENTILATION SITE
     MINE LIFTING AND WINDING STRUCTURE
     SPOIL HEAP
RT   COAL MINING SITE
     MINERAL RAILWAY

Mining Village
USE WORKERS VILLAGE

Ministers Cottage
USE MANSE

Minor Villa
USE VILLA (ROMAN)

MINOR WARSHIP
CL   MARITIME
BT   WARSHIP
NT   BOMB VESSEL
     CORVETTE
     CRUISER
     DESTROYER
     FIFTH RATE SHIP OF THE LINE
     FOURTH RATE SHIP OF THE LINE
     FRIGATE
     GALLEASSE

GALLEY
SIXTH RATE SHIP OF THE LINE
TORPEDO BOAT CARRIER

Minories
    USE FRANCISCAN FRIARY

MINSTER
    CL   RELIGIOUS, RITUAL AND FUNERARY
    BT   PLACE OF WORSHIP

MINT
    UF   Royal Mint
    CL   CIVIL
    RT   FOUNDRY

MINT
    UF   Royal Mint
    CL   INDUSTRIAL
    BT   NON FERROUS METAL PRODUCT SITE

MISSILE BASE
    CL   DEFENCE
    RT   EARLY WARNING STATION

MISSION CHURCH
    CL   RELIGIOUS, RITUAL AND FUNERARY
    BT   CHURCH
    RT   MISSION HALL

MISSION HALL
    CL   RELIGIOUS, RITUAL AND FUNERARY
    RT   ANGLICAN CHURCH
            CHILDRENS HOME
            HOMELESS HOSTEL
            MISSION CHURCH
            ORPHANAGE

MISSION HALL
    CL   HEALTH AND WELFARE

Mistal
    USE COW HOUSE

MITHRAEUM
    CL   RELIGIOUS, RITUAL AND FUNERARY
    BT   TEMPLE

MITRE LOCK
    CL   TRANSPORT
    BT   LOCK

MIXED BORDER
    CL   GARDENS, PARKS AND URBAN SPACES
    BT   BORDER
    RT   FLOWER BED

MIXED CEMETERY
    CL   RELIGIOUS, RITUAL AND FUNERARY
    BT   INHUMATION CEMETERY

MIXED WOODLAND
    CL   GARDENS, PARKS AND URBAN SPACES
    BT   WOODLAND

Mixing House
    USE GUNPOWDER MIXING HOUSE

MIXING HOUSE BARN
    CL   AGRICULTURE AND SUBSISTENCE
    BT   BARN
    RT   HORSE ENGINE HOUSE
            THRESHING BARN

Mizmaze
    USE MAZE

MOAT
    UF   Double Moated Garden

Homestead Moat
Moated Garden
Moated House
Moated Manor House
    SN   Use for moated sites, not defensive moats. Use
            with relevant site type where known, eg. MANOR
            HOUSE, GARDEN, etc.
    CL   DOMESTIC
    RT   DWELLING
            GARDEN

MOAT
    UF   Double Moated Garden
            Homestead Moat
            Moated Garden
            Moated House
            Moated Manor House
    SN   Use for moated sites, not defensive moats. Use
            with relevant site type where known, eg. MANOR
            HOUSE, GARDEN, etc.
    CL   WATER SUPPLY AND DRAINAGE
    RT   FISH POND
            GARDEN
            MANOR HOUSE

Moated Garden
    USE MOAT
            GARDEN
    SN   Use both terms.

Moated House
    USE HOUSE
            MOAT
    SN   Use both terms.

Moated Manor House
    USE MOAT
            MANOR HOUSE
    SN   Use both terms.

Model Cottage
    USE MODEL DWELLING

MODEL DWELLING
    UF   5% Industrial Dwellings
            Block Dwellings
            Exhibition Cottage
            Model Cottage
            Model Flats
            Peabody Flats
            Workers Flats
    SN   Flats or houses built by 19th century
            philanthropic societies as amodel to encourage the
            development of approved working class housing.
    CL   DOMESTIC
    BT   DWELLING

MODEL FACTORY
    CL   INDUSTRIAL
    BT   FACTORY <BY FORM>

MODEL FARM
    UF   Planned Farm
    CL   AGRICULTURE AND SUBSISTENCE
    BT   FARM

Model Flats
    USE MODEL DWELLING

Model Lodging House
    USE LODGING HOUSE

MODEL SETTLEMENT
    UF   Model Village
            Planned Town
            Planned Village
    CL   DOMESTIC
    BT   SETTLEMENT
    NT   CHARTIST LAND COLONY

ESTATE VILLAGE
GARDEN SUBURB
GARDEN VILLAGE
MORAVIAN SETTLEMENT
RESORT VILLAGE
UTOPIAN COMMUNITY VILLAGE
WORKERS VILLAGE

Model Village
USE MODEL SETTLEMENT

MOLE
SN A massive structure, usually of stone, serving as a pier or breakwater, or joining two places separated by water.
CL MARITIME
BT SEA DEFENCES
RT PIER

MONASTERY
UF Celtic Monastery
Convent
Monastery Barn
Monastery Bridge
Monastery Gatehouse
Monastery Gateway
Monastery Kitchen
Monastic Cathedral
Monastic Infirmary
SN Houses specifically of monks, canons or religious men but not friars.
CL RELIGIOUS, RITUAL AND FUNERARY
BT RELIGIOUS HOUSE
NT AUGUSTINIAN MONASTERY
BENEDICTINE MONASTERY
BONHOMMES MONASTERY
CARTHUSIAN MONASTERY
CISTERCIAN MONASTERY
CLUNIAC MONASTERY
GILBERTINE MONASTERY
GRANDMONTINE MONASTERY
PREMONSTRATENSIAN MONASTERY
SAVIGNIAC MONASTERY
TIRONIAN MONASTERY
TRINITARIAN MONASTERY
RT ABBEY
ABBOTS HOUSE
ALMONRY
CALEFACTORY
CAMERA
CATHEDRAL
CELL
CHAPTER HOUSE
CLOISTER
DORTER
DOUBLE HOUSE
FARM
FRATER
FRIARY
GATEHOUSE
GRANGE
GUEST HOUSE
HOSPITAL
INFIRMARY
KITCHEN
MANCIPLES HOUSE
MANOR
NUNNERY
PRECEPTORY
PRIORY
REFECTORY

Monastery Barn
USE MONASTERY
BARN
SN Use both terms.

Monastery Bridge
USE BRIDGE

MONASTERY
SN Use both terms.

Monastery Gatehouse
USE MONASTERY
GATEHOUSE
SN Use both terms.

Monastery Gateway
USE GATE
MONASTERY
SN Use both terms.

Monastery Kitchen
USE KITCHEN
MONASTERY
SN Use both terms.

Monastic Cathedral
USE CATHEDRAL
MONASTERY
SN Use both terms. Use specific type of monastery where known.

Monastic Grange
USE GRANGE

Monastic Infirmary
USE MONASTERY
INFIRMARY
SN Use both terms.

MONASTIC PRECINCT
CL RELIGIOUS, RITUAL AND FUNERARY
RT CATHEDRAL PRECINCT
PRECINCT

Monastic Vallum
USE RELIGIOUS HOUSE
SN Component. Use specific type of religious house where known.

MONKEY HOUSE
CL RECREATIONAL
BT ANIMAL HOUSE

Monolith
USE STANDING STONE

Montessori School
USE NURSERY SCHOOL

Monument
USE COMMEMORATIVE MONUMENT

Monumental Arch
USE COMMEMORATIVE MONUMENT
ARCH
SN Use both terms.

MONUMENTAL MOUND
SN Mound in excess of 150m in diameter. Late Neolithic and presumed ritual function, eg. Silbury Hill.
CL RELIGIOUS, RITUAL AND FUNERARY
RT MOUND
ROUND BARROW

MOORING BOLLARD
CL TRANSPORT
BT WATER TRANSPORT SITE
RT BOLLARD
CANAL WHARF
DOLPHIN
QUAY
WHARF

MOORING BOLLARD
CL MARITIME

BT   DOCK AND HARBOUR INSTALLATION
RT   BOLLARD
     DOLPHIN

MOORISH GARDEN
CL   GARDENS, PARKS AND URBAN SPACES
BT   GARDEN

MOORISH PAVILION
UF   Alhambra
CL   GARDENS, PARKS AND URBAN SPACES
BT   PAVILION

MOOT
UF   Folk Moot
SN   An outdoor meeting place.
CL   CIVIL
RT   MOOT HALL

MOOT HALL
UF   Court Of Speech
     Speech House
CL   CIVIL
BT   MEETING HALL
RT   ASSAY OFFICE
     COURT HOUSE
     GUILDHALL
     LEET HALL
     MOOT
     STEELYARD

MORAVIAN CHAPEL
UF   Moravian Church
CL   RELIGIOUS, RITUAL AND FUNERARY
BT   NONCONFORMIST CHAPEL

Moravian Church
USE MORAVIAN CHAPEL

Moravian School
USE CHURCH SCHOOL

MORAVIAN SETTLEMENT
SN   A community of German methodists.
CL   DOMESTIC
BT   MODEL SETTLEMENT
RT   CHURCH SCHOOL

MORT SAFE
CL   RELIGIOUS, RITUAL AND FUNERARY
BT   FUNERARY SITE

MORTAR MILL
CL   INDUSTRIAL
BT   PLASTER MANUFACTURING SITE

MORTAR MILL
CL   INDUSTRIAL
BT   MILL

MORTUARY
CL   RELIGIOUS, RITUAL AND FUNERARY
BT   FUNERARY SITE

MORTUARY CHAPEL
CL   RELIGIOUS, RITUAL AND FUNERARY
BT   CHAPEL
RT   CEMETERY
     CEMETERY CHAPEL
     CHARNEL HOUSE
     CREMATORIUM
     MORTUARY HOUSE

MORTUARY ENCLOSURE
UF   Long Mortuary Enclosure
CL   RELIGIOUS, RITUAL AND FUNERARY
BT   FUNERARY SITE
RT   BARROW
     ENCLOSURE

MORTUARY HOUSE
CL   RELIGIOUS, RITUAL AND FUNERARY
BT   FUNERARY SITE
RT   BARROW
     CHARNEL HOUSE
     MAUSOLEUM
     MORTUARY CHAPEL

MOSAIC
UF   Mosaic Pavement
CL   UNASSIGNED

Mosaic Pavement
USE MOSAIC

MOSQUE
CL   RELIGIOUS, RITUAL AND FUNERARY
BT   PLACE OF WORSHIP
RT   SYNAGOGUE
     TEMPLE

MOSS HOUSE
CL   GARDENS, PARKS AND URBAN SPACES
BT   GARDEN BUILDING

MOTEL
CL   COMMERCIAL
BT   HOTEL
RT   INN

MOTEL
CL   DOMESTIC
BT   HOTEL

MOTOR CYCLE FACTORY
CL   INDUSTRIAL
BT   MOTOR VEHICLE ENGINEERING SITE

MOTOR CYCLE FACTORY
CL   INDUSTRIAL
BT   FACTORY <BY PRODUCT>

MOTOR GUNBOAT
CL   MARITIME
BT   PATROL BOAT

Motor Repair Shop
USE GARAGE

Motor Repair Workshop
USE GARAGE

MOTOR TORPEDO BOAT
CL   MARITIME
BT   PATROL BOAT

Motor Track
USE RACING CIRCUIT

MOTOR VEHICLE ENGINEERING SITE
CL   INDUSTRIAL
BT   VEHICLE ENGINEERING SITE
NT   CAR FACTORY
     CARRIAGE WORKS
     COACH WORKS
     LORRY FACTORY
     MOTOR CYCLE FACTORY

MOTOR VEHICLE SHOWROOM
UF   Car Showroom
     Vehicle Showroom
CL   COMMERCIAL
BT   SHOWROOM
RT   GARAGE
     MULTI STOREY CAR PARK
     PETROL STATION

Motor Works

USE CAR FACTORY

MOTTE
- UF   Castle Motte
  - Castle Mound
  - Motte Castle
- CL   DOMESTIC
- BT   CASTLE
- RT   ADULTERINE CASTLE
  - BAILEY
  - MOTTE AND BAILEY
  - MOUND
  - RINGWORK
  - RINGWORK AND BAILEY

MOTTE
- UF   Castle Motte
  - Castle Mound
  - Motte Castle
- CL   DEFENCE
- BT   CASTLE
- RT   ADULTERINE CASTLE
  - BAILEY
  - MOTTE AND BAILEY
  - MOUND
  - RINGWORK

MOTTE AND BAILEY
- UF   Motte And Bailey Castle
- CL   DOMESTIC
- BT   CASTLE
- RT   BAILEY
  - MOTTE
  - RINGWORK
  - RINGWORK AND BAILEY

MOTTE AND BAILEY
- UF   Motte And Bailey Castle
- CL   DEFENCE
- BT   CASTLE
- RT   BAILEY
  - MOTTE
  - RINGWORK

Motte And Bailey Castle
USE MOTTE AND BAILEY

Motte Castle
USE MOTTE

MOULD LOFT
- SN   Used for the laying out and marking of the smaller parts of a ship prior to construction.
- CL   INDUSTRIAL
- BT   MARINE WORKSHOP   .
- RT   FABRICATION SHED
  - PATTERN SHOP

MOULD LOFT
- SN   Used for the laying out and marking of the smaller parts of a ship prior to construction.
- CL   MARITIME
- BT   MARINE WORKSHOP
- RT   PATTERN SHOP

MOULD STORE
- CL   INDUSTRIAL
- BT   POTTERY MANUFACTURING SITE
- RT   MOULDMAKERS SHOP

MOULDING HOUSE
- CL   INDUSTRIAL
- BT   BRICK AND TILEMAKING SITE

MOULDMAKERS SHOP
- CL   INDUSTRIAL
- BT   POTTERY MANUFACTURING SITE
- RT   CRATEMAKERS SHOP
  - MOULD STORE

TILEMAKING WORKSHOP

MOUND
- UF   Conical Mound
  - Toot
  - Tump
- CL   UNASSIGNED
- NT   BOUNDARY MOUND
- RT   ARTIFICIAL MOUND
  - BARROW
  - BURNT MOUND
  - EARTHWORK
  - FISHERY MOUND
  - GALLOWS MOUND
  - LONG MOUND
  - MONUMENTAL MOUND
  - MOTTE
  - PILLOW MOUND
  - PROSPECT MOUND
  - TREE MOUND
  - WINDMILL MOUND

Mount
USE ARTIFICIAL MOUND

Mount Pleasant Enclosure
USE HENGE ENCLOSURE

MOUNTING BLOCK
- UF   Horse Mounting Block
  - Horse Mounting Stone
  - Mounting Stone
- CL   GARDENS, PARKS AND URBAN SPACES
- BT   STREET FURNITURE
- RT   TETHERING POST

MOUNTING BLOCK
- UF   Horse Mounting Block
  - Horse Mounting Stone
  - Mounting Stone
- CL   TRANSPORT
- BT   ROAD TRANSPORT SITE
- RT   TETHERING POST

Mounting Stone
USE MOUNTING BLOCK

MOVING CRANE
- CL   TRANSPORT
- BT   CRANE <BY FORM>
- NT   MOVING QUAY CRANE

MOVING QUAY CRANE
- CL   TRANSPORT
- BT   MOVING CRANE

MOVING QUAY CRANE
- CL   TRANSPORT
- BT   QUAY CRANE

MUFFLE KILN
- SN   Muffle - flame proof lining of a pottery kiln.
- CL   INDUSTRIAL
- BT   POTTERY MANUFACTURING SITE
- RT   POTTERY KILN

MUG HOUSE
- CL   INDUSTRIAL
- BT   POTTERY MANUFACTURING SITE
- RT   HANDLING HOUSE
  - MARL PIT
  - POT HOUSE
  - THROWING HOUSE

Multi Span Bridge
USE BRIDGE

MULTI STOREY CAR PARK
- CL   TRANSPORT

BT   CAR PARK
RT   CAR RAMP
      GARAGE
      MOTOR VEHICLE SHOWROOM
      PETROL PUMP
      PETROL STATION

MULTI STOREY STABLE
CL   TRANSPORT
BT   STABLE

MULTIPLE DITCH SYSTEM
CL   DEFENCE
BT   ENCLOSED SETTLEMENT
RT   LINEAR EARTHWORK

MULTIPLE DWELLING
CL   DOMESTIC
BT   DWELLING
NT   CLUSTER BLOCK
      CLUSTER HOUSE
      FLATS
      MEWS
      ROW
      TENEMENT BLOCK
      TENEMENT HOUSE
      TERRACE

MULTIPLE ENCLOSURE FORT
SN   Hillslope forts with wide spaced ramparts.
CL   DOMESTIC
BT   HILLFORT

MULTIPLE ENCLOSURE FORT
SN   Hillslope forts with wide spaced ramparts.
CL   DEFENCE
BT   HILLFORT

MULTIVALLATE HILLFORT
UF   Large Multivallate Hillfort
      Small Multivallate Hillfort
CL   DOMESTIC
BT   HILLFORT

MULTIVALLATE HILLFORT
UF   Large Multivallate Hillfort
      Small Multivallate Hillfort
CL   DEFENCE
BT   HILLFORT

MUNGO MILL
SN   Low grade cloth made from ground-up heavy woollen
      rags.
CL   INDUSTRIAL
BT   TEXTILE MILL
RT   TEXTILE WAREHOUSE

MUNGO MILL
SN   Low grade cloth made from ground-up heavy woollen
      rags.
CL   INDUSTRIAL
BT   WOOL MANUFACTURING SITE
RT   FLOCK MILL
      SHODDY MILL

Municipal Baths
USE BATHS

Municipal Office
USE LOCAL GOVERNMENT OFFICE

MUNICIPIUM
CL   DOMESTIC
BT   TOWN

MUNICIPIUM
CL   CIVIL
BT   TOWN

MUNIMENT HOUSE

CL   CIVIL
RT   RECORD OFFICE

MUNITION HOUSE
CL   DEFENCE
BT   ARMAMENT STORE

Munitions Depot
USE ARMAMENT DEPOT

MUNITIONS FACTORY
SN   Manufacture of weapons, ammunition and military
      supplies.
CL   INDUSTRIAL
BT   FACTORY <BY PRODUCT>

MUNITIONS FACTORY
SN   Manufacture of weapons, ammunition and military
      supplies.
CL   INDUSTRIAL
BT   ARMAMENT MANUFACTURING SITE
RT   MAGAZINE
      ORDNANCE FACTORY

MUSEUM
CL   EDUCATION
RT   ART GALLERY
      CURATORS HOUSE
      EXHIBITION HALL

MUSEUM
CL   RECREATIONAL
BT   ART AND EDUCATION VENUE
RT   ART GALLERY
      CURATORS HOUSE
      EXHIBITION HALL

Music Academy
USE MUSIC SCHOOL

MUSIC AND DANCE VENUE
CL   RECREATIONAL
NT   BANDSTAND
      CONCERT HALL
      DANCE HALL
      DANCE STUDIO
      DISCOTHEQUE
      JAZZ CLUB
      MUSIC HALL
      OPERA HOUSE
      THEATRE

Music College
USE MUSIC SCHOOL

Music Conservatoire
USE MUSIC SCHOOL

MUSIC HALL
UF   Palace Of Varieties
      Peoples Palace
      Variety Theatre
CL   RECREATIONAL
BT   MUSIC AND DANCE VENUE
RT   CONCERT HALL
      THEATRE

Music House
USE CONCERT HALL

MUSIC SCHOOL
UF   Academy Of Music
      Military Music School
      Music Academy
      Music College
      Music Conservatoire
CL   EDUCATION
BT   TRAINING SCHOOL

MUSICAL INSTRUMENT FACTORY

CL INDUSTRIAL
BT FACTORY <BY PRODUCT>
NT ORGAN FACTORY
PIANO FACTORY

MUSTARD MILL
CL INDUSTRIAL
BT FOOD PRODUCTION SITE

MUSTARD MILL
CL INDUSTRIAL
BT MILL

Mynchery
USE NUNNERY

NAIL FACTORY
CL INDUSTRIAL
BT FACTORY <BY PRODUCT>
RT FORGE
NAIL SHOP
SCREW FACTORY
WIRE MILL

NAIL FACTORY
CL INDUSTRIAL
BT FERROUS METAL PRODUCT SITE

NAIL SHOP
CL INDUSTRIAL
BT FERROUS METAL PRODUCT SITE
RT FORGE
NAIL FACTORY
NAILERS ROW
SLITTING MILL

NAILERS ROW
CL INDUSTRIAL
BT CRAFT INDUSTRY SITE
RT NAIL SHOP
SMITHS COTTAGE

NAILERS ROW
CL DOMESTIC
BT ROW
RT SMITHS COTTAGE

NAMED TREE
CL COMMEMORATIVE
BT COMMEMORATIVE MONUMENT
RT HISTORICAL SITE
TREE

Narrow Gauge Railway
USE RAILWAY

NARROW RIDGE AND FURROW
CL AGRICULTURE AND SUBSISTENCE
BT RIDGE AND FURROW

National Debt Redemption Office
USE GOVERNMENT OFFICE

National School
USE CHURCH SCHOOL

National Society School
USE CHURCH SCHOOL

NATURAL FEATURE
SN Use only for natural features mistakenly assumed
to be archaeological or natural features with
archaeological significance.
CL UNASSIGNED
BT FEATURE
NT CAVE
FUNGUS RING
GEOLOGICAL MARKS
OXBOW LAKE

REED BED
ROCK BASIN
STONE
SUBMARINE FOREST
TREE
TREE HOLE
TREE STUMP

Naval Academy
USE NAVAL COLLEGE

Naval Architecture School
USE ARCHITECTURE SCHOOL

Naval Armament Depot
USE ARMAMENT DEPOT

Naval Arsenal
USE ARSENAL

Naval Asylum
USE MENTAL HOSPITAL

Naval Barracks
USE BARRACKS

NAVAL CAPTAINS HOUSE
CL DOMESTIC
BT MARITIME HOUSE

Naval Club
USE SERVICES CLUB

NAVAL COLLEGE
UF Naval Academy
Navigation School
Royal Merchant Navy School
CL EDUCATION
BT TRAINING COLLEGE
RT ARTILLERY SCHOOL
MILITARY COLLEGE

NAVAL COLLEGE
UF Naval Academy
Navigation School
Royal Merchant Navy School
CL MARITIME
RT ARTILLERY SCHOOL
MILITARY COLLEGE

NAVAL DOCKYARD
CL INDUSTRIAL
BT DOCKYARD

NAVAL DOCKYARD
CL MARITIME
BT DOCKYARD

NAVAL HOSPITAL
UF Seamens Hospital
CL HEALTH AND WELFARE
BT HOSPITAL

NAVAL OFFICERS HOUSE
CL DOMESTIC
BT MARITIME HOUSE
RT COMMANDER IN CHIEFS HOUSE
COMMISSIONERS HOUSE
NAVAL OFFICERS MESS

NAVAL OFFICERS MESS
CL MARITIME
RT NAVAL OFFICERS HOUSE
OFFICERS MESS
SERGEANTS MESS

NAVAL STOREHOUSE
UF Blockstone
Gun Carriage Store

Lay Apart Store
CL   MARITIME
RT   STOREHOUSE

NAVIGATION AID
CL   MARITIME
NT   BEACON
     COAST LIGHT
     COASTGUARD STATION
     COASTGUARD TOWER
     LANDMARK TOWER
     LIFEBOAT STATION
     LIGHTHOUSE
     SEA MARK
     TIMEBALL TOWER

Navigation Light
USE LIGHTHOUSE

Navigation School
USE NAVAL COLLEGE

Necessary House
USE PRIVY HOUSE

Necropolis
USE CEMETERY

NEEDLE FACTORY
CL   INDUSTRIAL
BT   FACTORY <BY PRODUCT>

NEEDLE MILL
CL   INDUSTRIAL
BT   MILL
RT   WIRE MILL

NEEDLE MILL
CL   INDUSTRIAL
BT   FERROUS METAL PRODUCT SITE
RT   PIN MILL
     WIRE MILL

Negative Lynchet
USE LYNCHET

Neighbourhood Centre
USE COMMUNITY CENTRE

NEPHROLOGY HOSPITAL
CL   HEALTH AND WELFARE
BT   SPECIALIST HOSPITAL

NERVOUS DISEASES HOSPITAL
CL   HEALTH AND WELFARE
BT   SPECIALIST HOSPITAL

NET FISHING VESSEL
CL   MARITIME
BT   FISHING VESSEL
NT   DRIFTER
     SEINER
     TRAWLER

NET HOUSE
SN   A free-standing building with enough space to hang
     and dry nets.
CL   AGRICULTURE AND SUBSISTENCE
BT   FISHING SITE

NET HOUSE
SN   A free-standing building with enough space to hang
     and dry nets.
CL   MARITIME
RT   FISHERMANS HOUSE
     NET LOFT
     RIGGING HOUSE

NET LOFT

SN   A component of another building (perhaps a house).
     Used for storing nets.
CL   AGRICULTURE AND SUBSISTENCE
BT   FISHING SITE
RT   NET HOUSE

NET LOFT
SN   A component of another building (perhaps a house).
     Used for storing nets.
CL   MARITIME
RT   NET HOUSE

NETBALL COURT
CL   RECREATIONAL
BT   SPORTS SITE

NEUROLOGY HOSPITAL
CL   HEALTH AND WELFARE
BT   SPECIALIST HOSPITAL

NEWSPAPER OFFICE
UF   Editorial Office
CL   COMMERCIAL
BT   COMMERCIAL OFFICE
RT   OFFICE
     PRINT SHOP
     PRINTING WORKS

NICKEL MINE
SN   Also use with other metal ores extracted and MINE
     where relevant.
CL   INDUSTRIAL
BT   MINE

NITRATE WORKS
SN   Type of fertiliser works producing nitrogen-rich
     fertiliser.
CL   INDUSTRIAL
BT   AGRICULTURAL CHEMICAL SITE
RT   FERTILISER WORKS

NITRE BED
SN   Constituent of gunpowder. Produced by the
     decomposition of vegetable matter and animal waste
     in large earthwork beds.
CL   INDUSTRIAL
BT   EXPLOSIVES SITE

NITROGLYCERINE WORKS
CL   INDUSTRIAL
BT   EXPLOSIVES SITE
RT   LABORATORY
     TESTING RANGE

Non Antiquity
USE SITE

NON FERROUS METAL EXTRACTION SITE
CL   INDUSTRIAL
BT   METAL INDUSTRY SITE
NT   ANTIMONY MINE
     ARSENIC MINE
     COPPER MINE
     COPPER WORKINGS
     GOLD MINE
     HUSH
     LEAD MINE
     LEAD WORKINGS
     MANGANESE MINE
     PROSPECTING PIT
     PROSPECTING TRENCH
     SILVER MINE
     STREAM WORKS
     TUNGSTEN MINE
     ZINC MINE

NON FERROUS METAL PROCESSING SITE
CL   INDUSTRIAL
BT   METAL INDUSTRY SITE

NT   BOUSE TEAM
      BUDDLE
      BUDDLE HOUSE
      CRAZING MILL
      CRUSHING CIRCLE
      CRUSHING FLOOR
      CRUSHING MILL
      KNOCK STONE
      MEERSTONE
      ORE STONE
      ORE WASHING PLANT
      SETTLING PIT
      STAMPING MILL
      STAMPS
      TIN MILL
      TIN WORKS
      TINNERS CACHE
      TINNERS HUT
      WASH KILN
      WASHING FLOOR

NON FERROUS METAL PRODUCT SITE
CL   INDUSTRIAL
BT   METAL INDUSTRY SITE
NT   ALUMINIUM SMELTER
      BATTERY MILL
      BELL CASTING PIT
      BELL FOUNDRY
      BRASS WORKS
      BRITANNIA METAL WORKS
      BRONZE FOUNDRY
      BRONZE WORKING SITE
      COPPER WORKING SITE
      COPPER WORKS
      GALVANIZING WORKSHOP
      GOLDSMITHS WORKSHOP
      JEWELLERY WORKS
      JEWELLERY WORKSHOP
      LEAD WORKS
      MINT
      PEWTER WORKS
      PLATING WORKS
      POLISHING SHOP
      SHOT TOWER
      SILVERSMITHS WORKSHOP
      TIN WORKS
      WATCHMAKERS WORKSHOP
      WHITESMITHS WORKSHOP
      ZINC WORKS

NON FERROUS METAL SMELTING SITE
CL   INDUSTRIAL
BT   METAL INDUSTRY SITE
NT   ARSENIC CALCINER
      BLOWING HOUSE
      BRASS FOUNDRY
      BRASS WORKS
      BRONZE WORKING SITE
      CONDENSING CHIMNEY
      CONDENSING FLUE
      COPPER WORKING SITE
      COPPER WORKS
      CUPOLA FURNACE (REVERBERATORY)
      LEAD WORKING SITE
      LEAD WORKS
      SILVER HEARTH
      SILVER WORKING SITE
      SLAG HEARTH
      SMELT MILL
      SMELTER
      SMELTERY
      ZINC WORKS
RT   ANNEALING FURNACE
      BLAST FURNACE
      BOLEHILL
      CUPELLATION FURNACE
      CUPOLA FURNACE (REVERBERATORY)
      ELECTRIC ARC FURNACE
      INDUCTION FURNACE

      LEAD FURNACE
      ORE HEARTH
      REVERBERATORY FURNACE
      ROASTING HEARTH
      SILVER HEARTH
      SLAG HEARTH

Non Parochial Chapel
      USE CHAPEL

Nonconformist Academy
      USE CHURCH SCHOOL

NONCONFORMIST CHAPEL
      UF   Dissenters Chapel
            Nonconformist Church
            Ranters Chapel
      CL   RELIGIOUS, RITUAL AND FUNERARY
      BT   CHAPEL
      NT   BAPTIST CHAPEL
            CONGREGATIONAL CHAPEL
            INDEPENDENT CHAPEL
            METHODIST CHAPEL
            MORAVIAN CHAPEL
            PRESBYTERIAN CHAPEL
            UNITARIAN CHAPEL
      RT   BAPTISTERY
            MEETING HOUSE OF JEHOVAHS WITNESSES
            NONCONFORMIST MEETING HOUSE

Nonconformist Church
      USE NONCONFORMIST CHAPEL

Nonconformist Hall
      USE NONCONFORMIST MEETING HOUSE

NONCONFORMIST MEETING HOUSE
      UF   Congregational Hall
            Dissenters Meeting House
            Gospel Hall
            Meeting House
            Methodist Central Hall
            Methodist Hall
            Nonconformist Hall
      CL   RELIGIOUS, RITUAL AND FUNERARY
      BT   PLACE OF WORSHIP
      NT   BRETHREN MEETING HOUSE
            FRIENDS MEETING HOUSE
            MEETING HOUSE OF JEHOVAHS WITNESSES
      RT   NONCONFORMIST CHAPEL

Nonconformist Proprietary School
      USE CHURCH SCHOOL

Nonconformist School
      USE CHURCH SCHOOL

NORTH LIGHT FACTORY
      SN   A type of single-storey factory building designed
            so that windows incorporated into the saw-tooth
            roof catch the available light.
      CL   INDUSTRIAL
      BT   FACTORY <BY FORM>
      RT   LIGHT ENGINEERING WORKS
            TEXTILE MILL

NUCLEAR BUNKER
      CL   DEFENCE
      RT   AIR RAID SHELTER
            UNDERGROUND MILITARY HEADQUARTERS
            UNDERGROUND STRUCTURE

NUCLEAR POWER STATION
      UF   Atomic Power Station
      CL   INDUSTRIAL
      BT   POWER STATION

NUNNERY
      UF   Celtic Monastery

Convent
Mynchery
Nuns Church
SN   Houses specifically of nuns/canonesses or
     religious women.
CL   RELIGIOUS, RITUAL AND FUNERARY
BT   RELIGIOUS HOUSE
NT   ANGLICAN NUNNERY
     AUGUSTINIAN NUNNERY
     BENEDICTINE NUNNERY
     CISTERCIAN NUNNERY
     CLUNIAC NUNNERY
     DOMINICAN NUNNERY
     FRANCISCAN NUNNERY
     PREMONSTRATENSIAN NUNNERY
     SISTERS OF ST JOHN NUNNERY
RT   ABBEY
     ALMONRY
     CAMERA
     CATHEDRAL
     CELL
     CHAPTER HOUSE
     CONVENT SCHOOL
     CURFEW BELL TOWER
     DOUBLE HOUSE
     FARM
     FRATER
     FRIARY
     GRANGE
     GUEST HOUSE
     MANOR
     MONASTERY
     PRECEPTORY
     PRIORY
     REFECTORY

Nuns Church
   USE CHURCH
       NUNNERY
   SN   Use both terms.

NURSERY
CL   HEALTH AND WELFARE
RT   CRECHE
     NURSERY SCHOOL

NURSERY GARDEN
UF   Plant Nursery
CL   GARDENS, PARKS AND URBAN SPACES
BT   GARDEN
RT   GLASSHOUSE
     GREENHOUSE

NURSERY GARDEN
UF   Plant Nursery
CL   AGRICULTURE AND SUBSISTENCE
BT   GARDEN
RT   GLASSHOUSE

NURSERY SCHOOL
UF   Montessori School
     Play School
CL   EDUCATION
BT   ELEMENTARY SCHOOL
RT   CRECHE
     NURSERY

Nurses Home
   USE NURSES HOSTEL

NURSES HOSTEL
UF   Nurses Home
CL   DOMESTIC
BT   RESIDENTIAL BUILDING
RT   HOSPITAL

Nurses School
   USE NURSES TRAINING SCHOOL

NURSES TRAINING SCHOOL

UF   Nurses School
     School For Nurses
CL   HEALTH AND WELFARE
RT   HOSPITAL

Nursing College
   USE MEDICAL COLLEGE

NURSING HOME
UF   Home For The Elderly
     Old Peoples Home
     Residential Home
     Rest Home
CL   HEALTH AND WELFARE
RT   CONVALESCENT HOME

NURSING HOME
UF   Home For The Elderly
     Old Peoples Home
     Residential Home
     Rest Home
CL   DOMESTIC
BT   RESIDENTIAL BUILDING
RT   CONVALESCENT HOME

NYMPHAEUM
SN   A grotto or shrine dedicated to the nymphs,
     composed of fountains designed to imitate a
     natural grotto.
CL   GARDENS, PARKS AND URBAN SPACES
BT   GROTTO

Oast
   USE OASTHOUSE

OASTHOUSE
UF   Oast
CL   INDUSTRIAL
BT   BREWING AND MALTING SITE
RT   HOP BARN
     HOP HOUSE
     HOP KILN
     HOP STORE

OASTHOUSE
UF   Oast
CL   INDUSTRIAL
BT   KILN <BY FUNCTION>

OASTHOUSE
UF   Oast
CL   AGRICULTURE AND SUBSISTENCE
BT   FOOD AND DRINK PROCESSING SITE
RT   HOP BARN
     HOP HOUSE
     HOP KILN
     HOP STORE

OBELISK
CL   GARDENS, PARKS AND URBAN SPACES
BT   GARDEN ORNAMENT
RT   COLUMN
     STATUE

OBELISK
CL   COMMEMORATIVE
BT   COMMEMORATIVE MONUMENT
RT   BUST
     COLUMN
     URN

OBSERVATORY
UF   Telescope Building
CL   EDUCATION
NT   TELESCOPE (CELESTIAL)
RT   CAMERA OBSCURA
     RESEARCH STATION
     SCHOOL

Occupation Site

USE SETTLEMENT

OCCUPATIONAL THERAPY UNIT
- CL HEALTH AND WELFARE

OCEAN LINER TERMINAL
- CL MARITIME
- BT SEA TERMINAL

Oceanographic Research Station
    USE RESEARCH STATION

OCHRE PIT
- CL INDUSTRIAL
- BT MINERAL EXTRACTION SITE
- RT UMBER WORKINGS

OCHRE PIT
- CL INDUSTRIAL
- BT DYE AND PIGMENT SITE

OCHRE PIT
- CL INDUSTRIAL
- BT EXTRACTIVE PIT
- RT MINERAL PIT

OCTAGONAL KILN
- CL INDUSTRIAL
- BT KILN <BY FORM>

OCTAGONAL TEMPLE
- CL GARDENS, PARKS AND URBAN SPACES
- BT GARDEN TEMPLE

ODDFELLOWS HALL
- CL INSTITUTIONAL
- BT MEETING HALL

OFF LICENCE
- CL COMMERCIAL
- BT SHOP
- RT LICENSED PREMISES

Offertorium
    USE CATHEDRAL

OFFICE
- UF Administration Block
  - Brewery Office
  - Dockyard Office
  - Estate Office
  - Headquarters
  - Land Stewards Office
  - Quarry Office
  - Sewer Commissioners Office
  - Shipyard Office
  - Water Board Office
  - Waterworks Office
  - Works Office
- CL UNASSIGNED
- BT BUILDING
- RT ARMY OFFICE
  - ASSAY OFFICE
  - BETTING OFFICE
  - BOOKING OFFICE
  - CABLE REPEATER OFFICE
  - CANAL OFFICE
  - CANTEEN
  - COMMERCIAL OFFICE
  - CONSTABLES OFFICE
  - COUNTING HOUSE
  - DOCKMASTERS OFFICE
  - DRAWING OFFICE
  - EXCISE OFFICE
  - GOVERNMENT OFFICE
  - HARBOUR MASTERS OFFICE
  - LEGAL OFFICE
  - LOCAL GOVERNMENT OFFICE
  - MARITIME OFFICE

    NEWSPAPER OFFICE
    PAY OFFICE
    PILOT OFFICE
    PORT AUTHORITY OFFICE
    POST OFFICE
    RAILWAY OFFICE
    RECORD OFFICE
    REGISTER OFFICE
    SORTING OFFICE
    TELEGRAPH OFFICE
    TIMEKEEPERS OFFICE
    UNIVERSITY ADMINISTRATION OFFICE

OFFICERS MESS
- CL DEFENCE
- RT ARMY CAMP
  - BARRACKS
  - COOKHOUSE
  - NAVAL OFFICERS MESS
  - SERGEANTS MESS

OGHAM STONE
- CL RELIGIOUS, RITUAL AND FUNERARY
- RT CROSS
  - GRAVESTONE
  - INSCRIBED STONE
  - RUNE STONE

OIL DISTILLERY
- CL INDUSTRIAL
- BT PETROCHEMICAL SITE
- RT SHALE QUARRY
  - WOOD CHEMICAL WORKS

OIL DISTILLERY
- CL INDUSTRIAL
- BT OIL REFINING SITE
- RT SHALE QUARRY

OIL ENGINE
- SN Internal combustion engine powered by the combustion of vapourised oil.
- CL INDUSTRIAL
- BT ENGINE

OIL FIRED POWER STATION
- CL INDUSTRIAL
- BT POWER STATION
- RT STEAM TURBINE POWER STATION

OIL FUEL BERTH
- SN Purpose built quay for supplying ships with fuel.
- CL MARITIME
- BT BERTH

OIL MILL
- CL INDUSTRIAL
- BT FOOD PROCESSING SITE

OIL MILL
- CL INDUSTRIAL
- BT MILL
- RT FARM BUILDING
  - GRINDSTONE
  - HORSE ENGINE
  - HORSE WHEEL
  - SOAP FACTORY

OIL PUMP
- CL INDUSTRIAL
- BT OIL REFINING SITE

OIL REFINERY
- CL INDUSTRIAL
- BT OIL REFINING SITE
- RT PIPE BRIDGE
  - PLASTICS FACTORY
  - TAR WORKS

OIL REFINING SITE

CL INDUSTRIAL
BT FUEL PRODUCTION SITE
NT OIL DISTILLERY
OIL PUMP
OIL REFINERY
OIL RIG
OIL SILO
OIL WELL

OIL RIG
CL INDUSTRIAL
BT OIL REFINING SITE

OIL SILO
CL INDUSTRIAL
BT OIL REFINING SITE

OIL WELL
CL INDUSTRIAL
BT OIL REFINING SITE

Old Peoples Asylum
USE ALMSHOUSE

Old Peoples Home
USE NURSING HOME

Omnibus Depot
USE BUS DEPOT

Omnibus Staton
USE BUS STATION

OPEN AIR THEATRE
CL GARDENS, PARKS AND URBAN SPACES
RT THEATRE

OPEN AIR THEATRE
CL RECREATIONAL
BT THEATRE

Open Cast Coal Workings
USE COAL WORKINGS

Open Cast Copper Workings
USE COPPER WORKINGS

Open Cast Iron Workings
USE IRONSTONE WORKINGS

OPEN CAST MINE
SN Use with product type where known.
CL INDUSTRIAL
BT MINE
RT CLAY MINE

Open Cast Tin Workings
USE TIN WORKS

Open Cast Workings
USE EXTRACTIVE PIT

OPEN FIELD
UF Irregular Open Field System
Regular Open Field System
Strip Cultivation
CL AGRICULTURE AND SUBSISTENCE
BT FIELD SYSTEM
RT PLOUGH HEADLAND
RIDGE AND FURROW
STRIP LYNCHET

OPEN HALL HOUSE
CL DOMESTIC
BT HALL HOUSE

OPEN HEARTH FURNACE
UF Siemens Furnace
SN A form of blast furnace. Steel is smelted in an
open hearth while the waste gases are used to
preheat the air blast.
CL INDUSTRIAL

BT METAL PRODUCTION FURNACE
RT BLAST FURNACE
CEMENTATION FURNACE
FERROUS METAL SMELTING SITE

Open Pit Mining
USE EXTRACTIVE PIT

OPEN PRISON
CL CIVIL
BT PRISON

Open Settlement
USE UNENCLOSED SETTLEMENT

OPEN SITE
UF Palaeolithic Open Site
SN As opposed to caves or rock shelters in early
prehistory.
CL DOMESTIC
BT SETTLEMENT

Open Work
USE EXTRACTIVE PIT

Opencast Lead Workings
USE LEAD WORKINGS

OPERA HOUSE
CL RECREATIONAL
BT MUSIC AND DANCE VENUE
RT CONCERT HALL
THEATRE

OPERATING THEATRE
UF Operating Theatre Block
CL HEALTH AND WELFARE
RT HOSPITAL

Operating Theatre Block
USE OPERATING THEATRE

Ophthalmic Department
USE EYE DEPARTMENT

Ophthalmic Hospital
USE EYE HOSPITAL

OPPIDUM
UF Belgic Oppidum
Territorial Oppidum
CL DOMESTIC
BT SETTLEMENT
NT ENCLOSED OPPIDUM
UNENCLOSED OPPIDUM
RT DYKE (DEFENCE)
HILLFORT

OPPIDUM
UF Belgic Oppidum
Territorial Oppidum
CL CIVIL
NT ENCLOSED OPPIDUM
UNENCLOSED OPPIDUM
RT HILLFORT

OPPIDUM
UF Belgic Oppidum
Territorial Oppidum
CL DEFENCE
BT ENCLOSED SETTLEMENT
RT DYKE (DEFENCE)
HILLFORT

ORANGERY
CL GARDENS, PARKS AND URBAN SPACES
BT GLASSHOUSE

Oratory

USE PRIVATE CHAPEL

ORCHARD
- CL GARDENS, PARKS AND URBAN SPACES
- BT WOODLAND

ORCHARD
- CL AGRICULTURE AND SUBSISTENCE
- BT LAND USE SITE

ORCHARD HOUSE
- SN A forcing house used for various types of fruit which first appeared in the 19th century. Lean-to houses were used for wall-grown fruit and free-standing houses for fruit grown in pots or for trees planted in the ground.
- CL GARDENS, PARKS AND URBAN SPACES
- BT GLASSHOUSE

ORDNANCE FACTORY
- UF Armaments Factory
      Gun Factory
      Rifle Factory
      Small Arms Factory
- SN Manufacture of weapons, particularly artillery pieces.
- CL INDUSTRIAL
- BT FACTORY <BY PRODUCT>
- RT ARMAMENT STORE
      ARSENAL

ORDNANCE FACTORY
- UF Armaments Factory
      Gun Factory
      Rifle Factory
      Small Arms Factory
- SN Manufacture of weapons, particularly artillery pieces.
- CL INDUSTRIAL
- BT EXPLOSIVES SITE

ORDNANCE FACTORY
- UF Armaments Factory
      Gun Factory
      Rifle Factory
      Small Arms Factory
- SN Manufacture of weapons, particularly artillery pieces.
- CL INDUSTRIAL
- BT ARMAMENT MANUFACTURING SITE
- RT FOUNDRY
      MUNITIONS FACTORY

ORDNANCE FACTORY
- UF Armaments Factory
      Gun Factory
      Rifle Factory
      Small Arms Factory
- SN Manufacture of weapons, particularly artillery pieces.
- CL DEFENCE
- RT ARMAMENT STORE
      ARSENAL
      FOUNDRY
      GUN TESTING SHOP

Ordnance Office
USE GOVERNMENT OFFICE

ORDNANCE STORE
- CL DEFENCE
- BT ARMAMENT STORE

ORDNANCE STOREKEEPERS HOUSE
- CL DOMESTIC
- BT MARITIME HOUSE

Ordnance Survey Office
USE GOVERNMENT OFFICE

ORDNANCE YARD
- SN Storage area usually for naval weapons and stores.
- CL INDUSTRIAL
- BT ARMAMENT MANUFACTURING SITE
- RT ARMAMENT DEPOT
      ARMOURY
      ARSENAL

Ore Crushing Mill
USE CRUSHING MILL

ORE HEARTH
- SN A furnace for smelting ore in which the fuel and ore are mixed.
- CL INDUSTRIAL
- BT METAL PRODUCTION FURNACE
- RT COPPER MINE
      CUPOLA FURNACE (REVERBERATORY)
      LEAD MINE
      NON FERROUS METAL SMELTING SITE

ORE STONE
- CL INDUSTRIAL
- BT NON FERROUS METAL PROCESSING SITE
- RT KNOCK STONE

ORE STORE
- CL INDUSTRIAL
- BT METAL INDUSTRY SITE

ORE WASHING PLANT
- SN Plant incorporating a range of ore processing operations such as buddles.
- CL INDUSTRIAL
- BT NON FERROUS METAL PROCESSING SITE
- RT BUDDLE
      SETTLING PIT
      WASHING FLOOR

ORGAN FACTORY
- UF Church Organ Factory
- CL INDUSTRIAL
- BT MUSICAL INSTRUMENT FACTORY
- RT PIANO FACTORY

ORIENTAL INSTITUTE
- CL EDUCATION
- BT INSTITUTE

ORIENTAL INSTITUTE
- CL INSTITUTIONAL
- BT INSTITUTE

Oriental Strangers Home
USE HOMELESS HOSTEL

Orillon
USE BASTION

ORNAMENTAL CANAL
- CL GARDENS, PARKS AND URBAN SPACES
- RT CANAL
      CASCADE
      ORNAMENTAL POND

ORNAMENTAL FOUNTAIN
- CL GARDENS, PARKS AND URBAN SPACES
- BT FOUNTAIN

ORNAMENTAL FOUNTAIN
- CL WATER SUPPLY AND DRAINAGE
- BT FOUNTAIN

ORNAMENTAL GARDEN
- CL GARDENS, PARKS AND URBAN SPACES
- BT GARDEN

ORNAMENTAL LAKE

CL   GARDENS, PARKS AND URBAN SPACES
BT   LAKE
RT   ORNAMENTAL POND

ORNAMENTAL POND
CL   WATER SUPPLY AND DRAINAGE
BT   POND
RT   ORNAMENTAL CANAL
      ORNAMENTAL LAKE

ORNAMENTAL POND
CL   GARDENS, PARKS AND URBAN SPACES

Ornamental Terrace
USE GARDEN TERRACE

Orphan Asylum
USE ORPHANAGE

Orphan Houses
USE ORPHANAGE

ORPHAN SCHOOL
UF   Foundling Hospital School
      Orphanage School
CL   EDUCATION
BT   FREE SCHOOL
RT   CHILDRENS HOME
      ORPHANAGE

ORPHANAGE
UF   Boys Home
      Boys Refuge
      Foundling Hospital
      Foundling Hospital Chapel
      Infant Orphans Asylum
      Little Boys Home
      Orphan Asylum
      Orphan Houses
      Orphanage Chapel
      Railway Orphanage
      Sailors Orphan Asylum
CL   HEALTH AND WELFARE
BT   CHILDRENS HOME
RT   ALMSHOUSE
      COTTAGE HOME
      HANDICAPPED CHILDRENS HOME
      MISSION HALL
      ORPHAN SCHOOL

ORPHANAGE
UF   Boys Home
      Boys Refuge
      Foundling Hospital
      Foundling Hospital Chapel
      Infant Orphans Asylum
      Little Boys Home
      Orphan Asylum
      Orphan Houses
      Orphanage Chapel
      Railway Orphanage
      Sailors Orphan Asylum
CL   DOMESTIC
BT   RESIDENTIAL BUILDING
RT   ALMSHOUSE
      COTTAGE HOME
      HANDICAPPED CHILDRENS HOME
      ORPHAN SCHOOL

Orphanage Chapel
USE CHAPEL
      ORPHANAGE
SN   Use both terms.

Orphanage School
USE ORPHAN SCHOOL

ORTHODONTICS DEPARTMENT
CL   HEALTH AND WELFARE

BT   HOSPITAL DEPARTMENT

ORTHODOX CHURCH
CL   RELIGIOUS, RITUAL AND FUNERARY
BT   CHURCH
NT   EASTERN ORTHODOX CHURCH
      SERBIAN ORTHODOX CHURCH

ORTHOPAEDIC DEPARTMENT
CL   HEALTH AND WELFARE
BT   HOSPITAL DEPARTMENT

ORTHOPAEDIC HOSPITAL
CL   HEALTH AND WELFARE
BT   SPECIALIST HOSPITAL

Orthostat
USE STANDING STONE

OSIER BED
CL   AGRICULTURE AND SUBSISTENCE
BT   LAND USE SITE

OSSUARY
SN   Container for bones of the dead.
CL   RELIGIOUS, RITUAL AND FUNERARY
BT   FUNERARY SITE
RT   BURIAL
      CINERARY URN
      CREMATION
      CREMATION CEMETERY

OUTBUILDING
SN   Use specific type where known, eg. DAIRY.
CL   UNASSIGNED
BT   BUILDING

Outer Bailey
USE BAILEY

OUTFALL SEWER
CL   WATER SUPPLY AND DRAINAGE
BT   SEWER

OUTFARM
CL   AGRICULTURE AND SUBSISTENCE
RT   FIELD BARN
      SHELTER SHED

OUTPATIENTS DEPARTMENT
CL   HEALTH AND WELFARE
BT   HOSPITAL DEPARTMENT

OVAL BARROW
CL   RELIGIOUS, RITUAL AND FUNERARY
BT   BARROW
RT   LONG BARROW
      ROUND BARROW

OVAL ENCLOSURE
CL   UNASSIGNED
BT   CURVILINEAR ENCLOSURE

OVEN
UF   Cooking Place
CL   UNASSIGNED
RT   COKE OVEN
      HEARTH
      KILN

Overhead Cableway
USE AERIAL ROPEWAY

OVERHEAD RAILWAY
CL   TRANSPORT
BT   RAILWAY
RT   FUNICULAR RAILWAY

Overlookers House

USE FOREMANS HOUSE

Overseers House
   USE FOREMANS HOUSE

Overshot Waterwheel
   USE OVERSHOT WHEEL

OVERSHOT WHEEL
   UF   Overshot Waterwheel
   CL   INDUSTRIAL
   BT   WATERWHEEL <BY FORM>

OX BOW STONE
   SN   Stone for holding ox yokes.
   CL   AGRICULTURE AND SUBSISTENCE

OXBOW LAKE
   CL   UNASSIGNED
   BT   NATURAL FEATURE

OXHOUSE
   CL   AGRICULTURE AND SUBSISTENCE
   BT   ANIMAL SHED

OYSTER BEDS
   CL   AGRICULTURE AND SUBSISTENCE
   BT   FISHING SITE

OYSTER DREDGER
   CL   MARITIME
   BT   FISHING DREDGER

PACKET
   CL   MARITIME
   BT   COMMUNICATIONS CRAFT

PACKHORSE BRIDGE
   CL   TRANSPORT
   BT   BRIDGE <BY FORM>
   RT   PACKHORSE ROAD

PACKHORSE BRIDGE
   CL   TRANSPORT
   BT   ROAD TRANSPORT SITE
   RT   JAGGERS HOSTEL
       PACKHORSE ROAD

PACKHORSE ROAD
   UF   Packhorse Track
   CL   TRANSPORT
   BT   ROAD
   RT   PACKHORSE BRIDGE

Packhorse Track
   USE PACKHORSE ROAD

PACKING HOUSE
   CL   INDUSTRIAL
   RT   CRATEMAKERS SHOP
       POTTERY WORKS
       POTTERY WORKSHOP

PAGODA
   CL   GARDENS, PARKS AND URBAN SPACES
   BT   GARDEN BUILDING

PAINT FACTORY
   CL   INDUSTRIAL
   BT   FACTORY <BY PRODUCT>

PAINT FACTORY
   CL   INDUSTRIAL
   BT   DYE AND PIGMENT SITE
   RT   BLACKING FACTORY

PAINT SHOP
   SN   Workshop for the painting of vehicles, machines, etc.
   CL   INDUSTRIAL

   BT   ENGINEERING INDUSTRY SITE
   RT   AGRICULTURAL ENGINEERING WORKS
       RAILWAY ENGINEERING WORKS

PALACE
   CL   DOMESTIC
   BT   DWELLING
   NT   ABBOTS SUMMER PALACE
       ARCHBISHOPS PALACE
       BISHOPS PALACE
       ROYAL PALACE
   RT   BANQUETING HOUSE
       COUNTRY HOUSE
       DOMESTIC CHAPEL
       MANOR HOUSE
       TOWN HOUSE

Palace Of Varieties
   USE MUSIC HALL

Palaeolithic Open Site
   USE OPEN SITE
   SN   Use specific site type, eg. KILL SITE, where known.

Pale
   USE PARK PALE

PALISADE
   SN   An enclosure of stakes driven into the ground for defensive purposes.
   CL   DEFENCE
   RT   PALISADED ENCLOSURE

PALISADED ENCLOSURE
   CL   DOMESTIC
   BT   SETTLEMENT
   NT   PALISADED HILLTOP ENCLOSURE
   RT   PALISADE
       PIT DEFINED ENCLOSURE

PALISADED ENCLOSURE
   CL   DEFENCE
   BT   ENCLOSED SETTLEMENT

PALISADED HILLTOP ENCLOSURE
   SN   Small, defended settlements dating to the Early Iron Age, located on spurs, promontories or hilltops. The defences are marked by single or double trenches which originally held substantial palisades.
   CL   DEFENCE
   BT   HILLTOP ENCLOSURE

PALISADED HILLTOP ENCLOSURE
   SN   Small, defended settlements dating to the Early Iron Age, located on spurs, promontories or hilltops. The defences are marked by single or double trenches which originally held substantial palisades.
   CL   DOMESTIC
   BT   PALISADED ENCLOSURE

PALISADED HILLTOP ENCLOSURE
   SN   Small, defended settlements dating to the Early Iron Age, located on spurs, promontories or hilltops. The defences are marked by single or double trenches which originally held substantial palisades.
   CL   DOMESTIC
   BT   HILLTOP ENCLOSURE

PALISADED HOMESTEAD
   CL   DOMESTIC
   BT   ENCLOSED SETTLEMENT

PALISADED SETTLEMENT
   CL   DOMESTIC
   BT   ENCLOSED SETTLEMENT

PALISSADE
- SN Originally a fence against which trees and shrubs were grown. Later used to describe a row of trees and shrubs forming a hedge clipped into a green wall.
- CL GARDENS, PARKS AND URBAN SPACES

PALM HOUSE
- UF Tropical House
- CL GARDENS, PARKS AND URBAN SPACES
- BT GLASSHOUSE
- RT BOTANIC GARDEN

Panels Office
USE RAILWAY OFFICE

PANORAMA
- CL RECREATIONAL
- BT ART AND EDUCATION VENUE
- RT DIORAMA

Pant
USE DRINKING FOUNTAIN

Pantechnicon
USE WAREHOUSE

PAPER INDUSTRY SITE
- SN Includes paper products.
- CL INDUSTRIAL
- NT BOARD MILL
  PAPER MILL
  PRINTING AND PUBLISHING SITE
  PULP MILL
  WALLPAPER FACTORY
- RT BARK MILL

PAPER MILL
- SN Use with power type where known.
- CL INDUSTRIAL
- BT MILL

PAPER MILL
- SN Use with power type where known.
- CL INDUSTRIAL
- BT PAPER INDUSTRY SITE
- RT ALUM WORKS
  FLOCK MILL

PARADE GROUND
- CL DEFENCE
- RT ARTILLERY GROUND
  BARRACKS
  FORT
  MILITARY CAMP

PARISH BOUNDARY
- UF Parish Stone
- CL CIVIL
- RT BOUNDARY

PARISH CHURCH
- CL RELIGIOUS, RITUAL AND FUNERARY
- BT CHURCH

Parish Hall
USE VILLAGE HALL

Parish Office
USE LOCAL GOVERNMENT OFFICE

Parish Room
USE VILLAGE HALL

PARISH SCHOOL
- CL EDUCATION
- BT SCHOOL

Parish Stone
USE PARISH BOUNDARY

Parish Watch House
USE WATCH HOUSE

PARK
- UF Parkland
- CL GARDENS, PARKS AND URBAN SPACES
- NT DEER PARK
  HUNTING PARK
  LANDSCAPE PARK
  PUBLIC PARK
  ROYAL PARK
- RT GARDEN
  PARK PALE
  PARK WALL

Park Lodge
USE GATE LODGE

PARK PALE
- UF Pale
- SN A wooden stake fence, often associated with deer hunting.
- CL GARDENS, PARKS AND URBAN SPACES
- RT DEER PARK
  PARK

PARK PALE
- UF Pale
- SN A wooden stake fence, often associated with deer hunting.
- CL AGRICULTURE AND SUBSISTENCE
- BT HUNTING SITE
- RT BOUNDARY
  DEER PARK
  PARK

Park Rangers Lodge
USE GATE LODGE

PARK SHELTER
- CL GARDENS, PARKS AND URBAN SPACES
- RT PUBLIC PARK

PARK WALL
- CL GARDENS, PARKS AND URBAN SPACES
- RT PARK

PARKING METER
- CL GARDENS, PARKS AND URBAN SPACES
- BT STREET FURNITURE

PARKING METER
- CL TRANSPORT
- BT ROAD TRANSPORT SITE

Parkland
USE PARK

Parliament House
USE HOUSES OF PARLIAMENT

PARROT HOUSE
- CL RECREATIONAL
- BT ANIMAL HOUSE

PARSONAGE
- CL DOMESTIC
- BT CLERICAL DWELLING

PARTERRE
- CL GARDENS, PARKS AND URBAN SPACES
- BT GARDEN
- RT FORMAL GARDEN
  GARDEN TERRACE

PARTICULAR BAPTIST CHAPEL
- CL RELIGIOUS, RITUAL AND FUNERARY

BT   BAPTIST CHAPEL

PASSAGE GRAVE
    CL   RELIGIOUS, RITUAL AND FUNERARY
    BT   CHAMBERED TOMB
    RT   CHAMBERED CAIRN

PASSENGER VESSEL
    CL   MARITIME
    BT   TRANSPORT CRAFT
    NT   CRUISE SHIP
         EMIGRANT SHIP
         FERRY
         LINER
         WATER TAXI

Patent Office
    USE GOVERNMENT OFFICE

PATH
    CL   TRANSPORT
    BT   PEDESTRIAN TRANSPORT SITE
    NT   GRAVEL PATH
    RT   PAVEMENT

PATHOLOGY DEPARTMENT
    CL   HEALTH AND WELFARE
    BT   HOSPITAL DEPARTMENT

PATIENTS VILLA
    CL   HEALTH AND WELFARE

PATIO
    CL   GARDENS, PARKS AND URBAN SPACES
    RT   COURTYARD
         GARDEN
         HOUSE

PATROL BOAT
    CL   MARITIME
    BT   WARSHIP
    NT   MOTOR GUNBOAT
         MOTOR TORPEDO BOAT

PATTERN SHOP
    SN   Workshop for the manufacture of master parts from
         working drawings which are then used as patterns
         for mass manufacture.
    CL   INDUSTRIAL
    BT   ENGINEERING INDUSTRY SITE
    RT   ASSEMBLY PLANT
         ENGINEERING WORKSHOP
         FOUNDRY
         MOULD LOFT

Pauper Lunatic Asylum
    USE MENTAL HOSPITAL

PAUPER SCHOOL
    CL   EDUCATION
    BT   FREE SCHOOL

PAVEMENT
    CL   UNASSIGNED
    NT   RAISED PAVEMENT
    RT   FOOTPATH
         PATH
         ROAD

PAVILION
    CL   GARDENS, PARKS AND URBAN SPACES
    NT   BOWLING GREEN PAVILION
         CHINESE PAVILION
         FISHING PAVILION
         MOORISH PAVILION
         REFRESHMENT PAVILION
         SPORTS PAVILION
         WATER PAVILION
    RT   CROQUET SHED

GARDEN BUILDING
GARDEN HOUSE

PAVILION WARD BLOCK
    SN   Detached block comprising one or more stories of
         wards.
    CL   HEALTH AND WELFARE
    BT   HOSPITAL BLOCK

Pawn Shop
    USE PAWNSHOP

PAWNSHOP
    UF   Pawn Shop
    CL   COMMERCIAL
    NT   PLEDGE DEPOT

PAY OFFICE
    CL   COMMERCIAL
    BT   COMMERCIAL OFFICE
    RT   COUNTING HOUSE
         FACTORY
         OFFICE
         SHIPYARD
         TIMEKEEPERS OFFICE

Paymaster Generals Office
    USE GOVERNMENT OFFICE

Peabody Flats
    USE MODEL DWELLING

PEAT CUTTING
    UF   Peat Tie
         Turbary Site
    CL   INDUSTRIAL
    BT   PEAT WORKINGS
    RT   PEAT STAND

Peat Drying Platform
    USE PEAT STAND

Peat House
    USE FUEL STORE

Peat Stack Platform
    USE PEAT STAND

PEAT STAND
    UF   Peat Drying Platform
         Peat Stack Platform
    CL   INDUSTRIAL
    BT   PEAT WORKINGS
    RT   PEAT CUTTING
         PEAT STORE
         TURF STACK

PEAT STORE
    CL   UNASSIGNED
    BT   FUEL STORE
    RT   BLOWING HOUSE
         FUEL STORE
         LEAD WORKING SITE
         PEAT STAND

Peat Tie
    USE PEAT CUTTING

PEAT WORKINGS
    CL   INDUSTRIAL
    BT   FUEL PRODUCTION SITE
    NT   PEAT CUTTING
         PEAT STAND

Pecking Mill
    USE FULLING MILL

Pedestal Monument
    USE TOMB

Pedestal Tomb
USE TOMB

Pedestrian Bridge
USE FOOTBRIDGE

PEDESTRIAN CROSSING
CL GARDENS, PARKS AND URBAN SPACES
BT STREET FURNITURE
NT ZEBRA CROSSING

PEDESTRIAN CROSSING
CL TRANSPORT
BT PEDESTRIAN TRANSPORT SITE
NT ZEBRA CROSSING

PEDESTRIAN PRECINCT
CL GARDENS, PARKS AND URBAN SPACES
BT URBAN SPACE

PEDESTRIAN TRANSPORT SITE
CL TRANSPORT
NT FOOTBRIDGE
FOOTPATH
PATH
PEDESTRIAN CROSSING
PEDESTRIAN TUNNEL
RIDGEWAY
STEPPING STONES
STEPS
STILE
SUBWAY

PEDESTRIAN TUNNEL
UF Foot Tunnel
CL TRANSPORT
BT PEDESTRIAN TRANSPORT SITE
RT SUBWAY
TUNNEL
UNDERPASS

PEDESTRIAN TUNNEL
UF Foot Tunnel
CL TRANSPORT
BT TRANSPORT TUNNEL
RT SUBWAY
TUNNEL
UNDERPASS

Peel Tower
USE PELE TOWER

PELE TOWER
UF Peel Tower
Rectory Pele
SN A strong fortified tower, built mainly in the
border country of the North up to the 17th
century.
CL DOMESTIC
BT FORTIFIED HOUSE
RT BARMKIN
TOWER

PELE TOWER
UF Peel Tower
Rectory Pele
SN A strong fortified tower, built mainly in the
border country of the North up to the 17th
century.
CL DEFENCE
BT FORTIFIED HOUSE
RT BARMKIN
TOWER

PEN
UF Pens
CL AGRICULTURE AND SUBSISTENCE
NT BOAR PEN

BULL PEN
RT POUND

PEN POND
SN Type of mill pond.
CL WATER SUPPLY AND DRAINAGE
BT POND
RT HAMMER POND
IRON WORKS

PEN POND
SN Type of mill pond.
CL INDUSTRIAL
BT WATER POWER PRODUCTION SITE
RT HAMMER POND
MILL POND

Penannular Enclosure
USE CURVILINEAR ENCLOSURE

PENGUIN POOL
CL RECREATIONAL
BT ANIMAL HOUSE

Penitentiary
USE PRISON

Pens
USE PEN

PENTECOSTALIST CHURCH
CL RELIGIOUS, RITUAL AND FUNERARY
BT CHURCH

PEOPLES COLLEGE
CL EDUCATION
BT TRAINING COLLEGE
RT CHURCH INSTITUTE
COLLIERY INSTITUTE
COOPERATIVE INSTITUTE
LITERARY AND SCIENTIFIC INSTITUTE
MECHANICS INSTITUTE
MINERS READING ROOM
WORKING MENS INSTITUTE

Peoples Palace
USE MUSIC HALL

PERCEE
SN A cutting through a wood to open up a view or
establish an allee.
CL GARDENS, PARKS AND URBAN SPACES
BT WALK

Perfume Distillery
USE HERB DISTILLERY

PERFUMERY
SN A place where perfume is sold, as well as
manufactured.
CL COMMERCIAL
BT SHOP

PERFUMERY
SN A place where perfume is sold, as well as
manufactured.
CL INDUSTRIAL
BT CHEMICAL PRODUCT SITE
RT HERB DISTILLERY

PERGOLA
UF Garden Archway
SN Timber or metal structure consisting of upright
and cross members designed to support climbing
plants.
CL GARDENS, PARKS AND URBAN SPACES
RT ARBOUR
LOGGIA
TRELLIS

PERIMETER TRACK
  CL   TRANSPORT
  BT   AIR TRANSPORT SITE

Pest House
  USE INFECTIOUS DISEASES HOSPITAL

Pet Cemetery
  USE ANIMAL CEMETERY

PETROCHEMICAL SITE
  CL   INDUSTRIAL
  BT   CHEMICAL PRODUCTION SITE
  NT   ETHER PLANT
       OIL DISTILLERY
       PLASTICS FACTORY

Petroglyph
  USE ROCK CARVING

PETROL PUMP
  CL   TRANSPORT
  BT   ROAD TRANSPORT SITE
  RT   GARAGE
       MULTI STOREY CAR PARK
       PETROL STATION
       SERVICE STATION

PETROL STATION
  UF   Filling Station
  CL   COMMERCIAL
  RT   GARAGE
       MOTOR VEHICLE SHOWROOM
       MULTI STOREY CAR PARK
       PETROL PUMP
       SERVICE STATION

PETROL STATION
  UF   Filling Station
  CL   TRANSPORT
  BT   ROAD TRANSPORT SITE
  RT   SERVICE STATION

Pewter Working Site
  USE PEWTER WORKS

PEWTER WORKS
  UF   Pewter Working Site
  CL   INDUSTRIAL
  BT   NON FERROUS METAL PRODUCT SITE

PHARMACEUTICAL CHEMICAL SITE
  CL   INDUSTRIAL
  BT   CHEMICAL PRODUCTION SITE
  NT   HERB DISTILLERY
       PHARMACEUTICAL WORKS

PHARMACEUTICAL WORKS
  CL   INDUSTRIAL
  BT   PHARMACEUTICAL CHEMICAL SITE
  RT   DISTILLATION PLANT
       ETHER PLANT
       LABORATORY

PHARMACY
  CL   HEALTH AND WELFARE
  RT   DISPENSARY

Pharos
  USE LIGHTHOUSE

PHILOLOGICAL SCHOOL
  CL   EDUCATION
  BT   TRAINING SCHOOL

Phoenix Unit
  USE FLOATING HARBOUR

PHOTOGRAPHIC GALLERY

CL   COMMERCIAL

PHOTOGRAPHIC GALLERY
  CL   RECREATIONAL
  BT   ART AND EDUCATION VENUE

PHYSIC GARDEN
  SN   A garden maintained for the study and cultivation
       of plants for medicinal purposes.
  CL   GARDENS, PARKS AND URBAN SPACES
  BT   GARDEN
  RT   BOTANIC GARDEN

Physicians College
  USE PROFESSIONAL INSTITUTE

PHYSIOTHERAPY DEPARTMENT
  CL   HEALTH AND WELFARE
  BT   HOSPITAL DEPARTMENT

PIANO FACTORY
  CL   INDUSTRIAL
  BT   MUSICAL INSTRUMENT FACTORY
  RT   ORGAN FACTORY

Piazza
  USE SQUARE

PICKER HOUSE
  SN   Working area for rag sorting and grading.
  CL   INDUSTRIAL
  BT   TEXTILE SITE <BY PROCESS/PRODUCT>
  RT   DYE HOUSE
       FULLING MILL
       SPINNING MILL

Picture House
  USE CINEMA

Picture Palace
  USE CINEMA

PIE AND MASH SHOP
  UF   Eel And Pie Shop
  CL   COMMERCIAL
  BT   SHOP

PIE AND MASH SHOP
  UF   Eel And Pie Shop
  CL   COMMERCIAL
  BT   EATING AND DRINKING ESTABLISHMENT

Piece Hall
  USE CLOTH HALL

PIER
  CL   MARITIME
  BT   LANDING POINT
  NT   LANDING PIER
  RT   MOLE
       PLEASURE PIER
       TELESCOPE (TERRESTRIAL)

PIER PAVILION
  CL   RECREATIONAL
  RT   PLEASURE PIER
       SEASIDE PAVILION
       TELESCOPE (TERRESTRIAL)

PIERMASTERS HOUSE
  CL   DOMESTIC
  BT   MARITIME HOUSE

Pig Cote
  USE PIGSTY

Pig Market
  USE LIVESTOCK MARKET

Pig Sty

USE PIGSTY

Pigeon House
USE DOVECOTE

PIGSTY
UF Pig Cote
Pig Sty
Swine Cote
CL AGRICULTURE AND SUBSISTENCE
BT ANIMAL SHED
RT BOAR PEN
HOGGERY

Pigswill Boiling House
USE BOILING HOUSE

PILE
SN Component: Use wider site type where known.
CL UNASSIGNED

PILE DWELLING
CL DOMESTIC
BT HOUSE <BY FORM>
RT CRANNOG

Pilgrims Rest House
USE GUEST HOUSE

PILLAR BOX
CL GARDENS, PARKS AND URBAN SPACES
BT LETTER BOX

PILLAR BOX
CL COMMUNICATIONS
BT POSTAL SYSTEM STRUCTURE

Pillar Stone
USE INSCRIBED STONE

PILLBOX
CL DEFENCE
RT AIR RAID SHELTER
BATTERY
BLOCKHOUSE
GUN EMPLACEMENT
SLIT TRENCH
TANK TRAP
UNDERGROUND MILITARY HEADQUARTERS

PILLORY
UF Jougs
CL CIVIL
BT PUNISHMENT PLACE
RT STOCKS
WHIPPING POST

PILLOW MOUND
CL AGRICULTURE AND SUBSISTENCE
RT MOUND
RABBIT WARREN

PILLOW STONE
CL RELIGIOUS, RITUAL AND FUNERARY
BT GRAVE

PILOT OFFICE
UF Dock Traffic Office
CL MARITIME
BT MARITIME OFFICE
RT CUSTOM HOUSE
OFFICE
PORT AUTHORITY OFFICE

PILOT VESSEL
CL MARITIME
BT SAFETY CRAFT

PIN FACTORY

CL INDUSTRIAL
BT FACTORY <BY PRODUCT>

PIN MILL
UF Pin Works
CL INDUSTRIAL
BT FERROUS METAL PRODUCT SITE
RT BRASS WORKS
GRINDSTONE
NEEDLE MILL
WIRE MILL

Pin Works
USE PIN MILL

PINERY
SN A glasshouse used for growing pineapples.
CL GARDENS, PARKS AND URBAN SPACES
BT GLASSHOUSE

PINETUM
SN An arboretum devoted mainly to the growing of conifers.
CL GARDENS, PARKS AND URBAN SPACES
BT GARDEN

Pinfold
USE POUND

PIPE BRIDGE
SN Bridge for carrying pipes between buildings or working areas.
CL INDUSTRIAL
BT CHEMICAL PRODUCTION SITE
RT DISTILLATION PLANT
LABORATORY
OIL REFINERY

Pipe Kiln
USE CLAY PIPE KILN

PIPE WORKSHOP
UF Claypipe Workshop
SN Use for clay tobacco pipes.
CL INDUSTRIAL
BT POTTERY MANUFACTURING SITE
RT FIRE CLAY WORKS
POTTERY WORKS
POTTERY WORKSHOP

PIPELINE
CL UNASSIGNED

PIT
UF Pit Dwelling
CL UNASSIGNED
RT BEAR PIT
BRINE PIT
BURIAL PIT
CESS PIT
COCKPIT
EXTRACTIVE PIT
HORNCORE PIT
PIT ALIGNMENT
PIT CIRCLE
PIT CLUSTER
PIT DEFINED ENCLOSURE
PLAGUE PIT
PREACHING PIT
RETTING PIT
RITUAL PIT
RUBBISH PIT
SAW PIT
SETTLING PIT
SOAKING PIT
STEEPING PIT
STORAGE PIT
TANNING PIT
VOTIVE PIT

WASHING PIT
WHEEL PIT

PIT ALIGNMENT
- CL UNASSIGNED
- RT BOUNDARY
  - PIT

PIT CIRCLE
- CL RELIGIOUS, RITUAL AND FUNERARY
- RT PIT
  - TIMBER CIRCLE

PIT CLUSTER
- SN Function unknown.
- CL UNASSIGNED
- RT PIT

PIT DEFINED ENCLOSURE
- CL UNASSIGNED
- BT ENCLOSURE
- RT PALISADED ENCLOSURE
  - PIT

Pit Dwelling
- USE PIT
- SN Previously interpreted as dwellings, now believed to be principally storage pits.

Pit Pony Stable
- USE MINE
  - STABLE
- SN Use both terms.

Pit Prop Shop
- USE COLLIERY
  - WORKSHOP
- SN Use both terms.

Pit Village
- USE WORKERS VILLAGE

PITCHBACK WHEEL
- CL INDUSTRIAL
- BT WATERWHEEL < BY FORM >

PITHEAD BATHS
- UF Colliery Baths
  - Miners Baths
- CL INDUSTRIAL
- BT MINE BUILDING

PITHEAD BATHS
- UF Colliery Baths
  - Miners Baths
- CL HEALTH AND WELFARE
- BT BATHS
- RT COLLIERY
  - LAMPHOUSE
  - MINERS CHANGING HOUSE

PLACE OF WORSHIP
- CL RELIGIOUS, RITUAL AND FUNERARY
- NT CATHEDRAL
  - CHAPEL
  - CHURCH
  - MINSTER
  - MOSQUE
  - NONCONFORMIST MEETING HOUSE
  - PREACHING PIT
  - SYNAGOGUE
  - TEMPLE

PLAGUE CEMETERY
- UF Plague Churchyard
- CL RELIGIOUS, RITUAL AND FUNERARY
- BT INHUMATION CEMETERY

Plague Churchyard

USE PLAGUE CEMETERY

Plague House
- USE INFECTIOUS DISEASES HOSPITAL

PLAGUE MEMORIAL
- CL COMMEMORATIVE
- BT COMMEMORATIVE MONUMENT

PLAGUE PIT
- CL RELIGIOUS, RITUAL AND FUNERARY
- BT BURIAL PIT
- RT PIT

PLAGUE STONE
- SN A stone on which plague victims placed vinegar-disinfected money to pay for food left for them by the townspeople.
- CL GARDENS, PARKS AND URBAN SPACES
- BT STREET FURNITURE
- RT STONE

PLAGUE STONE
- SN A stone on which plague victims placed vinegar-disinfected money to pay for food left for them by the townspeople.
- CL HEALTH AND WELFARE
- RT STONE

PLAIN AN GWARRY
- SN A Cornish Medieval amphitheatre used for the performance of mystery plays and sports.
- CL RECREATIONAL
- RT AMPHITHEATRE

PLAIN AN GWARRY
- SN A Cornish Medieval amphitheatre used for the performance of mystery plays and sports.
- CL RELIGIOUS, RITUAL AND FUNERARY
- RT AMPHITHEATRE
  - THEATRE

Plainsong School
- USE CHOIR SCHOOL

PLANETARIUM
- CL RECREATIONAL
- BT ART AND EDUCATION VENUE

PLANING MILL
- SN Mill for producing a smooth surface and edges on newly sawn timber.
- CL INDUSTRIAL
- BT MILL

PLANING MILL
- SN Mill for producing a smooth surface and edges on newly sawn timber.
- CL INDUSTRIAL
- BT TIMBER PROCESSING SITE
- RT BLOCK MILL
  - LUMBER MILL
  - SAW MILL

Plank Road
- USE WOODEN ROAD

Planned Farm
- USE MODEL FARM

Planned Town
- USE TOWN
  - MODEL SETTLEMENT
- SN Where plan refers to layout (eg. grid) rather than ideological concept (eg. Chartist land Colony).

Planned Village
- USE MODEL SETTLEMENT

Plant Nursery

USE NURSERY GARDEN

PLANTATION
CL   GARDENS, PARKS AND URBAN SPACES

PLANTATION
CL   AGRICULTURE AND SUBSISTENCE
BT   LAND USE SITE

PLANTATION BANK
UF   Plantation Circle
       Plantation Square
CL   AGRICULTURE AND SUBSISTENCE
BT   LAND USE SITE
RT   BOUNDARY
       WOOD BANK

Plantation Circle
USE PLANTATION BANK

Plantation Square
USE PLANTATION BANK

PLAQUE
UF   Commemorative Plaque
       Commemorative Tablet
       Wall Tablet
CL   UNASSIGNED
RT   DATE STONE

PLASTER MANUFACTURING SITE
CL   INDUSTRIAL
BT   MINERAL PRODUCT SITE
NT   MORTAR MILL
       PLASTER MILL
       PLASTER WORKS
       ROTARY KILN

PLASTER MILL
CL   INDUSTRIAL
BT   PLASTER MANUFACTURING SITE

PLASTER MILL
CL   INDUSTRIAL
BT   MILL
RT   GRINDSTONE

PLASTER WORKS
CL   INDUSTRIAL
BT   PLASTER MANUFACTURING SITE
RT   GYPSUM MINE

PLASTICS FACTORY
UF   Xylonite Works
SN   Production of plastics by chemical processes.
CL   INDUSTRIAL
BT   PETROCHEMICAL SITE
RT   CHEMICAL WORKS
       OIL REFINERY

PLASTICS FACTORY
UF   Xylonite Works
SN   Production of plastics by chemical processes.
CL   INDUSTRIAL
BT   FACTORY <BY PRODUCT>
RT   ASSEMBLY PLANT
       CHEMICAL WORKS

PLASTICS FACTORY
UF   Xylonite Works
SN   Production of plastics by chemical processes.
CL   INDUSTRIAL
BT   CHEMICAL PRODUCT SITE
RT   ARTIFICIAL TEXTILE FACTORY
       CHEMICAL WORKS

PLATE GLASS WORKS
SN   Thick flat glass used for shop window panes, etc.
       Produced by rolling and casting rather than
       traditional blowing.
CL   INDUSTRIAL

BT   GLASS WORKS
RT   TANK FURNACE

PLATE RACK
SN   Storage rack for sections of steel plate used in
       the construction of ships.
CL   INDUSTRIAL
BT   MARINE CONSTRUCTION SITE
RT   FABRICATION SHED
       PLATERS SHOP
       SHIP REPAIR WORKS
       SHIPHOUSE FRAME

PLATE RACK
SN   Storage rack for sections of steel plate used in
       the construction of ships.
CL   MARITIME
BT   MARINE CONSTRUCTION SITE

PLATERS SHOP
SN   Large covered spaces where the steel plate used
       for ship construction was cut and marked out,
       prior to being craned onto the hull, etc.
CL   INDUSTRIAL
BT   ENGINEERING INDUSTRY SITE
RT   BOILER SHOP
       BOILER WORKS

PLATERS SHOP
SN   Large covered spaces where the steel plate used
       for ship construction was cut and marked out,
       prior to being craned onto the hull, etc.
CL   INDUSTRIAL
BT   MARINE CONSTRUCTION SITE
RT   FABRICATION SHED
       PLATE RACK
       RIVET AND TOOL SHOP
       SHIP REPAIR WORKS
       SHIPHOUSE FRAME

PLATERS SHOP
SN   Large covered spaces where the steel plate used
       for ship construction was cut and marked out,
       prior to being craned onto the hull, etc.
CL   MARITIME
BT   MARINE CONSTRUCTION SITE

PLATEWAY
CL   TRANSPORT
BT   TRAMWAY

PLATFORM
SN   Unspecified. Use specific type where known.
CL   UNASSIGNED
NT   BUILDING PLATFORM
       CIRCULAR PLATFORM
RT   BARN PLATFORM
       HOUSE PLATFORM
       HUT PLATFORM

Platform House
USE HOUSE PLATFORM

PLATFORM SETTLEMENT
CL   DOMESTIC
BT   SETTLEMENT
NT   ENCLOSED PLATFORM SETTLEMENT
       UNENCLOSED PLATFORM SETTLEMENT

PLATING WORKS
UF   Electro Plating Works
       Silver Plating Works
       Tin Plating Works
CL   INDUSTRIAL
BT   NON FERROUS METAL PRODUCT SITE
RT   BRITANNIA METAL WORKS
       CUTLERY WORKS
       CUTLERY WORKSHOP
       SHEET METAL WORKS

TIN WORKS

Play School
    USE NURSERY SCHOOL

Playground
    USE CHILDRENS PLAYGROUND

PLAYGROUND SHELTER
    CL   RECREATIONAL
    RT   CHILDRENS PLAYGROUND

Playhouse
    USE THEATRE

PLAYING FIELD
    CL   RECREATIONAL
    BT   RECREATION GROUND
    NT   POLO FIELD

Pleasance
    USE GARDEN HOUSE

PLEASURE PIER
    CL   RECREATIONAL
    RT   PIER
            PIER PAVILION
            SEASIDE PAVILION
            TELESCOPE (TERRESTRIAL)

PLEDGE DEPOT
    SN   A municipal pawnshop.
    CL   COMMERCIAL
    BT   PAWNSHOP

PLOUGH HEADLAND
    CL   AGRICULTURE AND SUBSISTENCE
    BT   FIELD
    RT   OPEN FIELD
            RIDGE AND FURROW

PLOUGH MARKS
    UF   Ardmarks
    CL   AGRICULTURE AND SUBSISTENCE
    BT   CULTIVATION MARKS

Plumbago Mine
    USE GRAPHITE MINE

Plymouth Brethren Meeting House
    USE BRETHREN MEETING HOUSE

Pointed Bastion
    USE BASTION

POLICE BOX
    CL   GARDENS, PARKS AND URBAN SPACES
    BT   STREET FURNITURE
    RT   POLICE STATION
            POLICE TELEPHONE PILLAR
            TELEPHONE BOX
            WATCH HOUSE
            WATCHMANS BOX

POLICE BOX
    CL   COMMUNICATIONS
    BT   TELECOMMUNICATION STRUCTURE
    RT   POLICE STATION
            POLICE TELEPHONE PILLAR
            TELEPHONE BOX
            WATCH HOUSE

Police Headquarters
    USE POLICE STATION

Police Office
    USE POLICE STATION

POLICE STATION

    UF   Police Headquarters
            Police Office
            River Police Station
    CL   CIVIL
    BT   LEGAL SITE
    RT   CONSTABLES OFFICE
            POLICE BOX
            POLICE TELEPHONE PILLAR

Police Store
    USE STOREHOUSE

POLICE TELEPHONE PILLAR
    CL   GARDENS, PARKS AND URBAN SPACES
    BT   STREET FURNITURE
    RT   POLICE BOX
            POLICE STATION
            TELEPHONE BOX

POLICE TELEPHONE PILLAR
    CL   COMMUNICATIONS
    BT   TELECOMMUNICATION STRUCTURE
    RT   POLICE BOX
            POLICE STATION
            TELEPHONE BOX

Police Wireless Station
    USE RADIO STATION

POLISHING SHOP
    CL   INDUSTRIAL
    BT   ENGINEERING INDUSTRY SITE
    RT   WHITESMITHS WORKSHOP

POLISHING SHOP
    CL   INDUSTRIAL
    BT   NON FERROUS METAL PRODUCT SITE

POLITICAL CLUB
    UF   Conservative Club
            Labour Club
            Liberal Club
            Liberals Hall
    CL   INSTITUTIONAL
    BT   CLUB

POLO FIELD
    CL   RECREATIONAL
    BT   PLAYING FIELD

POLYGONAL ENCLOSURE
    CL   UNASSIGNED
    BT   RECTILINEAR ENCLOSURE

POLYTECHNIC
    CL   EDUCATION
    RT   FACULTY BUILDING
            HALL OF RESIDENCE
            STUDENTS UNION
            TRAINING COLLEGE
            UNIVERSITY

POND
    UF   Beast Pond
            Skating Pond
    SN   Use specifc type where known.
    CL   WATER SUPPLY AND DRAINAGE
    NT   DECOY POND
            DEWPOND
            DUCKING POND
            FISH POND
            FURNACE POND
            HAMMER POND
            LILY POND
            MAST POND
            MILL POND
            ORNAMENTAL POND
            PEN POND
            SWANNERY POND

TIMBER POND
RT   POND BAY

POND BARROW
CL   RELIGIOUS, RITUAL AND FUNERARY
BT   BARROW
RT   ROUND BARROW

POND BAY
SN   Form of dam, usually associated with ponds
      supplying water for blast furnaces.
CL   WATER SUPPLY AND DRAINAGE
RT   DAM
      HAMMER POND
      MILL
      MILL DAM
      POND
      WATERWHEEL

PONTOON
CL   MARITIME
BT   PONTOON BRIDGE

PONTOON
CL   MARITIME
BT   PONTOON PIER

PONTOON BRIDGE
CL   MARITIME
BT   UNMANNED CRAFT
NT   PONTOON

PONTOON PIER
CL   MARITIME
BT   UNMANNED CRAFT
NT   PONTOON

POOL
UF   Garden Pool
CL   GARDENS, PARKS AND URBAN SPACES
NT   SWIMMING POOL
RT   WATER GARDEN

Poor House
    USE WORKHOUSE

Poor Law Guardians Home
    USE COTTAGE HOME

Poor Law Guardians Office
    USE LOCAL GOVERNMENT OFFICE

Poor Law Infirmary
    USE WORKHOUSE
         INFIRMARY
SN   Use both terms.

Poor Law Institution
    USE WORKHOUSE

Poor Law Office
    USE LOCAL GOVERNMENT OFFICE

Poor Law Union Hospital
    USE WORKHOUSE
         INFIRMARY
SN   Use both terms.

POOR SOULS LIGHT
CL   RELIGIOUS, RITUAL AND FUNERARY

Porcelain Factory
    USE CHINA FACTORY

PORCELAIN SHOWROOM
CL   COMMERCIAL
BT   SHOWROOM

PORT

UF   Enclosed Port
CL   MARITIME
BT   DOCK AND HARBOUR INSTALLATION
NT   CANAL PORT
      RIVER PORT
      SEAPORT
RT   PORT ADMIRALS HOUSE
      PORT AUTHORITY OFFICE

PORT ADMIRALS HOUSE
CL   DOMESTIC
BT   MARITIME HOUSE
RT   PORT

PORT AUTHORITY OFFICE
CL   MARITIME
BT   MARITIME OFFICE
RT   OFFICE
      PILOT OFFICE
      PORT

PORTAL
UF   Adit Portal
CL   UNASSIGNED
RT   CANAL TUNNEL PORTAL
      GATE
      RAILWAY TUNNEL PORTAL
      ROAD TUNNEL PORTAL
      TRAMWAY TUNNEL PORTAL
      TUNNEL PORTAL

PORTAL DOLMEN
CL   RELIGIOUS, RITUAL AND FUNERARY
BT   CHAMBERED TOMB

PORTERS LODGE
UF   Lodge
CL   UNASSIGNED
BT   BUILDING
RT   GATE LODGE
      GATEHOUSE

Porters Office
    USE RAILWAY OFFICE

PORTERS REST
CL   GARDENS, PARKS AND URBAN SPACES

Positive Lynchet
    USE LYNCHET

POST BOX
CL   COMMUNICATIONS
BT   POSTAL SYSTEM STRUCTURE
RT   POST OFFICE
      SORTING OFFICE

POST HOLE
CL   UNASSIGNED

Post House
    USE POST OFFICE

Post Inn
    USE INN

POST MILL
CL   INDUSTRIAL
BT   WINDMILL <BY FORM>

POST OFFICE
UF   General Post Office
      Post House
      Post Office Headquarters
      Posting House
CL   COMMERCIAL
RT   OFFICE
      POST BOX
      SORTING OFFICE

POST OFFICE
- UF General Post Office
  - Post House
  - Post Office Headquarters
  - Posting House
- CL COMMUNICATIONS
- BT POSTAL SYSTEM STRUCTURE
- RT OFFICE
  - POST BOX
  - SORTING OFFICE

Post Office Headquarters
  USE POST OFFICE

Post Office Tower
  USE TELECOMMUNICATION BUILDING

POSTAL SYSTEM STRUCTURE
- CL COMMUNICATIONS
- NT MAIL BAG NET
  - PILLAR BOX
  - POST BOX
  - POST OFFICE
  - SORTING OFFICE

POSTERN
- UF Postern Gate
  - Sally Port
- CL DEFENCE
- RT CASTLE
  - GATE
  - TOWN GATE
  - WATER GATE

Postern Gate
  USE POSTERN

Posting House
  USE POST OFFICE

Pot Bank
  USE POTTERY WORKS

POT HAULER
- CL MARITIME
- BT FISHING VESSEL

POT HOUSE
- SN Pot Oven - entire kiln including both the hovel and the oven.
- CL INDUSTRIAL
- BT POTTERY MANUFACTURING SITE
- RT MUG HOUSE
  - POTTERS WORKSHOP
  - POTTERY WORKSHOP
  - THROWING HOUSE
  - WASTER TIP

POTASH KILN
- UF Lye Kiln
- SN Kiln used for the slow burning of vegetable matter to produce ashes.
- CL INDUSTRIAL
- BT AGRICULTURAL CHEMICAL SITE
- RT ELLING HEARTH
  - FERTILISER WORKS
  - GLASS WORKS
  - LEATHER FACTORY
  - POTASH MINE
  - SOAP FACTORY

POTASH KILN
- UF Lye Kiln
- SN Kiln used for the slow burning of vegetable matter to produce ashes.
- CL INDUSTRIAL
- BT KILN <BY FUNCTION>

POTASH MINE

- SN Potash is a deposit of potassium carbonate: the only example of a potash mine in the country is at Boulby in Cleveland.
- CL INDUSTRIAL
- BT AGRICULTURAL CHEMICAL SITE
- RT POTASH KILN

POTASH MINE
- SN Potash is a deposit of potassium carbonate: the only example of a potash mine in the country is at Boulby in Cleveland.
- CL INDUSTRIAL
- BT MINERAL EXTRACTION SITE
- RT POTASH KILN

POTASH MINE
- SN Potash is a deposit of potassium carbonate: the only example of a potash mine in the country is at Boulby in Cleveland.
- CL INDUSTRIAL
- BT MINE

POTTERS WORKSHOP
- CL INDUSTRIAL
- BT CRAFT INDUSTRY SITE
- RT POT HOUSE
  - POTTERY WORKS
  - SAGGAR MAKERS WORKSHOP

POTTERY KILN
- UF Biscuit Kiln
  - Glost Kiln
- CL INDUSTRIAL
- BT POTTERY MANUFACTURING SITE
- RT CLAY PIPE KILN
  - MUFFLE KILN
  - POTTERY WORKS

POTTERY KILN
- UF Biscuit Kiln
  - Glost Kiln
- CL INDUSTRIAL
- BT KILN <BY FUNCTION>
- RT BOTTLE KILN
  - CIRCULAR KILN
  - TUNNEL KILN

POTTERY MANUFACTURING SITE
- CL INDUSTRIAL
- BT MINERAL PRODUCT SITE
- NT BALL CLAY WORKS
  - BLUNGING PIT
  - CHINA CLAY WORKS
  - CHINA FACTORY
  - CLAY DRAINAGE PIPE WORKS
  - CLAY PIPE KILN
  - CLAY PIT
  - CLAY PUDDLING PIT
  - CLAY TOBACCO PIPE FACTORY
  - CRATEMAKERS SHOP
  - DECORATING SHOP
  - DIPPING HOUSE
  - FIRE CLAY WORKS
  - FLINT MILL
  - HANDLING HOUSE
  - MOULD STORE
  - MOULDMAKERS SHOP
  - MUFFLE KILN
  - MUG HOUSE
  - PIPE WORKSHOP
  - POT HOUSE
  - POTTERY KILN
  - POTTERY WORKS
  - POTTERY WORKSHOP
  - PUG MILL
  - SAGGAR MAKERS WORKSHOP
  - THROWING HOUSE
  - WASTER TIP
- RT CALCINING KILN

ENAMELLING KILN
TURNING SHOP
WASTER KILN

POTTERY WORKS
UF   Ceramics Factory
      Earthenware Works
      Majolica Works
      Pot Bank
CL   INDUSTRIAL
BT   POTTERY MANUFACTURING SITE
RT   CRATEMAKERS SHOP
      FIRE CLAY WORKS
      FLINT MILL
      HANDLING HOUSE
      MARL PIT
      PACKING HOUSE
      PIPE WORKSHOP
      POTTERS WORKSHOP
      POTTERY KILN
      POTTERY WORKSHOP
      SALT WORKS
      TERRACOTTA WORKS

POTTERY WORKSHOP
CL   INDUSTRIAL
BT   POTTERY MANUFACTURING SITE
RT   HANDLING HOUSE
      MARL PIT
      PACKING HOUSE
      PIPE WORKSHOP
      POT HOUSE
      POTTERY WORKS
      SAGGAR MAKERS WORKSHOP
      THROWING HOUSE
      TILEMAKING WORKSHOP

POTTING SHED
CL   GARDENS, PARKS AND URBAN SPACES
BT   GARDEN BUILDING
RT   GARDEN SHED
      SHED

POULTRY HOUSE
UF   Chicken House
      Fowl House
      Goose House
      Hen Cote
      Hen House
CL   AGRICULTURE AND SUBSISTENCE
BT   AGRICULTURAL BUILDING
RT   HEN BATTERY

Poultry Market
USE   LIVESTOCK MARKET

POUND
UF   Animal Pound
      Pinfold
      Village Pound
CL   AGRICULTURE AND SUBSISTENCE
NT   DEER POUND
RT   PEN
      SHEEP FOLD
      STOCK ENCLOSURE
      VILLAGE GREEN

POUND LOCK
CL   TRANSPORT
BT   LOCK
RT   CANAL

Powder House
USE   POWDER MAGAZINE

POWDER MAGAZINE
UF   Powder House
      Powder Store
SN   A place in which gunpowder and other explosives
      are stored in large quantities.
CL   INDUSTRIAL

BT   EXPLOSIVES SITE

POWDER MAGAZINE
UF   Powder House
      Powder Store
SN   A place in which gunpowder and other explosives
      are stored in large quantities.
CL   DEFENCE
BT   MAGAZINE

Powder Mill
USE   GUNPOWDER WORKS

Powder Store
USE   POWDER MAGAZINE

POWER GENERATION SITE
SN   Includes power transmission.
CL   INDUSTRIAL
NT   ANIMAL POWER SITE
      COAL GAS STRUCTURE
      ELECTRICITY PRODUCTION SITE
      ENGINE HOUSE
      HYDRAULIC POWER SITE
      STEAM POWER PRODUCTION SITE
      TRANSMISSION RODS
      WATER POWER PRODUCTION SITE
      WIND POWER SITE

POWER STATION
UF   Electric Generating Station
      Electric Light Works
      Electricity Plant
      Electricity Works
      Generating Station
      Hydraulic Power Station
CL   INDUSTRIAL
BT   ELECTRICITY PRODUCTION SITE
NT   COAL FIRED POWER STATION
      GAS FIRED POWER STATION
      HYDROELECTRIC POWER STATION
      NUCLEAR POWER STATION
      OIL FIRED POWER STATION
      REFUSE DESTRUCTOR STATION
      STEAM TURBINE POWER STATION
RT   CHIMNEY
      COOLING TOWER
      ELECTRICITY SUB STATION
      HYDRAULIC PUMPING STATION
      REFUSE DESTRUCTOR STATION
      TURBINE

PRACTICE CAMP
CL   DEFENCE
BT   TEMPORARY CAMP

Practice Trench
USE   SLIT TRENCH

Praetentura
USE   FORT
      LEGIONARY FORTRESS
SN   Use both terms.

Praetorium
USE   FORT
      LEGIONARY FORTRESS
SN   Use both terms.

Pre Conquest Inscribed Stone
USE   INSCRIBED STONE

PREACHING CROSS
CL   RELIGIOUS, RITUAL AND FUNERARY
BT   CROSS
RT   MARKET CROSS
      PREACHING PIT
      VILLAGE CROSS
      WAYSIDE CROSS

PREACHING PIT
- CL   RELIGIOUS, RITUAL AND FUNERARY
- BT   PLACE OF WORSHIP
- RT   PIT
       PREACHING CROSS

Prebendal House
   USE CLERGY HOUSE

Preceptors College
   USE PROFESSIONAL INSTITUTE

PRECEPTORY
- UF   Preceptory Of The Knights Of St Lazarus
- CL   RELIGIOUS, RITUAL AND FUNERARY
- BT   RELIGIOUS HOUSE
- NT   HOSPITALLERS PRECEPTORY
       TEMPLARS PRECEPTORY
- RT   ABBEY
       CAMERA
       CELL
       FARM
       FRIARY
       GRANGE
       HOSPITAL
       MANOR
       MANOR HOUSE
       MONASTERY
       NUNNERY
       PRIORY
       SISTERS OF ST JOHN NUNNERY
       TEMPLARS CHURCH

Preceptory Of The Knights Of St Lazarus
   USE PRECEPTORY

PRECINCT
- CL   UNASSIGNED
- RT   MONASTIC PRECINCT
       PRECINCT WALL

PRECINCT WALL
- UF   Abbey Wall
- CL   UNASSIGNED
- BT   WALL
- RT   ABBEY
       BOUNDARY WALL
       CATHEDRAL
       PRECINCT
       PRIORY

PREFAB
- CL   DOMESTIC
- BT   DWELLING

Premonstratensian Abbey
   USE ABBEY
       PREMONSTRATENSIAN MONASTERY
- SN   Use both terms.

PREMONSTRATENSIAN ALIEN CELL
- CL   RELIGIOUS, RITUAL AND FUNERARY
- BT   ALIEN CELL
- RT   PREMONSTRATENSIAN MONASTERY
       PREMONSTRATENSIAN NUNNERY

Premonstratensian Alien Priory
   USE PREMONSTRATENSIAN MONASTERY
       PREMONSTRATENSIAN NUNNERY
       ALIEN PRIORY
- SN   Use ALIEN PRIORY and PREMONSTRATENSIAN
       MONASTERY/NUNNERY.

PREMONSTRATENSIAN CELL
- UF   Premonstratensian Priory Cell
- CL   RELIGIOUS, RITUAL AND FUNERARY
- BT   CELL
- RT   PREMONSTRATENSIAN MONASTERY

PREMONSTRATENSIAN NUNNERY

PREMONSTRATENSIAN GRANGE
- CL   RELIGIOUS, RITUAL AND FUNERARY
- BT   GRANGE

PREMONSTRATENSIAN GRANGE
- CL   AGRICULTURE AND SUBSISTENCE
- BT   GRANGE

PREMONSTRATENSIAN MONASTERY
- UF   Premonstratensian Abbey
       Premonstratensian Alien Priory
       Premonstratensian Priory
- SN   Abbeys and Priories of Premonstratensian canons.
- CL   RELIGIOUS, RITUAL AND FUNERARY
- BT   MONASTERY
- RT   PREMONSTRATENSIAN ALIEN CELL
       PREMONSTRATENSIAN CELL
       PREMONSTRATENSIAN NUNNERY

PREMONSTRATENSIAN NUNNERY
- UF   Premonstratensian Alien Priory
       Premonstratensian Priory
- SN   Priories of Premonstratensian canonesses.
- CL   RELIGIOUS, RITUAL AND FUNERARY
- BT   NUNNERY
- RT   PREMONSTRATENSIAN ALIEN CELL
       PREMONSTRATENSIAN CELL
       PREMONSTRATENSIAN MONASTERY

Premonstratensian Priory
   USE PREMONSTRATENSIAN MONASTERY
       PREMONSTRATENSIAN NUNNERY
       PRIORY
- SN   Use PRIORY and PREMONSTRATENSIAN
       MONASTERY/NUNNERY.

Premonstratensian Priory Cell
   USE PREMONSTRATENSIAN CELL

PREPARATORY SCHOOL
- CL   EDUCATION
- BT   PRIVATE SCHOOL
- RT   ELEMENTARY SCHOOL

PRESBYTERIAN CHAPEL
- UF   Presbyterian Church
       Presbyterian Meeting House
- CL   RELIGIOUS, RITUAL AND FUNERARY
- BT   NONCONFORMIST CHAPEL
- NT   SCOTTISH PRESBYTERIAN CHAPEL
       WELSH PRESBYTERIAN CHAPEL

Presbyterian Church
   USE PRESBYTERIAN CHAPEL

Presbyterian Meeting House
   USE PRESBYTERIAN CHAPEL

PRESBYTERY
- CL   DOMESTIC
- BT   CLERICAL DWELLING
- RT   CHURCH
       PRIESTS HOUSE
       ROMAN CATHOLIC CHURCH

PRESS HOUSE
- SN   Building containing presses for the compaction of
       mill cake gunpowder as part of the gunpowder
       manufacturing process.
- CL   INDUSTRIAL
- BT   EXPLOSIVES SITE

PRESS SHOP
- CL   INDUSTRIAL
- BT   TEXTILE SITE <BY PROCESS/PRODUCT>
- RT   DYE HOUSE
       TENTER GROUND

PRIEST HOLE
- UF   Dean Hole
- CL   RELIGIOUS, RITUAL AND FUNERARY

PRIESTS HOUSE
- CL   DOMESTIC
- BT   CLERICAL DWELLING
- RT   PRESBYTERY

PRIMARY SCHOOL
- CL   EDUCATION
- BT   ELEMENTARY SCHOOL

PRIMITIVE METHODIST CHAPEL
- CL   RELIGIOUS, RITUAL AND FUNERARY
- BT   METHODIST CHAPEL

PRINT SHOP
- CL   INDUSTRIAL
- BT   PRINTING AND PUBLISHING SITE
- RT   BINDERY
-       NEWSPAPER OFFICE
-       PRINTING WORKS

PRINTING AND PUBLISHING SITE
- CL   INDUSTRIAL
- BT   PAPER INDUSTRY SITE
- NT   BINDERY
-       PRINT SHOP
-       PRINTING WORKS

PRINTING SHOP
- CL   INDUSTRIAL
- BT   TEXTILE FINISHING SITE

PRINTING WORKS
- CL   INDUSTRIAL
- BT   PRINTING AND PUBLISHING SITE
- RT   NEWSPAPER OFFICE
-       PRINT SHOP

PRIORS HOUSE
- UF   Priors Lodging
- CL   DOMESTIC
- BT   CLERICAL DWELLING
- RT   PRIORY

Priors Lodging
- USE   PRIORS HOUSE

PRIORY
- UF   Arrouiasian Priory
-       Augustinian Cathedral Priory
-       Augustinian Priory
-       Benedictine Cathedral Priory
-       Benedictine Priory
-       Carthusian Priory
-       Cathedral Priory
-       Cistercian Priory
-       Cluniac Priory
-       Convent Chapel
-       Conventual Chapel
-       Conventual Church
-       Dominican Priory
-       Farmery
-       Fontevraultine Priory
-       Gilbertine Priory
-       Grandmontine Priory
-       Holy Sepulchre Priory
-       Premonstratensian Priory
-       Priory Barn
-       Priory Church
-       Priory Gate
-       Priory Gatehouse
-       Priory Kitchen
-       Priory Wall
-       Sisters Of St John Priory
-       Tironian Priory

      Trinitarian Priory
      Victorine Priory
- SN   Use with narrow terms of DOUBLE HOUSE, FRIARY, MONASTERY or NUNNERY.
- CL   RELIGIOUS, RITUAL AND FUNERARY
- BT   RELIGIOUS HOUSE
- NT   ALIEN PRIORY
- RT   ABBEY
-       CATHEDRAL
-       CHAPTER HOUSE
-       CURFEW BELL TOWER
-       DOUBLE HOUSE
-       FRATER
-       FRIARY
-       GATEHOUSE
-       GUEST HOUSE
-       KITCHEN
-       MANCIPLES HOUSE
-       MONASTERY
-       NUNNERY
-       PRECEPTORY
-       PRECINCT WALL
-       PRIORS HOUSE
-       REFECTORY

Priory Barn
- USE   PRIORY
-       BARN
- SN   Use both terms.

Priory Cell
- USE   CELL

Priory Church
- USE   CHURCH
-       PRIORY
- SN   Use both terms.

Priory Gate
- USE   GATE
-       PRIORY
- SN   Use both terms.

Priory Gatehouse
- USE   PRIORY
-       GATEHOUSE
- SN   Use both terms.

Priory Kitchen
- USE   KITCHEN
-       PRIORY
- SN   Use both terms.

Priory Wall
- USE   WALL
-       PRIORY
- SN   Use both terms.

PRISON
- UF   Bridewell
-       Cage
-       Clink
-       County Gaol
-       Gaol
-       House Of Correction
-       Jail
-       Marshalsea
-       Penitentiary
-       Prison Garden
-       Prison Infirmary
- CL   CIVIL
- BT   LEGAL SITE
- NT   CELL BLOCK
-       DEBTORS PRISON
-       HIGH SECURITY PRISON
-       HOUSE OF DETENTION
-       JUVENILE PRISON
-       LOCK UP
-       OPEN PRISON

PRISON HULK
RT BOUNDARY WALL
    EXERCISE YARD
    INFIRMARY
    PRISON CHAPLAINS HOUSE
    PRISON GOVERNORS HOUSE
    PRISON TREADMILL
    PRISONER OF WAR CAMP

PRISON CHAPLAINS HOUSE
CL DOMESTIC
BT CLERICAL DWELLING
RT PRISON
    PRISON GOVERNORS HOUSE

Prison Garden
USE GARDEN
    PRISON
SN Use both terms.

PRISON GOVERNORS HOUSE
CL DOMESTIC
BT HOUSE <BY FUNCTION>
RT PRISON
    PRISON CHAPLAINS HOUSE

PRISON HULK
CL MARITIME
BT HULK

PRISON HULK
CL CIVIL
BT PRISON

Prison Infirmary
USE PRISON
    INFIRMARY
SN Use both terms.

PRISON TREADMILL
CL INDUSTRIAL
BT TREADMILL

PRISON TREADMILL
CL CIVIL
BT PUNISHMENT PLACE
RT PRISON

PRISONER OF WAR CAMP
CL DEFENCE
RT ARMY CAMP
    PRISON

Private Art Gallery
USE COMMERCIAL ART GALLERY

PRIVATE CHAPEL
UF Oratory
CL RELIGIOUS, RITUAL AND FUNERARY
BT CHAPEL

PRIVATE PATIENTS BLOCK
CL HEALTH AND WELFARE
BT HOSPITAL BLOCK

PRIVATE PATIENTS WARD BLOCK
CL HEALTH AND WELFARE
BT HOSPITAL BLOCK

PRIVATE SCHOOL
CL EDUCATION
BT SCHOOL
NT PREPARATORY SCHOOL
    PROPRIETARY SCHOOL
    PUBLIC SCHOOL
RT LADIES COLLEGE

PRIVATE SQUARE
CL GARDENS, PARKS AND URBAN SPACES

BT SQUARE

PRIVATEER
CL MARITIME
BT WARSHIP

Privy
USE PRIVY HOUSE

PRIVY HOUSE
UF Necessary House
    Privy
CL WATER SUPPLY AND DRAINAGE

PRODUCER GAS HOUSE
SN Producer gas is a mix of gases formed by passing
    compressed air through hot coke.
CL INDUSTRIAL
BT COAL GAS STRUCTURE
RT COKE OVEN

PROFESSIONAL INSTITUTE
UF Chartered Institute Office
    College Of Arms
    Heraldic Office
    Heralds College
    Physicians College
    Preceptors College
    Surgeons College
    Surgeons Institute
CL INSTITUTIONAL
BT INSTITUTE
RT ATHENAEUM
    CHURCH INSTITUTE

PROFESSIONAL INSTITUTE
UF Chartered Institute Office
    College Of Arms
    Heraldic Office
    Heralds College
    Physicians College
    Preceptors College
    Surgeons College
    Surgeons Institute
CL EDUCATION
BT INSTITUTE

PROMENADE
CL GARDENS, PARKS AND URBAN SPACES
BT WALK
RT TELESCOPE (TERRESTRIAL)

PROMENADE
CL MARITIME
BT DOCK AND HARBOUR INSTALLATION
RT BREAKWATER
    BULWARK
    CAUSEWAY
    TELESCOPE (TERRESTRIAL)

PROMONTORY FORT
CL DOMESTIC
BT ENCLOSED SETTLEMENT
NT CLIFF CASTLE
RT HILLFORT

PROMONTORY FORT
CL DEFENCE
BT ENCLOSED SETTLEMENT
NT CLIFF CASTLE
RT HILLFORT

Proof House
USE PROVING HOUSE

Property Boundary
USE BOUNDARY

PROPRIETARY SCHOOL

CL EDUCATION
BT PRIVATE SCHOOL

PROSPECT MOUND
CL GARDENS, PARKS AND URBAN SPACES
BT ARTIFICIAL MOUND
RT GAZEBO
MOUND
PROSPECT TOWER

PROSPECT TOWER
SN A tower built on a prominent part of an estate to
provide panoramic views of the surrounding
countryside.
CL GARDENS, PARKS AND URBAN SPACES
BT GARDEN BUILDING
RT BELVEDERE
PROSPECT MOUND
TOWER

PROSPECTING PIT
CL INDUSTRIAL
BT NON FERROUS METAL EXTRACTION SITE
RT PROSPECTING TRENCH

PROSPECTING TRENCH
CL INDUSTRIAL
BT NON FERROUS METAL EXTRACTION SITE
RT PROSPECTING PIT

Protestant Church
USE ANGLICAN CHURCH
FRENCH PROTESTANT CHURCH
SWISS PROTESTANT CHURCH
SN Use specific type where known.

Protestant School
USE CHURCH SCHOOL

Provender Store
USE FODDER STORE

PROVING HOUSE
UF Proof House
Testing Works
CL INDUSTRIAL
BT ARMAMENT MANUFACTURING SITE
RT ASSAY OFFICE
GUN TESTING SHOP

PROVOSTS HOUSE
CL DOMESTIC
BT CLERICAL DWELLING

Provosts Lodgings
USE COLLEGE LODGINGS

Psychiatric Hospital
USE MENTAL HOSPITAL

Psychiatric Unit
USE MENTAL HOSPITAL

Pub
USE PUBLIC HOUSE

Public Baths
USE BATHS

PUBLIC BUILDING
SN Use specific type of building where known.
CL CIVIL
NT ASSEMBLY ROOMS
MARKET HOUSE
MEETING HALL
RECORD OFFICE

PUBLIC CONVENIENCE
UF Public Lavatory

Public Toilet
Public Toilets
Public Urinal
Urinal
CL WATER SUPPLY AND DRAINAGE
RT TOILET

PUBLIC CONVENIENCE
UF Public Lavatory
Public Toilet
Public Toilets
Public Urinal
Urinal
CL HEALTH AND WELFARE
RT TOILET

Public Gallery
USE ART GALLERY

PUBLIC HALL
SN A purpose-built hall (usually 19th century) which
was available for public hire and could be used
for a variety of activities, eg. lectures,
meetings, balls and concerts.
CL CIVIL
BT MEETING HALL

PUBLIC HOUSE
UF Pub
Roadhouse
Tavern
CL COMMERCIAL
BT LICENSED PREMISES
NT WINE LODGE
RT ALE STORE
BEER SHOP
INN

PUBLIC HOUSE
UF Pub
Roadhouse
Tavern
CL RECREATIONAL
BT EATING AND DRINKING ESTABLISHMENT
RT ALE STORE
BEER SHOP
INN

Public Laundry
USE PUBLIC WASH HOUSE

Public Lavatory
USE PUBLIC CONVENIENCE

PUBLIC LIBRARY
UF Borough Library
County Library
District Library
Free Library
CL EDUCATION
BT LIBRARY

PUBLIC PARK
CL GARDENS, PARKS AND URBAN SPACES
BT PARK
RT BANDSTAND
BOATING LAKE
KIOSK
PARK SHELTER
REFRESHMENT PAVILION
TEA HOUSE

PUBLIC SCHOOL
CL EDUCATION
BT PRIVATE SCHOOL
RT LADIES COLLEGE

PUBLIC SQUARE
CL GARDENS, PARKS AND URBAN SPACES

BT SQUARE

Public Toilet
USE PUBLIC CONVENIENCE

Public Toilets
USE PUBLIC CONVENIENCE

Public Urinal
USE PUBLIC CONVENIENCE

PUBLIC WASH HOUSE
UF Public Laundry
CL HEALTH AND WELFARE
BT WASH HOUSE
RT BATHS

PUDDLING FURNACE
SN A reverberatory furnace used for forging wrought iron from pig iron using coal as fuel.
CL INDUSTRIAL
BT REVERBERATORY FURNACE

PUG MILL
SN Machine, frequently horse powered, for mixing raw clay into brick earth.
CL INDUSTRIAL
BT BRICK AND TILEMAKING SITE
RT CLAY MILL

PUG MILL
SN Machine, frequently horse powered, for mixing raw clay into brick earth.
CL INDUSTRIAL
BT POTTERY MANUFACTURING SITE
RT CLAY PUDDLING PIT

PUG MILL
SN Machine, frequently horse powered, for mixing raw clay into brick earth.
CL INDUSTRIAL
BT MILL

PULP MILL
SN Building housing the machinery for the shredding and grinding of wood in running water and pressing of the resulting fibres into a pulp.
CL INDUSTRIAL
BT WOOD PRODUCT SITE
RT SAW MILL
WOOD CHEMICAL WORKS

PULP MILL
SN Building housing the machinery for the shredding and grinding of wood in running water and pressing of the resulting fibres into a pulp.
CL INDUSTRIAL
BT PAPER INDUSTRY SITE

PUMP
CL WATER SUPPLY AND DRAINAGE
NT HAND PUMP
WATER PUMP
WAYSIDE PUMP
WIND PUMP
RT PUMP HOUSE
WELL

PUMP HOUSE
UF Dock Pumphouse
CL INDUSTRIAL
BT WATER POWER PRODUCTION SITE
RT PUMPING STATION
TURBINE MILL

PUMP HOUSE
UF Dock Pumphouse
CL WATER SUPPLY AND DRAINAGE
NT PUMP ROOM

RT CONDUIT HOUSE
ENGINE HOUSE
PUMP
WATERWORKS
WELL HOUSE

PUMP ROOM
SN A room or building where a pump is worked.
CL WATER SUPPLY AND DRAINAGE
BT PUMP HOUSE

PUMP ROOMS
CL RECREATIONAL
BT HEALTH ESTABLISHMENT
RT ASSEMBLY ROOMS
BATHS
HYDROPATHIC INSTITUTE
KURSAAL
MINERAL BATHS
SPA
SPA HOTEL
SPA PAVILION
THERMAL BATHS

PUMP ROOMS
CL HEALTH AND WELFARE
RT ASSEMBLY ROOMS
BATHS
HYDROPATHIC INSTITUTE
KURSAAL
MINERAL BATHS
SPA
SPA PAVILION
THERMAL BATHS

Pumping Shed
USE PUMPING STATION

PUMPING STATION
UF Dock Pumping Station
Drainage Works
Mine Pumphouse
Pumping Shed
CL WATER SUPPLY AND DRAINAGE
NT SEWAGE PUMPING STATION
WATER PUMPING STATION
RT BEAM ENGINE
CONDUIT HOUSE
ENGINE HOUSE
MINE PUMPING WORKS
PUMP HOUSE
WATER TOWER
WATERWORKS

PUNISHMENT PLACE
CL CIVIL
BT LEGAL SITE
NT DUCKING POND
DUCKING STOOL
EXECUTION SITE
PILLORY
PRISON TREADMILL
STOCKS
WHIPPING POST

Punt Shelter
USE BOAT HOUSE

PURIFIER
CL WATER SUPPLY AND DRAINAGE
RT FILTER BED
FILTER HOUSE
SEWAGE WORKS
WATERWORKS

PURIFIER HOUSE
CL INDUSTRIAL
BT COAL GAS STRUCTURE

Pye Kiln

USE LIME KILN

Pylon
    USE ELECTRICITY PYLON

PYRAMIDAL KILN
    CL INDUSTRIAL
    BT KILN <BY FORM>

QUADRANGULAR CASTLE
    CL DOMESTIC
    BT CASTLE

QUADRANGULAR CASTLE
    CL DEFENCE
    BT CASTLE

QUADRIGA
    SN A sculptured group comprising a chariot drawn by
        four horses.
    CL COMMEMORATIVE
    BT COMMEMORATIVE MONUMENT
    RT SCULPTURE
        STATUE

Quaker Burial Ground
    USE FRIENDS BURIAL GROUND

Quaker Graveyard
    USE FRIENDS BURIAL GROUND

Quaker Meeting House
    USE FRIENDS MEETING HOUSE

Quarriers Cottage
    USE WORKERS COTTAGE

QUARRY
    UF Quarry Office
    CL INDUSTRIAL
    BT STONE EXTRACTION SITE
    NT STONE QUARRY
    RT EXTRACTIVE PIT
        MILLSTONE WORKING SITE
        QUARRY HOIST

QUARRY HOIST
    CL INDUSTRIAL
    BT STONE EXTRACTION SITE
    RT QUARRY

Quarry Office
    USE QUARRY
         OFFICE
    SN Use both terms.

Quarrymans Cottage
    USE WORKERS COTTAGE

Quarters
    USE LODGINGS

QUASI AISLED HOUSE
    CL DOMESTIC
    BT AISLED HOUSE

QUAY
    UF Key
        River Quay
    CL TRANSPORT
    BT WATER TRANSPORT SITE
    RT CUSTOMS POST
        MOORING BOLLARD
        WHARF

QUAY
    UF Key
        River Quay
    CL MARITIME

    BT LANDING POINT
    NT FALSE QUAY
    RT CUSTOMS POST

QUAY CRANE
    CL TRANSPORT
    BT CRANE <BY FUNCTION>
    NT FIXED QUAY CRANE
        MOVING QUAY CRANE

Queen Eleanor Cross
    USE ELEANOR CROSS

Queristers House
    USE CHORISTERS HOUSE

QUERN WORKING SITE
    SN Manufacture of querns.
    CL INDUSTRIAL
    BT STONE WORKING SITE
    RT MILLSTONE WORKING SITE

QUINTAIN
    SN An object supported by a crosspiece on a post,
        used by knights as a target in tilting.
    CL RECREATIONAL
    BT SPORTS SITE
    RT TILTYARD
        TILTYARD TOWER

Quoit
    USE CHAMBERED TOMB

RABBIT TYPE
    SN Term applied to both the pit trap itself, and the
        walled enclosure containing pit trap(s).
    CL AGRICULTURE AND SUBSISTENCE
    RT RABBIT WARREN
        VERMIN TRAP

RABBIT WARREN
    UF Coney Garth
        Warren
    CL AGRICULTURE AND SUBSISTENCE
    RT PILLOW MOUND
        RABBIT TYPE

RACE TRACK
    SN For atheletes.
    CL RECREATIONAL
    BT SPORTS SITE

RACECOURSE
    SN For horse racing.
    CL RECREATIONAL
    BT SPORTS SITE
    RT GRANDSTAND
        RACECOURSE PAVILION
        RACING STABLE
        SPORTS PAVILION

RACECOURSE PAVILION
    CL RECREATIONAL
    BT SPORTS BUILDING
    RT CHANGING ROOMS
        GRANDSTAND
        RACECOURSE

RACING CIRCUIT
    UF Motor Track
        Racing Track
    SN For motor racing.
    CL RECREATIONAL
    BT SPORTS SITE

RACING CRAFT
    CL MARITIME
    BT LEISURE CRAFT

RACING STABLE

CL   RECREATIONAL
BT   SPORTS BUILDING
RT   RACECOURSE

Racing Track
   USE RACING CIRCUIT

RACKING ROOM
   CL   INDUSTRIAL
   BT   BREWING AND MALTING SITE
   RT   FERMENTING BLOCK

RADAR BEACON
   CL   COMMUNICATIONS
   BT   BEACON
   RT   RADAR STATION

RADAR STATION
   CL   DEFENCE
   RT   EARLY WARNING STATION
        RADAR BEACON.

Radio Beacon
   USE BROADCASTING TRANSMITTER

RADIO BROADCASTING STUDIO
   CL   COMMUNICATIONS
   BT   TELECOMMUNICATION STRUCTURE
   RT   BROADCASTING HOUSE
        TELEVISION STUDIO

Radio Mast
   USE BROADCASTING TRANSMITTER

RADIO STATION
   UF   Beam Station
        Police Wireless Station
        Wireless Station
   CL   COMMUNICATIONS
   BT   TELECOMMUNICATION BUILDING

RADIO STUDIO
   CL   COMMUNICATIONS
   BT   TELECOMMUNICATION STRUCTURE

RADIO TELESCOPE
   CL   COMMUNICATIONS
   BT   TELECOMMUNICATION STRUCTURE

RADIO VALVE WORKS
   UF   Electrical Valve Works
   CL   INDUSTRIAL
   BT   LIGHT ENGINEERING SITE

RADIUM INSTITUTE
   CL   HEALTH AND WELFARE

RAFT
   CL   MARITIME
   BT   UNASSIGNED CRAFT

RAG GRINDING MILL
   CL   INDUSTRIAL
   BT   TEXTILE MILL
   RT   RAG GRINDING SHED

RAG GRINDING SHED
   SN   Shed for grinding rags, eg. for use in mungo and
        shoddy mills.
   CL   INDUSTRIAL
   BT   TEXTILE SITE <BY PROCESS/PRODUCT>
   RT   RAG GRINDING MILL
        RAG MILL

RAG MILL
   SN   For grinding of all types of textile rags.
   CL   INDUSTRIAL
   BT   TEXTILE SITE <BY PROCESS/PRODUCT>
   RT   RAG GRINDING SHED

RAGGED SCHOOL
   CL   EDUCATION
   BT   FREE SCHOOL

RAILINGS
   CL   UNASSIGNED
   RT   BOUNDARY
        FENCE
        GATE

RAILWAY
   UF   Dock Railway
        Light Railway
        Narrow Gauge Railway
        Station Garden
   CL   TRANSPORT
   BT   RAILWAY TRANSPORT SITE
   NT   ATMOSPHERIC RAILWAY
        CLIFF RAILWAY
        COLLIERY RAILWAY
        DOCKYARD RAILWAY
        FUNICULAR RAILWAY
        MINERAL RAILWAY
        MINIATURE RAILWAY
        OVERHEAD RAILWAY
        UNDERGROUND RAILWAY
   RT   MILE PLATE
        MILEPOST
        MILESTONE

RAILWAY BRIDGE
   CL   TRANSPORT
   BT   BRIDGE <BY FUNCTION>
   RT   RAILWAY VIADUCT

RAILWAY BRIDGE
   CL   TRANSPORT
   BT   RAILWAY TRANSPORT SITE
   RT   RAILWAY EMBANKMENT
        RAILWAY VIADUCT

RAILWAY BUFFET
   UF   Station Buffet
   CL   COMMERCIAL
   BT   EATING AND DRINKING ESTABLISHMENT

RAILWAY BUFFET
   UF   Station Buffet
   CL   TRANSPORT
   BT   RAILWAY TRANSPORT SITE

Railway Carriage Shed
   USE RAILWAY SHED

RAILWAY CARRIAGE WORKS
   CL   INDUSTRIAL
   BT   RAILWAY ENGINEERING SITE

RAILWAY CARRIAGE WORKS
   CL   TRANSPORT
   BT   RAILWAY WORKS

Railway Crossing Keepers Cottage
   USE CROSSING KEEPERS COTTAGE

RAILWAY CUTTING
   CL   TRANSPORT
   BT   RAILWAY TRANSPORT SITE

RAILWAY EMBANKMENT
   CL   TRANSPORT
   BT   RAILWAY TRANSPORT SITE
   RT   RAILWAY BRIDGE
        RAILWAY VIADUCT

Railway Engine Shed
   USE ENGINE SHED

RAILWAY ENGINEERING SITE

CL   INDUSTRIAL
BT   ENGINEERING INDUSTRY SITE
NT   RAILWAY CARRIAGE WORKS
     RAILWAY ENGINEERING WORKS
     RAILWAY ENGINEERING WORKSHOP
     RAILWAY WAGON WORKS
     RAILWAY WORKS
     RAILWAY WORKSHOP
RT   BOILER SHOP
     FORGE
     TURNING SHOP

RAILWAY ENGINEERING WORKS
UF   Locomotive Works
CL   INDUSTRIAL
BT   RAILWAY ENGINEERING SITE
RT   CHAIN PROVING HOUSE
     PAINT SHOP

RAILWAY ENGINEERING WORKSHOP
CL   INDUSTRIAL
BT   RAILWAY ENGINEERING SITE

RAILWAY HOTEL
CL   COMMERCIAL
BT   HOTEL

RAILWAY HOTEL
CL   TRANSPORT
BT   RAILWAY TRANSPORT SITE

RAILWAY HOTEL
CL   DOMESTIC
BT   HOTEL

Railway Incline
     USE RAILWAY INCLINED PLANE

RAILWAY INCLINED PLANE
UF   Railway Incline
CL   TRANSPORT
BT   INCLINED PLANE

RAILWAY INCLINED PLANE
UF   Railway Incline
CL   TRANSPORT
BT   RAILWAY TRANSPORT SITE

RAILWAY JUNCTION
CL   TRANSPORT
BT   RAILWAY TRANSPORT SITE

Railway Level Crossing
     USE LEVEL CROSSING

RAILWAY LIFT
UF   Rolling Stock Hoist
CL   TRANSPORT
BT   LIFT

RAILWAY LIFT
UF   Rolling Stock Hoist
CL   TRANSPORT
BT   RAILWAY TRANSPORT SITE

RAILWAY LOOKOUT TOWER
SN   A semaphore signalling tower.
CL   COMMUNICATIONS
RT   SEMAPHORE STATION
     SIGNAL BOX

RAILWAY LOOKOUT TOWER
SN   A semaphore signalling tower.
CL   TRANSPORT
BT   RAILWAY TRANSPORT SITE

Railway Navvys Cottage
     USE RAILWAY WORKERS COTTAGE

RAILWAY OFFICE

UF   Goods Station Office
     Panels Office
     Porters Office
CL   TRANSPORT
BT   RAILWAY TRANSPORT SITE
RT   OFFICE

Railway Orphanage
     USE ORPHANAGE

RAILWAY PLATFORM
CL   TRANSPORT
BT   RAILWAY TRANSPORT SITE

Railway Provender Store
     USE RAILWAY STOREHOUSE

RAILWAY SHED
UF   Railway Carriage Shed
CL   TRANSPORT
BT   RAILWAY TRANSPORT SITE
RT   SHED

RAILWAY SIDING
UF   Railway Sidings
CL   TRANSPORT
BT   RAILWAY TRANSPORT SITE

Railway Sidings
     USE RAILWAY SIDING

RAILWAY SIGNAL
UF   Railway Signal Box
CL   TRANSPORT
BT   RAILWAY TRANSPORT SITE
RT   MAIL BAG NET
     SIGNAL BOX
     WATER POINT

RAILWAY SIGNAL
UF   Railway Signal Box
CL   COMMUNICATIONS
BT   SIGNALLING STRUCTURE
RT   MAIL BAG NET
     SIGNAL BOX
     WATER POINT

Railway Signal Box
     USE RAILWAY SIGNAL
          SIGNAL BOX
SN   Use both terms.

RAILWAY STABLE
CL   TRANSPORT
BT   RAILWAY TRANSPORT SITE
RT   GOODS YARD

RAILWAY STABLE
CL   TRANSPORT
BT   STABLE

RAILWAY STATION
UF   Halt
     Railway Terminus
CL   TRANSPORT
BT   RAILWAY TRANSPORT SITE
NT   UNDERGROUND RAILWAY STATION
RT   BOOKING OFFICE
     CATTLE DOCKS
     CROSSING KEEPERS COTTAGE

RAILWAY STOREHOUSE
UF   Railway Provender Store
CL   TRANSPORT
BT   RAILWAY TRANSPORT SITE
RT   RAILWAY WAREHOUSE
     STOREHOUSE

Railway Terminus

USE RAILWAY STATION

RAILWAY TRANSPORT SITE
- CL TRANSPORT
- NT ATMOSPHERIC RAILWAY ENGINE HOUSE
  ENGINE SHED
  GOODS SHED
  GOODS STATION
  GOODS YARD
  HOLDING SHED
  LEVEL CROSSING
  LEVEL CROSSING GATE
  LOCOMOTIVE DEPOT
  MAIL BAG NET
  MARSHALLING YARD
  RAILWAY
  RAILWAY BRIDGE
  RAILWAY BUFFET
  RAILWAY CUTTING
  RAILWAY EMBANKMENT
  RAILWAY HOTEL
  RAILWAY INCLINED PLANE
  RAILWAY JUNCTION
  RAILWAY LIFT
  RAILWAY LOOKOUT TOWER
  RAILWAY OFFICE
  RAILWAY PLATFORM
  RAILWAY SHED
  RAILWAY SIDING
  RAILWAY SIGNAL
  RAILWAY STABLE
  RAILWAY STATION
  RAILWAY STOREHOUSE
  RAILWAY TUNNEL
  RAILWAY TURNTABLE
  RAILWAY VIADUCT
  RAILWAY WORKS
  ROUNDHOUSE (RAILWAY)
  SIGNAL BOX
  TRAIN SHED
  TRANSIT SHED
  TRAVERSER
  WAGON SHED

RAILWAY TUNNEL
- CL TRANSPORT
- BT RAILWAY TRANSPORT SITE
- NT UNDERGROUND RAILWAY TUNNEL
- RT RAILWAY TUNNEL PORTAL
  TRAMWAY TUNNEL
  TUNNEL
  VENTILATION SHAFT

RAILWAY TUNNEL
- CL TRANSPORT
- BT TRANSPORT TUNNEL

Railway Tunnel Entrance
USE RAILWAY TUNNEL PORTAL

RAILWAY TUNNEL PORTAL
- UF Railway Tunnel Entrance
- CL TRANSPORT
- BT TUNNEL PORTAL
- RT PORTAL
  RAILWAY TUNNEL

RAILWAY TURNTABLE
- UF Turntable
- CL TRANSPORT
- BT RAILWAY TRANSPORT SITE
- RT TRAVERSER

RAILWAY VIADUCT
- CL TRANSPORT
- BT RAILWAY TRANSPORT SITE
- RT RAILWAY BRIDGE
  RAILWAY EMBANKMENT

RAILWAY VIADUCT

- CL TRANSPORT
- BT VIADUCT

RAILWAY WAGON WORKS
- CL INDUSTRIAL
- BT RAILWAY ENGINEERING SITE

RAILWAY WAREHOUSE
- CL COMMERCIAL
- BT WAREHOUSE
- RT GOODS YARD
  HOLDING SHED
  RAILWAY STOREHOUSE

Railway Water Tank
USE WATER POINT

RAILWAY WORKERS COTTAGE
- UF Railway Navvys Cottage
- CL DOMESTIC
- BT TRANSPORT WORKERS HOUSE
- RT CROSSING KEEPERS COTTAGE

RAILWAY WORKERS HOUSE
- CL DOMESTIC
- BT TRANSPORT WORKERS HOUSE

Railway Workers Village
USE WORKERS VILLAGE

RAILWAY WORKS
- CL INDUSTRIAL
- BT RAILWAY ENGINEERING SITE

RAILWAY WORKS
- CL TRANSPORT
- BT RAILWAY TRANSPORT SITE
- NT RAILWAY CARRIAGE WORKS

RAILWAY WORKSHOP
- UF Waggon Workshop
- CL INDUSTRIAL
- BT RAILWAY ENGINEERING SITE

RAINWATER HEAD
- SN The receptacle at the top of a rain-water pipe which gathers the water from one or more outlets or gutters on the roof.
- CL WATER SUPPLY AND DRAINAGE

RAISED BED
- CL GARDENS, PARKS AND URBAN SPACES
- BT FLOWER BED

RAISED PAVEMENT
- CL UNASSIGNED
- BT PAVEMENT
- RT EMBANKMENT

Raised Slab
USE TOMB

RAMP
- CL TRANSPORT
- BT ROAD TRANSPORT SITE
- NT CAR RAMP
  CARRIAGE RAMP

RAMPART
- CL DEFENCE
- RT GLACIS
  SCARP

Rams Hill Style Enclosure
USE ENCLOSED SETTLEMENT

RANCH BOUNDARY
- CL AGRICULTURE AND SUBSISTENCE
- BT LAND USE SITE

RT   BOUNDARY
      FIELD BOUNDARY
      LINEAR EARTHWORK
      REAVE

RANGERS HOUSE
CL   DOMESTIC
BT   HOUSE <BY FUNCTION>
RT   ESTATE COTTAGE
      VERDERERS COTTAGE

Ranters Chapel
   USE NONCONFORMIST CHAPEL

Ravelin
   USE BASTION OUTWORK

Rayon Factory
   USE ARTIFICIAL TEXTILE FACTORY

READING ROOM
CL   EDUCATION
NT   MINERS READING ROOM
RT   LIBRARY

REAVE
UF   Contour Reave
      Terminal Reave
      Watershed Reave
CL   AGRICULTURE AND SUBSISTENCE
BT   LAND USE SITE
RT   BOUNDARY
      FIELD BOUNDARY
      LINEAR EARTHWORK
      RANCH BOUNDARY

RECEIVING BLOCK
SN   In a workhouse, often includes porter's lodge,
      clothes store, washrooms, casual cells, etc.
CL   HEALTH AND WELFARE
BT   HOSPITAL BLOCK
RT   HOSPITAL
      WORKHOUSE

RECORD OFFICE
UF   State Paper Office
CL   CIVIL
BT   PUBLIC BUILDING
RT   GOVERNMENT OFFICE
      MUNIMENT HOUSE
      OFFICE

RECORDING STUDIO
UF   Studio
CL   COMMUNICATIONS
RT   TELEVISION STUDIO

RECREATION GROUND
CL   RECREATIONAL
BT   SPORTS SITE
NT   ADVENTURE PLAYGROUND
      ALL WEATHER PITCH
      CHILDRENS PLAYGROUND
      PLAYING FIELD
      SPORTS GROUND

RECREATIONAL
SN   This is the top term for the class. See
      RECREATIONAL Class List for narrow terms.

RECREATIONAL HALL
SN   For model estates, factories, flats etc.
CL   RECREATIONAL
RT   COMMUNITY CENTRE
      FACTORY
      FLATS
      GARDEN SUBURB
      GARDEN VILLAGE
      HOUSING ESTATE

      LODGING HOUSE
      TENANTS HALL

RECRUITING STATION
CL   DEFENCE
RT   ARMY OFFICE

RECTANGULAR ENCLOSURE
CL   UNASSIGNED
BT   RECTILINEAR ENCLOSURE

RECTILINEAR ENCLOSURE
UF   Wooton Style Enclosure
CL   UNASSIGNED
BT   ENCLOSURE
NT   GOAL POST ENCLOSURE
      POLYGONAL ENCLOSURE
      RECTANGULAR ENCLOSURE
      SQUARE ENCLOSURE
      TRAPEZOIDAL ENCLOSURE
RT   VIERECKSCHANZEN

RECTORY
UF   Rectory Pele
CL   DOMESTIC
BT   CLERICAL DWELLING

Rectory Pele
   USE PELE TOWER
       RECTORY
SN   Use both terms

RECUMBENT STONE
CL   RELIGIOUS, RITUAL AND FUNERARY
RT   RECUMBENT STONE CIRCLE
      STANDING STONE
      STONE

RECUMBENT STONE CIRCLE
CL   RELIGIOUS, RITUAL AND FUNERARY
BT   STONE CIRCLE
RT   RECUMBENT STONE

Red Hill
   USE SALTERN

Redan
   USE BASTION OUTWORK

REDEMPTIONISTS CHURCH
CL   RELIGIOUS, RITUAL AND FUNERARY
BT   CHURCH

Redoubt
   USE BASTION OUTWORK

REED BED
CL   UNASSIGNED
BT   NATURAL FEATURE

REELING SHED
SN   Boiling of silk worm cocoons to release the silk
      fibres.
CL   INDUSTRIAL
BT   SILK MANUFACTURING SITE
RT   SHED

REFECTORY
UF   Dining Hall
CL   DOMESTIC
RT   ABBEY
      CANTEEN
      FRATER
      FRIARY
      MONASTERY
      NUNNERY
      PRIORY
      RELIGIOUS HOUSE
      SCHOOL

REFERENCE LIBRARY
CL   EDUCATION
BT   LIBRARY

Reform Club
USE GENTLEMENS CLUB

REFRESHMENT PAVILION
CL   GARDENS, PARKS AND URBAN SPACES
BT   PAVILION
RT   COUNTRY HOUSE
      PUBLIC PARK
      REFRESHMENT ROOMS
      TEA HOUSE
      TEA ROOM

REFRESHMENT PAVILION
CL   RECREATIONAL
BT   EATING AND DRINKING ESTABLISHMENT
RT   COUNTRY HOUSE
      PUBLIC PARK
      REFRESHMENT ROOMS
      TEA HOUSE
      TEA ROOM

REFRESHMENT ROOMS
CL   COMMERCIAL
BT   EATING AND DRINKING ESTABLISHMENT
RT   REFRESHMENT PAVILION

REFRIGERATED FREIGHTER
CL   MARITIME
BT   FREIGHTER

REFRIGERATED STORE
SN   A storehouse using mechanical means of controlling
      temperature rather than ice or insulation.
CL   INDUSTRIAL
BT   FOOD PRESERVING SITE
RT   COLD STORE

REFUGE BEACON
CL   COMMUNICATIONS
BT   BEACON

REFUGE BEACON
CL   MARITIME
BT   BEACON

REFUGE BUOY
CL   MARITIME
BT   SAFETY CRAFT

REFUGE BUOY
CL   MARITIME
BT   UNMANNED CRAFT

REFUSE DEPOT
CL   INDUSTRIAL
BT   WASTE DISPOSAL SITE
NT   REFUSE TRANSFER DEPOT
RT   REFUSE DESTRUCTOR STATION
      REFUSE DISPOSAL PLANT
      REFUSE DISPOSAL SITE

REFUSE DESTRUCTOR STATION
SN   Power station using domestic refuse as its
      principal fuel.
CL   INDUSTRIAL
BT   POWER STATION
RT   INCINERATOR
      POWER STATION
      REFUSE DEPOT
      REFUSE DISPOSAL PLANT

REFUSE DESTRUCTOR STATION
SN   Power station using domestic refuse as its
      principal fuel.
CL   INDUSTRIAL

BT   WASTE DISPOSAL SITE
RT   INCINERATOR

REFUSE DISPOSAL PLANT
CL   INDUSTRIAL
BT   WASTE DISPOSAL SITE
RT   INCINERATOR
      REFUSE DEPOT
      REFUSE DESTRUCTOR STATION

REFUSE DISPOSAL SITE
UF   Rubbish Dump
CL   INDUSTRIAL
BT   WASTE DISPOSAL SITE
RT   REFUSE DEPOT

Refuse Pit
USE RUBBISH PIT

REFUSE TRANSFER DEPOT
CL   INDUSTRIAL
BT   REFUSE DEPOT

REFUSE TRANSFER DEPOT
CL   TRANSPORT

REGIMENTAL DEPOT
CL   DEFENCE
RT   ARMY CAMP

Regimental Hospital
USE MILITARY HOSPITAL

REGISTER OFFICE
UF   Registry Office
CL   CIVIL
RT   OFFICE

REGISTRARS HOUSE
CL   DOMESTIC
BT   HOUSE <BY FUNCTION>
RT   CEMETERY

Registry Office
USE REGISTER OFFICE

Regular Aggregate Field System
USE AGGREGATE FIELD SYSTEM

Regular Enclosed Field System
USE ENCLOSED FIELD SYSTEM

Regular Open Field System
USE OPEN FIELD

RELIGIOUS HOUSE
UF   Celtic Monastery
      Convent
      Monastic Vallum
CL   RELIGIOUS, RITUAL AND FUNERARY
NT   ABBEY
      CAMERA
      CELL
      DOUBLE HOUSE
      FRIARY
      GRANGE
      LAY BRETHREN SETTLEMENT
      MONASTERY
      NUNNERY
      PRECEPTORY
      PRIORY
RT   ALMONRY
      CHAPTER HOUSE
      HOSPITAL
      REFECTORY

RELIGIOUS, RITUAL AND FUNERARY
SN   This is the top term for the class. See RELIGIOUS,
      RITUAL AND FUNERARY Class List for narrow terms.

REPTILE HOUSE
  CL   RECREATIONAL
  BT   ANIMAL HOUSE

RESCUE TUG
  CL   MARITIME
  BT   SAFETY CRAFT

RESCUE TUG
  CL   MARITIME
  BT   TUG

Research Laboratory
  USE LABORATORY

RESEARCH STATION
  UF   Agricultural Research Station
       Experimental Research Station
       Meteorological Research Station
       Oceanographic Research Station
  CL   EDUCATION
  RT   LABORATORY
       MARINE LABORATORY
       OBSERVATORY

RESERVOIR
  CL   WATER SUPPLY AND DRAINAGE
  NT   CANAL RESERVOIR
  RT   CISTERN
       DAM
       HUSH
       RESERVOIR INSPECTION CHAMBER
       WATER TOWER
       WATERWORKS

RESERVOIR INSPECTION CHAMBER
  CL   WATER SUPPLY AND DRAINAGE
  RT   RESERVOIR

RESIDENTIAL BUILDING
  SN   Not permanent homes.
  CL   DOMESTIC
  NT   ALMSHOUSE
       BARRACKS
       BOTHY
       CHILDRENS HOME
       CONVALESCENT HOME
       COTTAGE HOME
       GUEST HOUSE
       HALL OF RESIDENCE
       HOSTEL
       HOTEL
       INN
       JUDGES LODGINGS
       LODGING HOUSE
       LODGINGS
       MAYORS RESIDENCE
       NURSES HOSTEL
       NURSING HOME
       ORPHANAGE
       SERVICES HOME
       TENANTS HALL
       WORKHOUSE
  RT   DWELLING

Residential Home
  USE NURSING HOME

Residentiary
  USE CLERGY HOUSE

RESORT VILLAGE
  SN   Model village built as a holiday resort.
  CL   DOMESTIC
  BT   VILLAGE

RESORT VILLAGE
  SN   Model village built as a holiday resort.
  CL   DOMESTIC

  BT   MODEL SETTLEMENT

Rest Home
  USE CONVALESCENT HOME
       NURSING HOME
  SN   Use both terms.

RESTAURANT
  UF   Brasserie
  CL   COMMERCIAL
  BT   EATING AND DRINKING ESTABLISHMENT
  RT   CANTEEN
       FISH AND CHIP SHOP

RETENTURA
  CL   DEFENCE

RETORT HOUSE
  SN   Central functional building of a gas works. Coal
       is roasted in retorts producing gas and coke.
  CL   INDUSTRIAL
  BT   COAL GAS STRUCTURE

RETTING PIT
  UF   Flax Retting Pit
  SN   Prolonged steeping of the flax plant in water to
       separate the fibres from the wood.
  CL   INDUSTRIAL
  BT   LINEN OR FLAX MANUFACTURING SITE
  RT   LINEN MILL
       PIT
       SCUTCHING MILL

REVENUE CUTTER
  CL   MARITIME
  BT   COASTGUARD CRAFT

REVERBERATORY FURNACE
  SN   A furnace in which the flame is turned back over
       the substance to be heated.
  CL   INDUSTRIAL
  BT   FURNACE
  NT   CUPOLA FURNACE (REVERBERATORY)
       PUDDLING FURNACE
       TANK FURNACE
  RT   FERROUS METAL SMELTING SITE
       GLASS WORKS
       NON FERROUS METAL SMELTING SITE

REVETMENT
  SN   A wall built to retain a bank of earth.
  CL   UNASSIGNED
  BT   WALL

Rhodonite Mine
  USE MANGANESE MINE

RIBBON FACTORY
  CL   INDUSTRIAL
  BT   FACTORY <BY PRODUCT>

RIBBON FACTORY
  CL   INDUSTRIAL
  BT   TEXTILE PRODUCT SITE

Ribbon Wall
  USE SERPENTINE WALL

Rick
  USE STACK STAND

RIDGE AND FURROW
  UF   Rig And Furrow
  CL   AGRICULTURE AND SUBSISTENCE
  BT   FIELD
  NT   BROAD RIDGE AND FURROW
       NARROW RIDGE AND FURROW
       STEAM PLOUGHED RIG
  RT   CORD RIG

OPEN FIELD
PLOUGH HEADLAND
STRIP LYNCHET

RIDGEWAY
  CL   TRANSPORT
  BT   PEDESTRIAN TRANSPORT SITE

Riding House
  USE RIDING SCHOOL

RIDING SCHOOL
  UF   Cavalry Riding School
       Riding House
       Riding Stables
  CL   EDUCATION
  BT   TRAINING SCHOOL
  RT   COUNTRY HOUSE
       STABLE
       TACK ROOM

RIDING SCHOOL
  UF   Cavalry Riding School
       Riding House
       Riding Stables
  CL   RECREATIONAL
  BT   SPORTS SITE
  RT   COUNTRY HOUSE
       SADDLERY
       STABLE
       TACK ROOM

Riding Stables
  USE RIDING SCHOOL

RIFLE BUTTS
  CL   DEFENCE
  BT   BUTTS

RIFLE BUTTS
  CL   RECREATIONAL
  BT   BUTTS

Rifle Factory
  USE ORDNANCE FACTORY

Rifle Range
  USE FIRING RANGE

Rig And Furrow
  USE RIDGE AND FURROW

RIGGING HOUSE
  UF   Cordage House
  CL   MARITIME
  BT   MARINE WORKSHOP
  RT   NET HOUSE

RIGGING HOUSE
  UF   Cordage House
  CL   INDUSTRIAL
  BT   MARINE WORKSHOP

RING BANK
  CL   UNASSIGNED
  BT   BANK (EARTHWORK)

RING BARROW
  CL   RELIGIOUS, RITUAL AND FUNERARY
  BT   BARROW
  RT   RING CAIRN

RING CAIRN
  CL   RELIGIOUS, RITUAL AND FUNERARY
  BT   BURIAL CAIRN
  RT   RING BARROW

RING DITCH
  SN   Circular or near circular ditches, usually seen as
       cropmarks, often ploughed out barrows.
  CL   UNASSIGNED

  RT   CURVILINEAR ENCLOSURE
       ROUND BARROW

Ring Enclosure
  USE CIRCULAR ENCLOSURE

RINGWORK
  CL   DOMESTIC
  BT   CASTLE
  RT   BAILEY
       ENCLOSURE
       MOTTE
       MOTTE AND BAILEY
       RINGWORK AND BAILEY

RINGWORK
  CL   DEFENCE
  BT   CASTLE
  RT   BAILEY
       ENCLOSURE
       MOTTE
       MOTTE AND BAILEY
       RINGWORK AND BAILEY

RINGWORK AND BAILEY
  CL   DOMESTIC
  BT   CASTLE
  RT   BAILEY
       MOTTE
       MOTTE AND BAILEY
       RINGWORK

RINGWORK AND BAILEY
  CL   DEFENCE
  BT   CASTLE

RIPE CHARGE HOUSE
  CL   INDUSTRIAL
  BT   EXPLOSIVES SITE
  RT   GUNPOWDER DRYING HOUSE

RISE LIFT
  CL   TRANSPORT
  BT   LIFT

RITUAL PIT
  CL   RELIGIOUS, RITUAL AND FUNERARY
  RT   PIT
       RITUAL SHAFT
       VIERECKSCHANZEN
       VOTIVE PIT
       VOTIVE SHAFT

RITUAL SHAFT
  CL   RELIGIOUS, RITUAL AND FUNERARY
  RT   RITUAL PIT
       SHAFT
       VIERECKSCHANZEN
       VOTIVE PIT
       VOTIVE SHAFT

River Bank
  USE FLOOD DEFENCES

River Defences
  USE FLOOD DEFENCES

RIVER DOCK
  CL   TRANSPORT
  BT   DOCK

River Embankment
  USE FLOOD DEFENCES

River Fishery
  USE FISHERY

RIVER INTAKE GAUGE
  CL   TRANSPORT

260

BT   WATER TRANSPORT SITE
RT   GAUGE HOUSE
     SLUICE GATE

RIVER LOCK
CL   TRANSPORT
BT   LOCK
RT   CANAL LOCK
     RIVER NAVIGATION

RIVER NAVIGATION
CL   TRANSPORT
BT   WATER TRANSPORT SITE
RT   CANAL
     MILE PLATE
     MILEPOST
     MILESTONE
     RIVER LOCK
     WEIR

River Police Station
USE POLICE STATION

RIVER PORT
CL   MARITIME
BT   PORT

River Quay
USE QUAY

River Sluice
USE SLUICE

River Stairs
USE LANDING STEPS

River Steps
USE LANDING STEPS

River Wall
USE FLOOD DEFENCES

River Weir
USE WEIR

RIVER WHARF
CL   TRANSPORT
BT   WHARF

RIVET AND TOOL SHOP
CL   INDUSTRIAL
BT   MARINE CONSTRUCTION SITE
RT   FABRICATION SHED
     MARINE ENGINEERING WORKS
     PLATERS SHOP
     RIVET AND TOOL STORE

RIVET AND TOOL SHOP
CL   MARITIME
BT   MARINE CONSTRUCTION SITE

RIVET AND TOOL STORE
CL   INDUSTRIAL
BT   MARINE CONSTRUCTION SITE
RT   RIVET AND TOOL SHOP

RIVET AND TOOL STORE
CL   MARITIME
BT   MARINE CONSTRUCTION SITE

ROAD
UF   Agger
     Boulevard
     Roman Road
     Street
CL   TRANSPORT
BT   ROAD TRANSPORT SITE
NT   ALLEY
     APPROACH ROAD

CARRIAGEWAY
COBBLED ROAD
DROVE ROAD
HOLLOW WAY
PACKHORSE ROAD
TOLL ROAD
TRACKWAY
WOODEN ROAD
RT   CAR RAMP
     CUL DE SAC
     FLYOVER
     MILE PLATE
     MILEPOST
     MILESTONE
     PAVEMENT
     ROAD BRIDGE
     ROAD JUNCTION
     ROAD SIGN
     ROAD TUNNEL
     ROAD VIADUCT
     SUSPENSION BRIDGE
     SWING BRIDGE
     UNDERPASS
     WAGONWAY

ROAD BRIDGE
CL   TRANSPORT
BT   BRIDGE <BY FUNCTION>
RT   FLYOVER
     ROAD
     UNDERPASS

ROAD BRIDGE
CL   TRANSPORT
BT   ROAD TRANSPORT SITE
RT   FLYOVER
     ROAD
     ROAD TUNNEL
     ROAD VIADUCT
     UNDERPASS

ROAD JUNCTION
CL   TRANSPORT
BT   ROAD TRANSPORT SITE
RT   CIRCUS (URBAN)
     FLYOVER
     ROAD
     ROND POINT

ROAD SIGN
CL   GARDENS, PARKS AND URBAN SPACES
BT   STREET FURNITURE
RT   ROAD

ROAD TRANSPORT SITE
CL   TRANSPORT
NT   AMBULANCE GARAGE
     AMBULANCE STATION
     BUS DEPOT
     BUS SHELTER
     BUS STATION
     CABMENS SHELTER
     CAR PARK
     CARRIAGE HOUSE
     CART SHED
     CLAPPER BRIDGE
     COACH HOUSE
     COACHING INN STABLE
     DIRECTION STONE
     FLYOVER
     FORD
     GARAGE
     GOODS CLEARING HOUSE
     HACKNEY STABLE
     HORSE TROUGH
     MEWS
     MOUNTING BLOCK
     PACKHORSE BRIDGE
     PARKING METER

PETROL PUMP
PETROL STATION
RAMP
ROAD
ROAD BRIDGE
ROAD JUNCTION
ROAD TUNNEL
ROAD VIADUCT
ROADSIDE LIGHTHOUSE
SEDAN CHAIR LIFT
SERVICE STATION
SIGNPOST
TERMINUS STONE
TETHERING POST
TOLL BOARD
TOLL BOUNDARY MARKER
TOLL BRIDGE
TOLL GATE
TOLL HOUSE
TOLLBOOTH
TRAMWAY TRANSPORT SITE
TRANSPORTER BRIDGE
TRAP HOUSE
UNDERPASS
RT   URBAN SPACE

ROAD TUNNEL
CL   TRANSPORT
BT   ROAD TRANSPORT SITE
RT   FLYOVER
ROAD
ROAD BRIDGE
ROAD TUNNEL PORTAL
TUNNEL
UNDERPASS
VENTILATION SHAFT

ROAD TUNNEL
CL   TRANSPORT
BT   TRANSPORT TUNNEL
RT   TUNNEL

ROAD TUNNEL PORTAL
CL   TRANSPORT
BT   TUNNEL PORTAL
RT   PORTAL
ROAD TUNNEL

ROAD VIADUCT
CL   TRANSPORT
BT   ROAD TRANSPORT SITE
RT   FLYOVER
ROAD
ROAD BRIDGE

ROAD VIADUCT
CL   TRANSPORT
BT   VIADUCT

Roadhouse
USE PUBLIC HOUSE

ROADSIDE LIGHTHOUSE
SN   eg. Dunston Pillar, Lincs.. Erected in 1751 to
guide travellers over the heath.
CL   GARDENS, PARKS AND URBAN SPACES
BT   STREET FURNITURE
RT   LIGHTHOUSE
MILEPOST
MILESTONE
TERMINUS STONE

ROADSIDE LIGHTHOUSE
SN   eg. Dunston Pillar, Lincs.. Erected in 1751 to
guide travellers over the heath.
CL   TRANSPORT
BT   ROAD TRANSPORT SITE
RT   LIGHTHOUSE
MILEPOST

MILESTONE
TERMINUS STONE

ROASTING HEARTH
SN   A hearth for roasting metallic ore, usually non
ferrous, before smelting.
CL   INDUSTRIAL
BT   METAL PRODUCTION FURNACE
RT   NON FERROUS METAL SMELTING SITE

ROBBER TRENCH
SN   Use broader site type where known
CL   UNASSIGNED

ROCK BASIN
CL   UNASSIGNED
BT   NATURAL FEATURE

ROCK BRIDGE
CL   GARDENS, PARKS AND URBAN SPACES
RT   GROTTO

ROCK CARVING
UF   Petroglyph
CL   RELIGIOUS, RITUAL AND FUNERARY
RT   CARVED STONE
CARVING
CUP AND RING MARKED STONE
CUP MARKED STONE

ROCK CUT CHAMBER
CL   UNASSIGNED
RT   CAVE
ROCK CUT DWELLING

ROCK CUT DWELLING
UF   Rock Cut House
Rock Dwelling
CL   DOMESTIC
BT   HOUSE <BY FORM>
RT   CAVE
ROCK CUT CHAMBER

Rock Cut House
USE ROCK CUT DWELLING

Rock Dwelling
USE ROCK CUT DWELLING

ROCK GARDEN
CL   GARDENS, PARKS AND URBAN SPACES
BT   GARDEN
RT   ALPINE GARDEN
ROCKERY

ROCK SHELTER
CL   DOMESTIC
BT   DWELLING
RT   CAVE

ROCKERY
CL   GARDENS, PARKS AND URBAN SPACES
RT   ALPINE GARDEN
ROCK GARDEN

ROCKET MOTOR FACTORY
SN   Manufacture of rocket motors for both civil and
military use.
CL   INDUSTRIAL
BT   AIRCRAFT ENGINEERING SITE
RT   EXPLOSIVES SITE

Rodway
USE TRANSMISSION RODS

ROLLING MILL
SN   Mill with a set of rollers to roll metal to set
thicknesses or shapes such as rails, beams or
rods.
CL   INDUSTRIAL

BT   MILL
RT   BRASS WORKS

ROLLING MILL
SN   Mill with a set of rollers to roll metal to set
     thicknesses or shapes such as rails, beams or
     rods.
CL   INDUSTRIAL
BT   METAL INDUSTRY SITE
RT   CHAFERY
     CUPOLA FURNACE (SHAFT)
     IRON WORKS
     SHEET METAL WORKS
     SLITTING MILL
     STEEL WORKS
     TUBE MILL
     WIRE MILL

Rolling Stock Hoist
USE RAILWAY LIFT

Rolls Office
USE GOVERNMENT OFFICE

Roman Barrow
USE ROUND BARROW
SN   Use Roman in a period field.

Roman Camp
USE TEMPORARY CAMP
SN   Use Roman in a period field.

ROMAN CATHOLIC CATHEDRAL
UF   Catholic Cathedral
CL   RELIGIOUS, RITUAL AND FUNERARY
BT   CATHEDRAL

ROMAN CATHOLIC CEMETERY
CL   RELIGIOUS, RITUAL AND FUNERARY
BT   INHUMATION CEMETERY

ROMAN CATHOLIC CHAPEL
UF   Catholic Chapel
CL   RELIGIOUS, RITUAL AND FUNERARY
BT   CHAPEL

ROMAN CATHOLIC CHURCH
UF   Catholic Church
CL   RELIGIOUS, RITUAL AND FUNERARY
BT   CHURCH
RT   PRESBYTERY

Roman Catholic College
USE THEOLOGICAL COLLEGE

Roman Catholic School
USE CHURCH SCHOOL

Roman Fort
USE FORT
SN   Use Roman in a period field.

Roman Fortlet
USE FORTLET
SN   Use Roman in a period field.

Roman Fortress
USE LEGIONARY FORTRESS
SN   Use Roman in a period field.

ROMAN KILN
CL   INDUSTRIAL
BT   KILN <BY FORM>

Roman Road
USE ROAD
SN   Use Roman in a period field.

Roman Vexillation Fortress

USE VEXILLATION FORT

ROND POINT
SN   An open circular area where avenues converge.
CL   GARDENS, PARKS AND URBAN SPACES
BT   URBAN SPACE
RT   CIRCUS (URBAN)
     ROAD JUNCTION

ROOF CRANE
CL   TRANSPORT
BT   CRANE <BY FORM>
NT   TRAVELLING ROOF CRANE

ROOT HOUSE
CL   GARDENS, PARKS AND URBAN SPACES
BT   GARDEN BUILDING
RT   ARBOUR
     HERMITAGE

Root Room
USE FODDER STORE

ROPE MANUFACTURING SITE
CL   INDUSTRIAL
BT   TEXTILE PRODUCT SITE
NT   ROPERY
     ROPEWALK
     TAR HOUSE
     YARN HOUSE

Rope Works
USE ROPERY

Ropehouse
USE ROPERY

ROPERY
UF   Double Ropehouse
     Rope Works
     Ropehouse
     Twine Works
CL   INDUSTRIAL
BT   ROPE MANUFACTURING SITE
RT   HATCHELLING HOUSE
     HEMP MILL
     HEMP STORE
     SAILMAKING WORKS

ROPEWALK
CL   INDUSTRIAL
BT   ROPE MANUFACTURING SITE
RT   HEMP STORE
     TAR HOUSE
     YARN HOUSE

ROSE BORDER
CL   GARDENS, PARKS AND URBAN SPACES
BT   BORDER

ROSE GARDEN
CL   GARDENS, PARKS AND URBAN SPACES
BT   FLOWER GARDEN

ROSTRAL COLUMN
CL   COMMEMORATIVE
BT   COMMEMORATIVE MONUMENT

ROTARY KILN
CL   INDUSTRIAL
BT   PLASTER MANUFACTURING SITE
RT   CEMENT KILN

ROTARY KILN
CL   INDUSTRIAL
BT   KILN <BY FORM>

ROTATIVE BEAM ENGINE
SN   An engine in which the oscillating motion of the
     beam is translated via gearing to a rotative
     motion.
CL   INDUSTRIAL

BT   BEAM ENGINE
RT   STEAM MILL
      STEAM WHIM

ROTUNDA
SN   An isolated building, circular on plan, generally
      consisting of one apartment with a domed roof, eg.
      Mausoleum at Castle Howard, Yorkshire.
CL   GARDENS, PARKS AND URBAN SPACES
BT   GARDEN BUILDING
NT   IONIC ROTUNDA
RT   GARDEN TEMPLE

ROUND
SN   Small Iron Age/Romano-British enclosed settlement
      found in SW England.
CL   DOMESTIC
BT   ENCLOSED SETTLEMENT

ROUND
SN   Small Iron Age/Romano-British enclosed settlement
      found in SW England.
CL   DEFENCE
BT   ENCLOSED SETTLEMENT

ROUND BARROW
UF   Roman Barrow
      Round Barrow Cemetery
CL   RELIGIOUS, RITUAL AND FUNERARY
BT   BARROW
NT   BELL BARROW
      BOWL BARROW
      CHAMBERED ROUND BARROW
      FANCY BARROW
RT   MONUMENTAL MOUND
      OVAL BARROW
      POND BARROW
      RING DITCH
      ROUND CAIRN

Round Barrow Cemetery
USE ROUND BARROW
       BARROW CEMETERY
SN   Use both terms.

ROUND CAIRN
UF   Cairn Circle
CL   RELIGIOUS, RITUAL AND FUNERARY
BT   BURIAL CAIRN
NT   CHAMBERED ROUND CAIRN
RT   ROUND BARROW

Round House (Domestic)
USE HUT CIRCLE

Round House (Horse Engine)
USE HORSE ENGINE HOUSE

Roundhouse (Lock Up)
USE LOCK UP

ROUNDHOUSE (RAILWAY)
CL   TRANSPORT
BT   RAILWAY TRANSPORT SITE
RT   ENGINE SHED

Route Marker
USE SIGNPOST

ROVING BRIDGE
CL   TRANSPORT
BT   BRIDGE < BY FUNCTION>
RT   AQUEDUCT
      CANAL BRIDGE
      TOWING PATH BRIDGE

ROVING BRIDGE
CL   TRANSPORT
BT   CANAL TRANSPORT SITE

RT   AQUEDUCT
      CANAL BRIDGE
      TOWING PATH BRIDGE

ROW
SN   A row of buildings built during different periods,
      as opposed to a TERRACE.
CL   DOMESTIC
BT   MULTIPLE DWELLING
NT   GALLERIED ROW
      NAILERS ROW
RT   TERRACE

ROW HOUSE
CL   DOMESTIC
BT   HOUSE < BY FORM >
NT   GALLERIED ROW HOUSE

ROWING CLUB
CL   RECREATIONAL
BT   SPORTS SITE
RT   BOAT HOUSE
      SAILING CLUB

Royal Air Force College
USE MILITARY COLLEGE

ROYAL AIR FORCE HOSPITAL
CL   HEALTH AND WELFARE
BT   HOSPITAL

ROYAL CHAPEL
CL   RELIGIOUS, RITUAL AND FUNERARY
BT   CHAPEL
RT   ROYAL PALACE

Royal Forest
USE HUNTING FOREST

Royal Hunting Lodge
USE HUNTING LODGE

Royal Institution
USE LEARNED SOCIETY BUILDING

Royal Merchant Navy School
USE NAVAL COLLEGE

Royal Mint
USE MINT

ROYAL PALACE
UF   Royal Pavilion
CL   DOMESTIC
BT   PALACE
RT   BANQUETING HOUSE
      COUNTRY HOUSE
      HUNTING LODGE
      ROYAL CHAPEL
      ROYAL PARK
      TILTYARD
      TILTYARD TOWER
      TOWN HOUSE

ROYAL PARK
CL   GARDENS, PARKS AND URBAN SPACES
BT   PARK
RT   ROYAL PALACE

Royal Pavilion
USE ROYAL PALACE

RUBBER WORKS
UF   Tyre Factory
CL   INDUSTRIAL
BT   CHEMICAL PRODUCT SITE

Rubbish Dump
USE REFUSE DISPOSAL SITE

RUBBISH PIT
- UF Refuse Pit
- CL DOMESTIC
- RT ASH PIT
  - MIDDEN
  - PIT

Rugby Football Stadium
  USE STADIUM

RUGBY PITCH
- CL RECREATIONAL
- BT SPORTS SITE

RUM WAREHOUSE
- CL COMMERCIAL
- BT WAREHOUSE

RUNE STONE
- UF Runic Stone
- CL RELIGIOUS, RITUAL AND FUNERARY
- RT CROSS
  - INSCRIBED STONE
  - OGHAM STONE

Runic Stone
  USE RUNE STONE

RUNWAY
- UF Landing Strip
- CL TRANSPORT
- BT AIR TRANSPORT SITE

RURAL INSTITUTE
- CL EDUCATION
- BT INSTITUTE
- RT AGRICULTURAL COLLEGE
  - HORTICULTURAL COLLEGE

RURAL INSTITUTE
- CL INSTITUTIONAL
- BT INSTITUTE

Russian Orthodox Church
  USE EASTERN ORTHODOX CHURCH

Sacred Well
  USE HOLY WELL

SACRISTY
- CL RELIGIOUS, RITUAL AND FUNERARY
- RT CHURCH
  - VESTRY

Saddle House
  USE SADDLERY

SADDLERY
- UF Saddle House
- CL DOMESTIC
- RT COUNTRY HOUSE
  - RIDING SCHOOL
  - STABLE
  - TACK ROOM

SAFETY CRAFT
- CL MARITIME
- BT MARITIME CRAFT
- NT CHANNEL CLEARANCE VESSEL
  - FIRE FIGHTING VESSEL
  - LIFEBOAT
  - LIGHT SHIP
  - PILOT VESSEL
  - REFUGE BUOY
  - RESCUE TUG

SAGGAR MAKERS WORKSHOP
- SN Saggar - fire clay box to protect ware from direct action of flame and gases during firing.
- CL INDUSTRIAL

- BT POTTERY MANUFACTURING SITE
- RT CLAY PUDDLING PIT
  - POTTERS WORKSHOP
  - POTTERY WORKSHOP

SAIL LOFT
- CL INDUSTRIAL
- BT MARINE WORKSHOP

SAIL LOFT
- CL MARITIME
- BT MARINE WORKSHOP

SAILING CLUB
- UF Yacht Club
- CL RECREATIONAL
- BT SPORTS SITE
- RT BOAT HOUSE
  - ROWING CLUB

SAILMAKING WORKS
- CL INDUSTRIAL
- BT TEXTILE MILL

SAILMAKING WORKS
- CL INDUSTRIAL
- BT TEXTILE PRODUCT SITE
- RT CANVAS WORKS
  - ROPERY

Sailors Chapel
  USE SEAMENS CHURCH

Sailors Church
  USE SEAMENS CHURCH

Sailors Cottage
  USE MARINERS COTTAGE

Sailors Exchange
  USE LABOUR EXCHANGE

Sailors Home
  USE ALMSHOUSE

Sailors Hostel
  USE LODGING HOUSE

Sailors Orphan Asylum
  USE ORPHANAGE

Sailors Registry
  USE LABOUR EXCHANGE

Sally Port
  USE POSTERN

Salmon Ladder
  USE FISH LADDER

SALT BATHS
- UF Brine Baths
- CL HEALTH AND WELFARE
- BT BATHS

Salt Evaporation Tank
  USE SALT WORKS

SALT MINE
- CL INDUSTRIAL
- BT MINERAL EXTRACTION SITE
- RT SALT WORKS
  - SALTERN

SALT MINE
- CL INDUSTRIAL
- BT MINE
- RT SALTERN

Salt Mound

USE SALTERN

Salt Pan
　USE SALT WORKS

Salt Shed
　USE SALT STORE

SALT STORE
　UF　Salt Shed
　　　Salt Warehouse
　　　Saltpie
　CL　INDUSTRIAL
　BT　CHEMICAL INDUSTRY SITE

Salt Warehouse
　USE SALT STORE

Salt Workings
　USE SALTERN

SALT WORKS
　UF　Salt Evaporation Tank
　　　Salt Pan
　　　Saltings
　CL　INDUSTRIAL
　BT　CHEMICAL PRODUCTION SITE
　RT　BRINE PIT
　　　COLOUR MILL
　　　FLINT MILL
　　　POTTERY WORKS
　　　SALT MINE

Saltcote
　USE SALTERN

SALTERN
　UF　Red Hill
　　　Salt Mound
　　　Salt Workings
　　　Saltcote
　CL　INDUSTRIAL
　BT　MINERAL EXTRACTION SITE
　RT　BRINE PIT
　　　SALT MINE

Saltings
　USE SALT WORKS

SALTPETRE STORE
　CL　INDUSTRIAL
　BT　EXPLOSIVES SITE

Saltpie
　USE SALT STORE

Saltway
　USE TRACKWAY

Saltworkers Cottage
　USE WORKERS COTTAGE

SALUTING BATTERY
　CL　DEFENCE
　BT　BATTERY

SALUTING BATTERY
　CL　MARITIME
　BT　MILITARY COASTAL DEFENCES

SALVAGE TUG
　CL　MARITIME
　BT　TUG

SALVAGE VESSEL
　CL　MARITIME
　BT　SERVICE CRAFT

Salvation Army Hostel

USE HOMELESS HOSTEL

SANATORIUM
　UF　Marine Sanatorium
　　　Seaside Sanatorium
　　　Tuberculosis Hospital
　　　Workhouse Sanatorium
　CL　HEALTH AND WELFARE
　BT　HOSPITAL
　RT　CONVALESCENT HOME
　　　CONVALESCENT HOSPITAL
　　　TUBERCULOSIS CHALET

SANCTUARY
　SN　Sacred area of land.
　CL　RELIGIOUS, RITUAL AND FUNERARY

Sanctuary Cross
　USE CROSS

SAND AND GRAVEL EXTRACTION SITE
　CL　INDUSTRIAL
　BT　MINERAL EXTRACTION SITE
　NT　GRAVEL PIT
　　　SAND PIT
　　　SAND WORKINGS

SAND PIT
　CL　INDUSTRIAL
　BT　SAND AND GRAVEL EXTRACTION SITE
　RT　CONCRETE WORKS
　　　GLASS WORKS
　　　MARL PIT

SAND PIT
　CL　INDUSTRIAL
　BT　EXTRACTIVE PIT
　RT　GRAVEL PIT

SAND WORKINGS
　CL　INDUSTRIAL
　BT　SAND AND GRAVEL EXTRACTION SITE

SANDSTONE QUARRY
　UF　Gritstone Quarry
　CL　INDUSTRIAL
　BT　STONE QUARRY
　RT　MILLSTONE WORKING SITE

SAP
　SN　A covered trench made for the purpose of
　　　approaching a besieged place under fire of the
　　　garrison.
　CL　DEFENCE
　BT　SIEGEWORK

SARCOPHAGUS
　CL　RELIGIOUS, RITUAL AND FUNERARY
　BT　COFFIN
　RT　CHURCHYARD
　　　GRAVE
　　　GRAVESTONE
　　　TOMBSTONE

Sarsen Stone
　USE STANDING STONE
　SN　Use stone where natural and not utilised by man.

SATELLITE DISH
　CL　COMMUNICATIONS
　BT　TELECOMMUNICATION STRUCTURE

SAUCER BARROW
　CL　RELIGIOUS, RITUAL AND FUNERARY
　BT　FANCY BARROW

Savigniac Abbey
　USE ABBEY
　　　SAVIGNIAC MONASTERY

SN Use both terms.

SAVIGNIAC MONASTERY
UF Savigniac Abbey
SN Abbey of Savigniac monks. Order merged with Cistercians c1147.
CL RELIGIOUS, RITUAL AND FUNERARY
BT MONASTERY
RT CISTERCIAN MONASTERY

SAW MILL
UF Gang Mill
CL INDUSTRIAL
BT MILL

SAW MILL
UF Gang Mill
CL INDUSTRIAL
BT TIMBER PROCESSING SITE
RT BOBBIN MILL
COOPERAGE
MATCH FACTORY
PLANING MILL
PULP MILL
SAW PIT

SAW PIT
CL INDUSTRIAL
BT TIMBER PROCESSING SITE
RT PIT
SAW MILL

SAXON SHORE FORT
CL DEFENCE
BT FORT

SAXON SHORE FORT
CL MARITIME
BT MILITARY COASTAL DEFENCES

SCAFFOLD
CL CIVIL
BT EXECUTION SITE

Scallage
USE LYCH GATE

Scallenge
USE LYCH GATE

SCARP
SN The bank or wall immediately in front of and below the rampart.
CL DEFENCE
RT RAMPART

SCAVELLMANS CABIN
SN A building used by labourers who clean and pump the docks, and in general, assist shipwrights.
CL MARITIME

SCHOOL
UF Academy
School Canteen
School Chapel
School Infirmary
School Laboratory
School Library
Workhouse School
CL EDUCATION
NT BOARD SCHOOL
BOARDING SCHOOL
CHARTIST COLONY SCHOOL
CHURCH SCHOOL
CONVENT SCHOOL
ELEMENTARY SCHOOL
PARISH SCHOOL
PRIVATE SCHOOL
SCHOOL FOR THE BLIND

SECONDARY SCHOOL
SUNDAY SCHOOL
TRAINING SCHOOL
VOLUNTARY SCHOOL
RT CANTEEN
CLASSROOM
EXAMINATION HALL
GYMNASIUM (SCHOOL)
HEADMASTERS HOUSE
HOPSCOTCH COURT
INFIRMARY
OBSERVATORY
REFECTORY
SCHOOL CLINIC
SCHOOL HOUSE
SCHOOLROOM
TEACHERS HOUSE

School Board Office
USE LOCAL GOVERNMENT OFFICE

School Canteen
USE SCHOOL
CANTEEN
SN Use both terms.

School Chapel
USE SCHOOL
CHAPEL
SN Use both terms.

SCHOOL CLINIC
CL HEALTH AND WELFARE
BT CLINIC
RT SCHOOL

School For Nurses
USE NURSES TRAINING SCHOOL

SCHOOL FOR THE BLIND
UF Blind School
CL EDUCATION
BT SCHOOL

SCHOOL HOUSE
CL EDUCATION
RT SCHOOL
SCHOOLROOM

School Infirmary
USE SCHOOL
INFIRMARY
SN Use both terms.

School Laboratory
USE SCHOOL
LABORATORY
SN Use both terms.

School Library
USE SCHOOL
LIBRARY
SN Use both terms.

School Of Arts And Crafts
USE ART SCHOOL

School Of Industry
USE INDUSTRIAL SCHOOL

School Teachers House
USE TEACHERS HOUSE

Schoolmasters House
USE TEACHERS HOUSE

SCHOOLROOM
CL EDUCATION
NT CLASSROOM

RT SCHOOL
    SCHOOL HOUSE

SCIENTIFIC INSTITUTE
CL EDUCATION
BT LITERARY AND SCIENTIFIC INSTITUTE

SCONCE
UF Artillery Mound
SN A small protective fortification, such as an
    earthwork.
CL DEFENCE
RT ARTILLERY FORT
    BASTION
    BATTERY
    FORTRESS
    SIEGEWORK
    TOWN DEFENCES

SCOOP WHEEL
CL INDUSTRIAL
BT WATERWHEEL <BY FORM>

Scooped Enclosure
USE SCOOPED SETTLEMENT

SCOOPED SETTLEMENT
UF Scooped Enclosure
CL DOMESTIC
BT SETTLEMENT

SCOTCH BAPTIST CHAPEL
CL RELIGIOUS, RITUAL AND FUNERARY
BT BAPTIST CHAPEL

SCOTCH KILN
CL INDUSTRIAL
BT KILN <BY FORM>
RT UPDRAUGHT KILN

Scottish National School
USE CHURCH SCHOOL

Scottish Office
USE GOVERNMENT OFFICE

SCOTTISH PRESBYTERIAN CHAPEL
CL RELIGIOUS, RITUAL AND FUNERARY
BT PRESBYTERIAN CHAPEL

SCOUT HUT
CL RECREATIONAL
RT YOUTH CLUB

SCRAP YARD
CL INDUSTRIAL
BT FERROUS METAL PRODUCT SITE
RT IRON FOUNDRY

SCRATCH DIAL
CL UNASSIGNED
RT SUNDIAL

Screen Wall
USE CURTAIN WALL

SCREENING PLANT
SN For sizing, sorting and washing of coal.
CL INDUSTRIAL
BT COAL MINING SITE
RT COAL CRUSHER HOUSE

SCREENS HOUSE
CL WATER SUPPLY AND DRAINAGE
RT SEWAGE WORKS

SCREW FACTORY
CL INDUSTRIAL
BT FACTORY <BY PRODUCT>

SCREW FACTORY
CL INDUSTRIAL
BT FERROUS METAL PRODUCT SITE
RT NAIL FACTORY
    SCREW MILL

SCREW MILL
UF Wood Screw Mill
CL INDUSTRIAL
BT FERROUS METAL PRODUCT SITE
RT SCREW FACTORY

SCREW MILL
UF Wood Screw Mill
CL INDUSTRIAL
BT MILL

SCRIBBLING MILL
UF Slubbing Mill
SN Preparation of raw fleece etc, for spinning by a
    coarse form of carding.
CL INDUSTRIAL
BT TEXTILE MILL
RT COMBING SHED
    SPINNING MILL
    WEAVING MILL
    WILLEY SHED

SCRIBBLING MILL
UF Slubbing Mill
SN Preparation of raw fleece etc, for spinning by a
    coarse form of carding.
CL INDUSTRIAL
BT TEXTILE SITE <BY PROCESS/PRODUCT>
RT FULLING MILL
    SPINNING MILL
    WEAVING MILL

SCULPTURE
CL GARDENS, PARKS AND URBAN SPACES
BT GARDEN ORNAMENT
NT BUST
    STATUE
RT HERM
    QUADRIGA
    SCULPTURE GARDEN
    SPHINX

SCULPTURE GARDEN
CL GARDENS, PARKS AND URBAN SPACES
BT GARDEN
RT SCULPTURE

SCUTCHING MILL
SN Removal by mechanical means of the dried wood of
    the flax plant after retting.
CL INDUSTRIAL
BT TEXTILE MILL
RT FLAX DRY SHED
    FLAX MILL
    RETTING PIT

SCUTCHING MILL
SN Removal by mechanical means of the dried wood of
    the flax plant after retting.
CL INDUSTRIAL
BT LINEN OR FLAX MANUFACTURING SITE

SCYTHE MILL
CL INDUSTRIAL
BT MILL
RT GRINDSTONE

SCYTHE MILL
CL INDUSTRIAL
BT FERROUS METAL PRODUCT SITE
RT EDGE TOOL WORKS
    FORGE

SEA BATHING HOSPITAL
  CL   HEALTH AND WELFARE
  BT   SPECIALIST HOSPITAL

SEA BEACON
  CL   COMMUNICATIONS
  BT   BEACON

SEA BEACON
  CL   MARITIME
  BT   BEACON

SEA DEFENCES
  SN   Non-military maritime flood and erosion defences.
  CL   MARITIME
  NT   BREAKWATER
       BULWARK
       GROYNE
       MOLE
  RT   FLOOD DEFENCES

SEA LION POOL
  CL   RECREATIONAL
  BT   ANIMAL HOUSE

SEA MARK
  CL   MARITIME
  BT   NAVIGATION AID

Sea Mill
  USE TIDEMILL

SEA TERMINAL
  UF   Terminal Building
  CL   MARITIME
  BT   DOCK AND HARBOUR INSTALLATION
  NT   CONTAINER TERMINAL
       FERRY TERMINAL
       HOVERCRAFT TERMINAL
       OCEAN LINER TERMINAL

SEAL FISHERIES VESSEL
  CL   MARITIME
  BT   FISHING VESSEL

Seamans Hostel
  USE LODGING HOUSE

SEAMENS CHURCH
  UF   Dockyard Church
       Mariners Church
       Sailors Chapel
       Sailors Church
  CL   RELIGIOUS, RITUAL AND FUNERARY
  BT   CHURCH

SEAMENS CHURCH
  UF   Dockyard Church
       Mariners Church
       Sailors Chapel
       Sailors Church
  CL   MARITIME

Seamens Hospital
  USE NAVAL HOSPITAL

SEAPORT
  CL   MARITIME
  BT   PORT

SEARCHLIGHT BATTERY
  CL   DEFENCE
  BT   BATTERY

SEASIDE PAVILION
  CL   RECREATIONAL
  RT   PIER PAVILION

Seaside Sanatorium
  USE SANATORIUM

SECOND RATE SHIP OF THE LINE
  CL   MARITIME
  BT   SHIP OF THE LINE

SECOND RATE SHIP OF THE LINE
  CL   MARITIME
  BT   CAPITAL WARSHIP

SECONDARY MODERN SCHOOL
  CL   EDUCATION
  BT   SECONDARY SCHOOL

SECONDARY SCHOOL
  UF   Higher Elementary School
  CL   EDUCATION
  BT   SCHOOL
  NT   COMPREHENSIVE SCHOOL
       GRAMMAR SCHOOL
       HIGHER GRADE SCHOOL
       SECONDARY MODERN SCHOOL

SECULAR CATHEDRAL
  CL   RELIGIOUS, RITUAL AND FUNERARY
  BT   CATHEDRAL

SECULAR HALL
  UF   Ethical Society Hall
  CL   INSTITUTIONAL
  BT   MEETING HALL

SEDAN CHAIR LIFT
  CL   GARDENS, PARKS AND URBAN SPACES
  BT   STREET FURNITURE

SEDAN CHAIR LIFT
  CL   TRANSPORT
  BT   ROAD TRANSPORT SITE

SEINER
  CL   MARITIME
  BT   NET FISHING VESSEL

Semaphore
  USE SEMAPHORE STATION

SEMAPHORE STATION
  UF   Semaphore
       Semaphore Tower
  SN   Pre-electrical telegraphy, c1800.
  CL   DEFENCE
  BT   SIGNAL STATION
  RT   RAILWAY LOOKOUT TOWER
       TELEGRAPH STATION

SEMAPHORE STATION
  UF   Semaphore
       Semaphore Tower
  SN   Pre-electrical telegraphy, c1800.
  CL   COMMUNICATIONS
  BT   SIGNAL STATION
  RT   RAILWAY LOOKOUT TOWER
       SHUTTER TELEGRAPH STATION

Semaphore Tower
  USE SEMAPHORE STATION

Semi Detached Cottage
  USE SEMI DETACHED HOUSE

SEMI DETACHED HOUSE
  UF   Double Cottage
       Semi Detached Cottage
  CL   DOMESTIC
  BT   HOUSE <BY FORM>

Senate House
USE UNIVERSITY ADMINISTRATION OFFICE

SENTRY BOX
CL DEFENCE
RT WATCH HOUSE
WATCHMANS BOX

SEPTIC TANK
CL WATER SUPPLY AND DRAINAGE
RT SEWAGE WORKS

Sepulchral Cross
USE CROSS

SERBIAN ORTHODOX CHURCH
CL RELIGIOUS, RITUAL AND FUNERARY
BT ORTHODOX CHURCH

SERGE FACTORY
SN Serge is a heavy woollen cloth.
CL INDUSTRIAL
BT TEXTILE MILL

SERGE FACTORY
SN Serge is a heavy woollen cloth.
CL INDUSTRIAL
BT WOOL MANUFACTURING SITE

SERGEANTS MESS
CL DEFENCE
RT ARMY CAMP
BARRACKS
COOKHOUSE
NAVAL OFFICERS MESS
OFFICERS MESS

Serjeants Inn
USE LEGAL CHAMBERS

SERPENTINE PATH
CL GARDENS, PARKS AND URBAN SPACES
BT WALK

SERPENTINE WALK
CL GARDENS, PARKS AND URBAN SPACES
BT WALK

SERPENTINE WALL
UF Crinkle Crankle Wall
Ribbon Wall
SN A wall for growing fruit, dating in England from
the mid-18th century, whose curving lines gave
added strength, thus doing away with the need for
buttressing.
CL GARDENS, PARKS AND URBAN SPACES
RT WALL

SERPENTINE WALL
UF Crinkle Crankle Wall
Ribbon Wall
SN A wall for growing fruit, dating in England from
the mid-18th century, whose curving lines gave
added strength, thus doing away with the need for
buttressing.
CL AGRICULTURE AND SUBSISTENCE
RT WALL

SERVICE CRAFT
CL MARITIME
BT MARITIME CRAFT
NT ANCHOR HANDLING CRAFT
BARRAGE BALLOON VESSEL
DIVING SUPPORT VESSEL
FUELER
HARBOUR SERVICES VESSEL
HOSPITAL SHIP
SALVAGE VESSEL

SURVEY VESSEL
TENDER
TUG
VICTUALLER
WATER CARRIER

SERVICE STATION
SN Use for complexes where services (eg. restaurants,
shops) are provided in addition to facilities for
buying petrol.
CL COMMERCIAL
RT PETROL STATION

SERVICE STATION
SN Use for complexes where services (eg. restaurants,
shops) are provided in addition to facilities for
buying petrol.
CL TRANSPORT
BT ROAD TRANSPORT SITE
RT PETROL PUMP
PETROL STATION

Servicemens Club
USE SERVICES CLUB

SERVICES CLUB
UF Army And Navy Club
British Legion Club
Cavalry Club
Naval Club
Servicemens Club
CL INSTITUTIONAL
BT CLUB
RT BRITISH LEGION HALL

SERVICES CLUB
UF Army And Navy Club
British Legion Club
Cavalry Club
Naval Club
Servicemens Club
CL RECREATIONAL
BT CLUB
RT BRITISH LEGION HALL

SERVICES HOME
CL DOMESTIC
BT RESIDENTIAL BUILDING

SETTLEMENT
UF Cave Settlement
Habitation Site
Occupation Site
CL DOMESTIC
NT CONSTRUCTION CAMP
ENCLOSED SETTLEMENT
HAMLET
HOUSING ESTATE
HUT CIRCLE SETTLEMENT
LINEAR SETTLEMENT
MODEL SETTLEMENT
OPEN SITE
OPPIDUM
PALISADED ENCLOSURE
PLATFORM SETTLEMENT
SCOOPED SETTLEMENT
SQUATTER SETTLEMENT
TENEMENT
TOWN
UNENCLOSED SETTLEMENT
VICUS
VILL
VILLAGE
RT DWELLING

SETTLING PIT
SN Pit for the depostion of ore sediment from waste
water collected from ore washing.
CL INDUSTRIAL

BT NON FERROUS METAL PROCESSING SITE
RT BUDDLE
    BUDDLE HOUSE
    ORE WASHING PLANT
    PIT
    WASHING FLOOR

SETTLING RESERVOIR
CL MARITIME
BT WATER REGULATION INSTALLATION

SETTLING TANK
CL INDUSTRIAL

SEVENTH DAY ADVENTISTS CHURCH
CL RELIGIOUS, RITUAL AND FUNERARY
BT CHURCH

SEWAGE DUMPING VESSEL
CL MARITIME
BT WASTE DISPOSAL VESSEL

Sewage Farm
  USE SEWAGE WORKS

SEWAGE PUMPING STATION
CL WATER SUPPLY AND DRAINAGE
BT PUMPING STATION
RT SEWAGE WORKS

Sewage Treatment Works
  USE SEWAGE WORKS

SEWAGE WORKS
UF Sewage Farm
    Sewage Treatment Works
CL WATER SUPPLY AND DRAINAGE
RT FILTER BED
    FILTER HOUSE
    PURIFIER
    SCREENS HOUSE
    SEPTIC TANK
    SEWAGE PUMPING STATION
    SEWER

SEWER
UF Sewer Vent
CL WATER SUPPLY AND DRAINAGE
NT INTERCEPTOR
    OUTFALL SEWER
RT CESS PIT
    CESS POOL
    CULVERT
    DRAIN
    SEWAGE WORKS
    UNDERGROUND STRUCTURE

Sewer Commissioners Office
  USE OFFICE

Sewer Vent
  USE SEWER

SHAFT
UF Flue
    Funnel
SN Use only if function unknown, otherwise use
    specific type.
CL UNASSIGNED
NT AIR SHAFT
    VENTILATION SHAFT
RT ADIT
    MINE SHAFT
    RITUAL SHAFT
    TUNNEL
    UNDERGROUND STRUCTURE
    VOTIVE SHAFT
    WELL

SHAFT FURNACE

SN A furnace constructed as a shaft with the fire at
    the bottom and the fuel and ore added from the
    top.
CL INDUSTRIAL
BT METAL PRODUCTION FURNACE
NT BLOOMERY
    CUPOLA FURNACE (SHAFT)
RT FERROUS METAL SMELTING SITE

SHAFT KILN
CL INDUSTRIAL
BT KILN < BY FORM >
NT SPLIT SHAFT KILN
RT CEMENT KILN

SHALE QUARRY
UF Shale Workings
CL INDUSTRIAL
BT STONE QUARRY
RT ALUM QUARRY
    OIL DISTILLERY

SHALE WORKING SITE
CL INDUSTRIAL
BT STONE WORKING SITE

Shale Workings
  USE SHALE QUARRY

Sham Castle
  USE FOLLY

Sham Ruin
  USE FOLLY

SHAMBLES
CL COMMERCIAL
RT ABATTOIR
    MEAT MARKET

Shealing
  USE SHIELING

SHED
UF Implement Shed
CL UNASSIGNED
BT BUILDING
RT ANIMAL SHED
    BRICK DRYING SHED
    CART SHED
    COAL SHED
    COMBING SHED
    CROQUET SHED
    DRESSING SHED
    ENGINE SHED
    FABRICATION SHED
    FLAX DRY SHED
    GARDEN SHED
    GOODS SHED
    GRASS DRYING SHED
    HOLDING SHED
    LEATHER DRYING SHED
    MILKING SHED
    POTTING SHED
    RAILWAY SHED
    REELING SHED
    SHEEP SHEARING SHED
    SHELTER SHED
    SLIP SHED
    SPINNING SHED
    STOREHOUSE
    TIMBER SEASONING SHED
    TRAIN SHED
    TRANSIT SHED
    WAGON SHED
    WAREHOUSE
    WILLEY SHED
    WOOD SHED

Sheep Cote

USE SHEEP FOLD

SHEEP DIP
UF Sheep Wash
CL AGRICULTURE AND SUBSISTENCE
BT ANIMAL WASH
RT SHEEP FOLD
    SHEEP HOUSE
    SHEEP SHEARING SHED
    WASHFOLD

SHEEP FOLD
UF Hogg Cote
    Sheep Cote
CL AGRICULTURE AND SUBSISTENCE
RT BIELD
    POUND
    SHEEP DIP
    SHEEP HOUSE
    SHEEP SHEARING SHED
    SHEPHERDS HUT
    SHIELING
    WASHFOLD

SHEEP HOUSE
UF Bercarie
    Hogg House
CL AGRICULTURE AND SUBSISTENCE
BT ANIMAL SHED
RT SHEEP DIP
    SHEEP FOLD
    SHEEP SHEARING SHED
    SHEPHERDS HUT

SHEEP SHEARING SHED
CL AGRICULTURE AND SUBSISTENCE
BT ANIMAL SHED
RT SHED
    SHEEP DIP
    SHEEP FOLD
    SHEEP HOUSE
    SHEPHERDS HUT

Sheep Wash
USE SHEEP DIP

SHEER HULK
SN Old ship hull used as a base for lifting tackle.
CL INDUSTRIAL
BT MARINE CONSTRUCTION SITE
RT MAST HOUSE
    MASTING SHEAR
    MILL POND

SHEER HULK
SN Old ship hull used as a base for lifting tackle.
CL MARITIME
BT HULK
RT MAST POND

SHEER HULK
SN Old ship hull used as a base for lifting tackle.
CL MARITIME
BT MARINE CONSTRUCTION SITE

SHEER LEGS
SN Lifting tackle comprising three legs forming a
    tripod and set of pulleys and a winch.
CL INDUSTRIAL
BT MARINE CONSTRUCTION SITE
RT DERRICK
    MAST HOUSE
    MAST POND
    MASTING SHEAR
    MILL POND

SHEER LEGS
SN Lifting tackle comprising three legs forming a
    tripod and set of pulleys and a winch.
CL MARITIME

BT MARINE CONSTRUCTION SITE

SHEET METAL WORKS
CL INDUSTRIAL
BT FERROUS METAL PRODUCT SITE
RT CAR FACTORY
    HYDRAULIC ENGINE HOUSE
    PLATING WORKS
    ROLLING MILL
    STEEL WORKS

SHEILA NA GIG
CL RELIGIOUS, RITUAL AND FUNERARY

Sheiling
USE SHIELING

SHELL BRIDGE
CL GARDENS, PARKS AND URBAN SPACES
RT BRIDGE

SHELL FOUNTAIN
CL GARDENS, PARKS AND URBAN SPACES
BT FOUNTAIN

SHELL FOUNTAIN
CL WATER SUPPLY AND DRAINAGE
BT FOUNTAIN

SHELL GROTTO
CL GARDENS, PARKS AND URBAN SPACES
BT GROTTO

SHELL KEEP
UF Shell Keep Castle
CL DEFENCE
BT KEEP

SHELL KEEP
UF Shell Keep Castle
CL DOMESTIC
BT KEEP

Shell Keep Castle
USE SHELL KEEP

SHELL MIDDEN
CL DOMESTIC
BT MIDDEN

SHELL MIDDEN
CL AGRICULTURE AND SUBSISTENCE
BT MIDDEN

SHELTER
CL UNASSIGNED
NT LABOURERS SHELTER
RT CABMENS SHELTER
    CATTLE SHELTER

SHELTER SHED
SN An open-sided building known to have been used for
    sheltering animals other than cattle.
CL AGRICULTURE AND SUBSISTENCE
BT ANIMAL SHED
RT CATTLE SHELTER
    FIELD BARN
    HOVEL
    OUTFARM
    SHED

SHEPHERDS HUT
CL DOMESTIC
BT HUT
RT FARM
    SHEEP FOLD
    SHEEP HOUSE
    SHEEP SHEARING SHED
    SHIELING

TRANSHUMANCE HUT

SHEPHERDS HUT
    CL   AGRICULTURE AND SUBSISTENCE
    BT   AGRICULTURAL BUILDING
    RT   FARM
          SHEEP FOLD
          SHEEP HOUSE
          SHEEP SHEARING SHED
          SHIELING
          TRANSHUMANCE HUT

Shiel
    USE SHIELING

Shielding
    USE SHIELING

SHIELING
    UF   Shealing
          Sheiling
          Shiel
          Shielding
    SN   Pasture to which animals were driven for grazing,
          with associated temporary huts for domestic or
          agricultural use.
    CL   DOMESTIC
    RT   FARM
          FARM BUILDING
          HUT
          SHEPHERDS HUT
          STACK STAND
          TRANSHUMANCE HUT

SHIELING
    UF   Shealing
          Sheiling
          Shiel
          Shielding
    SN   Pasture to which animals were driven for grazing,
          with associated temporary huts for domestic or
          agricultural use.
    CL   AGRICULTURE AND SUBSISTENCE
    BT   LAND USE SITE
    RT   FARM
          FARM BUILDING
          HUT
          SHEEP FOLD

Shifted Medieval Village
    USE SHIFTED VILLAGE
    SN   Use Medieval in a period field.

SHIFTED VILLAGE
    UF   Shifted Medieval Village
    CL   DOMESTIC
    BT   VILLAGE

SHIFTING HOUSE
    CL   MARITIME
    BT   DOCK AND HARBOUR INSTALLATION
    RT   ARSENAL
          FORTRESS

SHIP
    SN   A vessel of uncertain function over 30 metres
          long.
    CL   MARITIME
    BT   CRAFT

SHIP BISCUIT SHOP
    CL   MARITIME
    RT   CHANDLERY

SHIP BURIAL
    SN   Use with barrow type where necessary.
    CL   RELIGIOUS, RITUAL AND FUNERARY
    BT   BURIAL
    RT   BOAT BURIAL

SHIP CANAL
    CL   TRANSPORT
    BT   CANAL
    RT   CANAL

Ship Chandlery
    USE CHANDLERY

SHIP OF THE LINE
    CL   MARITIME
    BT   WARSHIP
    NT   FIFTH RATE SHIP OF THE LINE
          FIRST RATE SHIP OF THE LINE
          FOURTH RATE SHIP OF THE LINE
          SECOND RATE SHIP OF THE LINE
          SIXTH RATE SHIP OF THE LINE
          THIRD RATE SHIP OF THE LINE

SHIP REPAIR WORKS
    CL   INDUSTRIAL
    BT   MARINE CONSTRUCTION SITE
    RT   CHAIN WORKS
          DRY DOCK
          FLOATING CRANE
          GRIDIRON
          MARINE ENGINEERING WORKS
          PLATE RACK
          SHIPWRIGHTS WORKSHOP

SHIP REPAIR WORKS
    CL   MARITIME
    BT   MARINE CONSTRUCTION SITE

Shipbuilding Works
    USE SHIPYARD

SHIPHOUSE FRAME
    SN   An open metalwork structure supporting either a
          fabrication shed or the runners for an overhead
          crane.
    CL   INDUSTRIAL
    BT   MARINE CONSTRUCTION SITE
    RT   FABRICATION SHED
          PLATE RACK
          PLATERS SHOP

SHIPHOUSE FRAME
    SN   An open metalwork structure supporting either a
          fabrication shed or the runners for an overhead
          crane.
    CL   MARITIME
    BT   MARINE CONSTRUCTION SITE

Shipping Insurance Office
    USE COMMERCIAL OFFICE

Shippon
    USE COW HOUSE

SHIPWRECK GRAVE
    SN   Graves known to be of shipwreck victims buried
          close to their site of discovery, as was customary
          until the 19th century, rather than in consecrated
          ground.
    CL   RELIGIOUS, RITUAL AND FUNERARY
    BT   GRAVE

SHIPWRECK GRAVE
    SN   Graves known to be of shipwreck victims buried
          close to their site of discovery, as was customary
          until the 19th century, rather than in consecrated
          ground.
    CL   MARITIME
    RT   GRAVE

SHIPWRIGHTS WORKSHOP
    CL   INDUSTRIAL
    BT   MARINE WORKSHOP

RT SHIP REPAIR WORKS

SHIPWRIGHTS WORKSHOP
  CL MARITIME
  BT MARINE WORKSHOP

SHIPYARD
  UF Shipbuilding Works
      Shipyard Office
  CL INDUSTRIAL
  BT MARINE CONSTRUCTION SITE
  RT BOILER SHOP
      CRANE
      DOCK WORKERS COTTAGE
      DOCKYARD
      PAY OFFICE
      SLIPWAY

SHIPYARD
  UF Shipbuilding Works
      Shipyard Office
  CL INDUSTRIAL
  BT TIMBER PRODUCT SITE
  RT CARPENTERS WORKSHOP
      MARINE WORKSHOP

SHIPYARD
  UF Shipbuilding Works
      Shipyard Office
  CL MARITIME
  BT MARINE CONSTRUCTION SITE
  RT BOILER SHOP
      CRANE
      DOCK WORKERS COTTAGE
      DOCKYARD
      PAY OFFICE
      SLIPWAY

Shipyard Office
  USE SHIPYARD
       OFFICE
  SN Use both terms.

SHIRE HALL
  CL CIVIL
  BT MEETING HALL
  RT CIVIC CENTRE
      COUNTY HALL

SHODDY MILL
  SN Poor quality woollen cloth made from fibres
      produced by grinding light woollen rags.
  CL INDUSTRIAL
  BT TEXTILE MILL

SHODDY MILL
  SN Poor quality woollen cloth made from fibres
      produced by grinding light woollen rags.
  CL INDUSTRIAL
  BT WOOL MANUFACTURING SITE
  RT FLOCK MILL
      MUNGO MILL

Shoddy Warehouse
  USE TEXTILE WAREHOUSE

SHOE FACTORY
  UF Boot And Shoe Factory
  CL INDUSTRIAL
  BT FACTORY <BY PRODUCT>
  RT CURRIERY
      LEATHER WORKERS SHOP

SHOE FACTORY
  UF Boot And Shoe Factory
  CL INDUSTRIAL
  BT CLOTHING INDUSTRY SITE
  RT CURRIERY
      LEATHER WORKERS SHOP

Shooting Box
  USE HUNTING LODGE

Shooting Butt
  USE SHOOTING STAND

Shooting Lodge
  USE HUNTING LODGE

SHOOTING STAND
  UF Shooting Butt
  SN Position often screened by earth or stone from
      which game is shot.
  CL RECREATIONAL
  BT HUNTING SITE
  RT HUNTING LODGE

SHOOTING STAND
  UF Shooting Butt
  SN Position often screened by earth or stone from
      which game is shot.
  CL AGRICULTURE AND SUBSISTENCE
  BT HUNTING SITE
  RT HUNTING LODGE

SHOP
  UF Emporium
  CL COMMERCIAL
  NT BAKERS SHOP
      BARBERS SHOP
      BEER SHOP
      BOOKSHOP
      BUTCHERS SHOP
      CHEMISTS SHOP
      CLOCK SHOP
      CLOTHING SHOP
      CONFECTIONERS SHOP
      COOKSHOP
      COOPERATIVE STORE
      DELICATESSEN
      DEPARTMENT STORE
      DRAPERS SHOP
      FISHMONGERS SHOP
      FLORISTS SHOP
      GENERAL STORE
      GREENGROCERS SHOP
      GROCERS SHOP
      HAIRDRESSERS SALON
      HARDWARE SHOP
      MILLINERS SHOP
      OFF LICENCE
      PERFUMERY
      PIE AND MASH SHOP
      SUPERMARKET
      TAILORS SHOP
      TAKE AWAY
      TOBACCONISTS SHOP
      WIGMAKERS SHOP
  RT KIOSK
      SHOPPING ARCADE
      SHOPPING CENTRE
      SHOPPING PARADE
      SHOPPING PRECINCT
      SHOWROOM

SHOPPING ARCADE
  UF Bazaar
      Street Arcade
  SN Late 18th/19th century. A covered shopping street,
      sometimes with galleries.
  CL COMMERCIAL
  RT SHOP
      SHOPPING CENTRE
      SHOPPING PARADE
      SHOPPING PRECINCT

SHOPPING CENTRE
  CL COMMERCIAL

RT KIOSK
    SHOP
    SHOPPING ARCADE
    SHOPPING PARADE
    SHOPPING PRECINCT
    SUPERMARKET

Shopping Mall
  USE SHOPPING PRECINCT

SHOPPING PARADE
  SN A purpose-built terrace of shops.
  CL COMMERCIAL
  RT SHOP
      SHOPPING ARCADE
      SHOPPING CENTRE
      SHOPPING PRECINCT

SHOPPING PRECINCT
  UF Shopping Mall
  CL GARDENS, PARKS AND URBAN SPACES
  BT URBAN SPACE
  RT SHOP
      SHOPPING ARCADE
      SHOPPING CENTRE
      SHOPPING PARADE

SHOPPING PRECINCT
  UF Shopping Mall
  CL COMMERCIAL
  RT SHOP
      SHOPPING ARCADE
      SHOPPING CENTRE
      SHOPPING PARADE

SHOT TOWER
  SN In which shot is made from molten lead poured
      through sieves at top and falling into water at
      bottom.
  CL INDUSTRIAL
  BT ARMAMENT MANUFACTURING SITE
  RT TOWER

SHOT TOWER
  SN In which shot is made from molten lead poured
      through sieves at top and falling into water at
      bottom.
  CL INDUSTRIAL
  BT NON FERROUS METAL PRODUCT SITE

SHOWROOM
  UF Showrooms
  CL COMMERCIAL
  NT MOTOR VEHICLE SHOWROOM
      PORCELAIN SHOWROOM
  RT SHOP

Showrooms
  USE SHOWROOM

SHRINE
  CL RELIGIOUS, RITUAL AND FUNERARY
  RT ALTAR
      CHURCH
      HOLY WELL
      TEMPLE

SHRUB BORDER
  CL GARDENS, PARKS AND URBAN SPACES
  BT BORDER

SHRUBBERY
  CL GARDENS, PARKS AND URBAN SPACES
  NT BOSQUET

Shrunken Medieval Village
  USE SHRUNKEN VILLAGE
  SN Use Medieval in a period field.

Shrunken Settlement

USE SHRUNKEN VILLAGE

SHRUNKEN VILLAGE
  UF Shrunken Medieval Village
      Shrunken Settlement
  CL DOMESTIC
  BT VILLAGE

SHUTTER TELEGRAPH
  SN Pre-semaphore.
  CL COMMUNICATIONS
  BT SIGNAL STATION
  RT SHUTTER TELEGRAPH STATION

SHUTTER TELEGRAPH STATION
  SN Pre-semaphore.
  CL COMMUNICATIONS
  BT SIGNAL STATION
  RT SEMAPHORE STATION
      SHUTTER TELEGRAPH
      TELEGRAPH STATION

Shutting Stile
  USE STILE

Sick Childrens Hospital
  USE CHILDRENS HOSPITAL

Sick House
  USE INFIRMARY
  SN Use INFIRMARY with appropriate complex type (eg.
      SCHOOL).

SIEGE CASTLE
  CL DEFENCE
  BT CASTLE

SIEGE CASTLE
  CL DEFENCE
  BT SIEGEWORK

SIEGEWORK
  UF Circumvallation
      Civil War Defences
      Civil War Siegework
      Contravallation
  CL DEFENCE
  NT SAP
      SIEGE CASTLE
  RT BATTERY
      SCONCE

Siemens Furnace
  USE OPEN HEARTH FURNACE

SIGNAL BOX
  UF Railway Signal Box
  CL TRANSPORT
  BT RAILWAY TRANSPORT SITE
  RT RAILWAY LOOKOUT TOWER
      RAILWAY SIGNAL

SIGNAL BOX
  UF Railway Signal Box
  CL COMMUNICATIONS
  BT SIGNALLING STRUCTURE
  RT RAILWAY LOOKOUT TOWER
      RAILWAY SIGNAL
      TRAFFIC LIGHTS

SIGNAL STATION
  CL DEFENCE
  NT SEMAPHORE STATION
  RT BEACON
      FORTLET
      FRONTIER DEFENCE
      TELEGRAPH STATION
      WATCH TOWER

SIGNAL STATION

CL   COMMUNICATIONS
BT   SIGNALLING STRUCTURE
NT   SEMAPHORE STATION
      SHUTTER TELEGRAPH
      SHUTTER TELEGRAPH STATION
RT   BEACON
      LIGHTHOUSE
      TELEGRAPH STATION
      WATCH TOWER

SIGNAL TOWER
CL   COMMUNICATIONS
BT   SIGNALLING STRUCTURE
NT   TIMEBALL TOWER
RT   TOWER

SIGNALLING STRUCTURE
CL   COMMUNICATIONS
NT   BEACON
      LIGHTHOUSE
      RAILWAY SIGNAL
      SIGNAL BOX
      SIGNAL STATION
      SIGNAL TOWER
      TRAFFIC LIGHTS

SIGNPOST
UF   Finger Post
      Guide Plate
      Guide Post
      Guide Stone
      Guidepost
      Route Marker
      Way Marker
CL   TRANSPORT
BT   ROAD TRANSPORT SITE
RT   DIRECTION STONE
      MILE PLATE
      MILEPOST
      MILESTONE

SILK MANUFACTURING SITE
CL   INDUSTRIAL
BT   TEXTILE SITE <BY PROCESS/PRODUCT>
NT   REELING SHED
      SILK MILL
      THROWING MILL

SILK MILL
CL   INDUSTRIAL
BT   TEXTILE MILL
RT   LOOMSHOP

SILK MILL
CL   INDUSTRIAL
BT   SILK MANUFACTURING SITE

Silk Weavers Cottage
    USE WEAVERS COTTAGE

Silk Weavers Workshop
    USE WEAVERS WORKSHOP

SILKWORM FARM
CL   AGRICULTURE AND SUBSISTENCE
BT   FARM

Silo
    USE GRAIN SILO

SILVER HEARTH
SN   Ore hearth specifically for the refining of
      silver.
CL   INDUSTRIAL
BT   METAL PRODUCTION FURNACE
RT   ELLING HEARTH
      NON FERROUS METAL SMELTING SITE
      SLAG HEARTH

SILVER HEARTH

SN   Ore hearth specifically for the refining of
      silver.
CL   INDUSTRIAL
BT   NON FERROUS METAL SMELTING SITE
RT   LEAD WORKING SITE
      NON FERROUS METAL SMELTING SITE

SILVER MINE
SN   Use with other minerals extracted and MINE where
      relevant, eg. ZINC MINE.
CL   INDUSTRIAL
BT   NON FERROUS METAL EXTRACTION SITE
RT   LEAD MINE
      ZINC MINE

SILVER MINE
SN   Use with other minerals extracted and MINE where
      relevant, eg. ZINC MINE.
CL   INDUSTRIAL
BT   MINE
RT   ZINC MINE

Silver Plating Works
    USE PLATING WORKS

SILVER WORKING SITE
CL   INDUSTRIAL
BT   NON FERROUS METAL SMELTING SITE

SILVERSMITHS WORKSHOP
CL   INDUSTRIAL
BT   CRAFT INDUSTRY SITE
RT   ASSAY OFFICE
      CUPELLATION FURNACE
      GOLDSMITHS WORKSHOP
      JEWELLERY WORKS
      JEWELLERY WORKSHOP

SILVERSMITHS WORKSHOP
CL   INDUSTRIAL
BT   NON FERROUS METAL PRODUCT SITE

SINGLE AISLED HOUSE
CL   DOMESTIC
BT   AISLED HOUSE

Single Ended Hall
    USE SINGLE ENDED HALL HOUSE

SINGLE ENDED HALL HOUSE
UF   Single Ended Hall
CL   DOMESTIC
BT   CROSS WING HOUSE
RT   DOUBLE ENDED HALL HOUSE

SINGLE ENDED WEALDEN HOUSE
UF   Half Wealden House
SN   Differences between occurrences of term may be at
      a higher broad term level than that displayed
      here. See DOMESTIC Class List for context.
CL   DOMESTIC
BT   WEALDEN HOUSE

SINGLE ENDED WEALDEN HOUSE
UF   Half Wealden House
SN   Differences between occurrences of term may be at
      a higher broad term level than that displayed
      here. See DOMESTIC Class List for context.
CL   DOMESTIC
BT   WEALDEN HOUSE

Single Mens Hostel
    USE LODGING HOUSE

Single Span Bridge
    USE BRIDGE

Sink House
    USE WASH HOUSE

SISTERS HOUSE
CL   DOMESTIC
BT   HEALTH WORKERS HOUSE

SISTERS OF ST JOHN NUNNERY
UF   Sisters Of St John Priory
SN   Priories of female Order of Knights Hospitallers.
CL   RELIGIOUS, RITUAL AND FUNERARY
BT   NUNNERY
RT   CAMERA
     HOSPITALLERS CAMERA
     HOSPITALLERS PRECEPTORY
     PRECEPTORY

Sisters Of St John Priory
USE SISTERS OF ST JOHN NUNNERY
      PRIORY
SN   Use both terms.

SITE
UF   A P Site
     Crop Mark
     Non Antiquity
     Soil Mark
     Unclassified Site
SN   Unclassifiable site with minimal information.
     Specify site type wherever possible.
CL   UNASSIGNED

SIXTH RATE SHIP OF THE LINE
CL   MARITIME
BT   SHIP OF THE LINE

SIXTH RATE SHIP OF THE LINE
CL   MARITIME
BT   MINOR WARSHIP

Skating Pond
USE POND

SKATING RINK
UF   Ice Rink
     Ice Skating Rink
CL   RECREATIONAL
BT   SPORTS SITE

Skeleton
USE INHUMATION
      HUMAN REMAINS
SN   Use INHUMATION for articulated skeleton, HUMAN
     REMAINS for unarticulated remains.

SKIN DISEASE HOSPITAL
CL   HEALTH AND WELFARE
BT   SPECIALIST HOSPITAL

Skin Market
USE LEATHER MARKET

SLAG HEAP
UF   Iron Slag Heap
SN   Use for iron slag heap only. Otherwise use SPOIL
     HEAP.
CL   INDUSTRIAL
BT   FERROUS METAL SMELTING SITE
RT   SPOIL HEAP
     STEEL WORKS

SLAG HEARTH
SN   Used for the reheating of metal slag to extract
     further metal.
CL   INDUSTRIAL
BT   METAL PRODUCTION FURNACE
RT   NON FERROUS METAL SMELTING SITE
     SMELT MILL

SLAG HEARTH
SN   Used for the reheating of metal slag to extract
     further metal.
CL   INDUSTRIAL

BT   NON FERROUS METAL SMELTING SITE
RT   LEAD WORKING SITE
     NON FERROUS METAL SMELTING SITE
     SILVER HEARTH

Slate Mine
USE SLATE QUARRY

SLATE QUARRY
UF   Slate Mine
     Slate Works
CL   INDUSTRIAL
BT   STONE QUARRY

Slate Works
USE SLATE QUARRY

Slaughter House
USE ABATTOIR

Slight Univallate Hillfort
USE UNIVALLATE HILLFORT

Slip
USE SLIPWAY

SLIP SHED
CL   INDUSTRIAL
BT   MARINE WORKSHOP
RT   BOAT HOUSE
     DOCKYARD
     SHED
     SLIPWAY

SLIP SHED
CL   MARITIME
BT   MARINE WORKSHOP
RT   BOAT HOUSE
     DOCKYARD
     SHED
     SLIPWAY

SLIPPER BATHS
CL   HEALTH AND WELFARE
BT   BATHS

SLIPWAY
UF   Slip
CL   TRANSPORT
BT   WATER TRANSPORT SITE
RT   CAUSEWAY
     LIFEBOAT STATION
     SLIP SHED

SLIPWAY
UF   Slip
CL   MARITIME
RT   BOAT YARD
     CAUSEWAY
     DOCKYARD
     SHIPYARD
     SLIP SHED

SLIT TRENCH
UF   Practice Trench
CL   DEFENCE
BT   TRENCH
RT   PILLBOX

SLITTING MILL
SN   Mill with machinery used to cut slabs of metal
     into rods or thin sections for use in nail making
     or wire drawing.
CL   INDUSTRIAL
BT   MILL
RT   BRASS WORKS

SLITTING MILL
SN   Mill with machinery used to cut slabs of metal
     into rods or thin sections for use in nail making
     or wire drawing.
CL   INDUSTRIAL

BT   METAL INDUSTRY SITE
RT   FORGE
      IRON WORKS
      NAIL SHOP
      ROLLING MILL
      WIRE MILL

Slubbing Mill
   USE SCRIBBLING MILL

SLUICE
UF   Clow
      River Sluice
SN   A dam which can be raised or lowered to regulate
      the flow of water.
CL   WATER SUPPLY AND DRAINAGE
RT   CULVERT
      DRAIN
      SLUICE GATE
      WEIR

SLUICE
UF   Clow
      River Sluice
SN   A dam which can be raised or lowered to regulate
      the flow of water.
CL   MARITIME
BT   WATER REGULATION INSTALLATION

SLUICE GATE
CL   WATER SUPPLY AND DRAINAGE
RT   RIVER INTAKE GAUGE
      SLUICE

Small Arms Factory
   USE ORDNANCE FACTORY
SN   Manufacture of hand held weapons such as rifles,
      pistols, etc.

Small Multivallate Hillfort
   USE MULTIVALLATE HILLFORT

Small Stone Circle
   USE STONE CIRCLE

SMALLHOLDING
CL   AGRICULTURE AND SUBSISTENCE
BT   LAND USE SITE
RT   ALLOTMENT
      CROFT
      FARM
      MESSUAGE
      TOFT

Smallpox Hospital
   USE INFECTIOUS DISEASES HOSPITAL

SMELT MILL
UF   Copper Mill
      Copper Smelting Works
      Lead Mill
      Lead Smelting Mill
      Smelting Works
SN   Manufacturing complex incorporating furnaces,
      calciner and condenser flues.
CL   INDUSTRIAL
BT   NON FERROUS METAL SMELTING SITE
RT   SLAG HEARTH
      SMELTER
      SMELTING HOUSE

SMELT MILL
UF   Copper Mill
      Copper Smelting Works
      Lead Mill
      Lead Smelting Mill
      Smelting Works
SN   Manufacturing complex incorporating furnaces,
      calciner and condenser flues.
CL   INDUSTRIAL

BT   MILL

Smelt Mill Chimney
   USE CONDENSING CHIMNEY

Smelt Mill Flue
   USE CONDENSING FLUE

SMELTER
CL   INDUSTRIAL
BT   NON FERROUS METAL SMELTING SITE
NT   ALUMINIUM SMELTER
RT   SMELT MILL
      SMELTING HOUSE
      ZINC WORKS

SMELTERY
SN   Where ores are smelted. Use more specific site
      type where known.
CL   INDUSTRIAL
BT   NON FERROUS METAL SMELTING SITE
NT   SMELTING HOUSE

SMELTING HOUSE
CL   INDUSTRIAL
BT   SMELTERY
RT   CONDENSING CHIMNEY
      SMELT MILL
      SMELTER

Smelting Works
   USE SMELT MILL

Smithery
   USE BLACKSMITHS WORKSHOP

SMITHS COTTAGE
UF   Blacksmiths Cottage
      Sword Cutlers Cottage
CL   DOMESTIC
BT   INDUSTRIAL HOUSE
RT   BLACKSMITHS WORKSHOP
      FORGE
      NAILERS ROW
      WORKERS COTTAGE

SMITHS COTTAGE
UF   Blacksmiths Cottage
      Sword Cutlers Cottage
CL   INDUSTRIAL
BT   INDUSTRIAL HOUSE

Smithy
   USE BLACKSMITHS WORKSHOP

SMOCK MILL
CL   INDUSTRIAL
BT   WINDMILL <BY FORM>

SMOKE HOUSE
UF   Fish Curing House
      Fish Smoking House
      Kippering Shed
      Smoking House
CL   INDUSTRIAL
BT   ANIMAL PRODUCT SITE
RT   ABATTOIR
      CURING HOUSE
      FISH HOUSE
      FISH WAREHOUSE

SMOKE HOUSE
UF   Fish Curing House
      Fish Smoking House
      Kippering Shed
      Smoking House
CL   INDUSTRIAL
BT   FOOD PRESERVING SITE
RT   ABATTOIR

CURING HOUSE
FISH HOUSE
FISH WAREHOUSE
ICEHOUSE

Smoking House
USE SMOKE HOUSE

SMUGGLERS CACHE
CL COMMERCIAL
RT CACHE

Snack Bar
USE CAFE

SNUFF MILL
CL INDUSTRIAL
BT MILL

SNUFFER
UF Light Snuffer
CL GARDENS, PARKS AND URBAN SPACES
BT STREET FURNITURE
RT GAS LAMP
LAMP POST
LIGHT HOLDER

SOAKING PIT
CL INDUSTRIAL
BT ANIMAL PRODUCT SITE
RT PIT
STEEPING PIT
TANNING PIT
WASHING PIT

SOAP FACTORY
CL INDUSTRIAL
BT ANIMAL PRODUCT SITE
RT ELLING HEARTH
TALLOW FACTORY

SOAP FACTORY
CL INDUSTRIAL
BT CHEMICAL PRODUCT SITE
RT OIL MILL
POTASH KILN
SODA WORKS

SOAP FACTORY
CL INDUSTRIAL
BT FACTORY <BY PRODUCT>

Soccer Stadium
USE STADIUM

SOCIAL CLUB
CL RECREATIONAL
BT CLUB

SOCIAL CLUB
CL INSTITUTIONAL
BT CLUB

SODA KILN
CL INDUSTRIAL
BT CHEMICAL PRODUCTION SITE
RT GLASS WORKS
SODA WORKS

SODA KILN
CL INDUSTRIAL
BT KILN <BY FUNCTION>

SODA WORKS
SN Production of sodium bicarbonate, soda ash or
caustic soda.
CL INDUSTRIAL
BT CHEMICAL PRODUCTION SITE
RT ACID TOWER

BLEACH WORKS
GLASS WORKS
SOAP FACTORY
SODA KILN

Soil Mark
USE SITE
SN Use specific type of site where known.

Solicitors Office
USE LEGAL OFFICE

Song School
USE CHOIR SCHOOL

SORTING OFFICE
CL COMMUNICATIONS
BT POSTAL SYSTEM STRUCTURE
RT OFFICE
POST BOX
POST OFFICE

Sough
USE DRAINAGE LEVEL

Sough Tunnel
USE DRAINAGE LEVEL

Sound Dish
USE LISTENING POST

Sound Mirror
USE LISTENING POST

SOUP KITCHEN
CL HEALTH AND WELFARE

SOUTERRAIN
SN An underground chamber, store room or passage.
CL DOMESTIC
RT FOGOU
HULL
UNDERGROUND STRUCTURE

SPA
UF Spa Building
Spa Well
CL WATER SUPPLY AND DRAINAGE
RT BATHS
HYDROPATHIC INSTITUTE
PUMP ROOMS

SPA
UF Spa Building
Spa Well
CL HEALTH AND WELFARE
RT BATHS
HYDROPATHIC INSTITUTE
MINERAL BATHS
PUMP ROOMS
SPA HOTEL
SPA PAVILION
THERMAL BATHS
WELL

Spa Building
USE SPA

SPA HOTEL
CL COMMERCIAL
BT HOTEL
RT BATHS
SPA
SPA PAVILION

SPA HOTEL
CL HEALTH AND WELFARE
RT BATHS
HYDROPATHIC INSTITUTE

KURSAAL
MINERAL BATHS
PUMP ROOMS
SPA
SPA PAVILION
THERMAL BATHS

SPA HOTEL
CL DOMESTIC
BT HOTEL
RT BATHS
    SPA

SPA PAVILION
CL RECREATIONAL
BT HEALTH ESTABLISHMENT
RT PUMP ROOMS
    SPA
    SPA HOTEL

SPA PAVILION
CL HEALTH AND WELFARE
RT PUMP ROOMS
    SPA HOTEL

Spa Well
    USE SPA

Spade And Shovel Works
    USE EDGE TOOL WORKS

Spade Forge
    USE EDGE TOOL WORKS

Spale Makers Workshop
    USE BASKET MAKERS WORKSHOP

SPECIALIST HOSPITAL
    SN   A hospital providing medical, surgical or
         psychiatric testing and treatment for patients
         with specific illnesses or injuries.
    CL   HEALTH AND WELFARE
    BT   HOSPITAL
    NT   CANCER HOSPITAL
         CHEST HOSPITAL
         CHILDRENS HOSPITAL
         DENTAL HOSPITAL
         EAR HOSPITAL
         EAR NOSE AND THROAT HOSPITAL
         EYE AND EAR HOSPITAL
         EYE HOSPITAL
         FOOT HOSPITAL
         GERIATRIC HOSPITAL
         HEART HOSPITAL
         HOMOEOPATHIC HOSPITAL
         HOSPITAL FOR FISTULA AND RECTAL DISEASES
         HOSPITAL FOR URINARY DISEASES
         INFECTIOUS DISEASES HOSPITAL
         LEPER HOSPITAL
         LOCK HOSPITAL
         MATERNITY HOSPITAL
         MINERAL WATER HOSPITAL
         NEPHROLOGY HOSPITAL
         NERVOUS DISEASES HOSPITAL
         NEUROLOGY HOSPITAL
         ORTHOPAEDIC HOSPITAL
         SEA BATHING HOSPITAL
         SKIN DISEASE HOSPITAL
         WOMEN AND CHILDRENS HOSPITAL
         WOMENS HOSPITAL

SPECTACLE ENCLOSURE
CL UNASSIGNED
BT CURVILINEAR ENCLOSURE

Speech House
    USE COURT HOUSE
         MOOT HALL
    SN   Use both terms.

Spelk Makers Workshop
    USE BASKET MAKERS WORKSHOP

Spelter Factory
    USE ZINC WORKS

Spelter Works
    USE ZINC WORKS

SPHINX
CL GARDENS, PARKS AND URBAN SPACES
BT GARDEN ORNAMENT
RT BUST
    SCULPTURE
    STATUE

Spike
    USE WORKHOUSE

SPINNING MILL
UF Spinning Works
CL INDUSTRIAL
BT TEXTILE MILL
RT DOUBLING MILL
    TWIST MILL

SPINNING MILL
UF Spinning Works
CL INDUSTRIAL
BT TEXTILE SITE <BY PROCESS/PRODUCT>
RT FULLING MILL
    PICKER HOUSE
    SCRIBBLING MILL
    SPINNING SHED
    THROWING MILL
    WEAVING MILL

SPINNING SHED
CL INDUSTRIAL
BT TEXTILE SITE <BY PROCESS/PRODUCT>
RT SHED
    SPINNING MILL
    SPINNING SHOP

SPINNING SHOP
CL INDUSTRIAL
BT TEXTILE SITE <BY PROCESS/PRODUCT>
RT LOOMSHOP
    SPINNING SHED

Spinning Works
    USE SPINNING MILL

Spital
    USE LEPER HOSPITAL

Spittle House
    USE LEPER HOSPITAL

SPLIT LEVEL HOUSE
CL DOMESTIC
BT HOUSE <BY FORM>

SPLIT SHAFT KILN
CL INDUSTRIAL
BT SHAFT KILN
RT CEMENT KILN

SPOIL HEAP
UF Coal Tip
CL INDUSTRIAL
BT MINING INDUSTRY SITE
RT COLLIERY
    MINE
    SLAG HEAP

Spoon Factory
    USE CUTLERY WORKS

SPORTS BUILDING
CL   RECREATIONAL
BT   SPORTS SITE
NT   BOWLING GREEN PAVILION
     CRICKET PAVILION
     CROQUET SHED
     FENCING SCHOOL
     GRANDSTAND
     GYMNASIUM (SPORTS)
     RACECOURSE PAVILION
     RACING STABLE
     SPORTS CENTRE
     SPORTS PAVILION
     TILTYARD TOWER

SPORTS CENTRE
CL   RECREATIONAL
BT   SPORTS BUILDING
RT   SQUASH COURT
     SWIMMING POOL
     TENNIS COURT

SPORTS GROUND
CL   RECREATIONAL
BT   RECREATION GROUND
NT   CRICKET GROUND
     FOOTBALL GROUND

SPORTS PAVILION
UF   Games Pavilion
CL   RECREATIONAL
BT   SPORTS BUILDING
RT   CHANGING ROOMS
     CRICKET GROUND
     GRANDSTAND
     RACECOURSE

SPORTS PAVILION
UF   Games Pavilion
CL   GARDENS, PARKS AND URBAN SPACES
BT   PAVILION
RT   CHANGING ROOMS
     GRANDSTAND
     RACECOURSE

SPORTS SITE
CL   RECREATIONAL
NT   ATHLETICS TRACK
     BOWLING CLUB
     BOWLING GREEN
     BOXING ARENA
     BUTTS
     CHANGING ROOMS
     CROQUET LAWN
     FIRING RANGE
     FIVES COURT
     FOOTBALL PITCH
     FOOTBALL TERRACE
     GOLF CLUB
     GOLF COURSE
     HOCKEY PITCH
     HOPSCOTCH COURT
     NETBALL COURT
     QUINTAIN
     RACE TRACK
     RACECOURSE
     RACING CIRCUIT
     RECREATION GROUND
     RIDING SCHOOL
     ROWING CLUB
     RUGBY PITCH
     SAILING CLUB
     SKATING RINK
     SPORTS BUILDING
     SQUASH COURT
     STADIUM
     SWIMMING POOL
     TENNIS CLUB

     TENNIS COURT
     TILTYARD
     WATER CHUTE

Sports Stadium
USE STADIUM

SPRING
UF   Spring Head
CL   WATER SUPPLY AND DRAINAGE
RT   HOLY WELL

SPRING GARDEN
CL   GARDENS, PARKS AND URBAN SPACES
BT   GARDEN

Spring Head
USE SPRING

SPRING SHOP
CL   INDUSTRIAL
BT   ENGINEERING INDUSTRY SITE
RT   ERECTING SHOP

SPRING SHOP
CL   INDUSTRIAL
BT   FERROUS METAL PRODUCT SITE
RT   SPRING WORKS

SPRING WORKS
CL   INDUSTRIAL
BT   FERROUS METAL PRODUCT SITE
RT   SPRING SHOP

Springfield Style Enclosure
USE ENCLOSED SETTLEMENT

SQUARE
UF   Piazza
CL   GARDENS, PARKS AND URBAN SPACES
BT   URBAN SPACE
NT   PRIVATE SQUARE
     PUBLIC SQUARE
RT   CIRCUS (URBAN)
     CRESCENT

SQUARE BARROW
UF   Square Barrow Cemetery
CL   RELIGIOUS, RITUAL AND FUNERARY
BT   BARROW
RT   CART BURIAL

Square Barrow Cemetery
USE SQUARE BARROW
     BARROW CEMETERY
SN   Use both terms.

SQUARE CAIRN
CL   RELIGIOUS, RITUAL AND FUNERARY
BT   BURIAL CAIRN

SQUARE ENCLOSURE
CL   UNASSIGNED
BT   RECTILINEAR ENCLOSURE

SQUASH COURT
CL   RECREATIONAL
BT   SPORTS SITE
RT   SPORTS CENTRE

SQUATTER SETTLEMENT
CL   DOMESTIC
BT   SETTLEMENT

SQUATTERS COTTAGE
CL   DOMESTIC
BT   HOUSE <BY FUNCTION>

STABLE

UF Brewery Stable
Dockyard Stable
Loose Box
Pit Pony Stable
CL AGRICULTURE AND SUBSISTENCE
BT ANIMAL SHED
RT COACH HOUSE
COACHMANS COTTAGE
GROOMS COTTAGE
MEWS
RIDING SCHOOL
SADDLERY
STABLEHANDS LODGINGS
STALLION HOUSE
TACK ROOM

STABLE
UF Brewery Stable
Dockyard Stable
Loose Box
Pit Pony Stable
CL TRANSPORT
NT COACHING INN STABLE
HACKNEY STABLE
LIVERY STABLE
MULTI STOREY STABLE
RAILWAY STABLE
TRAMWAY STABLE
RT BREWERY
COACH HOUSE
COACHMANS COTTAGE
COUNTRY HOUSE
DOCKYARD
GROOMS COTTAGE
MEWS
RIDING SCHOOL
SADDLERY
TACK ROOM
TRAP HOUSE

STABLEHANDS LODGINGS
CL DOMESTIC
BT LODGINGS
RT GROOMS COTTAGE
MEWS
STABLE

STACK STAND
UF Rick
CL AGRICULTURE AND SUBSISTENCE
RT BARN PLATFORM
FARM
SHIELING

STACK YARD
CL AGRICULTURE AND SUBSISTENCE

STADDLE STONE
UF Straddle Stone
SN Mushroom-shaped stones used as a base to lift off
ground timber-built barns, granaries, etc.
CL AGRICULTURE AND SUBSISTENCE
RT BARN
GRANARY

STADIUM
UF Football Stadium
Rugby Football Stadium
Soccer Stadium
Sports Stadium
CL RECREATIONAL
BT SPORTS SITE
RT CRICKET GROUND
FOOTBALL GROUND
GRANDSTAND

STAINED GLASS WORKSHOP
CL INDUSTRIAL
BT GLASSMAKING SITE

RT GLASS WORKING SITE
GLASS WORKS

STAINED GLASS WORKSHOP
CL INDUSTRIAL
BT CRAFT INDUSTRY SITE
RT GLASS WORKS
STONEMASONS YARD

STAITH
UF Coal Staith
Coal Staithe
Jetty Staith
Staithe
SN A waterside depot for coals brought from the
collieries for shipment, furnished with staging
and chutes for loading vessels.
CL TRANSPORT
BT WATER TRANSPORT SITE
RT CANAL DOCKYARD
CANAL WHARF
COAL DROP
COAL JETTY
COALING CRANE

STAITH
UF Coal Staith
Coal Staithe
Jetty Staith
Staithe
SN A waterside depot for coals brought from the
collieries for shipment, furnished with staging
and chutes for loading vessels.
CL MARITIME
BT LANDING POINT
RT CANAL WHARF
COAL JETTY

Staithe
USE STAITH

STALLION HOUSE
CL AGRICULTURE AND SUBSISTENCE
BT ANIMAL SHED
RT STABLE

STAMPING MILL
UF Knocking Mill
SN Building or structure housing a form of ore
crushing device associated with tin mines.
CL INDUSTRIAL
BT NON FERROUS METAL PROCESSING SITE
RT CRAZING MILL
CRUSHING FLOOR
CRUSHING MILL
STAMPS
TIN MILL

STAMPING MILL
UF Knocking Mill
SN Building or structure housing a form of ore
crushing device associated with tin mines.
CL INDUSTRIAL
BT MILL

STAMPS
UF Drop Forge Stamps
SN Form of ore crushing machinery associated with tin
mines often wooden and water-powered.
CL INDUSTRIAL
BT NON FERROUS METAL PROCESSING SITE
RT BUDDLE
BUDDLE HOUSE
CRUSHING FLOOR
STAMPING MILL
TIN MILL
TIN MINE
TIN WORKS

Stanch

USE STAUNCH

Stand
USE GRANDSTAND

Standing
USE BELVEDERE

Standing Cross
USE CROSS

STANDING STONE
UF   Long Stone
      Megalith
      Menhir
      Monolith
      Orthostat
      Sarsen Stone
CL   RELIGIOUS, RITUAL AND FUNERARY
RT   COVE
      RECUMBENT STONE
      STONE
      STONE ALIGNMENT
      STONE AVENUE
      STONE CIRCLE
      STONE SETTING

Standpipe Tower
USE WATER TOWER

STANNARY COURT
CL   CIVIL
BT   LAW COURT
RT   COINAGE HALL
      TIN MINE

Staple Enclosure
USE GOAL POST ENCLOSURE

STAR FORT
CL   DEFENCE
BT   FORT
RT   ARTILLERY CASTLE
      BASTION TRACE FORT

STARCH MILL
CL   INDUSTRIAL
BT   MILL

State Paper Office
USE RECORD OFFICE

Station Buffet
USE RAILWAY BUFFET

Station Garden
USE GARDEN
      RAILWAY
SN   Use both terms.

Station House
USE LOCK UP

STATION MASTERS HOUSE
CL   DOMESTIC
BT   TRANSPORT WORKERS HOUSE
RT   CROSSING KEEPERS COTTAGE

STATIONAL MONUMENT
CL   RELIGIOUS, RITUAL AND FUNERARY

Statuary
USE STATUE

STATUE
UF   Equestrian Statue
      Statuary
CL   GARDENS, PARKS AND URBAN SPACES
BT   SCULPTURE

RT   BUST
      COLUMN
      HERM
      OBELISK
      QUADRIGA
      SPHINX
      URN

Statue Factory
USE STATUE FOUNDRY

STATUE FOUNDRY
UF   Statue Factory
CL   INDUSTRIAL
BT   CRAFT INDUSTRY SITE
RT   STONEMASONS YARD
      TERRACOTTA WORKS

STAUNCH
UF   Stanch
CL   TRANSPORT
BT   WATER TRANSPORT SITE
RT   FLASH LOCK

Steading
USE FARMSTEAD

Steam Baths
USE TURKISH BATHS

Steam Cooperage
USE COOPERAGE

STEAM CRANE
CL   TRANSPORT
BT   CRANE < BY FUNCTION >

STEAM ENGINE
CL   INDUSTRIAL
BT   ENGINE
RT   ATMOSPHERIC ENGINE HOUSE
      ATMOSPHERIC RAILWAY ENGINE HOUSE
      BLOWING ENGINE HOUSE
      CHIMNEY
      FACTORY
      HAULAGE ENGINE HOUSE
      TEXTILE MILL
      TURBINE HOUSE
      WORKS

STEAM ENGINE
CL   INDUSTRIAL
BT   STEAM POWER PRODUCTION SITE
NT   BEAM ENGINE
      COMPOUND STEAM ENGINE
      HORIZONTAL STEAM ENGINE
      TRACTION STEAM ENGINE
      VERTICAL STEAM ENGINE
RT   BOILER HOUSE
      HELVE HAMMER
      STEAM MILL
      STEAM PLANT
      STEAM PUMP
      STEAM TURBINE
      STEAM WHIM
      STEAM WINDER

STEAM ENGINE HOUSE
CL   INDUSTRIAL
BT   ENGINE HOUSE
NT   BEAM ENGINE HOUSE
RT   ATMOSPHERIC RAILWAY ENGINE HOUSE
      STEAM POWER PRODUCTION SITE

STEAM MILL
CL   INDUSTRIAL
BT   MILL

STEAM MILL

CL INDUSTRIAL
BT STEAM POWER PRODUCTION SITE
RT ROTATIVE BEAM ENGINE
    STEAM ENGINE

STEAM PLANT
CL INDUSTRIAL
BT STEAM POWER PRODUCTION SITE
RT STEAM ENGINE
    SUGAR REFINERY

STEAM PLOUGHED RIG
CL AGRICULTURE AND SUBSISTENCE
BT RIDGE AND FURROW

STEAM POWER PRODUCTION SITE
CL INDUSTRIAL
BT POWER GENERATION SITE
NT BOILER HOUSE
    COMPRESSOR HOUSE
    ECONOMISER HOUSE
    STEAM ENGINE
    STEAM MILL
    STEAM PLANT
    STEAM PUMP
    STEAM TURBINE
    STEAM WHIM
    STEAM WHIM HOUSE
    STEAM WINCH
    STEAM WINDER
    TURBINE HOUSE
RT STEAM ENGINE HOUSE

STEAM PUMP
CL INDUSTRIAL
BT STEAM POWER PRODUCTION SITE
RT BEAM ENGINE
    STEAM ENGINE

STEAM TURBINE
CL INDUSTRIAL
BT TURBINE

STEAM TURBINE
CL INDUSTRIAL
BT STEAM POWER PRODUCTION SITE
RT STEAM ENGINE
    STEAM TURBINE POWER STATION

STEAM TURBINE POWER STATION
CL INDUSTRIAL
BT POWER STATION
RT COOLING TOWER
    GAS FIRED POWER STATION
    OIL FIRED POWER STATION
    STEAM TURBINE
    TURBINE
    TURBINE HOUSE

STEAM WHIM
UF Whimsey
SN A steam-powered machine used for raising ore or
    water from a mine.
CL INDUSTRIAL
BT STEAM POWER PRODUCTION SITE
RT MINE
    ROTATIVE BEAM ENGINE
    STEAM ENGINE
    STEAM WHIM HOUSE
    STEAM WINDER

STEAM WHIM HOUSE
UF Whimsey House
CL INDUSTRIAL
BT STEAM POWER PRODUCTION SITE
RT MINE
    STEAM WHIM

STEAM WINCH

CL INDUSTRIAL
BT STEAM POWER PRODUCTION SITE

STEAM WINDER
SN Steam powered colliery (or other mine) winding
    gear.
CL INDUSTRIAL
BT MINE LIFTING AND WINDING STRUCTURE

STEAM WINDER
SN Steam powered colliery (or other mine) winding
    gear.
CL INDUSTRIAL
BT STEAM POWER PRODUCTION SITE
RT STEAM ENGINE
    STEAM WHIM

Steel Forge
    USE FORGE

Steel House
    USE STEEL WORKS

Steel Mill
    USE STEEL WORKS

Steel Workers Village
    USE WORKERS VILLAGE

STEEL WORKS
UF Steel House
    Steel Mill
CL INDUSTRIAL
BT FERROUS METAL PRODUCT SITE
NT CEMENTATION STEEL WORKS
    CRUCIBLE STEEL WORKS
RT BELLOWS HOUSE
    COKE OVEN
    CUTLERY WORKS
    CUTLERY WORKSHOP
    FOUNDRY
    LIME KILN
    ROLLING MILL
    SHEET METAL WORKS
    SLAG HEAP
    WORKERS VILLAGE

STEELYARD
SN A portable balance or scale suspended off centre
    from above.
CL COMMERCIAL
RT GUILDHALL
    MOOT HALL
    TOLL HOUSE
    TRINITY HOUSE
    WEIGH HOUSE

STEEPING PIT
SN Pit for soaking animal hides as part of the
    tanning process.
CL INDUSTRIAL
BT LEATHER INDUSTRY SITE
RT PIT
    SOAKING PIT
    TANNING PIT
    WASHING PIT

STEEPING TANK
CL INDUSTRIAL
BT ALUM WORKS

STEPPED TERRACE
CL DOMESTIC
BT TERRACE

STEPPING STONES
CL TRANSPORT
BT PEDESTRIAN TRANSPORT SITE
RT FORD

STEPS
UF Grees
      Gryse
CL TRANSPORT
BT PEDESTRIAN TRANSPORT SITE
RT FOOTPATH
      GARDEN STEPS

Stew
  USE FISH POND

STEWARDS HOUSE
CL DOMESTIC
BT HOUSE < BY FUNCTION >

Stews
  USE FISH POND

Stick House
  USE STOREHOUSE

Stiddy
  USE BLACKSMITHS WORKSHOP

STILE
UF Closing Stile
      Shutting Stile
CL TRANSPORT
BT PEDESTRIAN TRANSPORT SITE
RT KISSING GATE

Still
  USE DISTILLERY

STILL HOUSE
CL INDUSTRIAL
BT DISTILLING SITE
RT MASH HOUSE

STILLING HOUSE
CL DOMESTIC
RT BREWHOUSE

Stithy
  USE BLACKSMITHS WORKSHOP

STOCK ENCLOSURE
CL AGRICULTURE AND SUBSISTENCE
RT ENCLOSURE
      POUND

STOCK EXCHANGE
CL COMMERCIAL
BT EXCHANGE

Stock House
  USE ANIMAL SHED

Stock Shed
  USE ANIMAL SHED

STOCKADED ENCLOSURE
SN Rare site type of Neolithic date.
CL RELIGIOUS, RITUAL AND FUNERARY
RT ENCLOSURE

Stockingers Cottage
  USE HOSIERS COTTAGE

STOCKS
CL CIVIL
BT PUNISHMENT PLACE
RT PILLORY
      WHIPPING POST

STONE
SN Use only where stone is natural or where there is
      no indication of function.
CL UNASSIGNED

BT NATURAL FEATURE
RT BOUNDARY STONE
      CARVED STONE
      INSCRIBED STONE
      PLAGUE STONE
      RECUMBENT STONE
      STANDING STONE
      STONE BLOCK

STONE ALIGNMENT
UF Stone Row
SN Single row of stones.
CL RELIGIOUS, RITUAL AND FUNERARY
RT STANDING STONE
      STONE AVENUE
      STONE SETTING

STONE AVENUE
UF Avenue
SN Multiple rows of stones.
CL RELIGIOUS, RITUAL AND FUNERARY
RT STANDING STONE
      STONE ALIGNMENT
      STONE SETTING

STONE AXE FACTORY
UF Axe Factory
CL INDUSTRIAL
BT EXTRACTIVE PIT

STONE AXE FACTORY
UF Axe Factory
CL INDUSTRIAL
BT STONE WORKING SITE

STONE BLOCK
CL UNASSIGNED
RT STONE
      STONE EXTRACTION SITE

STONE BREAKING YARD
SN Associated with workhouses.
CL HEALTH AND WELFARE
NT BUNK
RT WORKHOUSE

STONE CIRCLE
UF Concentric Stone Circle
      Large Irregular Stone Circle
      Large Regular Stone Circle
      Large Stone Circle
      Small Stone Circle
CL RELIGIOUS, RITUAL AND FUNERARY
NT EMBANKED STONE CIRCLE
      FOUR POSTER STONE CIRCLE
      RECUMBENT STONE CIRCLE
RT COVE
      HENGIFORM MONUMENT
      STANDING STONE
      STONE SETTING
      TIMBER CIRCLE

STONE CRUSHING PLANT
CL INDUSTRIAL
BT STONE EXTRACTION SITE

STONE DISPATCH BUILDING
UF Limestone Dispatch Building
CL INDUSTRIAL
BT STONE EXTRACTION SITE

STONE DRESSING FLOOR
CL INDUSTRIAL
BT STONE EXTRACTION SITE

STONE EXTRACTION SITE
SN Includes preparation processes.
CL INDUSTRIAL
BT MINERAL EXTRACTION SITE

NT QUARRY
   QUARRY HOIST
   STONE CRUSHING PLANT
   STONE DISPATCH BUILDING
   STONE DRESSING FLOOR
   STONE GRUBBING SITE
   STONE WORKING SITE
   STONE WORKS
RT DRESSING FLOOR
   DRESSING MILL
   DRESSING SHED
   STONE BLOCK

STONE GRUBBING SITE
SN Small scale extraction and working of surface
   boulders.
CL INDUSTRIAL
BT STONE EXTRACTION SITE

Stone Hut Circle
   USE HUT CIRCLE

Stone Mine
   USE STONE QUARRY

STONE QUARRY
UF Chalk Quarry
   Stone Mine
CL INDUSTRIAL
BT QUARRY
NT GRANITE QUARRY
   GYPSUM QUARRY
   LIMESTONE QUARRY
   MARBLE QUARRY
   SANDSTONE QUARRY
   SHALE QUARRY
   SLATE QUARRY
RT GRINDSTONE

Stone Row
   USE STONE ALIGNMENT

STONE SETTING
CL RELIGIOUS, RITUAL AND FUNERARY
RT COVE
   STANDING STONE
   STONE ALIGNMENT
   STONE AVENUE
   STONE CIRCLE

STONE WORKING SITE
CL INDUSTRIAL
BT STONE EXTRACTION SITE
NT FLINT WORKING SITE
   JET WORKING SITE
   MILLSTONE WORKING SITE
   QUERN WORKING SITE
   SHALE WORKING SITE
   STONE AXE FACTORY
   STONEMASONS YARD

STONE WORKS
UF Marble Works
CL INDUSTRIAL
BT STONE EXTRACTION SITE

STONEMASONS YARD
CL INDUSTRIAL
BT STONE WORKING SITE
RT STAINED GLASS WORKSHOP
   STATUE FOUNDRY

STOP LOCK
CL TRANSPORT
BT LOCK

STORAGE HULK
CL MARITIME
BT HULK

STORAGE PIT
CL AGRICULTURE AND SUBSISTENCE
NT GRAIN STORAGE PIT
RT PIT

Store
   USE STOREHOUSE

Store Building
   USE STOREHOUSE

STOREHOUSE
UF Police Store
   Stick House
   Store
   Store Building
   Tackle House
CL UNASSIGNED
BT BUILDING
RT FERTILISER STOREHOUSE
   NAVAL STOREHOUSE
   RAILWAY STOREHOUSE
   SHED
   SUGAR HOUSE
   WAREHOUSE

STORESHIP
CL MARITIME
BT TRANSPORT CRAFT

Stowce
   USE STOWE

STOWE
UF Stowce
SN A type of windlass for drawing up ore.
CL INDUSTRIAL
BT MINE LIFTING AND WINDING STRUCTURE
RT MINE
   WINDER HOUSE
   WINDLASS

Straddle Stone
   USE STADDLE STONE

Straw Hat Factory
   USE HAT FACTORY

STREAM
CL WATER SUPPLY AND DRAINAGE
BT WATERCOURSE

STREAM WORKS
SN Tin extraction site.
CL INDUSTRIAL
BT NON FERROUS METAL EXTRACTION SITE
RT GOLD MINE
   LEAT

STREAM WORKS
SN Tin extraction site.
CL INDUSTRIAL
BT TIN WORKS

Street
   USE ROAD

Street Arcade
   USE SHOPPING ARCADE

STREET FURNITURE
CL GARDENS, PARKS AND URBAN SPACES
NT BENCH
   BOLLARD
   BOOT SCRAPER
   BUS SHELTER
   CANNON
   CANNON BOLLARD

COAL HOLE COVER
DUTY POST
FIRE HYDRANT
FLAGPOLE
HOARDING
INN SIGN
LAMP BRACKET
LAMP POST
LETTER BOX
LIGHT HOLDER
MILEPOST
MILESTONE
MOUNTING BLOCK
PARKING METER
PEDESTRIAN CROSSING
PLAGUE STONE
POLICE BOX
POLICE TELEPHONE PILLAR
ROAD SIGN
ROADSIDE LIGHTHOUSE
SEDAN CHAIR LIFT
SNUFFER
STREET LAMP
TELEGRAPH POLE
TELEPHONE BOOTH
TELEPHONE BOX
TELEPHONE POLE
TELESCOPE (TERRESTRIAL)
TETHERING POST
TRAFFIC LIGHTS
TRAM SHELTER
TROUGH
WATCHMANS BOX
WAYSIDE PUMP
WEIGHING MACHINE
RT   URBAN SPACE

STREET LAMP
CL   GARDENS, PARKS AND URBAN SPACES
BT   STREET FURNITURE
NT   GAS LAMP

STREET TRAMWAY
CL   TRANSPORT
BT   TRAMWAY

STRICT BAPTIST CHAPEL
CL   RELIGIOUS, RITUAL AND FUNERARY
BT   BAPTIST CHAPEL

String Hearth
USE BLOOMERY

Strip Cultivation
USE OPEN FIELD

STRIP LYNCHET
CL   AGRICULTURE AND SUBSISTENCE
BT   LYNCHET
RT   CULTIVATION TERRACE
     OPEN FIELD
     RIDGE AND FURROW

STRUCTURE
SN   Unknown function use specific type where known.
CL   UNASSIGNED
NT   UNDERGROUND STRUCTURE
RT   BUILDING

Students Hostel
USE HALL OF RESIDENCE

STUDENTS UNION
CL   EDUCATION
RT   POLYTECHNIC
     TRAINING COLLEGE
     UNIVERSITY

Studio

USE FILM STUDIO
     RECORDING STUDIO
     TELEVISION STUDIO
     DANCE STUDIO
SN   Use appropriate term.

STUDIO HOUSE
UF   Artists House
CL   DOMESTIC
BT   HOUSE < BY FORM >

STUDIO THEATRE
UF   Theatre Workshop
CL   RECREATIONAL
BT   THEATRE

Stump
USE TREE STUMP
     BOLLARD
SN   Use appropriate term.

SUB CIRCULAR ENCLOSURE
CL   UNASSIGNED
BT   CURVILINEAR ENCLOSURE

Sub Station
USE ELECTRICITY SUB STATION

SUBDEANERY
CL   DOMESTIC
BT   CLERICAL DWELLING
RT   DEANERY

SUBMARINE
CL   MARITIME
BT   WARSHIP
NT   FLEET SUBMARINE
     HOLLAND SUBMARINE
     MIDGET SUBMARINE
     MINE LAYING SUBMARINE
     SUBMARINE SEAPLANE CARRIER

SUBMARINE FOREST
CL   UNASSIGNED
BT   NATURAL FEATURE

SUBMARINE SEAPLANE CARRIER
CL   MARITIME
BT   SUBMARINE

Subscription Library
USE LENDING LIBRARY

Subscription School
USE VOLUNTARY SCHOOL

SUBWAY
CL   TRANSPORT
BT   PEDESTRIAN TRANSPORT SITE
RT   PEDESTRIAN TUNNEL
     UNDERPASS

SUCTION DREDGER
CL   MARITIME
BT   DREDGER

SUGAR HOUSE
CL   INDUSTRIAL
BT   FOOD PROCESSING SITE
RT   STOREHOUSE
     SUGAR REFINERY

SUGAR REFINERY
CL   INDUSTRIAL
BT   FOOD PROCESSING SITE
RT   CONFECTIONERY WORKS
     STEAM PLANT
     SUGAR HOUSE

SULPHUR STORE

CL INDUSTRIAL
BT EXPLOSIVES SITE

SUMMERHOUSE
UF Casino (Garden)
SN A building in a garden or park designed to provide
a shady retreat from the heat of the sun.
CL GARDENS, PARKS AND URBAN SPACES
BT GARDEN BUILDING

SUNDAY SCHOOL
CL EDUCATION
BT SCHOOL
RT CHURCH

SUNDIAL
CL GARDENS, PARKS AND URBAN SPACES
BT GARDEN ORNAMENT
RT SCRATCH DIAL
SUNSHINE RECORDER

Sunken Featured Building
USE GRUBENHAUS

Sunken Floored Building
USE GRUBENHAUS

SUNKEN GARDEN
CL GARDENS, PARKS AND URBAN SPACES
BT GARDEN

Sunken Wall
USE HA HA

SUNSHINE RECORDER
CL GARDENS, PARKS AND URBAN SPACES
BT GARDEN ORNAMENT
RT SUNDIAL

SUPERMARKET
UF Hypermarket
Superstore
CL COMMERCIAL
BT SHOP
RT SHOPPING CENTRE

SUPERPHOSPHATE FACTORY
CL INDUSTRIAL
BT FACTORY <BY PRODUCT>

SUPERPHOSPHATE FACTORY
CL INDUSTRIAL
BT FERTILISER WORKS

Superstore
USE SUPERMARKET

Surgeons College
USE PROFESSIONAL INSTITUTE

Surgeons Institute
USE PROFESSIONAL INSTITUTE

SURGERY
UF Dental Surgery
Doctors Surgery
Veterinary Surgery
Vets Surgery
CL HEALTH AND WELFARE

SURVEY TOWER
CL TRANSPORT
RT BRIDGE
TOWER

SURVEY VESSEL
CL MARITIME
BT SERVICE CRAFT

Surveyors Office

USE DRAWING OFFICE

SUSPENSION BRIDGE
UF Chain Bridge
CL TRANSPORT
BT BRIDGE <BY FORM>
RT ROAD

Swanneck Crane
USE FAIRBAIRN JIB CRANE

SWANNERY
CL AGRICULTURE AND SUBSISTENCE

SWANNERY POND
CL WATER SUPPLY AND DRAINAGE
BT POND

Swedenborgian Chapel
USE SWEDENBORGIAN CHURCH
CHAPEL
SN Use both terms.

SWEDENBORGIAN CHURCH
UF Swedenborgian Chapel
CL RELIGIOUS, RITUAL AND FUNERARY
BT CHURCH

Swill Makers Workshop
USE BASKET MAKERS WORKSHOP

Swimming Baths
USE BATHS

SWIMMING POOL
CL GARDENS, PARKS AND URBAN SPACES
BT POOL
RT SPORTS CENTRE
WATER CHUTE

SWIMMING POOL
CL RECREATIONAL
BT SPORTS SITE
RT SPORTS CENTRE

Swine Cote
USE PIGSTY

SWING BRIDGE
CL TRANSPORT
BT BRIDGE <BY FORM>
RT ROAD

SWISS COTTAGE
CL GARDENS, PARKS AND URBAN SPACES
BT GARDEN BUILDING

SWISS GARDEN
CL GARDENS, PARKS AND URBAN SPACES
BT GARDEN

SWISS PROTESTANT CHURCH
UF Protestant Church
CL RELIGIOUS, RITUAL AND FUNERARY
BT CHURCH

SWITCH HOUSE
SN Building housing switch gear to control
electricity supply either to the National Grid,
industrial or domestic premises.
CL INDUSTRIAL
BT ELECTRICITY PRODUCTION SITE
RT TRANSFORMER STATION

Sword Cutlers Cottage
USE SMITHS COTTAGE

SWORD FACTORY
CL INDUSTRIAL

BT   FACTORY <BY PRODUCT>

SWORD FACTORY
CL   INDUSTRIAL
BT   FERROUS METAL PRODUCT SITE
RT   TILT HAMMER

Symphony Hall
USE CONCERT HALL

SYNAGOGUE
UF   Jewish Temple
CL   RELIGIOUS, RITUAL AND FUNERARY
BT   PLACE OF WORSHIP
RT   MOSQUE
       TEMPLE

SYNODAL HALL
SN   Used for church government.
CL   RELIGIOUS, RITUAL AND FUNERARY
RT   BISHOPS PALACE
       CHAPTER HOUSE

Synthetic Textile Factory
USE ARTIFICIAL TEXTILE FACTORY

Tabernacle
USE CHAPEL

TABLE TOMB
CL   RELIGIOUS, RITUAL AND FUNERARY
BT   TOMB

TACK ROOM
CL   DOMESTIC
RT   COUNTRY HOUSE
       MEWS
       RIDING SCHOOL
       SADDLERY
       STABLE

Tackle House
USE STOREHOUSE

TAIL RACE
SN   Water channel leading from water wheel.
CL   WATER SUPPLY AND DRAINAGE
BT   MILL RACE
RT   MILL POND
       TUMBLING WEIR
       WATERCOURSE
       WATERMILL

TAIL RACE
SN   Water channel leading from water wheel.
CL   INDUSTRIAL
BT   MILL RACE

Tailoring Factory
USE CLOTHING FACTORY

TAILORS SHOP
CL   COMMERCIAL
BT   SHOP
RT   CLOTHING SHOP
       CLOTHING WORKSHOP
       TAILORS WORKSHOP

TAILORS WORKSHOP
CL   INDUSTRIAL
BT   CLOTHING INDUSTRY SITE
RT   TAILORS SHOP

TAKE AWAY
CL   COMMERCIAL
BT   SHOP
NT   FISH AND CHIP SHOP

TALLOW FACTORY

SN   Where tallow is produced, ie. solid animal fat
       that has been separated by heating, usually for
       making candles.
CL   INDUSTRIAL
BT   FACTORY <BY PRODUCT>

TALLOW FACTORY
SN   Where tallow is produced, ie. solid animal fat
       that has been separated by heating, usually for
       making candles.
CL   INDUSTRIAL
BT   ANIMAL PRODUCT SITE
RT   CANDLE FACTORY
       CURRIERY
       SOAP FACTORY

Tammy Hall
USE CLOTH HALL

Tan Pit
USE TANNING PIT

Tan Yard
USE TANNERY

TANK FURNACE
CL   INDUSTRIAL
BT   REVERBERATORY FURNACE
RT   PLATE GLASS WORKS

TANK TRAP
UF   Anti Tank Block
CL   DEFENCE
RT   BATTERY
       GUN EMPLACEMENT
       PILLBOX

TANKER
CL   MARITIME
BT   CARGO VESSEL

TANNERY
UF   Hide And Skin Works
       Tan Yard
CL   INDUSTRIAL
BT   LEATHER INDUSTRY SITE
RT   ABATTOIR
       ALUM WORKS
       BARK HOUSE
       BARK MILL
       FLEECING SHOP
       GLUE FACTORY
       LEATHER DRYING SHED
       LEATHER FACTORY
       TANNING PIT
       WASHING PIT

TANNING PIT
UF   Tan Pit
CL   INDUSTRIAL
BT   LEATHER INDUSTRY SITE
RT   PIT
       SOAKING PIT
       STEEPING PIT
       TANNERY
       WASHING PIT

TAPE MILL
CL   INDUSTRIAL
BT   TEXTILE PRODUCT SITE

TAPE MILL
CL   INDUSTRIAL
BT   TEXTILE MILL

TAPESTRY MILL
CL   INDUSTRIAL
BT   TEXTILE MILL

TAPESTRY WEAVING WORKSHOP

CL INDUSTRIAL
BT CRAFT INDUSTRY SITE
RT CARPET WEAVERS WORKSHOP

Tar Cellar
USE TAR HOUSE

TAR HOUSE
UF Tar Cellar
CL INDUSTRIAL
BT ROPE MANUFACTURING SITE
RT HATCHELLING HOUSE
ROPEWALK

Tar Tunnel
USE ADIT

TAR WORKS
CL INDUSTRIAL
BT CHEMICAL PRODUCT SITE
RT COKE OVEN
OIL REFINERY

TARGET
UF Firing Target
CL DEFENCE

TARGET CRAFT
CL MARITIME
BT UNMANNED CRAFT

Tarpaulin Drying Shed
USE DRYING HOUSE

Tarred Yarn House
USE YARN HOUSE

Tavern
USE PUBLIC HOUSE

TAXIWAY
CL TRANSPORT
BT AIR TRANSPORT SITE

TEA HOUSE
UF Tearoom Pavilion
CL RECREATIONAL
BT EATING AND DRINKING ESTABLISHMENT
RT BANDSTAND
COUNTRY HOUSE
GARDEN
PUBLIC PARK
REFRESHMENT PAVILION
TEA ROOM

TEA ROOM
CL COMMERCIAL
BT EATING AND DRINKING ESTABLISHMENT
RT REFRESHMENT PAVILION
TEA HOUSE

TEA WAREHOUSE
CL COMMERCIAL
BT WAREHOUSE

TEACHER TRAINING COLLEGE
CL EDUCATION
BT TRAINING COLLEGE

TEACHERS CENTRE
CL EDUCATION

TEACHERS HOUSE
UF School Teachers House
Schoolmasters House
Tutors House
CL DOMESTIC
BT HOUSE <BY FUNCTION>
RT SCHOOL

TEACHING HOSPITAL
CL HEALTH AND WELFARE
BT HOSPITAL

TEAGLE
CL TRANSPORT
BT HOIST

Tearoom Pavilion
USE TEA HOUSE

TEAZLE SHOP
SN Raising the fibres on new woollen cloth by
brushing it with teazle heads.
CL INDUSTRIAL
BT WOOL MANUFACTURING SITE
RT FULLING MILL
HANDLE HOUSE

TECHNICAL COLLEGE
UF Engineering College
CL EDUCATION
BT TRAINING COLLEGE
RT TECHNICAL SCHOOL

TECHNICAL SCHOOL
CL EDUCATION
BT TRAINING SCHOOL
RT TECHNICAL COLLEGE

TECHNOLOGY INSTITUTE
CL EDUCATION
BT INSTITUTE

TECHNOLOGY INSTITUTE
CL INSTITUTIONAL
BT INSTITUTE

Teetotal Public House
USE TEMPERANCE PUBLIC HOUSE

TELECOMMUNICATION BUILDING
UF Post Office Tower
CL COMMUNICATIONS
NT BROADCASTING HOUSE
RADIO STATION
TELEGRAPH OFFICE
TELEGRAPH STATION
TELEPHONE EXCHANGE
TELEPHONE REPEATER STATION

TELECOMMUNICATION STRUCTURE
CL COMMUNICATIONS
NT BROADCASTING CONTROL ROOM
BROADCASTING TRANSMITTER
POLICE BOX
POLICE TELEPHONE PILLAR
RADIO BROADCASTING STUDIO
RADIO STUDIO
RADIO TELESCOPE
SATELLITE DISH
TELEGRAPH POLE
TELEPHONE BOOTH
TELEPHONE BOX
TELEPHONE POLE
TELEVISION STUDIO

TELEGRAPH OFFICE
CL COMMUNICATIONS
BT TELECOMMUNICATION BUILDING
NT CABLE REPEATER OFFICE
RT HOTEL
OFFICE
TELEGRAPH STATION

TELEGRAPH POLE
CL GARDENS, PARKS AND URBAN SPACES
BT STREET FURNITURE

RT TELEPHONE POLE

TELEGRAPH POLE
CL COMMUNICATIONS
BT TELECOMMUNICATION STRUCTURE
RT TELEPHONE POLE

TELEGRAPH SHIP
CL MARITIME
BT COMMUNICATIONS CRAFT
RT TELEGRAPH STATION

TELEGRAPH STATION
UF Telegraph Tower
SN Electrical telegraphy.
CL COMMUNICATIONS
BT TELECOMMUNICATION BUILDING
RT CABLE REPEATER OFFICE
SEMAPHORE STATION
SHUTTER TELEGRAPH STATION
SIGNAL STATION
TELEGRAPH OFFICE
TELEGRAPH SHIP

Telegraph Tower
USE TELEGRAPH STATION

TELEPHONE BOOTH
CL GARDENS, PARKS AND URBAN SPACES
BT STREET FURNITURE
RT TELEPHONE BOX

TELEPHONE BOOTH
CL COMMUNICATIONS
BT TELECOMMUNICATION STRUCTURE

TELEPHONE BOX
UF Telephone Kiosk
CL GARDENS, PARKS AND URBAN SPACES
BT STREET FURNITURE
RT POLICE BOX
POLICE TELEPHONE PILLAR
TELEPHONE BOOTH

TELEPHONE BOX
UF Telephone Kiosk
CL COMMUNICATIONS
BT TELECOMMUNICATION STRUCTURE
RT POLICE BOX
POLICE TELEPHONE PILLAR
TELEPHONE EXCHANGE

TELEPHONE EXCHANGE
CL COMMUNICATIONS
BT TELECOMMUNICATION BUILDING
RT TELEPHONE BOX

Telephone Kiosk
USE TELEPHONE BOX

TELEPHONE POLE
CL GARDENS, PARKS AND URBAN SPACES
BT STREET FURNITURE
RT TELEGRAPH POLE

TELEPHONE POLE
CL COMMUNICATIONS
BT TELECOMMUNICATION STRUCTURE
RT TELEGRAPH POLE

TELEPHONE REPEATER STATION
CL COMMUNICATIONS
BT TELECOMMUNICATION BUILDING

TELESCOPE (CELESTIAL)
CL EDUCATION
BT OBSERVATORY

TELESCOPE (TERRESTRIAL)

CL RECREATIONAL
RT PIER
PIER PAVILION
PLEASURE PIER
PROMENADE

TELESCOPE (TERRESTRIAL)
CL GARDENS, PARKS AND URBAN SPACES
BT STREET FURNITURE

Telescope Building
USE TELESCOPE DOME
OBSERVATORY
SN Use both terms.

TELESCOPE DOME
UF Telescope Building
CL EDUCATION

Television Mast
USE BROADCASTING TRANSMITTER

TELEVISION STUDIO
UF Studio
CL COMMUNICATIONS
BT TELECOMMUNICATION STRUCTURE
RT BROADCASTING HOUSE
FILM STUDIO
RADIO BROADCASTING STUDIO
RECORDING STUDIO

Telling House
USE COUNTING HOUSE

TEMPERANCE HALL
SN Meeting hall of Temperance Society.
CL INSTITUTIONAL
BT MEETING HALL
RT TEMPERANCE HOTEL
TEMPERANCE PUBLIC HOUSE

TEMPERANCE HOTEL
CL COMMERCIAL
BT HOTEL
RT TEMPERANCE HALL
TEMPERANCE PUBLIC HOUSE

TEMPERANCE HOTEL
CL DOMESTIC
BT HOTEL

TEMPERANCE PUBLIC HOUSE
UF Cocoa Tavern
Coffee Palace
Coffee Public House
Coffee Tavern
Teetotal Public House
CL COMMERCIAL
BT EATING AND DRINKING ESTABLISHMENT
RT TEMPERANCE HALL
TEMPERANCE HOTEL

TEMPERATE HOUSE
CL GARDENS, PARKS AND URBAN SPACES
BT GLASSHOUSE

TEMPLARS CAMERA
UF Knights Templars Camera
CL RELIGIOUS, RITUAL AND FUNERARY
BT CAMERA
RT TEMPLARS PRECEPTORY

TEMPLARS CHURCH
UF Knights Templars Church
CL RELIGIOUS, RITUAL AND FUNERARY
BT CHURCH
RT HOSPITALLERS CHURCH
PRECEPTORY

TEMPLARS GRANGE

CL   RELIGIOUS, RITUAL AND FUNERARY
BT   GRANGE

TEMPLARS GRANGE
CL   AGRICULTURE AND SUBSISTENCE
BT   GRANGE

TEMPLARS PRECEPTORY
UF   Knights Templars Preceptory
SN   Includes the mother house styled the Temple, London.
CL   RELIGIOUS, RITUAL AND FUNERARY
BT   PRECEPTORY
RT   HOSPITALLERS PRECEPTORY
      TEMPLARS CAMERA

TEMPLE
SN   Use for places of worship. For later landscape features use, eg. GARDEN TEMPLE.
CL   RELIGIOUS, RITUAL AND FUNERARY
BT   PLACE OF WORSHIP
NT   BUDDHIST TEMPLE
      MITHRAEUM
RT   GARDEN TEMPLE
      IONIC TEMPLE
      MOSQUE
      SHRINE
      SYNAGOGUE

TEMPORARY CAMP
UF   Roman Camp
CL   DEFENCE
NT   MARCHING CAMP
      PRACTICE CAMP
RT   FORT

Tenaille
    USE BASTION OUTWORK

Tenaillon
    USE BASTION OUTWORK

TENANTS HALL
SN   A communal room or building attached to flats.
CL   DOMESTIC
BT   RESIDENTIAL BUILDING
RT   COMMUNITY CENTRE
      FLATS
      LODGING HOUSE
      RECREATIONAL HALL

TENDER
CL   MARITIME
BT   SERVICE CRAFT

TENEMENT
SN   A parcel of land.
CL   DOMESTIC
BT   SETTLEMENT
RT   DWELLING

TENEMENT BLOCK
SN   Use for speculatively built 19th century "model dwellings", rather than those built by a philanthropic society.
CL   DOMESTIC
BT   MULTIPLE DWELLING
RT   FLATS
      LODGING HOUSE
      MAISONETTE
      TENEMENT HOUSE

TENEMENT FACTORY
UF   Flatted Factory
CL   INDUSTRIAL
BT   FACTORY <BY FORM>

TENEMENT HOUSE
SN   Originally built as a family house. Converted into flats during the 19th or 20th century.
CL   DOMESTIC

BT   MULTIPLE DWELLING
RT   FLATS
      LODGING HOUSE
      TENEMENT BLOCK

TENNIS CLUB
CL   RECREATIONAL
BT   SPORTS SITE
RT   TENNIS COURT

TENNIS COURT
CL   RECREATIONAL
BT   SPORTS SITE
RT   SPORTS CENTRE
      TENNIS CLUB

TENTER GROUND
SN   Field or area of ground where washed new cloth is stretched out to dry.
CL   INDUSTRIAL
BT   TEXTILE SITE <BY PROCESS/PRODUCT>
RT   BLEACHFIELD
      CLOTH DRY HOUSE
      FLAX BEATING STONE
      FLAX DRY HOUSE
      FULLING STOCKS
      PRESS SHOP
      TENTER POST
      WEAVERS COTTAGE
      WOOL DRY HOUSE
      WOOL WALL
      YARN DRY HOUSE

Tenter House
    USE CLOTH DRY HOUSE

TENTER POST
SN   Posts with hooks attached to allow drying new cloth to be stretched out between them.
CL   INDUSTRIAL
BT   TEXTILE SITE <BY PROCESS/PRODUCT>
RT   FLAX BEATING STONE
      TENTER GROUND
      WEAVERS COTTAGE
      WOOL WALL

Term
    USE HERM

Terminal Building
    USE BUILDING
         SEA TERMINAL
    SN   Use both terms.

Terminal Figure
    USE HERM

Terminal Reave
    USE REAVE

TERMINUS STONE
SN   To mark the end of a turnpike road.
CL   TRANSPORT
BT   ROAD TRANSPORT SITE
RT   MILEPOST
      MILESTONE
      ROADSIDE LIGHTHOUSE
      TOLL ROAD

TERRACE
CL   DOMESTIC
BT   MULTIPLE DWELLING
NT   BACK TO BACK TERRACE
      BACK TO EARTH TERRACE
      BLIND BACK TERRACE
      STEPPED TERRACE
      WEALDEN TERRACE
RT   CRESCENT
      ROW

TERRACED HOUSE

TERRACED GARDEN
CL   GARDENS, PARKS AND URBAN SPACES
BT   GARDEN
RT   GARDEN TERRACE
     TERRACED LAWN
     TERRACED WALK

TERRACED GROUND
CL   UNASSIGNED
RT   CULTIVATION TERRACE

TERRACED HOUSE
CL   DOMESTIC
BT   HOUSE <BY FORM>
NT   BACK TO BACK HOUSE
     BACK TO EARTH HOUSE
     BLIND BACK HOUSE
RT   CLUSTER HOUSE
     TERRACE

TERRACED LAWN
CL   GARDENS, PARKS AND URBAN SPACES
BT   LAWN
RT   TERRACED GARDEN

TERRACED WALK
CL   GARDENS, PARKS AND URBAN SPACES
BT   WALK
RT   TERRACED GARDEN

TERRACOTTA WORKS
CL   INDUSTRIAL
BT   MINERAL PRODUCT SITE
RT   BRICKWORKS
     POTTERY WORKS
     STATUE FOUNDRY
     TILE WORKS

Territorial Oppidum
USE OPPIDUM

TESSELATED FLOOR
CL   UNASSIGNED
BT   FLOOR

TEST HOUSE
UF   Airport Test House
CL   TRANSPORT
BT   AIR TRANSPORT SITE
RT   CONTROL TOWER
     FOG DISPERSAL PLANT

Tester Tomb
USE CANOPIED TOMB

TESTING RANGE
CL   INDUSTRIAL
BT   EXPLOSIVES SITE
RT   NITROGLYCERINE WORKS

Testing Works
USE PROVING HOUSE

TETHERING POST
UF   Tethering Ring
CL   GARDENS, PARKS AND URBAN SPACES
BT   STREET FURNITURE
RT   MOUNTING BLOCK

TETHERING POST
UF   Tethering Ring
CL   TRANSPORT
BT   ROAD TRANSPORT SITE
RT   MOUNTING BLOCK

Tethering Ring
USE TETHERING POST

TEXTILE CONDITIONING HOUSE
SN   Building for testing the condition and strength of
     textiles.
CL   INDUSTRIAL
BT   TEXTILE FINISHING SITE

Textile Factory
USE TEXTILE MILL

TEXTILE FINISHING SITE
SN   Includes bleaching, dressing, dyeing and printing.
CL   INDUSTRIAL
BT   TEXTILE SITE <BY PROCESS/PRODUCT>
NT   BEETLING MILL
     BLEACHERY
     BLEACHFIELD
     CALENDER MILL
     CALICO PRINTING WORKS
     CLOTH DRESSING MILL
     CLOTH DRY HOUSE
     COLOUR HOUSE
     COLOUR MILL
     DYE HOUSE
     DYE WORKS
     FINISHING HOUSE
     FINISHING WORKS
     PRINTING SHOP
     TEXTILE CONDITIONING HOUSE
     TOPSHOP
     WASHING SHOP
     WEAVERS WORKSHOP
     WEAVING MILL
     WEAVING SHED
RT   TEXTILE MILL

TEXTILE INDUSTRY SITE
SN   Includes all stages of production process of
     textiles, eg. wool, cotton, linen, etc, and
     textile products.
CL   INDUSTRIAL
NT   TEXTILE MILL
     TEXTILE PRODUCT SITE
     TEXTILE SITE <BY PROCESS/PRODUCT>

TEXTILE MILL
UF   Fabric Mill
     Textile Factory
CL   INDUSTRIAL
BT   TEXTILE INDUSTRY SITE
NT   ALPACA MILL
     ARTIFICIAL TEXTILE FACTORY
     BEETLING MILL
     BLANKET MILL
     BOMBASINE MILL
     CALENDER MILL
     CALICO MILL
     CALICO PRINTING WORKS
     CANVAS WORKS
     CARDING MILL
     CARPET MILL
     CLOTH DRESSING MILL
     COMBING WORKS
     COTTON MILL
     CREPE MILL
     DOUBLING MILL
     DRABBET FACTORY
     FELT MILL
     FINISHING WORKS
     FLAX DRESSING SHOP
     FLAX MILL
     FLOCK MILL
     FULLING MILL
     HEMP MILL
     JUTE MILL
     LACE FACTORY
     LINEN MILL
     MUNGO MILL
     RAG GRINDING MILL

SAILMAKING WORKS
SCRIBBLING MILL
SCUTCHING MILL
SERGE FACTORY
SHODDY MILL
SILK MILL
SPINNING MILL
TAPE MILL
TAPESTRY MILL
THROWING MILL
TWEED MILL
TWIST MILL
WEAVING MILL
WOOLLEN MILL
WORSTED MILL
YARN MILL
RT CLOTHING FACTORY
     DRYING HOUSE
     FIREPROOF BUILDING
     FIREPROOF FACTORY
     HANDLE HOUSE
     HOSIERY FACTORY
     MANAGERS HOUSE
     NORTH LIGHT FACTORY
     TEXTILE FINISHING SITE
     TEXTILE PRODUCT SITE
     TEXTILE SITE <BY PROCESS/PRODUCT>
     TEXTILE WAREHOUSE
     TUMBLING WEIR
     WEIR
     WORKERS VILLAGE

TEXTILE MILL
UF Fabric Mill
     Textile Factory
CL INDUSTRIAL
BT MILL
RT CHIMNEY
     ECONOMISER HOUSE
     ENGINE HOUSE
     STEAM ENGINE

TEXTILE PRODUCT SITE
SN Sites making products other than cloth.
CL INDUSTRIAL
BT TEXTILE INDUSTRY SITE
NT BLANKET MILL
     CARPET MANUFACTURING SITE
     FLOCK MILL
     LACE MANUFACTURING SITE
     RIBBON FACTORY
     ROPE MANUFACTURING SITE
     SAILMAKING WORKS
     TAPE MILL
RT CLOTHING INDUSTRY SITE
     TEXTILE MILL

TEXTILE SITE <BY PROCESS/PRODUCT>
SN Site for the production of textiles.
CL INDUSTRIAL
BT TEXTILE INDUSTRY SITE
NT CARDING MILL
     COMBING SHED
     COMBING WORKS
     COTTON MANUFACTURING SITE
     CREPE MILL
     DOUBLING MILL
     LINEN OR FLAX MANUFACTURING SITE
     LOOMSHOP
     PICKER HOUSE
     PRESS SHOP
     RAG GRINDING SHED
     RAG MILL
     SCRIBBLING MILL
     SILK MANUFACTURING SITE
     SPINNING MILL
     SPINNING SHED
     SPINNING SHOP
     TENTER GROUND

TENTER POST
TEXTILE FINISHING SITE
TWIST MILL
WILLEY SHED
WOOL MANUFACTURING SITE
YARN DRY HOUSE
YARN MILL
RT TEXTILE MILL

TEXTILE WAREHOUSE
UF Shoddy Warehouse
CL COMMERCIAL
BT WAREHOUSE
RT MUNGO MILL
     TEXTILE MILL

Theater
USE THEATRE

THEATRE
UF Playhouse
     Theater
CL RECREATIONAL
BT MUSIC AND DANCE VENUE
NT OPEN AIR THEATRE
     STUDIO THEATRE
RT AMPHITHEATRE
     ARTS CENTRE
     CINEMA
     CONCERT HALL
     KIOSK
     MUSIC HALL
     OPEN AIR THEATRE
     OPERA HOUSE
     PLAIN AN GWARRY

Theatre Pay Box
USE KIOSK

Theatre School
USE DRAMA SCHOOL

Theatre Workshop
USE STUDIO THEATRE

Theatrical School
USE DRAMA SCHOOL

THEOLOGICAL COLLEGE
UF Anglican College
     Baptist College
     Catholic College
     Congregational College
     Jesuit College
     Methodist College
     Roman Catholic College
CL EDUCATION
BT TRAINING COLLEGE
RT DIVINITY SCHOOL

THEOSOPHICAL COLLEGE
CL EDUCATION
BT TRAINING COLLEGE

Therm
USE HERM

THERMAL BATHS
CL HEALTH AND WELFARE
BT BATHS
RT MINERAL BATHS
     PUMP ROOMS
     SPA
     SPA HOTEL

THIMBLE MILL
CL INDUSTRIAL
BT MILL

THIRD CLASS CRUISER

CL   MARITIME
BT   CRUISER

THIRD RATE SHIP OF THE LINE
  CL   MARITIME
  BT   SHIP OF THE LINE

THIRD RATE SHIP OF THE LINE
  CL   MARITIME
  BT   CAPITAL WARSHIP

THRESHING BARN
  CL   AGRICULTURE AND SUBSISTENCE
  BT   BARN
  RT   HORSE ENGINE HOUSE
       MIXING HOUSE BARN
       THRESHING MILL

THRESHING FLOOR
  SN   Use where there is no building.
  CL   AGRICULTURE AND SUBSISTENCE
  RT   BARN
       THRESHING MILL

THRESHING MILL
  CL   INDUSTRIAL
  BT   MILL

THRESHING MILL
  CL   AGRICULTURE AND SUBSISTENCE
  BT   FARM BUILDING
  RT   THRESHING BARN
       THRESHING FLOOR

THROUGH BY LIGHT
  CL   DOMESTIC
  BT   BACK TO BACK HOUSE
  RT   CLUSTER HOUSE

THROWING HOUSE
  CL   INDUSTRIAL
  BT   POTTERY MANUFACTURING SITE
  RT   HANDLING HOUSE
       MARL PIT
       MUG HOUSE
       POT HOUSE
       POTTERY WORKSHOP

THROWING MILL
  SN   Twisting and doubling of thread to provide
       material strong enough to be spun and woven.
  CL   INDUSTRIAL
  BT   TEXTILE MILL
  RT   FLAX MILL
       SPINNING MILL

THROWING MILL
  SN   Twisting and doubling of thread to provide
       material strong enough to be spun and woven.
  CL   INDUSTRIAL
  BT   SILK MANUFACTURING SITE

Ticket Office
  USE BOOKING OFFICE

TIDAL BASIN
  CL   MARITIME
  BT   WATER REGULATION INSTALLATION

Tidal Canal Lock
  USE TIDAL LOCK

TIDAL DOOR
  CL   TRANSPORT
  BT   WATER TRANSPORT SITE
  RT   TIDAL LOCK
       TIDE GAUGE

TIDAL DOOR

CL   MARITIME
BT   WATER REGULATION INSTALLATION

TIDAL LOCK
  UF   Tidal Canal Lock
  CL   TRANSPORT
  BT   LOCK
  RT   TIDAL DOOR
       TIDE GAUGE

TIDAL LOCK
  UF   Tidal Canal Lock
  CL   MARITIME
  BT   WATER REGULATION INSTALLATION

TIDE GAUGE
  CL   TRANSPORT
  BT   WATER TRANSPORT SITE
  RT   GAUGE HOUSE
       TIDAL DOOR
       TIDAL LOCK

TIDE GAUGE
  CL   MARITIME
  BT   WATER REGULATION INSTALLATION

Tide Gauge House
  USE GAUGE HOUSE

TIDEMILL
  UF   Sea Mill
  SN   Watermill, powered by retaining seawater at high
       tide and then releasing it at low tide via the
       water wheel.
  CL   INDUSTRIAL
  BT   MILL
  RT   CORN MILL
       TUMBLING WEIR
       WATERWHEEL

TIDEMILL
  UF   Sea Mill
  SN   Watermill, powered by retaining seawater at high
       tide and then releasing it at low tide via the
       water wheel.
  CL   INDUSTRIAL
  BT   WATER POWER PRODUCTION SITE
  RT   CORN MILL
       TUMBLING WEIR
       WATERWHEEL

Tied Cottage
  USE ESTATE COTTAGE

TILE BURIAL
  CL   RELIGIOUS, RITUAL AND FUNERARY
  BT   BURIAL

TILE KILN
  CL   INDUSTRIAL
  BT   KILN <BY FUNCTION>
  RT   BOTTLE KILN
       CLAMP KILN

TILE WORKS
  UF   Tilery
  CL   INDUSTRIAL
  BT   BRICK AND TILEMAKING SITE
  RT   CLAY MILL
       TERRACOTTA WORKS

TILEMAKING WORKSHOP
  CL   INDUSTRIAL
  BT   BRICK AND TILEMAKING SITE
  RT   MOULDMAKERS SHOP
       POTTERY WORKSHOP

TILEMAKING WORKSHOP
  CL   INDUSTRIAL

BT   CRAFT INDUSTRY SITE

Tilery
   USE TILE WORKS

TILT HAMMER
   SN Early form of powered hammer, usually wooden, used
        primarily in the iron industry.
   CL   INDUSTRIAL
   BT   HAMMER
   RT   CHAIN SHOP
        FINERY
        SWORD FACTORY

TILTYARD
   UF   Catadrome
   CL   RECREATIONAL
   BT   SPORTS SITE
   RT   QUINTAIN
        ROYAL PALACE
        TILTYARD TOWER

TILTYARD TOWER
   CL   RECREATIONAL
   BT   SPORTS BUILDING
   RT   QUINTAIN
        ROYAL PALACE
        TILTYARD

TIMBER CIRCLE
   UF   Wooden Circle
   CL   RELIGIOUS, RITUAL AND FUNERARY
   RT   HENGIFORM MONUMENT
        PIT CIRCLE
        STONE CIRCLE

Timber Drying Shed
   USE TIMBER SEASONING SHED

TIMBER FRAMED HOUSE
   CL   DOMESTIC
   BT   HOUSE <BY FORM>
   NT   BOX FRAME HOUSE
        CRUCK HOUSE
        JETTIED HOUSE
        WEALDEN HOUSE

TIMBER MARKET
   CL   COMMERCIAL
   BT   MARKET

TIMBER POND
   SN Pond for storing cut lengths of timber to prevent
        them becoming seasoned.
   CL   WATER SUPPLY AND DRAINAGE
   BT   POND

TIMBER PROCESSING SITE
   CL   INDUSTRIAL
   BT   WOOD PROCESSING SITE
   NT   LUMBER MILL
        PLANING MILL
        SAW MILL
        SAW PIT
        TIMBER SEASONING SHED
        TIMBER YARD

TIMBER PRODUCT SITE
   SN Manufacture of timber products.
   CL   INDUSTRIAL
   BT   WOOD PROCESSING SITE
   NT   BLOCK MILL
        BOBBIN MILL
        CARPENTERS WORKSHOP
        CLOG MILL
        COOPERAGE
        FURNITURE FACTORY
        JOINERS SHOP
        MATCH FACTORY

        SHIPYARD
        WHEEL MOULD
        WHEELWRIGHTS WORKSHOP
   RT   TURNING SHOP

TIMBER SEASONING SHED
   UF   Timber Drying Shed
   CL   INDUSTRIAL
   BT   TIMBER PROCESSING SITE
   RT   BLOCK MILL
        COOPERAGE
        SHED
        TIMBER YARD
        WOOD DRYING KILN
        WOOD SHED

Timber Shed
   USE WOOD SHED

TIMBER YARD
   UF   Balk Yard
   CL   INDUSTRIAL
   BT   TIMBER PROCESSING SITE
   RT   BUILDERS YARD
        TIMBER SEASONING SHED

Time Office
   USE TIMEKEEPERS OFFICE

TIMEBALL TOWER
   SN A structure for visually communicating the exact
        time to ships in anchorage. A ball slides down a
        mast at the top of the tower, usually at noon or
        one o'clock exactly.
   CL   COMMUNICATIONS
   BT   SIGNAL TOWER
   RT   BEACON
        LIGHTHOUSE

TIMEBALL TOWER
   SN A structure for visually communicating the exact
        time to ships in anchorage. A ball slides down a
        mast at the top of the tower, usually at noon or
        one o'clock exactly.
   CL   MARITIME
   BT   NAVIGATION AID

TIMEKEEPERS OFFICE
   UF   Time Office
   CL   COMMERCIAL
   BT   COMMERCIAL OFFICE
   RT   COUNTING HOUSE
        FACTORY
        MILL
        OFFICE
        PAY OFFICE

TIN MILL
   SN Unspecified type used for crazing, stamping or
        smelting ("blowing") of tin ore.
   CL   INDUSTRIAL
   BT   NON FERROUS METAL PROCESSING SITE
   RT   CRAZING MILL
        STAMPING MILL
        STAMPS
        TIN MINE
        WASHING FLOOR

TIN MILL
   SN Unspecified type used for crazing, stamping or
        smelting ("blowing") of tin ore.
   CL   INDUSTRIAL
   BT   MILL

TIN MINE
   SN Use with other metals extracted and MINE where
        necessary, eg. COPPER MINE.
   CL   INDUSTRIAL
   BT   MINE

RT   COINAGE HALL
       COPPER MINE
       CRAZING MILL
       MANGANESE MINE
       STAMPS
       STANNARY COURT
       TIN MILL
       TIN WORKS
       TINNERS CACHE
       TINNERS HUT
       TUNGSTEN MINE

Tin Plating Works
   USE PLATING WORKS

Tin Workers Cottage
   USE WORKERS COTTAGE

Tin Working Site
   USE TIN WORKS

TIN WORKS
   UF   Open Cast Tin Workings
         Tin Working Site
   CL   INDUSTRIAL
   BT   NON FERROUS METAL PROCESSING SITE
   NT   STREAM WORKS
   RT   BLOWING HOUSE
         CRAZING MILL
         PLATING WORKS
         TIN MINE
         TINNERS HUT

TIN WORKS
   UF   Open Cast Tin Workings
         Tin Working Site
   CL   INDUSTRIAL
   BT   NON FERROUS METAL PRODUCT SITE
   RT   STAMPS
         TINNERS HUT

TINNERS CACHE
   CL   INDUSTRIAL
   BT   NON FERROUS METAL PROCESSING SITE
   RT   CACHE
         TIN MINE

TINNERS HUT
   CL   INDUSTRIAL
   BT   NON FERROUS METAL PROCESSING SITE
   RT   TIN MINE
         TIN WORKS

Tinworkers Cottage
   USE WORKERS COTTAGE

Tippler
   USE COAL TIPPLER

Tironensian Abbey
   USE ABBEY
        TIRONIAN MONASTERY
   SN   Use both terms.

Tironian Abbey
   USE ABBEY
        TIRONIAN MONASTERY
   SN   Use both terms.

TIRONIAN ALIEN CELL
   UF   Tironian Alien Priory Cell
         Tironian Cell
   CL   RELIGIOUS, RITUAL AND FUNERARY
   BT   ALIEN CELL
   RT   TIRONIAN MONASTERY

Tironian Alien Priory
   USE TIRONIAN MONASTERY
        ALIEN PRIORY

   SN   Use both terms.

Tironian Alien Priory Cell
   USE TIRONIAN ALIEN CELL

Tironian Cell
   USE TIRONIAN ALIEN CELL

TIRONIAN GRANGE
   CL   RELIGIOUS, RITUAL AND FUNERARY
   BT   GRANGE

TIRONIAN GRANGE
   CL   AGRICULTURE AND SUBSISTENCE
   BT   GRANGE

TIRONIAN MONASTERY
   UF   Tironensian Abbey
         Tironian Abbey
         Tironian Alien Priory
         Tironian Priory
   SN   Abbeys and Priories of monks of Tiron.
   CL   RELIGIOUS, RITUAL AND FUNERARY
   BT   MONASTERY
   RT   TIRONIAN ALIEN CELL

Tironian Priory
   USE TIRONIAN MONASTERY
        PRIORY
   SN   Use both terms.

TITHE BARN
   CL   AGRICULTURE AND SUBSISTENCE
   BT   BARN
   RT   GRANGE BARN

TOBACCO FACTORY
   UF   Cigarette Factory
   CL   INDUSTRIAL
   BT   FACTORY <BY PRODUCT>

TOBACCO WAREHOUSE
   CL   COMMERCIAL
   BT   WAREHOUSE

TOBACCONISTS SHOP
   CL   COMMERCIAL
   BT   SHOP

TOFT
   CL   DOMESTIC
   BT   HOUSE <BY FORM>
   RT   CROFT
         FARM
         HOUSE PLATFORM
         MESSUAGE
         SMALLHOLDING

TOILET
   UF   Cludgie
         Garderobe
         Gong
         Jakes
         Jube
         Lavatory
   CL   WATER SUPPLY AND DRAINAGE
   RT   LATRINE
         PUBLIC CONVENIENCE

Toll Bar Cottage
   USE TOLL HOUSE

TOLL BOARD
   UF   Toll Sign
   CL   TRANSPORT
   BT   ROAD TRANSPORT SITE
   RT   TOLL GATE
         TOLL HOUSE
         TOLLBOOTH

TOLL BOUNDARY MARKER
- UF   Turnpike Boundary Marker
- CL   TRANSPORT
- BT   ROAD TRANSPORT SITE
- RT   BOUNDARY MARKER
         COAL TAX POST
         TOLL ROAD

TOLL BRIDGE
- UF   Turnpike Bridge
- CL   TRANSPORT
- BT   BRIDGE <BY FUNCTION>
- RT   TOLL GATE
         TOLL HOUSE
         TOLL ROAD
         TOLLBOOTH

TOLL BRIDGE
- UF   Turnpike Bridge
- CL   TRANSPORT
- BT   ROAD TRANSPORT SITE
- RT   TOLL GATE
         TOLL ROAD

TOLL GATE
- UF   Turnpike Gate
- CL   TRANSPORT
- BT   ROAD TRANSPORT SITE
- RT   GATE
         TOLL BOARD
         TOLL BRIDGE
         TOLL HOUSE
         TOLL ROAD
         TOLLBOOTH

TOLL HOUSE
- UF   Canal Toll House
         Canal Tollhouse
         Toll Bar Cottage
         Tollhouse
         Turnpike House
- CL   DOMESTIC
- BT   TRANSPORT WORKERS HOUSE
- RT   STEELYARD
         TOLL BOARD
         TOLL BRIDGE
         TOLL GATE
         TOLL ROAD
         TOLLBOOTH
         WEIGH HOUSE

TOLL HOUSE
- UF   Canal Toll House
         Canal Tollhouse
         Toll Bar Cottage
         Tollhouse
         Turnpike House
- CL   TRANSPORT
- BT   ROAD TRANSPORT SITE
- RT   STEELYARD
         TOLL BOARD
         TOLL BRIDGE
         TOLL GATE
         TOLL ROAD
         TOLLBOOTH
         WEIGH HOUSE

TOLL ROAD
- UF   Turnpike Road
- CL   TRANSPORT
- BT   ROAD
- RT   TERMINUS STONE
         TOLL BOUNDARY MARKER
         TOLL BRIDGE
         TOLL GATE
         TOLL HOUSE
         TOLLBOOTH

Toll Sign
USE TOLL BOARD

TOLLBOOTH
- CL   TRANSPORT
- BT   ROAD TRANSPORT SITE
- RT   TOLL BOARD
         TOLL BRIDGE
         TOLL GATE
         TOLL HOUSE
         TOLL ROAD

Tollhouse
USE TOLL HOUSE

Tolstoyan Community Village
USE UTOPIAN COMMUNITY VILLAGE

TOMB
- UF   Pedestal Monument
         Pedestal Tomb
         Raised Slab
- CL   RELIGIOUS, RITUAL AND FUNERARY
- BT   FUNERARY SITE
- NT   ALTAR TOMB
         CANOPIED TOMB
         CHEST TOMB
         TABLE TOMB
         TOMBSTONE
- RT   CENOTAPH
         CHURCHYARD
         MAUSOLEUM
         WAR MEMORIAL

Tomb Chest
USE CHEST TOMB

TOMBSTONE
- CL   RELIGIOUS, RITUAL AND FUNERARY
- BT   TOMB
- RT   CHURCHYARD
         SARCOPHAGUS

Toot
USE MOUND

Topiary
USE TOPIARY GARDEN

TOPIARY AVENUE
- CL   GARDENS, PARKS AND URBAN SPACES
- RT   TOPIARY GARDEN

TOPIARY GARDEN
- UF   Topiary
- CL   GARDENS, PARKS AND URBAN SPACES
- BT   GARDEN
- RT   TOPIARY AVENUE

TOPSHOP
- UF   Attic Workshop
- SN   Attic workshop for textile manufacture, usually weaving.
- CL   INDUSTRIAL
- BT   CRAFT INDUSTRY SITE
- RT   FRAMEWORK KNITTERS COTTAGE
         HOSIERY WORKSHOP
         LACE DRYING HOUSE
         LOOMSHOP
         WEAVERS COTTAGE

TOPSHOP
- UF   Attic Workshop
- SN   Attic workshop for textile manufacture, usually weaving.
- CL   INDUSTRIAL
- BT   TEXTILE FINISHING SITE
- RT   FRAMEWORK KNITTERS COTTAGE
         HOSIERY WORKSHOP
         LACE DRYING HOUSE

LOOMSHOP
WEAVERS COTTAGE

TOR CAIRN
    CL   RELIGIOUS, RITUAL AND FUNERARY
    BT   BURIAL CAIRN

TORPEDO BOAT CARRIER
    CL   MARITIME
    BT   MINOR WARSHIP

Tour En Bec
    USE BASTION

TOW PATH
    CL   TRANSPORT
    BT   WATER TRANSPORT SITE
    RT   CANAL
          FOOTPATH

Towbridge
    USE TOWING PATH BRIDGE

TOWER
    UF   Dock Tower
    SN   Use specific type where known.
    CL   UNASSIGNED
    BT   BUILDING
    NT   CLOCK TOWER
    RT   ANGLE TOWER
          BELL TOWER
          BELVEDERE
          BOOM TOWER
          HYDRAULIC ACCUMULATOR TOWER
          MARTELLO TOWER
          PELE TOWER
          PROSPECT TOWER
          SHOT TOWER
          SIGNAL TOWER
          SURVEY TOWER
          TURRET
          WATCH TOWER
          WATER TOWER

TOWER BLOCK
    UF   High Rise Block
    CL   UNASSIGNED
    BT   BUILDING

TOWER HOUSE
    UF   Vicars Pele
    CL   DOMESTIC
    BT   FORTIFIED HOUSE
    RT   BARMKIN

TOWER HOUSE
    UF   Vicars Pele
    CL   DEFENCE
    BT   FORTIFIED HOUSE
    RT   BARMKIN

TOWER KEEP
    UF   Tower Keep Castle
    CL   DEFENCE
    BT   KEEP

TOWER KEEP
    UF   Tower Keep Castle
    CL   DOMESTIC
    BT   KEEP

Tower Keep Castle
    USE TOWER KEEP

TOWER MILL
    CL   INDUSTRIAL
    BT   WINDMILL <BY FORM>

TOWING PATH BRIDGE
    UF   Towbridge
    CL   TRANSPORT
    BT   BRIDGE <BY FUNCTION>
    RT   CANAL BRIDGE
          ROVING BRIDGE

TOWING PATH BRIDGE
    UF   Towbridge
    CL   TRANSPORT
    BT   WATER TRANSPORT SITE
    RT   CANAL BRIDGE
          ROVING BRIDGE

TOWN
    UF   Planned Town
    CL   DOMESTIC
    BT   SETTLEMENT
    NT   CIVITAS CAPITAL
          COLONIA
          MUNICIPIUM
    RT   BURH
          TOWN CROSS
          TOWN DEFENCES

TOWN
    UF   Planned Town
    CL   CIVIL
    NT   CIVITAS CAPITAL
          COLONIA
          MUNICIPIUM
    RT   BURH
          TOWN CROSS
          TOWN DEFENCES

Town Cellars
    USE CELLAR

TOWN CROSS
    UF   City Cross
    CL   RELIGIOUS, RITUAL AND FUNERARY
    BT   CROSS
    RT   MARKET CROSS
          TOWN

TOWN DEFENCES
    UF   City Defences
    CL   DEFENCE
    NT   TOWN GATE
          TOWN WALL
    RT   BARBICAN
          BASTION
          FORTRESS
          MILITARY CANAL
          SCONCE
          TOWN
          WALL

TOWN GATE
    UF   Bar
          Bar Gate
          City Gate
          Town Gatehouse
    CL   DEFENCE
    BT   TOWN DEFENCES
    RT   GATE
          GATEHOUSE
          POSTERN
          TOWN WALL
          WATER GATE

Town Gatehouse
    USE TOWN GATE

TOWN HALL
    UF   Borough Hall
          City Hall
          Civic Hall
          Vestry Hall
    CL   CIVIL

BT   MEETING HALL
RT   CHURCH HOUSE
      CIVIC CENTRE
      COUNTY HALL
      GUILDHALL
      LOCAL GOVERNMENT OFFICE
      MARKET HOUSE
      MARRIAGE FEAST HOUSE

TOWN HOUSE
UF   Town Mansion
CL   DOMESTIC
BT   HOUSE <BY FORM>
RT   COUNTRY HOUSE
      GREAT HOUSE
      MANOR HOUSE
      PALACE
      ROYAL PALACE

Town Mansion
USE TOWN HOUSE

TOWN WALL
UF   City Wall
CL   DEFENCE
BT   TOWN DEFENCES
RT   TOWN GATE
      WALL

TOY FACTORY
CL   INDUSTRIAL
BT   FACTORY <BY PRODUCT>

TRACKWAY
UF   Brushwood Trackway
      Corduroy Road
      Saltway
CL   TRANSPORT
BT   ROAD
NT   BRIDLEWAY

Trackway Field System
USE FIELD SYSTEM

Traction Engine Works
USE ENGINEERING WORKS

TRACTION STEAM ENGINE
SN   Small mobile steam engine.
CL   INDUSTRIAL
BT   STEAM ENGINE

TRADE SCHOOL
CL   EDUCATION
BT   TRAINING SCHOOL

TRADES UNION BUILDING
CL   INSTITUTIONAL
RT   TRADES UNION HALL

TRADES UNION HALL
UF   Coalminers Union Hall
      Miners Hall
      Miners Union Hall
CL   INSTITUTIONAL
BT   MEETING HALL
RT   TRADES UNION BUILDING

Trading Estate
USE INDUSTRIAL ESTATE

TRAFFIC LIGHTS
CL   GARDENS, PARKS AND URBAN SPACES
BT   STREET FURNITURE
RT   SIGNAL BOX

TRAFFIC LIGHTS
CL   COMMUNICATIONS
BT   SIGNALLING STRUCTURE

RT   SIGNAL BOX

TRAIN SHED
CL   TRANSPORT
BT   RAILWAY TRANSPORT SITE
RT   SHED

TRAINING CENTRE
CL   EDUCATION

TRAINING COLLEGE
UF   College
      College Library
CL   EDUCATION
NT   AGRICULTURAL COLLEGE
      COMMERCIAL COLLEGE
      FURTHER EDUCATION COLLEGE
      HORTICULTURAL COLLEGE
      LADIES COLLEGE
      MEDICAL COLLEGE
      MILITARY COLLEGE
      NAVAL COLLEGE
      PEOPLES COLLEGE
      TEACHER TRAINING COLLEGE
      TECHNICAL COLLEGE
      THEOLOGICAL COLLEGE
      THEOSOPHICAL COLLEGE
      VILLAGE COLLEGE
      WORKING MENS COLLEGE
RT   FACULTY BUILDING
      POLYTECHNIC
      STUDENTS UNION
      UNIVERSITY

TRAINING SCHOOL
SN   For specialist skills.
CL   EDUCATION
BT   SCHOOL
NT   ARCHITECTURE SCHOOL
      ART SCHOOL
      ARTILLERY SCHOOL
      BALLET SCHOOL
      CHOIR SCHOOL
      COMMERCIAL TRAVELLERS SCHOOL
      DENTAL SCHOOL
      DIVINITY SCHOOL
      DOMESTIC SCIENCE SCHOOL
      DRAMA SCHOOL
      EXAMINATION SCHOOL
      FENCING SCHOOL
      INDUSTRIAL SCHOOL
      MUSIC SCHOOL
      PHILOLOGICAL SCHOOL
      RIDING SCHOOL
      TECHNICAL SCHOOL
      TRADE SCHOOL

TRAINING SHIP
CL   MARITIME
BT   MARITIME CRAFT
NT   CADET TRAINING SHIP

TRAM DEPOT
UF   Tram Shed
      Tramshed
CL   TRANSPORT
BT   TRAMWAY TRANSPORT SITE
RT   TRAM TRANSFORMER STATION
      TRAMWAY STABLE

Tram Shed
USE TRAM DEPOT

TRAM SHELTER
CL   TRANSPORT
BT   TRAMWAY TRANSPORT SITE
RT   BUS SHELTER

TRAM SHELTER

CL GARDENS, PARKS AND URBAN SPACES
BT STREET FURNITURE
RT BUS SHELTER

TRAM TRANSFORMER STATION
SN Building housing transformers to convert AC electricity supply to DC supply for use by tramcars.
CL INDUSTRIAL
BT TRANSFORMER STATION
RT TRAM DEPOT

TRAM TRANSFORMER STATION
SN Building housing transformers to convert AC electricity supply to DC supply for use by tramcars.
CL TRANSPORT
BT TRAMWAY TRANSPORT SITE

Tram Tunnel
USE TRAMWAY TUNNEL

Tramp Ward
USE CASUAL WARD BLOCK

Tramshed
USE TRAM DEPOT

TRAMWAY
CL TRANSPORT
BT TRAMWAY TRANSPORT SITE
NT PLATEWAY
STREET TRAMWAY
WAGONWAY
RT TRAMWAY BRIDGE
TRAMWAY TUNNEL

TRAMWAY BRIDGE
CL TRANSPORT
BT BRIDGE <BY FUNCTION>
RT TRAMWAY
TRAMWAY EMBANKMENT

TRAMWAY BRIDGE
CL TRANSPORT
BT TRAMWAY TRANSPORT SITE
RT TRAMWAY EMBANKMENT

TRAMWAY EMBANKMENT
CL TRANSPORT
BT TRAMWAY TRANSPORT SITE
RT TRAMWAY BRIDGE

TRAMWAY REVERSING TRIANGLE
CL TRANSPORT
BT TRAMWAY TRANSPORT SITE

TRAMWAY STABLE
CL TRANSPORT
BT STABLE
RT TRAM DEPOT

TRAMWAY STABLE
CL TRANSPORT
BT TRAMWAY TRANSPORT SITE

TRAMWAY TRANSPORT SITE
CL TRANSPORT
BT ROAD TRANSPORT SITE
NT TRAM DEPOT
TRAM SHELTER
TRAM TRANSFORMER STATION
TRAMWAY
TRAMWAY BRIDGE
TRAMWAY EMBANKMENT
TRAMWAY REVERSING TRIANGLE
TRAMWAY STABLE
TRAMWAY TUNNEL
TRAMWAY TUNNEL PORTAL

TRAMWAY TUNNEL
UF Tram Tunnel
CL TRANSPORT
BT TRANSPORT TUNNEL
RT RAILWAY TUNNEL
TRAMWAY
TUNNEL

TRAMWAY TUNNEL
UF Tram Tunnel
CL TRANSPORT
BT TRAMWAY TRANSPORT SITE
RT TRAMWAY TUNNEL PORTAL

Tramway Tunnel Entrance
USE TRAMWAY TUNNEL PORTAL

TRAMWAY TUNNEL PORTAL
UF Tramway Tunnel Entrance
CL TRANSPORT
BT TUNNEL PORTAL
RT PORTAL
TRAMWAY TUNNEL

TRAMWAY TUNNEL PORTAL
UF Tramway Tunnel Entrance
CL TRANSPORT
BT TRAMWAY TRANSPORT SITE

TRANSEPTED GALLERY GRAVE
CL RELIGIOUS, RITUAL AND FUNERARY
BT GALLERY GRAVE

TRANSFORMER BOX
CL INDUSTRIAL
BT ELECTRICITY PRODUCTION SITE

TRANSFORMER STATION
CL INDUSTRIAL
BT ELECTRICITY PRODUCTION SITE
NT TRAM TRANSFORMER STATION
RT ELECTRICITY SUB STATION
SWITCH HOUSE

TRANSHUMANCE HUT
CL DOMESTIC
BT HUT
RT SHEPHERDS HUT
SHIELING

TRANSIT SHED
CL TRANSPORT
BT RAILWAY TRANSPORT SITE
RT BONDED WAREHOUSE
SHED

TRANSMISSION RODS
UF Rodway
SN The line of a flat rod system transmitting power from an engine or waterwheel.
CL INDUSTRIAL
BT POWER GENERATION SITE

TRANSPORT
SN This is the top term for the class. See TRANSPORT Class List for narrow terms.

TRANSPORT CRAFT
CL MARITIME
BT MARITIME CRAFT
NT CARGO VESSEL
CEREMONIAL CRAFT
PASSENGER VESSEL
STORESHIP
TROOP SHIP

Transport Office
USE LOCAL GOVERNMENT OFFICE

TRANSPORT TUNNEL
    CL   TRANSPORT
    NT   CANAL TUNNEL
          HORSE TUNNEL
          PEDESTRIAN TUNNEL
          RAILWAY TUNNEL
          ROAD TUNNEL
          TRAMWAY TUNNEL
          UNDERGROUND RAILWAY TUNNEL
    RT   TUNNEL

TRANSPORT WORKERS HOUSE
    CL   DOMESTIC
    BT   HOUSE <BY FUNCTION>
    NT   BRIDGE KEEPERS COTTAGE
          CANAL WORKERS COTTAGE
          COACHMANS COTTAGE
          CROSSING KEEPERS COTTAGE
          FERRYKEEPERS COTTAGE
          INCLINE KEEPERS COTTAGE
          LENGTHMANS COTTAGE
          LOCK KEEPERS COTTAGE
          RAILWAY WORKERS COTTAGE
          RAILWAY WORKERS HOUSE
          STATION MASTERS HOUSE
          TOLL HOUSE
          WHARFINGERS COTTAGE
    RT   GAUGE HOUSE

TRANSPORTER BRIDGE
    CL   TRANSPORT
    BT   BRIDGE <BY FORM>

TRANSPORTER BRIDGE
    CL   TRANSPORT
    BT   ROAD TRANSPORT SITE

TRANSVERSE ARCH KILN
    CL   INDUSTRIAL
    BT   KILN <BY FORM>

TRAP HOUSE
    UF   Wainhouse
    CL   TRANSPORT
    BT   ROAD TRANSPORT SITE
    RT   CARRIAGE HOUSE
          COACH HOUSE
          STABLE

TRAPEZOIDAL ENCLOSURE
    CL   UNASSIGNED
    BT   RECTILINEAR ENCLOSURE

TRAVELLING CRANE
    CL   TRANSPORT
    BT   CRANE <BY FORM>
    NT   TRAVELLING OVERHEAD CRANE
          TRAVELLING ROOF CRANE

TRAVELLING OVERHEAD CRANE
    SN   Crane suspended from running rails in the roof of
          an engineering workshop or similar establishment.
    CL   TRANSPORT
    BT   TRAVELLING CRANE
    RT   ENGINEERING INDUSTRY SITE

TRAVELLING ROOF CRANE
    CL   TRANSPORT
    BT   ROOF CRANE

TRAVELLING ROOF CRANE
    CL   TRANSPORT
    BT   TRAVELLING CRANE

TRAVERSER
    CL   TRANSPORT
    BT   RAILWAY TRANSPORT SITE
    RT   RAILWAY TURNTABLE

TRAWLER
    CL   MARITIME
    BT   NET FISHING VESSEL

TREADMILL
    CL   INDUSTRIAL
    BT   ANIMAL POWER SITE
    NT   PRISON TREADMILL
    RT   TREADWHEEL

TREADWHEEL
    CL   INDUSTRIAL
    BT   ANIMAL POWER SITE
    RT   CRANEWHEEL
          TREADMILL
          TREADWHEEL CRANE

TREADWHEEL CRANE
    CL   TRANSPORT
    BT   CRANE <BY FORM>
    RT   CRANEWHEEL
          TREADWHEEL

TREASURERS HOUSE
    CL   DOMESTIC
    BT   HOUSE <BY FUNCTION>
    RT   CATHEDRAL
          CLERGY HOUSE

Treasurers Office
    USE LOCAL GOVERNMENT OFFICE

Treasury
    USE GOVERNMENT OFFICE

Treasury Office
    USE GOVERNMENT OFFICE

TREE
    SN   Natural feature with no historic association (see
          NAMED TREE).
    CL   UNASSIGNED
    BT   NATURAL FEATURE
    RT   NAMED TREE
          TREE HOLE
          TREE STUMP

TREE AVENUE
    UF   Avenue
    CL   GARDENS, PARKS AND URBAN SPACES

Tree Circle
    USE TREE RING

TREE ENCLOSURE RING
    UF   Tree Ring Enclosure
    CL   GARDENS, PARKS AND URBAN SPACES
    RT   ENCLOSURE
          TREE RING
          WOODLAND

TREE HOLE
    CL   UNASSIGNED
    BT   NATURAL FEATURE
    RT   TREE

TREE HOUSE
    SN   Ornamental garden building constructed within the
          branches of trees.
    CL   GARDENS, PARKS AND URBAN SPACES
    BT   GARDEN BUILDING

TREE MOUND
    CL   GARDENS, PARKS AND URBAN SPACES
    RT   MOUND
          WOODLAND

TREE RING

302

UF   Tree Circle
SN   Trees planted in an ornamental circle. For
     earthwork surrounding trees use TREE ENCLOSURE
     RING.
CL   GARDENS, PARKS AND URBAN SPACES
RT   TREE ENCLOSURE RING
     WOODLAND

Tree Ring Enclosure
USE TREE ENCLOSURE RING

TREE STUMP
UF   Stump
CL   UNASSIGNED
BT   NATURAL FEATURE
RT   TREE

TREE TRUNK COFFIN
CL   RELIGIOUS, RITUAL AND FUNERARY
BT   COFFIN

TRELLIS
CL   GARDENS, PARKS AND URBAN SPACES
NT   BERCEAU
RT   ARBOUR
     PERGOLA

TRENCH
UF   Entrenchment
CL   DEFENCE
NT   SLIT TRENCH
RT   BLOCKHOUSE
     BREASTWORK

Tribunal
USE COURT HOUSE

TRICK FOUNTAIN
UF   Automata
SN   An automata or water device which surprises the
     unwary onlooker with water. A feature of 16th and
     17th century gardens.
CL   GARDENS, PARKS AND URBAN SPACES
BT   FOUNTAIN

TRICK FOUNTAIN
UF   Automata
SN   An automata or water device which surprises the
     unwary onlooker with water. A feature of 16th and
     17th century gardens.
CL   WATER SUPPLY AND DRAINAGE
BT   FOUNTAIN

TRINITARIAN MONASTERY
UF   Trinitarian Priory
SN   Priories or houses of Trinitarian brethren also
     named Maturins.
CL   RELIGIOUS, RITUAL AND FUNERARY
BT   MONASTERY

Trinitarian Priory
USE TRINITARIAN MONASTERY
     PRIORY
SN   Use both terms.

TRINITY HOUSE
CL   MARITIME
RT   CUSTOM HOUSE
     GUILDHALL
     STEELYARD

TRINITY HOUSE
CL   CIVIL
RT   CUSTOM HOUSE
     GUILDHALL
     STEELYARD

TRIUMPHAL ARCH
CL   COMMEMORATIVE

BT   COMMEMORATIVE MONUMENT
RT   ARCH

Trolleybus Depot
USE BUS DEPOT

TROOP SHIP
CL   MARITIME
BT   TRANSPORT CRAFT

Tropical Diseases Hospital
USE INFECTIOUS DISEASES HOSPITAL

Tropical House
USE PALM HOUSE

TROUGH
UF   Drinking Trough
CL   GARDENS, PARKS AND URBAN SPACES
BT   STREET FURNITURE
NT   DOG TROUGH
     HORSE TROUGH

TROUGH
UF   Drinking Trough
CL   AGRICULTURE AND SUBSISTENCE
NT   CATTLE TROUGH
     HORSE TROUGH

TROUGH
UF   Drinking Trough
CL   WATER SUPPLY AND DRAINAGE
NT   CATTLE TROUGH
     DOG TROUGH
     HORSE TROUGH

Trout Farm
USE FISH FARM

TUBE MILL
CL   INDUSTRIAL
BT   MILL
RT   BLOWING HOUSE
     BRASS WORKS

TUBE MILL
CL   INDUSTRIAL
BT   FERROUS METAL PRODUCT SITE
RT   ROLLING MILL

Tube Station
USE UNDERGROUND RAILWAY STATION

Tube Tunnel
USE UNDERGROUND RAILWAY TUNNEL

TUBERCULOSIS CHALET
CL   HEALTH AND WELFARE
RT   SANATORIUM

Tuberculosis Hospital
USE SANATORIUM

Tuck Mill
USE FULLING MILL

Tucking Mill
USE FULLING MILL

TUDOR GARDEN
SN   A 19th century Tudor revival garden.
CL   GARDENS, PARKS AND URBAN SPACES
BT   GARDEN

TUG
CL   MARITIME
BT   SERVICE CRAFT
NT   FIRE FIGHTING TUG
     RESCUE TUG

SALVAGE TUG

TUMBLING WEIR
- CL INDUSTRIAL
- BT WEIR
- RT FORGE
  HEAD RACE
  MILL RACE
  TAIL RACE
  TEXTILE MILL
  TIDEMILL
  WATERMILL

TUMBLING WEIR
- CL TRANSPORT
- BT WEIR
- RT FORGE
  HEAD RACE
  MILL RACE
  TAIL RACE
  TEXTILE MILL
  TIDEMILL
  WATERMILL

Tump
USE MOUND

Tumulus
USE BARROW

Tun Hall
USE VAT HALL

Tun Room
USE VAT HALL

TUNGSTEN MINE
- SN Use with other mineral ores extracted and MINE,
  eg. TIN MINE.
- CL INDUSTRIAL
- BT NON FERROUS METAL EXTRACTION SITE
- RT TIN MINE

TUNGSTEN MINE
- SN Use with other mineral ores extracted and MINE,
  eg. TIN MINE.
- CL INDUSTRIAL
- BT MINE
- RT TIN MINE

TUNNEL
- SN Use specific type where known.
- CL UNASSIGNED
- RT ADIT
  CANAL TUNNEL
  HORSE TUNNEL
  PEDESTRIAN TUNNEL
  RAILWAY TUNNEL
  ROAD TUNNEL
  SHAFT
  TRAMWAY TUNNEL
  TRANSPORT TUNNEL
  TUNNEL PORTAL
  UNDERGROUND RAILWAY TUNNEL
  UNDERGROUND STRUCTURE
  WATER TUNNEL

TUNNEL ARBOUR
- CL GARDENS, PARKS AND URBAN SPACES
- BT ARBOUR

TUNNEL CHAMBER
- CL UNASSIGNED
- RT ADIT
  MINE SHAFT
  VENTILATION SHAFT

TUNNEL KILN
- CL INDUSTRIAL

- BT KILN <BY FORM>
- RT CHIMNEY
  DOWNDRAUGHT KILN
  POTTERY KILN

TUNNEL PORTAL
- CL TRANSPORT
- NT CANAL TUNNEL PORTAL
  RAILWAY TUNNEL PORTAL
  ROAD TUNNEL PORTAL
  TRAMWAY TUNNEL PORTAL
- RT PORTAL
  TUNNEL

Turbary Site
USE PEAT CUTTING

TURBINE
- CL INDUSTRIAL
- BT ENGINE
- NT GAS TURBINE
  STEAM TURBINE
  WATER TURBINE
- RT HYDROELECTRIC POWER STATION
  POWER STATION
  STEAM TURBINE POWER STATION

TURBINE HOUSE
- CL INDUSTRIAL
- BT ENGINE HOUSE
- RT STEAM ENGINE
  STEAM TURBINE POWER STATION

TURBINE HOUSE
- CL INDUSTRIAL
- BT STEAM POWER PRODUCTION SITE

TURBINE MILL
- CL INDUSTRIAL
- BT WATER POWER PRODUCTION SITE
- RT PUMP HOUSE
  WATER TURBINE
  WATERMILL

Turf Accountants
USE BETTING OFFICE

Turf House
USE FUEL STORE

TURF MAZE
- CL RELIGIOUS, RITUAL AND FUNERARY
- BT MAZE

TURF MAZE
- CL GARDENS, PARKS AND URBAN SPACES
- BT MAZE

TURF STACK
- CL AGRICULTURE AND SUBSISTENCE
- RT PEAT STAND

TURFED SEAT
- CL GARDENS, PARKS AND URBAN SPACES
- BT GARDEN SEAT

TURFED STEPS
- CL GARDENS, PARKS AND URBAN SPACES
- BT GARDEN STEPS

TURKISH BATHS
- UF Steam Baths
- CL HEALTH AND WELFARE
- BT BATHS

TURNING SHOP
- SN For completing the shape of a product or part by
  turning on a lathe or wheel.
- CL INDUSTRIAL

BT ENGINEERING INDUSTRY SITE
RT AIRCRAFT ENGINE FACTORY
    ENGINEERING WORKSHOP
    FITTERS WORKSHOP
    HEAVY ENGINEERING SITE
    MACHINE SHOP
    POTTERY MANUFACTURING SITE
    RAILWAY ENGINEERING SITE
    TIMBER PRODUCT SITE

Turnpike Boundary Marker
    USE TOLL BOUNDARY MARKER

Turnpike Bridge
    USE TOLL BRIDGE

Turnpike Gate
    USE TOLL GATE

Turnpike House
    USE TOLL HOUSE

Turnpike Road
    USE TOLL ROAD

Turntable
    USE RAILWAY TURNTABLE

TURRET
    SN Roman.
    CL DEFENCE
    BT FRONTIER DEFENCE
    RT TOWER

Tutors House
    USE TEACHERS HOUSE

Tutors Lodgings
    USE COLLEGE LODGINGS

TWEED MILL
    CL INDUSTRIAL
    BT TEXTILE MILL
    RT WEAVING MILL

TWEED MILL
    CL INDUSTRIAL
    BT WOOL MANUFACTURING SITE
    RT WEAVERS COTTAGE
    WOOL WALL

Twine Works
    USE ROPERY

TWIST MILL
    CL INDUSTRIAL
    BT TEXTILE MILL

TWIST MILL
    CL INDUSTRIAL
    BT TEXTILE SITE <BY PROCESS/PRODUCT>
    RT DOUBLING MILL
    SPINNING MILL
    WEAVING MILL
    YARN MILL

Tyre Factory
    USE RUBBER WORKS

UMBER WORKINGS
    CL INDUSTRIAL
    BT MINERAL EXTRACTION SITE
    RT MANGANESE MINE
    OCHRE PIT

UNASSIGNED
    SN This is the top term for the class. See UNASSIGNED
    Class List for narrow terms.

UNASSIGNED CRAFT

CL MARITIME
BT MARITIME CRAFT
NT CANOE
    CORACLE
    CRAFT
    LOGBOAT
    RAFT

Unclassified Site
    USE SITE

UNDERCROFT
    SN Use wider site type where known.
    CL UNASSIGNED

UNDERGROUND CAR PARK
    CL TRANSPORT
    BT CAR PARK

UNDERGROUND MILITARY HEADQUARTERS
    UF Bunker
    CL DEFENCE
    RT AIR RAID SHELTER
    NUCLEAR BUNKER
    PILLBOX

UNDERGROUND RAILWAY
    CL TRANSPORT
    BT RAILWAY

UNDERGROUND RAILWAY STATION
    UF Tube Station
    Underground Station
    CL TRANSPORT
    BT RAILWAY STATION

UNDERGROUND RAILWAY TUNNEL
    UF Tube Tunnel
    CL TRANSPORT
    BT RAILWAY TUNNEL
    RT TUNNEL
    VENTILATION SHAFT

UNDERGROUND RAILWAY TUNNEL
    UF Tube Tunnel
    CL TRANSPORT
    BT TRANSPORT TUNNEL
    RT TUNNEL

Underground Station
    USE UNDERGROUND RAILWAY STATION

UNDERGROUND STRUCTURE
    CL UNASSIGNED
    BT STRUCTURE
    RT ADIT
    AIR RAID SHELTER
    DRAIN
    FOGOU
    HULL
    NUCLEAR BUNKER
    SEWER
    SHAFT
    SOUTERRAIN
    TUNNEL
    WELL

UNDERPASS
    CL TRANSPORT
    BT ROAD TRANSPORT SITE
    RT FLYOVER
    PEDESTRIAN TUNNEL
    ROAD
    ROAD BRIDGE
    ROAD TUNNEL
    SUBWAY

Undershot Waterwheel
    USE UNDERSHOT WHEEL

UNDERSHOT WHEEL
  UF   Undershot Waterwheel
  CL   INDUSTRIAL
  BT   WATERWHEEL <BY FORM>

Unenclosed Cremation Cemetery
  USE CREMATION CEMETERY

UNENCLOSED HUT CIRCLE SETTLEMENT
  UF   Unenclosed Stone Hut Circle Settlement
  CL   DOMESTIC
  BT   HUT CIRCLE SETTLEMENT

UNENCLOSED HUT CIRCLE SETTLEMENT
  UF   Unenclosed Stone Hut Circle Settlement
  CL   DOMESTIC
  BT   UNENCLOSED SETTLEMENT

UNENCLOSED OPPIDUM
  CL   DOMESTIC
  BT   OPPIDUM

UNENCLOSED OPPIDUM
  CL   CIVIL
  BT   OPPIDUM

UNENCLOSED OPPIDUM
  CL   DOMESTIC
  BT   UNENCLOSED SETTLEMENT

UNENCLOSED PLATFORM SETTLEMENT
  CL   DOMESTIC
  BT   PLATFORM SETTLEMENT

UNENCLOSED PLATFORM SETTLEMENT
  CL   DOMESTIC
  BT   UNENCLOSED SETTLEMENT

UNENCLOSED SETTLEMENT
  UF   Open Settlement
  SN   Use specific type where known.
  CL   DOMESTIC
  BT   SETTLEMENT
  NT   LAKE VILLAGE
       UNENCLOSED HUT CIRCLE SETTLEMENT
       UNENCLOSED OPPIDUM
       UNENCLOSED PLATFORM SETTLEMENT

Unenclosed Stone Hut Circle Settlement
  USE UNENCLOSED HUT CIRCLE SETTLEMENT

Unenclosed Urnfield
  USE URNFIELD

Union House
  USE WORKHOUSE

UNION ROOM
  SN   Area in a brewery used for the production of beer
       by the Burton Union method.
  CL   INDUSTRIAL
  BT   BREWING AND MALTING SITE

UNITARIAN CHAPEL
  UF   Unitarian Church
       Unitarian Meeting House
  CL   RELIGIOUS, RITUAL AND FUNERARY
  BT   NONCONFORMIST CHAPEL

Unitarian Church
  USE UNITARIAN CHAPEL

Unitarian Meeting House
  USE UNITARIAN CHAPEL

UNITED REFORMED CHURCH
  CL   RELIGIOUS, RITUAL AND FUNERARY
  BT   CHURCH

UNIVALLATE HILLFORT
  UF   Large Univallate Hillfort
       Slight Univallate Hillfort
  CL   DOMESTIC
  BT   HILLFORT

UNIVALLATE HILLFORT
  UF   Large Univallate Hillfort
       Slight Univallate Hillfort
  CL   DEFENCE
  BT   HILLFORT

UNIVERSITY
  UF   University Chapel
       University Church
       University Library
  CL   EDUCATION
  RT   FACULTY BUILDING
       GRADUATE HOUSE
       HALL OF RESIDENCE
       POLYTECHNIC
       STUDENTS UNION
       TRAINING COLLEGE
       UNIVERSITY ADMINISTRATION OFFICE
       UNIVERSITY COLLEGE

UNIVERSITY ADMINISTRATION OFFICE
  UF   Convocation House
       Senate House
       University Office
  CL   EDUCATION
  RT   OFFICE
       UNIVERSITY

University Chapel
  USE UNIVERSITY
       CHAPEL
  SN   Use both terms.

University Church
  USE UNIVERSITY
       CHURCH
  SN   Use both terms.

UNIVERSITY COLLEGE
  UF   College
       College Library
  CL   EDUCATION
  RT   UNIVERSITY

University Library
  USE LIBRARY
       UNIVERSITY
  SN   Use both terms.

University Office
  USE UNIVERSITY ADMINISTRATION OFFICE

UNMANNED CRAFT
  CL   MARITIME
  BT   MARITIME CRAFT
  NT   BLOCK SHIP
       BOOM DEFENCE
       PONTOON BRIDGE
       PONTOON PIER
       REFUGE BUOY
       TARGET CRAFT

UPDRAUGHT KILN
  CL   INDUSTRIAL
  BT   KILN <BY FORM>
  RT   BOTTLE KILN
       DOWNDRAUGHT KILN
       SCOTCH KILN

Upper Floor Hall House
  USE FIRST FLOOR HALL HOUSE

Urban District Office

USE LOCAL GOVERNMENT OFFICE

URBAN SPACE
- CL GARDENS, PARKS AND URBAN SPACES
- NT CIRCUS (URBAN)
  MARKET PLACE
  PEDESTRIAN PRECINCT
  ROND POINT
  SHOPPING PRECINCT
  SQUARE
- RT ROAD TRANSPORT SITE
  STREET FURNITURE

Urinal
USE PUBLIC CONVENIENCE

URN
- CL GARDENS, PARKS AND URBAN SPACES
- BT GARDEN ORNAMENT
- RT CINERARY URN
  COLUMN
  OBELISK
  STATUE
  VASE

Urned Cremation
USE CINERARY URN

URNFIELD
- UF Unenclosed Urnfield
- CL RELIGIOUS, RITUAL AND FUNERARY
- BT CREMATION CEMETERY
- NT ENCLOSED URNFIELD
- RT CINERARY URN

UTOPIAN COMMUNITY VILLAGE
- UF Tolstoyan Community Village
- CL DOMESTIC
- BT VILLAGE
- RT CHARTIST LAND COLONY

UTOPIAN COMMUNITY VILLAGE
- UF Tolstoyan Community Village
- CL DOMESTIC
- BT MODEL SETTLEMENT
- RT CHARTIST LAND COLONY

VACCARY
- CL AGRICULTURE AND SUBSISTENCE
- RT BANK BARN
  CATTLE SHELTER
  COMBINATION BARN
  COW HOUSE
  FIELD BARN
  LAITHE
  LINHAY

VALLUM
- CL DEFENCE
- BT FRONTIER DEFENCE

VALVE TOWER
- CL WATER SUPPLY AND DRAINAGE

Variety Theatre
USE MUSIC HALL

VASE
- CL GARDENS, PARKS AND URBAN SPACES
- BT GARDEN ORNAMENT
- RT URN

VAT HALL
- UF Brewery Vat Hall
  Tun Hall
  Tun Room
  Vat House
  Vinegar Vat Hall
- CL INDUSTRIAL

- BT BREWING AND MALTING SITE

Vat House
USE VAT HALL

VAULT
- SN Use wider site type where known.
- CL UNASSIGNED

VEGETABLE GARDEN
- CL GARDENS, PARKS AND URBAN SPACES
- BT GARDEN
- RT ALLOTMENT

VEHICLE ENGINEERING SITE
- SN Excludes railway vehicles. See also RAILWAY
  ENGINEERING SITE.
- CL INDUSTRIAL
- BT ENGINEERING INDUSTRY SITE
- NT AIRCRAFT ENGINEERING SITE
  BICYCLE FACTORY
  MOTOR VEHICLE ENGINEERING SITE
- RT AGRICULTURAL ENGINEERING WORKS
  ASSEMBLY PLANT

Vehicle Repair Shop
USE GARAGE

Vehicle Repair Workshop
USE GARAGE

Vehicle Showroom
USE MOTOR VEHICLE SHOWROOM

Velvet Cutters Workshop
USE CLOTH CUTTERS WORKSHOP

VENEREAL DISEASE UNIT
- CL HEALTH AND WELFARE

Venison House
USE GAME LARDER

Venison Larder
USE GAME LARDER

Ventilating Fanhouse
USE EXHAUSTER HOUSE

VENTILATION CHIMNEY
- UF Ventilation Tower
- CL INDUSTRIAL
- BT CHIMNEY
- RT VENTILATION SHAFT

VENTILATION FURNACE
- SN Small furnace, used to create an upward draught of
  air in mine workings.
- CL INDUSTRIAL
- BT FURNACE
- RT MINE DRAINAGE AND VENTILATION SITE

Ventilation House
USE VENTILATION SHAFT

VENTILATION SHAFT
- UF Air Shaft Tower
  Air Vent House
  Ventilation House
- CL UNASSIGNED
- BT SHAFT
- RT EXHAUSTER HOUSE
  MINE SHAFT
  RAILWAY TUNNEL
  ROAD TUNNEL
  TUNNEL CHAMBER
  UNDERGROUND RAILWAY TUNNEL
  VENTILATION CHIMNEY

Ventilation Tower

USE VENTILATION CHIMNEY

VERDERERS COTTAGE
CL DOMESTIC
BT HOUSE <BY FUNCTION>
RT RANGERS HOUSE
VERDERERS HALL

VERDERERS HALL
CL CIVIL
BT MEETING HALL
RT VERDERERS COTTAGE

VERGERS HOUSE
CL DOMESTIC
BT CLERICAL DWELLING

VERMIN TRAP
CL AGRICULTURE AND SUBSISTENCE
RT RABBIT TYPE

VERTICAL STEAM ENGINE
SN An engine in which a vertical piston rod supplies
energy via a crankshaft directly to the flywheel
suspended above the cylinder. Extensively used as
mine winding engines.
CL INDUSTRIAL
BT STEAM ENGINE
RT BEAM ENGINE
WINDING ENGINE

VESTRY
CL RELIGIOUS, RITUAL AND FUNERARY
RT CHURCH
SACRISTY

Vestry Hall
USE TOWN HALL

VETERINARY HOSPITAL
UF Veterinary Infirmary
CL HEALTH AND WELFARE
BT ANIMAL WELFARE SITE
NT HORSE HOSPITAL

Veterinary Infirmary
USE VETERINARY HOSPITAL

Veterinary Surgery
USE SURGERY

Vets Surgery
USE SURGERY

VEXILLATION FORT
UF Roman Vexillation Fortress
CL DEFENCE
BT FORT
RT LEGIONARY FORTRESS

VIADUCT
CL TRANSPORT
NT RAILWAY VIADUCT
ROAD VIADUCT
RT AQUEDUCT
BRIDGE
CANAL

VICARAGE
CL DOMESTIC
BT CLERICAL DWELLING

Vicars Pele
USE TOWER HOUSE

Victorine Abbey
USE ABBEY
AUGUSTINIAN MONASTERY
SN Use both terms.

Victorine Priory
USE AUGUSTINIAN MONASTERY
PRIORY
SN Use both terms.

VICTUALLER
CL MARITIME
BT SERVICE CRAFT

VICUS
SN A Roman village or suburb.
CL DOMESTIC
BT SETTLEMENT
RT FORT

VICUS
SN A Roman village or suburb.
CL CIVIL

VIERECKSCHANZEN
SN Rectilinear ritual enclosure of Iron age date.
CL RELIGIOUS, RITUAL AND FUNERARY
RT RECTILINEAR ENCLOSURE
RITUAL PIT
RITUAL SHAFT

VILL
SN Small discreet rural settlements which do not
provide the commercial, legal or ecclesiastical
services typically found within medieval urban
areas.
CL DOMESTIC
BT SETTLEMENT
RT FARM
FARMSTEAD
VILLAGE

VILLA (NON ROMAN)
CL DOMESTIC
BT HOUSE <BY FORM>
RT COUNTRY HOUSE

VILLA (ROMAN)
UF Corridor Villa
Courtyard Villa
Major Villa
Minor Villa
Winged Corridor Villa
SN A rural house, usually consisting of farm
buildings and residential quarters around a
courtyard, with associated land. Roman period.
CL AGRICULTURE AND SUBSISTENCE
BT LAND USE SITE
RT FARM

VILLA (ROMAN)
UF Corridor Villa
Courtyard Villa
Major Villa
Minor Villa
Winged Corridor Villa
SN A rural house, usually consisting of farm
buildings and residential quarters around a
courtyard, with associated land. Roman period.
CL DOMESTIC
BT HOUSE <BY FORM>
RT FARM

VILLAGE
UF Inhabited Medieval Village
Medieval Village
Village Kitchen
CL DOMESTIC
BT SETTLEMENT
NT AGGREGATE VILLAGE
DESERTED VILLAGE
GARDEN VILLAGE
MIGRATED VILLAGE

RESORT VILLAGE
SHIFTED VILLAGE
SHRUNKEN VILLAGE
UTOPIAN COMMUNITY VILLAGE
WORKERS VILLAGE
RT COMMUNAL BAKEHOUSE
    HAMLET
    VILL

VILLAGE COLLEGE
SN 1930s building type, found in Cambridgeshire, for
    example.
CL EDUCATION
BT TRAINING COLLEGE

VILLAGE CROSS
CL RELIGIOUS, RITUAL AND FUNERARY
BT CROSS
RT MARKET CROSS
    PREACHING CROSS
    WAYSIDE CROSS

VILLAGE GREEN
CL GARDENS, PARKS AND URBAN SPACES
RT POUND

VILLAGE HALL
UF Parish Hall
    Parish Room
CL CIVIL
BT MEETING HALL
RT CHURCH HALL

Village Kitchen
USE KITCHEN
     VILLAGE
SN Use both terms.

Village Pound
USE POUND

VINEGAR BREWERY
UF Vinegar Distillery
    Vinegar Factory
    Vinegar Works
CL INDUSTRIAL
BT BREWERY

Vinegar Distillery
USE VINEGAR BREWERY

Vinegar Factory
USE VINEGAR BREWERY

Vinegar Vat Hall
USE VAT HALL

Vinegar Works
USE VINEGAR BREWERY

VINERY
CL GARDENS, PARKS AND URBAN SPACES
BT GLASSHOUSE

VINEYARD
CL AGRICULTURE AND SUBSISTENCE
BT LAND USE SITE

Vista Closer
USE FOLLY

Vivarium
USE FISH POND

Voluntary Hospital
USE GENERAL HOSPITAL

VOLUNTARY SCHOOL
UF Subscription School

CL EDUCATION
BT SCHOOL

VOTIVE PIT
CL RELIGIOUS, RITUAL AND FUNERARY
RT PIT
    RITUAL PIT
    RITUAL SHAFT
    VOTIVE SHAFT

VOTIVE SHAFT
CL RELIGIOUS, RITUAL AND FUNERARY
RT RITUAL PIT
    RITUAL SHAFT
    SHAFT
    VOTIVE PIT

Waggon Workshop
USE RAILWAY WORKSHOP

Wagon Burial
USE CART BURIAL

WAGON SHED
CL TRANSPORT
BT RAILWAY TRANSPORT SITE
RT CART SHED
    SHED

Wagon Stable
USE CART SHED

Wagon Weighing Machine
USE WEIGHBRIDGE

WAGONWAY
SN Transportation of freight by wagons on rails on a
    road. An early form of railway.
CL TRANSPORT
BT TRAMWAY
RT ROAD

Wainhouse
USE TRAP HOUSE

WAITING ROOM
CL TRANSPORT
RT BOOKING OFFICE
    BUS STATION

WALK
CL GARDENS, PARKS AND URBAN SPACES
NT ALLEE
    ETOILE
    LIME WALK
    PERCEE
    PROMENADE
    SERPENTINE PATH
    SERPENTINE WALK
    TERRACED WALK
    YEW WALK

Walk Mill
USE FULLING MILL

WALL
UF Churchyard Wall
    Dock Wall
    Field Wall
    Priory Wall
    Wharf Wall
SN Use specific type where known.
CL UNASSIGNED
NT BOUNDARY WALL
    PRECINCT WALL
    REVETMENT
RT BOUNDARY
    CURTAIN WALL
    GARDEN WALL

GATE
HA HA
HEATED WALL
SERPENTINE WALL
TOWN DEFENCES
TOWN WALL
WALLED GARDEN
WOOL WALL

WALL CRANE
CL TRANSPORT
BT CRANE <BY FORM>

WALL MONUMENT
CL COMMEMORATIVE
BT COMMEMORATIVE MONUMENT

WALL PAINTING
CL UNASSIGNED

Wall Tablet
USE PLAQUE

WALLED GARDEN
CL GARDENS, PARKS AND URBAN SPACES
BT GARDEN
RT WALL

WALLPAPER FACTORY
CL INDUSTRIAL
BT FACTORY <BY PRODUCT>

WALLPAPER FACTORY
CL INDUSTRIAL
BT PAPER INDUSTRY SITE

WAR MEMORIAL
UF War Memorial Chapel
War Memorial Cloister
War Memorial Garden
CL COMMEMORATIVE
BT COMMEMORATIVE MONUMENT
RT CENOTAPH
MILITARY CEMETERY
TOMB

War Memorial Chapel
USE CHAPEL
WAR MEMORIAL
SN Use both terms.

War Memorial Cloister
USE WAR MEMORIAL

War Memorial Garden
USE GARDEN
WAR MEMORIAL
SN Use both terms.

War Office
USE GOVERNMENT OFFICE

WARD BLOCK
SN Non-pavilion type of attached ward block.
CL HEALTH AND WELFARE
BT HOSPITAL BLOCK
RT HOSPITAL

WAREHOUSE
UF Canal Depository
Depository
Dock Warehouse
Freestore
Pantechnicon
CL COMMERCIAL
NT BONDED WAREHOUSE
FISH WAREHOUSE
GRAIN WAREHOUSE
LEATHER WAREHOUSE

RAILWAY WAREHOUSE
RUM WAREHOUSE
TEA WAREHOUSE
TEXTILE WAREHOUSE
TOBACCO WAREHOUSE
WHOLESALE WAREHOUSE
WOOL WAREHOUSE
RT CHANDLERY
COLD STORE
SHED
STOREHOUSE

Warren
USE RABBIT WARREN

WARSHIP
CL MARITIME
BT MARITIME CRAFT
NT AIRCRAFT CARRIER
AMPHIBIOUS OPERATIONS VESSEL
CAPITAL WARSHIP
DECOY VESSEL
DUMMY WARSHIP
ESCORT
FIRESHIP
MINELAYER
MINESWEEPER
MINOR WARSHIP
PATROL BOAT
PRIVATEER
SHIP OF THE LINE
SUBMARINE

WASH HOUSE
UF Sink House
CL DOMESTIC
RT BATH HOUSE
LAUNDRY

WASH HOUSE
UF Sink House
CL HEALTH AND WELFARE
NT PUBLIC WASH HOUSE
RT BATH HOUSE
LAUNDRY

WASH KILN
CL INDUSTRIAL
BT NON FERROUS METAL PROCESSING SITE

Washery
USE COAL CLEANING PLANT

WASHFOLD
CL AGRICULTURE AND SUBSISTENCE
BT ANIMAL WASH
RT SHEEP DIP
SHEEP FOLD

WASHING FLOOR
SN Open-air area often terraced on which a range of ore processing operations are carried out.
CL INDUSTRIAL
BT NON FERROUS METAL PROCESSING SITE
RT BUDDLE
CRAZING MILL
KNOCK STONE
ORE WASHING PLANT
SETTLING PIT
TIN MILL

WASHING PIT
CL INDUSTRIAL
BT LEATHER INDUSTRY SITE
RT PIT
SOAKING PIT
STEEPING PIT
TANNERY
TANNING PIT

WASHING SHOP
CL   INDUSTRIAL
BT   TEXTILE FINISHING SITE
RT   CLOTH DRESSING MILL

WASTE DISPOSAL SITE
CL   INDUSTRIAL
NT   INCINERATOR
      REFUSE DEPOT
      REFUSE DESTRUCTOR STATION
      REFUSE DISPOSAL PLANT
      REFUSE DISPOSAL SITE

WASTE DISPOSAL VESSEL
CL   MARITIME
BT   MARITIME CRAFT
NT   SEWAGE DUMPING VESSEL

WASTER KILN
UF   Kiln Waster
CL   INDUSTRIAL
BT   KILN < BY FUNCTION >

WASTER KILN
UF   Kiln Waster
CL   INDUSTRIAL
BT   MINERAL PRODUCT SITE
RT   GLASS CONE
      GLASSMAKING SITE
      POTTERY MANUFACTURING SITE

WASTER TIP
CL   INDUSTRIAL
BT   POTTERY MANUFACTURING SITE
RT   CLAY TOBACCO PIPE FACTORY
      POT HOUSE

WATCH HOUSE
UF   Dock Watch House
      Parish Watch House
      Watchmans Hut
CL   CIVIL
RT   CHURCHYARD
      FACTORY
      GUARDHOUSE
      LOCK UP
      POLICE BOX
      SENTRY BOX
      WATCHMANS BOX

Watch Office
USE CONTROL TOWER

WATCH TOWER
CL   DEFENCE
RT   BEACON
      CUSTOMS LOOKOUT
      FRONTIER DEFENCE
      GUARDHOUSE
      LIGHTHOUSE
      MARTELLO TOWER
      SIGNAL STATION
      TOWER

WATCH TOWER
CL   COMMUNICATIONS
RT   BEACON
      CUSTOMS LOOKOUT
      FRONTIER DEFENCE
      GUARDHOUSE
      LIGHTHOUSE
      MARTELLO TOWER
      SIGNAL STATION
      TOWER

Watchmakers Shop
USE WATCHMAKERS WORKSHOP

WATCHMAKERS WORKSHOP

UF   Watchmakers Shop
CL   INDUSTRIAL
BT   CRAFT INDUSTRY SITE
RT   INSTRUMENT ENGINEERING WORKS
      JEWELLERY WORKSHOP
      LOCKSMITHS WORKSHOP

WATCHMAKERS WORKSHOP
UF   Watchmakers Shop
CL   INDUSTRIAL
BT   NON FERROUS METAL PRODUCT SITE

WATCHMANS BOX
CL   GARDENS, PARKS AND URBAN SPACES
BT   STREET FURNITURE
RT   POLICE BOX
      SENTRY BOX
      WATCH HOUSE

Watchmans Hut
USE WATCH HOUSE

Water Board Office
USE OFFICE

WATER CARRIER
CL   MARITIME
BT   SERVICE CRAFT

WATER CHANNEL
UF   Dike
      Dyke (Water)
CL   WATER SUPPLY AND DRAINAGE
BT   WATERCOURSE
NT   GULLY
      LEAT
RT   AQUEDUCT
      CANAL
      CONDUIT
      MILL RACE
      WEIR

WATER CHUTE
CL   RECREATIONAL
BT   SPORTS SITE
RT   SWIMMING POOL

WATER GARDEN
CL   GARDENS, PARKS AND URBAN SPACES
BT   GARDEN
RT   CASCADE
      CASCADE HOUSE
      FOUNTAIN
      FOUNTAIN HOUSE
      POOL
      WATER PAVILION
      WATERFALL

WATER GATE
CL   DEFENCE
RT CASTLE
      GATE
      GATE TOWER
      POSTERN
      TOWN GATE

WATER GATE
CL   TRANSPORT
BT   WATER TRANSPORT SITE
RT CASTLE
      GATE
      GATE TOWER
      POSTERN
      TOWN GATE

WATER LILY HOUSE
CL   GARDENS, PARKS AND URBAN SPACES
BT   GLASSHOUSE

WATER MEADOW

CL   AGRICULTURE AND SUBSISTENCE
BT   FIELD SYSTEM

WATER PAVILION
CL   GARDENS, PARKS AND URBAN SPACES
BT   PAVILION
RT   CASCADE HOUSE
      FISHING LODGE
      FISHING PAVILION
      FOUNTAIN HOUSE
      WATER GARDEN

WATER PIPE
CL   WATER SUPPLY AND DRAINAGE
BT   WATERCOURSE
RT   CISTERN

Water Plant
USE WATERWORKS

WATER POINT
UF   Railway Water Tank
      Watering Standard
CL   WATER SUPPLY AND DRAINAGE
RT   MAIL BAG NET
      RAILWAY SIGNAL
      WATER TANK
      WATER TOWER

WATER POWER PRODUCTION SITE
CL   INDUSTRIAL
BT   POWER GENERATION SITE
NT   DAM
      DRAINAGE MILL
      HAMMER POND
      LEAT
      MILL POND
      MILL RACE
      PEN POND
      PUMP HOUSE
      TIDEMILL
      TURBINE MILL
      WATER TURBINE
      WATERCOURSE
      WATERMILL
      WATERWHEEL
      WEIR
      WHEEL HOUSE
      WHEEL PIT

WATER PUMP
UF   Hydrant
CL   WATER SUPPLY AND DRAINAGE
BT   PUMP
RT   HAND PUMP
      WAYSIDE PUMP

Water Pumphouse
USE WATER PUMPING STATION

WATER PUMPING STATION
UF   Water Pumphouse
CL   WATER SUPPLY AND DRAINAGE
BT   PUMPING STATION
RT   CONDUIT
      ENGINE HOUSE
      WATERWORKS
      WELL HOUSE

WATER REGULATION INSTALLATION
CL   MARITIME
NT   BALANCE BEAM
      CULVERT
      DOCK BASIN
      DOCK GATE
      GAUGE HOUSE
      IMPOUNDING STATION
      LOCK
      LOCK CHAMBER

      LOCK GATE
      LOCK SILL
      SETTLING RESERVOIR
      SLUICE
      TIDAL BASIN
      TIDAL DOOR
      TIDAL LOCK
      TIDE GAUGE

Water Softening Plant
USE WATERWORKS

Water Sulphurisation Plant
USE WATERWORKS

WATER SUPPLY AND DRAINAGE
SN   This is the top term for the class. See WATER
      SUPPLY AND DRAINAGE Class List for narrow terms.

WATER TANK
CL   WATER SUPPLY AND DRAINAGE
NT   CISTERN
RT   WATER POINT
      WATER TOWER
      WATERWORKS

WATER TAXI
CL   MARITIME
BT   PASSENGER VESSEL

WATER TOWER
UF   Manometer Tower
      Standpipe Tower
CL   WATER SUPPLY AND DRAINAGE
RT   CONDUIT HOUSE
      PUMPING STATION
      RESERVOIR
      TOWER
      WATER POINT
      WATER TANK
      WATERWORKS
      WELL HOUSE

WATER TRANSPORT SITE
CL   TRANSPORT
NT   AQUEDUCT
      BALANCE BEAM
      BAULK
      BOAT HOUSE
      BOAT LIFT
      BOAT YARD
      CANAL TRANSPORT SITE
      DOCK
      DOCKYARD
      GAUGE HOUSE
      HARBOUR
      JETTY
      LANDING PIER
      LANDING STAGE
      LANDING STEPS
      LOCK
      LOCK CHAMBER
      LOCK GATE
      LOCK SILL
      MOORING BOLLARD
      QUAY
      RIVER INTAKE GAUGE
      RIVER NAVIGATION
      SLIPWAY
      STAITH
      STAUNCH
      TIDAL DOOR
      TIDE GAUGE
      TOW PATH
      TOWING PATH BRIDGE
      WATER GATE
      WEIR
      WHARF
RT   LOCK KEEPERS COTTAGE

Water Treatment Plant
USE WATERWORKS

WATER TUNNEL
  CL WATER SUPPLY AND DRAINAGE
  BT WATERCOURSE
  RT TUNNEL
      WATERWORKS

WATER TURBINE
  CL INDUSTRIAL
  BT WATER POWER PRODUCTION SITE
  RT TURBINE MILL

WATER TURBINE
  CL INDUSTRIAL
  BT TURBINE

WATERCOURSE
  CL INDUSTRIAL
  BT WATER POWER PRODUCTION SITE
  RT MILL RACE

WATERCOURSE
  CL WATER SUPPLY AND DRAINAGE
  NT AQUEDUCT
      CANAL
      STREAM
      WATER CHANNEL
      WATER PIPE
      WATER TUNNEL
  RT HEAD RACE
      MILL
      TAIL RACE
      WATERMILL

WATERCRESS BED
  CL AGRICULTURE AND SUBSISTENCE
  BT LAND USE SITE

WATERFALL
  CL GARDENS, PARKS AND URBAN SPACES
  RT CASCADE
      WATER GARDEN

Watering Standard
USE WATER POINT

WATERMILL
  UF Horizontal Watermill
  SN Use with product type where known.
  CL INDUSTRIAL
  BT MILL
  RT CORN DRYING KILN
      CORN DRYING OVEN
      CORN MILL
      MILL DAM
      MILL POND
      MILL RACE
      TUMBLING WEIR
      WATERCOURSE

WATERMILL
  UF Horizontal Watermill
  SN Use with product type where known.
  CL INDUSTRIAL
  BT WATER POWER PRODUCTION SITE
  RT CORN MILL
      HEAD RACE
      MILL DAM
      MILL POND
      MILL RACE
      TAIL RACE
      TUMBLING WEIR
      TURBINE MILL
      WATERWHEEL
      WEIR

Watershed Reave

USE REAVE

WATERWHEEL
  UF Millwheel
  CL INDUSTRIAL
  BT WATER POWER PRODUCTION SITE
  NT WATERWHEEL <BY FORM>
  RT HEAD RACE
      HELVE HAMMER
      MILL DAM
      POND BAY
      TIDEMILL
      WATERMILL
      WHEEL HOUSE
      WHEEL PIT

WATERWHEEL <BY FORM>
  CL INDUSTRIAL
  BT WATERWHEEL
  NT BREASTSHOT WHEEL
      OVERSHOT WHEEL
      PITCHBACK WHEEL
      SCOOP WHEEL
      UNDERSHOT WHEEL

WATERWORKS
  UF Water Plant
      Water Softening Plant
      Water Sulphurisation Plant
      Water Treatment Plant
      Waterworks Office
  CL WATER SUPPLY AND DRAINAGE
  RT AQUEDUCT
      CONDUIT HOUSE
      ENGINE HOUSE
      FILTER BED
      FILTER HOUSE
      PUMP HOUSE
      PUMPING STATION
      PURIFIER
      RESERVOIR
      WATER PUMPING STATION
      WATER TANK
      WATER TOWER
      WATER TUNNEL
      WATERWORKS COTTAGE
      WELL HOUSE

WATERWORKS COTTAGE
  CL DOMESTIC
  BT HOUSE <BY FUNCTION>
  RT WATERWORKS

Waterworks Office
USE WATERWORKS
    OFFICE
  SN Use both terms.

Waulk Mill
USE FULLING MILL

WAX FACTORY
  CL INDUSTRIAL
  BT FACTORY <BY PRODUCT>

WAX FACTORY
  CL INDUSTRIAL
  BT CHEMICAL PRODUCT SITE
  RT CANDLE FACTORY
      CANDLE WORKS

Way Marker
USE SIGNPOST

WAYSIDE CROSS
  CL RELIGIOUS, RITUAL AND FUNERARY
  BT CROSS
  RT MARKET CROSS
      PREACHING CROSS

VILLAGE CROSS

WAYSIDE PUMP
- CL   WATER SUPPLY AND DRAINAGE
- BT   PUMP
- RT   HAND PUMP
      WATER PUMP

WAYSIDE PUMP
- CL   GARDENS, PARKS AND URBAN SPACES
- BT   STREET FURNITURE

WEALDEN HOUSE
- CL   DOMESTIC
- BT   HALL HOUSE
- NT   SINGLE ENDED WEALDEN HOUSE
- RT   WEALDEN TERRACE

WEALDEN HOUSE
- CL   DOMESTIC
- BT   TIMBER FRAMED HOUSE
- NT   SINGLE ENDED WEALDEN HOUSE
- RT   WEALDEN TERRACE

Wealden Row
  USE WEALDEN TERRACE

WEALDEN TERRACE
- UF   Wealden Row
- CL   DOMESTIC
- BT   TERRACE
- RT   WEALDEN HOUSE

WEAVERS COTTAGE
- UF   Silk Weavers Cottage
- CL   DOMESTIC
- BT   INDUSTRIAL HOUSE
- RT   FLAX BEATING STONE
      LOOMSHOP
      TENTER GROUND
      TENTER POST
      TOPSHOP
      TWEED MILL

WEAVERS COTTAGE
- UF   Silk Weavers Cottage
- CL   INDUSTRIAL
- BT   CRAFT INDUSTRY SITE
- RT   FLAX BEATING STONE
      LOOMSHOP
      TENTER GROUND
      TENTER POST
      TOPSHOP

WEAVERS COTTAGE
- UF   Silk Weavers Cottage
- CL   INDUSTRIAL
- BT   INDUSTRIAL HOUSE

WEAVERS WORKSHOP
- UF   Silk Weavers Workshop
- CL   INDUSTRIAL
- BT   CRAFT INDUSTRY SITE

WEAVERS WORKSHOP
- UF   Silk Weavers Workshop
- CL   INDUSTRIAL
- BT   TEXTILE FINISHING SITE

WEAVING MILL
- CL   INDUSTRIAL
- BT   TEXTILE MILL
- RT   BLANKET MILL
      CARPET MILL
      LOOMSHOP
      SCRIBBLING MILL
      SPINNING MILL
      TWEED MILL
      TWIST MILL

WEAVING SHED
WORSTED MILL

WEAVING MILL
- CL   INDUSTRIAL
- BT   TEXTILE FINISHING SITE
- RT   WEAVING SHED

WEAVING SHED
- CL   INDUSTRIAL
- BT   TEXTILE FINISHING SITE
- RT   WEAVING MILL

WEIGH HOUSE
- CL   TRANSPORT
- RT   ASSAY OFFICE
      STEELYARD
      TOLL HOUSE

WEIGHBRIDGE
- UF   Wagon Weighing Machine
- SN   A platform scale, flush with the road, for weighing vehicles, cattle, etc.
- CL   TRANSPORT
- RT   BRIDGE KEEPERS COTTAGE

Weighbridge House
  USE BRIDGE KEEPERS COTTAGE

WEIGHING MACHINE
- CL   GARDENS, PARKS AND URBAN SPACES
- BT   STREET FURNITURE

Weights And Measures Office
  USE GOVERNMENT OFFICE

WEIR
- UF   River Weir
- CL   INDUSTRIAL
- BT   WATER POWER PRODUCTION SITE
- NT   TUMBLING WEIR
- RT   CANAL
      DAM
      MILL DAM
      MILL RACE
      WATERMILL

WEIR
- UF   River Weir
- CL   TRANSPORT
- BT   WATER TRANSPORT SITE
- NT   TUMBLING WEIR
- RT   CANAL
      DAM
      EEL TRAP
      FISH LADDER
      FLASH LOCK
      FORD
      MILL RACE
      RIVER NAVIGATION
      SLUICE
      WATER CHANNEL

WEIR
- UF   River Weir
- CL   WATER SUPPLY AND DRAINAGE
- RT   CANAL
      DAM
      EEL TRAP
      FISH LADDER
      FLASH LOCK
      FORD
      FORGE
      MILL POND
      MILL RACE
      RIVER NAVIGATION
      SLUICE
      TEXTILE MILL
      WATER CHANNEL

WATERMILL

WELL
CL   WATER SUPPLY AND DRAINAGE
NT   DIPPING WELL
RT   DONKEY WHEEL
      DRINKING FOUNTAIN
      HAND PUMP
      HOLY WELL
      PUMP
      SHAFT
      SPA
      UNDERGROUND STRUCTURE
      WELL COVER
      WELL HEAD
      WELL HOUSE
      WELL SHAFT

WELL COVER
CL   WATER SUPPLY AND DRAINAGE
RT   WELL
      WELL HEAD
      WELL HOUSE

WELL HEAD
CL   WATER SUPPLY AND DRAINAGE
RT   WELL
      WELL COVER
      WELL HOUSE

WELL HOUSE
CL   WATER SUPPLY AND DRAINAGE
RT   CONDUIT HOUSE
      DONKEY WHEEL
      HYDRAULIC PUMPING STATION
      PUMP HOUSE
      WATER PUMPING STATION
      WATER TOWER
      WATERWORKS
      WELL
      WELL COVER
      WELL HEAD

WELL SHAFT
CL   WATER SUPPLY AND DRAINAGE
RT   WELL

WELSH PRESBYTERIAN CHAPEL
UF   Welsh Presbyterian Church
CL   RELIGIOUS, RITUAL AND FUNERARY
BT   PRESBYTERIAN CHAPEL

Welsh Presbyterian Church
USE WELSH PRESBYTERIAN CHAPEL

WESLEYAN METHODIST CHAPEL
CL   RELIGIOUS, RITUAL AND FUNERARY
BT   METHODIST CHAPEL

WESTWORK
CL   RELIGIOUS, RITUAL AND FUNERARY
RT   CHURCH

Wet Cooperage
USE COOPERAGE

WET DOCK
CL   INDUSTRIAL
BT   MARINE CONSTRUCTION SITE

WET DOCK
CL   MARITIME
BT   DOCK

WET DOCK
CL   MARITIME
BT   MARINE CONSTRUCTION SITE

WHALE CATCHER

CL   MARITIME
BT   WHALER

WHALE PROCESSING SHIP
CL   MARITIME
BT   FACTORY SHIP

WHALE PROCESSING SHIP
CL   MARITIME
BT   WHALER

WHALER
CL   MARITIME
BT   FISHING VESSEL
NT   WHALE CATCHER
      WHALE PROCESSING SHIP

WHARF
UF   Gun Wharf
      Wharf Wall
CL   TRANSPORT
BT   WATER TRANSPORT SITE
NT   CANAL WHARF
      RIVER WHARF
RT   MOORING BOLLARD
      WHARFINGERS COTTAGE

WHARF
UF   Gun Wharf
      Wharf Wall
CL   MARITIME
BT   LANDING POINT
RT   DOCK
      QUAY

Wharf Managers House
USE WHARFINGERS COTTAGE

Wharf Wall
USE WALL
      WHARF
SN   Use both terms.

WHARFINGERS COTTAGE
UF   Wharf Managers House
CL   DOMESTIC
BT   MARITIME HOUSE
RT   BRIDGE KEEPERS COTTAGE
      CANAL
      CANAL DOCKYARD
      CANAL GATEHOUSE
      CANAL OFFICE
      INCLINE KEEPERS COTTAGE
      LENGTHMANS COTTAGE
      WHARF

WHARFINGERS COTTAGE
UF   Wharf Managers House
CL   DOMESTIC
BT   TRANSPORT WORKERS HOUSE

Wheel Cross
USE CROSS

WHEEL HOUSE
CL   INDUSTRIAL
BT   WATER POWER PRODUCTION SITE
RT   WATERWHEEL
      WHEEL PIT

WHEEL MOULD
CL   INDUSTRIAL
BT   TIMBER PRODUCT SITE
RT   WHEELWRIGHTS WORKSHOP

WHEEL PIT
CL   INDUSTRIAL
BT   WATER POWER PRODUCTION SITE
RT   PIT

WATERWHEEL
WHEEL HOUSE

WHEELWRIGHTS WORKSHOP
CL INDUSTRIAL
BT TIMBER PRODUCT SITE
RT JOINERS SHOP
WHEEL MOULD

Whim Gin
USE HORSE ENGINE

Whim House
USE HORSE ENGINE HOUSE

Whimsey
USE STEAM WHIM

Whimsey House
USE STEAM WHIM HOUSE

WHIPPING POST
CL CIVIL
BT PUNISHMENT PLACE
RT PILLORY
STOCKS

Whips Office
USE GOVERNMENT OFFICE

White Cloth Hall
USE CLOTH HALL

WHITE GARDEN
CL GARDENS, PARKS AND URBAN SPACES
BT GARDEN

White Horse
USE HILL FIGURE

White Market
USE MEAT MARKET

White Yarn House
USE YARN HOUSE

WHITESMITHS WORKSHOP
SN Workshop with a forge for the melting and working
of white metal, ie. low-melting alloys. Also used
for a smith specialising in decorative or finely
finished wrought iron work.
CL INDUSTRIAL
BT HEAVY ENGINEERING SITE
RT ENGINEERING WORKSHOP
POLISHING SHOP

WHITESMITHS WORKSHOP
SN Workshop with a forge for the melting and working
of white metal, ie. low-melting alloys. Also used
for a smith specialising in decorative or finely
finished wrought iron work.
CL INDUSTRIAL
BT NON FERROUS METAL PRODUCT SITE

WHOLESALE MARKET
CL COMMERCIAL
BT MARKET

WHOLESALE WAREHOUSE
CL COMMERCIAL
BT WAREHOUSE

Wiccamical Prebendaries House
USE CLERGY HOUSE

Widows Home
USE ALMSHOUSE

WIGMAKERS SHOP

CL COMMERCIAL
BT SHOP

WILD GARDEN
CL GARDENS, PARKS AND URBAN SPACES
BT GARDEN

WILLEY SHED
SN Beating of wool/cotton to clean and separate the
fibres.
CL INDUSTRIAL
BT TEXTILE SITE <BY PROCESS/PRODUCT>
RT COMBING SHED
COMBING WORKS
SCRIBBLING MILL
SHED
YARN MILL

WINCH
CL TRANSPORT
BT LIFTING AND WINDING STRUCTURE
NT BARGE WINCH
ELECTRIC WINCH

WIND ENGINE
CL INDUSTRIAL
BT WIND POWER SITE

WIND ENGINE
CL INDUSTRIAL
BT ENGINE

WIND POWER SITE
CL INDUSTRIAL
BT POWER GENERATION SITE
NT WIND ENGINE
WIND PUMP
WINDMILL
WINDMILL MOUND

WIND PUMP
CL WATER SUPPLY AND DRAINAGE
BT PUMP
RT DRAINAGE MILL
WINDMILL

WIND PUMP
CL INDUSTRIAL
BT WIND POWER SITE

WINDER HOUSE
UF Beam Winder House
Colliery Winding House
Koepe Winding Tower
Winding Engine House
Winding House
CL INDUSTRIAL
BT MINE LIFTING AND WINDING STRUCTURE
RT HAULAGE ENGINE HOUSE
MAN ENGINE
MINE
STOWE

WINDING CIRCLE
UF Gin Circle
Horse Walk
CL INDUSTRIAL
BT MINE LIFTING AND WINDING STRUCTURE
RT ANIMAL POWER SITE
HORSE WHIM
MINE

WINDING ENGINE
CL TRANSPORT
BT LIFTING AND WINDING STRUCTURE
NT INCLINE WINDING ENGINE
RT LIFT SHAFT
VERTICAL STEAM ENGINE

Winding Engine House

USE WINDER HOUSE

WINDING GEAR
UF Headgear
    Headstock
SN Machinery for raising and lowering men and
    materials to and from the surface of a mine.
CL INDUSTRIAL
BT MINE LIFTING AND WINDING STRUCTURE
RT HAULAGE ENGINE HOUSE
    HEAPSTEAD
    HORSE WHIM

Winding Gear Shop
USE MINE
     WORKSHOP
SN Use both terms.

Winding House
USE WINDER HOUSE

WINDLASS
CL INDUSTRIAL
BT MINE LIFTING AND WINDING STRUCTURE
RT STOWE

WINDLASS
CL INDUSTRIAL
BT ANIMAL POWER SITE

WINDMILL
UF Air Mill
SN Use with product type where known.
CL INDUSTRIAL
BT MILL
RT CORN MILL
    DRAINAGE MILL
    WIND PUMP
    WINDMILL MOUND

WINDMILL
UF Air Mill
SN Use with product type where known.
CL INDUSTRIAL
BT WIND POWER SITE
NT WINDMILL <BY FORM>
RT CORN MILL
    WIND PUMP
    WINDMILL MOUND

WINDMILL <BY FORM>
CL INDUSTRIAL
BT WINDMILL
NT HORIZONTAL AIR MILL
    POST MILL
    SMOCK MILL
    TOWER MILL

WINDMILL MOUND
UF Mill Mound
CL INDUSTRIAL
BT WIND POWER SITE
RT MOUND
    WINDMILL

WINE AND CIDERMAKING SITE
CL INDUSTRIAL
BT FOOD AND DRINK INDUSTRY SITE
NT CIDER FACTORY
    CIDER MILL
    CIDER PRESS
    CIDER VAULT
    WINE PRESS
    WINERY

WINE BAR
CL COMMERCIAL
BT LICENSED PREMISES

WINE CELLARS

UF Catacomb (Wine Storage)
SN Commercial complex of wine cellars.
CL COMMERCIAL
RT CELLAR

WINE LODGE
UF Lodge
CL COMMERCIAL
BT PUBLIC HOUSE

WINE PRESS
CL INDUSTRIAL
BT WINE AND CIDERMAKING SITE
RT CIDER MILL
    CIDER PRESS
    WINERY

WINERY
CL INDUSTRIAL
BT WINE AND CIDERMAKING SITE
RT WINE PRESS

Winged Corridor House
USE HOUSE

Winged Corridor Villa
USE VILLA (ROMAN)

WINTER GARDEN
SN Originally ground planted with conifers for winter
    display. Otherwise use CONSERVATORY.
CL GARDENS, PARKS AND URBAN SPACES
BT GARDEN

WIRE MILL
UF Wire Works
CL INDUSTRIAL
BT MILL
RT BRASS WORKS
    COMB MILL
    NAIL FACTORY
    NEEDLE MILL
    PIN MILL
    ROLLING MILL
    SLITTING MILL

WIRE MILL
UF Wire Works
CL INDUSTRIAL
BT METAL INDUSTRY SITE
RT COMB MILL
    NAIL FACTORY
    NEEDLE MILL
    PIN MILL
    ROLLING MILL
    SLITTING MILL

Wire Works
USE WIRE MILL

Wireless Station
USE RADIO STATION

WITHERITE MINE
SN When secondary mineral, use with term for product,
    eg. LEAD MINE.
CL INDUSTRIAL
BT MINERAL EXTRACTION SITE
RT BARYTES MINE
    LEAD MINE

WITHERITE MINE
SN When secondary mineral, use with term for product,
    eg. LEAD MINE.
CL INDUSTRIAL
BT MINE
RT BARYTES MINE
    LEAD MINE

WITHY BOILER

SN   Used for boiling sections of willow for basket
     making, etc.
CL   INDUSTRIAL
BT   WOOD PRODUCT SITE

WOMEN AND CHILDRENS HOSPITAL
CL   HEALTH AND WELFARE
BT   SPECIALIST HOSPITAL

WOMENS HOSPITAL
CL   HEALTH AND WELFARE
BT   SPECIALIST HOSPITAL

WOOD
CL   AGRICULTURE AND SUBSISTENCE
BT   WOODLAND
RT   HUNTING FOREST
     WOOD BANK

WOOD BANK
UF   Wood Boundary
     Woodland Earthworks
CL   AGRICULTURE AND SUBSISTENCE
BT   LAND USE SITE
RT   BOUNDARY
     PLANTATION BANK
     WOOD

Wood Boundary
USE   WOOD BANK

WOOD CHEMICAL WORKS
SN   Production of turpentine, wood alcohol and similar
     chemicals by the distillation of pulped wood.
CL   INDUSTRIAL
BT   CHEMICAL PRODUCT SITE
RT   CHARCOAL PRODUCTION SITE
     DISTILLATION PLANT
     OIL DISTILLERY

WOOD CHEMICAL WORKS
SN   Production of turpentine, wood alcohol and similar
     chemicals by the distillation of pulped wood.
CL   INDUSTRIAL
BT   WOOD PRODUCT SITE
RT   LOGWOOD MILL
     PULP MILL

WOOD DRYING KILN
CL   INDUSTRIAL
BT   DRYING KILN

WOOD DRYING KILN
CL   INDUSTRIAL
BT   WOOD PRODUCT SITE
RT   TIMBER SEASONING SHED

Wood House
USE   WOOD SHED

WOOD PROCESSING SITE
SN   Includes processing and manufacturing of all forms
     of wood.
CL   INDUSTRIAL
NT   TIMBER PROCESSING SITE
     TIMBER PRODUCT SITE
     WOOD PRODUCT SITE

WOOD PRODUCT SITE
SN   Manufacture and use of wood side products, ie.
     unprocessed wood rather than processed timber.
CL   INDUSTRIAL
BT   WOOD PROCESSING SITE
NT   BARK HOUSE
     BARK MILL
     BARK PEELERS HUT
     BASKET MAKERS WORKSHOP
     BOARD MILL
     BRUSH FACTORY

BRUSHMAKERS WORKSHOP
COPPICE BARN
LOGWOOD MILL
PULP MILL
WITHY BOILER
WOOD CHEMICAL WORKS
WOOD DRYING KILN
WOODWORKERS HUT
WOODWORKING SITE

Wood Screw Mill
USE   SCREW MILL

WOOD SHED
UF   Timber Shed
     Wood House
CL   UNASSIGNED
RT   FUEL STORE
     SHED
     TIMBER SEASONING SHED

Wood Turners Shop
USE   CARPENTERS WORKSHOP

Wooden Circle
USE   TIMBER CIRCLE

WOODEN ROAD
UF   Plank Road
CL   TRANSPORT
BT   ROAD

WOODLAND
CL   GARDENS, PARKS AND URBAN SPACES
NT   BELT
     CONIFEROUS WOODLAND
     COPSE
     DECIDUOUS WOODLAND
     GROVE
     MIXED WOODLAND
     ORCHARD
RT   TREE ENCLOSURE RING
     TREE MOUND
     TREE RING
     WOODLAND GARDEN

WOODLAND
CL   AGRICULTURE AND SUBSISTENCE
BT   LAND USE SITE
NT   WOOD

Woodland Earthworks
USE   WOOD BANK

WOODLAND GARDEN
CL   GARDENS, PARKS AND URBAN SPACES
BT   GARDEN
RT   WOODLAND

WOODWORKERS HUT
CL   INDUSTRIAL
BT   WOOD PRODUCT SITE
RT   BARK PEELERS HUT
     WOODWORKING SITE

WOODWORKERS HUT
CL   DOMESTIC
BT   HUT
RT   INDUSTRIAL HOUSE

Woodworking Shop
USE   CARPENTERS WORKSHOP

WOODWORKING SITE
CL   INDUSTRIAL
BT   WOOD PRODUCT SITE
RT   BARK PEELERS HUT
     WOODWORKERS HUT

WOOL BARN

CL INDUSTRIAL
BT WOOL MANUFACTURING SITE
RT HANDLE HOUSE
   WOOL STOVE

WOOL DRY HOUSE
CL INDUSTRIAL
BT WOOL MANUFACTURING SITE
RT DRY HOUSE
   TENTER GROUND

WOOL EXCHANGE
CL COMMERCIAL
BT EXCHANGE
RT WOOL WAREHOUSE

Wool Hall
USE WOOL STAPLE

WOOL MANUFACTURING SITE
SN Includes worsted and other wool-related textiles.
CL INDUSTRIAL
BT TEXTILE SITE <BY PROCESS/PRODUCT>
NT ALPACA MILL
   BOMBASINE MILL
   FELT MILL
   FULLING MILL
   FULLING STOCKS
   GREASE WORKS
   HANDLE HOUSE
   MUNGO MILL
   SERGE FACTORY
   SHODDY MILL
   TEAZLE SHOP
   TWEED MILL
   WOOL BARN
   WOOL DRY HOUSE
   WOOL STOVE
   WOOL WALL
   WOOLCOMBERS SHOP
   WOOLLEN MILL
   WORSTED MILL

WOOL STAPLE
UF Wool Hall
SN A market appointed for the sale of wool.
CL COMMERCIAL
BT MARKET

WOOL STOVE
CL INDUSTRIAL
BT WOOL MANUFACTURING SITE
RT HANDLE HOUSE
   WOOL BARN

WOOL WALL
CL INDUSTRIAL
BT WOOL MANUFACTURING SITE
RT CLOTHIERS WORKSHOP
   FLAX BEATING STONE
   TENTER GROUND
   TENTER POST
   TWEED MILL
   WALL

WOOL WAREHOUSE
CL COMMERCIAL
BT WAREHOUSE
RT WOOL EXCHANGE
   WOOLLEN MILL

WOOLCOMBERS SHOP
CL INDUSTRIAL
BT WOOL MANUFACTURING SITE
RT COMBING WORKS

Woollen Carding Mill
USE CARDING MILL

WOOLLEN MILL

CL INDUSTRIAL
BT TEXTILE MILL
RT CARPET MILL
   FLOCK MILL
   WOOL WAREHOUSE

WOOLLEN MILL
CL INDUSTRIAL
BT WOOL MANUFACTURING SITE

Wooton Style Enclosure
USE RECTILINEAR ENCLOSURE

Wootton Hill Style Enclosure
USE ENCLOSED SETTLEMENT

WORKERS COTTAGE
UF Brickworkers Cottage
   Coal Miners Cottage
   Ironworkers Cottage
   Lead Miners Cottage
   Mill Workers Cottage
   Miners Cottage
   Quarriers Cottage
   Quarrymans Cottage
   Saltworkers Cottage
   Tin Workers Cottage
   Tinworkers Cottage
   Workers House
SN Industrial worker's house which has been purpose
   built by an employer, as opposed to the workshop
   houses used by artisans.
CL DOMESTIC
BT INDUSTRIAL HOUSE
RT BOTHY
   FOREMANS HOUSE
   MANAGERS HOUSE
   MINE CAPTAINS HOUSE
   SMITHS COTTAGE
   WORKERS VILLAGE

WORKERS COTTAGE
UF Brickworkers Cottage
   Coal Miners Cottage
   Ironworkers Cottage
   Lead Miners Cottage
   Mill Workers Cottage
   Miners Cottage
   Quarriers Cottage
   Quarrymans Cottage
   Saltworkers Cottage
   Tin Workers Cottage
   Tinworkers Cottage
   Workers House
SN Industrial worker's house which has been purpose
   built by an employer, as opposed to the workshop
   houses used by artisans.
CL INDUSTRIAL
BT INDUSTRIAL HOUSE

Workers Flats
USE MODEL DWELLING

WORKERS HOSTEL
CL DOMESTIC
BT HOSTEL
RT BOTHY
   INDUSTRIAL HOUSE

Workers House
USE WORKERS COTTAGE

WORKERS VILLAGE
UF Coal Miners Village
   Colliery Village
   Factory Model Village
   Industrial Housing Estate
   Industrial Model Village
   Mill Workers Village

Miners Village
Mining Village
Pit Village
Railway Workers Village
Steel Workers Village
CL DOMESTIC
BT VILLAGE
RT COLLIERY INSTITUTE
INDUSTRIAL HOUSE
WORKERS COTTAGE

WORKERS VILLAGE
UF Coal Miners Village
Colliery Village
Factory Model Village
Industrial Housing Estate
Industrial Model Village
Mill Workers Village
Miners Village
Mining Village
Pit Village
Railway Workers Village
Steel Workers Village
CL DOMESTIC
BT MODEL SETTLEMENT
RT COLLIERY
COLLIERY INSTITUTE
FACTORY
INDUSTRIAL HOUSE
MINE
MINERS READING ROOM
STEEL WORKS
TEXTILE MILL
WORKERS COTTAGE

WORKHOUSE
UF House Of Industry
House Of Institution
Poor House
Poor Law Infirmary
Poor Law Institution
Poor Law Union Hospital
Spike
Union House
Workhouse Chapel
Workhouse Infirmary
Workhouse Mental Ward Block
Workhouse Sanatorium
Workhouse School
CL HEALTH AND WELFARE
RT ALMSHOUSE
CASUAL WARD BLOCK
EXERCISE YARD
INFIRMARY
MENTAL HOSPITAL
RECEIVING BLOCK
STONE BREAKING YARD
WORKHOUSE MASTERS HOUSE

WORKHOUSE
UF House Of Industry
House Of Institution
Poor House
Poor Law Infirmary
Poor Law Institution
Poor Law Union Hospital
Spike
Union House
Workhouse Chapel
Workhouse Infirmary
Workhouse Mental Ward Block
Workhouse Sanatorium
Workhouse School
CL DOMESTIC
BT RESIDENTIAL BUILDING
RT WORKHOUSE MASTERS HOUSE

Workhouse Chapel
USE CHAPEL

WORKHOUSE
SN Use both terms.

Workhouse Infirmary
USE WORKHOUSE
INFIRMARY
SN Use both terms.

WORKHOUSE MASTERS HOUSE
CL DOMESTIC
BT HEALTH WORKERS HOUSE
RT WORKHOUSE

Workhouse Mental Ward Block
USE WORKHOUSE
MENTAL WARD BLOCK
SN Use both terms.

Workhouse Sanatorium
USE WORKHOUSE
SANATORIUM
SN Use both terms.

Workhouse School
USE SCHOOL
WORKHOUSE
SN Use both terms.

Working Ladies Hostel
USE LODGING HOUSE

WORKING MENS CLUB
CL RECREATIONAL
BT CLUB

WORKING MENS CLUB
CL INSTITUTIONAL
BT CLUB

WORKING MENS COLLEGE
CL EDUCATION
BT TRAINING COLLEGE
RT CHURCH INSTITUTE
COLLIERY INSTITUTE
COOPERATIVE INSTITUTE
LITERARY AND SCIENTIFIC INSTITUTE
MECHANICS INSTITUTE
MINERS READING ROOM
PEOPLES COLLEGE
WORKING MENS INSTITUTE

Working Mens Hostel
USE LODGING HOUSE

WORKING MENS INSTITUTE
UF Workmans Institute
CL EDUCATION
BT INSTITUTE
RT MINERS READING ROOM
PEOPLES COLLEGE
WORKING MENS COLLEGE

WORKING MENS INSTITUTE
UF Workmans Institute
CL INSTITUTIONAL
BT INSTITUTE
RT MINERS READING ROOM
PEOPLES COLLEGE
WORKING MENS COLLEGE

Working Mens Lodgings
USE LODGING HOUSE

Workmans Institute
USE WORKING MENS INSTITUTE

WORKS
SN Unknown function. Use specific type where known.
CL INDUSTRIAL

RT ASSEMBLY PLANT
    ENGINE HOUSE
    FACTORY
    INDUSTRIAL ESTATE
    INDUSTRIAL SITE
    LIGHT ENGINEERING SITE
    LIGHT ENGINEERING WORKS
    MILL
    STEAM ENGINE
    WORKSHOP

Works Canteen
  USE CANTEEN

Works Managers House
  USE MANAGERS HOUSE

Works Office
  USE OFFICE

WORKSHOP
  UF Cage Shop
     Colliery Repair Shop
     Pit Prop Shop
     Winding Gear Shop
  SN Use more specific term where possible.
  CL INDUSTRIAL
  RT BRUSHMAKERS WORKSHOP
     CARPENTERS WORKSHOP
     CLOTH CUTTERS WORKSHOP
     WORKS

WORSTED MILL
  CL INDUSTRIAL
  BT TEXTILE MILL

WORSTED MILL
  CL INDUSTRIAL
  BT WOOL MANUFACTURING SITE
  RT COMBING SHED
     COMBING WORKS
     GREASE WORKS
     WEAVING MILL

Xylonite Works
  USE PLASTICS FACTORY

Yacht Club
  USE SAILING CLUB

Yachting Lodge
  USE BOAT HOUSE

YARD
  CL UNASSIGNED
  RT BACKYARD
     COURTYARD

Yard House
  USE COURTYARD HOUSE

YARN DRY HOUSE
  CL INDUSTRIAL
  BT TEXTILE SITE <BY PROCESS/PRODUCT>
  RT DRY HOUSE
     TENTER GROUND

YARN HOUSE
  UF Black Yarn House
     Tarred Yarn House
     White Yarn House
  CL INDUSTRIAL
  BT ROPE MANUFACTURING SITE
  RT HATCHELLING HOUSE
     ROPEWALK

Yarn Market
  USE CLOTH MARKET

YARN MILL

CL INDUSTRIAL
BT TEXTILE MILL
RT DOUBLING MILL
    TWIST MILL

YARN MILL
  CL INDUSTRIAL
  BT TEXTILE SITE <BY PROCESS/PRODUCT>
  RT COMBING SHED
     WILLEY SHED

Yelling House
  USE BREWHOUSE

YEW GARDEN
  CL GARDENS, PARKS AND URBAN SPACES
  BT GARDEN
  RT YEW WALK

YEW WALK
  CL GARDENS, PARKS AND URBAN SPACES
  BT WALK
  RT YEW GARDEN

Yielding House
  USE BREWHOUSE

Ymca Hostel
  USE CHRISTIAN ASSOCIATION HOSTEL

YOUTH CLUB
  UF Boys Club
     Girls Club
  CL RECREATIONAL
  BT CLUB
  RT YOUTH HOSTEL

YOUTH CLUB
  UF Boys Club
     Girls Club
  CL INSTITUTIONAL
  BT CLUB
  RT SCOUT HUT
     YOUTH HOSTEL

Youth Custody Centre
  USE JUVENILE PRISON

YOUTH HOSTEL
  CL RECREATIONAL
  RT YOUTH CLUB

YOUTH HOSTEL
  CL DOMESTIC
  BT HOSTEL
  RT YOUTH CLUB

Ywca Hostel
  USE CHRISTIAN ASSOCIATION HOSTEL

ZEBRA CROSSING
  CL GARDENS, PARKS AND URBAN SPACES
  BT PEDESTRIAN CROSSING

ZEBRA CROSSING
  CL TRANSPORT
  BT PEDESTRIAN CROSSING

ZINC MINE
  SN Use with other metal ores extracted and MINE where
     necessary, eg. LEAD MINE.
  CL INDUSTRIAL
  BT NON FERROUS METAL EXTRACTION SITE
  RT CALAMINE MINE
     FLUORSPAR MINE
     LEAD MINE
     SILVER MINE

ZINC MINE

SN   Use with other metal ores extracted and MINE where
       necessary, eg. LEAD MINE.
CL   INDUSTRIAL
BT   MINE
RT   CALAMINE MINE
       FLUORSPAR MINE
       LEAD MINE
       SILVER MINE

ZINC WORKS
UF   Spelter Factory
       Spelter Works
CL   INDUSTRIAL
BT   NON FERROUS METAL SMELTING SITE
RT   SMELTER

ZINC WORKS
UF   Spelter Factory
       Spelter Works
CL   INDUSTRIAL
BT   NON FERROUS METAL PRODUCT SITE

ZOO
UF   Menagerie
       Zoological Garden
CL   RECREATIONAL
BT   ANIMAL DWELLING

ZOO
UF   Menagerie
       Zoological Garden
CL   GARDENS, PARKS AND URBAN SPACES
RT   BOTANIC GARDEN

Zoological Garden
   USE ZOO